THE HANDBOOK OF
HUMAN RESOURCE
DEVELOPMENT

THE HANDBOOK OF HUMAN RESOURCE DEVELOPMENT

LEONARD NADLER, EDITOR

A Wiley-Interscience Publication
JOHN WILEY & SONS
New York   Chichester   Brisbane   Toronto   Singapore

Copyright © 1984 by John Wiley & Sons, Inc.

This publication is designed to provide accurate and
authoritative information in regard to the subject
matter covered. It is sold with the understanding that
the publisher is not engaged in rendering legal, accounting,
or other professional service. If legal advice or other
expert assistance is required, the services of a competent
professional person should be sought. *From a Declaration
of Principles jointly adopted by a Committee of the
American Bar Association and a Committee of Publishers.*

ISBN 0-471-89234-3

Printed in the United States of America

10 9 8 7 6 5 4 3 2 1

Contributors

ARACELY BALDIZON, Organizational Consultant, CENSA (Pepsi), Mexico City, Mexico

DOUGLAS J. BARNEY, Staff HRD Consultant, Link Simulation Systems, The Singer Company, Columbia, Maryland

CHIP R. BELL, Consultant, Charlotte, North Carolina

ELLIS BERNE, Consultant, Potomac, Maryland

LAWRENCE G. BROWN, Administrator of Co-operative Education and Engineering Personnel Liaison, Rockford, Illinois

LANNIE J. BROWN, Assistant to the Director for Program Planning and Development, Janet Wattles Mental Health Center, Rockford, Illinois

JULIO C. CASAS, Julio C. Casas, Associates, Caracas, Venezuela

NEAL CHALOFSKY, Assistant Professor of Education, Virginia Polytechnic Institute and State University, Blacksburg, Virginia

VIRGIL E. COLLINS, Director of Human Resource Development, Akron City Hospital, Akron, Ohio

STEPHEN H. CONFER, Director, National Training Fund for the Communications Industry, Communication Workers of America, Washington, D.C.

STANLEY CONNELL III, President, Productive Concepts Systems, Inc., Rockville, Maryland

ABRAHAM DANTUS, Dantus y Asociados, S.C., Mexico City, Mexico

RICHARD W. DAVIS, Bell System Center for Technical Education, Lisle, Illinois

COLEMAN FINKEL, National Conference Center, East Windsor, New Jersey

DAVID GETTER, Executive Vice President, Factor Humano, Caracas, Venezuela

RALPH R. GLAZER, Fairfax County Public School System, Fairfax, Virginia

CRISPIN GREY-JOHNSON, Economic Affairs Officer, United Nations Economic Commission for Africa, Addis Ababa, Ethiopia

DANIEL F. GULIANO, Assistant Professor, School of Education and Human Development, The George Washington University, Washington, D.C.

THOMAS G. GUTTERIDGE, Dean, College of Business and Administration, Southern Illinois University, Carbondale, Illinois

PEGGY G. HUTCHESON, Atlanta Consulting Associates, Atlanta, Georgia

TOM JAAP, Director, Human Resource Associates, London, England

DAVID W. JAMIESON, Jamieson Consulting Group, Los Angeles, California. President (1984), American Society for Training and Development, Washington, D.C.

DEBORAH BACH KALLICK, Union Bank, Los Angeles, California

MALCOLM S. KNOWLES, Consultant, Raleigh, North Carolina

C. EDWARD KUR, Vice President, Phoenix Associates, Phoenix, Arizona

GORDON LIPPITT, Professor of Behavior Science, The George Washington University, Washington, D.C.

RONALD LIPPITT, Professor Emeritus in Sociology and Psychology, University of Michigan, Ann Arbor, Michigan

FRANCIS X. MAHONEY, Vice President, Institute for Management Improvement, Houston, Texas

ELLEN WEISBERG MALASKY, Consultant, Washington, D.C.

MICHAEL J. MARQUARDT, USDA Graduate School, Washington, D.C.

LEONARD NADLER, Professor of Adult Education and Human Resource Development, The George Washington University, Washington, D.C.

NEAL NADLER, President, Neal Nadler Associates, Washington, D.C.

ZEACE NADLER, Vice President, Neal Nadler Associates, Washington, D.C.

ELIZABETH OLSON, Consultant, Washington, D.C.

JACK J. PHILLIPS, Manager, Administration, Vulcan Material Company, Birmingham, Alabama

LEONARD B. POULIOT, President International Consulting Associates, Arlington, Virginia

ANTHONY O. PUTMAN, Management Support Technology, Inc., Ann Arbor, Michigan

VANKATRAM K. RAMCHANDRAN, Consultant, Madras, India

ANGUS STUART REYNOLDS, Senior Human Resource Development Consultant, Control Data Education Technology Center, Rockville, Maryland

AUGUST K. SPECTOR, Supervisory and Management Development Specialist, U.S. Nuclear Regulatory Commission, Washington, D.C.

EDWARD A. SCHROER, Assistant Director for Training, U.S. Office of Personnel Management, Washington, D.C.
    Vice President for Professional Development, American Society for Training and Development, Washington, D.C.

GARLAND D. WIGGS, Associate Professor of Adult Education and Human Resource Development, The George Washington University, Washington, D.C.

Preface

The field of human resource development (HRD) has been with us for a long time, but it grew and expanded under a variety of labels including: *training, training and development, industrial training, adult education, employee education*, and so forth. Although we have not yet reached total agreement on nomenclature, that is evolving.

As can be expected, the growth of the field has produced a burgeoning of publications. Some have contributed to growth and understanding, while many have served only to confuse both those in the field and the organizations they serve.

This handbook has been planned to eliminate some of the confusion and to contribute to a clarification of some of the models and concepts in HRD. One method of providing such clarity is through the use of the glossary. Each of the contributors received this glossary, reviewed it, and agreed to write their chapters using the words as defined in it. This was not easy, as HRD terminology has tended to be somewhat imprecise. The contributors have done an excellent job, and you will find that HRD terminology has the same meaning in every chapter. (Any exception is indicated in the chapter opening.) This is a unique innovation in a HRD handbook, or in a book of HRD readings, for that matter. It will greatly facilitate reading the book and using the material.

Let me share with you the organization of this handbook, as reflected in the various sections.

Section One—The Field of Human Resource Development

Chapter 1 provides an overview of the field, including a history, and presents a model that clearly defines HRD and relates it to other areas of human resources. A distinction is also made among three different kinds of HRD experiences labeled: *training, education,* and *development.* This is followed by models related to the roles of HRD people.

In Chapter 2, we discuss managing the HRD function. The contributor discusses where HRD fits into the organization. The model of the subroles of the HRD Manager, presented in Chapter 1, is used as the framework for this chapter. There is new material on the HRD Manager and policy, a growing area of concern. As management is increasing the use of the strategic planning process, it is also incumbent upon the HRD Manager to explore this area and to learn how to relate HRD to strategic planning.

Although HRD is concerned with learning, it is important for HRD practitioners to understand the financial aspects of HRD, as discussed in Chapter 3. The contributor presents a model that includes both program development and program delivery and explores how they differ. Budgeting by HRD managers has generally been woefully inadequate, and many HRD programs have built in their own failure through lack of competence in the budgeting process.

It is important that there be the proper environment for learning, and this is presented in Chapter 4. The contributor of this chapter has a long and successful record in the field of HRD and the allied field of meetings. In this chapter, he presents some common elements and focuses on how the environment can contribute to learning. If your organization is planning its own learning facility, his discussion of the frequent mistakes made in such planning will prove extremely helpful. You may be faced with making decisions about using external facilities, and you will find useful information in this chapter. The contributor also provides a glimpse of future uses for technology in learning environments.

The term *consultant* is too frequently used merely to label a person coming from outside the organization. Actually, consulting is a process, and there are internal consultants as well as external consultants. The contributors to Chapter 5 have extensive experience in *consulting*—in the true sense of the term. They differentiate between internal and external consultants and identify the behavioral roles of the consultant. They explore the skills needed by a consultant and how consulting is used in HRD. In addition to discussing current practices, they also provide information regarding how consultants can invent and innovate. They conclude the chapter by identifying what you need to do to develop yourself as a consultant.

HRD is concerned with adults and learning, and the contributor to Chapter 6 provides material on the theory and practice of adult learning. He discusses some of the various theories of adult learning and how they relate to HRD. If you have heard about *androgogy* but were never sure what it was, the contributor provides background and examples of this concept of adult learning. He concludes by suggesting that learning should be accomplished in a climate of collaboration, rather than of competition. This may sound unrealistic, but his work is being used successfully in many leading organizations in the private sector.

Learning can be either incidental or intentional. As is explained in Chapter 7, HRD practitioners are concerned with intentional learning, so it becomes necessary to discuss how learning programs are designed. Learning in HRD, in contrast to the usual forms of adult education, begins with the intent of the organization and the learner. The contributor shares two different models, the critical events model, and the instructional systems development model. By no means are these the only models, but if you understand them you will be in a better position to make decisions regarding the models you can use in designing learning programs. The contributor also focuses on the competencies required by the HRD practitioner who wants to be an instructional designer.

Too frequently, the organization views the HRD practitioner as being a stand-up instructor. Of course, the delivery of the learning program is a crucial task, particularly where it is instructor mediated rather than machine mediated. In Chapter 8, the contributor discusses the roles of the instructor as a facilitator in the learning process and the classroom techniques necessary for succesful instruction. Actually, the instructor should not be a presenter but a real facilitator in the learning/teaching transaction. As the instructor has a direct relationship to the learner, the instructor must know what motivates people to learn and what factors inhibit the learning process. Learning should be evaluated to produce results without fear. The contributor also examines the emerging use of technology in the learning situation.

Facilitators of learning use a variety of different instructional strategies to make the learning as effective as possible. The term *instructional strategies* is meant to include all the methods, techniques, and devices that are used in the learning situation. There is a lack of agreement regarding those three terms, and the impact of electronic and computer resources has made differentiating among them an exercise in futility. Therefore, the term *instructional strategies* has arisen as the encompassing designation.

For this handbook, I have chosen to divide the strategies into two chapters. This does not mean that the strategies are not used together. Indeed, a good learning situation will use a variety of the strategies discussed in both chapters.

Chapter 9 deals with nonmedia strategies. The contributor provides a long list of these strategies, and even that does not cover them all. The strategies selected for inclusion are those that are most commonly used.

There is a staggering amount of media available for HRD programs, as described in Chapter 10. It is a specialized field, and the contributor begins by examining its terminology. This is followed by a discussion of some general characteristics of audiovisual instructional materials. A distinction is made between *hardware* and *software*, as applied to instructional media, and a comparison of the different media is provided. A much needed glossary concludes the chapter.

Chapter 11 focuses on computer-based learning. This is more than just another media form. As it is the newest, it will probably be less familiar to you. In addition, it is a unique form of instructional strategy, hence a separate chapter. The contributor helps you to understand the new HRD environment and the specialized vocabulary of the world of learning with and by the computer. He differentiates very specifically among computer-based learning, computer-assisted instruction, computer-managed instruction, and computer-supported learning resources and defines the differences among hardware, software, and courseware. He then discusses the computer as an instructional strategy within organizations and explains cost benefit analysis. The future workplace and the computer are also examined. Finally, there is a much needed glossary at the end of this chapter.

You are probably familiar with the adage, "We are all concerned about evaluation but do very little about it." This need not be the case. In Chapter 12, the contributor provides material on evaluation that can be useful immediately. The focus is on quantitative evaluation, and it is unfortunate that I could not locate a single person to write on qualitative evaluation and HRD. There are people who know qualitative evaluation, but they were not prepared to apply it to HRD—at least not yet. In this chapter, the contributor provides specific information on how to prepare for evaluation. This is necessary for if there has been no preparation of all concerned, there may be hostility and opposition to the evaluation effort. Various evaluation methods are discussed, and the chapter closes with material on that important issue of measuring the return.

In Chapter 13, still looking at the overview of the field, you can move into looking at yourself and your colleagues. This chapter deals with professional growth for those who are directly involved in providing HRD. The contributor provides an overview of this kind of professional development and then discusses some of the formal learning resources available. He emphasizes the need for self-directed learning for HRD practitioners as well as other learners.

Section Two—Program Areas of HRD

In Section 2 we look at some of the major program areas in HRD. Of course, there are many more than are listed here, but the purpose is to provide you with some information and insight into those that are most widely used. The order of presentation of these areas does not denote a hierarchy. There is no way or need to develop that mode of approach.

In Chapter 14, the contributor discusses programs related to the sales area. The chapter contains material that is relevant to sales activities regardless of the organization, the product, or the consumer. The contributor defines sales and sales management training (he does mean *training*, and not *education*) and its place in the HRD scheme. He provides insights into the evolution of sales HRD programs and the responsibilities of the sales HRD practitioner. He also discusses *education*—the preparation of people to enter the sales field. In that field, sales managers are crucial, and he discusses learning programs for sales managers. There are a variety of people involved in sales, such as distributors, dealers, and other customer contact personnel. All have HRD needs, and they are discussed in this chapter. As with many other fields, sales is changing; the contributor discusses programs to meet the future needs of sales people and sales managers.

It is generally agreed that the most active program area in HRD is the one that deals with those in executive, management, and supervisory positions. In Chapter 15, the contributor provides an overview of this program area and of the competencies required by people at management levels. He includes material on right-brain, left-brain research and how that material relates to HRD for managers. He provides a general design for building an HRD program for those levels and for designing an organization-specific program.

The technical area is sometimes considered to be at the opposite end of the spectrum from managers and executives. That is not entirely true. Many executives and managers come out of a technical background. In Chapter 16, the contributor provides a brief history of the field, with particular reference to HRD. He describes several technical HRD programs and how they function. The relationship to higher education is explored, for there is a close tie. The chapter ends with a look at the future of technical HRD, to the extent one can foresee it at this time.

The U.S. federal government is very involved in HRD. As one of our largest employers, it is important to know what is happening. Also, as taxpayers, you should be interested in how the government spends its HRD dollars. This is akin to being a stockholder in a private company, and we should all be just as interested. In Chapter 17, the contributor examines the philosophy, policies, and organization of HRD in the federal government. He provides some demographic data on HRD people (called *Employee Development Specialists*) and how they use learning technology. The total situation is viewed from the perspective of the government (employer) as well as of the individual.

Chapter 18 is unique, as it identifies a new area of HRD activity. Our public schools have provided learning experiences for teachers, administrators, custodians, and others for many years. Until the middle 1970s, however, the HRD activity was essentially one of sending employees to universities or to others who would provide some form of academic credit or similar recognition. With the significant changes in student enrollment and a slowdown in hiring teachers and administrators, the picture has changed. One result is the emerging role of the Staff Developer (HRD person) who is employed directly by the school system. In this chapter, the contributor discusses the evolving concepts and how HRD relates to organizational patterns in school systems. Based on his own research, he shares with us the emerging role of the Staff Developer and the future of HRD in school systems.

It was difficult finding a good title for Chapter 19—*special populations.* In the past, some of the designations would have been: *minorities, disadvantaged, underemployed, ethnic groups.* While this chapter deals with all of these, the focus is on how HRD has helped and can continue to help people in the United States improve their economic and social status. The designations may change, but it appears that the problem will be with us for many years to come. The contributors list some of the legislation and then focus on some specific examples of how HRD is used for various special populations. Rather than a theoretical treatment, this chapter focuses on actual experiences of the public and the private sectors.

There has been very little written about organized labor and HRD. The material in Chapter 20 relates to unions in any field of activity. In this chapter, a leading practitioner in the field provides a model of HRD activities in the labor movement. He describes current activities and discusses how important organized labor will be in the future, as it takes a more active role in HRD activities of employers, particularly in relation to productivity.

People from outside the United States are amazed at the volume of volunteering we do. While we take it for granted, to them, it is staggering. Most of the large voluntary organizations have some kind of HRD staff, ranging from one person to a very large central office and field office staff. Chapter 21 provides a discussion of the general management of voluntary organizations. This will probably be new material for many readers—particularly the movement of top management in voluntary organizations toward some form of strategic management. The contributor shares with us some ideas on how voluntary organizations have built effective HRD units. Specifically, there is a presentation of some of the key functions of the HRD unit as well as critical targets and programs. The chapter concludes with a look at how voluntary organizations are changing and how the HRD effort is responding to those changes.

Section Three—International Areas of HRD

When planning this book, there was a great deal of discussion on whether or not to include this section. My involvement in international HRD since 1959 may have influenced my insistence on its conclusion.

We are a *big blue marble, one world,* and *spaceship earth.* At one time, perhaps, we in the United States did have the edge on HRD and could help people in other countries learn how to use it. This is no longer the situation, for there is much we can learn from each other about HRD. Also, HRD efforts in one country can have many implications for other countries.

Chapter 22 begins with a discussion of global awareness. This is directly tied to HRD efforts, including the unique HRD program in which the unemployed learn how to be unemployed. This may be a harbinger of similar future efforts, though the term *unemployed* may be readily replaced by *underemployed.*

Chapter 23 is designed for those who are interested in working internationally. The contributor discusses culture and how it affects learning in the United States and in other countries. Specifically, he focuses on international HRD employment opportunities and the competencies needed by a successful HRD practitioner in the international field.

The next four chapters examine HRD efforts in specific parts of the world. The segments presented in this book are for convenience of organization. In practical terms, there is no way to segment the international scene without reference to other parts of the globe.

There were five contributors to Chapter 24, an attempt to get a number of different sources for HRD in Latin America. The various national efforts are examined, and their extent will probably come as a surprise to many of you. The efforts have been going on for years aned are vast. Political, social, and economic factors have in some cases impeded the progress that seemed possible through the national efforts.

In Chapter 25, the HRD efforts in Africa are examined. I called upon a United Nations expert in HRD to give us some insight into this continent's very complicated HRD situation. You will learn of the role of human resources in developmental strategies in Africa and the staggering need for HRD.

Asia is equally diverse. Therefore, Chapter 26 has been divided into three parts. The first deals with Asia in general and the Asian Productivity Organization. There is also material on the various national productivity organizations that are some of the major resources in providing HRD in their countries.

The second part of this chapter deals with HRD in Japan. Obviously, Japan has such a unique culture and economy that it is not helpful to deal with it as just another Asian country. In this part of the chapter, the background of HRD in Japan, particularly since World War II, is examined. The unique Japanese employment system, as it relates to HRD, is discussed. The changes that Japanese sources see for HRD in Japan are explored also.

Although smaller in size than the other areas discussed, Europe is also a diverse continent. Western Europe is discussed in Chapter 27. The contributor is from the United States, as I had great difficulty in finding a European who was willing or able to write about the whole area. This chapter's contributor interviewed a great many Europeans from many countries and synthesized the material into a brief chapter. He begins by presenting the trends, practices, and issues. (He found a good deal of agreement on definitions of HRD, as set forth in this book.) He examines learning in the Western European context and the emphasis on support systems. He also explores the vast array of skill-building HRD provided by employers. In many Western European countries, the government supports learning programs for adults, particularly those preparing to enter the work force. Some innovative practices are described in this chapter, and the impact of the future on HRD professionals in Western Europe is also discussed.

Section Four—Human Resource Areas Related to HRD

This book is focused, of course, on Human Resource Development. As noted in Chapter 1, there are other human resource activities in organizations. They are and should be related, but they provide different services—not *learning* as in HRD. Practitioners in these related areas require different competencies than those required of the HRD practitioner.

In Chapter 28, the focus is on Human Resource Management. The term *management*, is used for a variety of human resource activities, including a major focus on what is generally thought of as personnel. The contributor discusses these aspects as well as the relationship of HRM to organizational performance.

There is no question that Organization Development (OD) and Human Resource Development are related areas. In Chapter 29, the contributors examine the roots and realities of these different but related fields. They view both areas as necessary to contemporary organizations. There has been specialization in both fields, but there is also the need for cooperation between the fields. Both must consider technology, the changing nature of the work force, and the culture of the organization. Both have a great deal to contribute to organizations and individuals. The contributors present a case for cooperation between OD and HRD.

A related field that has grown significantly in the past and is likely to grow further is presented in Chapter 30—Career Development. Because there are many different interpretations of the field, the contributors provide an overview of the career development process. They show the components of a career development system and how HRD relates to that system. They indicate how career development can be used as a planning tool for HRD in identifying the need for individualized training, education, and development.

Section Five—The Future of HRD

As might be expected, the handbook concludes with a look at the future of HRD. There are many ways to do this, and the contributors to Chapter 31 present a unique and different approach. They first look at projections— one of the common ways to examine the future. They then stimulate our thinking by presenting paradoxes and paradigms.

Finally, a personal note. Bringing this handbook together has been a labor of love, with many of the frustrations one finds in a love affair. There have been disappointments and surprises.

It was not an easy task to obtain the contributions from the leaders in the field. They are all, obviously, very busy. Generally, they met deadlines and responded positively to the feedback on their original submissions.

Behind the scenes and only appearing as the editor of one chapter has been my wife Zeace. Those of you who know her are aware that we have worked together professionally for many years. She has an uncanny knack for simplifying and unravelling involved professional concepts and models. She has personally reviewed each chapter in detail. If you find this book readable as well as valuable, it is due in great part to her efforts.

College Park, Maryland   *Leonard Nadler*
March, 1984

Contents

Glossary

This glossary was provided to each of the contributors to this handbook. As a result, you will find that the words defined here are used the same way in each chapter. In a few instances, variations were necessary, and these have been indicated in the introduction to the specific chapter.

Adult Education—the field of adult learning that usually consists of programs conducted by schools, communities, and so forth. In a sense, Adult Education and Human Resource Development can be used interchangeably. At present, however, those working in business and industry do not see themselves as being in *Adult Education* and, therefore, prefer the term *Human Resource Development*.

Andragogy—a concept of how adults learn. (See Chapter 6 by Malcolm S. Knowles.)

Consultant—person who actually *consults*, whether internally or externally. It should not be used to designate anybody external to the organization who provides a specific *learning* program.

Development—learning that is not job-related, although it may have some impact on a present or future job.

Education—learning provided to improve performance on a future job.

Hierarchy of Needs—concept introduced by Abraham Maslow (see his book *Motivation and Personality*, Harper & Row, 1954). Essentially, Maslow helped us understand that there is a hierarchy of needs: physiological, security, social, ego, and self-actualization.

Human Resource Development (HRD)—organized learning, over a given period of time, to provide the possibility of performance change.

HRD Practitioner—general term used for those who work in the field of HRD.

HRD Manager—person in charge of the HRD unit within an organization.

International—programs that involve people from more than one country. It includes organizations that are sometimes labeled *transnational* or *multinational*.

Instructor of Instructors—traditionally termed *trainer of trainers*. Generally, this has been incorrect as there is no acceptable definition of a *trainer*. Does it include designing, managing, and so forth? Usually, it means the instruction of those who instruct others.

Learner—generic term for people in the learning situation. It includes such terms as: *student, participant,* and *trainee*.

Off-the-Shelf—term used for many companies (i.e., vendors) that develop good learning programs and market them broadly. There is nothing wrong with this, and the purchaser (i.e., internal HRD person) can benefit from the ability of the vendor to produce a program that would be much more costly if produced by the internal HRD staff. It is, however, a question of *caveat emptor*—let the buyer beware. There is little in the way of criteria that can be applied to discern the quality of the programs.

On-the-Job Training (OJT)—term coined during World War I. The concept has been extended since then and generally is applied to those learning activities conducted informally on the job site, usually by a supervisor or some person delegated that function by the supervisor.

School—term used to identify institutions from kindergarten to senior high school level.

Theory X and Theory Y—basic assumptions that people have of the workplace and people in it. The terms come from the work of Douglas McGregor (*The Human Side of Enterprise*, McGraw-Hill, 1959), which has been quoted and misquoted through the years.

Training—learning that is provided in order to improve performance on the present job.

Vendor—consultant. Frequently, the term *consultant* is inappropriately applied to those who are selling a product or service (e.g., conducting a training program). As consultants prefer that designation to *vendor*, it is unlikely that this will change—even though the term *vendor* provides more clarity regarding what is involved.

THE FIELD OF HUMAN RESOURCE DEVELOPMENT

CHAPTER ONE

Human Resource Development

LEONARD NADLER

The title of this handbook and all the material in it relate to human resource development (HRD), either directly or indirectly. Therefore, if readers start with this chapter, they will more readily understand the concepts presented.

This chapter deals in concepts rather than semantics. Unfortunately, we do have to get into some "wordsmithing" because of historical developments. When the author first presented the term *human resource development* in 1969, it did not immediately receive international acceptance. Actually, it was used infrequently, and then not in relation to the field that is the essence of this book. Over the years, many people have begun to use the term, without studying the concepts. The result is that HRD is now a commonly used term that has different meanings for different people.

In this chapter, we go back to its origin, in relation to what has been called the field of training and development to see how the concepts have evolved and changed. This chapter provides models for use in understanding HRD concepts and for identifying HRD practitioners.

Leonard Nadler (Ed.D.) is professor of adult education and human resource development, School of Education and Human Development, The George Washington University. He has been involved in the fields of HRD and adult education since 1938, except for three years working for an accounting company and two years as a cost accountant in an industrial plant. Prior to coming to GWU, he was a training officer with the Agency for International Development in Japan and Ethiopia. He works internationally in HRD and has worked in 31 different countries. He was a national board member of ASTD for five years and has served as president of three chapters. He has published five books and over 125 articles.

This chapter will set forth the framework of the field, as evidenced by the chapters that follow. Thus it would be useful for readers to begin here. Of course, some readers will prefer immediately to search out the chapters that meet a current need and then turn to this chapter.

OVERVIEW

Let us start by taking a look at the field of human resource development. This is not easy, for the term human resource development has become so attractive that some people are now using it to cover concepts other than those originally intended. I first introduced this term at the conference of the American Society for Training and Development (ASTD) in Miami in 1969. Rather than get into an involved argument as to who coined the term, I can only relate the historical fact noted in the previous sentence.

Definition

Some persons contend that there is no definition for HRD. I suggest they look at *Developing Human Resources*.[1] One need not agree to this definition, but there has in fact been a definition in print since 1970. It has been somewhat modified over the years, but the essence of it still holds true.

We need a definition if we are to communicate about the field. Since the middle 1970s there has been an influx of many new people into HRD and it has been a disservice to these people that too few of the leadership have sought to define the field. (Of course, the process of definition also means putting limits on what is included.)

Because we do have a definition (which follows), it has been possible to organize this handbook and evolve the glossary that is included. As a result the reader can turn to any chapter in this book and find that the words (e.g., *training, education*) mean the same thing.

Human resource development is defined as:

organized learning experiences
in a definite time period
to increase the possibility of:
    improving job performance
    growth

There are some people in a related field, adult education (AE), who will find that this definition does not differ markedly from the one used in

AE. In part, this is true. Both fields are concerned with adult learning. Rather than become involved, at this point, in differentiating between the fields, we can say that HRD is concerned mainly with learning provided by employers to their employees or by organizations to nonemployees, according to the goals of the organization (e.g., labor unions, associations).

Let us look more closely at each element of this definition and consider how the definition has been modified over the years.

"Organized learning experiences." People learn in a variety of ways. Some of them are *incidental*. You can learn by reading a newspaper, talking to a colleague, reading a book, watching television, traveling. Usually those activities are done for recreational purposes or to acquire information, in which case you do not have specific learning objectives, nor do you evaluate your experience to see if learning has taken place.

There are many other forms of incidental learning that take place in work situations. "Bull sessions," the grapevine, and people just traveling in the same carpool can all produce a variety of forms of incidental learning.

In HRD we are concerned with *intentional* learning, in which the learner has purposely engaged in a learning experience with objectives, a plan, and provision for evaluation.

Intentional learning is organized, but can be either formal or informal. When *formal*, it involves the use of facilities, equipment, and materials. Most often it is conducted in a group situation, though this is not essential.

It is also possible to have *informal* learning. But informal does not mean unorganized. Informal learning simply tends to be more individualized than formal learning. Many adults engage in such learning activities.[2] As our work force becomes composed of more individuals with high levels of schooling, we can expect the amount of informal learning to increase.

Informal learning is not limited to those who have high levels of schooling. On-the-job training (OJT) is a prime example of this kind of HRD. To be effective, OJT must be organized. By definition, however, it is conducted right on the job and usually on a one-to-one basis. The supervisor, or a member of the work unit designated by the supervisor, will be responsible for providing informal learning to those in the unit who need it in order to meet the output or production standards of that unit.

"In a definite time period." The time element is important, whether the learning is formal or informal. This part of the definition includes several factors. First, if a person is to learn, it is essential that a clearly identified and definite period be set aside for that learning. The period may vary from 15 minutes to a year or more, but the learner and those involved should all have a mutual expectation as to how long that learning period will be.

In the world of work, the time periods are usually less than a year. They will more often last either a few days or several hours a day over a period of several weeks. As the learner is in the work force, provision must be made for releasing the learner from the work situation. This can mean altering production schedules, providing for replacements, and making other necessary arrangements.

If the learner is to be sent away from the work site, there are other factors to be considered. Most of the adult learners involved in HRD will be married and may have dependents (children or parents who need attention). If the learner must change schedules or physically leave that geographic area for the learning, adequate provision must be made to cover the nonwork obligations. Obviously, the amount of time the learner will be away from work and home must be determined and specified at the outset.

Learning should be evaluated. To provide for this, there must be an identified point at which a particular phase of the learning has been completed. It is then possible to evaluate whether learning took place. This does not mean that all learning has stopped, only that a particular phase has been completed.

"To increase the possibility of."   Here we must pause, for there are two "possibilities" to be examined in the following sections. Before proceeding to them, let us first consider this phrase. HRD cannot and should not promise that as a result of the learning experience performance will change. This may sound like a radical statement until we look at the false promises that some in HRD have made.

Performance is affected by many forces, most of which are outside the control of the HRD people—and should be. HRD people do not supervise those outside the HRD unit. The supervisor is a prime factor in influencing employee performance. HRD people can provide the learning, but the translation into changed performance is beyond the scope of HRD. It is a function of the supervisor. Therefore, through HRD we can "increase the possibility," but the actuality lies in the area of supervision.

"Improving job performance."   Most of HRD is directly concerned with job performance—either the present job or a future job. It is job oriented, and the organization provides resources to HRD essentially to affect job performance. This is the major and most common use of HRD by an organization.

"Growth."　There are two elements of growth. The first is *growth in the organization*. That is, an organization can provide learning for employees that is not directly related to the present job or a future job. Rather, it is to help the individual grow so as to move generally with the organization. It does not mean career development, as that activity is usually related to future jobs in the organization. Rather, it is the recognition that change is constantly with us and that there are some people in the organization who should be stimulated to think of non–job-related growth, so they will be ready to move with the organization in any number of unpredictable directions.

The second element is *individual growth*. This area enlarges and shrinks depending upon the economy and the nature of the work force. In essence, it concerns a variety of non–job-related learning experiences people seek to achieve inner satisfaction. Whether it is the responsibility of the employing organization to provide this is arguable, however. It is a decision that will reflect the culture of the country and the organization as well as the availability of resources for this kind of learning.

History

There are still those who think that HRD is a new field or one with a short history. Of course, this will depend upon the definition one uses. Given the definition discussed earlier, HRD has been around since the first caveman took his son aside and taught him how to tie a sharpened piece of obsidian to a piece of straight wood to make a spear. True, it was not an employer-employee relationship, but it was certainly job related—related to the job of the caveman at that dawn of history.

HRD has a long history, but it is generally imbedded in other fields under a variety of other names.[3] The reason, perhaps, is that only since the early 1940s has there been sufficient concern about the field, and only since that time can we find written material directly related to the field.

A search of the literature will indicate that one must look for terms such as *training, vocational education,* and *apprenticeship*. Despite the plethora of written material directly related to HRD, let us take a quick trip through history to see how the field evolved. I will call it "HRD from the beginning," although the term was not applied to the field until 1969. This approach will be easier than trying to deal with the myriad terms that will be encountered.

Ancient Times.   We can move very quickly through the history of human beings from the beginning to about 1800. This does not mean that there was no HRD, but that the changes were comparatively insignificant when viewing the total picture. The main large organizations using HRD were the religious groups, the military, and governments. In each of these, there was a well-organized HRD activity, though the documentation is sparse.

For some occupations, HRD did exist, commonly in a one-on-one situation. A new seaman on a ship would be taught his various tasks by serving alongside an older, experienced, seaman. This was the common practice in many occupations. Slowly the practice became more formalized into an apprenticeship program, particularly in those occupations requiring craft skills.

Even as that period ended and the era of mercantilism began, newly required arithmetic and record-keeping skills, were mostly still taught by having the new worker serve under an older and presumably more skilled worker.

Factory System.   About 1800 we emerged into an era that has been labeled the Industrial Revolution. For our purposes, this meant the emergence of manufacturing systems—that is, the tendency to group a number of people within the same building, doing related work. It also meant a breakdown of some of the previous types of work relationships that had been built on "cottage industries."

We need not go through the whole history of the nineteenth century, but in the early years a phenomenon developed that is not unlike what we are experiencing today. New technology was introduced, and it was no longer possible to have the new worker learn merely by being assigned to an older worker. The older worker did not have the competencies required to work on the new machinery and processes. It became necessary to introduce a more formal type of learning for new workers. The older workers also required learning if they were to retain their jobs.

In the United States, we saw the development of mechanics and mercantile institutes. They were new institutions and the forerunners of the schools for adults that are part of our modern HRD history. These new institutions catered to young men who had not yet entered the work force. Employers who needed skilled workers, in larger numbers than ever before, could no longer afford the practice of providing their own. Thus they turned to these new institutions to provide workers with skills that probably did not previously exist within their own work force.

Although at this time, we lack documentation, it is probable that some employers began to designate some in-company people to devote a significant portion of their time to instructing others. They were the pioneers of HRD in the workplace.

By the middle of the nineteenth century, the Industrial Revolution made its impact on agriculture in the form of machinery that had not previously existed. This, in addition to other advances in agriculture, produced the same situation as that in the factories. It became more difficult for a farmer to exist with only the knowledge he had gained from his father. He had to seek outside help if he was to farm effectively and competitively.

This situation was one of the many reasons for the Morrill Land Grant Act of 1862. This monumental piece of legislation established the A & M (agricultural and mechanical) colleges in each state. Soon thereafter came the County Extension agents in agriculture. In a way they were also HRD people: a significant part of their task was to help the farmers improve their methods of agricultural production.

1900–1920.   This period saw the major thrust in industrial production in the United States. As was to be expected, it also brought with it an increase in HRD. As more and more of the population began to work in large factories, it was possible for employers to provide the necessary learning for employees—new and old. HRD was still, however, a fairly low-key function. The waves of immigration provided continual sources of new labor. In some cases, the United States was very fortunate, for we received skilled labor from some of the European countries. In the steel industry, for example, the "older" immigrants (sometimes having arrived only a year earlier) instructed the newer immigrants who came from the same country.

During this period we also saw the development of learning programs by unions. Essentially, they were HRD programs to make the officers more efficient and to help the members understand the function of the union. Many of the unions were craft oriented. This meant that the worker had to achieve a satisfactory competency level before being allowed to join the union. Therefore, few of the HRD efforts of unions were devoted to job skills.

By the end of this period, we had experienced World War I. One of the major outcomes, from the viewpoint of HRD, was the recognition that work-related activities could be taught quickly and effectively. It was the first national recognition of the contribution that HRD could make to the workplace.

1920–1940. This period is marked by many significant events related to HRD. First, there was the postwar situation, followed by serious work that had an impact on HRD, and then the Great Depression.

After World War I, some employers recognized the possibilities of HRD and began to provide programs. The federal government was very active in this area, and in 1938 the importance of HRD was recognized when President Roosevelt signed an executive order stating that the government, as an employer, should provide HRD for its employees.

In the private sector at that time, given the understanding of industrial relations that existed, HRD was seen essentially as a tool of the company: there was comparatively little concern for the individual. A major concern was to make production both more efficient and effective. To this end, some companies began to bring in outside people to provide some answers. At that time, they were called "researchers" though today we might call them "consultants." They were asked to consider various ways in which the workplace, including people, could be manipulated to increase production.

Among the most famous of these efforts were the Hawthorne studies[4] conducted at the Hawthorne Plant of the Western Electric Company in Cicero, Illinois. Without going into detail, this series of studies started out by examining the physical aspects of the workplace (e.g., color of the walls) and then moved into the psychological aspects (e.g., breaks, group pressure). The studies gave rise to a field that today is called *industrial psychology*.

There was much in the studies, limited as they were, that had implications for the HRD field. The studies, however, were terminated toward the end of the decade of the 1920s, at about the time we entered the Great Depression. During the Depression few companies did much about HRD. There were plenty of skilled workers available, and few companies would spend very limited resources on HRD when they could get the skills they needed by firing some workers and hiring others.

The activity around HRD moved from the private sector to the public sector. Although no program had a *single* objective, the Civilian Conservation Corps (CCC) did have job skills as part of its program. Many of the Work Projects Administration (WPA) projects were designed not only to provide jobs but also to provide workplace skills to a work force with more than 25% unemployment.

Toward the end of this period, as we became the "arsenal for democracy" (Franklin Roosevelt's words), jobs became more available. Rather than conjecture on what might have happened, let us confine ourselves to history.

World War II. This period of five years had a tremendous impact on HRD. In the private sector it became necessary for industry to expand rapidly. At the same time the usual work force began to shrink. At first it was the young men who were drafted. When hostilities broke out on December 7, 1941, there was an even more significant impact. Just when we needed to increase production, fewer young males were available.

We turned to alternative sources of labor. Among these were women, the traditionally unemployed, and older men. Previously, each of these groups had not been in the work force in significant numbers. This may seem unusual to the reader of today, so allow me a brief digression that could be helpful.

The concept of women working in the United States, outside of agriculture, was comparatively unknown. This does not mean there were no women in the work force, but they were usually young women who worked until they married. Employers were loathe to hire women for any but the most menial and low-paying jobs. There was certainly little thought of careers or even jobs that required significant skills.

The economists used to estimate, and some still do, that about 3% of the work force would always be unemployed or underemployed. These would be people, it was thought, who would work only until they had some money to spend. Then they would leave the work force and only re-enter it when their money ran out. This group included many of the ethnic and racial groups who were the victims of discrimination.

"Older" men meant anybody over 40. It may seem peculiar to us today, but at that period in our history it was the general practice not to hire a man over 40. Therefore, if for any reason a man became unemployed after 40, he had practically no possiblitiy of getting another meaningful job. He would revert to the underemployed or unemployed category—not because he did not want to work, but because few companies would hire him.

With the war effort, it became necessary to recruit workers from these traditionally unemployed groups who had been discriminated against. It was a move founded in desperation. Indeed, our government at first tried to meet the labor shortage by granting deferments to those working in "war industries." It soon became evident, however, that the cost in manpower lost to the armed forces required other approaches. We had to look to these alternative workers.

It became obvious, very rapidly, that the three groups discussed earlier could make a vital contribution to production. It became even more obvious when HRD was provided. These three groups previously had very little opportunity to learn work-related skills. Or, as in the case of the over-40 group, their skills were obsolete. Teachers were recruited out of vocational programs in the secondary schools and put to work teaching specific job-related skills. HRD had really arrived. It became obvious that most of the people in these groups could learn and could become productive members of the organization.

As more people became involved in providing HRD, they felt the need to speak to others in similar jobs with related problems. Local and state HRD organizations were formed. By 1942 there were many such active organizations, and they came together to form the American Society of Training Directors (ASTD). It was not really a membership organization, but rather a confederation of some of the local and state organizations. There were enough of such organizations, however, that they formed and built an organization that today is the American Society for Training and Development. (Some of the state organizations still exist—some of which still feel they are part of a confederation.)

1945–1960.   After the end of World War II, there was a slight decline in HRD, as other matters had higher priority. The setback was only temporary, however, since a lesson had been learned. Those in management positions, as well as those in first-line supervision in the private sector, had firsthand experience with HRD and the contribution it could make to an organization. There were vast opportunities for making HRD an important part of the operations of every large organization.

Unfortunately, this development did not take place. It is possible to conjecture about this, but documentation is lacking. It is probable that the HRD people in organizations had some limitations. Some of them who had come from the school systems never fully understood the workplace. They stayed but retained some of their previous behavior. For example, they reported their activities in terms of "students," "hours of instruction," and similar school-oriented expressions. They printed brochures and catalogs and scheduled regular times for enrolling in courses. This is not meant to be overly critical: that was simply the stage of development of the field.

Those who came from the staff or line could not wait to get back to their former positions. Particularly the line people rushed to return. The cost-accounting terminology of that period was to break the work force down into two categories: productive and nonproductive. The latter were the staff people, including HRD. Management could be considered nonproductive, but when HRD people (and those in similar activities) were put into that category, to them it meant second-class citizenship in the organization.

As if to emphasize this, many HRD units were given a unique and special task in the 1950s. They were asked to develop programs in "human relations." At that time, those programs focused on getting people to like each other. The thinking was that if people liked each other they would work together in a more efficient manner. It was also the period of the introduction of "sensitivity training"[5] into the workplace. Some HRD units devoted vast resources to such activities.

In general, by the end of this period, HRD was viewed as a soft area within an organization. It did not, in some cases, seem to make much of a contribution to the organization—although it was a nice thing to have.

1960–1973. This was the period of rapid movement in high technology in the United States. We reacted to the Soviet sputnik with massive efforts to achieve some kind of leadership in the space race. HRD efforts increased as we moved into project groups and task forces to cope with the challenge of the new technology.

At the same time, there was an increase in other, completely non-technological, programs. One attempted to take behavioral science into the workplace, and a new term appeared—*applied* behavioral science. It also provoked an effort that later became called *organization development* (OD). This was, in part, a reaction to HRD programs that appeared to be effective but made little or no impact on the workplace.

Put another way, people could learn but then found that there were inhibiting factors in the workplace that minimized or wiped out any possibility of applying that learning. Attention began to be focused on efforts to change the workplace as one way of improving performance. It was accompanied by increased interest in people, as well as in the technical aspects of organization.

At the start of this period we also were influenced by Douglas McGregor[6] and others who were espousing participative management. As a result, there were many HRD programs that contained the work of McGregor and others, but by the end of this period such programs were receiving strong criticism—to such an extent that it became difficult to find many significant examples of the use of the participative approach.

At just about the same time, the influence of the Japanese in the international marketplace became an important factor. Productivity had increased phenomenally in Japan while decreasing in many other industrializied countries. U.S. executives and managers were trying to probe the secret of Japan's productivity. Unfortunately, too few attempts were made to try to understand the Japanese system in terms of culture and history, including the history of more than 5000 Japanese coming to the United States in the decade of 1955–1965.[7]

On the domestic front, we saw increased efforts focused on programs related to the "disadvantaged" and to equal employment opportunity. The range of programs included Manpower Development and Training Administration (MDTA), Economic Opportunity Act (which included the Job Corps), and the Comprehensive Employment and Training Administration (CETA). These were government-led and -funded activities. Within the private sector, there were also efforts. It is unfortunate that we cannot report that many HRD leaders took note of these programs at that time or tried to work with them despite the fact that all of these programs were based on HRD.

1973 to the present. Significant changes began to occur at the start of this period, and we can expect some of them to continue well into the 1980s. The year 1973 was selected as the start of this period because it marked the beginning of a new era. The era does not yet have a name, although we can be sure that future historians will give it a label.

The Organization of Petroleum Exporting Countries (OPEC) was organized in the early 1960s, but it was not until October, 1973, that OPEC made itself felt in a political move that had vast economic repercussions: the oil embargo. The price of petroleum soared, and world economies shook. In the space of about a week, power had shifted from petroleum-consuming nations to petroleum-producing nations. In the decade that followed, there were shifts back and forth, and the power of the OPEC countries was tested many times. Even if OPEC should fall, however, few predict that we will return to the pre-1973 situation.

At first, the economic repercussions produced recessions in many developed countries. HRD programs, as well as other activities, felt the pinch. As we move through the later years, we find an interesting phenomenon. The OPEC situation had caused increased interest in physical and financial resources and less concern about human resources. After the first impact, however, we find an *increasing* interest in the human resources.

It is difficult to pinpoint the exact reasons for this change. Some conjectures rely upon demographics. The first wave of the post-World War II baby boom was entering the labor force. With it came different concerns than had previously been known.[8] There were probably other factors that are yet to be uncovered by research. It is known, however, that more organizations became concerned about HRD, as evidenced by the increase in positions available and the significant increase in the membership of ASTD.

HRD was not the only area affected. The whole field of human resources felt the influence. New positions began to emerge, such as vice president for human resources, director of HRD, and human resource manager.

HUMAN RESOURCES IN ORGANIZATIONS

As can be expected, the increased concern about human resources has brought about a proliferation of titles and an overlap in operational areas. It is not possible, therefore, to provide a set of definitions that will stand the test of time. Part of this development is positive, for increased concern with human resources is important for all organizations. There is also a negative aspect, in that the constant changes make it difficult for us to communicate among ourselves as well as with management.

Human Resource Activities

There have been many attempts to categorize the field, but few have achieved general recognition. In 1983 ASTD pictured the field but it can be expected that this vision will change.

ASTD still uses the term *training and development*. It would be useless to try to identify the reasons for retaining this archaic and inadequate title when Human Resources Development includes training, education, and development. (A distinction among these terms will be discussed later in this chapter.) Extremely significant is the definition, or focus, as it is called: Developing—*through learning*—key competencies and motivations of the work force for current and future jobs. (The emphasis is mine.)

This is the first time that ASTD has officially recognized that the unique contribution of HRD is based on *learning*.

This does not mean that others do not use learning to accomplish their goals within the organization. It does mean that they are encouraged to look to the HRD unit to provide professional assistance when learning is a factor. This definition of the field is crucial, but not yet fully appreciated. By accepting this definition, we can also accept that the major role of HRD in the organization is to provide for learning, but not necessarily to do the actual instruction.

There is an interdependency among the human resource activities within an organization that requires some knowledge of the work that each does in order to recognize the unique and special contribution of each to the goals of the organization and the individuals. Unfortunately, interdependency can also foster competition. This is wasteful and should be avoided, although that is not always possible.

The reality of organizational life is that there is still the tendency for empire building. This is observed in terms of the number of people reporting to a particular individual, the size of the budget, or the amount of floor space in the plant or office. Therefore, some of the human resource units tend to try to include all the functions possible so as to have the biggest empire.

We can see this in the struggle for control of work force planning within the organization. Traditionally, this has been within the purview of the *personnel* office (although the titles have been changing). For a variety of reasons that need not be discussed here, the human resource planning function now crops up in a variety of units, including HRD. There is no question that the HRD unit has a strong and vital role to play in the process of human resource planning and the implementation of the plans. But is it a human resource *development* function? I do not believe so, for it is possible to do human resource *planning* without any learning. The implementation probably cannot take place without learning unless the plan is to fire the existing work force and recruit and select new people.

Another factor that adds reality to the confusion deals with the people involved in the human relation functions—their own perceptions and concepts. There are still those who believe that HRD is part of the personnel operation. More recently, "personnel" has been called human resource *management*, though even here there is a lack of agreement. Some use this term in place of *personnel*, while others use it to encompass the entire range of human resource activities. These varying perceptions, unless clearly expressed, lead to guerrilla warfare within an organization and to a dissipation of resources.

One approach is to identify the competencies needed for each HRD activity. Of course there are some overlaps, as all are focused on people. More important, however, are the areas where the competencies are unique to that one segment. An organization that does not have people with the appropriate competencies will have difficulty achieving the benefits of that segment. The labels can change at will, but if the competencies are missing the organization has been deprived.

Unfortunately, that is exactly what happens when HRD is seen merely as part of one of the other segments rather than as an activity unto itself. It is easy, then, to give somebody the title but not to look for the competencies.

This has given rise to the criticism that managers do not understand HRD. Of course, if we do not take the time to give them a specific definition and examples, we should not be amazed or alarmed at their confusion. Also, if the people doing HRD lack the necessary competencies, the impression is spread that there are no competencies and that nobody can do HRD because it is not an identifiable field.

The view in this handbook is that human resource development has a unique and identifiable function. It provides learning to employees and nonemployees in order to help organizations and individuals achieve their goals.

ACTIVITY AREAS IN HRD

There are specific areas of activity within HRD. As will become clear in this discussion, it is important to make the distinctions. This too emphasizes the need for some clarity in labels. By using *training and development*, one is forced to ask: Where is education? The answer can only be found in defining the three terms and distinguishing among them.

Distinguishing among Them

The three activity areas are learning for

Improved performance on the present job of the individual;
Preparation of an individual for an identified job in the not-too-distant future; and
General growth not related to any specific job.

As will be seen, these are three distinct and separate learning activities. When they are not identified or separated, the learning is less effective.[9]

For purposes of facilitating communication, a label is applied to each as follows:

Training = learning related to present job
Education = learning to prepare the individual for a different but identified job
Development = learning for growth of the individual but not related to a specific present or future job

Let us not waste time and energy on contesting the labels. Some purists will go back to the Latin derivations, but that has little use for us in this situation. There are those who contend that, given the definitions, the sequence should be training, development, education. If that helps them make the distinction, they should by all means use it.

If you have glanced at the glossary in this handbook, you know that the terms have been defined, and you can have confidence that they are being used within those definitions by all the contributors. One benefit becomes obvious—no matter which chapter you read, you know what the author is saying when using those terms. It would be so helpful if we could find similar agreement in the workplace to facilitate communication among HRD people and with others in the organization.

Returning to the definitions, there are many benefits to be derived from making these distinctions.[10] Let us look at only three at this time, although others will be discussed later.

1. *Objectives.* The objectives are vastly different when one looks at the definitions. This helps the managers and HRD people make a decision. If the goal is to improve performance on the present job, then training must be conducted, and evaluation should be made in terms of improved performance. If education is the goal, then we cannot evaluate performance until the individual moves to the new job. If the objective is development, we should not expect a change in performance as, by definition, development is not job related.

2. *Mutual Expectations.* This leads us directly into exploring the expectations of all concerned. To begin with, if the HRD people do not know the specific objective, as distinguished above, it becomes very difficult to design or select the appropriate learning program. If the intent is development, then job skills are not relevant to that particular learning program. If the intent is education, then provision must be made for reinforcement, as the learner will not be using the learning immediately but at some future time. Without reinforcement there will be fade-out. We have often heard from a participant, "I don't know why I'm here. I was just told to show up." Minimally, the participant, supervisor, and HRD practitioner should be in agreement as to whether the learning is for training, education, *or* development.

3. *Responsibility.* It is too easy to say that the responsibility for learning rests with the learner. As the organization is allocating resources for the learning, somebody in the organization must assume some responsibility. Given the definitions above, it becomes obvious that

responsibility for training will be with the immediate supervisor. That is the person who is directly concerned with the current level of performance of the employee. Responsibility for education will rest with those at the managerial level, for they are the ones who know the future direction of the organization and the human resource needs. It is also a policy matter. "Do we promote from within or meet our needs by external recruitment?" If the policy is internal movement, then education is essential. If the policy is external recruitment, then there will be fewer resources allocated to education. Development should be the concern of the higher managerial or executive levels. They should be concerned with the general tenor of their work force at all levels and interested in providing growth for the long range. Development, for a variety of reasons, is not well understood. More will be said specifically about this area in a later section.

Now let us look more closely at each of the activity areas.

Training

As noted earlier, training is defined as *learning related to the present job*. It may be asked why an organization should provide learning related to the present job for somebody who is already working on that job? There are a variety of reasons.

Purpose.   Let us assume that the human resource office concerned with recruitment has done a good job in obtaining new employees. Those employees will have the necessary competencies, but these may still need to be "fine tuned" to the specific organization. The same kind of job, in various organizations, will have differences. A good salesperson may have all the competencies required, but in a new organization different forms and procedures must be learned if the new employee is to be effective.

For those already working for the organization, there are also reasons for providing training. It is all too easy for even a good employee to lose some skills over a period of time. This becomes very evident when an experienced employee is no longer working up to standard. Without training, it is probable that the employee will fall further and further below standard. This can result in the firing of a good employee when all that was required was training.

Another reason for training employees on their present jobs is the impact of technology. The job may be essentially unchanged, but new techniques, processes, and materials require appropriate training to respond to those changes.

In general, training is needed when there is a problem to which learning is an appropriate response.[11] Of course, not all problems faced by managers call for a training response—but many do.

Learners.   Learners for training should be selected by the immediate supervisor, who knows the problem and who is seeking the results.

Too often, training is seen as either a reward or a punishment. As a reward, the supervisor may be sending the learner off to a pleasant experience at some off site location. Neither the supervisor nor the employee expects much to happen in relation to the job. This is usually the case when there is no identified problem or need.

As punishment, an employee may be sent to a learning experience "to get your head screwed on straight." Obviously, this does not present a workable learning objective. It implies that the training program will do something to the employee whether the employee agrees or not.

Support System.   It is essential that the learner, supervisor, and HRD people are all in agreement as to the purpose of the training. It is equally important that the supervisor build in the supports to ensure that the learning will be used on the job as soon as possible. Without that, fade-out occurs.

Evaluation.   There is constant concern about evaluation. When using this model, evaluation becomes much more specific. If the purpose is training, as defined, then the evaluation should be in terms of improved performance on the job. It should be possible to see immediate changes. If not, two basic questions should be asked: Was the purpose training or something else? What was the nature of the improved performance that was expected?

To evaluate training effectively, the supervisor must be directly involved. Without that involvement, it is not possible to evaluate whether or not the expected change took place.

Education

As defined earlier, education is *learning to prepare the individual for a different but identified job.* The distinction between training and education is that the former is for the present job, the latter for a different job.

In this context, it is a different job within a reasonable period of time. As the work to be done within an organization changes, education should be provided for a job for which the performance is identified and specified.

Purpose.   Education is designed to enable an employee to learn about a different job within the same organization. Generally, the different job is a promotion, but not always. Given what we are learning about burnout, it is apparent that there are people who are seeking a different job within the same organization, but not necessarily a promotion. That does not mean that they would not like to be promoted but that there are other alternatives. This is sometimes referred to as *internal mobility*. Provision is made for employees to move to other jobs, laterally, rather than to other organizations. It also keeps the organization from having to seek new employees from outside.

A great deal has been said about technology, but one aspect has not received sufficient attention. One impact of technology is that new jobs are being created that did not exist before. Of course, it is possible to place an employee in a new job and then provide training. At that point, it may be discovered that the employee is not suitable for the new job and may not even like it. It is much more efficient and much less costly to provide education before the employee is moved into the new job.

During downsizing, another purpose arises for providing education. The plan may be to move an employee to a lower-level job. This cost saving may be lost if the employee cannot function effectively on that lower-level job. By providing education, it may be possible to determine that possibility before the change has been made.

Usually, education should be provided for those moving either upwards or laterally in the organization.

Learners.   Learners for education should be selected in a very different fashion from those selected for training. For education, the organization should seek those who are being actively considered for the new job. If this point has not been made clear to the employee and supervisor, the results are confusion and wasted resources. In addition, the HRD function develops a poor reputation, and deservedly so.

Providing education does not necessarily produce the *crown prince* (or *princess*) effect. That is, being sent to a learning experience, clearly identified as education, does not mean that a job change will result. It does provide the opportunity for a tryout by the identified employee and perhaps even some kind of assessment by the organization as to how that employee might function in the different job. Either or both may decide that a job movement would be inappropriate.

In education, all parties should realize that the learning is not designed to improve performance on the present job. This does not mean that some of what is learned might not be useful, but that is not the purpose. The learner is encouraged to think in terms of the future job.

Providing education for potential supervisors, for example, can be extremely helpful to the individual and the organization. Moving from subordinate to supervisor is probably the most traumatic move in the work force. It is the first step at which one is no longer responsible only for one's own output, but rather for the output of others. The measure of effectiveness is how well the others being supervised perform.

If used incorrectly, education can produce exactly the wrong results. Picture a supervisor who has an employee, X, who is not particularly productive. The HRD unit sends out a list of courses available, and the supervisor recognizes that this is a good way to minimize the poor production of employee X. It is no great loss to the unit if employee X is not present, and it can look good on the supervisor's record that an employee was sent to a learning experience. This is particularly true if the budget resides in the HRD unit rather than in the line unit.

After several such experiences, somebody in personnel looks at the record of employee X and notices that the organization has invested money in employee X by providing education. The investment can pay off only if employee X is promoted. The result—a low-performing employee gets promoted by having been sent to several education programs. Thus it is essential that education be used more effectively by the supervisors and HRD people in the organization.

Support System. The support system for education is different and more difficult than for training. The principal difference is that, in training, the present supervisor of the employee is known and can be directly involved in supporting the training.

An education program requires more work on the part of the HRD practitioner and the supervisor, but the results will be well worth the effort. There are essentially two possible situations: (1) the future supervisor of the learner is known, and (2) the future supervisor is not known.

In the first situation, the learner is being prepared for a specific vacancy, and it is usually only a matter of time before the learner will be placed on that specific job. The future supervisor is waiting for that person to come to the job. All the elements about the new job are known, such as where it will be located, who the other employees will be, and so forth. In this situation, building a support system for education is not too difficult. The HRD practitioner can provide reinforcing materials so that there will be no significant loss of learning between the time the learning is completed and the time the learner actually moves into the new job. The HRD practitioner can also arrange for meetings between the learner and the future supervisor. These can be reinforcing, and might even identify additional learning needs for that specific situation.

In the second situation, the learner is being prepared for a new job, but it has not been possible to identify the specific new supervisor. This happens when there are many possibilities, and it depends on which job opens up first. In this situation, there should be some minimal reinforcement by the HRD practitioner to minimize or avoid fade-out of learning.

Evaluation.   Education must be evaluated in a very different way from training. Where the HRD people do not make the distinction between these two kinds of learning, they have built an evaluation trap for themselves.

As the purpose of education is a future job, it is not really possible to evaluate performance until the employee moves into that future job. We can, of course, evaluate whether the employee has learned. We can even build in simulations and other learning strategies to test out the possibility of performance in the new and different situation. However, until the employee actually gets on the job, we cannot really evaluate the HRD program. There are too many job variables that cannot be accounted for in an artificial situation, no matter how well constructed.

An added difficulty in evaluation is the fact that the supervisor of the employee in the new situation is different from the supervisor who originally sent the employee. The receiving supervisor may have had little choice in selecting the employee and may have little interest in evaluation. It may seem to the receiving supervisor that what is being evaluated is the supervisor, not the learner or the application of the learning. This can be a delicate situation, and the HRD practitioner is advised to involve the receiving supervisor in evaluation as soon as possible.

Development

As defined earlier, development is *learning for growth of the individual but not related to a specific present or future job.* The important distinction is that development is *not* job related. As with other learning, this does not mean that what is learned during development cannot be applied to a present or future job. It is just not the essential purpose.

As development is not job related, it proves to be an area of confusion for organizations—and HRD practitioners. It is important that the latter group understand this type of learning activity, for it does have much to offer in keeping organizations and individuals on the cutting edge.

Purpose. Development is designed to help individuals grow, through learning in general, not necessarily in specific directions. It relates to two areas: (1) the organization and (2) the individual.

Organizations are constantly growing and changing. It is necessary that they do so if they are to remain alive and well. It is generally not possible to foretell the future directions and needs of organizations, just as no one can accurately foretell the future. Rather, to be vital and strong, it is essential for organizations to employ people with an understanding of possible futures. This can be done through appropriate learning.

Individuals are also constantly growing and changing. Most individuals need challenges and opportunities to grow through learning. If the organization does not provide such opportunities, individuals may seek them elsewhere, or they may join an organization that does provide growth through learning.

It is unfortunate that the word *development* is used too loosely and therefore does not have the impact it should. You will find writers and speakers using the term *management development* when they really mean training or education for managers.

We know that those adults who are in a constant learning posture are more likely to learn, whatever the subject matter. As indicated in other parts of this handbook, we have many *theories* of adult learning. There does appear to be some agreement that learning is a skill. The more one practices that skill, the easier it is to learn. Keeping employees of an organization in a state of learning readiness can have many benefits for the individual and the organization.

Learners. It is not as easy to identify who should be involved in development as it is with training and education. In development, there is no sharp focus as to need or subject matter, as in the other two learning activity areas.

Development should not be exclusively for top-level employees. Through development, it is possible for an organization to identify employees at all levels who have great potential for learning and for using that learning.

Of course, one would expect to find more development offered to upper-level employees—particularly the learning that is related to possible organizational futures.

Support System. It is not necessary to build a support system for development, as there is no intention to support the learner on the present or future job. We should ensure, however, that there is not a destructive system. The employee should not return to the job from development and be asked to apply that learning to the job. Neither should development be looked upon as a vacation or a perk from the organization. Rather, development is a firm and positive indication of the commitment of the organization to growth for many, if not all, of its employees. Development should become the norm and be generally accepted. It is part of the *quality of work life* that has become such an important issue in the workplace.

Evaluation. It is possible to evaluate if learning took place in a development program. This element of evaluation is possible in any HRD activity. For development it is not possible to evaluate change in job performance, for that is not the objective of development. If job performance, present or future, is a purpose, then the appropriate activity is training or education and should be handled in that fashion.

The lack of evaluation should not be a deterrent to providing development. Obviously, it is a limitation, because there is a tendency to try to evaluate most aspects of organizational life, particularly in the quantitative mode. Consider evaluating development qualitatively. As we develop measures for that type of evaluation, perhaps it will be possible to apply some of those techniques to development. That has not yet happened.

HRD PEOPLE—ROLES

Let us turn our attention to those who serve in HRD capacities within their organizations. The material presented here focuses on the internal people. That does not mean that there are no external people—there are many of them, but probably not as many as internal. Also, we have substantial research on internal people that is lacking when we look at the external people.

As will be seen from the model presented here and used throughout the handbook, some of the roles can be readily filled by external people.

Research

There is significant research dating back to at least 1955.[12] My own work was done in 1958 when I tried to identify what colleges and universities could do for "training directors" (the term in use at that time).[13]

In 1964, I was asked to join the faculty of The George Washington University, School of Education (now Education and Human Development), to implement my study. The university had been offering courses and degrees in *employee training*, but had never had a full-time professor. I became the first.

At about the same time, I was asked to make a presentation at the annual meeting of the Training Officers Conference in Washington, D.C. My friend and colleague Gordon Lippitt was also asked to be on the program. We reviewed some of my research, and others', on what training directors do. We found that we needed some way of communicating the total picture to others. I had researched what training directors do. The grouping produced a series of roles and subroles.[14] I had also researched the "know-how" of training directors. Today this is referred to as "competency."

I am not maintaining that my original research of 1958 is still completely valid today. It has been supplemented by the research of others and through my own experiences. The basic model, modified and updated, is valid and valuable.

There are two important factors to keep in mind in reviewing and using this model. The first is that it is a pragmatic model. That is, it is based on the real world of work as it is. The model does not deal with wishful thinking. It does not deal with the "ideal" situation. This model has stood the test of time specifically because it does change to reflect the changes in the real world of work.

The second factor is that the model focuses on the internal HRD practitioner. This does not mean that it cannot be used, with modification, by an external person. The model in its present form, however, has been researched and used in connection with internal HRD practitioners.

The Roles Model

The model, as revised up to the present, indicates three major roles and twelve subroles. They are:

Learning specialist.
Facilitator of learning

Designer of learning programs

Developer of instructional strategies

Manager of HRD.

Developer of HRD policy

Supervisor of programs

Maintainer of relations

Developer of HRD personnel

Arranger of facilities and finance

Consultant.

Expert

Advocate

Stimulator

Change agent

The order of presentation is not meant to reflect any hierarchy. Usually when presenting this schema in learning situations, I use a circle to avoid the notion that any role is more important than any other role. The presentation here generally represents the historical order in which the roles emerged.

Before proceeding to a fuller discussion of the roles and subroles, however, we should look at another model.

The ASTD Model

In 1983, the American Society for Training and Development (ASTD) completed a study (commonly referred to as the *competency study* or the *McLagan study*, for Pat McLagan who was the study director).[15]

That study group selected the fifteen key training and development roles and used that listing with the 300 respondents in the study. It is interesting to note what we find when we compare this with the model cited earlier. For purposes of clarifying the two models, I shall refer to the *Nadler model* and ask your forebearance if that sounds self-aggrandizing.

Let us look now at the starred items.

The *individual development counselor* is responsible for planning career actions. Including this as an HRD function raises the issue of where in the organization is the best place for the function of counseling individual employees about career goals. One point of view is that to be effective the counselor must be in a position to know where the openings

ASTD Model	Nadler Model
Evaluator	Supervisor of programs
Group facilitator	Facilitator of learning
Individual development counselor	*
Instructional writer	Instructional strategist
Instructor	Facilitator of learning
Manager of training and development	Administrator/Manager
Marketer	*
Media specialist	Instructional strategist
Needs analyst	Designer of programs
Program administrator	Arranger of facilities and finance
Program designer	Designer of programs
Strategist	*
Task analyst	Designer of programs
Theoretician	*
Transfer agent	Supervisor of programs

will occur; otherwise, the counseling can effectively direct the employee out of the organization. Generally, the information on staffing and future vacancies is not generated within the HRD unit, although the unit may have some of that information. For this and other reasons, it is certainly debatable and highly doubtful whether career counseling is an HRD function.[16]

The role of *marketer* in the ASTD study is defined as "selling Training and Development...outside one's own work unit." We can assume that this means *selling* HRD within the organization. Generally, it can be said that HRD should be an effective management tool to solve present or anticipated problems. If so, then *selling* (as used in the ASTD model) is inappropriate. If the HRD unit engages in selling, individuals within the unit can expect to be treated as salespeople, dealing with the usual sales resistance that occurs. If the HRD unit is viewed as a resource to management for problem solving, selling is obviously not necessary. Note, however, that there is the subrole of *maintainer of relations* in the Nadler model that does not appear in the ASTD model. That subrole comes closer to the concept of HRD as a service unit within the organization.

The role of *strategist* is interesting and may well develop into a new role or subrole, but it is too early to tell. We are finding some indication that HRD managers are being invited into strategic planning sessions. Also, in recent years, we find more HRD managers being called upon to develop policy regarding HRD. As a result, the Nadler model has been modified to include this as a subrole under *manager*.

What the ASTD model calls *theoretician* is more commonly referred to as *researcher*. Although this position is important, there are too few organizations prepared to pay somebody to devote a significant amount of time to that activity. In some large organizations (e.g., Xerox, IBM, Ford) there have been research units in the past, and it is hoped that they will be continued and even expanded. There is much about learning we still need to know.

As noted above, most of the roles identified in the ASTD study already exist in the Nadler model. Therefore, let us continue with further discussion on that model that has existed for many years, been researched, tested, and found useful.

Learning Specialist

Within the role of *learning specialist* there are three subroles: *facilitator of learning, designer of programs*, and *developer of instructional strategies*. There are times when one person will fill all three subroles, and this is most common where the HRD staff is small. Such cases require, however, that the individual filling all three subroles have sufficient competency in each of them.

In large organizations, it is not unusual to find at least three different people, one in each subrole. In very large organizations there may be three separate units!

In the discussion that follows, I will deal with each subrole as if it were handled by a single individual. When there are several individuals, differences will occur in relation to supervising the unit and understanding the unique competencies that each person brings to the subrole.

Facilitator of Learning.   This is the subrole of those who work directly with the learner. This ranges from the person who gives direct instruction, sometimes referred to as the *stand-up instructor*, to machine-mediated instruction where the facilitator serves mainly as a coach and resource.

The facilitator uses a wide variety of approaches to make learning available. Generally, the facilitator uses outlines and lesson plans provided by the designer of programs. There are many variables to consider. One is the competency and self-image of the facilitator. If the facilitator has been professionally prepared and is experienced, a wide variety of instructional strategies can be utilized. When the facilitator is essentially not a professional in the field, there will be greater reliance on the designer of programs and the instructional materials provided.

Facilitators, if competent, may use a variety of small group techniques and other sophisticated learning strategies. It is important that there be congruence between the design, strategies, and the competency of the facilitator.

Designer of Learning Programs. The designer must be highly competent in learning theory and its application to adults in work situations. Also the designer must be familiar with a variety of models for designing and be prepared to select the one, or combination of several, that is appropriate for the particular program being designed.

Identification of organizational problems and analysis of learning needs are essential competencies for the designer. Therefore, it is also essential that the designer have competencies in interpersonal relationships. Designing cannot be done sitting in an office and having no contact with the work situation or those in it (e.g., supervisor, learner).

Frequently, the designer also functions as the facilitator. Therefore, the designer must be able to produce lesson plans and other documentation that will be utilized by others. The form and content of these materials are crucial. The designer must either know the facilitator personally or maintain contacts with facilitators to ensure that the material provided by the designer is understood and used effectively. The designer should not supervise the facilitator, but should serve as a resource to the facilitator as needed.

Designers do not need to know subject matter. This is an area that needs much clarification. The designer's competency should be in the area of learning theory and design—how adults learn. When it comes to the content—what they should learn—the designer should be able to utilize Subject Matter Specialists (SMS) (also sometimes called Subject Matter Experts [SME]). The SMS can come from within the organization, usually from the line or operational units. The SMS can also come from a research and development unit. It is also common to call upon an SMS from outside the organization. Such external SMSs can come from universities, trade organizations, or particular specialties.

Developer of Instructional Strategies. The term *strategies* requires clarification. It includes methods, materials, techniques, and devices, and there is a lack of generally acceptable meanings for the individual terms.

Also, the use of the various approaches constitutes a strategy for facilitating learning.

Many designers prefer to develop their own strategies, and for some of them, it may be possible. These will generally be strategies that do not require the development of any special competencies, such as lecture, simple role plays, flip chart. Some strategies have been brought together in source books that are available from several publishers.

When it is desirable to develop strategies based on the particular situation or organization, the services of the developer are needed. For example, writing case studies is much more difficult than many realize, and there are also variations of the essential case study. It no longer need be presented by written pages, but can be produced on videotape for greater impact, particularly when the case concerns people rather than things.

It is essential that the designer and the developer work together in an almost symbiotic relationship. They need each other and should not feel competitive. Each brings particular resources to the learning situation. Both must also work with the facilitator to ensure that the strategies selected and developed are used effectively.

Let us take one example to indicate the need for a competent developer. The overhead projector is one of the most frequently used visual devices. Producing the transparencies for that device requires competence in several areas. For example, how large should the letters be? A frequent mistake made by those lacking the competency is to put too much material on a single transparency. What colors are best used, given the material and the learners? What about overlays and provision for stripping? It is also possible for the competent developer to create transparencies that can show motion.

This is only one example from one strategy—the overhead projector. Considering the large variety of strategies, it becomes obvious that developing strategies has evolved as a special area of competency within the HRD field.

As technology has become a part of the learning scene, the subrole of the developer has become even more important. Few facilitators or designers can devote the time and energy needed to keep up with the latest in technology as applied to learning. Using the computer for learning is almost a specialty in itself. As the computer is coupled with video, slides, and other technologies, the range of competencies required increases. It even raises the question as to whether any one individual can be expected to have all the competencies required.

A new aspect of the designer's competencies is working with people outside the organization. One group includes those who have the special competencies the internal developer may lack. This is not a reflection on the internal developer, but rather a reflection of the rapid changes in the wide variety of strategies available.

One significant weakness in choosing learning strategies is that we lack sufficient research evidence as to which strategies are most effective for a particular learning situation. We have some models, but they are based on only two sources. One is the particular interest or assumptions of the model builder. The other source includes studies that ask learning specialists their perceptions of the strategies as related to learning objectives. Little useful research has been done to give the designer a sound basis for selecting particular strategies. Therefore, developers must be ready and willing to work with researchers—who are generally external.

Manager of HRD Unit

Managing the HRD unit has become an increasingly important function. Before 1980 this role was not considered too significant. In the early 1970s, as consulting became significant, some managers chose to become *consultants*. Indeed, in some organizations, the internal HRD consultant had more prestige and a higher salary than the manager.

As we entered the 1980s, this began to change. There was increased recognition of the total field of human resources and the need for leadership in that area within organizations. The HRD manager had to be concerned with more than just setting up courses and arranging for tuition reimbursement. The need emerged for an individual who could be an effective manager in the HRD area.

Underlying this change in the role of the manager are several trends.

1. *HRD is a responsibility of the entire organization.* Although the HRD unit appears to provide the programs or courses (the words are generally used interchangeably), every person in the organization has some responsibility. Therefore, the HRD unit is a service group to everybody in the organization—to provide the possibility of learning within, or sponsored by, the organization.

2. *HRD does more than provide a school within the organization.* It has been the practice in the past, and in some organizations it still persists, to reflect the activity of the HRD unit through the catalogs or announcements it produces. Some managers indicate the "success" of their endeavors through such publications. If the HRD catalog of courses

is thicker this year than last, then the assumption is that there is more HRD being offered. Of course, this also carries the assumption that "more is better."

3. *Quantification is not the only way to report on HRD.* It has been customary to report on the work of the HRD unit in terms of quantity— that is, charts showing the number of courses or number of students. Actually, it tells little or nothing about the changes HRD has brought about in the organization.

The alternative that developed was to try to tie the HRD activity into cost benefit, return on investment, and similar criteria. The assumption here is that learning is an isolated factor that alone can bring about changes. In some limited situations it can, but as we are dealing with people and organizations, usually no one factor is responsible for change.

There are other trends, but these are sufficient to indicate the changes in the activities of the manager. As a result, the manager of HRD has emerged as a real manager of a staff function serving the entire organization in a unique way. This has been reflected by more HRD units being taken out of the traditional placement in the personnel function. The trend is to set up the HRD unit as a separate unit, reporting to a vice president for human resources or some other generic human resource executive.

There is another movement that both confuses and reinforces the role of the manager of HRD. As recognition of the importance of HRD has increased, some organizations have placed an HRD person at fairly high levels in the organization. That person usually functions as a consultant rather than a manager. As the term *internal consultant* or *consultant* is still viewed with suspicion in some organizations, that person has been designated as a manager. Actually, the *manager* at that level does little in the way of management.

Some organizations centralize the HRD function, and the manager is discernible and highly visible. Where the HRD function is decentralized, there will be many HRD units, and each will probably have its own manager.

As with the discussion of the learning specialist, it should be noted that one person may fill all the subroles that follow, there may be combinations, or there may be separate units for each of these subroles. The order of discussion that follows is not meant to indicate any hierarchy of subroles. All are important and could be depicted on a diagram in a circular fashion. In writing, however, they can only be presented one after another.

Developer of HRD Policy. This is the newest of the subroles. It is a reflection of the changing role of the manager. Previously, the manager was concerned more with operational matters than policy. With the increased concern over human resources and HRD, however, this subrole has emerged.

As this subrole is new, we need more experience with it to be able to indicate specifics. Earlier, some of what is now in this subrole was in other places. For example, somewhere in the organization *policy* was made regarding tuition reimbursement. It was the function of the HRD unit merely to arrange for the necessary paperwork to facilitate payments. It has become recognized that the paperwork is only incidental to the policy, and sometimes there was no policy although there was practice.

This is only one example of the need for a policy. There are many others, such as what kinds of HRD should be provided (i.e., training, education, development); where the responsibility lies for providing HRD; how HRD should relate to other functions in the organization. At this time, too little is known about policy and HRD. A study is under way which will not be completed before this book is published. It focuses on policy statements for HRD that are suggested by the literature, recommended by organizations, and actually exist. If it is completed successfully, it will contribute to our understanding of policy areas in HRD.

Supervisor of Programs. If the HRD unit is large enough, the manager may be able to delegate some of the subroles to others. The supervisor is one of those subroles that can be readily delegated.

This is the subrole that is directly related to the learning specialist. The supervisor is the link between the HRD unit and the various subroles of the learning specialist. For example, when a problem has been identified and referred to the HRD unit, the supervisor may do the initial exploration as to whether or not learning is an appropriate response. If so, the supervisor will assign it to a designer. The designer will then report to the supervisor on the progress of the project.

The supervisor may also be responsible for selecting or assigning the facilitators to specific programs. It may also be the responsibility of the supervisor to make sure that all the needed steps are taken to implement the program. This may include working with line supervisors to identify and select the appropriate learners and generally *oversee* (i.e., supervise) the delivery of the learning program.

Providing for the evaluation of learning lies within the scope of the designer. The supervisor must provide for the evaluation of the program as well as the application of the learning in the work situation. The supervisor should be the continuing link between the learning specialist and the organization.

Maintainer of Relations.   This is an important subrole that is generally not delegated It has so many aspects that there are times when the manager will call upon the competencies of others in the HRD unit.

Some call this a *marketing* role. In one sense it is, if marketing is concerned with image building. It is certainly not a *selling* role, but if the manager is not careful it can be perceived as such in the organization.

The essential purpose of this role is communication—to keep lines open between the HRD unit and individuals and groups both within and external to the organization.

Let us first examine the internal dimensions. The manager should strive to help others in the organization understand the unique contribution of HRD to the organization. This can be done in myriad ways. One is for the manager to maintain constant contact with others in the organization. This can be accomplished in a formal sense by arranging for invitations to attend staff meetings of other units, reviewing reports from other units, and inviting others to meet with HRD personnel.

The manager must be out of the office frequently on *walk arounds*.[17] These may be done only for the sake of visibility, but more for keeping the manager familiar with what is physically happening in the organization. In addition, such walk arounds make the manager readily available to supervisors who might hesitate to call in the HRD manager.

The astute manager identifies the various groups and subgroups (e.g., those who eat together) and tries to relate to them without becoming part of any one group.

On the external side, the manager essentially focuses on two areas. One is to maintain relations with those who could be resources for HRD, such as universities, vendors, and professional societies. In these situations, the manager is trying to understand them. The other area focuses on the same populations and/or organizations, but the purpose is to have them understand HRD in the organization. This is sometimes accomplished by the HRD manager writing articles or chapters for books such as this or making presentations.

Another activity of this subrole is the HRD advisory committee. It has been suggested that there should be at least one such committee in an organization. Usually there are several, depending upon the scope of the HRD operation. There may be a special advisory committee for tuition reimbursement and another for those programs that will take the employee off the job for any period beyond a week. The number and types of advisory committees will depend upon the HRD operation and on the perception of the manager as to the purpose and functions of these committees.

Developer of HRD Personnel.   Although the manager may delegate part of this subrole, it is not possible to delegate it all. The reason is that this subrole relates to evaluation of the HRD personnel and plans for growth of the individuals.

Essentially there are two kinds of personnel: those assigned full time to the HRD unit and those who are temporary. Although the latter group should have learning experiences made available to them, that can be accomplished by delegating the responsibility to another member of the HRD staff.

For full-time personnel, the manager must assume the prime responsibility. The problem is that too often the energies of the HRD unit are focused on providing growth for everybody else in the organization, but not the HRD personnel. Unless the manager makes sure that this subrole is filled, it is unlikely that the needs of HRD personnel will be met.

As with any other manager, the HRD manager must know what is expected in performance, evaluate that performance, and provide learning, as appropriate, to make up for deficiencies in performance. In addition, it is important that all HRD personnel keep up with the *state of the art*. This may be done by the manager ensuring that appropriate professional publications are made available to the HRD people. The manager may also have to arrange for attendance at meetings of various groups who have programs related to HRD.

The manager should encourage HRD staff to be active in the variety of professional societies and other organizations in the field of HRD or related to it. This would include, but not be limited to, American Society for Training and Development, National Society for Performance and Instruction, American Association for Adult and Continuing Education, and the Association for Education and Technology.

Arranger of Facilities and Finance.   This is a subrole that many managers prefer to delegate to others. As with any delegation, the manager should not be completely removed from the situation, as this is an area where practice can conflict with policy.

If the HRD unit does not have its own learning center—that is, classrooms, equipment, and materials for learning—then facilities may not be a great concern to the manager.

There has been a growing tendency for large organizations to develop their own *conference* facilities or *learning centers*. There is no agreement on the name for such facilities, but they fall into two categories. The first category includes those facilities owned by the organization and managed by the HRD unit. It may be one facility or many, depending upon the size and scope of the organization. IBM, for example, has such facilities in various parts of the United States as well as in other countries. Although the facility is owned by the organization, it may be rented out to other groups for learning purposes. This became the practice of the Xerox Learning Center in Leesburg, Virginia in the early 1980s. In part, this was due to owning a fabulous facility that was being underutilized.

The second category includes those facilities that are rented either in whole or part for the organization's HRD programs. This may require even more effort on the part of the arranger than if the facility is owned by the organization.

In all this, the arranger has a variety of functions related to facilities that must be carefully coordinated in terms of the policy regarding HRD and the use of facilities, as well as how others who are in the organization but not part of the HRD unit can utilize the facilities.

When the arranger deals with finance, the situation becomes complicated. It depends upon how the HRD unit is organized (budget center, cost center, profit center), the accounting systems in the organization, and all the various factors concerned with budgeting and availability of funds.

Too often in the past, the HRD manager focused primarily on learning, problem solving, and the like. That is fine and just what needs to be done. If, however, the manager does not pay sufficient attention to the financial aspects, much of the activity of the HRD unit can be controlled by others outside the unit.

Just like any other manager, the HRD manager must be prepared to become directly involved in the internal financial concerns of the organization. To do less is to be perceived as being "outside" of the organization or lacking in cost consciousness. Such perceptions build unnecessary barriers with other managers.

Emerging Roles.   We can anticipate that there will always be changes in the roles and subroles. For example, the Nadler model has been in existence since 1964, and there have been several changes. Some have been internal, within a major role, such as a changing and strengthening of the subrole of developer of instructional strategies under the major role of learning specialist.

There has been a title change from administrator to manager to reflect the changing terminology in the workplace. A significant addition to this role, presented here for the first time, is the addition of the subrole of developer of HRD policy.

Emerging roles are sometimes difficult to identify. They may represent only a temporary change or the emergence of another field that then develops its own identity (e.g., organization development, career development).

Researcher. As this is being written, a new role has been emerging, and it may well become a part of the model. There is no question about the need for research in HRD. This is not to belittle the contribution made to HRD by research in other fields, but recognizes that too little direct research in HRD has been conducted in the past.

Some large organizations have their own HRD research unit. In other organizations a personnel research unit is concerned with any research about employees at all levels. The number of these research units has been growing.

It appears (note my cautious approach) that researcher may well be an emerging role. (Recall the earlier statement that the model focuses on internal practitioners.) There have always been external practitioners doing research for a variety of reasons. Sometimes the organization has hired an external person or group to research a particular part of HRD. With the increase in graduate programs in HRD, we can expect that there will be more doctoral students looking for dissertation topics and hence more research. All of this is good, but it has not produced, and will not produce, an internal role.

The emergence of the role of researcher must come from within the organization. The organization must be prepared to pay and support an individual whose major function (i.e., role or subrole) is to do research. It may well happen, and we should be sensitive to this possibility.

Consultant. This role can be difficult to understand. The major reason is that the term has been used to describe a wide range of roles in a variety of situations. There are internal and external consultants, just as there are internal and external learning specialists. Our major focus here is on the internal consultant. (More on the external consultant can be found in Chapter 5 by Ronald Lippitt and Gordon Lippitt.)

Consulting is a process. There are some general models regarding this process. One major difference among consultants is the subject of their consultation. In this chapter, we are focusing on the person consulting about HRD matters.

There are four different types of consultant behavior and, in this model, they are called *subroles.* The subroles are: expert, advocate, stimulator, and change agent.

The *expert* is expected to be just that—a person with expertise or competency in broad areas of HRD. In general, this would include all the areas reflected in the subroles discussed earlier. In addition, the expert should have substantial knowledge of other human resource areas, although the consultant may not necessarily be "expert" in them.

The expert is expected to respond to management's needs—how HRD can be used to solve problems in the organization, how to build on opportunities, and how to plan using HRD to avoid possible problems. As HRD is not an exact science, the expert should be able to offer the client a range of possible solutions to the particular situation. This means that to function as an expert, the consultant should not espouse a particular point of view, but rather should present a variety of options, including some conflicting or contradictory approaches. For each, the expert should be able to point out the advantages and limitations. The final decision, in this mode of consulting, should be made by the client, after receiving substantial input from the expert consultant.

A more limited approach is taken by the *advocate.* The consultant in this subrole provides a specific response to the identified situation. The client should understand that not all alternatives are being presented— only those that the advocate suggests as the appropriate response. The advocate must have sufficient competency to make the recommendation.

The difference between these two subroles is that the expert is being asked to respond by providing information based on experience, research, and practice, without espousing any particular approach. In the case of the advocate, management is asking the advocate consultant to recommend a decision, rather than exploring the alternatives themselves.

In both subroles, consultant is content oriented and reactive. The client expects the consultant to have a high level of competency in the content area of HRD and to be able to relate that competency specifically to the situation at hand. In the past, the term *reactive* has too often been seen as negative. It is not. There are times when the client wants specific help and seeks a consultant who can react to the identified problem or concern.

The next subrole is that of *stimulator.* In this situation, the client is seeking outside help to assist in clarifying a problem or a situation. There is still the need for the stimulator consultant to know HRD, but not to the degree required in the consultant subroles of expert and advocate. As a stimulator, the client expects the consultant to raise questions, facilitate management's exploration of problem areas related to HRD, and generally help the client think. The stimulator is not expected to have answers, and the client should not rely too heavily on the stimulator to provide content input. Rather, the stimulator should focus on stimulating the thinking of the client, which could be a group, as the problem or situation is being explored.

The consultant can also function as a change agent. The term *change agent* is not used as frequently today as it was in the past, although the activity still exists. In this subrole, the consultant does not actually bring about change. That is the responsibility of the manager within the organization. Rather, the consultant change agent helps the client identify the need for change, the direction of change, the anticipated result of the change, and, perhaps, even the methodology for bringing about the change. There are other consultants who do this as well, and they are sometimes called *consultants in organizational behavior* or *consultants in organization development* (OD). The unique contribution of HRD consultants is their ability to focus on those aspects of change for which HRD can be useful and helpful.

In the consultant subroles of stimulator and change agent, the HRD consultant is process oriented and proactive. As differentiated from the earlier subroles of expert and advocate, the focus is on the process of stimulation or bringing about change. To function in these subroles requires competency in the process. These subroles also require that the consultant be *proactive*, which means keeping ahead of the current situation rather than just reacting to it. If the client is seeking this kind of help, then the advice of a consultant is appropriate and helpful.

HRD PEOPLE—CATEGORIES

In the previous discussion, HRD people were treated as if they were all the same except for their subroles and competencies. There is another dimension that must also be considered.

The model that follows is based on work done in viewing professional fields or occupations emerging as professions. As this is being written, research of this model is in progress.

Basis for the Categories

Some of the original work in this area was done in the late 1950s. At that time, there was an effort to change behavior in hospitals so that the service providers (medical doctors, nurses, medical technologists, etc.) would work as a team. When the efforts were less than successful, attention was focused on finding out why.

It was found that there were essentially two kinds of people in the fields. One group looked to their professional society for leadership as to how they should function, and they were referred to as *cosmopolitans*. Another group looked to their own institutions for this leadership, and they were called *locals*.

In 1973, Zeace, my closest professional colleague and my wife, and I were doing some work for Ford Motor Company. In endeavoring to identify the specific need for the program under consideration, we discussed the HRD people at various levels in Ford. During the consultation, one aspect became clear when we compared the anticipated time on a particular job. It worked out as follows:

Plant level—one year
Department level—one to three years
Corporate level—three to five years

Of course, there were some who did not move under this plan. This led us to look at the differences. We recalled the earlier research in the health field and found that it provided us with a way of looking at this situation.

We then began to examine the research in the other organizations we were serving. I also explored the concept with the graduate students in our MA and EdD programs in HRD at The George Washington University. They tested out the concept within their employing organizations or their client organizations. From this emerged the model discussed here, modified over more than a decade of use.

The Three Categories

The following are the three categories. Once again, the order of listing should not be perceived as a hierarchy, and no one category is more or less important. Each category is an important part of the HRD activities in an organization.

Category 1—professionally identified
Category 2—organizationally identified
Category 3—collateral duties

Within these three categories, there are subcategories that will be discussed in later sections. It is important to reiterate that this is a model that still needs further investigation and research. For the time being, however, the model can be helpful and will clarify some issues related to HRD in organizations.

Category 1—Professionally Identified

The assumption here is that the individual's self-perception is that of being in the field of HRD, as defined earlier. One way of looking at this is to ascertain how long the individual has been in the field and whether the individual plans to remain in the field.

Generally, the individual should have been in the field at least two years before being able to respond. The two-year stipulation is a bit arbitrary, but will have to suffice until we get more data. Generally, I have found, in many organizations, that people who are not interested in HRD as a career field will not stay longer than two years. This has been found to be the case in many organizations and with many individuals. Of course, this can vary within the organization, as the Ford example cited earlier shows.

At the other end, the individual should be planning to stay in the field for several years. Note that it is not possible to say "for the rest of my career." For a variety of reasons, a person may opt to leave the field. What is important is for the individual to determine whether the present assignment in HRD is intended as a launching pad (it used to be called a "stepping stone") to another job or career or whether the individual plans to stay in HRD for the present employer or a different one.

The category 1 person will also probably be active in various professional societies but not by just attending meetings. The category 1 individuals will probably seek office in those societies or in some other ways increase their identification with the HRD field.

Another way of indicating an intention to stay and grow in the field is by enrolling in academic study. This is more than just attending an occasional workshop in a particular area. There is nothing wrong with that kind of learning experience, but it does not distinguish between category 1 and category 2. The category 1 employee will seek to study the field in depth, and generally that can only be done through a well-planned academic experience. With the increase in the number of universities offering degrees in HRD, this is less difficult for a category 1 person than it had been in the past when The George Washington University was one of the very few granting such a degree.

Category 2—Organizationally Identified

In this category we find those people who work for an organization and are moved from one department or unit to another. This practice is common among those organizations that see their employees as long term and having a strong identification with the organization.

The category 2 person might be one who is perceived as being a general manager. As a manager that person is perceived as being able to manage anything, including the HRD function. Although this may be debatable, this is not the place to debate that point. The practice is prevalent among large organizations and should be accepted.

Using the same criterion as with category 1, the category 2 employee is a person who has not previously been in HRD, is there for a current assignment, but does not intend to remain in HRD. This is resented by some HRD people who do not understand this kind of movement. It is not a result of seeing HRD as a low-level function that anybody can perform. Quite the contrary, it is seen as an important function that should have the benefit of a professional manager in charge.

This approach is a mixed blessing. The professional manager, functioning as a manager of HRD, may not take the time or make the effort to fully understand HRD. In addition, the professional manager is only in HRD as a temporary assignment. Therefore, long-range planning for HRD does not receive the attention it deserves.

As a professional manager, the category 2 individual will seek to be as successful as possible—that means short-range programs and readily discernible successes. This may be good for that manager, but is considerably less helpful to the overall growth and utility of the HRD unit.

Of course, HRD is not the only unit receiving these transient (in the positive sense) managers. This happens in many units in the organization. A difference, however, is that the category 2 manager may have studied finance, purchasing, or any of the other areas concerned with traditional management. Few schools of management include anything about HRD as part of the curriculum. The study of people, by managers, relates to motivation and similar behavioral science topics. They learn very little in MBA programs about HRD as a management tool.

There are other category 2 people. For example, a good salesperson may be assigned to the HRD unit to be involved in training and education programs for salespeople. The implication, if not the statement, is that if that salesperson does a good job in the HRD unit, there will be a promotion to district sales manager, regional sales manager, or some similar position.

There are other reasons for assigning people to HRD on a temporary basis. Too often, the category 1 people see the category 2 people as interlopers and as an attempt to dilute the HRD operation. Quite the contrary. These category 2 people will either return to their former positions or move on and up to higher positions in the organization. This is a prime opportunity for the category 1s to help the category 2s understand what HRD is and how it relates to the goals and objectives of the organization and individuals. The time spent in the HRD unit should be seen as a learning experience for the category 2 employees in addition to the work they are expected to perform.

Category 3—Collateral Duties

These are people who usually do not actually work in the HRD unit, but who have HRD responsibilities. The HRD people should not see them as competition, but rather as part of the whole HRD system in the organization that goes beyond just the HRD unit.

The most common group includes the line supervisors and managers who are expected to use learning with their subordinates. This can range from on-the-job training (OJT) to developmental-learning experiences to increase potential in designated employees.

It is also possible for the line people to be directly involved, preferably when serving as an SMS or even a facilitator. Essentially, that is what the supervisor is—a facilitator of learning—when providing OJT.

There are other units that also use HRD, although they may not be part of the HRD unit. The director of safety may provide training and education without any direct contact with the HRD unit. This does not make it any less HRD, and the HRD people are well advised to relate to such HRD safety programs without taking them over.

Using the Categories

When the categories are applied to a particular organization, some of the conflicts within the HRD unit may become understandable. The model can also help the organization make some decisions about staffing the function.

There is no simple formula as to how many of each category should be employed in the HRD unit. Rather, this determination should represent some agreement in organization policy regarding human resources as related to HRD. If the organization is seeking to build a cadre of managers with a long-time relationship to the organization, then category 2s are not only acceptable, but necessary. If, however, the organization staffs its HRD unit entirely with category 2s, it should come as no surprise that there is little long-range or strategic planning. The competency levels can be expected to be lower among category 2s since it is not in their interest to devote too many resources to building competencies. That takes time and does not have immediate payoffs.

CONCERNS

It is not possible to close this chapter without some discussion about the concerns of HRD in the general workplace. We know that the workplace is changing. This is not an attempt to look at the future; there is an excellent chapter at the end of this handbook that does that. Rather, let us look at three concerns that are indicative of trends. They will continue, although the form may change.

Productivity.   Increasing productivity is a worldwide concern of all industrialized nations. HRD is a major factor in productivity, although certainly not the only one.

The basic relationship is that training can contribute directly to productivity. Education may have some relevance particularly as old jobs are disappearing and new ones are emerging. When education is provided, employees can become productive sooner than if they are placed in the new jobs and then trained.

For development, it is difficult to identify how HRD activity can directly contribute to productivity. In a general sense, it might. We can conjecture that employees who feel that the organization is concerned about them as individuals will tend to be high producers. Unfortunately, there is little research that allows us to make that generalization.

The problem is that the concentration on training and education, because of productivity concerns, may deprive an organization of the benefits of development. It is important for an organization to weigh the relative elements and not push only for productivity.

To complicate the situation further, there is general agreement that some industrialized countries (e.g., the United States and Japan) are moving from manufacturing to service. We are just beginning to understand how to measure productivity in manufacturing. It is doubtful if those measures can be directly transferred into measuring productivity in service areas.

HRD people should be aware of these trends and concerns and be prepared to identify how HRD relates to them.

Quality of Work Life

We have heard and will continue to hear about that vague area referred to as *quality of work life*. It is still in the process of definition, but there are some general areas of agreement.

Part of the area of quality of work life is found in the question: Is work enough? People who spend most of their waking hours working, and that includes most of us, are still questioning whether the main purpose of life is to work. It is not an objection to working, but rather an attempt to make work a more positive aspect of one's total life scheme. From the viewpoint of the employer, the intent is to make the workplace a positive and healthy environment.

It sounds easy when stated in that fashion, but we know it is complicated. We do not know enough about what people want from work, although we are accumulating studies that give us clues.

There are thoughts about making the workplace become a lifeplace. It is a place where people do more than just produce—they live there. This is not a return to the old "company town," for quality of work life assumes that the employees at all levels will be able to influence and build the kind of workplace they want.

Alternatives

Life is full of alternatives and options that many of us never exercise. There are two sets of alternatives that are emerging in the workplace and have a direct impact on HRD.

The first is alternative work *scheduling*. Most people are familiar with flexitime and the positive results it has provided for individuals and organizations. Extensions of that concept go to flexiday, -week, -month, -year. We have already seen some examples of these.[18]

Couple with this, alternative work *sites*. Alvin Toffler has referred to the "electronic cottage."[19] That is, through the use of technology some people can work at home rather than going to the office. Experiences with this have been mixed, but the trend is apparent. A variation is also developing that I call "satellite stations." That is, the organization sets up small offices on the periphery of large cities where it is convenient for clusters of employees who work at home to gather when they so wish. This relates to the *high tech/high touch need* that Naisbitt has discussed.[20]

These alternatives mean that HRD will have to respond by finding alternative ways of delivering learning. The designer may have to use computer conferencing as one way of identifying needs of small groups of people who are in scattered locations.

HRD people have the resources and competencies to respond to these concerns if they recognize them and react accordingly.

CONCLUSION

This has been a brief discussion of human resource development. The references contain additional sources, and you may choose to go to them for more detail.

It is hoped that the reader will now be more informed about some of the history, models, and concerns in the field. They will change, of course, but rather than "rediscovering the wheel" it is now possible to build up on what we have known and done before.

Above all, perhaps we can help each other and our organizations recognize the unique contributions that human resource development can make in reaching individual and organizational goals.

NOTES

1. See Leonard Nadler, *Developing Human Resources*, 2d ed. (Austin, Texas: Learning Concepts, 1979).
2. See Allen Tough, *The Adult's learning Projects* (Toronto: Ontario Institute for Studies in Education, 1971). This was the original report of his research. There have been subsequent reports, notably Allen Tough, *International Change: A Fresh Approach to Helping People Change* (Chicago: Follett, 1982).
3. See Malcolm Knowles, *The Modern Practice of Adult Education* (New York: Association Press, 1970). His numerous other publications present these ideas as well.
4. These studies are described in F.J. Roethlisberger and William J. Dickson, *Management and the Worker* (Cambridge, Mass.: Harvard University Press, 1939).
5. See Lee Bradford, Jack R. Gibb, and Kenneth D. Benne, *T-Group Theory and Laboratory Method* (New York: Wiley, 1964).
6. See Douglas McGregor, *The Human Side of Enterprise* (New York: McGraw-Hill, 1960).
7. This is from my personal knowledge as a training officer with the Agency for International Development in Japan from 1959–1962.
8. See David A. Nadler, *The Now Employee* (Houston: Gulf Publishing Company, 1971).
9. See Leonard Nadler, *Corporate Human Resource Development* (New York: Van Nostrand, 1980).
10. See Leonard Nadler, "Implications of the HRD Concept," *Journal of ASTD* (1974).
11. See Leonard Nadler, "HRD—Helping Managers Solve Problems," *Journal of ASTD*, 35 (1981): 46–48.
12. A list of these research studies is available from the author of this chapter.
13. See Leonard Nadler, "A Study of the Needs of Selected Training Directors in Pennsylvania Which Might Be Met by Professional Education Institutes" (Ph.D. diss., Columbia University, 1962). The original research was completed in 1958, but completion of the dissertation was delayed until returning home from serving as a training officer with the Agency for International Development in Japan. Although the dissertation was not published, some of the material was used in Leonard Nadler, *Developing Human Resources*, 1st ed. (Houston: Gulf Publishing Company, 1970).

14. Gordon L. Lippitt and Leonard Nadler, "Emerging Roles of the Training Director," *Training and Development Journal*, 21 (1967): 2–10.
15. American Society for Training and Development, *Models for Excellence: The Conclusions and Recommendations of the ASTD Training and Development Competency Study* (ASTD, 1983).
16. For more on this topic, see Chapter 31 by Gutteridge and Hutcheson.
17. The "walk around" is described in Leonard Nadler, *Personal Skills for the Manager* (Homewood, IL: Dow Jones-Irwin, 1983), p. 15.
18. For comments on flexitime and other aspects of quality of work life, see Donald N. Scobel, *Creative Worklife* (Houston: Gulf Publishing Company, 1981).
19. See Alvin Toffler, *The Third Wave* (New York: William Morrow, 1980), p. 26.
20. This is discussed in John Naisbitt, *Megatrends: Ten New Directions Transforming Our Lives* (New York: Warner, 1982), Chapter 2.

BIBLIOGRAPHY

American Society for Training and Development. *Models for Excellence: The Conclusions and Recommendations of the ASTD Training and Development Competency Study*, Washington, D.C.: ASTD, 1983.

Bradford, Lee, Jack R. Gibb, and Kenneth D. Benne. *T-Group Theory and Laboratory Method.* New York: John Wiley & Sons, 1964.

Knowles, Malcolm. *The Modern Practice of Adult Education.* Association Press, 1970.

Lippitt, Gordon L., and Leonard Nadler. "Emerging Roles of the Training Director." *Training and Development Journal*, 21 (1967).

McGregor, Douglas. *The Human Side of Enterprise.* New York: McGraw-Hill, 1960.

Nadler, David A. *The Now Employee.* Houston: Gulf Publishing Company, 1971.

Nadler, Leonard. *Corporate Human Resource Development.* New York: Van Nostrand, 1980.

Nadler, Leonard. *Developing Human Resources*, 2nd ed. Austin: Learning Concepts, 1979.

Nadler, Leonard. "HRD—Helping Managers Solve Problems." *Journal of ASTD*, 35 (1981): 46–48.

Nadler, Leonard. *Personal Skills for the Manager.* Homewood, IL: Dow Jones-Irwin, 1983.

Nadler, Leonard. "A Study of the Needs of Selected Training Directors in Pennsylvania Which Might Be Met by Professional Education Institutions." Ph.D. Dissertation, Columbia University, 1962.

Naisbitt, John. *Megatrends: Ten New Directions Transforming Our Lives.* New York: Warner, 1982.

Roethlisberger, F.J., and William J. Dickson. *Management and the Worker.* Cambridge, Mass.: Harvard University Press, 1939.

Scobel, Donald N. *Creative Worklife.* Houston: Gulf Publishing Company, 1981.

Tough, Allen. *The Adult's Learning Projects.* Toronto: Ontario Institute for Studies in Education, 1971.

Tough, Allen. *Intentional Change: A Fresh Approach to Helping People Change.* Chicago: Follett, 1982.

CHAPTER TWO

Managing the HRD Function

ELLIS BERNE

Of all the activities performed by HRD practitioners, it appears that being an HRD manager is becoming the most important. There are a variety of reasons for this, and Berne shares them with us.

Essentially, there are an increasing number of organizations recognizing the importance of HRD. In part, it is a repetition of what happened in the late 1940s. During World War II, U.S. industry relied more heavily on HRD than ever before in order to meet the demands of increased wartime production. The lesson was clear then—HRD could contribute significantly to the organization. HRD managers emerged.

Over the years, attention shifted. First, in the 1960s, attention turned to the new learning technologies that emerged. Then, in the 1970s, there was increased emphasis on internal consulting by HRD practitioners, rather than on managing.

In the early 1980s, we found an increased need for people to manage the HRD function, even though the extent of that management was not clear. In this chapter, Berne helps us look specifically at the HRD manager.

Ellis Berne had a long and distinguished career with the federal government before retiring in 1982. Toward the end of his career, he rose to the senior executive rank—one of the few HRD people in the federal government to reach that high level. During his career, he was HRD director for a number of large federal departments and agencies. Since his retirement, he has provided HRD service to a variety of organizations in the public and private sectors and has served as a part-time instructor in the HRD program at The George Washington University.

A casual glance at the shelves of a library area designed "management" will reveal literally hundreds of volumes devoted to the subject. On closer look, the reader will find that these many handbooks, texts, and tomes concern skills, functions, or disciplines of management. Why then another chapter on managing the HRD function?

HRD, which is generally conducted in a business or industry setting, is an organized learning experience, over a given period of time, that provides the possibility of performance change on the part of the participant. There is a host of specific considerations, arising from the nature of the HRD function, that will affect the success or failure of the program. Unless the HRD manager is aware of, and sensitive to, these issues, there is increased risk of failure.

For example, in response to the request of a bureau head, an HRD manager arranged for a valued employee to get several weeks of learning. Unfortunately, the HRD manager did not verify with the bureau head that the proper foundation had been laid, that is, that the employee and the organization had mutual expectations. Instead of the employee seeing the learning as a career enhancement, it was perceived as a setback. Others in the organization saw it as criticism of the employee. That employee started looking for another position. It was only by chance that the HRD director became aware of the situation and with the bureau director was able to correct a potentially negative situation.

WHERE DOES HRD FIT IN THE ORGANIZATION?

In the past, the HRD function in organizations had generally been associated with the personnel function. More recently, some organizations have established the HRD unit as a staff office reporting to a senior executive. Thus, evolutionary development parallels the history of other emerging professional activities within organizations. The personnel function, which emerged in the 1930s, was, in many cases, initially an area of office services. Labor relations as a function was, and in some cases still is, attached to a personnel office. With the increasing importance of labor relations, there are many situations in which the labor relations function is independent of the personnel function.

Similarly, when HRD began to emerge as a new professional function in the 1940s, it was most frequently made a part of existing personnel offices. Many personnel officials would still argue that the so-called "training function" should be a part of the personnel function. Learning professionals see how the many benefits of an identifiable HRD function contribute to the success of the organization. The issue of organizational location of the HRD function is treated more extensively elsewhere in this book, therefore, a final remark—How well is the HRD function likely to fare in the apportionment of staff and dollar resources where such distribution is made by individuals who believe that HRD has a lower priority than classification or staffing?

THE HRD MANAGER AS DEVELOPER OF HRD PERSONNEL

"The shoemaker's children go barefoot, the dairyman's children drink no milk, and HRD staff get no learning." These are the words to a tuneless little melody often heard plaintively murmured in the halls of organizations.

By contrast, the HRD manager recognizes that a critical requirement for success is developing the capabilities of the HRD staff itself. In a sense, the HRD manager may use the HRD staff as a microcosm for testing out the methods and techniques that could be used throughout the rest of the organization. Pretesting of programs can reveal problem areas and unanticipated difficulties that can be resolved before the programs are exported for larger scale use.

Normally, an HRD staff will have personnel ranging from entry level to senior. How do the manager and the staff go about the process of developing these resources?

In a very real sense, the development process used by the manager for HRD personnel should be a showcase for the rest of the organization. This, of course, must be handled with scrupulous fairness so that the rest of the organization does not feel that a disproportionate amount of resources (human, physical, or financial) is used for the HRD staff. Developing the human resource begins with a clear understanding of the macro and micro objectives of the organization. What is the overall organization attempting to accomplish? Is it a high-tech organization with primary emphasis on keeping its members on the cutting edge of technology? Is it a service organization where continuing attention must be given to effective, efficient, and courteous interaction with clientele? Each organization, depending on its product, will have its own unique mix of requirements for training, education, and development and an HRD group designed to best serve the needs of the organization. In a large HRD group there will be clerical, administrative, entry level professional, journey, senior, supervisory, managerial, and executive staff levels. Each of these levels is not only deserving of HRD services but absolutely requires them if the group is to be as highly effective as it should be.

For each employee in the HRD unit there should be a profile that includes information on formal and informal learning experiences and work history with some detail. This suggested profile will sound to many readers like a personnel folder. However, most traditional personnel folders do not contain adequate information for HRD documentation or planning. Traditional personnel folders assure that authorizations for HRD expenditures are proper and that such authorized learning has been completed. There are many public jurisdictions in which only learning accomplished within the department is documented. Consequently, the personnel folder will not reflect courses taken in other departments, unless the employee voluntarily chooses to inform the home department. With the increased use of automated data processing equipment, record keeping hopefully will become easier, more comprehensive, and accurate. In the meantime, an HRD record, producing the type of information the HRD group needs, is an important adjunct to effective planning.

HRD may often be conducted effectively in connection with career planning. Where is the employee now? Where is the employee going? What does the organization need? Are these objectives mutually complementary? However surprising it may be, there are a significant number of employees who will not be interested in career development opportunities. They are content with what they are currently doing. They may not want to invest the additional time or effort necessary to acquire new or expanded skills. In some cases, such individuals will be involved in second jobs or vocational interests that are time and energy consuming. In any event, opportunities should be made available, if possible, to all employees. Where such opportunities are rejected, such rejections should be documented, since they may be relevant at some future date.

For those HRD employees participating in the program, it will have to be made clear that this program operates within available resources. Unless there are unlimited resources, or more reasonably, unless resources are not an issue in the particular case, choices have to be made and priorities assigned. Generally, after a program has been in place for some time, it should be possible to project future costs with a high degree of accuracy so that adequate budgeting can take place. As in many other situations, the HRD manager must balance the needs of the organization, organizational priorities, available resources, and unexpected developments against commitments made, employee expectations, benefits to organization, damage to organization image if expectations are not met, and employee morale. On balance, only the most extreme circumstances should involve disrupting previously made commitments to HRD for staff considerations.

Until now, we have been discussing HRD for permanent full-time and part-time employees. What about HRD for temporary full-time and part-time employees? According to conventional wisdom, an organization should expend or invest as little as possible in temporary employees, whether they work full time or part time. There is a superficial attractiveness in this position as a cost-saving measure. Yet there are circumstances where training, education, and even development may be cost effective. For example, many health organizations, faced with severe shortages of nursing personnel, have been willing to reexamine their traditional eight-hour shifts, 40-hour weeks. Even though it complicates personnel record keeping, these organizations have been willing to consider any four hour bloc of time that a nurse may have. Similar arrangements have been used for other shortage category personnel. In the human resource development field, there are many instances where temporary or part-time employees are exposed to learning. For example, a temporary instructor may have to be put through a production process learning experience because there has been a change since the original course was developed; or a part-time registrar accustomed to a manual system of monitoring program participants will require learning when the system undergoes automation. Individuals in these categories, if they are to provide high quality service, will require reasonable amounts of training to enhance present performance; education, if they are to undertake new duties and responsibilities; and even development, as part of the mind stretch that all employees need from time to time.

On balance, it would seem that the issue is not whether the employee is a permanent, temporary, full-time, or part-time worker. The decision process should revolve around the best interests of the organization. Intelligent use of HRD techniques produces far better results than slavish adherence to policies that do not cover the situation.

THE HRD MANAGER AS
MAINTAINER OF COMMUNITY RELATIONS

Communication effectiveness is considered one of the critical elements in the success of a manager. What then does the HRD manager communicate to colleagues in management? Where the HRD function is relatively new to the organization, the HRD manager will have to develop, among colleagues, an understanding of and interest in how HRD services can help solve performance problems. As in other staff functions, unless operating officials "buy in" to the idea that help can be obtained from HRD, little or nothing will be achieved. The HRD group can have excellent analysts, curriculum developers, audiovisual support, and classroom instructors, but without participants and support from colleagues, little will happen.

Frequently, an HRD effort will have begun because of a perceived problem. Success with a beginning program will lay the groundwork for further, systematic efforts. Such success will permit an HRD manager to develop the necessary rapport with other managers, so that HRD issues may be discussed without the HRD manager being viewed as "wasting" the time of busy line officials.

Many different techniques have been developed over the years to facilitate better communication among managers. Some HRD managers hold periodic briefings of managers on the status of programs and plans and invite further contacts. This is a relatively formal procedure and suggests a large, hierarchical organization. Almost as formal a method is the issuance of an informational memorandum to colleagues. Being alert to organizational issues is frequently a basis for interaction. Developing a network of HRD-oriented individuals within the organization is a productive technique.

A distinguished psychologist once defined life as "the continual reception of stimuli." This definition is particularly apt in organizational life. The HRD manager who has a finger on the pulse of an organization can be an effective and productive member. This means not only communicating problems and concerns but also sharing successes and accomplishments. By contrast, the individual who waits in the office for other managers to bring in their problems may eventually find the result is unemployment. It is a source of surprise to many new professionals to discover how little professionals in other fields know about HRD. It is a continuing responsibility of all professionals, including HRDers, to inform others and, without being burdensome, help them develop insight into ways they can be of assistance.

Having stated the case for excellent communication with one's peers, let me sound a note of caution. If the HRD manager is too positive or persuasive, colleagues may begin to see HRD as a panacea, or even worse, will make use of HRD to solve non-HRD problems. Typically, an organization will have an employee who is a "problem." It is not that the employee is technically incompetent, instead, he or she may not get along with other colleagues. So the manager sends the employee to training. This decision buys the manager some time. The manager also hopes that perhaps the employee will find another job.

This situation arises all too frequently. It is not a training problem. The training solution bears no relation to the problem. Counseling, discipline, or separation may be far more appropriate. Without suggesting what the appropriate course of action is, the HRD manager must be sensitive to the pitfalls of providing "no win" training solutions to nontraining problems. Great sensitivity must be displayed with colleagues when dealing with such issues, since line managers will often believe they are "helping a colleague" with a difficult situation.

THE HRD MANAGER AS MAINTAINER OF RELATIONS WITH THOSE TO BE SERVED

The HRD manager must maintain credibility in order to maintain relations with others. Never promise more than you can deliver, and deliver what you promise. In many other fields of endeavor there are tangibles that the user can judge. In the field of HRD, we often deal with future-oriented outcomes. It is only in training that there is an immediate and visible result. In the case of education, even a successful learning experience cannot be demonstrated until the individual enters upon the new position. This issue becomes far more complicated when one deals with a "program" rather than a single occurrence. When there is a supervisory development program, or a management development program, or an executive development program that usually involves a series of formal learning experiences, interspersed with a variety of different work experiences over the period of a year or more, the question of credibility becomes critically imporant. A participant will frequently ask, "Is this program for real?" Explicitly, does the organization intend to reward those individuals who are successful in the program?

Credibility is the question. Is an organization going to follow through for those who succeed in programs? While we are on the issue of rewards for accomplishment, it is worth noting that the HRD manager should not be trapped by the commonly held belief that the only reward for good work is promotion and more money. Of course, just about everyone can use more money, and promotion is seen as an avenue to such a monetary increase. But realistically, the Frederic Herzberg formulation that money is a "satisfier" and not a "motivator" is extremely important in its practical implications. Assuming that basic monetary requirements are met, an increase in monetary reward does not result in better performance. Instead, the reward for success may be more responsibility, different or more interesting assignments, opportunities for professional development, or recognition. On balance, unless those who are to be served have trust and confidence in the programs offered, little success can be expected in the HRD operation.

THE HRD MANAGER AS MAINTAINER OF RELATIONS WITH OUTSIDE GROUPS

All professions consider an informed public important to their continued acceptance and support. Many organizations make speakers available and carry on other informational activities, such as the issuing of press releases on new developments. The HRD manager, as a professional, is implicitly responsible for making the public aware of what HRD is and how it can contribute to the success of groups and organizations. As we have already noted, many of the HRD manager's colleagues within the organization will not have a clear idea of the value and contributions of HRD to organizational effectiveness. Think how much more this is true in groups and organizations where there is no HRD function or where HRD is carried on as a collateral duty, usually by a personnel professional, and consists of signing up participants in likely sounding HRD programs on a hit-or-miss basis.

The HRD manager should, as part of overall professional responsibility, welcome invitations to speak on HRD before various groups. In addition, the HRD manager should participate in a local group, such as ASTD, to help foster professional awareness and growth. Where no such group exists, as is all too often the case, the manager should at least maintain a national professional group affiliation. Further, if circumstances permit, the manager should lend energy and knowledge to the establishment of a local group to help bring about professional interaction in the area.

THE HRD MANAGER AS PLANNER

Planning carries a wide range of connotations to those who use the word. For some, it is as trivial as organizing the next hour's or day's activities to make them efficient and effective. For others, it may be as elaborate as the USSR's State Planning Commission, which has attempted, on a multiyear basis, to plan all production activity within the country. This range of possibilities points to the wisdom of the physical scientists. They attempt to reduce phenomena to mathematical formulations in order to discourage the fuzzing and obliteration of precision, since different individuals use the same terms with different meanings.

Similarly, with regard to planning, while daily work, staff, and budget planning are all of significance, and will, in greater or lesser degree, be discussed here and elsewhere, the focus of this discussion will be on strategic planning and planning HRD programs for the organization.

Most organizations have a yearly plan. For convenience' sake, this plan is often tied to the budget year. The convenience here is for the budget and financial managers who, if at all possible, like to have beginning and ending points for their operations. Yearly plans are usually driven by a set of assumptions set forth by top management. These assumptions can be economic—"assume a growth rate of 5%"; they can be technological—"assume our new personal computer will capture 20% of the available market for personal computers"; they can be demographic—"assume that there will be a 12% increase in first-time social security claimants"; or they can be political, to cite a few of the possible areas of consideration.

The managers of the various organizational functions will factor these assumptions into their projections of what they hope to accomplish and what it will take in personnel, material, and money to do so. In an organization with an effective HRD operation, managers will have been sensitized to ways that HRD efforts can help them attain their goals. Basic considerations include questions such as, "What training does my present staff need to enhance its present job performance?" "What education does my staff need to prepare for near future assignments?" "Are those employees who show promise on career tracks with an appropriate mix of different work assignments and formal learning experiences?"

Beyond basic issues, varieties of factors enter, such as "Is the organization growing, or is it stable?" "Are resources tight, moderate, or readily available?" "Is this a high-tech organization which must be in the forefront of developments?" "Is this a service organization concentrating on successful interaction with clientele?" Not the least important factor is the vision and future view of the organization and its HRD manager.

For example, in recent years we have seen very imaginative training and education efforts extended by high-tech computer companies to the purchasers of their equipment. The perception that consumers who are comfortable with your product are more likely to buy it, use it, and recommend it to others has not been lost on the marketing community.

During the planning phase, the HRD manager will be involved in frequent discussions with peers regarding what is likely, feasible, and potentially productive in HRD activities.

At the same time, the HRD manager should act as a functional manager in planning for the HRD operation. If size and scope of HRD staff permits, it is desirable for the HRD staff member next in responsibility to the HRD manager to carry out the advisory-consultant role to the manager in developing plans for the HRD operation. In this way, there is a staff development opportunity, and the HRD manager gets an additional point of view regarding the operation.

THE HRD MANAGER AND POLICY DEVELOPMENT

Thomas Edison is alleged to have said that genius is 98% perspiration and 2% inspiration. Instead of talking about "inventing," he could just as well have been talking about HRD. HRD is a subject of intense interest to many people within an organization. Employees want to know how they can be promoted. Supervisors are interested in seeing that they have the best available staff. Union officials want to be sure that their members are getting everything they are entitled to. Managers wish to be seen as powerful. Securing learning experiences for themselves and their senior staff is viewed by their colleagues as an indication of power. Budgeters want to be sure that, "we aren't going overboard with this do-gooder stuff." Financial managers want to be sure that the learners are not living at the Ritz or eating caviar and drinking champagne for breakfast, lunch, and dinner.

The circle of interested onlookers and participants seems to be endless and ever growing. This is all to the good, since it is an indication that the HRD manager is making an impact on a lot of people in the organization. As a result, it also generates a great deal of unsolicited advice and guidance.

This intense interest leads to the generation of policy and, by necessity, policy statements. Contrary to popular opinion, policy statements do not set policy. At best, they confirm it. And in this statement lies the problem with many policy issuances by organizations. Policies are frequently issued to deal with a specific situation that has arisen. An employee wishes to take a course at a local university. Will the company reimburse the employee for taking the course? In whole or in part? Must the employee achieve a certain grade in order to be reimbursed? Does the company pay in advance or at the successful conclusion? These and many other details must be worked through. Some organizations pursue a policy clearance process in which proposed policy statements are circulated in draft with a request for comments and/or concurrence within a time limit. Comments are considered, conformed, and then, if there is a consensus, a final proposed policy statement is generated. In many cases, such policy statements will be discussed with union representatives or affected employee groups.

This is not to suggest that policies must always be generated by a democratic, pluralistic method. Most organizations are hierarchical, and the decision-making authority is reserved to the various levels of the organization. What is suggested is that the HRD manager, in developing policy, is dealing with another facet of the credibility issue. Before the HRD policy is issued, the HRD manager should be aware of all the implications, impacts, and alternatives to the policy that is being established.

THE HRD MANAGER AS STRATEGIC PLANNER

In recent years HRD managers have been participating increasingly in strategic planning.

Most managers are accustomed to the process of working on an annual plan with goals, objectives, and accountability. With the advent of computers, reports that once took weeks to assemble are now available overnight. The idea of instant reporting and analysis has become so pernicious that many CEOs survive from quarterly report to quarterly report. A less than profitable report can lead to rapid replacement. This trend has led to shifts in the survival strategy for CEOs and to criticism by analysts who see large U.S. organizations increasingly sacrificing such areas as research and development to the search for quick, visible profits.

There has been a countertrend in the last 20 years. While Alfred P. Sloan of General Motors is credited with much of the early thinking in this area, it is the Japanese who are credited with making strategic planning a cornerstone of their obvious economic success.

What is strategic planning? In some respects it is easier to say what it is not, a practice that has become quite common. For example, health is defined as the absence of illness. This easy understanding substitutes for the more complex (and mostly unknown) requirement specifying the composition and acceptable normal parameters of blood, tissue, cells, and organ systems.

Strategic planning is not predicting the future. While some very good guesses have been made over the years, most future projections do not anticipate what cannot be anticipated. Unanticipated changes in technological, social, and political relationships have made forecasting the future very difficult. As has been noted, "The problem with the future is that it is not what it used to be."

Strategic planning is not the application of statistics, computers, or other sophisticated devices to analyze the future. Some of these methodologies may be used to assure the process, but they are not necessary. Strategic planning is a decision-making process. As long as decision making involves an element of judgment, it will be a less than precise art.

Strategic planning involves answers to intriguing questions, such as: "What is our business?" "What will it be in X time (5–10 years)?" Normally one sees strategic plans in periods of five years or longer, because fewer than five years brings the plan within the operational planning range. But the length of time to be considered in strategic planning is itself a variable. Currently, in the computer industry, hardware and software are being generated at such a rate as to become obsolete almost as they are issued. In such circumstances, long-range planning may be six months into the future and strategic planning may be two years into the future. Therefore, short-range planning accounts for what must be done soon and long-range planning accounts for what must be done later. Strategic planning deals with making present decisions that are implemented by short-range and long-range planning so that the organization may survive in the uncertain future.

The third question to be answered is: "What should our business be?" When these questions are answered systematically, with the best knowledge that one can bring to bear on the subject, decisions can be made on how to get there. In effect, what decisions and actions have to be taken today to maximize the likelihood of getting there tomorrow? By monitoring results through systematic feedback, appropriate adjustments can be made as knowledge improves and situations become clearer.

HRD is an important element in short-range and long-range planning. HRD may be the key element in the strategic planning process. Change, modification, and evolution are all necessary for successful survival. Doing nothing or doing more of the same generally leads to nonsurvival.

Changes in technology, methodology, and organization require ever-increasing attention to HRD functions, if success is to be achieved. This is particularly true as changes accelerate. Organizations could literally become "learning communities" in order to meet the challenges of rapidly evolving technology, methodology, and organization.

By the same token, HRD becomes a key element in the strategic planning process because of the very nature of strategic planning. The basic assumption is that the future will be different. Therefore, the organization can successfully arrive in the future only by preparing employees to move with the organization as it develops, changes, and grows. Efforts at organizational renewal, exchange programs, and think tank activities are examples of the HRD developmental process. While these activities do not guarantee success, they increase its probability.

WHAT ROLE DOES THE HRD MANAGER PLAY IN STRATEGIC PLANNING?

There is evidence to suggest that the strategic planner is an emerging role in HRD that will be increasingly important in the years to come.

Consider the three questions we associated with strategic planning and the ancillary considerations that follow. First, "What is our business?" This question prompts further considerations. Who are our employees—demographically, educationally? What learning experiences are necessary to prepare them to produce our product and to function effectively? What changes in technology are we prepared to deal with— the increased use of self-paced learning, computer-assisted learning, videodiscs? A basic assumption in the analysis of what is our business is that our business is probably not what we think it is.

Second, "What will our business be?" Again, this question involves possible changes in preparation or delivery. What skills, knowledge, and abilities will be necessary for the staff to perform successfully? Can we develop these skills, knowledge, and abilities internally, or will we have to seek outside help? The product today may bear little or no relationship to the product of the future. Consider the circumstance of the successful horse collar manufacturer who at the time of the introduction of the horseless carriage was blissfully projecting slow but steady growth in the need for his product.

The third question is: "What should the business be?" Who foresaw the emergence of women into the labor market following World War II? Who foresaw the major economic progress that blacks would make when Martin Luther King first started his movement? Who foresaw the impact of the rise in oil prices under the pressure of the OPEC countries? What the business should be is not, as indicated, an exercise in future forecasting. Rather, the question is what decisions have to be made, and when, so that there is a future? Strategic planning for the HRD manager offers the opportunity to provide a flexible, multipurpose resource to the organization that is prepared and confident, and thus, able to respond to the unexpected.

It has been aptly stated that a human is still the least expensive 180-lb nonlinear, multipurpose, flexible computer available. HRDers have been saying for years that employee development is concerned with preparing the employee so that he or she can move with the organization as it develops, changes and grows.

The HRD manager, as part of the top management's strategic planning effort, can assist with knowledge, vision, and wit in making decisions and taking action that will provide prepared and developed employees and permit success. There are few endeavors that offer as much excitement and satisfaction in work life.

Financial Aspects of HRD

RICHARD W. DAVIS

We have often heard that everybody talks about evaluation, but few do anything about it. That statement applies even more strongly to the financial aspects of HRD.

It is possible to conjecture about that situation. Many HRD practitioners come from a background in behavioral and social sciences and have little academic work in finance. Even if the practitioner comes from a management background, there has been little encouragement to apply financial principles to HRD.

In this chapter, Davis has entered virtually uncharted territory. He has taken some accepted financial principles and applied them to HRD. While the chapter's emphasis on developing and delivering projects and programs may be familiar to the reader, the process of financial analysis itself may be new and, for some, difficult territory.

HRD is in the marketplace, however, and to survive in that environment it is necessary that HRD practitioners study and feel comfortable with budgeting and other aspects of the financial picture.

Richard W. Davis (Ph.D.) is in the Processor and Software Systems Division of AT&T Technologies. He has been involved in developing HRD applications for AT&T's UNIX computer system. Previously, he was a district manager of development with the Bell System Center for Technical Education. Prior to entering the Bell System, he was on the graduate faculty of the University of Minnesota. His doctorate, from Indiana University, is in instructional systems technology.

FINANCIAL ANALYSIS

The career of many HRD professionals begins with one of two kinds of preparation—academic degree programs or staff positions within a corporation. Few HRD managers have extensive experience with project management, at least to the extent required by an HRD assignment. Neither the academic background nor the corporate staff experience provides a solid grounding in the management of project funds. Most HRD managers learn budget and financial analysis in "the school of hard knocks." More than one HRD manager has expressed frustration over winning the instructional battles while losing the financial ones. This chapter is intended to provide an introduction to the financial processes underlying HRD projects. The hope is that the material will give HRD managers a good start in examining the financial nature of their own activity. Today, HRD is not only a business, it is a big business. Current estimates suggest that more than $40 billion are spent annually on HRD in the private sector in the United States alone.[1] The total cost of all HRD functions together is, of course, even larger than that. This enormous amount of money is beginning to attract attention.

Not only has HRD become important in itself, but HRD impacts the total financial performance of many organizations today, including governments and entire industries. It should not be a surprise, then, that HRD increasingly comes under the same financial scrutiny given any other aspect of a large organization. But the cost of HRD to the organization is not an answer to the question, "Why is project finance important to human resource development?" Organizations now view HRD as an integral staff function basic to their success. Because it takes that view, the organization expects HRD to operate under the same financial rules that apply to the rest of the firm. In those particular firms that have chosen to treat the HRD function as a profit center or line of business (as many companies have done in the recent past), financial analysis becomes particularly important. Financial analysis provides the only means by which a profit center can determine how well it meets its organizational objective to return a profit on the resources invested in its activity. Some HRD organizations may not work under the strict accounting and budgeting rules of a profit center or line of business. They still benefit, however, from the rigor and control that financial analysis of their work provides.

Certainly factors other than financial performance alone are important in assessing organizational effectiveness. Still, more and more managers view financial results as the single most important index of a group's overall performance—profit center or not. The number of job advertisements seeking a "bottom line, results-oriented manager" in HRD provides evidence of the priority that firms place on financial performance.

How Much Does It Cost?

Effective financial analysis of HRD activity is difficult. To dramatize the problem, consider these two questions: "How much does it cost to make a widget?" "How much does it cost to teach someone to fix it?"

If one were to ask the first question of a general manager of a large factory, one would expect a detailed answer. "On what day?" is a typical response. For example, on one particular day, the cost to manufacture a particular product in a particular plant was $44.35; the next day it was $44.32. Why? The price of copper went down. The manager might explain that manufacturing costs vary because of changes in costs of material, in the number of units produced, and in the labor cost associated with different components of each unit. The manager is aware not only of the cost of the product but of the factors to which cost is sensitive. Now consider the second question. Ask the same manager about the cost of HRD, and the typical response is, "I don't know." The answer is rarely given as a dollar amount.

Before this example pushes the discussion into a corner, one point should be made clear. The differences between HRD and manufacturing are neither wrong nor bad. Rather, the difference should be somewhat comforting, since HRD professionals, as a group, tend to reject mechanistic models for training and education. Few HRD practitioners subscribe to views that suggest strong similarities between the two processes. The whole concept of andragogy in HRD is seen by many as antithetical to mechanistic models of learning. Thus, the argument that a manager cannot spit out some figure for the cost of HRD, as could be done for the cost of manufacture, should not be viewed narrowly as a problem of HRD. An organization's inability to give HRD activity precise financial description does, however, present a problem. But it is probably best viewed as a problem of management. The question of "How much does it cost to train someone?" requires a good answer, even though that answer may be different than for other kinds of organizational activity.

Financial analysis is important for yet another reason as well. If, as stated earlier, management needs financial analysis to make HRD efforts effective, why is this so? If one looks at the HRD profession's own teachings about effective human performance and focuses specifically on the idea that people achieve optimum performance only when they get appropriate feedback, the answer becomes clearer. At its best, financial analysis provides formal and precise feedback. If the goals, resources, products, services, and activities in a given human performance system can be represented as money, then the organization can obtain feedback expressed as money. Even when the organization cannot reduce everything to dollars and cents—and obviously there are things one does not want to measure that way—financial analysis provides an extremely effective means of communicating about organizational performance. The idea that the major purpose of financial analysis is to provide feedback about organizational performance is fundamental to any discussion of financial analysis.

Some Beginning Assumptions

To introduce the discussion of financial analysis of HRD activity, one can make a few key assumptions.

All HRD efforts may be viewed as either projects or programs.

All HRD effort takes place inside organizations.

Financially, the development and delivery of HRD efforts are two different matters.

A brief discussion of each of these three points will help ensure clarity.

Everything Is a Project or a Program.   By choosing to view every HRD effort as either a project or a program, the HRD manager establishes an organizational structure in which to establish financial control. The project or program approach provides the basic unit of financial analysis. The HRD manager takes the position that the business of human resources development consists of developing projects that identify needs, creating programs to deal with those needs, and then implementing the programs. The results or outcomes of those individual programs and projects is the feedback the HRD manager requires.

The alternative to analysis by programs is to view HRD as an ongoing process—the continuous flow of resource and activity. While such an approach may appear easier and even more natural, given how HRD units operate, it is financially disastrous. The process approach limits two critical elements of a functioning financial system. It permits neither tight linking of particular costs with particular activities nor the coupling of financial information to direct management action.

The problem becomes clearer if one compares a process and a program, each designed to achieve the same goal. Green Inc. and Blue Co. each orient new employees. Green sees this activity as part of the overall hiring process and gives its personnel department money for orientation based on the number of new employees hired. Blue Co., on the other hand, has created a new-hire program within its HRD group. Periodically, the program director prepares a new budget describing the performance of the program and describes how the expenditure of those funds will support the stated goal of orienting new hires.

Without going into a detailed analysis of which organization does the better job, one could argue that the Blue Co. effort is probably easier to control. At regular intervals, the organization reviews what has occurred to meet the specific goal and what should occur next. The review focuses on the project's financial activity. Managing the HRD activity as a program or project does not automatically make the product better than when it is viewed as a process: instead, viewing the effort as a project makes financial analysis easier and more useful. Blue Co. has every reason to expect, therefore, that HRD management will use the good financial information provided to meet the organization's goals more effectively.

You Are Working Inside an Organization.   Human resources development has as its fundamental objective the improvement of human performance in organizations. The HRD practitioner is accountable to the organization being served. Certainly, accountability covers much more than financial performance alone, but finance constitutes the principal focus of accountability. Accountability, then, is an argument:

1. The HRD manager's responsibility for programs comes from the organization.
2. The organization entrusts resources to the manager for use in achieving goals.
3. The financial analysis becomes the method the organization uses to communicate with the manager about achievement of those goals.

Program Development and Program Delivery Are Financially Different.   To observe the financial differences between development[2] and delivery, one need only consider a list of expenses for the two. Program development might include such items as needs analysis, materials design, measurement instrument validation, and design consultant fees. Program delivery would include none of those things. Similarly, delivery would include reproduction of materials, and perhaps audiovisual equipment rental or transportation expense, but development probably would not.

The two differ, however, in more fundamental ways. During project development, the organization has committed resources to a project with the expectation that the effort will produce later savings, profits, or both.[3] There is always some risk, however, that the project will not be able to achieve established goals. To help ensure success, the organization wants to know how project resources are being used. Specifically, it wants to know whether or not the resources are being applied toward the project goals in an effective manner. Generally, this is done by assigning the project a budget based on a detailed plan of activities and then tracking those activities. The project represents a risk to the organization and bears major similarities to any other research and development activity.

Delivery of an HRD program cannot be described easily in such terms. Delivery does not fit the definition of research and development activity. It best fits the traditional definition of a *service*, an activity performed by an individual or organization for another for a fee. In the new-hire program example used earlier, neither Green Inc. nor Blue Co. could predict precisely how many new employees they would hire in a given period of time. Budgeting for delivery, therefore, is expressed often as a schedule. The schedule establishes targets for delivery volume, together with budgets expressed as the cost for particular levels of delivery volume.

But differences in the use the organization makes of financial information for project control determine the separation of development from delivery. In development, HRD management controls total project cost by seeking alternative strategies. In delivery, on the other hand, the management reduces unit expense to minimize the cost of implementing the program. Generally stated, development managers seek to minimize overall project cost within the constraints of overall project goals, while delivery managers seek to minimize unit costs while maintaining program effectiveness and quality. In practice, the differences between development and delivery become dramatic, with contention for resources between them being common.

To summarize the three assumptions, let us reexamine the question, "How much does it cost?" Any attempt to analyze the cost of human resource development efforts must focus on projects or programs undertaken by organizations. Furthermore, the analysis must discriminate between the development of the project and its delivery.

Goals of Effective Finance and Budgeting

The view of finance and budgeting put forward here is utilitarian. Feedback has already been cited as the principal function of financial analysis. But all too often, HRD managers think of accountability as the only concern of financial analysis. Not until the managers use financial analysis as a tool in managing their own projects does the system of budgets help the whole organization. In other words, if the manager views financial control as imposed from above, then the manager will not be able to use financial information effectively within his or her own group. However, if the manager views budget and finance as a basic part of project management, then the manager is likely to use the information from analysis for effective decision making aimed at improving performance.

E.C. Dykeman calls the budget one of the most effective techniques used to accomplish the objectives of management and lists five major aspects of the budgeting process.[4]

The budget expresses managerial capacity.

The budget is a coordination device.

The budget expresses a plan of action.

The budget is a communications device.

The budget is the basis for comparisons and evaluations.

The discussion here focuses on the last three of these points.

What Does It Cost? Versus What Do We Charge?   As an example of how the manager might use financial information to improve performance, consider the problem of charging tuition. Universal to training and education, this problem extends into virtually every aspect of HRD as well. It is most easily observed in state-supported universities. Sociology 101 makes a lot of money on most college campuses. If one fills a lecture hall with 250 students paying more than $500 per course, the gross revenue from one semester exceeds $125,000. Offered twice a year, this one course alone could produce more than $250,000 per year in tuition income. One large midwestern university routinely teaches its introductory sociology course to no fewer than 2000 undergrads a year. Tuition revenue for the one course approaches $1 million.

Now, contrast Sociology 101 with a senior physics course such as Crystalography of SubMicron Physical Structures. Taught by a senior faculty member, the course's tuition income from the 15 students enrolled totals $15,000 (the tuition charged is the same as for Sociology 101). That does not pay for professor time, let alone for the expensive laboratory equipment and its operation. The example here is not intended to dramatize the difference in revenue alone. A key point is that the school's administration has no idea how much either course actually costs to run. Independent of how much the institution chooses to charge for courses, it cannot hope to manage its resources effectively unless it knows how much a course costs. This point has been a recurring theme in institutions of higher education since the 1960s. Now the problem has appeared in business and industry as well. The uninformed HRD manager says, "I am going to charge $50 for this service, because I think that is what it is worth to our clients. I have no idea what it really costs." The informed HRD manager argues, "This service really costs $65, but I am only going to charge $40, because the organization is willing to pay a $25 subsidy."

Once questions about programs are put in such terms, the decisions that managers face become much clearer and better defined. The HRD manager can show the source of the cost (accountability) and help decide how to derive benefit from the project (manageability). Thus financial control contributes directly to the project's effectiveness.

What Managers Require.   While the contrast between college tuition and the true cost of instruction seems dramatic, it may be hard to see how that specific issue relates to all HRD activity. What makes the example broadly applicable is that no matter what organizational environment the HRD manager works in, resources are scarce. Nobody has a blank check for HRD. So the manager makes tradeoffs. In making those tradeoffs, the HRD manager ties resources to projects. The manager's purpose is to obtain the greatest organizational benefit from the available resources. But only when good financial information about the resources and projects is available can the manager actually make decisions about the best application of resources. Viewed from the perspective of the manager, financial information about project resources is itself a resource.

However, like all other resources, financial information has its own costs. Staff time, documentation, and the manager's own time are required to gather and process the information needed to prepare the financial reports. So a good question is, "How much financial information does the manager really need?" It should be no surprise that sometimes there is too much information and sometimes there is too little. Neither is it surprising that effective managers learn the decision-making process and accountability through experience.

Fortunately, it is possible to generalize about the essential requirements common to all financial reporting approaches. These generalizations emerge as a set of key requirements for effective financial systems.

How Do You Budget?

The Basic Budget Cycle.   Within any organization, projects and their budgets acquire a natural cycle. Development projects in particular take on a seasonal pattern of conception, fetal growth, and birth. For example, project funds are proposed in October, approved in January, used in the spring, and bear fruit in the summer. The budget process parallels the project and, in particular, ties itself to this "life cycle" of the project.

Even in mature projects, such as large industrial HRD programs, the cycle is evident. Estimates of demand for a course arrive twice a year; capital funds are approved in September; project reports are due in November. The fiscal year marches on. Built into this budget cycle are complex management expectations about growth, continuity, acquisition of capital, and other financial matters. So as the HRD manager begins the budget process, the organization has already established a context or environment for the financial performance of the HRD group—an environment to which the manager must be acutely sensitive. The budget's first requirement, then, is to meet expectations. Only rarely does a well-planned budget surprise supervisors.

Defining the Project.   Regardless of the organizational environment or management's expectations, project definition is the initial activity in preparing a budget. This makes sense, since a front-end project definition is a natural first step in any HRD activity. As in any project analysis, the manager identifies an overall aim or goal for the effort and then works to achieve that end. The focus here on budget and finance points toward an additional front-end activity. Effective financial analysis requires that managers begin to associate monetary amounts with project goals early in the project. Amounts do not need to be precise. Estimates simply cannot be more precise than the goals they describe. Still, managers will find it useful to estimate the financial size of the program goal right from the project's inception. Is it a $1,000 goal, a $10,000 goal, or a $100,000 goal? Roughly how much total dollar effort is being considered?

Thinking in financial terms from project start yields a twofold advantage. First, the exercise conditions the manager to the habit of thinking financially. At the same time, the project receives an immediate "reality test." "Will $5,000 train all supervisors in a new manufacturing technology?" Management would reject that as a ridiculously low figure. "Will $500,000 be realistic for a program on letter writing?" Far too much money for the effort. The manager quickly gauges the project's scale against supervisory expectations and thereby begins the management communication process as early in the project as possible. Jack S. Jenness points out that a "budget climate" exists in organizations, and the HRD manager must be aware of it.[5]

Estimate the Financial Performance. Once the general project plans are reviewed and accepted, managers must specify how the project's financial resources will be employed. This process of analyzing, or breaking down projects into steps and activities, is what most people refer to as "making a budget," although the word *budget* is used much more broadly in this discussion.

The work done at this stage produces a detailed estimate of financial activity, for a definite period of time, for a particular project. It states, in dollars, the expected resources and expenses for the project. The budget has now become a communication from the HRD manager to the next level of management that states: "Here is what my group and I expect to be doing." In the discussion and review of the estimate, the HRD manager hopes to show the next management level how the project will meet its goals within the resource restrictions applied to the project. The manager's motto should be, "Help stamp out surprises," because if budgeting is done right, there will be no financial surprises when the project is completed.

Through analysis and review, the organization will produce a financial estimate. That estimate becomes the statement of the work to be done. This statement of work objectives represents a contract, whereby the manager agrees to work within the budget. For external consultants, the estimate might actually be part of the contract. Any organization will use the financial performance of its managers and contractors to evaluate them.

Track Expenses. One aspect of financial analysis and budgeting for which the analogy between a personal budget and a business budget works well is expense tracking. In general, both the "head of household" and the manager have concerns about budget exceptions. For both of them, this fundamental rule applies: If the budget estimate proves wrong, action must follow. When the project expense underruns the budget (estimate exceeds actual expense), the unused resources must be reallocated. Reallocation is the action generally prompted by a budget underrun. Since extra funds usually mean money was saved somewhere, managers tend to be pleased with underruns. That attitude, however, may be short sighted. Budget underruns generally show that the original estimates were not correct and that the organization has "extra" resources. Unless the manager can quickly reapply the resources saved, they may be lost or wasted. Furthermore, frequent or large budget underruns typically point to poor initial planning and should be causes for concern.

Budget overruns, especially large ones, signal an event requiring management attention—again, an exception. An overrun represents increased risk that the organization might not complete a project satisfactorily. In extreme cases, an overrun in a critical area of a project might even mean that the project cannot be completed at all. More often, however, the overrun simply signals managers to let them know that one element of a project has become more expensive. The manager must correct the problem by limiting the overrun, going to an alternate project plan, or reassigning resources from underruns in other areas. So the general rule applies again—overruns require the manager to exercise control and correct problems.

Learn, Manage, and Control.   In expense tracking, the tight relationship between financial analysis and management control is made clear. The financial analysis (tracking) identifies unexpected variances (exceptions) between the project plan and the project itself. Management uses its financial information when it makes decisions to alter the project from the original plan. This process is perhaps the best example of the concept of management control.

The benefit of financial analysis and management control is not limited to a single project. Managers and the organization are able to learn. Writers often cite this ability to learn as a key characteristic of successful organizations. Because projects are likely to share many essential features—especially financial features—managers can generalize about financial activity. The financial history of projects, then, becomes an important part of the information the organization employs in planning and control, because that is the data the organization uses as it learns. Just as the collective financial performance of all projects determines the overall health of an organization, the collective experience of its managers is the best basis the organization has for planning and control.

There is a danger inherent in exception reporting and management control. It relates to an insidious financial conservatism that argues: Since exceptions mean managers must intervene to deal with deviations from plans, a good project is one with no exceptions.

An obvious example of a good exception is one created through aggressive attempts to control cost or through the development of a better approach after the project plan has been established. So the argument that budgets were meant to be followed simply does not hold up in organizations trying to improve their own performance. Effective organizations learn and improve as they manage and control. The rule that says all financial exceptions require action in no way says that all financial exceptions are bad or are to be avoided.

Report Financial Performance. The financial analysis of a project comes down to a single exception report—the overall project budget figure. The manager hopes that the planning and control activities in the project have put the exception on the underrun list, but the manager has confidence that the actions taken, when exceptions did occur, were appropriate. The manager is both accountable and responsible. The organization requires that the manager show clearly what was done with the organization's resources and why, and the financial report becomes the principal mechanism for doing this. With the final report, the budget cycle on the project is closed.

Direct Versus Indexed Approaches to Budgeting

Do not run to a book on financial analysis in organizations to look up *direct* and *indexed* budgeting. They are not there. What is being put forward here is a fundamental concept—not an accounting principle—of how managers view resources.

The direct approach to resource management represents a perfectly natural and ordinary way of looking at projects. So does the opposite, or indexed approach. Both are such general concepts that they become metaphors and require some definition before we can use them as working terms.

There is no better example of the difference between the two views than the difference between a billed service and a tax. When a city provides a service, such as garbage pick up, it generally charges for that service through a tax. It argues, "Everybody uses the service. Everyone will share in the cost. Each person's share will be determined by how much property they own, how much they earn locally, or some other index." Hence, the name *indexed*. A commercial refuse service takes a different approach. It cannot charge those who do not use the service, so it establishes a charge for the service. The firm bills its customers directly for the services they use. The disposal service uses a direct charge, while the city uses an indexed charge.

Direct Approaches to Budgeting and Finance.   In budgeting as well as in most other things, *direct* is a synonym for straightforward. But at the same time, the direct approach to anything is not necessarily the fastest or easiest approach. Direct budgeting is straightforward in that it seeks to assign a specific value to each identifiable budget item. It is pure analysis at its best and often appeals to HRD managers who are familiar with task analysis and systems analysis. But as projects become complex, encompassing large numbers of individual tasks, the direct approach to budgeting grows cumbersome. For many projects, a purely direct budgeting system becomes too complex to manage. That is primarily because direct budgeting requires estimating the cost of every activity within the project down to a fine level of detail. The more activities a project has, the more complex the budget analysis. The more complex the budget analysis, the greater the likelihood of omissions or inaccuracies.

Before discussing the alternative to direct estimating, it is important to discuss what the direct estimate produces and how the estimating is done. Activity pricing represents a challenge to any manager, because it requires judgment. The rewards for the manager who is able to make accurate activity price estimates are the ability to plan effectively and relief from the burden of work created by the need to respond to overruns and underruns.

Once a project has been analyzed or broken down into steps or activities, the manager attempts to put a price on each of those separate steps. The price of the project is the sum of the prices of all the separate activities. In theory, pricing individual steps should be easier to accomplish than pricing the entire project. But in practice, the job may still be difficult. There are four basic approaches to activity pricing with virtually infinite variations. The four are:

Expert views based on history and experience ("guestimating")
Comparison to baseline or "classic" activities
Reduction of the project to smaller activities
Analysis of unit costs

Often managers generate reliable estimates of activity cost based principally on their experience. In making such estimates, the expert relies on complex logic and many interrelated pieces of information—trends, history, time of year, external pressures, and even weather may figure in the expert's forecast. Such estimates are good places to start the budgeting process, since they are typically easy to obtain and, depending on the expert, should be reasonably accurate. Each of the other approaches may be best viewed as an effort to improve on the expert's "guestimate." Regardless of how the direct estimate is obtained, the idea behind all direct approaches is the same. The manager defines the cost of the project as the sum of the cost of each of its components.

Indirect Approaches to Financial Analysis.   Mired down in the tedium of trying to do a direct financial analysis of a project with many activities, one sees the attractiveness of the indirect approach to budgeting. In a set of similar activities, such as producing artwork for various media, costs will be closely related to each other. If a way of comparing activities on some common basis can be found—such as the size of the artwork or the number of slides to be produced—then producing a good estimate of cost will be simple. The information used in the comparison represents an index of project cost. The key idea in indexing is that some easily counted or observed aspect of the project is used to calculate the estimated expense of an activity that is hard to count or observe.

While inflation has altered this example, it was once true that bulldozers cost $1.00 per pound. A small, 10,000-lb. bulldozer cost about $10,000, while a huge, 20-ton monster cost $40,000. Clearly, many more things contribute to the cost of bulldozers than their weight, but the idea of using the cost per pound as an index of total expense makes sense. Cost per pound, however, is an inappropriate index for an HRD project. Still, managers often find that indexes provide fast and remarkably accurate ways of estimating HRD project expenses. Here are some examples of commonly used indexes and the rationale behind them.

Index.   Student weeks of instruction.
Rationale.   All delivery costs are tied to student attendance.
Index.   Pages of course material.
Rationale.   The number of pages of material per unit of instruction is nearly constant, and pages are easy to count.
Index.   Behavioral objectives.

Rationale.   If a careful task analysis is performed, all objectives should be the same level of difficulty, and a good quick estimate of project cost could be based on them.

Index.   Minutes of video tape.

Rationale.   For a good quick estimate of media expense, many organizations use a dollars-per-minute figure based on previous budget performance.

Indexing, or indirect expense accounting, has two broad applications. In the first of these, indexing helps managers deal with expenses too complex or too small to treat as direct expenses within the organization's accounting system. The cost of photocopying, for example, is hard to track for each project activity. A common approach taken in accounting is to assign such distributed costs proportionately to projects across an entire organizational unit. The index used to assign the expense is the direct expense of each project itself, a practice commonly called *pro-rating.* The indexed expense can be said to be prorated over the direct expense. Such use of prorated expense accounting is of more than passing interest to the HRD project manager. Not only does it suggest the need to include prorated expenses in the project budget when estimates are being made, but it suggests a second, more useful application of indexes and multipliers.

The real power of indexed budget estimating is its ability to provide managers with reasonable, quick, easily obtained estimates of project expenses for planning purposes. If an appropriate index is available, the manager can estimate a project budget almost entirely on the basis of historical data regarding average or unit costs. The estimating process then consists of multiplying the index by the units of indexed activities (e.g., the number of pages of output) to be produced in the project. The whole estimate of even a complex project can be produced in minutes on a pocket calculator. If nothing else, the indexed approach to budget estimating provides an excellent cross-check for direct analytical estimating methods.

An Example.   The best way to dramatize the interplay of the two estimating approaches is to provide an example. The HRD manager used the direct budgeting method to identify the following expenses for a program to administer a management skills inventory to the staff of a small corporation.

Test instruments	$2,500
Test scoring	1,750
Analysis and writing	3,150
Management notification	1,250
Project administration	2,000
Miscellaneous expense	1,000
Total project budget	$11,650

The manager had another way to estimate the cost of the project. On previous measurement projects with similar characteristics, project expenses had been close to five times the cost of the test instruments. So the alternative, index-based budget for the project is:

Test instruments	$2,500
Historical index	× 5.0
Total project budget	$12,500

A few points need to be made. Notice that in the indexed example, the dollar units are not in the index but in the units of project measurement. Also, consider the figure of $2,000 for administration in the direct estimate. That number might be based on an estimate of two and one-half weeks of time at a $20 loaded hourly wage. But the figure is not an indexed estimate. It still represents the real expense the manager expects the project to generate. Even the miscellaneous expense category is simply a collective heading for specific expense items.

Both the direct and indexed methods of forecasting provide estimates of future financial performance and needs, but which of the estimates is correct? Both may be; either may be; neither may be. Correctness means, narrowly, that one estimate will come closer to the actual budget performance of the project than the other. What the manager really wants to know is which estimate is going to be more helpful in suggesting ways the manager can plan and control. The answer depends, of course, on what the manager does with the estimates. Through analysis of the information contained in the estimates and the assumptions behind them, the HRD manager will learn what financial forces are at work on the project. Knowledge gained in the analysis, not just the dollar figure in the estimate, will be the basis for effective project management.

Comparing Direct and Indirect Budgets.   Perhaps the most useful way of answering the question regarding which method provides the best estimates is to compare them, pointing out the relative strengths and weaknesses of each.

Budget Method Comparison

	Direct	Indexed
Organization size	Works for various sized organizations; detail required increases with size of firm	More appropriate for large organizations
Project size	Easier for small HRD projects	Easier for large projects
Manager control	Associated with tight control and feedback	Appropriate in projects with delegation or light control
Responsibility	Clearly but narrowly defined	Loosely but broadly defined
Big advantage	Easy to understand	Easy to calculate
Blind spot	Requires that all project activities are identified up front; unforeseen expenses are not counted	May not point to areas of potential savings, since many small steps get lumped together

   In addition to these generalized characteristics of the two basic methods, one needs to consider that all HRD projects are not created equal. Of all the possible variations and distinctions, perhaps the most important is the one raised earlier between development and delivery. The distinction is important and can be stated as a general rule: Development activities usually require direct budget estimates; delivery activities can be adequately estimated through an index if enough historical data exist.

   Development activities may be characterized as varying widely, subject to rapidly changing forces, and organizationally complex. Each development project is a custom effort with significant differences from any other development project. Only in the largest human resource development organizations can enough historical data be gathered to permit the definition of reasonable indexes. So it is not surprising that direct budget methods dominate cost estimating for development projects. While indexed budget methods may be used and can provide useful cross-checks and supplementary information, direct budget analysis is the fundamental tool of the developer.

Delivery activities, on the other hand, submit to different analytical approaches. Many costs are tied closely to either students or instructors. Thus the most important elements of the project—the people—provide useful and convenient indexes for estimating overall project performance. For project delivery, the index method of estimating works so well that the project manager might be tempted to forsake direct methods completely and depend on the easier index approach. The risk, and it is a considerable one, is that exceptional expenses, gradual changes to projects, and organizational pressures will never get recognized—a dilemma for management.

What the organization requires is that budget estimates reflect reality. But reality is dynamic. So neither the direct nor the indexed budgeting approach reflect reality perfectly. People often ask where the creativity lies in management. One excellent answer is that the judgments the manager makes in estimating or selecting the right plan represents creativity of the first order.

A BUDGET CASE EXAMPLE:
WHAT'S IN A BUDGET?

So far the discussion of HRD project budgeting and finance has been purely abstract. However, since the budget process itself is anything but abstract, some good examples are needed. Following are two budgets— one for development and another for delivery—each one small but annotated to illustrate and further develop the points made earlier.

A Development Project

Figure 3.1 represents the budget of a small, formal development project. While the specific nature of the project does not affect the form of the budget, a brief narrative may make the project more real. This budget comes from the HRD department of a moderately-sized, heavy equipment manufacturer. The proposal covers the training needed to provide the skills and knowledge required to operate a new, computer-controlled (numerical control) milling machine. A significant part of the budget deals with the development of job aids to be used with the machine.

Expense Item	Amount
Personnel[1]	
Professional staff	$18,000
Clerical staff	5,000
Other support staff	3,000
Subject matter specialists	—
Facilities	2,000[2]
Materials production	
Printing	7,500
Graphics	6,000
Photography	3,000
Video	—
Computer programming[3]	—
Project administration and overhead	4,500[4]
Transportation	—
Total	$49,000

[1]This represents a loaded wage; that is, salary plus benefits and administrative expense such as workman's compensation taxes.

[2]The facilities expense includes rent, utilities, and insurance for HRD prorated across active projects.

[3]The specific itemization of computer expense is becoming increasingly common.

[4]Administrative expense was estimated at 10% of all other expense.

Figure 3.1. Proposed training development budget for Chambers LINK-24 training project.

Sources of Development Funds.   The funds for the development project may not all come from the same source. Multiple divisions of the company may participate in the project and contribute from their resources. In Figure 3.2 some project funds are tied to the new machine, while others come from general training sources. Furthermore, the income funds are exactly the same dollars that will be applied to the expense budget and thus require the same level of management attention and control.

With the expense and income planning budgets, the project is ready to proceed. In reality, there would be some adjustments to the budgets at the planning meeting, but in this example, one can assume that everything was approved without change.

Development Project Tracking and Control.   The project starts, and the budget becomes the key tool in the project tracking process. Project tracking, in this example, becomes the principal responsibility of the HRD manager. At several points in the project, the HRD manager will need to know several key pieces of information about the project's budget.

Source of Funds	Amount
Division operating budgets	
Houston	$11,000
Phoenix	11,000
St. Louis	11,000
Milwaukee	0[1]
Training organization	
New development funds	5,000[2]
Reassigned from LINK-16B	6,000[3]
Technology impact fund	13,000[4]
Total	$57,000

[1]Milwaukee will not be using the LINK-24 and will not contribute to development.

[2]These funds will be used in project administration and interaction with the vendor.

[3]These funds are reassigned from a project which underran its budget and which is closely related to the LINK-24 project.

[4]These funds are indirectly contributed by the operating divisions and marketing.

Figure 3.2.   Proposed funding sources for LINK-24 training development.

Specifically, for each item in the budget, the manager will need to know whether the expenses for the project fit the overall budget plan. It will also be useful to know what happened in the recent past—typically the last month—if management is to identify exceptions and take action. Finally, it would be useful to forecast what the total project expense is going to be, given the exceptions and actions that have occurred so far.

Figure 3.3, often called a spreadsheet, describes the current financial position of the project. The items listed are the same as were set out in the plan—a concession to making a good example. This status report describes the project at just past the midpoint. The manager now has enough data to see trends in expenses and plan a "midcourse correction."

Analysis of the Budget Status Report.   If one simply looks at the totals, the project appears to be moving forward largely as planned. The project has a $4,800 overrun to this point ($24,700 minus $19,900).

However, more detailed analysis reveals several difficulties. These difficulties appear to be of the type the manager needs to control. The most significant problem is the forecast budget overrun itself. This overrun seems particularly alarming since the report assumes that no more overruns will occur in the remainder of the project—an assumption the manager knows to be incorrect. In analyzing the project as described in the budget status report, the manager makes observations and formulates plans to deal with problems.

	A	B	C	D	E	F
	Expense for May		Total expense through May		Expense to end	
(Budgeted/Actual)	Budget	Actual	Budget	Actual	Budget	Projected[1]
Personnel						
Professional staff	2.0	3.0	9.0	9.3	18.0	18.3
Clerical staff	0.6	0.5	2.0	3.6	5.0	6.6
Support staff	0.3	0.4	1.5	1.8	3.0	3.3
Facilities expense	0.2	0.5	1.0	2.3	2.0	3.3
Materials production expense						
Printing	1.0	1.3	3.5	1.4	7.5	5.4
Graphics	0.5	0.2	2.0	5.3	6.0	9.3
Photography	0.3	0.0	1.0	1.0	3.0	3.0
Administration and overhead					4.5	4.5
Total	4.9	5.9	20.0	24.7	49.0	53.7

[1] Projected expense (column F) refers to an estimate of total project expenses. This estimate is the sum of actual expenses to date (column D) plus expenses budgeted for the rest of the project (column E minus column C).

Figure 3.3.   Project budget status report; Project LINK-24 report for May (in thousands of dollars).

Analyzing columns A and B.   Total expense for the month is more than 20% over budget, largely because of heavy staff activity. This extra activity came about because of some early slippage in the schedule. Next month will also be heavy, but the project end figure of $18,000 is still about right. No action required.

The facilities expense overrun is a much more serious problem. At about $300 for May, this item has overrun every month of the project and could produce a total overrun much higher than the modest $1,300 overrun projected in the status report. The manager thinks a $4,500 overrun will occur if the flow is not checked. The problem has two causes. First, utilities and building rent went up. Second, two other projects originally planned were dropped, causing loadings for building expenses to be spread across three projects instead of five. That, in effect, nearly doubles the facilities expense, even though no change has occurred in the project. The manager will request additional funding to cover the increased facilities expense.

Analyzing columns C and D.   The "project to date" figures look good. Personnel expense is close to the figure planned. Facilities expense

Adjusted Project Budget Estimate: May

Expense Item	Current Budget	Original Budget
Personnel		
Professional staff	$18,000	$18,000
Clerical staff	6,000	5,000
Other support staff	3,500	3,000
Facilities	3,800	2,000
Materials production		
Printing	7,800	7,500
Graphics	10,000	6,000
Photography	2,500	3,000
Project administration and overhead	2,800	4,500
Total	$54,400	$49,000

Figure 3.4. Revised project expense budget.

looks terrible for the reasons cited above. Printing and graphics have both drifted away from their original estimates. Printing is low because the development staff was slow in producing the written materials. While that slippage does not place the overall project schedule in jeopardy, a small amount of overtime pay will be needed to get the product out. The manager's best estimate of total expense on that item is $7,800 for the total project. Graphics has seriously overrun its budget. Some work was done early, but the cost was much higher than predicted. The manager will need to consult with project staff to find ways to control the high graphics expense.

Analyzing columns E and F.   The manager recalculates estimates of the project expense budget (Figure 3.4) based on this midproject report and personal perspective on what remains to be done on the project.

The project manager has discovered ways of adjusting some of the more serious problems and of controlling the project's expenses. An overrun will occur, and the need for more funds is communicated to upper-level management early. While this is a simple example, it illustrates the key features of a development project expense budget, an income budget, and budget tracking spreadsheet.

A Delivery Activity

Rather than tracking a complete delivery budget as in the case of the development example, the discussion of delivery budgets will focus on the idea, introduced earlier, that development budgets involve indexed categories of both income and expense.

Sources of Delivery Funds.   The most obvious example of indexing is tuition itself. Whether the money comes directly from the individual student, as in a proprietary school, or from the organization for which the individual works, as in the military, the HRD organization's funding is often indexed to the delivery of the program to the individual. Virtually all money coming to any HRD delivery project arrives on a "per head" basis—per test, per interview, per lesson, per worker, per day, per anything. Financing by indexed income has two attractive features. First, income forecasting is simple, because one need estimate only the total delivery activity to estimate income. And second, since all delivery costs are tied into the delivery index, it should be easy to adjust budget items in response to changing delivery. That, at least, is the theory.

In practice, however, forecasting delivery income based on delivery volume is difficult. HRD units must plan delivery in advance and cannot adjust to large, rapid variations in the demand for service. A delivery forecast becomes more and more accurate the closer one gets to the delivery date. But adjusting to changes in an estimate of delivery volume becomes harder and harder. Planning for facilities, staff, and support for the delivery of HRD programs may need to begin months or even years in advance. The precision of plans cannot exceed the accuracy of the demand forecast.

The organizational response to this problem is twofold. First, the manager makes intermediate estimates—successive approximations to the true load, each with less variability or risk than the previous estimate. In large organizations with big budgets, this process may become intensely formal. The organization seeks to provide managers with the best available estimate of a future condition. An example follows:

Estimates of Participation in Quality Circles Program
Allied Tektonics, Inc.

Date of Estimate	Estimate	Variability
July	400 employees	within 100 employees
October	320 employees	within 20 employees
December	337 employees	within 5 employees[1]

[1]Actual number of employees on January 14: 334 employees

The second approach to dealing with planning limits in HRD units is to keep the program's response to changing levels of demand as flexible as possible. The classic means of accomplishing this goal is for the manager to minimize fixed or nondiscretionary costs within a program. Then variations in program demand can be met with minimal change to the unit cost of the project. *Nondiscretionary costs* are those costs over which an individual manager has little or no control. The organization is committed to those expenses regardless of what the manager does.

Examples of Management Control.   A brief example will show how the manager can work toward minimizing nondiscretionary expenses. Monon Transportation Industries discovers that the Interstate Commerce Commission has introduced a new safety rule affecting no less than 50% of Monon's workers. Within three weeks, Monon must have a document on file showing that each employee involved in handling freight has participated in a program explaining the new ruling and that each employee has passed a simple, 10-item quiz about changed procedures resulting from the new rule.

The HRD manager studies alternative ways to support the program. Although the program could be conducted internally, the manager contracts with external HRD professionals to handle this "one-shot" load. The key point is that external organizations and facilities are used not just to help out in an emergency but as a basic way of keeping fixed costs low.

J.P. Yaney and others have explored the financial implications of using external contractors on nondiscretionary expenses.[6] To further explore this idea, consider what happens to two fast food companies with different fixed costs for HRD delivery when their programs slow down. Hodap's Pizza is a national chain of pizza parlors known for their thin crust and thick cheese. They conduct an HRD program to develop store managers, and the program has attracted national attention. Hodap's owns an office building next to one of their largest pizza parlors and runs an HRD center there. They employ 10 staff full time at the center. Another chain, The Salty Dog, also has a large HRD program, but they do not operate a development center as such. Their program operates out of corporate headquarters and uses hotels near their restaurants for classrooms. Leaders are borrowed from the field on rotating assignments and are given special leader effectiveness training. The quality of the programs is about equal.

In the following example, the ratio of discretionary to total expenses is compared for the two firms at two different levels of operation. The impact of fixed costs on the programs is the key point to be gained from the comparison. The interesting result is Salty Dog does better in an economic downturn. Salty has lower fixed or nondiscretionary costs. So the increase in expense per new manager brought on by reduced program demand is less for Salty than for the competition. Salty Dog is financially more flexible than Hodap. This financial flexibility translates directly into an increased ability to meet organizational needs. In this instance, the need is simply to save money during a slowdown.

Management Development Program Expense Per Year: Two Firms at Full Operation (250 trainees)

	Hodap	Salty Dog
Discretionary costs	$300,000	$800,000
Nondiscretionary costs	700,000	200,000
Total cost	$1,000,000	$1,000,000
New managers in program	250	250
Cost per new manager	$4,000	$4,000

Management Development Program Expense Per Year: Two Firms at Reduced Operation (150 trainees)

	Hodap	Salty Dog
Discretionary costs		
(60% reduced)	$180,000	$480,000
Nondiscretionary costs	700,000	200,000
Total cost	$880,000	$680,000
New managers in program	150	150
Cost per new manager	$5,867	$4,533

Sources of Delivery Expense. The assumption made in discussing delivery expense has been that all expenses can be indexed based on historical data about the relationship of delivery volume to total costs. Exceptional expenses, such as the added expense of labs in a training course or of travel in a management development program, provide examples of expenses that may be hard to index.

Indexed budgeting is of little value, furthermore, on the first project an organization undertakes. Therefore, management must fall back on the project budget approach described for development. The management is safe in arguing that the first delivery effort is a development project. One goal of that intitial project is to establish a financial pattern for future projects.

A Summary of Budget and Control.   If one returns to the earlier considerations about why managers prepare budgets and about what budgets do (i.e., ideas about feedback and learning), then all the budget details and all the control begins to make sense. A budget is a model of the project. The activities in the project or program have financial properties—costs, expenses, incomes, and overheads that actually exist. The budget models the financial features of the project so the manager can plan and control it. The categories and relationships important to the reality of the project become important in the simulated categories and relationships of the model as well. The categories of costs that the manager chooses to reflect in the budget are those that contribute to a valid model and describe aspects of the project important to the manager. They are the big ones, organized into classes the manager can describe easily; they are the ones the manager can control, organized into classes of management action. For each manager, differences in management approach, background, and purpose yield differences in budget planning and control. Good results may be achieved by pursuing many different paths.

SPECIAL TOPICS IN BUDGET AND FINANCE

For many managers, the budgeting process stands among the most important activities in each project. Because of the importance given budgets and financial analysis, managers generally work hard to integrate budgeting into the mainstream of their activities. Furthermore, tools such as systems analysis and microcomputers have provided managers with specialized approaches that make budgeting easier and more useful. An introduction to these topics will conclude the discussion here.

The Tie to Accounting

Up to this point there has been no discussion of accounting—the formal discipline of analyzing, verifying, and reporting the financial results of an organization. It is important that the two—budgeting and accounting—

be kept separate, even though they share many features. Budgeting is a tool for managers to use in planning and controlling projects and programs. G.C. Hentschke sees accounting as having three principal uses, one of which is that routine internal reporting aspect of budgeting. The other two uses of accounting he cites are nonroutine internal reporting and external reporting as to stockholders or government agencies.[7] What is alike about the two is that both rely on the same information—the financial activity of the organization—for their input. The budget process will rely heavily on the accounting system. The historical data used in calculating indexes for budget planning will almost always come from accounting. The categories the manager tracks through a project may be determined by accounting. So even though the two are different, they are never widely separated.

Accrual Accounting.   Some accounting principles are important for budget analysis and financial planning. Among these are accruals and cash flow. Accounting has changed a great deal since double-entry bookkeeping was invented by Florentine merchants and bankers in the fifteenth century. For 500 years, accountants have worked to solve problems, as they arose, with available tools.

One problem accountants must deal with is *liabilities*—the idea that even though money has not actually moved from one place to another, an individual or organization has taken an action that means money will change hands at a later time. For example; an HRD manager needs slides for a presentation and sends out 20 sketches to a firm on April 10. The slides and a bill arrive on April 20. As the manager's company and the slide maker have an agreement that bills do not have to be paid for 60 days, the company does not pay the bill until June 19. The difficulty is that the manager wants to count the expense against the budget plan for April, but the company wants to count the expense against the bill actually paid in June. Accrual accounting deals with this dilemma. An *accrual* is a short-term liability or debt based on a financial commitment that will be paid off shortly. "Shortly" simply means the commitment cannot be complicated by leases or interest, etc. So the accounting department sees the bill in April and says that the HRD manager's account has an expense accrued to it. The accountant knows the bill has not been paid (but it will be), and the manager knows that for planning purposes the money was spent in April, just as the budget indicated. Accrual accounting is, in fact, the only sensible way to manage the changing, complicated budgets that HRD managers create.

Cash Flow.   Another problem of mutual concern to the manager and the accounting office is cash flow. The problem is so fundamental to HRD development that all HRD managers are certain to have thought about it, whether they have used the term *cash flow* or not.

In its simplest terms, cash flow is a cycle in which money moves into and out of the organization as income and expense.[8] For example, the money to develop an HRD project comes in as income at the start of the project and is used as the project progresses. Any money remaining at the end of the project becomes profit or is used for additional work on other projects. That is the project level definition.

Obviously, things do not happen that way. Sometimes the project gets well under way before any money arrives. In that case, the project temporarily borrows money from other projects to get going. If money is not available inside the organization to cover the project's expenses across the period during which expense exceeds income, the organization may go to a lending institution or bank to borrow money. Our society has become sophisticated in the way it allows organizations to deal with cash flow problems.

But cash flow looks different from the accountant's perspective. To the accountant, cash flow must be planned for and incorporated into the financial planning of the entire organization. The accountant and financial manager may be concerned with those factors that directly impact the budget planning of the HRD manager. One such factor is the availability of funds, tied to the expense-before-income scenario described above. There may be times, especially in smaller organizations, when insufficient money is available to permit work to progress on a project as rapidly as the HRD manager would want. The financial manager may temporarily restrict spending on a project because of the limited amount of cash moving, or flowing, into the organization.

But the principal problem the financial manager must solve is how to keep the financial position of the firm strong. In the largest organizations or in government-sponsored organizations, the solution may be hard to see, but it is there in one form or another.

The money a firm expects to receive for a project is an *asset*— something another firm owes it. The firm is established on *capital*— money people have invested in the firm to make it work. The critical number that tells those people how much their firm is worth right now is a figure called *the current ratio*. Without turning this into an elementary accounting text, one point should be understood. As long as current assets—such as contracts for projects—increase, while everything else stays fairly constant, the current ratio worsens. That, in turn, limits the firm's ability to borrow or to attract additional investors.

Therefore, HRD projects can cause serious difficulties for the financial manager. For this and other economic and accounting reasons, program development is financially painful to the organization. Program delivery may be expensive, but it is more straightforward from the accountant's point of view.

Balance Sheets

As HRD becomes widely accepted in industry, it is increasingly important that HRD managers be able to speak the language of the firm's operations and financial managers. The financial language they speak is largely centered on the balance sheet. Rather than provide a detailed introduction to reading a balance sheet, this discussion will focus on what a balance sheet is and how it is important to the HRD manager.

The Balance Sheet.   The *balance sheet* is a financial description of the firm and its relationship to the financial community outside the firm—especially those people who have invested money in the hope that the firm will earn a profit. Traditionally, this situation is described at a point in time, since a primary consideration of the firm's investors is the growth or change in the business. At that point in time, often the end of the year, the firm describes its assets and debts (also called liabilities or claims on assets).

Income Statements.   The balance sheet is not, however, the entire story. The income statement provides a somewhat more direct picture of what the firm did during the previous year. Again, ratios are important. With the additional information provided by the income statement, the firm is able to determine two more types of financial results:

Activity ratios, which measure how efficiently the firm is using its resources, especially its capital

Profitability ratios, which express how much money the firm has made in relationship to other important figures, especially sales or income

The firm's profitability is the information most important to the individual manager and to the stockholder. "How much money did the firm make doing what it did?" "How did that relate to income (sales) and to capital?" These are the questions answered by the firm's two chief financial documents.

The Bottom Line. If one looks up *bottom line* in the index of a reputable text on financial management, disappointment is almost guaranteed. The term will not be there; it is slang. Bottom line refers specifically to the last or next to the last line of the firm's income statement. The line is usually labeled "net income after taxes"—in short, profit. So the bottom-line-oriented manager is solely, or at least principally, concerned with increasing profits. This attitude is often associated with the Harvard Business School, which sought to educate managers to focus on things they could control—their own bottom line. This begs an obvious question. What else is there? Many other goals motivate organizations. Stability, public service, quality of work life for the employees, and environmentalism are all reasonable goals for firms but will not maximize profits. However, there is an even more fundamental answer.

In past years, the United States has faced competition from foreign industries. Some have succeeded dramatically in moving into traditional U.S. markets and performing significantly better than established U.S. firms. Part of the view propounded in the resulting self-criticism of U.S. firms is that maximizing profits should not mean maximizing profits in the current year. The tendency in HRD projects and income statements alike is to focus on one year at a time. This practice leads to a dangerous form of managerial myopia in which the manager foregoes long-range opportunities for growth and profit in order to maximize profits in the current year. In HRD projects, for example, the manager may pursue a strategy that makes this year's budget look good but which might at the same time make long-term projects more expensive.

So the bottom line is best treated as a metaphor for short-term, profit maximizing strategies, rather than as a management philosophy or a general budget or accounting goal.

Tools of Analysis

The practice of managerial science has produced several tools that can help managers conduct more effective financial analysis. While many of these techniques require sophisticated mathematical analysis and considerable effort, some are quite straightforward.

Sensitivity Analysis. In any project, some factors can be estimated with only limited accuracy. Sensitivity analysis is designed to help the manager identify which factors will influence the outcome of the project most if varied from the manager's estimate.[9] For a project where costs are simply additive, a technique such as sensitivity analysis is scarcely worthwhile. For large or complex projects, in which several indexed costs come together, sensitivity analysis may mean the difference between a successful project and a disastrous one.

In a simple application of the technique, the manager first calculates a budget based on all the fixed and easily estimated costs. Then, for each of the "risky" cost factors, the manager calculates a budget based on three different estimates for that expense item—typically a high, low and "best guess." If there are three different "risky" factors in a particular project, the analysis would require 27 ($3 \times 3 \times 3$) different budgets—one for each level of each factor. Among these 27 budgets would be one that is highest, one that is lowest, and a large group somewhere in the middle. Examining these results, the manager can say with some confidence that the actual outcome lies somewhere between the extreme guesses and is most likely to be near the mean value of all 27 guesses. Computers help reduce the tedium of calculating the 27 different budgets.

Even more useful is the information the manager gains regarding how the budget behaves (remember that it is a model) as each factor varies. For example, the manager may observe that the budget total varies little for factor A. The clear implication is that the manager need not expend much effort to control factor A since the overall effect is slight. But noting that variations in factor B produce enormous changes in overall project budget figures, the manager can immediately plan the strategies to be employed in controlling it. In conducting the analysis, the manager learns about the sensitivity of the project outcome to individual factors in it, hence, the name of the technique.

"What-if" Games.   The microcomputer revolution has been a revolution not only of machines but of software applications as well. Among the most widely used of the new programs are the electronic spreadsheets. In these programs, which commonly include the syllable "calc" or "plan" somewhere in their names, the manager has a powerful new tool for budgeting and financial analysis.

In the spreadsheet program, the manager sets up a table with column and row headings just as would be done on paper. In those cells of the table for which the manager has data, the numbers are entered into the computer. For those cells calculated from other data in the table, the manager puts the formula for computing that value.

The computer instantly calculates all the values of all the entries in the cells from the initial data provided. When a new piece of data is entered into the table, the computer recalculates. Without a demonstration or hands-on experience, it is difficult to visualize what a powerful tool the computer-based spreadsheet can be for financial planning. However, if one supposes that the HRD manager is trying to plan how to adjust the budget after looking at midproject results, then the usefulness becomes apparent. The manager can think, "What if I were to reduce the number of clerical staff working on the project from four people to three and increase the number of management staff from two to three the following month?" One needs to perform 50 calculations to determine the budget impact of that simple personnel change. So even with a pocket calculator the "what-if" game is hard to play. With a spreadsheet program, however, the manager need change only two numbers and make no new calculations. The "what-if" game becomes simple and productive. Electronic spreadsheets may be among the best new tools available to the HRD manager.

Conclusion.   Spreadsheets are, in fact, an appropriate topic on which to end this discussion. The discussion began by developing the notion of utility in budgeting and financial planning—the idea that the budget is a tool for the manager. The discussion ends by suggesting that spreadsheet programs and similar microcomputer utilities are tools for budgeting.

The HRD manager who uses these tools to become actively involved in the budgeting process has the opportunity to become more effective. Penny-pinching is not the point. The real payoff is the planning and control discipline made available through the modeling and feedback aspects of the budget and financial analysis processes. The irony here is that so many HRD managers see the budget process as foreign, when in fact it has much in common with the disciplines underlying HRD itself. These include systems analysis, needs analysis, and formal planning models. As HRD grows in importance to the organization, the need for effective project control through budgeting and financial analysis will grow as well.

NOTES

1.   A.J. Carnevale, "Human Capital: The Future For Private Training," *Training and Development*, 36(1): 41–48.

2. In this chapter, *development* refers to program development, such as the activity of an HRD organization involved in creating a new program offering. *Development* used in this way does not refer to a particular mode of the training, education, development model discussed elsewhere in this handbook.

3. W.E. Becker and R.W. Davis, "An Economic Model of Training in an Industrial Setting," *Journal of Instructional Development*, 6(2):6–14.

4. E.C. Dykeman, *Financial Reporting Systems and Techniques* (Englewood Cliffs, N.J.: Prentice-Hall, 1968), p. 27.

5. Jack S. Jenness, "Budgeting and Controlling Training Costs," in *Training and Development Handbook: A Guide to Human Resource Development*, ed. Robert L. Craig (New York: McGraw-Hill, 1976), p. 4.6–4.12.

6. J.P. Yaney, "Cost Reductions and Control for Program Development," in *Managing the Instructional Programming Effort*, ed. G. Rummler, W. Schrader, and J. Yaney. (Ann Arbor, Michigan: Bureau of Industrial Relations, 1976), p. 274–276.

7. G.C. Hentschke, *Management Operations in Education* (Berkeley, Cal.: McCutchaen Publishing, 1975), p. 3.

8. J.F. Weston and E.F. Brigham, *Managerial Finance*, 5th ed. (Hinsdale, Ill.: Dryden Press, 1975), p. 75–78.

9. G.H. Fisher, *Cost Considerations in Systems Analysis* (New York: American Elsevier, 1971), p. 12.

BIBLIOGRAPHY

Becker, W.E., and R.W. Davis. "An Economic Model of Training in an Industrial Setting." *Journal of Instructional Development*, 6 (2): 26–32. It is nearly the only economic model that highlights the dichotomy between development and delivery.

Davies, Ivor K. *Objectives in Curriculum Design*. New York: McGraw-Hill, 1976. His influence on the idea of goal setting is a fundamental part of HRD program management.

Dykeman, E.C. *Financial Reporting Systems and Techniques*. Englewood Cliffs, N.J.: Prentice-Hall, 1968. A "textbook" reference, particularly for budget purposes.

Fisher, G.H. *Cost Considerations in Systems Analysis*. American Elsevier, 1971. Contains a very thorough treatment of systems analysis approaches to budgeting, especially sensitivity analysis.

Hentschke, G.C. *Management Operations in Education*. Berkeley, Cal.: McCutchaen Publishing, 1975. A major reference that could have been cited in several places. Unfortunately, it is largely university and school oriented.

Jenness, Jack S. "Budgeting and Controlling Training Costs." In *Training and Development Handbook: A Guide to Human Resource Development*, 2d ed., edited by Robert L. Craig. New York: McGraw-Hill, 1976. Discusses the idea that the organization is investing with a hope of return, a concept that Jenness states particularly well.

Weston, J.F., and E.F. Brigham. *Managerial Finance*, 5th ed. Hinsdale, Ill.: Dryden Press, 1975. A good general financial text.

Yaney, J.P. "Cost Reductions and Control for Program Development." In *Managing The Instructional Programming Effort*, edited by G. Rummler, W. Schrader, and J. Yaney. Ann Arbor, Michigan: Bureau of Industrial Relations, 1967. A classic book in the field, with emphasis on programmed instruction.

The Learning Environment: Its Critical Importance to Successful Meetings

COLEMAN FINKEL

There is disagreement among HRD personnel regarding the role meetings play in the HRD field. There is no lack of agreement, however, that the learning environment is an essential element of any group activity. The physical facility can enhance or hamper the learning activity.

Whether you have your own facilities or utilize some external facility, you need to be aware of the advantages and limitations of hotels, motels, and conference facilities. Finkel, from his vast experience in the field, helps us understand the factors to consider when building or renting a facility for a learning environment.

Coleman Finkel is an owner of the National Conference Center in East Windsor, New Jersey. The center was built after he had conducted four years of research into learning environments, equipment, and ambiance. As a result, his services have been requested by major organizations as they developed their own learning centers. He is the author of two books on conference planning and the recipient of many awards including the Torch Award of ATD. Coleman Finkel is also CEO of Conference Center Development Corporation.

Life-long learning is crucial for coping with the ever-changing conditions of the work world. As never before, organizations require and value the acquisition of new information and skills. The meeting—a unique, pervasive, and superior group process—stands as one means of imparting information and developing skills.

To increase the learning levels inherent in meetings, every facet of the meeting should be examined. There are, or should be, learning goals in every type of meeting, whether held for purposes of training, problem solving, communication of information, or motivation. "Learning" is a process that results in the acquisition of knowledge—an understanding of its meaning; insights into its uses; and, in a training program, the development of skills in its application.

FOUR INGREDIENTS OF A SUCCESSFUL MEETING

There are four ingredients essential to a successful meeting:

1. *Program*—identification of the right subjects and development of a creative meeting design
2. *Communicators*—use of effective instructors, speakers, or chairpersons
3. *Administration*—efficient execution of administrative details
4. *Learning environment*—appropriate design of an environment within which a program takes place

This discussion will concentrate on the importance of the learning environment. Is there a specific environment more conducive to learning than any other? The answer is a resounding "yes." Only by applying advanced learning-environment concepts to the design of meeting facilities will organizations receive the greatest return on the time and money they invest in meetings. For too long we have minimized, ignored, and accepted inadequate meeting facilities. We must challenge traditional thinking and recognize that significant differences in meeting results can occur when new concepts are applied to the planning of a modern learning environment.

In the context of this article, I will deal with a small group meeting composed of 10 to 50 persons and held for training purposes. This meeting will be held in an outside facility and will involve at least one overnight stay. These concepts can, of course, be adapted to accommodate shorter meetings of larger numbers of people, without overnight requirements, held for purposes other than training.

THE GOAL AND DEFINITION OF A LEARNING ENVIRONMENT

In an advertisement for *The New York Times*, a picture showed a clutter of billboards on Times Square in New York City. The headline read, "Every message is at the mercy of its environment." This idea is particularly pertinent to a meeting. The messages we communicate in a meeting are affected, often subconsciously, by even the smallest detail of the physical environment.

B.F. Skinner, in *Beyond Freedom and Dignity*, observes that we are all simply a product of the stimuli we get from the external world. He further points out that if you specify the environment completely enough, you can exactly predict the individual's actions. What are the implications of that principle applied to a learning environment? Determine the emotions and attitudes you want to generate in a meeting to develop positive feelings toward the learning experience. Ascertain the participant actions you desire to achieve the goals of your meeting. Using these inputs, specify the design of your environments completely, and the successful results of your meeting will be predictable.

The design approach for an office, school, home, or plant is not viable for a learning environment. It therefore becomes necessary to think of a completely fresh approach—one in which the learning areas in the environment are personalized, defined, and planned to maximize the inherent opportunities for learning. We have to design learning places and spaces for people, not for magazine covers.

HOW THE ENVIRONMENT CONTRIBUTES
TO PARTICIPANT LEARNING

The planners of a learning environment must create specific surroundings that will best meet the needs of program participants and the requirements of their learning. Most settings for meetings make it difficult to help participants learn. Such arrangements survive because few question them. A responsive environment, in the context of a meeting, should be designed totally around an understanding of the learning process. Unfortunately, such insights are not part of the study or experience of many planners of a learning facility.

The beneficial results that a participant gains from a meeting can be significantly improved by understanding the role of the environment in contributing to greater learning.

Role 1—Provide a Transition

The meeting facility should be a place where participants can free themselves of the pressures, anxieties, and problems of the outside world. It should make them feel they are stepping into a different and welcoming world created specifically to enhance their learning and emotional transition to a different task—a task of introspection, meditation, and exploration. The role the participant plays is more passive than the active part one takes in the workplace. The environment is a key in helping participants make the role adjustment to learner, thinker, prober. Once this transition is made, it should be sustained through the 24 hours of a meeting day. This important adjustment of attitude and mind can be lost if the participant must move to one location for the meeting, a second place for meals, and a third site for sleeping. Once the important transition has been made, all the activities of the meeting should, optimally, be held within one complex. I call it "the total immersion environment."

Role 2—Improve Concentration of Participants

Learning in the more structured programs of human resource development, conferences, or planning meetings is often not an easy job for adults who are beyond their formalized schooling days. Their attention span is short. Adult learners have not only lost the discipline needed to concentrate for long periods, but there is a carryover of negative attitudes from the rigid teaching approaches too often followed in many schools and colleges.

Thus the environment should be organized so that a person can maintain maximum concentration. The properly designed environment is a major factor in assisting participants to think more deeply. However, to do so, we must consider how the environment can be planned to keep minds from wandering and to prevent disturbances from interfering with the flow of thought. To improve the concentration of participants, we should find ways to reduce the fatigue level of participants and to eliminate distractions from the environment.

Reduce Fatigue Level of Participants.   Many elements in an environment contribute to the participant's fatigue, impairing alertness and the thinking process. The following examples illustrate how fatigue can be reduced by proper planning of a learning environment:

A lighting system in a meeting room should provide even illumination of sufficient intensity to allow one to see with ease. Lighting should not produce high spots and low shadowing on walls—a condition which will add to eye strain.

The walls in many meeting rooms are painted white, gray, or tan— lifeless, sterile colors that are tiring after prolonged viewing. Rather, paint the walls in cheerful shades of blue, green, yellow, or orange.

Chairs are often bought for the wrong reason (i.e., they are pretty, stackable, soft, or cheap). Do not judge a meeting room chair solely on the fact that it feels most comfortable after sitting for a few moments. A good chair should permit a person to maintain good posture and relieve strain, change positions easily so different muscles can be used, give support to back muscles, and avoid pressure on thighs and the backs of knees. We have actually designed our own special meeting room chairs at The National Conference Center.

Reflective surfaces in a meeting room (i.e., chrome, crystal, and mirrors) should be avoided. Their glare has a hypnotic effect that lowers perceptual levels.

Eliminate distractions.   It is difficult to achieve participant concentration if there are distracting factors in the environment that interfere with thinking. We must concern ourselves with the factors that create "static" for the eye and ear.

Windows do not belong in a meeting room. Among other negative factors, it is too easy for the eye to be distracted by the activities outside or for the mind to be led astray by the weather outdoors.

If passers-by are able to look into a meeting room through a glass window, it is not only distracting to participants, but is conducive to feelings of anxiety.

Pictures or clocks in a meeting room are undesirable.

Any distracting noises such as voice leakage from adjacent rooms, air conditioning, kitchen, vehicular traffic, heels clicking on a hard floor surface outside of the meeting room should be eliminated. Noise is a distraction that must be counted as an information input. The human mind is capable of processing only a limited amount of information at one time. Noise distractions reduce the information that the mind can receive and process.

Role 3—Encourage Increased Participant Interaction

Because the physical environment impinges so much on the group interaction, facilities should work toward the blending of spaces and people. The environment is an active ingredient in encouraging the nature and amount of social interaction. If there is an increase in the time—both formal and informal occasions—that groups spend together, there will be a corresponding increase in the exchange of ideas among them. It is through discussions with others in the same group that one gains most from a meeting. Therefore, participants from the same group should be kept together as much as possible throughout a meeting and not be influenced by other groups. In order for this group "togetherness" to be most productive, privacy and the design of interior space must be considered.

The Importance of Privacy.   A group develops closeness and cohesiveness as they share the same experiences in a learning situation. It is within the one group that trust levels are established. Thus each person feels free and is encouraged to speak openly—to discuss ideas, clarify information, and test applications—in terms relevant to the individual's work. To the degree possible, therefore, each group's activities—both formal and informal—should take place apart from other groups.

The mixing of groups from different sessions, even in the same organization, introduces outside influences. Such intermingling will reduce the freedom with which any one group feels it can share thoughts. In addition, the greater the number of people concentrated in one area, the more arousing and disquieting the environment becomes. Think small and private.

Proxemics.   The specialized study of space and of how individuals use space is embodied in a field called "proxemics." We use proxemics to organize interior space and to enhance interaction among people. I have found in the informal interaction among participants, for example, that the space within which individuals feel most comfortable to exchange ideas is two to six feet. Space of two feet or less is private space. When our private space is invaded, we are likely to react with discomfort, anxiety, and resentment.

The three examples that follow are activities to which the concepts of proxemics and privacy are relevant.

1. *At Breaks.* Every group should be assigned a private area—if possible a room adjacent to the meeting room—where the group can gather exclusively. In so doing, the informal exchanges among participants are more likely to result in meeting-related discussion—extending, clarifying, and relating information. If these breaks are held in a corridor or in a common area with other groups, the same kind of intensive discussion will not occur.

2. *Informal Socializing.* There are many opportunities for members of a group to talk informally between sessions, after meals, in the evening. Once again, if there is a private room dedicated to one group, the individuals are more likely to go to this special and exclusive area. At such times, discussions are held most typically in groups of two, three, or four. Therefore, seating should be arranged in clusters of these numbers, maintaining the two to six feet relationship for most comfortable interchange.

There are other considerations to weigh during the times of informal socializing. For example, we have learned that people do not want to sit on a sofa that seats three, because they do not want to be touched by others. Also, seats should not be permanently fixed but should be the type that can be easily moved about.

3. *At Meals.* In order to maximize the likelihood of program-related discussions at meals, we have found that tables for six to eight people are preferable—not tables for two, four, or ten. Tables should also be designated for the exclusive use of individuals in the same group. In addition, ample space between tables should be provided.

Role 4—Permit Relaxation and Exercise

The learning environment should provide opportunities for participants to get away, even momentarily, from the discussion of meeting-related issues. The opportunity to unwind will improve the productiveness of those times when concentration is required.

In studying the types of exercise and recreation used by participants at a training meeting and the numbers of people using each type, I have made the following evaluation (presuming the various amenities are available). I have averaged the use, by participants, for all kinds of meetings, although a particular type of meeting may show different use patterns. (For example, a top management meeting that combines work and play will show different use patterns.)

1. Indoor game rooms   30%
2. Racquet sports (tennis, racquetball, platform tennis)   15%
3. Golf   12%
4. Jogging   10%
5. Sauna   5%
6. Exercise room   3%
7. Indoor swimming   2%

Role 5—Help the Communicator Be More Effective

The meeting leadership (HRD practitioners, speakers, chairpersons, coordinator) is the center around which the direction and quality of a program revolves. It is particularly important that the planners of a learning environment understand the ways in which these key individuals operate on the firing line.

Additional study is needed on the relationship of the physical setting to the communication requirements between the meeting leadership and participants. HRD professionals must not be trapped into merely accepting awkward arrangements.

There are many details to consider in a learning environment that will make the communicators' work easier. If they are more comfortable in their role and can perform it more efficiently, the quality of their leadership will improve, and, ultimately, the program will become more effective.

Some examples:

1. Light switches should be available for immediate control—both dimmers and overhead.
2. The room structure should be squared, as opposed to long, narrow rooms which separate participants in the rear from the communicator.
3. Finger-tip off-on control should be available for 35mm slide and 16mm movie projection.
4. A special instructor chair should be provided to reduce fatigue; it should be high enough to permit easy viewing of the group when the instructor is sitting.
5. Air conditioning controls should be installed in each room for easy adjustment by the leader.

There should also be a range of practical devices, equipment, audio-visual systems, etc., to stimulate the communicators to design more innovative programs (i.e., audience response, data lines for computer gaming, closed-circuit television to sleeping rooms as a change of pace for meeting-related films or talks).

MOST FREQUENT MISTAKES MADE BY ORGANIZATIONS IN PLANNING A MEETING FACILITY

The Council of Education Facility Planners, in a brochure titled, "What Went Wrong," observed that it is a tragedy that even now educational facilities are being planned on the basis of antiquated theories and false conceptions. The brochure further pointed out that complacency and contentment with the status quo are incompatible with good plant building.

It is evident that these facility planners recognize that the traditional designs followed in educational settings are not generally conducive to good learning. Yet, too frequently, in an industrial application, we have permitted ourselves to follow the school model. Such an approach is even now being questioned by school administrators. I have found that it is also inappropriate for planning for adult learners.

Organizations hold many types of meetings in their own facilities, from short committee meetings to longer HRD programs. One on-site conference room or an entire area is devoted to meeting rooms. More recently, a few groups have planned a "stand-alone" meeting facility, with or without a hotel.

Frequently, people ask questions about in-house learning facilities. Many of the individuals have little knowledge about the specialized qualities needed for a learning environment. They do not tackle the basic, strategic question: What is the purpose, nature, and concept of how the meeting environment can contribute to an increase in participant learning levels?

As an example, the vice president for purchasing of a company had been given the responsibility, by his president, for planning an in-house conference room. The only instruction the president gave was, "It better be good." In another instance, company management was thinking about building a conference center and hotel for its own use. When questioned about the nature of the learning objectives that management had established for this complex, an employee boasted, "We're going to have a facility for the year 2000." Period.

In both of these illustrations, there are built-in handicaps. They are imposed by the concepts on which the facilities will be built. These limitations will be reflected also in the criteria for evaluating how well the planners of a meeting facility have done their job. Management too often looks at the "window dressing" because these factors are easy to see and to demonstrate.

1. The beauty and impressiveness of the building and its interiors. Management's concentration is on the "look" of the facility and whether it projects an attractive, quality image.
2. The state of the art in audiovisual systems. Management might be led to believe that the company is in the forefront of meeting facilities just because the center can display and has incorporated all the latest advances in equipment and audiovisual devices.

In judging the quality of these two factors, management may conclude, superficially, that the enormous amount of money invested by the company has been spent wisely.

The design of a modern meeting center involves far greater subtleties and incorporates more complex considerations than these factors. It is understandable that management is unaware of other considerations. Management has no experience in the design of a meeting facility, and many other matters occupy their time. Yet, management should look more closely at a meeting facility, since the fundamental considerations of design strongly influence whether participants achieve value from a meeting that goes beyond the beauty or audiovisual sophistication of the facility. Other factors, when included in facility planning, provide a more realistic prediction of the true measure of return the company can expect from its substantial investment in a meeting center.

Beauty and the incorporation of appropriate audiovisual systems are not incompatible with productive learning. However, these two elements must fit into the myriad details that relate to the more important issues of achieving greater productivity from the time spent in meetings.

I have visited numerous meeting facilities and have talked with HRD practitioners, speakers, meeting planners, plant engineers, architects, and interior designers. My research indicates that many organizations make mistakes when designing a meeting facility.

Mistake 1—HRD professionals feel they
should know how to design meeting facilities.

There are many complexities and subtleties that go into the design of a learning facility and they extend beyond the typical experiences of training professionals or the studies they have been able to make. HRD input is obviously essential. However, the knowledge and skills needed to design a learning environment are different from those needed to manage an HRD department or design and instruct a program. After all, it is the rare golf professional who has the qualifications to design a golf course.

With sufficient study and experience, an HRD professional could certainly learn the nuances of designing a learning environment. Unfortunately, sufficient time is seldom available for the necessary orientation.

Certainly, a knowledge of how participants learn, study, relax, move, interact, and spend time in a meeting is essential. However, the assignment to plan a meeting facility generally comes only once in the career of an HRD professional. Hence, it is unlikely that the company executive assigned the job of planning a facility has gained the necessary knowledge, skill, or exposure to effectively carry out this specialized task.

Mistake 2—Architects and interior designers
are given primary responsibility for
defining the needs of an HRD activity.

Professional designers tend to emphasize the creation of an aesthetically attractive facility. Although beauty is certainly desirable and important, the identification and inclusion of functional standards and objectives should be achieved first. The architect and interior designer make vital contributions to the success of a facility, but it is important that these contributions be made in appropriate sequence.

The company must not forget that the basis for the design of any meeting environment starts with an understanding of the learning process. Only within this framework should subsequent steps be taken. The initial step is to spell out the specifications for making the meeting spaces maximally functional for the psychological, physical, and mental needs of participants. The architect can then create a beautiful structure. Organizations should guard against being so impressed with the attractiveness of a learning facility that they overlook its fundamental role—to optimize the time spent in meetings.

Mistake 3—There is an overemphasis on incorporating the most sophisticated audiovisual systems.

The reasoning behind this emphasis is that the more sophisticated the audiovisual system, the more advanced the center will be considered. Exotic systems are frequently included because they represent a new or faddish approach to audiovisual communications. These sophisticated systems are often unnecessary. They are neither used nor wanted by instructors. Anyone who plans meeting facilities should certainly keep abreast of the developments in interconnection and telecommunications, but applications must be practical, economical, and integrated into the total learning experience. We have found, for example, that 90% of the leaders of small groups use only one piece of visual equipment—the overhead projector.

Much money is wasted on unused audiovisual systems. Management, in looking at its wonderland of available equipment, may feel satisfied that its facility is truly modern and ahead of the times. But it would be prudent to look beyond such advances and determine whether the equipment is really needed or wanted by facility users.

Mistake 4—Decisions on meeting rooms are based on a tour of existing facilities.

When an organization is thinking of building or renovating meeting space, visits are often made to structures that already exist. The presumption is that others have taken an objective look at new concepts and have thus been guided in their design programs. Seldom, it turns out, have other organizations challenged conventional approaches. They, too, have not considered such relevant information as developments in proxemics, environmental psychology, strobe hypnosis, human factors engineering, suggestopaedia—and their impact on how learning is realized as a factor of a specific environment. Thus rooms have been designed on traditional concepts that are perpetuated by the visiting company.

Visitors to present facilities are generally accorded a cordial welcome and provided with answers to almost any questions. In extolling the virtues of a facility and projecting a progressive image for the company, the guide may fail to point out its drawbacks.

Mistake 5—The learning facility is viewed simplistically.

Insufficient thought is often given to the basic question of what the nature and purpose of a meeting area or facility should be. The question may sound simple, but it is not. The answer goes to the heart of how meeting spaces can contribute to increased learning. Designing a "perfect" conference room or meeting facility means attending to a multitude of details. The planning of an environment for meetings should accomplish a singular mission—to contribute to an increase in the learning level of every participant and to the successful results of each program held in the facility.

If the simplistic and superficial approach is taken merely to "provide space" or emphasize the design of attractive areas, maximum educational effectiveness will not take place.

Mistake 6—The research and evaluation of the meetings held by a company have insufficient depth.

In translating the research into specifications, too little weight is given to the implications of information gathered. These gaps in information limit meeting space flexibility, maximum utilization, and allowance for growth or changes. Typically, a company will send questionnaires to potential users of a meeting facility. The responses are then summarized and analyzed. The results form the program for user needs. There is an illusion that such research and evaluation are definitive. They are not. The information too frequently has limitations: the respondents will interpret questions differently or give hasty and superficial answers, while questioners fail to probe in depth for meaning or ask questions only in the more obvious areas. In fact, respondents do not know what they want.

The gathering, evaluation, and synthesis of an extensive amount of information are fundamental to the development of a facility. However, it is a job that has certain requirements: objectivity, skill in research, and the ability to "read between the lines." Further, in order to interpret and apply the information to an effective physical structure, specialized experience in learning facility design and operation is needed.

Mistake 7—The primary emphasis of top management is to produce an "image-building," prestigious-looking facility.

The important goal of planning an environment that will increase meeting productivity is emphasized less than the beauty of the facility. Top management is typically preoccupied with creating a "showplace" for customers, colleagues, friends and stockholders. There is justifiable pride in the facility's visual impact, symbolic of management's progressiveness. But do not stop there, and certainly do not start there. Pride can obscure many shortcomings.

There is no conflict between a facility of beauty and one of total "learning effectiveness." However, it is essential that top management be oriented early to what the true goals and priorities of the learning facility should be. The first step is to establish the functions and specifications that will best achieve maximum learning levels and participant impact. Then, and only then, should the creative inputs of the architect and other professionals be made.

USERS WHO ARE BUILDING THEIR OWN STAND-ALONE FACILITY—AN EVALUATION

Organizations today are concentrating more extensively on human resource development. This emphasis has often resulted in a related increase in the number of meetings held, many in outside facilities. This latter growth has led management, in some organizations, to evaluate every aspect of those off-site meetings: cost, effectiveness, types, number, and administrative problems.

A few organizations have elected to build their own tailor-made facility in which to centralize many programs. A handful of these firms have included full hotel accommodations, although the facility is not open to the public. Most organizations cannot afford or will not even want to build a separate meeting center. However, the following analysis of my research will be of value in planning a conference room or a meeting area and even in selecting an outside facility for a meeting. This analysis is a summary of the rationale for and against the building of an in-house, stand-alone meeting facility with or without a hotel. (Keep in mind that no organization mentioned all of the reasons under either category.)

1. *Reasons given by organizations for building a stand-alone meeting facility.*
   a. *To Gain Prestige.*   The facility represents a symbol of the leadership that the organization wishes to project. It is a place that management can show off to stockholders and customers.
   b. *To Save Money on Meetings.*   In analyzing the money spent on outside facilities, organizations have calculated that they can save money by building and using their own structure.
   c. *To Ensure Availability of Space.*   Organizations can assure themselves there will always be room for their meetings; they are not at the mercy of hotels, where they might be competing for space with others.
   d. *To Consolidate Meeting Facilities.*   While not all meetings will take place in the meeting facility, national programs can be centralized there. Directives are often issued, strongly suggesting that the various meeting instructors try to conduct their programs in the organization's facility first.
   e. *To Build Morale and Aid in Retaining Staff.*   Employees are proud of their own facility and consider it a privilege to attend programs there. The facility represents a commitment to the staff that the organization is a progressive firm interested in helping its employees improve.
   f. *To Control Program Quality.*   The quality of outside facilities is perceived as uneven. By tailoring an environment entirely to their needs, management can assure themselves that their meetings will be held in a facility of uniform high quality.
   g. *To Recruit Better Employees.*   The building stands as a commitment to training. As such, it can be a persuasive symbol to desirable college graduates, for whom there is competition from other companies. The building's existence shows that the organization is concerned about human resource development.
   h. *To Please the President.*   If the chief executive officer feels a

stand-alone facility is desirable, for whatever reason, there
will be justification found to build one.

2. *Reasons organizations do not build a facility or abandon one they
   have erected.*

   a. *Facilities Become Out of Date.* Apparently, the initial
      planning was not as thorough as it should have been. The
      organization soon learns that changes must be made, additions
      are required, or there is not the flexibility for different
      programs.

   b. *Prestige Wears Off.* Organizations find that the prestige
      afforded by the meeting facility is not as important as they
      thought, and even when prestige does exist, it eventually
      wears thin.

   c. *Not As many Meetings Are Held As Expected.* Although
      individuals in an organization are urged to use the facility,
      many find reasons not to do so. As a result, facility use does not
      reach expected levels. In some cases, in slow months, the
      company may have tried to sell open time to outside users.
      When that occurs, the company is suddenly involved in a
      totally different business.

   d. *The Facility Cannot Accommodate All Users.* In the premi-
      um meeting months, the facility cannot take care of all who
      want to use it. Those who cannot use it are forced to use outside
      facilities.

   e. *People Want a Change.* Even though users may be satisfied,
      they often do not want to come back to the same place year
      after year.

   f. *The Staff That Runs the Facility Grows More Rapidly Than
      Anticipated.* Operation costs increase more than expected.

   g. *The Facility Is More Expensive to Build and Equip Than Had
      Been Projected.* Inevitably, there are cost overruns or
      additions that cause the initial budget to be exceeded.

   h. *Meetings Are Developed Just to Keep the Facility Busy.*
      Management wants to be certain that the facility is being used
      to the fullest extent. At times, meetings have been developed
      solely for the purpose of giving the impression of high
      utilization.

   i. *Capital Is Diverted From the Principal Business of the
      Organization.* The meeting facility is a different business

from the organization's principal product or service. Many people feel that the money to build a facility would be better used in the organization's own field, rather than in the seemingly unrelated "hospitality" field. The facility becomes a business totally divorced from the organization's principal line and thus a diversion of capital and management attention.

j. *Management in Subsequent Years Has a Different Philosophy.* The reasons that one president built a facility may not make as much sense to a new CEO. The chief executive, in subsequent years, may think the facility is no longer desirable or needed and decide to sell or close it down.

k. *HRD Philosophy Changes.* Organizations that once centralized their training decide subsequently to regionalize programs. Thus the number of meetings in a centralized facility declines considerably.

l. *The Organization Moves Its Headquarters, and a Nearby Center Is No Longer Viable.* The HRD staff who planned programs and the headquarters executives who participated in them are frequently moved to the new location. They no longer find it convenient to use the old facility. So meetings are shifted to the area in which the headquarters is now located. The use of the old center falls off dramatically.

Generally, it is the largest companies in the country that have already built meeting places or are exploring the possibility. They spend millions of dollars annually, using outside hotels. For these organizations, a company-owned meetings facility may make sense. However, they will probably still hold many meetings in off-site locations.

Unfortunately, in several cases, organizations have constructed a separate meeting building, carried away by a euphoria of initial enthusiasm that permeates the organization. In such instances, the organization turned opposition aside. The pitfalls were obscured in the excitement of establishing an organization's leadership with its own building. At the time, it was "unpatriotic" to question the decision to build. Yet it is mandatory that an objective analysis of every facet of building be conducted to determine how valid and appropriate are the

reasons for establishing a stand-alone, organization-owned facility—
emotions aside.

SELECTING THE PROPER OUTSIDE MEETING FACILITY
MATCHING ENVIRONMENT TO LEARNING GOALS

Although organizations maintain internal facilities for meetings, they
may still use outside places. There is a range of such facilities from which
to choose. It is important that thought be given to matching need to a
particular setting.

Each meeting exists in an environment—good or bad. Every detail of
the meeting can limit or maximize its results. The design and selection of
an environment for a particular type of meeting requires careful
consideration of two factors: (1) the kind of work that goes on in the
meeting, and (2) the range of activities that occur during the 24-hour
meeting day. The environment should be seen as an integrated whole, as
opposed to a random assembly of spaces. People can adapt to any meeting
environment, but it may be at the cost of learning effectiveness.

Outside meeting facilities can be classified into four general categories:

1. City hotels—located within city limits, usually large and in
   downtown areas
2. Suburban hotels—located outside of a city on heavily traveled
   roads or in quiet, rural settings
3. Airport hotels—adjacent to or near an airport
4. Resorts—located generally in isolation with emphasis on relaxation and recreational amenities

Before selecting a particular facility, five primary factors must be
weighed:

1. *How long is the program?*
   If the meeting lasts a day or less, a nearby easily accessible facility
   should be considered, such as an airport or city hotel. If the
   meeting lasts several days, travel time is of less importance.
2. *What is the purpose of the meeting in terms of program intensity?*
   Within this factor are three broad categories. Although a partic-

ular meeting may not fall exactly into a particular category, make a choice that is closest in purpose. Is the meeting highly intensive work, study, and discussion; a combination of work and play; or most recreational and entertaining?

3. *What is the level and mix of attendees?*

Top level executives expect the best. Entry-level employees can be placed in facilities that are less expensive. If spouses are in attendance, the facility should be of higher quality.

4. *How many people will be in attendance?*

Hotels can be classified by size into these categories: 299 rooms or less, 300–500 rooms, 501–1000 rooms, and over 1000 rooms. As you go up the scale, fewer hotels are available, and reservations must often be made further in advance. As a general rule, meetings of under 100 people should be held at smaller hotels (under 300 rooms). Your group is more likely to be the principal occupant and will thus be given better service.

5. *What is the design of the program, its schedule, and its activities?*

What requirements are there for needs such as break-out rooms, social functions, audiovisual equipment, recreation, and sightseeing? Once these requirements have been determined, other guidelines must be followed. These guidelines establish the parameters within which you can select from several possible sites. Then other criteria may be used to select, from your narrowed hotel choices, the optimum facility for your meeting.

SELECTION CRITERIA FOR AN OUTSIDE FACILITY

When several possible meeting sites have been identified, your job is to select the one that best suits your program. Two factors should be considered: (1) the activities in which participants will engage, and (2) the appropriate environments within which the activities will occur.

I have identified 11 activities which could conceivably take place in the 24 hours of a participant's day. All meetings will have some of them, a few will include all. The activities have been related to seven environments. Ideally, these seven environments should be contained within one complex.

For greatest effectiveness, select a facility that provides a total environment: eliminating distractions, enhancing concentration, encouraging interaction and providing a pressure-free atmosphere conducive to relaxed learning.

THE MEETING ACTIVITIES IN WHICH PARTICIPANTS ENGAGE

The first step is to review the 11 activities listed below for a specific meeting. Indicate in the right-hand column the hours that your group will be spending, on the average, per day.

Activities	Hours
Presentation and discussion in main meeting room	_____
Work in small groups	_____
Meals	_____
Coffee break	_____
Cocktail parties	_____
Informal socializing with other participants	_____
Recreation and exercise	_____
Individual work related to program	_____
Personal: washing, dressing, watching TV	_____
Doing business work	_____
Sleeping	_____

Figure 4.1. Time analysis of participant activities.

Examine the activities engaged in by your participants. Relate these activities to the environments in which they take place (see Figure 4.2). Consider how you can find or create the right environments in which to place the activities.

THE ENVIRONMENTS IN WHICH MEETING ACTIVITIES OCCUR

Whatever the activity may be, its success is facilitated or limited by a particular setting. The activities of participants occur within seven particular environments at a meeting. Each of these seven environments should be planned separately and differently. Each should be evaluated for its contribution toward the learning effectiveness of the various activities within that environment.

Whether your meeting is held in your own facility or one outside, consider whether separate areas or rooms for each of the environments exist or can be arranged. By ensuring that these different areas exist in a facility, learning and participant satisfaction will be greatly enhanced. In the right-hand column of the following figure, there is a numbered listing. The numbers relate to the activities from Figure 4.1. As you will note, some environments can be used for more than one activity (and have to be designed accordingly).

Environments	Activities that take place in these environments (see Figure 4.1)
1. Environment of the meeting room in which the principal instruction, talks, discussions take place	1
2. Environment of the break-out room in which project work occurs in small groups	2, 6, 8
3. Environment of the room which represents the "home" of the participant: where the person sleeps, relaxes, may meet with others, does individual study and work	6, 8, 9, 10, 11
4. Environment of the indoor and outdoor areas where the participant takes part in recreation or exercise	6, 7
5. Environment where participants relax, take breaks, and informally socialize, drink, talk with other members of the group	2, 3, 4, 5, 6, 8
6. Environment for the three meals	3
7. Environment presented by the exterior building and outside setting	2, 4, 5, 6, 7, 8

Figure 4.2.   Environment analysis for participant activities.

THE TOTAL IMMERSION LEARNING
ENVIRONMENT OF THE FUTURE:
A SUMMARY

What is needed today is a radically different way of examining how a physical facility can make a vital contribution to the productive results of a meeting. The emotional, physical, and intellectual impact on individuals, created by a meeting environment, must be recognized, categorized, and matched with the activities occurring in that environment.

From the time a participant enters a meeting facility, there should be a total immersion of mind and attitude in a different lifestyle—one removed from the everyday, decision-making role, freeing the person to shift to a calm frame of mind, suitable for learning. A change is necessary to provide fertile ground for skill development and improvement, intellectual impact and growth, attitude challenge and change, and information absorption and gain.

How do you create a completely new environment for learning? Many people are questioning what is now available in meeting facilities. For example, Kenniston Lord, an HRD consultant for more than 20 years, points out, in *The Design of the Industrial Classroom*, that he had often wondered what it would be like to have a facility designed to accommodate the participants, rather than have a physical facility to which the participants and instructors must adjust. He indicates that there are those who view a classroom as merely another room or converted office space. Lord expresses frustration at trying to learn in an inadequate facility that actually negates the learning process. Alvin Toffler, in *Future Shock*, reinforced this idea by pointing out that our educational structures are racing toward obsolescence, with very little being done to save or replace them.

We do not need more know-how in the building of structures. We require greater recognition and insights into how to incorporate people within an environment that is totally dedicated and designed for learning.

REVIEW

Here is a review of the requirements that should be incorporated into the planning or selection of a "total immersion" environment—one that is supportive of higher levels of learning and more effective meetings.

Requirement 1—Understand the learning process

We should start with the premise that the primary mission of any meeting is to achieve the full scope of learning potential inherent in that meeting. The facility planner or the person selecting a meeting place should never lose sight of that fundamental goal. Whether deciding on an off-site location or planning an in-house facility, the involved person should study how people act in a learning environment—how they move, listen, socialize, interact, study, relax, adjust, play, and think. It is important to be sensitive to the real and underlying needs of people in a meeting. Only then can we address the question: "In what ways can those needs be translated into the physical environment?"

Requirement 2—Use the environment to achieve a positive impact

I do not know of anyone else who has defined, specifically, the environment that is particularly hospitable for learning. Today, many disciplines focus on how individuals are affected by factors in their environment in general—not a learning environment in particular.

Dr. Harold Proshansky, a former dean at New York University, has studied how an individual's actions and attitudes are affected by the environment. He calls the field *environmental psychology.*

Ergonomics ("ergo," work and "nomos," natural law) is a scientific discipline that focuses on a person's skills, limitations, and capabilities and examines how they interact with the tools, furniture, and equipment within the specific environment. *Human engineering* is another name for this discipline.

The psychological influence of the environment can cover a range of emotions. Feelings developed can be described as: warmth, comfort, welcome, relaxation, unhurried, calming, pleasant, happy, private, special. If we know the emotions and attitudes that we want to project, as Dr. Skinner observed, every detail in the environment can be designed to achieve certain objectives. No one element in an environment exists in isolation, so the psychological contribution of each to the whole must be considered.

Requirement 3—Appreciate and support the work of the communicators

The productive results of any meeting reflect the competence of its leadership. A good meeting facility should present every opportunity to support the efforts of the communicators (speakers, instructors, chairpersons).

The modern facility should achieve three principal objectives to help the communicators perform their responsibilities effectively.

1. Provide all the tools, equipment, and devices necessary to make it easy for them to work with minimum fatigue and trouble.
2. Create a layout of the physical spaces to permit the program and schedule to flow smoothly.
3. Relieve the leadership of all administrative details, so that their minds and energies can be devoted completely to their professional responsibilities.

Requirement 4—Select, train, and educate a special staff to operate the facility

As important as the physical facility and its accouterments are, the specialized staff that is responsible for the learning environment is equally important. This staff should be separate from hotel personnel. The organization, procedures, and policies of this trained staff are dedicated to anticipating the needs of participants and communicators and providing an instant and courteous response to requests for information and assistance. In training this special staff, management of the center should emphasize the staff's role in helping meetings run without a hitch.

Requirement 5—Study and create approaches that contribute to greater learning effectiveness

A meeting facility equal to the demands of the future is part of the learning field. As such, it will carve out the "learning environment" ingredient to successful meetings as its particular area of specialization. To do so, it must break away from conventional thinking as such thinking allows little room for adaptation to a set of needs for people who participate in a learning program.

The facility of the future will have planners whose role will be to observe what participants and communicators do and how they study, interact, learn, and relax. Then the planners will seek to innovate procedures and systems that can help meetings function more effectively.

The facility will view its objective as stimulating the program designers of meetings to develop more creative programs by offering a range of innovations: data lines, closed circuit television, teleconference rooms, and television studios for role playing.

CONCLUSION

Whether their meetings are held on-site or off-site, organizations must be more attentive to the impact that the properly designed learning environment can have on program outcome. A reassessment is long overdue.

Two typical approaches are followed today: the conventional and traditional practice of just providing space and the practice of developing spectacular audiovisual systems and a facility of surpassing beauty. Neither approach will do. Primary concentration on these two approaches misses those elements that are far more basic to planning a learning environment that will achieve its singular mission—to contribute to increased participant learning levels and successful completion of each meeting held in the environment.

We must recognize the complex roles of environment in contributing to the success of a meeting. The environment must meet the subtle and overt needs of the whole person and consider all of the activities of a participant. The environment must *not* be a single, unvarying design, but one in which seven different environmental approaches are required. A new level of meeting effectiveness will result when we consider a learning environment in terms of these more critical and fundamental decisions.

The Consulting Function of the Human Resource Development Professional

GORDON LIPPITT
RONALD LIPPITT

Consulting is one of the roles of the human resource developer. In the past few years, consulting has grown in importance and will probably continue to grow in the future.

The authors of this chapter have been closely identified with consulting for more than 30 years. Their writings have been reproduced, reprinted, and quoted in the United States and many other countries. The material presented here is a fresh look at consulting as it applies to the HRD practitioner.

Particular attention should be paid to the material on "influence power." This is an area that is too often overlooked. Also, note the section on "skills." It goes far beyond what is usually considered when discussing consulting skills. Of course, reading the material will not build skills for a consultant—that takes guided practice and feedback.

Gordon Lippitt (Ph.D.) is professor of behavior science in the School of Government and Business Administration, The George Washington University, and a diplomate of the American Board of Professional Psychology. He also serves as president of Organization Renewal, Inc. He was program director of the National Training Laboratories (1950–1960) and president of the ASTD (1969). He has published over 300 articles, pamphlets, and books. Among his recent books are: Systems Thinking (coeditor, 1981) and Organization Renewal (revised, 1982).

Ronald Lippitt (Ph.D.) is professor emeritus in sociology and psychology, University of Michigan. Before retiring, he served for 30 years as research program director, Institute for Social Research and Research Center for Group Dynamics, Michigan Institute of Technology and the University of Michigan. He was cofounder of the National Training Laboratories Institute for Applied Behavioral Science in 1947. He has provided services related to HRD and planned change efforts and organizational renewal for private companies, higher education institutions, school systems, health systems, human service agencies, and communities. He is executive officer of Organization Renewal Inc. and initiator of Lippitt Professional Support Network. He has published many books and articles.

In the current contexts of organizational complexity, productivity concerns, quality control, and "doing more with less," the need for technical help from the HRD specialist becomes ever more critical. As decentralization of accountability spreads through organizations, more managers at more levels need help in assessing ways to utilize employee skills, experience, energy, motivation, and time more productively.[1]

CHALLENGES FOR CONSULTANTS

In a recent conference on human energy utilization, the participants identified the following issues and challenges for the HRD professional:

Overload

Underuse

Waste, misuse

Maldistribution

Redirection

New sources

Conversion from one use to another

Renewal

Refining

Updating

It is necessary to identify a few of the challenges that occur in the operations of most organizations that present intervention opportunities for the HRD consultant, internal or external.

Assessing the Task

One of the most significant contributions to high productivity and innovation is having the right persons teamed at the right time with the needed support. The major blocks to achieving this are the lack of flexibility of personnel teaming and inadequate analysis of the human resource needs of particular tasks. There is a strong tendency and tradition in organizations to divide into subunits—departments, sections, divisions—with the assumption and expectation that these units have a portfolio of task assignments (e.g., marketing, research and development, manufacturing, accounting, etc.).

With each passing decade, the problems to be solved and decisions to be made by management become more complex. This increasing complexity requires the effective use of a more diverse set of skills and consideration of a wider range of variables. Most tasks require a different variety of knowledge, competencies, and disciplines for creative problem solving. So the same heads in the same departments cannot be expected necessarily to be the appropriate heads for the flow of tasks and decisions with which they are confronted. One of the great challenges for the HRD practitioner is to provide technical leadership in the procedures of task analysis, in order to establish the range and types of knowledge, skills, personality styles, and experiences needed to tackle a particular task creatively and successfully in the optimum time. Such task analysis must precede any recruiting or assigning of people and should provide them with the appropriate learning for the task.

Locating the Needed Resources

Every HRD professional faces the challenge of helping develop an appropriate human resource bank or inventory to serve as the basis for creating problem-solving teams or task forces. In one small organization, the CEO has a matrix chart on the wall with the names of the employees down the side and the types of skills and experiences needed for different tasks across the top. In the cells, the skills and experiences of each employee are checked. When a new task is defined (e.g., explore a new product idea, assess a competitor's product, investigate a new trend, consider a new policy), the CEO and his top management team assess the human resource requirements of the task and identify the mix of persons, from the chart, that seems to meet the need. Alternates are also chosen in case some person cannot be released, even temporarily, from ongoing responsibilities.

One social service organization has its bank on McBee cards, and more and more have the human resource bank computerized, which provides maximum flexibility in rapidly identifying the right people.[2]

Recruiting the Right Leaders

To achieve human resource use flexibility, an organization must develop the norms and reward procedures to support "temporary system" teaming. Such a system may be for temporary, full-time involvement, part-time work, or even for the "one-shot" effort of a single brainstorming session or advisory conference.

Two factors challenge the skill of the HRD practitioner in helping recruit the right leaders. First, the right leaders may not feel motivated, may be committed to more important priorities, or may feel overloaded. One effective procedure is to select two potential persons for each needed slot and to offer the challenge, "We need you for this task because of your particular skills (or experience), but if for some reason you feel you cannot accept, we have identified an alternate." The presentation should explain the need rather than be a heavy-handed mandate.

The second challenge is to secure the sanction and support of the unit supervisor, by presenting the need, the potential payoffs for the department as well as the person, a realistic assessment of the time involved, and clarification of the continuing line relationship of the employees to their supervisors. Neglecting these two factors often decreases the effectiveness of the matrix use of human resources.

Building Effective Teamwork

It is incorrect to assume that "putting the right heads together" will ensure a creative and productive outcome. Actually, the more diverse and specialized the heads, the more difficulty they will have working together. So the HRD practitioner must facilitate teamwork development of diverse personnel.

From our work in such situations, two guidelines emerge for the HRD practitioner. The first is that technical, task-oriented personnel tend to reject "being trained" and "playing games." Our most successful intervention has been working with them on designing effective participative meetings and win-win procedures of conflict resolution as well as the simple techniques of five-minute "how are we doing" stop sessions, to share data on "how we're doing" and "how we could work more productively."[3]

The second guideline is to be cautious about any separate training of task force leaders without the involvement of the rest of the group. The leaders are usually peer specialists in some technical discipline and run a risk of "behaving differently" from the other members of the group. The group needs to define its goals and criteria for productivity, then group members can legitimize their needs for and expectations of leadership. So we usually start by consulting the group rather than training the leader.

Designing for Support and Motivation

A good start in any problem-solving process is critical, but if there is to be payoff, there must be the basis for continuing motivation and support from top management and the needed support services of assistance, secretaries, etc.

There are several important interventions that can help ensure vitality and success:

Breaking the task down into a series of very concrete tasks with clear criteria of progress

Setting deadlines about which there is concensus and commitment

Defining some types of shared celebration when steps of progress have been achieved

Establishing norms and procedures for asking for help as a sign of strength rather than weakness

Learning the techniques of rehearsal, simulation or pilot tryouts so that confidence and competence can be developed before "playing for keeps"

Identifying "early warning signals" so there can be preventive review and revision before too much time and energy are wasted

Keeping top management informed so their sanction can be active, informed support

These interventions should help the client (internal or external) take a proactive, action research-oriented posture toward problem solving and human resource utilization, rather than a reactive, constricted, coping-oriented posture toward traditions and precedents.

Teaming People with Computers

Perhaps the most rapidly growing area of human resource mobilization is helping people to extend their capabilities through the use of computer hardware and software. All HRD practitioners need to project learning goals for themselves in this area. These represent some key areas where the HRD professional can function as a professional "helper" consultant to management.

The role of the HRD consultant should be examined in two ways. First, examine whether the consultant is inside or outside the system in which the consultation is taking place. Second, examine the behavioral roles of the consultant on a directive to nondirective continuum.

Using these two complementary approaches will allow us to see the many ways an HRD consultant functions to meet the needs we have identified.

INTERNAL AND EXTERNAL CONSULTANTS

Definitions

The Internal Consultant. A helper (professional or nonprofessional) who is considered a member of the client system or a closely related system.

The External Consultant. A helper (usually professional) who has minimal or no organizational/political relationship with the client system.

The Internal-External Consultant. A helper (usually professional) who is located at the headquarters of an organization and is "sent out" to field units for consultant work. The consultant is an "insider" to the total system but an outsider to the client system.

Why might a discussion of similarities and differences between internal and external consulting situations be important? There are three answers to this question:

1. The consultants' effectiveness depends primarily on their professional behavior. An internal consultant may behave quite differently from an external consultant—even when working in the same consulting situation. For example, the internal consultant may exercise extreme caution because of "having to live with the client." The external person has the option to leave and thus can behave in a more objective, assertive manner.

2. Consulting behavior can be adjusted appropriately if the consultant is aware of the situational differences (and the major reasons for those differences) between the internal and external types.

3. The most effective consultation occurs when external and internal consultants "team consult." In these situations, awareness of similarities and differences is critical in order to match and complement each other's strengths and limitations in team consultation situations.[4]

Role Similarities

Whether external or internal, consulting roles are similar in these ways:

1. Both are helpers.
2. They must get their job done through others who do not report to them organizationally.
3. They work with and through client system members.
4. They can be called in by the client or imposed upon the client by forces outside the client system.
5. They can both play multiple consulting roles.
6. They both want to be successful.

Situational Differences

The differences between internal and external consultant types are due to the unique situations each must confront. Figure 5.1 outlines some of these situational differences.

Suggested Behavior/Action for the Internal HRD Consultant[5]

1. *Behave like an external consultant.* This requires a careful role clarification between consultant and client. In addition, a strong psychological contract characterized by mutual trust and openness is a must before entering any consulting relationship.

2. *Do some outside (external) consulting.* Whether done for a fee or free, external experience can broaden perspective, increase internal credibility, and increase consultant confidence. Outside experience provides an arena for experimentation. In some instances, it can provide a significant part of the financial security required to support the internal consultant when it is found appropriate to confront the internal client system.

3. *Be proactive and aggressive at least 25% of the time.* It is important for the internal consultant to introduce ideas for change as well as to help clients respond to unplanned change. "Influence power" accrues to the consistent, responsible innovator.

4. *Focus on the job to be done.* The internal consultant survives and grows in direct proportion to the client's effectiveness in getting the job done. All consulting activities—even career consulting—must focus on the job to be done and must use a results-oriented approach.

Internal Consultant	External Consultant
As part of the system, usually knows the language and background of the problem	Usually has more "influence" with client system
As part of the system, may be a part of the problem	Usually has more varied experiences; broader perspective
Usually will give more time to the client because of availability and costs	Usually more objective about the client and the problem—he's independent of the client power structure
Sometimes encounters resistance because of vested interests and organizational politics	Pay and continued use are usually tied to results
Sub-system tends to tell the IC that things are "o.k."	Is usually aware of other resources that might be helpful to client
Usually knows the norms and political realities better than someone from outside	Client tends to be more open with the external consultant about needing help
An internal consultant is not seen as a "prophet" in his own organization. May lack a power base	Free to leave the situation when consultation is complete
Internal consultant knows more about potential "linkage" with other parts of system	Client usually has high expectations that may verge on inappropriate dependency
Usually identifies with the system's needs/pains/aspirations	Free to reject the consulting assignment
A "known quantity"	In a position to introduce "new" things into the client system
May lack perspective	
May not have required special knowledge or skill	
May have to live down past failure or affiliations	

Figure 5.1. Situational differences of internal and external consultants. D. Swartz, *Journal of European Training,* 4(5):259–260. Reprinted with permission.

5. *Be your own person.* No one else owns you. No one manipulates you. No one can change you any more than you can change them. Be courageous, competent, skilled, diagnostic, and professional.

Suggested Behavior/Action for the External HRD Consultant

1. *Do not take on an assignment if your gut says "no."* Feelings about the client and client system norms, values, and methods should be

allowed to surface. This means precontract data gathering and face-to-face meeting(s) with the client. Then, trust your gut.

2. *Study the client system; learn the "language."* Empathy for the client system is critical to building trust with the client. Empathy is best achieved when the consultant understands and appreciates the culture of the client system. The external consultant may get along famously with the client but fail to get close to the system if the consultant "cannot speak the language."

3. *Do not bypass internal helpers (personnel, organization development, HRD, etc.).* Involve internal helpers as early as possible in contacts with the client. Encourage the client to keep these helpers "clued in." External consultants are a natural threat to internal helpers. Without the internal helpers' understanding and, at the very least, their neutrality, the external consultant's work could be subtly sabotaged.

4. *Collaborate with internal consultants.* If a qualified internal helper is not apparent, encourage the client to help find one. A collaborative working relationship between internal and external consultants is valuable. It is a powerful and necessary approach if the positive changes sought through consultative intervention are to be gained and sustained.

5. *Leave the inside consultant with increased power.* A major contribution external consultants make to client systems is to help them gain strength to cope with their problems without outside help. A skilled internal consultant in a legitimatized helper role is essential to the client system's ability to self-renew. The external consultant should be constantly helping the internal counterpart to gain credibility within the organization.

6. *Be human.* External consultants are expected to be pros; they are not expected to be gods. The external consultant should take the calculated risk, occasionally leave the comfort of a "proven technique" to respond more effectively to unique client system needs, and say forthrightly, "I goofed! Now what can we learn from that?" Freedom to fail is the block. Celebrate your learnings, for they give you freedom as an internal consultant and as an external consultant.

BEHAVIORAL ROLES OF THE CONSULTANT

The consultant, in carrying out his or her professional role, will not work from a power base, as is typical of a line manager. Instead, the consultant works as a resource person using *influence power* that comes from four sources:

Influence by competence

Influence by ideas

Influence by acceptance

Influence by one's role (legitimization)

These influence methods have to be "earned" by the consultant. Influence power will not emerge without demonstrated skills and professionalism. As Beckhard put it:

> The consultant (or person in a helping role) always enters such a relationship as a person with authority—achieved either through position or role in the organization or through the possession of specialized knowledge.
>
> To achieve an effective consultative relationship, it is essential that they understand the nature of this power and develop skills to use it in a way which will be viewed as helpful by the person receiving help.
>
> A person entering a consulting or helping relationship must have the ability to diagnose the problem and goals of the person being helped, and be able to assess realistically their own motivations for giving the help. A consultant must also recognize the limits of their own resources to help in the particular situation.[6]

In carrying out a "helping" relationship to management, consultants will find themselves operating along a continuum of consulting roles. Figure 5.2 illustrates some of these major helping relationships, from directive to primarily nondirective consultations. Directive refers to those behaviors in which the consultant assumes a leadership position or initiates activity. In the nondirective role, the consultant provides data for the client's use.

Situational roles are not mutually exclusive; they may manifest themselves in many ways in a particular client relationship. These roles are "spheres of influence," rather than a static continuum of isolated behavior. These different role choices in response to the client's need should be examined.

Advocate Role

In an advocate role, the consultant endeavors to influence the client. There are two quite different types of advocacy. *Positional* or *content advocacy* is a role posture of trying to influence the client to choose particular goals or to accept particular values. *Methodological advocacy* is a role posture of trying to influence the client to become a problem

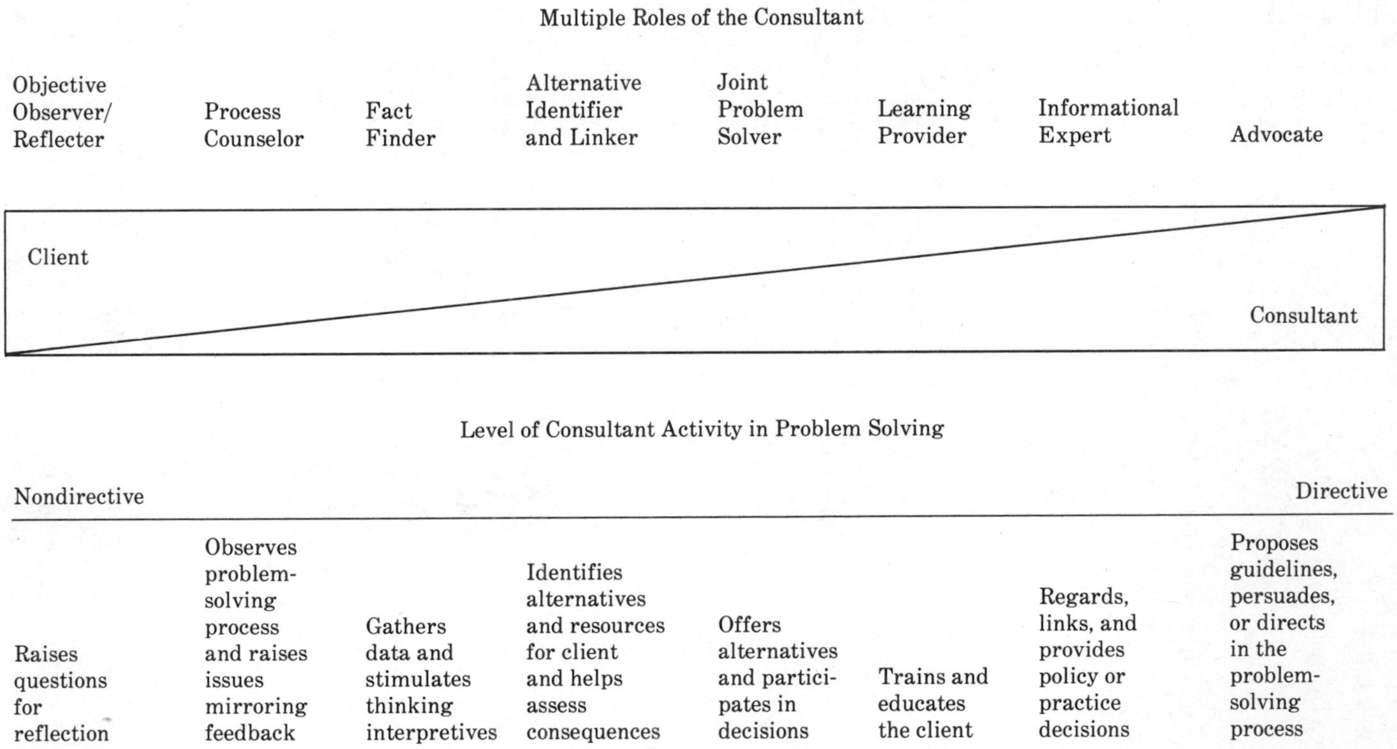

Multiple Roles of the Consultant

Objective Observer/ Reflecter	Process Counselor	Fact Finder	Alternative Identifier and Linker	Joint Problem Solver	Learning Provider	Informational Expert	Advocate

Client — Consultant

Level of Consultant Activity in Problem Solving

Nondirective — Directive

Raises questions for reflection	Observes problem-solving process and raises issues mirroring feedback	Gathers data and stimulates thinking interpretives	Identifies alternatives and resources for client and helps assess consequences	Offers alternatives and partici-pates in decisions	Trains and educates the client	Regards, links, and provides policy or practice decisions	Proposes guidelines, persuades, or directs in the problem-solving process

Figure 5.2. Description of the consultant's role on a directive and nondirective continuum.

solver and to use certain methods of problem solving. The consultant must be careful not to become an advocate for any particular solution (which would be positional advocacy). In this role, the behavior of the consultant is derived from a "believer" or "valuer" stance about a content or methodological matter.

Informational Expert

One of the roles of a consultant is that of an information expert or technical specialist. The more traditional role of a consultant is that of a specialist who, through special knowledge, skill, and professional experience, is engaged, either by internal employment or contract, in providing a unique service to a client. Within this realm of augmenting client expertise, the client is mainly responsible for defining the problem and the objectives of the consultation. Thereafter, the consultant assumes a directive role until the client is comfortable with the particular approach selected. Later in the relationship, the consultant may act as a catalyst in implementing the recommendations that were developed.

Either the internal or the external consultant may be a content specialist working on the client's problem or a process specialist working on how to cope with a problem. This particular role demonstrates the consultant's substantive knowledge.

Learning Provider

Innovative consultation frequently may require the use of periodic or continuous training and education within the client system. In this aspect of the helping relationship, the consultant may advise which learning process can best be employed critically and creatively, depending on the situation and the need. The consultant may be a designer of learning experiences or a direct teacher. In a sense, this role requires the consultant to have the skill of a learning methodologist (i.e., learning specialist).

Joint Problem Solver

The helping role assumed by the consultant in the problem-solving mode utilizes a synergistic approach to complement and collaborate with the client in the perceptual, cognitive, and action-taking process needed to solve the problem. The consultant helps to maintain objectivity while stimulating conceptualization during the defining of the problem.

Additionally, the consultant must help to isolate and define the "real" dependent and independent variables that influenced the problem's cause and, ultimately, its solution. The consultant also assists in weighing alternatives, aids in sorting out salient causal relationships that may affect alternatives, and synthesizes and develops a course of action for an effective resolution. The consultant in this role is involved in decision making as a peer member.

Alternative Identifier and Linker

There are direct costs associated with decision making. While the value of a decision depends on the attainment of a given set of objectives, several alternatives and their attendant risks can be proposed when selecting an appropriate solution to a problem. The alternatives, either for economic or other identifiable reasons, should be discovered jointly by the client and the consultant. In this helping relationship, the consultant must establish relevant criteria for assessing alternatives and develop cause-effect relationships for each alternative, along with an appropriate set of strategies. In this particular situational role, however, the consultant is not a participant in decision making itself but a retriever of appropriate alternatives facing the problem solver.

Fact Finder

Fact finding is an integral part of the consulting process, whether it be for developing a data base or for resolving intricate client problems. It is perhaps the most critical area and often the one that receives the least attention in actual problem solving and decision making. This role first requires the development of criteria and guidelines to be used in the performance of the actual fact-finding process and related analysis. It ends when all available facts have been analyzed and synthesized. Then the problem-solving information is given to the client. Fact-finding can be as simple as listening or as complex as a formal survey utilizing a number of techniques. In this role, the consultant is functioning basically as a researcher.

A Process Counselor

In this role, the consultant attempts to help the client be more effective and responsive. The consultant must be specifically concerned with the work process itself as a way of achieving client adaptability.

As a process counselor or specialist, the consultant must sharpen all multiple role skills to help the client. The consultant works on developing joint client-consultant diagnostic skills for addressing specific and relevant problems, in order to focus on how things are done, rather than on what tasks are performed. The consultant helps the client integrate interpersonal and group skills and events with task-oriented activities and observes the best match of relationships. In this role, the consultant functions as a "feedbacker."

Objective Observer/Reflector Role

When operating in the mode of a reflector, the consultant stimulates the client to make decisions by asking reflective questions that may help clarify, modify, or change a given situation. In utilizing this attribute, the consultant may be an arbitrator, an integrator, or an empathetic respondent who experiences, along with the client, those blocks which provided the structure and provoked the situation initially. In this role, the consultant functions as an "overviewer" and a philosopher.

SKILLS AND THE CONSULTING FUNCTION

What kind of person is able to perform these multiple roles appropriately? Such a person must possess the proper combination of knowledge, skills, and attitudes.

The effective development of the resources of an organization is essential to its continued growth and viability and requires competent HRD professionals. What qualifications must this kind of person have? Must one be a behavioral scientist? Does one need to be an expert on communication systems? Must one be so courageous or personally active in initiating change, as to risk one's own job? What unusual psychological maturity is required?

Whoever is responsible for initiating better resource utilization and development will need to manifest professional behavior and leadership. Any list of the profesional capabilities of such a consultant is extensive.

The qualities a consultant needs fall into two broad categories: distinctly intellectual abilities and distinctly personal attributes.[8]

Dilemma Analysis Ability

Intellectually, the consultant needs what we call, "the ability to make a dilemma analysis," because an organization that uses a consultant is probably faced with a situation that appears insoluble. If the difficulty could be solved easily by the operating manager, a consultant would not be needed. The consultant must recognize that a dilemma, whether real or not, exists in the minds of those within the organization. The consultant's role is to help discover the nature of the dilemma and determine the real causes of it, rather than what are thought to be the causes.

To accomplish this, the consultant must have a special type of diagnostic skill. The consultant should approach a study of the organization's dilemma by means of an existential pragmatism[9] that takes into account the total client setting and all situational variables. Through skillful examination of the organization's fabric, one can see the structural relationships between the various subsystems that make up the total organization and the interdependent nature of its individuals, groups, substructures, and environment.

To make this kind of dilemma analysis, insight or perception and intuition are necessary. Insight or perception is vital, because the problem and solution to almost any dilemma requiring outside assistance will be part of a very complex situation. The ability to penetrate the complexity and isolate the key situational variables is the toughest task. Unless the important factors can be sifted from the maze of detail and the cause separated from the symptoms, accurate diagnosis is impossible.

Sense of "Organizational Climate"

Intuition or "sensing" must be coupled with perception in order to assess the nature of power and politics in the organization. Bureaucratic structures, both public and private, are not optimally functional. Underlying the functional operations that the organization performs are the crucial dynamics of internal power and politics. Invariably, people compete for organizational influence or for some internal political reason. Very often, the consultant has been asked to help provide needed assistance and to serve as an instrument of a strategy designed to secure an influence objective.

Unless the consultant has the intuition to sense the organizational climate, there is the risk of being nothing but a pawn in a game of organizational politics. If consultants can recognize and understand the dynamics of the internal power and political relationship, they can creatively utilize these abilities to pursue whatever change objectives the client and consultant conclude are appropriate.

Apart from the diagnostic abilities, the consultant needs implementation skills. Obviously, the consultant must have some basic knowledge of the behavioral sciences and the theories and methods of one's own discipline. But more than these, the individual needs imagination and experimental flexibility. "Dilemma dissolving" is essentially a creative enterprise. No real life situation is going to fit perfectly within the model suggested by typical techniques or textbook methods. Diversity and unique circumstances will almost always exist. The consultant must have imagination enough to innovate adaptations and to tailor concepts to meet real demands.

The consultant must be able to visualize the impact or the ultimate outcome of the actions proposed or implemented.[10] But, like most things, this is as much a process of experimental trial and error as it is of a priori solutions. The courage to experiment and the flexibility to discard as many approaches as needed to solve the problem are important ingredients in the practitioner's makeup.

Integrity Is Essential

The other qualities of a successful consultant are personal attributes. Above all, the consultant must be professional in attitude and behavior. To be successful, one must be as sincerely interested in helping the organization as any good doctor is interested in helping the patient. Consultants must not conceive of themselves as, or project the image of, being a huckster of patent medicines. The consulting role is no different from that of any other profession. If the prime concern of a consultant is to make an impression or build an "empire" and only secondarily to help the organization, the organization leaders will soon recognize the individual as a phony and act accordingly. Generally, people in management are astute individuals. They can identify objectivity, honesty, and, above all, integrity.

When entering a client system, a strong tolerance for ambiguity is important. Often, the first acquaintance with an organizational problem is marked by a certain amount of bewilderment. It takes time to figure out the situation, and during this time, one will experience a certain amount of confusion. One must expect this and not worry about it.

Coupled with this type of tolerance must be patience and a high frustration level. Helping a client is likely to be a long and trying experience. Quick results, full cooperation, and complete success are unlikely, in the short run. Inevitably, attempts to change people's relationships and behavior patterns will be met with resistance, resentment, and obstructionism by those who are, or think they may be, adversely affected. It is important for consultants to have the kind of maturity and realism to recognize that much of their work will meet with resistance. Such maturity is necessary to avoid the reaction of defeatism and withdrawal that commonly accompanies the frustration of a person's sincere efforts to help others.

Sense of Timing

Finally, the consultant should have a good sense of timing, a stable personality, and good interpersonal skills. Timing can be crucial. The best conceived and articulated plans for change can be destroyed if introduced at the wrong time. Timing is linked to a knowledge of power and of the political realities that exist in the change situation and to the kind of patience that overrides the enthusiasm surrounding a newly conceived idea or learning intervention that one cannot wait to try out.

Obviously, consulting involves people dealing with people, more than people dealing with machines or mathematical solutions. The consultant must have good interpersonal skills and must be able to communicate and deal with people in an atmosphere of tact, trust, politeness, friendliness, change, and stability. This is important, because the impact of the practitioner's personality must be minimized to keep it from becoming another variable in the existential setting that contributes to the existing complexity. Beyond this, success will depend on the persuasiveness and tact of the consultant in confronting the interpersonal contact on which the helping situation is based.

As the HRD professional's role in today's organization and society changes, so do the kinds of consultant interventions.

CONTEXTS FOR HRD CONSULTATION INTERVENTION

Several different goal contexts guide HRD practitioners in their choice of appropriate interventions. We believe it is important for the practitioner to be able to define or choose these goal contexts and to have a repertoire of tools and techniques to provide help to the client.

We have identified these goal contexts as:

1. Preventing or reversing the process of entropy ("running down")
2. Coping with downsizing ("doing more with less")

3. Complying with regulations and mandates
4. Improving quality of services and productivity
5. Inventing and innovating new practices
6. Disseminating successful practices

The challenge for the HRD practitioner in each of these areas of need for professional help should be examined.

Preventing or Reversing Deterioration

The basic notion here is that many practices and procedures that are established tend to "run down" or deteriorate by becoming habituated and depersonalized. This process of entropy—loss of energy and quality—may result from complacency, loss of meaning of the activity, or routinization of performance.

The challenge for the HRD practitioner in such situations is to find ways of maintaining or restoring the quality of the procedure or performance. In most human service or product situations, deterioration can be reversed (e.g., by confrontation, awareness, learning experiences, consultation, motivating, etc.), and much can be done, by monitoring feedback and performance review, to prevent deterioration.

Examples of significant HRD interventions in this goal context are:

1. As newcomers were assigned to a job, an "old-timer" team was asked to plan and conduct the briefing and demonstration. This reactivated their awareness and motivation and ensured continuity for the newcomers.
2. Quarterly review of feedback data was instituted.
3. An annual "visiting committee" of outside consultants was employed to review progress and explore improvements.
4. Periodic group interviews with clients were instituted to keep staff oriented to "where our clients are."
5. Each new employee was asked to review the procedures manual and to make recommendations for revision.

Coping with Downsizing[11]

Cutbacks in budget, personnel, or other resources are frequent aspects of our current organizational life. Many problems are activated by this situation—competitive rivalries, turf protecting, defensive withdrawal, constricted thinking and defensive problem solving.

The challenge for the HRD practitioner is to stimulate proactive, imaginative thinking about alternatives, to search for duplication of services and unused, misused, and new resources, and to simplify tasks and procedures.

In work with our clients, brainstorming sessions have led to identification of differences between a proactive and a reactive response to downsizing requirements. These are compared in Figure 5.3.

Proactive Initiatives	Reactive Responses
Image potential gains	Focus on pain (problems)
Assume alternatives can be found	Assume "it's beyond me," helpless
Reprioritize	Across the board cutback "nibble" (e.g., 10%)
Involve everyone in ideas for saving	"Closet decisions" at the top
Explore collaborative exchange and sharing of resources	Jealously guard turfdom
Restructure roles with involvement training and education	Assign overloads
Explore alternative sources of support	Blame regular sources for problem
Preserve problem-solving resourcefulness in reducing personnel	Cut the most vulnerable personnel (e.g., trainers)
Explore new markets	Cut back on innovation resources
Utilize and expand volunteer and part-time resources	Cut coordinator of volunteers and marginal part-time workers (i.e., young, etc.)
Search for innovative models that simplify and economize	Skimp on our regular methods

Figure 5.3.   Differences between proactive and reactive responses.

The HRD practitioner can be especially useful in helping to collect information about successful practices in other organizations, to convene separate units for collaborative problem solving, and to obtain positive recognition for creative efforts that demonstrate that downsizing need not mean downgrading.

Complying with Regulations and Mandates

All workers, at all levels, must adapt and respond to a variety of external impacts on their thinking and practices. There are always new regulations, new policies, mandated behaviors, new technology, and revised administrative mandates. The challenge for the HRD practitioner is to help workers understand the rationale of the regulations and regulators, deal with resistance motivations, and explore options and alternatives of compliance and feasible strategies of feedback. How to constructively and effectively "influence upward" is one of the most important skills of any subordinate in a complex organization.

Examples of effective interventions by HRD colleagues include:

1. Staff brainstorming of all the alternative ways to implement a regulation and discussing the criteria for choosing one or another alternative for different client situations.

2. Staff discussions of their interpretations of a mandate, to check out and make a contribution to clarification.

3. Staff task force development of a proposed revision of a regulation and rehearsal of a presentation of the proposal to those "upstairs" in the system.

4. Inviting in representatives of the regulatory agency for an exploration of rationale, interpretation, and degree of flexibility.

5. Initiating a workshop with a consultant on "how to influence upward in bureaucratic systems."

Improving Quality and Productivity

There typically seem to be two different reasons for initiating improvement efforts. One of these is the realization of some problem or pain (e.g., drop in quality of product or service). The second reason for a push toward improvement is an *image of potential* of how things could be better, how they are better someplace else—the realization that there are new practices and technologies that are better or that a competitor is doing better than we are.

The challenges for the HRD practitioner are sometimes to stimulate images of potential where there is complacency. Or the job may be to convert "pain" into concrete goals and motivations for improvement and to reduce the depression and frustration that prevent improvement efforts.

From our combined 60 years of helping organizations make improvement efforts, we have concluded there are key strategies of the change-effort that the HRD practitioner needs to be able to facilitate to ensure a successful improvement in productivity or quality of service or work life. There are also several key traps the consultant must be able to help avoid.

Strategy	Trap
Allow those who will be affected to participate in defining need for change and direction of improvement	Small group makes decisions about what changes are needed and what to do
Actively explore images of desired outcomes before defining specific goals for improvement	Reactive focus on present problem pains as basis for defining change goals
Accept doubts, "resistance" as normal and as sources of important data for realistic change efforts	Label people and groups as resistors to be overcome
Put the right leaders together as project teams to plan or carry out action	Assume those heads will work productively without help on team-work and effective meeting skills
Provide support and reward for risk-taking efforts and for follow-through on good intentions	Assume good ideas can be sold on merits alone or can be ordered into action
Have stepwise plans, with documentation of progress and plans for recognition, celebration	Too big steps, no documentation, "duty posture"
Have coordinating and sanctioning support of a resource/consultation team, usually combining inside key persons with external resources	Get things started with no mechanism for continuous concern for quality of process and support for deadlines

Figure 5.4.   Strategies and traps in improving productivity, quality of service, or work life.

Inventing and Innovating New Practices

In every organization there are creative inventors who, when faced with problem situations, create new approaches, new ways of responding to needs, and new techniques for solving problems. Some staff members have modified and perfected procedures developed by others. The fact is that most of these significant innovations remain unknown and unused by others.

The challenge for the HRD practitioner is to help identify, document, and spread these innovations and to help the top leadership recognize and reward these creative contributions to the quality of operations.

In most fields of social practice, such as education, social work, business management, health care, and political action, probably 75% of the social inventions—new practices that are created by an innovative practitioner, or group, or organization and will be important in the future—are already being used someplace. But the tragedy is that most of these practices do not spread beyond the inventor. There are many reasons why significant practices do not spread.[12]

There is actually a great readiness to share and learn about new practices. One of the important skills of the HRD practitioner is the designing and leading of an exchange of successful practice sessions, within and among organizations. A brief vignette of such a session will illustrate this important HRD function.

Thirty middle managers are seated at tables of five. The HRD coordinator explains the idea of successful social inventions as a method of responding to complaints or motivating a worker. Two brainstorming sessions tackle the following questions: "Why, when we develop a way of doing some part of our job, don't we go around telling others about it?" "Why, when we have heard somebody seems very successful at something, don't we go and ask them how they do it?" A dozen responses are called out immediately.

The leader then proposes that in the next hour and a half the group try to overcome both of these handicaps to productivity by willingly sharing ideas and asking questions. The leader then tells each person that he or she has 30 seconds to *identify*, not explain, what could be shared that might be of interest to the group. Each table selects two of these practices to document, based on those they feel might be of greatest interest and value for the total group.

Each table is given a documentation interview schedule[13] and several ditto masters and is asked to use the schedule to probe the individuals and document the two practices they have selected. The ditto machine in the corner of the room reproduces the masters and copies are placed on the "pick up table." In an hour, 15 documented practices have been duplicated and placed on the table. In the last 30 minutes of this session everyone picks up and scans the practices and has brief consultation conversations with the two or three persons whose ideas they most want to try.

Follow-up research several months later indicated a significant use of new practices. Variations of this procedure should be in the repertoire of every HRD practitioner.

Disseminating Successful Practice

New technologies and practices are being invented continuously—in research programs and in the experimentation of creative practitioners in every organization. Dissemination of these discoveries is very slow. The challenge for the HRD practitioner is to help search for the new products and practices, evaluate their potential payoff, and initiate the process of imparting and adopting the new resource, or more frequently, to help adapt the new practice to the particular needs and capabilities of the local situation.

The skills of searching and retrieving are usually neglected as part of the job description for HRD personnel. Here are a few examples of these skills in practice:

1.   A computer search was initiated, for the employee relations unit of the ERIC system, to find abstracts and reports on recent studies of employee counseling, employee feedback practices, and employee survey procedures. These abstracts led to telephone contacts with several of the most interesting programs.

2.   Several staff members agreed to scan a different journal or newsletter for relevant reports and to share information at a monthly lunch meeting.

3.   The HRD practitioner invited an innovative professional from another organization (the practitioner had heard of the professional at an ASTD chapter meeting) to describe his practice at a brown bag seminar lunch.

4.   A task force of four, working on ways to improve the annual merit review procedure, spent a day visiting colleagues in another organization who had reported a favorable evaluation of a new procedure.[14]

5.   The HRD practitioner received nominations for several successful quality circle projects. A one-hour telephone conference interview was arranged for the task force and the coordinators of four of these projects. All of them appreciated the chance to listen to each other and to respond to the questions from the task force.

Remarkably small amounts of the tremendous resources of human inventiveness are disseminated. This is a very significant challenge for any HRD program.

GROWING AND DEVELOPING AS AN HRD PRACTITIONER

The more rapid the rate of change in organizational structure and function, the greater the challenge to the HRD practitioner to develop new job skills and continue to grow professionally. Our late colleague, Ed Lindeman, often commented that every professional practitioner these days had to become "at least 10% futurist" to stay in touch with societal and organizational change and to stay at the cutting edge of his or her professional specialty. Clearly, one of the new cutting edges, for all of us, is the computer technology that is making it possible for us to stay informed, even though the area of relevant knowledge is becoming more complex.[15]

The frustrations of information overload ready the HRD practitioner for the challenge of simplification and integration that comes from giving more priority to reflection, participation in seminars and workshops, and meaningful discussions with a few colleagues. Some examples of growth and development activities in the lives of creative HRD colleagues are:

1. Helping form small colleague support groups that agree to read, explore resources, and share at regular meetings (e.g., once a month, for an evening).
2. Helping each other identify professional growth interests and needs, and developing a yearly plan of learning experiences to pursue
3. Arranging a computer literacy learning program for oneself.
4. Becoming a member of the World Future Society and sharing important information from the *Futurist* with colleagues and clients.
5. Becoming an active member of the local ASTD chapter or other interdisciplinary associations of professionals.
6. Designating time for reading, in a wide range of fields.
7. Budgeting for two or three annual professional meetings per year.
8. Finding a colleague to coauthor a professional article that helps you conceptualize and organize your thinking.

Personal Development of Consulting Skills

It is a prerequisite for effective consulting that those practicing such a role manifest professional and mature behavior. This cannot be merely an outgrowth of the acquisition of degrees. It must be a manifestation of appropriate knowledge, skills, and attitudes in our day-to-day work in and for organizations. In this sense, the following guidelines are helpful:

Focus on the problem-solving approach to learning and change; use data, not just hunches.

Develop interdependence with others, not independency.

Practice what we preach in the field of our specialized knowledges.

Diagnose situations, rather than merely treat symptoms.

Understand ourselves so thoroughly that we do not let our personal needs get in the way of helping people and organizations develop.

Communicate on a reality level in an "open" fashion.

Admit mistakes and learn from failure.

Develop interests and skills so as to be able to work with people in a noncontrolling manner.

Be willing to experiment and innovate.

Develop a personal philosophy about working and developing people and organizations.

Be capable of saying, "I don't know."

Be willing to learn and change.

These criteria may not be the most important or the only criteria for professional consultant role behavior, but they are some we value highly. Unfortunately, we are unable to achieve these standards as consistently as we wish. While we want to increase the professionalization of the consultation field, the real goal is not only to acquire certain areas of knowledge but also to acquire the professional styles of competent behavior each of us demonstrates in our responsibility to help others.

NOTES

1. R. Capelle, *Changing Human Systems* (Toronto: International Human Systems Distributor, 1979).
2. R. Lippitt, "Effective Use of Human Resources," *Human Resource Development Journal*, 4(1): 1980, 3–7.
3. E. Schindler-Rainman and R. Lippitt, *Taking Your Meetings Out of the Doldrums*, (San Diego: University Associates, 1975).
4. According to unpublished reports of consulting practices—successes and failures: Gordon Lippitt, Jerry B. Harvey and Leslie This, 1980.
5. D. Swartz, "Similarities and Differences of Internal and External Consultants," *Journal of European Training*, 4(5):258–262, 1977. Adapted with permission.
6. R. Beckhard, *Leader Looks at the Consultative Process* (Washington, D.C.: Leadership Resources, Inc., 1971), p. 3.
7. This section was adapted from a portion of a book by G. Lippitt and R. Lippitt, *The Consulting Process in Action* (San Diego: University Associates, 1978).
8. This next section is adapted from a portion of an article by G. Lippitt, "Criteria for Selecting, Evaluating, and Developing Consultants," *ASTD Journal* (August, 1972), 62–68.

9. G. Lippitt, *Organization Renewal* (Englewood Cliffs, N.J.: Prentice-Hall, 1982), p. 18.
10. G. Lippitt, *Visualising Change* (Bethesda, Md.: Development Publications, 1983, Rev. Ed.).
11. G. Lippitt and R. Lippitt, "Downsizing—How to Manage More with Less," *Management Review*, 71(3):9, March, 1982.
12. R. Lippitt and E. Schindler-Rainman, *Identifying, Sharing, Exchanging Successful Practice*, (Bethesda, Md.: Development Publications, 1981).
13. R. Lippitt and E. Schindler-Rainman, *The Group Interview: A Tool for Organization Diagnosis and Action Research*, (Bethesda, Md.: Development Publications, 1982).
14. R. Lippitt, "Effective Use of Human Resources," *Human Resource Development Journal*, 4(4):2, 1980.
15. R. Lippitt, *The Dynamics of Planned Change*, (New York: Harcourt, Brace, & World, 1958).

BIBLIOGRAPHY

Beckhard, R. *Leader Looks at the Consultative Process*. Washington, D.C.: Leadership Resources, Inc., 1971.

Capelle, R. *Changing Human Systems*. Toronto: International Human Systems Distributor, 1979.

Lippitt, G. "Criteria for Selecting, Evaluating, and Developing Consultants." *ASTD Journal* (1972), August, 62–68.

Lippitt, G. *Organization Renewal*. Englewood Cliffs, N.J.: Prentice-Hall, 1982.

Lippitt, G. *Visualising Change*. Bethesda, Md.: Development Publications, 1973.

Lippitt, G., and R. Lippitt. *The Consulting Process in Action*. San Diego: University Associates, 1978.

Lippitt, G., and R. Lippitt. "Downsizing—How to Manage More with Less." *Management Review*, 71(3):9.

Lippitt, R. *The Dynamics of Planned Change*. New York: Harcourt, Brace, & World, 1958.

Lippitt, R. "Effective Use of Human Resources." *Human Resource Development Journal* 4(1):3.

Lippitt, R., and E. Schindler-Rainman. *The Group Interview: A Tool for Organization Diagnosis and Action Research*. Bethesda, Md.: Development Publications, 1982.

Lippitt, R., and E. Schindler-Rainman. *Identifying, Sharing, Exchanging Successful Practice*. Bethesda, Md.: Development Publications, 1981.

Schindler-Rainman, E., and R. Lippitt. *Taking Your Meetings Out of the Doldrums*. San Diego: University Associates, 1975.

Swartz, D. "Similarities of Internal and External Consultants." *Journal of European Training* 4(5):258–60.

Adult Learning: Theory and Practice

MALCOLM S. KNOWLES

HRD is based in learning, and every HRD practitioner, no matter what the role or subrole, should be competent in the area of adult learning theory. There are several people who, in recent years, have contributed to our understanding of adult learning theory. One of the most significant is the author of this chapter.

In this chapter, Knowles provides a broad overview of the background of adult learning and discusses some of the most prevalent theories. He does not opt for one over another; rather, he indicates when the different theories would be most appropriate.

Knowles also discusses andragogy, and who is better suited to do this? He is credited with bringing the andragogy concept into the field of learning in the United States.

Knowles brings all of his expertise together and relates it specifically to human resource development.

Malcolm S. Knowles (Ph.D.) has retired from his last academic position but is busier than ever conducting workshops and consulting with a wide variety of organizations in the United States and abroad. The major focus of these HRD activities is on modern concepts of adult learning and their implications for HRD. In his long career, he has held numerous positions including: director of training, National Youth Administration, Massachusetts; director of education for various YMCAs; executive director of the Adult Education Association; and professor of adult education at Boston University and then at North Carolina State University. He has a long list of very popular publications.

A HISTORICAL PERSPECTIVE

Would it surprise you if I told you that the earliest thinking about the nature of learning concerned learning for adults? All of the great teachers of ancient times were teachers of adults, not children. In ancient China, Confucius and Lao Tse were teachers of adults, not children. The Hebrew prophets and Jesus were teachers of adults, not children. The ancient Greeks—Socrates, Plato, Aristotle—were teachers of adults, not children. The great teachers in ancient Rome—Cicero, Quintilian, and Euclid—were teachers of adults, not children. Since their experiences were with adults, they perceived learning very differently than teachers later came to perceive it. To the teachers of ancient times learning was a process of active inquiry on the part of the learners, and they invented techniques for involving the learners in active inquiry. The ancient Chinese and Hebrews invented what we would now call the *case method*. One member of a study group (not necessarily the leader) would present a paradox—often in the form of a parable—and the group would examine its background and explore possible resolutions. The ancient Greeks used what we now call the method of the *Socratic Dialogue*, in which a member of the study group would pose a question, and the group would pool their resources to arrive at an answer.

With the fall of Rome in the second and third centuries A.D., the writings of these ancient great teachers were deposited in the archives of European monasteries and largely forgotten. When schools for children became systematically organized between the seventh and twelfth centuries—first in the cathedrals and monasteries and later in secular institutions—a different perception of the nature and purpose of learning gained prominence. The concepts *teachers* and *teaching* were invented, and *learning* was defined as a process of transmitting content (mostly knowledge and skills) from teachers to students. This was often known as the "empty vessel" theory, since the teachers saw themselves as filling the empty vessels of students from their own reservoirs of content.

This approach to learning came to be labeled *pedagogy*, a term derived from the Greek words *paid*, meaning "child" and *agogus*, meaning "leader of." Because the experiences of the teachers of this era were exclusively with young children, and because they were concerned primarily with teaching the basic skills of reading, writing, and arithmetic, they made very different assumptions about the learning process than those made by the ancient great teachers. They assigned to the role of teacher full responsibility for making all decisions about what should be learned, how it should be learned, when it should be learned, and if it had been learned—leaving the students pretty much in the role of passive, dependent recipients of the teachers' transmissions. When public schools were established in the early nineteenth century, this pedagogical model was the only one school people of that time had to follow, and so our entire school system was established on the basis of the pedagogical model.

Unfortunately, when adult education was organized systematically during the first quarter of this century, the pedagogical model was the only model teachers of adults had as well. As a result, most adults have been taught as if they were children. This is the primary cause of many of the problems adult education teachers have encountered—problems such as high drop-out rate, low motivation, and poor performance. Until recently, this same affliction had characterized much of the human resource development programs in business and industry.

THE BEGINNING OF THEORIZING ABOUT ADULT LEARNING

In 1926, the first book attempting to explain the unique characteristics of adults as learners was published. Eduard C. Lindeman's *The Meaning of Adult Education* is still one of the most insightful and inspiring works in the literature of adult education. In the following quotation he captured what later research has shown to be the essence of adult learning:

> I am conceiving adult education in terms of a new technique for learning, a technique as essential to the college graduate as to the unlettered manual worker.... It represents a process by which the adult learns to become aware of and to evaluate his experience. To do this he cannot begin by studying "subjects" in the hope that some day this information will be useful. On the contrary, he begins by giving attention to situations in which he finds himself, to problems which include obstacles to his self-fulfillment. Facts and information from the differentiated spheres of knowledge are used, not for the purpose of accumulation, but because of need in solving problems. In this process the teacher finds a new function. He is no longer the oracle who speaks from the platform of authority, but rather the guide, the pointer-outer who also participates in learning in proportion to the vitality and relevancy of his facts and experiences. In short, my conception of adult education is this: a cooperative venture in nonauthoritarian, informal learning, the chief purpose of which is to discover the meaning of experience; a quest of the mind which digs down to the roots of the preconceptions which formulate our conduct; a technique of learning for adults which makes education coterminous with life and hence elevates living itself to the level of adventurous experiment.[1]

In 1928 Edward L. Thorndike published his classic study of adult intelligence, *Adult Learning.* He posited that the ability to learn did not decline until age 35, and then it declined only 1% per year—thus rebutting the prevalent folklore of that time that "you can't teach old dogs new tricks." (However, research by Thorndike's successors showed that it was the speed of learning, not the power to learn, that declined.) During the next 30 years, reports by successful teachers of adults appearing in the periodical literature described how teachers were forced to depart from the pedagogical model to maintain interest and retain their students. Research-based knowledge about adult learning was contributed from other social science disciplines: clinical psychology added knowledge about the process of behavioral change; social psychology, about the effects of environment on learning; sociology, about the consequences of institutional policies and procedures, norms, and reward systems; and developmental psychology, about the stages of development during the adult years.

By the late 1950s, European adult educators felt the need for a term that would enable them to discuss this growing body of knowledge about adult learners in parallel with pedagogy. They coined the word "andragogy," derived from the Greek word *anere*, for adult, and *agogus*, meaning "the art and science of helping students learn." Although this term has not yet appeared in any of the standard dictionaries, it is now widely used by adult educators around the world to describe a theory of adult learning.

THE MEANING AND PRACTICAL USE OF THEORIES

A theory, as described here, is a set of principles or propositions that attempt to explain and, it is hoped, predict phenomena. A theory can, therefore, provide guidelines for action. As the great social scientist, Kurt Lewin, is said to have stated, "There is nothing as practical as a good theory." Presumably, if we have a "good" theory about an HRD situation, we will know what learning strategies to use in dealing with it.

But how do we know if we have a good theory? Since all theories are derived from models of the phenomena they are trying to explain, it helps to know what model of reality a given theory is using so that we can determine if the particular model is realistic for the particular situation.

For example, Newton derived his theory of energy ($E=m$) from a model of the universe in a stable state. Given that model, it was reasonable to define energy and mass as interchangeable. But toward the end of the last century when more powerful telescopes determined that the universe was not stable but was expanding at a rapid rate, a new ingredient, velocity, had to be added to the theory. Einstein did it with his formula ($E=mc^2$), and the whole new world of atomic energy was opened up to us.

Since we are concerned with the learning of human beings, we need to determine the model of "man" from which each theory is derived. Then we can decide whether that model is realistic for the particular situation. Essentially, there are three groups of learning theories which stem from three different models of man:

1. *Mechanistic (or Behaviorist) Theories.* These theories equate man with machine, in that, as with machines, if you introduce an input (stimulus) into a human being and control how that input is processed (operant conditioning), you will get a predetermined output (response). According to this set of theories, the purpose of education is to produce prescribed behaviors—the behaviors the teacher decides the learners should perform. These are commonly known as "S-R" (stimulus-response) theories.

2. *Cognitive Theories.* These theories equate man with brain, based on the proposition that the one thing that distinguishes human beings from other living things is that they possess brains that are capable of critical thinking and problem solving. The purpose of learning, accordingly, is to teach the brain to engage in such critical thinking and problem solving.

3. *Organismic (or Humanistic) Theories.* These theories hold that human beings, like all living organisms, have their own genetically determined, unique, individual potential. The purpose of learning, therefore, is to encourage each individual to develop to his or her full, unique potential.

Each model prescribes its own preferred strategies of learning. The mechanistic model prescribes programmed instruction, teaching machines, behavioral modification, linear computer-assisted instruction, teaching to terminal behaviors, and drills. The cognitive model prescribes didactic instruction, rote memorization of information or procedures (e.g., steps in problem solving), and standardized testing of "right solutions" to preset problems. The organismic model prescribes discovery methods, individualized learning projects, and self-directed learning.

The proponents of each set of theories tend to present them as absolute, excluding the validity of any other theories. Thus the behaviorists (or mechanistic theorists)—Pavlov, Thorndike, Watson, Skinner, Mager, and others—hold that learning occurs only when a learner is conditioned to give the "right" response to a given stimulus. The cognitive theorists—Piaget, Bruner, Gagne, and others—hold that learning occurs only when learners acquire the time-tested principles and strategies of critical thinking and problem solving. And the humanistic theorists—as epitomized by Carl Rogers—hold that learning occurs only when learners have the "freedom to learn" what is particularly relevant to their personal life situation.

Each theory is appropriate under particular conditions, since each of us behaves like a machine, a brain, and a living organism under different circumstances. When we want to learn a mechanical operation, such as how to operate a strange machine, the behaviorists are in touch with that reality, and behaviorist strategies, such as operant conditioning, are appropriate. When we want to learn to analyze a document critically, then instruction in procedures of critical analysis is appropriate. And when we want to develop our unique style, increase our self-understanding, or enhance any other aspect of our "selves," then humanistic strategies, such as self-directed inquiry, are appropriate.

Let me illustrate this position by applying it to what I am doing now—writing a chapter for a book. The first thing I had to learn was how to use a typewriter by touch. Actually, I learned this in high school, when my typing teacher told me which fingers should hit which keys. While I practiced, she hovered over me tapping my fingers with a little rod each time I hit a wrong key. She had announced at the beginning that the terminal behavior objective for the class was for each student to type 60 words a minute with a maximum of three errors per page. By conditioning us with punishments and rewards, we achieved that objective.

Having learned to operate the machine efficiently, I wanted to learn how to use it to write term papers, letters, and, eventually, articles and books. I took courses that taught me to think logically, to read critically, to use acceptable standard forms for letters and papers, and many other cognitive operations.

But I wanted to learn to use my typewriter to write creative essays, poetry, and original books in a style of my own. I did this by reading many essays, poems, and books, comparing the styles of different authors to determine which aspects of their styles felt best to me, experimenting, and getting people's reactions to what I wrote.

Applying this position to business operations, behaviorist strategies are preferred in situations where employees need to learn basic skills. When cognitive operations are involved, didactic teaching is preferred. But when more complex and self-developmental operations are involved, humanistic strategies are preferred.

THE ANDRAGOGICAL THEORY OF LEARNING

What do we know at this point about the characteristics of adults as learners and the adult learning process? Since adult learning is a relatively new subject of scientific investigation, much of what we think we know about it is based upon intuitive experience with adult learners. An increasing volume of our knowledge is, however, derived from rigorous research. Consequently, the theoretical framework for thinking about adult learning consists of "assumptions" or "concepts" rather than of "knowledge." So far, most of what we have learned through experience has been borne out by research.

Here are the most important assumptions we now make about adults as learners:

1. *The Need to Know.* Adults learn more effectively if they understand why they need to know or be able to do something. We have a dictum in adult learning that the first task of the teacher is to create an awareness of "the need to know" on the part of the learners. When adults undertake to learn something on their own, they explore the benefits of learning versus the costs of not learning before they invest their time and energy. In HRD programs, those employees who choose to participate in a learning activity may already have a good idea as to how it will benefit them. But employees who are "sent" to a learning activity by their supervisors or managers or who otherwise feel that they are participating under compulsion are not likely to understand the benefits and so will not have a deep commitment, in fact, may even be resistant, to learning. Hence, it is important that a strong case be made for the personal benefits they will gain. The more directly they can experience or see the benefits, in contrast to merely being told about them, the more strongly they will feel "the need to know."

2. *The Need to Be Self-Directing.* Adults have a deep psychological need to take responsibility for their own lives—to be self-directing. In fact, the psychological definition of *adult* is "one who has arrived at the self-concept of being in charge of one's life, being responsible for one's own decisions and actions." This is a self-concept that starts forming quite early in life and is accelerated as we become aware of being biologically mature (able to reproduce), legally mature (able to get a driver's license, vote, buy liquor, etc.), and socially mature (start performing such adult roles as those of worker, spouse, parent, etc.). The process of developing a self-concept of adultness can be facilitated by

cultural conditions that encourage individuals to take increasing responsibility for themselves, or it can be retarded by cultural conditions that keep individuals dependent on others to make their decisions for them (as is the case in many home and school cultures in our society). Accordingly, some individuals who come from home and school experiences that encourage them to take responsibility for themselves arrive at the self-concept of adultness earlier than others.

At some point in our lives, however, each of us becomes aware that we are fully adult—that we are capable of being self-directing. At that point we experience a deep psychological need to be perceived and treated by others as being capable of taking responsibility for ourselves. From then on, whenever we find ourselves in situations in which we feel that others are making our decisions for us—whether supervisors, teachers, or organizational leaders—we experience a resentment of and resistance to that situation.

This psychological reality presents a special problem to those of us in HRD and adult education. When adults enter into any activity that is labeled "education" or "training" or any of their synonyms, they revert back to their previous experiences in school, put on their dunce hats of dependency, sit back, fold their arms, and say "Teach me." They have been conditioned to perceive the role of student as a dependent role, and they expect the teacher to direct them.

Over the last several years, it has become increasingly apparent that this is a problem. Examples of innovative strategies that try to help adults make the transition from dependent learners to self-directing learners are described in Boud,[2] Griffith,[3] and Knowles.[4] Adults need to be prepared for a first experience with self-directed learning through an orientation experience, before being plunged into it. This orientation can be as brief as one hour or extended to five days, depending on the time available and the complexity of the learning experience. In either case, the critical components of an orientation to self-directed learning are: (1) an exposure to the ideas that differentiate being taught from learning;[5] (2) a relationship-building and resource-identification exercise;[6] and (3) some practice exercises to sharpen skills in self-directed learning.[7] Adults who are asked to take some responsibility for their own learning for the first time will experience a degree of confusion, tension, and anxiety initially. But as they start working on their own self-planned learning projects, they get "turned on" to learning and invest more energy in self-directed inquiry than could ever be required of them in didactic instruction.

Self-directed learning does not mean learning in isolation or learning without help. The most effective self-directed learners are highly skillful in getting help from peers, teachers, printed materials, audiovisual aids, and every other kind of resource. The key distinction between learning and being taught is the locus of responsibility; in didactic teaching the locus of responsibility is in the teacher, whereas in self-directed learning it is in the learner. When learners take some responsibility in the learning process, they learn more, retain what they learn longer, and learn more efficiently.

3. *Greater Volume and Quality of Experience.* Adults, by virtue of having lived longer, accumulate a greater volume and a different quality of experience than children and youth. The greater volume is self-evident—they have done more things, and the longer they have lived, the more things they have done. The different quality of experience stems from their having performed such roles as full-time worker, spouse, parent, and responsible citizen, which children and youth do not usually perform.

Several consequences flow from these differences of experience. First, it assures that every group of adults will be heterogeneous and that the greater the mix of ages and backgrounds in the group, the greater the heterogeneity will be. Hence, the emphasis in adult learning is on the individualization of "instruction"—the provision for a wide choice of learning strategies and resources and the extensive use of subgroups or networks linking people with similar backgrounds (when that is appropriate). Important as it is to take into account individual differences in providing learning for children and youth, it is much more necessary to take them into account in providing learning for adults.

Second, since adults enter into a learning situation with more experience, they are a richer source for learning—for themselves and for one another. In fact, for many kinds of learning the richest resources are often the learners. This is why, in adult learning, so much emphasis is placed on experiential techniques that tap into the experience of the learners or provide them with experiences from which they can learn (e.g., group discussion, simulation exercises, field experiences), and less emphasis is placed on transmittal techniques.

A third consequence of their greater experience is that adults may have developed habit patterns, preconceptions, prejudices, and rigid ways of thinking that may interfere with their learning. This danger can be minimized by building into the learning designs some mind-opening or "unfreezing" activities, such as a "mini" sensitivity-training session.

Perhaps the most important, if most subtle, consequence of adults' greater experience is that whereas children and youth derive their self-identity primarily from external sources (their parents, their peer group, their school, their youth organization), adults derive their self-identity primarily from their experience; they are their experience. Accordingly, if we ignore or undervalue their experience in a learning session, it is not just their experience that they feel is being rejected; they feel rejected as persons.

4. *Readiness to Learn.* Whereas youth have been well conditioned to be ready to learn what they are told they should or have to learn, adults become ready to learn those things that they perceive will bring them greater satisfaction or success in life. One of the chief sources of "readiness to learn" is the developmental stages or "transitions" we pass through during the adult years. For example, as we move from being a student to becoming a full-time worker, we ready ourselves to learn the necessary skills to get and hold a job. As we move toward marriage, we become ready to learn about marital relations. As we move toward being a parent, we become ready to learn about infant care. As we move from being a worker to becoming a supervisor, we ready ourselves to learn about supervision, and so on.

Several implications for HRD flow from this concept of "readiness to learn." Perhaps the most important implication has to do with the timing of our offerings. Learning opportunities that are timed to coincide with the learners' readiness to learn are more likely to be effective than those that are out of step with it. In fact, some of the great errors in HRD have occurred as a result of individuals being pushed into learning programs for which they were not ready. Workers are not ready to learn about supervision, for example, until they feel that they have mastered the jobs they will be supervising.

We do not, however, have to sit by passively and wait for readiness to develop naturally; there are things we can do to stimulate it. We can expose people to "a better life" or a more satisfying performance through audiovisual presentations, simulation exercises, linkage with role models, career-planning programs, counseling, self-diagnostic procedures, and performance appraisal processes for needs assessment rather than screening purposes.

5. *Orientation to Learning.* Whereas children and youth have been conditioned to enter into a learning activity with a subject-centered orientation to learning, adults have a life-centered, task-centered, or problem-centered orientation. While young people see the purpose of

learning as accumulating subject matter so as to pass a test or earn credit toward a diploma or degree, adults see the purpose of learning as acquiring competencies that will enable them to cope more effectively with life, perform life tasks, or solve real problems. This difference in orientation toward learning has several implications for HRD.

One central implication has to do with how we organize the curriculum. We do not have subject-centered courses, such as Composition I, Composition II, and Composition III. Instead, we have Writing Better Business Letters, Writing Clearer Reports, and Communicating with the Public. It is not just that the titles of our offerings are different; the way we design the learning experiences is different. In Composition I the learners memorize the rules of grammar; in "Writing Better Business Letters" they write a variety of business letters and, by critiquing them, generate skills in grammatical writing. When teaching literacy skills to undereducated adults, do not give them courses in reading, writing, and arithmetic, instead help them learn the skills of reading, writing, and computing that they need to have in order to be able to cope more effectively with their real life problems in the world of work, the world of local government and community service, the world of health care, the world of the consumer, and so on.

During this past year I have been trying to learn to use a microcomputer to write letters, articles, and books, and I have been having a difficult time. The instructional manuals and software programs are written by engineers who do not understand that adults are task-oriented learners. So they instruct me to memorize information about how the machine works and the commands that will make it work. I spent hours memorizing information I had no idea how to use, and I proceeded to forget most of it. Then I started teaching myself how to use the computer to write letters, articles, and books, and although the manuals were not very helpful, I eventually was able to get the microcomputer to do the work I needed. I would have learned much faster and more easily if the manuals and software programs had been organized around life tasks (i.e., How to write a letter, how to write a report, how to personalize form letters, etc.).

Examine your orientation programs to see if they are organized around the real questions and problems new workers confront as they prepare to enter into a strange workplace, or are they merely transmitting information about the organizational structure, personnel policies, products, market, and financial practices of the company? Examine your programs in basic skills, communications, human relations, supervision, management, and the rest of your human resources development programs against the criterion of their task-centeredness.

APPLYING THE ANDRAGOGICAL MODEL

The mission of traditional teachers of both the behaviorist and cognitive theoretical persuasions is to transmit content, and so they employ a *content model* in planning and conducting their programs. They are dogmatic and ideological in their attitudes toward their respective theories. To a behaviorist, the stimulus-response-operant conditioning strategy is the only valid method. To the cognitive practitioners, didactic instruction is the exclusive solution to all learning situations. The andragogical model, on the other hand, is a *process model* that can incorporate principles and technologies from various theories and still maintain its own integrity.

In traditional learning, the teacher (or instructor, the curriculum committee, etc.) decides in advance what knowledge or skills need to be transmitted, arranges this body of content into logical units, selects the most efficient means for transmitting this content (lectures, assigned readings, films, tapes, programmed instruction, etc.), and then develops a plan for transmitting these content units in a logical sequence. In contrast, the andragogical teacher (facilitator, consultant, change agent) prepares in advance a set of procedures for facilitating the acquisition of content by the learners. It is not that content is important to one and not to the other; it is that the transmission of the content is what is important to the pedagog and the acquisition of the content by the learners is what is important to the andragog. Andragogs see their role as twofold: first as the designers and managers of the processes for facilitating learning and as content resources. Even in this secondary role, they see themselves as not only direct content resources but also as the link to many other content resources (in a way, as educational brokers).

Establishing a Climate Conducive to Learning

Just as in the past decade or more we have witnessed a growing concern for the quality of environments for living, so during the same period has there been increasing concern among educators for the quality of environments for learning. Valuable information about the effects of the physical properties of environment on learning has come from the ecological psychologists. The social psychologists have uncovered important effects of the human environment—especially the influence of the quality of interpersonal relations. And from the industrial psychologists and sociologists have come many useful insights about the effects of the organizational environment—the structure, policies, procedures, and norms of the institutions in which learning takes place.

In developing a process design consider two aspects of climate: the physical climate and the psychological climate.

In designing a physical environment, the fertile brain of man could not possibly create one that is less conducive to learning than the typical classroom—with chairs in rows facing a lectern in front. That design announces to anyone entering the room that the name of the game here is one-way transmission; the appropriate role for the learners is to sit passively and dependently and absorb the transmission from the lectern. I make a point of going to an assigned room and "casing the joint." When I find it set up as a classroom (which is the only way most custodians know how to set it up), I move the lectern to a distant corner and rearrange the chairs in one big circle, if that is possible or, if not, in several small circles, preferably around tables. The room's design should announce that the name of the game here is active participation. Of course, provision must be made for creature comforts, such as temperature, ventilation, easy access to rest rooms, breaks for refreshments, comfortable chairs, adequate light, and good acoustics.

As important as physical climate is, psychological climate is even more important. The following are the characteristics of a psychological climate that is conducive to learning:

A Climate of Mutual Respect.   People who feel respected are more open to learning. If they feel that they are being talked down to, that their experience is being ignored or denigrated, that they are regarded as not being capable of taking responsibility and making decisions for themselves, they will dwell on these feelings.

To create a climate of mutual respect, have the participants use bold felt pens to make large name tents on folded 5″ × 8″ cards; people feel more respected if they are addressed by name. Arrange groups of five or six people and have them share things about themselves: what they are (their positions and work background); who they are as unique human beings (one thing about themselves that will enable others to see them as unique); what special resources they are bringing with them from their previous experience that others might tap into; and what questions, problems, and concerns they are hoping will be dealt with in this session. Be a role model by presenting this information about yourself. This will establish a "human" relationship with the participants from the outset. Ask one person in each group to volunteer to give a summary of the information generated in the table discussions, or shorten the time required by calling out categories of their "whats" (institutional settings, roles) and resources and have the table reporters give only the questions, problems, and concerns. Listen very carefully to what participants say. If there is any doubt in your mind as to what they mean, repeat what you think they said in your own words and ask if that is what they meant. This conveys respect for their contributions.

A Climate of Collaborativeness, Not Competitiveness.   Creating such a climate is difficult because adults have been conditioned by all of their previous school experience to perceive the proper relationship among students to be that of competitors. The norm-referenced grading system, in which each learner's performance is compared with that of others, automatically induces a rivalrous attitude. Indeed, in many situations in school, one student helping another is defined as cheating. In adult learning, often the richest resources for learning are within the group of learners, therefore peer helping and sharing are critical. The group-sharing exercise described above helps to set the standard that it is expected that learners will help one another.

A Climate of Supportiveness.   Adults often enter into a learning activity with some anxiety. If they did not do well in earlier schooling, or if they have not been exposed to formal instruction for some time, they may also have a negative self-concept as learners; they may worry about being embarrassed in front of their peers by asking dumb questions or giving dumb answers. Therefore, it is important that the teacher be a supportive person, accepting all contributions as being worthwhile and building on them so as to enhance their significance. The teacher should make frequent use of peer support groups or networks and schedule times for students to check things out with one another.

A Climate of Mutual Trust.   Creating such a climate is also difficult because of previous school experience. Teachers are overwhelmingly presented by their institutions as authority figures who have power over students—the power to give grades, fail students, assign work, and criticize. We learn early that people who have power over us do not always use that power fairly or constructively, and so we have a built-in tendency to mistrust authority figures. Teachers should try to minimize this tendency by presenting themselves as caring human beings and describing their role as facilitators or helpers. Teachers should also behave in ways that show they convey trust to the students.

A Climate of Active Inquiry.   I have a rule-of-thumb that in the opening session there is never more than 10 minutes of front-end talk before actively involving the participants in building relationships and sharing concerns, as in the exercise described previously. It is important to begin with the understanding that learning is a process of active inquiry, not a process of passive reception of transmitted information.

A Climate of Openness.   Some people have a tendency, when put into a learning situation, to play the role of traditional student, which involves showing off, pretending to know things they do not, and being defensive. Learning is enhanced if people feel free to be natural, to act authentically. The teacher can induce such a climate by being an open, natural, and authentic role model.

Another aspect that affects the quality of learning is the organizational climate of the larger social system in which the learning takes place. The notion of an organizational climate involves several sets of ideas. One set has to do with the policy framework undergirding the HRD program. In some organizations, HRD is relegated to the peripheral status in the policy framework, and therefore there is not much reinforcement of motivation to engage in it. Other organizations—especially in the high-tech industries—assign HRD a central role in the achievement of organizational goals and make this explicit in their policy statements.

Another set of ideas regarding organizational climate involves management philosophy. A "Theory X" management philosophy (manager as controller) provides an organizational climate that induces disrespect, competitiveness, threat, defensiveness, and pedagogical strategies. A "Theory Y" management philosophy (manager as facilitator) provides an organizational climate that is more congenial to andragogical strategies.

A third aspect of organizational climate, closely related to the second and possibly a part of it, is the structure of the organization. A number of studies have shown that in hierarchically structured organizations there is less motivation for self-improvement and more blocks to learning (e.g., high anxiety) than in organizations more functionally structured, such as by interlinked work groups or by project task forces or quality circles.

Organizational climate is also affected by financial policies. At the most primary level, the sheer amount of financial resources made available to HRD influences attitudes toward HRD at all levels. When employees see that their organization values HRD highly enough to support it liberally, they are likely to value it as well. If, in times of austerity, HRD is the first budget to be cut, it will come to be seen as a peripheral activity. Perhaps the ultimate sign that an organization has a deep commitment to human resource development is when the HRD budget is handled as an asset (like new machinery), rather than as an operating cost.

Finally, a most crucial determinant of climate is the reward system. All learning theorists would jump on the stimulus-response theorists' bandwagon in acknowledging that those behaviors that are rewarded are likely to be maintained. Accordingly, in those organizations in which participation in the HRD program is given obvious weight in wage and salary increases, promotion, and other job emoluments, the climate will certainly be more conducive to learning than in organizations in which the attitude is that learning should be its own reward.

Climate setting is probably the single most crucial element in the whole process of HRD. If the climate is not really conducive to learning, if it does not convey that an organization considers human beings its most valuable asset and their development its most productive investment, then all the other elements in the process are jeopardized. There is little likelihood of having a first-rate program of human resource development in an environment that is not supportive of learning.

Creating a Mechanism for Mutual Planning

One aspect of learning that most sharply differentiates the pedagogical from the andragogical, the mechanistic from the organismic, and the "teaching" from the "facilitating of learning" schools of thought is the role of the learner in planning. In the first of each of the above pairs, responsibility for planning is assigned almost exclusively to an authority figure (teacher, programmer, instructor), but this practice is glaringly in conflict with the adult's need to be self-directing. Therefore, a cardinal principle of andragogy is that a mechanism must be provided to involve all the parties concerned with a learning enterprise—learners, teachers or instructors, line supervisors or managers, clients or customers. Social science research indicates that people tend to feel committed to a decision or activity in direct proportion to their participation in or influence on the making of a decision or the planning of an activity. The reverse of this "law of human nature" is even more relevant to HRD; people tend to feel uncommitted to any decision or activity to the extent that they have not had an opportunity to influence it.

For this reason, the most successful HRD programs almost always have planning committees (or councils or task forces) for every level of activity: one for organization-wide programs, one for each departmental or functional group program, and one for each course, seminar, or workshop. Merely having mechanisms for mutual planning is not enough, however. They must be treated in good faith, with real delegation of responsibility and real influence in decision making, or they can backfire.

Diagnosing the Needs for Learning

There are several levels of depth and objectivity at which learning needs can be assessed. At the lowest level, and often the best one with which to start, is asking the individuals themselves what they want or think they need to learn in order to be more productive and happier in their work. The next level is to ask functional work groups what they think their learning needs are as a group; quality circles are being used increasingly for this purpose. The next level is to obtain data from line supervisors and managers as to what they think the learning needs of their workers are; the management-by-objectives process is being used by a number of corporations and agencies to generate this kind of information. Other sources of organizational data about learning needs include systems analyses, performance analyses, and analyses of such internal documents as safety reports, productivity records, quality control reports, personnel appraisals, and cost/effectiveness studies.

Another approach gaining rapidly in popularity is the use of competency models as a basis for self- or group-diagnosis. Many organizations have created models of the competencies required for performing various roles by having task forces composed of people who are experienced in those roles, pool their thinking about which competencies create superior performance. Individuals assess the gaps between where they are now and where the model says they need to be in performing the specified competencies. Usually these self-assessments are then checked out with peers and supervisors. Knowles provides detailed descriptions of how this approach works and provides some examples.[8,9]

Formulating Program Objectives

The purpose of program objectives is to provide program planners with some guidelines as to broad goals for which they will be held accountable and to provide consumers (including supervisors and workers) with a basis for selecting those aspects of the program that would be relevant to them. The first purpose is served by statements of the general goals of the whole HRD program that generally appear in personnel manuals and corporate policy pronouncements.The second purpose is served by statements of the objectives of particular units of the HRD program, such as courses, seminars, and workshops that generally appear in the announcements of these activities.

There is somewhat of a battle going on in all of education regarding how the objectives of particular HRD activities should be stated. At one end of the battlefield are the behaviorists, who maintain that an objective must describe a "terminal behavior that can be observed and measured."[10] At the other end are the humanists, who hold that most human learning is too complex to be described by a terminal behavior that can be observed and measured, and that objectives should therefore describe directions of growth in terms of knowledge, skill, attitudes, and values. Both forms of stating objectives are appropriate for different situations. Where the operations being learned are basic skills, such as how to operate a new machine, behavioral objectives probably give the best guidance to the learner. Where the operations being learned are highly complex, such as decision making, critical thinking, better human relations, and gaining self-confidence, more holistic statements of objectives probably give the best guidance to the learner. According to the andragogical model, which places emphasis on learning, the function of objectives is to provide guidance for the learner, as contrasted with the pedagogical model, which places emphasis on teaching, with objectives serving as an instrument of control and evaluation by the teacher.[11]

Designing and Operating a Learning Resource System

Three years ago this section would have been titled, "Designing A Comprehensive Program,"[12] and the following section would have been titled, "Operating a Comprehensive Program."[13] Until that time HRD was generally conceptualized as only a program of activities—courses, seminars, workshops, institutes, multimedia-packaged programs, and the like. The role of the training staff consisted of managing the logistics of operating this program—performing needs assessment, planning learning sequences, recruiting resource people, drafting budgets, scheduling activities, and promoting the program.

But with the increasing application of systems theory to dealing with organizational affairs in the late 1970s, a new approach to HRD began to emerge. The starting point of this new way of thinking is to conceptualize an organization as a system of learning resources. Once we perceive it as a system of learning resources then we must ask a very different set of questions about the role and operation of HRD than ever asked before.

The first question is: "What are *all* of the resources for learning in this organization and its environment?" We would usually come up with a list that looks something like this:

All the instructional activities scheduled under the auspices of the HRD department

All the line supervisors and managers

All functional work groups

All daily experience on the job

Printed materials, audiovisual aids, and multimedia packages in the library or media center.

Specialists who are using their expertise for work but not as a resource for others' learning

Community resources—schools, colleges, commercial vendors of learning programs, consultants, and retired persons

Effective techniques for identifying all these resources and storing information about them so it can be retrieved quickly (via a computer, for example) have been developed by the "educational brokering" agencies that are spreading like wildfire across the country.[14]

A second question has to be asked: "How well are these resources being used for learning and how might they be used more effectively?" You probably would arrive at the answer that most of them are not being used very systematically and that they would be used more effectively if the following actions were taken:

1.   Substantial blocks of time should be built into the supervisory training and management training development programs exposing the line managers to modern concepts of adult learning and providing them with skill practice exercises on how to serve as facilitators of learning for their subordinates. After all, most current supervisors and managers have had no instruction in learning and know about it only from how they were taught as children and youth. They do not understand that adults learn differently from the way *they* have been taught.

2.   The job descriptions of supervisors and managers should be modified so as to put heavy emphasis on their responsibility to be *people developers* as well as *work managers*. The personnel appraisal system should provide brownie points for the results achieved in developing their personnel through learning.

3.   Functional work groups should be given guidelines and tools for assessing not only their productivity but also their learning needs. For example, it has been found in several corporations that quality circle

participants need to improve their competencies in planning and decision making to be effective in improving their productivity.

4. Information needs to be disseminated, and frequently updated, about the materials, audiovisual aids, and multimedia packages available in the library and media center and how and when they can be used by employees for personal development as self-directed learners.

5. A process needs to be devised for helping employees make use of these resources for continuous, systematic self-development. The single most potent tool for accomplishing this purpose is the *learning contract*.[15] It is a device which enables individuals to construct a plan that involves: stating learning objectives, identifying appropriate learning resources for each objective, specifying a target date for accomplishing each objective, describing what evidence will be collected to demonstrate the accomplishment of each objective, and indicating how that evidence will be validated.

This approach to HRD has many implications for redefining the nature and role of HRD in an organization. It places the primary responsibility for HRD in the line, and it places a heavy responsibility on the professional HRD personnel to serve as consultants to the line supervisors and managers in carrying out their people-development functions. It shifts the role of the HRD personnel from primarily managers of the logistics of instructional activities to managers of a system of learning resources. In effect, their new role is that of systems engineers.

Evaluating the Outcomes of an HRD System

Of all of the aspects of adult learning, there is not one that causes more of a sense of inadequacy, guilt, and dissatisfaction than evaluation. I know of nobody in our field who is secure and happy with the state of the art in evaluation. There is a simple explanation. We have been living for the last 40 years in a mythical world that has laid a burdensome load of unrealistic expectations on us—the world of quantitative measurement. The assumption that the significant effects of learning can be measured and reported quantitatively is simply not true.

Fortunately, we are at a turning point in our theory and practice of evaluation. We are moving from the "quantitative binge" we have been on for several decades to a new emphasis on *qualitative evaluation*. The central theme of this new approach is that if we really want to find out what the effects of our HRD efforts are, we need to get inside the people involved (learners, supervisors, clients, and public) and find out how they feel and what they are doing about it. This approach requires a completely different set of techniques from the traditional pretests and post-tests of recall and statistical tests of significance of difference. It requires such qualitative techniques as participant observation, in-depth interviews, case studies, personal diaries, analyses of performance changes, and others. The contemporary leaders of qualitative evaluation are Patton,[16] Guba and Lincoln,[17] and Cronbach.[18]

NOTES

1. R. Gessner, ed., *The Democratic Man: Selected Writings of Edward C. Lindeman* (Boston: Beacon Press, 1956), p. 160.
2. D. Boud, ed., *Developing Student Autonomy in Learning* (New York: Nichols Publishing Co., 1981), pp. 135–44.
3. G. Griffith, A. Tough, W. Barnard, and D. Brundage, *The Design of Self-Directed Learning* (Toronto: Ontario Institute for Studies in Education, 1980).
4. M.S. Knowles, *Self-Directed Learning: A Guide for Learners and Teachers* (Chicago: Follet Publishing Co., 1975).
5. Ibid., pp. 14–28.
6. Ibid., pp. 71–74.
7. Ibid., pp. 105–109.
8. M.S. Knowles, *The Modern Practice of Adult Education: From Pedagogy to Andragogy* (Chicago: Follet, 1980), pp. 227–32.
9. M.S. Knowles, *The Adult Learning: A Neglected Species* (Houston: Gulf Publishing Company, 1978), pp. 180–93.
10. R. Mager, *Preparing Instructional Objectives* (Belmont, Cal.: Fearon, 1962).
11. Knowles, *The Adult Learner: A Neglected Species*, pp. 117–21.
12. Knowles, *The Modern Practice of Adult Education: From Pedagogy to Andragogy*, pp. 127–54.
13. Ibid., pp. 155–97.
14. J.M. Heffernan, F.L. Macy, and D.F. Vickers, *Educational Brokering: A New Service for Adult Learners* (Syracuse, N.Y.: National Center for Educational Brokering, 1976).
15. Knowles, *The Adult Learning: A Neglected Species*, pp. 127–28, 198–203.
16. M.Q. Patton, *Qualitative Evaluation Methods* (Beverly Hills, Cal.: Sage Publications, Inc., 1980).
17. E.G. Guba and Y.S. Lincoln, *Effective Evaluation* (San Francisco: Jossey-Bass Inc., Publishers, 1981).
18. L.J. Cronbach, *Toward Reform of Program Evaluation* (San Francisco: Jossey-Bass Inc., Publishers, 1980).

BIBLIOGRAPHY

Boud, D., ed. *Developing Student Autonomy in Learning.* New York: Nichols Publishing Co., 1981.

Cronbach, L.J. *Toward Reform of Program Evaluation.* San Francisco: Jossey-Bass Inc., Publishers, 1980.

Gessner, R., ed. *The Democratic Man: Selected Writings of Eduard C. Lindeman.* Boston: Beacon Press, 1956.

Griffith, G., A. Tough, W. Barnard, and D. Brundage. *The Design of Self-Directed Learning.* Toronto: Ontario Institute for Studies in Education, 1980.

Guba, E.G., and Y.S. Lincoln. *Effective Evaluation.* San Francisco: Jossey-Bass Inc., Publishers, 1981.

Heffernan, J.M., F.L. Macy, and D.F. Vickers. *Educational Brokering: A New Service for Adult Learners.* Syracuse, N.Y.: National Center for Educational Brokering, 1976.

Knowles, M.S. *The Adult Learner: A Neglected Species.* Houston: Gulf Publishing Company, 1978.

Knowles, M.S. *The Modern Practice of Adult Education: From Pedagogy to Andragogy.* Chicago: Follett Publishing Co., 1975.

Knowles, M.S. *Self-Directed Learning: A Guide for Learners and Teachers.* Chicago: Follett Publishing Co., 1975.

Mager, R. *Preparing Instructional Objectives.* Belmont, Cal.: Fearon, 1962.

Patton, M.Q. *Qualitative Evaluation Methods.* Beverly Hills, Cal.: Sage Publications, Inc., 1980.

Designing Learning Programs

GARLAND D. WIGGS

Most HRD practitioners who are not HRD managers or consultants devote a great deal of time to designing learning programs. Many organizations have found that although it is certainly possible to contract out for both the design and conduct of learning programs, the results of the externally designed and conducted programs often fail to meet the desired objectives. Therefore, it is important for HRD practitioners to know how to design effective and efficient learning programs.

As Wiggs points out in this chapter, it is essential that the designer understand how adults learn. Without that basic competency, it is doubtful whether the designer can be successful.

It is no longer necessary for the designer to start anew each time a learning program has to be designed. There are now numerous published models that a designer can adopt or adapt for use in developing a learning program. They generally fall into two types: prescriptive or descriptive, sometimes referred to as closed and open systems models. Wiggs discusses these and provides examples of a commonly used model in each category.

Garland D. Wiggs (Ed.D.) is professor of adult education and human resource development in the School of Education and Human Development, The George Washington University. He also serves a variety of clients in the private and public sectors. Before joining the university, he served as associate director, Educational Service Bureau, *The Wall Street Journal;* education director, Ohio Petroleum Marketers Association; and dealer trainer, Texaco. He is a past president of the Washington, D.C. chapter of ASTD and a member of the National Society for Performance and Instruction.

Since HRD deals with organized learning, the use of instructional design models is an effective way to organize that learning. Although there are other chapters in this handbook on how adults learn and on evaluation, a brief overview regarding the implications of cognition and learning is needed before discussing the design of learning and conceptual models for program design.

FOCUS ON LEARNING AND THE LEARNER'S/ORGANIZATION'S INTENT

"If you don't know where you are going, any road will take you there."

Lewis Carroll in
Alice's Adventures in Wonderland (1865)

What is learning? When one says, "I really learned something from that experience," just what is meant?

I recall vividly my learning experiences in three college undergraduate courses and two university graduate courses in statistics—a total of five college courses aimed at learning statistics. Although I received passing grades in all five, what did I actually learn? I learned an important fact: when faced with any complex manipulation of numerical data, I should hire a statistician.

The key question remains: When does someone really learn something? How does the learner, the designer, or facilitator of the learning transaction, or for that matter, the sponsor of the learning program, know when the learner has actually learned what was intended to be learned?

The answers to these key questions are critical to the design of effective and efficient learning programs. This chapter, therefore, begins by focusing on learning and on the learner's and sponsoring organization's intent for the specific learning transactions.

Learning Defined

Recognizing the fact that there are as many different definitions of the terms "learning" and "to learn" as there are definers, it seems most important here to establish some working definitions of the terms used by designers of learning programs.

Webster's New Collegiate Dictionary defines the term *learning*: (1) the act or experience of one that learns; (2) knowledge or skill acquired by instruction or study; (3) modification of a behavioral tendency by experience (as exposure to conditioning). Webster's defines the term *learn:* to gain knowledge of or understanding of a skill by study, instruction, or experience. These definitions imply that individuals can learn (i.e., change their behavior) either through vicarious or experiential learning transactions.

Many individuals state that their best learnings come from experiencing (by doing) that which they are striving to learn. They are prone to say experience is the best teacher. Those with an opposing view say classroom instruction, media-directed self-study, or other vicarious learning modes are by far more effective and efficient learning methods.

For purposes of designing learning programs, Webster's definitions, as well as numerous others' attempts to define learning, fail to provide sufficient guidance or direction to the designers of learning programs. I prefer a definition of learning that offers more specificity for design purposes: Learning is a process of internalizing skills, knowledge, or attitudes which provide a relatively permanent change of behavior.

Learning should always imply change. Changes in behavior should result from every learning transaction, if the learner has accomplished the learning goals. Without such behavioral change, one might seriously question whether learning has, in fact, taken place. It is true that learners often learn some things without expressing overt behavioral changes. However, the covert behaviors are learned new behaviors, even though they cannot be seen externally.

The learning process described herein acknowledges that there are recognizable learning levels, determined by the intent of the learner and/or by the sponsor of the learning activity. For example, in the case of learning the skills required of a new job, the learner is expected to internalize the required skills, knowledge, and/or attitudes sufficiently in depth to perform the job.

Learning on the job continues after the learning activity, as the new employee gains the additional skills, knowledge, and attitudes required to perform the job. This is done through on-the-job continuing training and more hands-on experience in doing the tasks associated with the job. The levels of learning in such cases are an ever-increasing growth experience, until such time as the employee has internalized the activities associated with doing the job. The internalization process continues to take place within the learner until doing the job tasks are well-established habits. When the learner-trainee no longer needs to use job aids, and does not have to continually ask questions of the job supervisor or lead person regarding the job, that learner has accomplished a high level of learning.

It is often just as true that the intent of a learning episode is only to gain some degree of familiarization or comprehension about a skill or knowledge, a specific topic, or some needed bit of information. Recalling my learning transactions in college statistics courses, I never intended to become a statistician. However, I did want to understand the use of statistics and to become familiar with the wide variety of statistical techniques used in quantitative research methods, conducted in HRD. I achieved this goal at a relatively low learning level.

Many times, a learning program sponsor does not intend for the learners to make major behavioral changes as a result of their experience in the learning episode. For example, a company's HRD department may offer an annual series of Equal Employment Opportunity (EEO) workshops for all supervisors in the firm. The purpose of the workshops is to make the supervisors aware of their continued need to be responsible in dealing with matters of affirmative action and equal employment opportunity. The supervisors are not expected to change their behavior if they have established an excellent EEO/AA record in the firm. The intent of the workshop is to provide additional encouragement for them to maintain their good records in this important arena. This, too, is an example of a relatively low level of learning.

Before leaving this discussion of my operational definition of learning, one additional point must be made. The definition states: "...a relatively permanent change of behavior." Admittedly, without continuous opportunities to practice new behaviors, the learner may forget what has been learned. The adage, "Use it or lose it!" applies so well. Therefore, on-the-job transfer of learning must be available upon completion of the learning activity. In case of training, for example, the learning program can enable a person to do something better and can result in that person having every intention of doing so. However, the actual doing, on the job, can fail to occur for a variety of reasons which have little or nothing to do with ability or intention. Removal of those roadblocks to on-the-job applications by the learner-trainee is a key management responsibility—not a part of the learning program as such.

LEARNING INTENTS

There have been numerous books and articles written about learning objectives in recent years,[1,2] the majority of which describe the need for and construct of learner behavioral terminal objectives. By far, the majority of these authors ignore the legitimacy of other forms of statements regarding learning intent or objectives.

Although I am firmly convinced that learner behavioral objectives are mandatory for identifying learner performance objectives in job skills training programs, I am not at all convinced that designers of these or other learning programs can reject other forms of learning intent (objectives) statements. For purposes of design, it is crucial for the designer to know the intent of the learning program. Behaviorally stated, learner objectives alone do not convey the intent of the learning program sufficiently for design purposes.

Overall Course Goal or Purpose

These general statements, which are often referred to as course objectives, describe the broad purposes or goals of the program. They reflect the identified learner's and organization's needs and priorities (the problem), the learner's backgrounds and learning or performance conditions (the setting), and the available resources and target date for completion of the learning (the constraints).

The designer of a learning program must have a clear understanding of the problem, the setting, and the constraints relative to the proposed learning activity in order to design a learning program that will accomplish its goals or purposes. Again one is reminded of the sage advice of Lewis Carroll, "If you don't know where you are going, any road will take you there!"

Instructional Objectives
Behavioral Terminal Objectives

These are detailed, specific statements of what will be expected of the learner at the conclusion of the learning experience. The statement includes not only the identified performance but also the conditions under which the learner is to peform and the criteria (standard) of acceptable performance.

Instructional Objectives
Nonbehavioral Terminal Objectives

These are statements of instructional intent, describing the expected learning outcomes by the learner but not in behavioral terms. For example, a safety training program might have as its instructional objective: The learner will acquire insight into and a positive attitude about the rules of the road and safe driving practices on the job.

Organizational Improvement Objectives

These are statements reflecting the desired results of the learning experience for, in, or on an organization.

These informational objectives are useful to both the designer of the learning program and to the target group toward whom the program is directed, for their understanding of why it is being offered.

Ultimate Value Objectives

These statements are another type of informational objective, focusing on the anticipated, final results that are achieved after a series of intermediate results. The ultimate value objective statements are also useful to the designer of the learning program and to the sponsoring organization's management team, in their strategic planning interventions.

Before proceeding, the designer of learning programs must have a clear understanding of "What is learning?" and "What is the intent of the learning transactions?" Without that understanding, the learning program will most certainly be ineffective at best and doomed to failure at worst.

A FOCUS ON DESIGN MODELS

When we were children, many of us built model airplanes, collected model automobiles, or played with model train sets, G.I. Joes or Barbie dolls. Those models were important to our young lives.

Today, we use a variety of models which have also become important to our lives. Models help us plan and do our work, keep us healthy, build our homes, offices, and factories, and help us enjoy our free time. We would not think of embarking on a cross-country automobile trip without first obtaining a road map to help plan our journey and guide us once under way. Maps are a type of model that graphically depict the routes of the highways crisscrossing our nation.

Models help us design effective and efficient learning programs.

Learning Program Design Models

Just as a road map helps guide us to our destination, learning program design models help designers ensure that the learners and sponsors of the learning programs will achieve their learning intents.

Design models for learning programs can vary in form and layout from extremely complex to very simple. Some model builders take elaborate steps to make their designs represent their author's theoretical concepts of how a learning program should achieve the learner's and/or sponsor's intent. Just as the various definitions of the term, learning, reflect their definers' views, so do the many different published learning design models present their authors' view of a desirable model.

Regretfully, there does not exist, and most likely never will, a perfect design model for all learning programs. Design models are based on ideal conditions (as identified by the model's author) that will provide the greatest possibility of potential success when used by designers of learning programs. Unfortunately, very few designers find ideal conditions for either the design or the conduct of learning programs where they work. More often, the many variables involved in designing learning programs cause far less than ideal conditions to prevail. And yet, a learning program is designed, the program is implemented, and learning intents are accomplished. Usually, the people involved are satisfied that the experience was a good one; and it may have been accomplished without any specific design model in mind. So why all this discussion about design models?

Does the above suggest we should reject the use of theory-based design models or deny their validity for providing designers with a foundation for their work? No! The cognitive learning theorists who describe how human beings learn and provide us with conceptual design models offer excellent guidance and direction for the design of effective learning programs. Their learning theories and models serve to establish a much needed background of theory foundations and to suggest alternative design and instructional strategies. A model is only as good as its conceptual foundations—the theoretical base and assumptions upon which it is built. So, too, is the design of a learning program.

A design model can be viewed as depicting a system of interacting and independent variables that impact on, or actually form, the learning program itself. For example, every learning program has these interrelated variables:

Objectives
Learners
Instructional materials or aids
Program sponsors
Content

Instructional strategies

Learning facilities or aids

Instructors/Instructional media

Most often a learning program will also have some major, independent variables that must be considered, even when the designer of that learning has no control over them. For example, it is not unusual for some of the following independent variables to impact on the program or its learners:

Organizational climate

Reductions in force/layoffs

Job design workflow problems

Wage/Salary issues

Employee-Supervisor conflicts

Job mechanization/Technology changes

The design process entails orchestrating these and numerous other variables throughout the life of the learning program. Design does not end with the completion of a plan of instruction, lesson plans, or course materials; it is an ongoing process. The design models provide step-by-step checkpoints that are helpful during the design process and throughout the learning program.

Types of Design Models

Design models are constructed, by their authors, to be either descriptive or prescriptive in nature. They either describe the design procedures and the variables related to the learning program, or they prescribe the step-by-step procedures the designer must follow in implementing the learning program.

A descriptive design model describes the many variables to be considered by the designer during the total design process. The authors of this type of model acknowledge the fact that the designer may not be required to follow a given sequence of steps, but the designer should be made aware of the interacting and independent variables associated with the learning program throughout its design, implementation, and conclusion.

A prescriptive design model prescribes the detailed, specific steps in the design process, as the many different interacting and independent variables are addressed by the designer of the learning program.

The term *systems approach* to instructional design has been used extensively during the past 25 years in the professional literature. It refers to the concept of systems engineering applied to the design of an instructional program.[3] Each of the interacting variables is conceived as being a subsystem of the entire learning program.

In any design model, the learners in the proposed program would be a subsystem to be considered by the designer when working through the design process. The designer who uses a prescriptive design model must check the learners' needs most carefully prior to building the curriculum content. On the other hand, the designer using a descriptive design model may already know exactly what the learners' needs are and not have to do any data collection or analysis regarding this subsystem in the learning program design process. When using a prescriptive design model, the designer has no choice in the matter. The designer must investigate the learners' needs prior to building the curriculum content.

A prescriptive design model forces the designer to complete each and every step, in sequence, as depicted in the model. There is no leeway for modification or adaptation in the model. The proponents of prescriptive models suggest they are most appropriate for designing learning programs in which the learning intent demands mastery of specific skills, knowledge, and/or attitudes required for performance of a task or job.

Design models are often referred to as being open or closed systems models. A descriptive/open systems design model refers to the options a designer has in implementing the design process. In a prescriptive/closed systems model, the designer has no options but must follow each and every step prescribed in the model.

Proponents of learning design models suggest that these systems approaches to instructional design provide the necessary discipline the designers of learning programs need to achieve the learning intents. The advantages of both the open and closed design models for learning programs are many:

1. Learning is job centered for it is based on defined, specific job(s)/task(s)/skills, knowledge, and/or attitudes.
2. Learning programs have precisely stated objectives. The learners must achieve precise levels of proficiency, and sponsors can depend on the results.

3. Learners are provided instruction that has resulted from systematic, precise design of curricula. The instructional materials, methods, and media are geared to the instructional objectives. The instruction is based on the learners' needs derived through analysis.

4. There is a greater possibility of active learner participation and motivation because the emphasis throughout the learning program is on developing specific job/task skills, knowledge and/or attitudes. The program emphasis is on the learners, helping them achieve their learning intent or perform better.

5. Efficiency of learning is encouraged by maximizing learning while minimizing learning time by focusing on prioritizing the must-knows, should-knows, and nice-to-knows as the learning program is designed.

6. The instructor's role is made more effective and efficient because of the confidence generated by using proven instructional materials and methods. The instructor can concentrate more on learning facilitation.

The flexibility allowed in the descriptive/open systems design models does acknowledge the reality of many design environments. It is not unusual for the designer to be provided data regarding several of the interacting variables related to the proposed learning program. For example, the management team of the sponsoring organization may provide what they believe to be factual and complete data regarding one or more of the variables related to the proposed target learners or other important interdependent variables. Data might come from the personnel department, the marketing department, or the manufacturing department. Other types of data may come from the comptroller's office, or it is even likely that in many cases the designer is so close to the situation that the learners' needs may be known without having to perform a formal needs assessment.

An open systems model permits the elimination of certain steps in the design process when the needs assessment or some other step has already been accomplished and is furnished to the designer. By far, the majority of designers follow an open systems design model, for obvious reasons. Most designers, as was pointed out earlier, do not have ideal conditions under which they design learning programs, so they often do not have the leeway within the sponsoring organization to follow the process requirements of the closed system design models.

The conditions for designing competency-based learning programs using prescriptive/closed systems models are most often ideal, because of the total organizational support that is evident throughout the design and implementation phases of the learning programs. Such learning programs are most often given high priority, because the learners' performance on the job translates into productivity and profits for the organization. The learning is directly measurable, for it is peformance-based. The learning intents are criterion-referenced for ease of identifying the direct payoffs to the sponsoring organization.

THE CRITICAL EVENTS MODEL

An example of a descriptive/open systems design model is the "Critical Events Model" (CEM).[4] Nadler's model depicts the steps in the design process as critical events the designer must follow when planning a learner program (see Figure 7.1). He highlights the importance of evaluation and feedback throughout the design process, by stressing the importance of information gathering and analysis at every step in the design model.

The CEM is most applicable for the design of learning programs where the learner's/sponsor's intents are specific and the interdependent and independent variables associated with the learning program are identifiable. Before proceeding with the design process, the designer using the CEM should have the cooperation and support of the sponsor's management team and subject matter experts (SMEs) and a clear understanding of the organizational needs and priorities.

The CEM offers the designer logical, step-by-step procedures to ensure that the learning program will accomplish the learning intents and that those learnings do, in fact, meet the needs of the sponsoring organization and the learners.

Needs of the Organization

The initial step in the CEM requires that the designer determine if the proposed learning program will accomplish the identified needs of the organization. Will the learning program solve an organizational problem or exploit an opportunity? Regretfully, learning programs have been designed and conducted that have compounded, not resolved, organizational problems. They should not have been designed in the first place, because they addressed symptoms rather than problems.

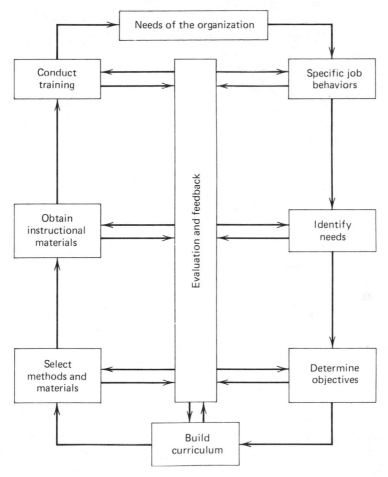

Figure 7.1. The CEM Model. Leonard Nadler, *Designing Training Programs,* © 1982, Addison-Wesley, Reading, Massachusetts. Reprinted with permission of publisher.

For example, when an organizational problem is identified by members of a management team as requiring a learning program, the designer must ascertain if a change in skills, knowledge, or attitudes of the proposed learners will help resolve the problem. If not, then an intervention other than training is more appropriate to resolve the problem. The deficiency in performance might be caused by a workflow problem, a supervisory problem, or some other variable in the work unit that has nothing to do with the acquiring of new skills, knowledge, or attitudes to change the behaviors of the proposed learners.

Needs of organizations can also be associated with the needs of decision makers. For example, it would not be unrealistic to acknowledge that if one is requested by the CEO, to design a learning program for a specific target group, that learning program will be designed—regardless of the organizational needs. The CEO's perceived need most certainly suffices (if the designer wishes to maintain employment).

Learning program needs can also be derived from requests of participants in previous learning programs. It is very common for the participants in one learning program to identify additional learning needs they wish to address in future learning programs.

Before the designer proceeds to the next step in the CEM, the decision whether or not to initiate the design of a learning program must be made. That decision should always be based on the data gathered from within the organization and be thoroughly analyzed by all parties involved in the design process.

Job Behaviors

As the designer of a learning program begins this step of the CEM, the decision of whether or not to initiate the learning program is only tentative until the job/task analysis has been completed. The designer may determine that there are more cost-effective solutions for the organizational need than implementation of a learning program.

The terms, such as job analysis, task analysis, work analysis, position analysis, and skills, attitudes, knowledge profiles at times are inter-changeable. There is no universally accepted terminology to describe the functions performed in determining exactly what skills, knowledge, or attitudes are required in the performance of a specific job or task.

Different analysis techniques, however, use basically four types of methods either singly or in combination.

1. *Observation Task Analysis.* The person(s) doing the job or task is observed while performing all the functions associated with its accomplishment. The observer records each step in the process of doing the job or task under actual working conditions and standards of performance. The job/task data are then compiled, analyzed, and synthesized to identify specific psychomotor skills, background knowledge and attitudes required in performance.

2. *Simulated Task Analysis.* An individual or group skilled in the job/task simulate performing the functions required of the job/task under working conditions and standards of performance as close

as possible to the actual work environment. The job/task data are compiled, analyzed with inputs from the skilled performers, and then the SKAs are synthesized to ascertain their importance and frequency in performance of the job/task.

3. *Content Analysis.* Another task analysis method used frequently is content analysis. The operating manual or the specifications/technical manual related to the job/task is analyzed to determine the SKAs associated with performing the job/task. A detailed breakdown of each operating step is made to determine exactly what actions the worker must take as well as what the results of those actions are in performing the job/task.

4. *Interview Analysis.* The interview analysis technique is most likely used in combination with other methods due to the human fallacy of forgetfulness. An individual worker who is experienced and skilled in performing a job/task will often forget to mention crucial steps in doing the functions required. The worker has done that particular step so often that it is internalized and often fails to acknowledge doing it! The interview analysis technique is often used to validate data gathered by other techniques.

The different methods of task analysis approach the work from different perspectives. Some emphasize the actions workers perform and/or the results of those actions. Others focus on developing extensive task inventories to determine critical tasks, frequency of performance of the tasks, and to identify common skills, knowledge, and/or attitudes found in the various tasks.

Regardless of which task analysis method the designer chooses, the data gathered must reflect the specific job/tasks and their SKAs, as well as the expected job behaviors or standards of performance in accomplishing the job.

The resulting job/task inventory lists not only provide the designer with data about the job or tasks appropriate for the proposed learning program, but they also provide some important clues regarding possible instructional strategies for learning various categories of tasks or SKAs required in the job.

It is important here to recognize that not all of the job/tasks or required SKAs associated with doing the particular job are necessarily included in the proposed learning program.

Once a job/task analysis is completed, it often becomes obvious to the designer that certain aspects of a job will best be learned through vicarious learning methods. This is especially true if the task or SKA is critical, is difficult to learn, and/or is essential in the performance of another task or tasks required on the job.

Other job/tasks or SKAs required in doing the job may be better learned experientially, either through on-the-job training, practice in performing the task with job aids, or by performance under the guidance of a supervisor or lead person. In these instances, formal, vicarious learning activities would not be required at all.

One must acknowledge that there will always be some trade-off considerations to be made in design of learning programs. Although somewhat overused by many people, the terms *effective* and *efficient* should always prevail in instructional design work. A learning program can be designed to be highly effective and yet be far too costly; that is, it is not efficient. A guiding principle for all HRD programming is to seek the most effective program within acceptable costs while meeting the learning intents.

HRD learning programs begin with the identification of an organization problem or opportunities for growth and can be considered successful only if the problem is solved or the opportunities are exploited—all else is academic. By far the majority of organizations competing in the world today, regardless of their size or wealth, can ill afford the conduct of academic exercises or faddish learning programs that fail to meet either the learners' or sponsors' needs.

The true assessment of HRD learning programs comes in terms of their impact on reduced costs, increased productivity, fewer employee grievances, improved product-service quality, fewer customer complaints, and on the abilities of individuals prepared to accept more responsibilities. These are the real world indices of success in organizations today.

Regretfully, it is not uncommon to find HRD programs being assessed in other terms: numbers of learners enrolled, numbers of learning activities conducted, how well the participants liked the program, the instructional materials, or the instructor. An HRD professional should acknowledge the fact that learning programs are but a means to an end—not an end in themselves.

Identify Learner Needs

In the next step in the CEM, the designer must gather information about the proposed learners. Much of the target population data is essential and most is useful when making decisions relative to a proposed learning program.

The population data categories might include all or some of the following:

Anticipated number of learners

Location(s) of the learners

Education/training/work experience backgrounds of the learners

Experience in present or related job

Job performance requirements versus learners' present skill levels (i.e., learning deficiency ranges)

Language or cultural differences of learners

Motivations of learners

Physical or mental characteristics of learners

Specific interests or biases of learners

Using the data gathered and analyzed from both the task analysis and the target population categories, the designer can fairly well determine the learners' needs. The intent of this important step in the CEM is to describe, as clearly as possible, what the learning needs are for the specific learners.

Working closely with the SMEs, the designer must ascertain the "must-knows," "should-knows," and "nice-to-knows" pertaining to the particular job/task. When these are identified, the decisions relative to depth and scope of topical coverage in the learning program can be made. Again, the issues of effectiveness and efficiency are raised, and decisions must be made by the program sponsors.

Determine Objectives

It is in this step of the CEM that the designer establishes the overall learning program objectives, the general instructional objectives, and specific learner objectives for the learning program.

The written objectives statements should reflect the identified organization's and learners' needs and explicitly describe the learning intents of the program.

The general instructional objectives for the learning program focus on its design and facilitation. They are more detailed and specific than are the overall program objectives established to inform decision makers and to ascertain the usefulness of the program to the target population.

The specific learner objectives contain three major components:

Tasks:

>Use appropriate action verbs to identify performance of the task(s)
>
>Describe the observable performance or product

Conditions:

>Describe the actual conditions under which the performance of the task(s) will occur or be observed
>
>Identify the tools, procedures, materials, aids, or facilities to be used in performing the task(s)

Standards:

>State the level of acceptable performance of the task(s), in terms of quantity, quality, time limitations, etc.

One should recognize that task performance may not meet the actual on-the-job standard immediately upon completion of a learning program. Additional on-the-job training or practice on the job, under direction of a supervisor or lead person, may be required before attainment of the actual standard of performance is accomplished.

This most certainly depends on the nature of the learning content and the learners' and sponsors' intent. As a frequent airline passenger, I fervently pray that airline pilots' training is based upon nothing less than 100% accomplishment of actual on-the-job flight standards. I am not nearly as particular about other types of learning standards.

Build Curriculum

Again, working closely with subject matter experts (SMEs), the designer organizes the learning content into meaningful instructional sequences during this step in the CEM.

There are several options available to build a curriculum for the learning program.

Psychological Order. The content is organized according to ease of learning:

>old to new
>
>simple to complex
>
>familiar to unknown
>
>concrete to abstract
>
>practical to theoretical
>
>present to future

Job Performance Order. Subject matter content is organized according to the sequences in which the job or task is actually performed.

Logical Order. The subject matter content is presented according to its difficulty or its logical arrangement in a predetermined prescribed sequential operation.

Problem-Centered Order. Using an inductive approach to learning, the content is delivered only after the learners utilize a diagnostic, problem-centered technique. Most commonly used in supervisory-management training and human relations training, the approach encourages learners to move from the specific to the general and from examples to development of resolutions and general rules.

This last curriculum design method was also employed in apprenticeship and craft education in the Job Corps. For example, a young person wanting to learn carpentry would be given a saw, a piece of lumber, a set of blueprints, and carpenter's rule. The learner would be told to cut the board according to the specific requirements layed out in the blueprint. Needless to say, the young person soon determined a need for skills in blueprint reading, how to use a carpenter's ruler, some basic mathematical knowledge, as well as how to hold the saw when making the cut on the board. Only when the individual learner acknowledges these learning needs is the subject matter content offered.

Select Methods and Materials

After the learning program subject matter content has been identified, it is time to determine the appropriate delivery methods for the learning program. In this step of the CEM, the designer must identify, select, and/or develop the specific methods and materials. Some factors to consider when deciding these matters include:

1. *Instructional/Learner Objectives.* The overriding consideration in the selection and development of either methodology or instructional materials should always be the learning intent and instructional objectives.
2. *Program Subject Matter Content.* The nature of the subject matter content affects the appropriateness of methods and materials selected for instruction.
3. *Instructors.* The number, quality, and individual competencies of the available instructors has a direct bearing on the selection of the instructional methods and materials.

4. *Target Learner Population.*   The size of the learner group, their school level, cultural and language backgrounds, reading and mathematical abilities must be appropriate for the methods and materials selected.

5. *Classroom Facilities and Equipment.*   The availability of required classroom and laboratory space facilities and equipment must be available for the instructional methods and materials selected.

6. *Time.*   The time necessary for using the selected method or materials is available.

7. *Costs.*   The costs associated with the development or acquisition of the instructional materials to be utilized is available.

Regretfully, designers of learning programs often select specific methods or materials because they are available, rather than because they are the most appropriate for a given learning activity. For example, one finds videotaping frequently being used in a learning program only because the designer had the video camera and recording equipment available—not because the method was actually the most appropriate for the given learning situation.

Once the appropriate methods and materials have been identified as being ideally suited for delivery of the learning content, the designer must take the next important step in the CEM—obtain the instructional resources.

Obtain Instructional Resources

Although by far the majority of learning programs are designed and conducted within previously established budgets, Nadler's CEM encourages the designer to delay that critical event to this step in the design process. The premise is sound, albeit somewhat idealistic, because a designer really does not know the instructional resource requirements for the specific learning program until this time. Without having worked through to this step in the CEM, the designer will only be "guestimating" the actual instructional resources needed: staff, media, materials, facilities, and budgets.

It is important to recognize that the selection of the appropriate methods and materials for a particular learning program in the previous CEM step should have identified those that would ensure accomplishment of the learners' and program interests. If instructional resources for those appropriate methods and materials cannot be obtained designer must rework previous events to reduce the expected lea. objectives and the depth and scope of content coverage, and/or the designer must admit to a somewhat lessened standard of performance by the learner upon completion of the learning program.

If the designer defers making arrangements for the instructional resources until previous events of the CEM are completed, the necessary data will then be available to make a most effective budget and instruction resources request. Otherwise, the learning program can suffer from lack of appropriate instructional resources.

Conduct Training

Although the conduct of a learning program is the final important step in the CEM, one should recognize the importance of ongoing design processes that must occur during the event. While the designer of a learning program has diligently worked through all the previous steps in the CEM, redesign work will continue to be done by the learning facilitator and the participants as they go through the experience. Planned learning events will often take more time than allocated in the design; techniques that worked in a pilot program may fail in the later programs; equipment fails to arrive on time at the learning site; or other unforeseen situations come into play while the learning program is under way. All such instances will call for the redesign of the learning program on an "as needed" basis.

With this in mind, the designer should always document every instructional activity or event throughout the program to formulate data necessary for its internal and external evaluation.

The internal evaluation of the learning program focuses on the process of accomplishing the learning objectives. Were the planned learning strategies actually appropriate to accomplish the learner's and sponsor's intents for the learning program? Was the program effective?

An external evaluation of the learning program focuses on its accomplishments of the learner's and sponsor's intents. Did the planned instructional program meet the organization's or learner's needs? Was the program efficient in terms of its return on investment and its objectives? For a more complete discussion of evaluating learning programs, there are other chapters in this handbook.

The ultimate evaluation of any HRD learning program should always be: "Did the result of the learner's new behaviors resolve the problem?" If the learner's results were positive, the program was successful. If not, both the designer and sponsor of the learning program would have good reason to question the worth of the endeavor.

The CEM provides designers of learning programs with a framework upon which they can build successful learning programs—even in organizational environments that are less than ideal. The model helps the designers ask the "right kinds of dumb questions"—questions that will provide good answers to the many interrelated and independent variables that impact on both design and conduct of effective and efficient learning programs.

THE INSTRUCTIONAL SYSTEMS DEVELOPMENT MODEL

Today there are numerous examples available of published instructional design models that focus on performance-based, criterion-referenced learning.[5,6,7,8] They represent good examples of prescriptive/closed systems design process models.

The ISD (Instruction Skills Development) Model is most appropriate for designing learning programs in work environments where:

Specific job/task data is obtainable

Uniformity of job/task performance is required

Standards of performance of the job are absolute

The ISD model selected for discussion in this chapter is probably the most extensively used instructional design model in use today. The ISD model was established by the U.S. Department of Defense (DOD) for the U.S. military organizations.[9] In the mission-oriented military organizations, many of the jobs of the military (enlisted and officer personnel) require identical performance, to absolute standards, wherever and whenever the job is performed, regardless of who is doing it. A specific military job may require that it be performed 24 hours per day, seven days a week, manned by many different individuals on shift work. They must all perform the job/task in the same way, so their learning programs must ensure such performance. In addition, since military personnel assignments are based on one- to three-year cycles, the replacement personnel must be trained to perform the job/task in a like manner. A competency-based learning program provides the only practical solution to such work environments. Each of the armed forces has adopted its own version of the five-phased DOD ISD model.

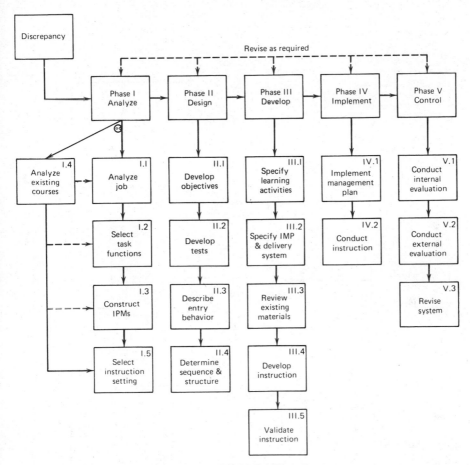

Figure 7.2. ISD Model Flowchart.

The U.S. Navy ISD model flowchart (see Figure 7.2) is published in a three volume document for U.S. Navy learning program design groups and the managers of navy education and training activities.[10]

The five phases of the ISD model include the key processes of analysis design, development, implementation, and control required for design of all learning programs. However, the ISD model focuses on competency learning leading to mastery of SKAs required for performance.

The focus of Phase I (see Figure 7.3) is on job information after the organization problem or performance discrepancy has been identified. If a new job, it must be thoroughly analyzed. If the discrepancy in

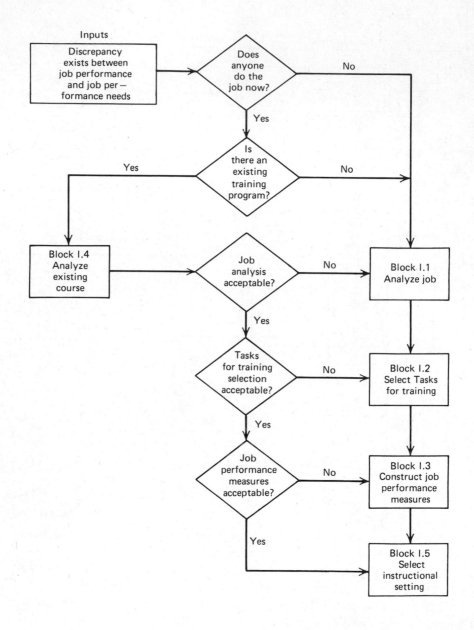

Figure 7.3. Phase I of the ISD Model: Analyze.

performance is related to an existing job, any current learning programs for that job must be analyzed to determine whether a job task analysis had been done earlier, by someone else, following the ISD model guidelines. If the job task analysis was not done or if the job task had been significantly changed, a new task analysis must be completed.

Once the job task inventory has been compiled and its SKAs identified, the inventory must be validated by SMEs. The designers and SMEs then divide the tasks into three groups: those that are to be included for instruction in the formal learning program, those that are to be included in on-the-job training, and, finally, those for which no formal or on-the-job training will be required.

It is also during the Phase I process that performance standards for the identified tasks are determined. Job site observations and interviews of job incumbents and supervisors provide performance standards data that is verified by the SMEs.

A final step in Phase I is to determine the most appropriate instructional setting and delivery system for the tasks selected for formal and on-the-job learning.

The actual instructional design work begins in Phase II, using the job and performance analysis from Phase I of the model.

The first step in Phase II is to develop specific, terminal learning objectives for each of the tasks selected in the learning program (see Figure 7.4). Each terminal objective is analyzed to determine whether it requires one or more enabling objectives and to identify the actual learning steps required for mastery of the task.

It is also in Phase II of the ISD model that the important criterion-referenced test items are designed to match each of the learning objectives. The ISD model is designed to produce performance-based, criterion-referenced instruction, so test items must be developed to determine the learner's acquisition of the skills, knowledge, and attitudes required to perform the task.

A sample of the learner target population is tested during Phase II to determine whether the sample's entry behaviors (SKAs) match the level of proposed instruction. If not, the designers of the learning program will have to adjust the proposed learning objectives to meet the needs of the learners.

A final product of Phase II is the determination of the sequence and structure of the learning program to ensure accomplishment of the learning objectives.

The instructional development phase of the ISD model (see Figure 7.5) focuses on selecting appropriate instructional strategies required for

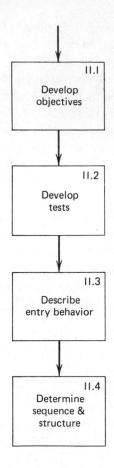

Figure 7.4. Phase II of the ISD Model: Design.

accomplishing the learning objectives for the program. The designer begins this analysis by identifying the classifications of learning objectives for each job/task by its learning category:

Mental skills
Information
Physical skills
Attitudes

The designer should be guided in the selection of instructional methodology and techniques by determining: What is the best way to assist in the learning process? What media will provide the most effective learning stimulus?

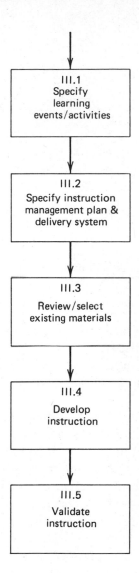

Figure 7.5. Phase III of the ISD Model: Develop.

Once determined, the instructional media and learning materials/aids are then selected and/or developed to be packaged for presentation in the learning program. Such factors as the instructional settings (selected in Phase I of the ISD model) for the learning program, media characteristics, instructor abilities, and costs, must be taken into account at this phase. It is most important here to review existing instructional

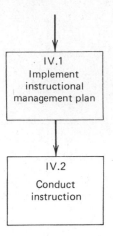

Figure 7.6. Phase IV of the ISD Model: Implement.

materials, if available, to determine whether they can be adopted, redesigned, or perhaps discarded, relative to the new learning program. Whenever possible, the duplication of available instructional materials must be avoided to contain costs associated with learning program development.

Plans of managing the learning program are established by the program sponsor and designer during this important phase of the ISD model. The management plan must address the allocation and management of all resources needed to adequately support the learning program, including: budgets, schedules, instructors, learners, facilities, media and materials, and housing and transportation (if required).

During this important phase, a final design process step is to develop a comprehensive plan of instruction for the learning program that includes the curriculum outline, unit, modules, lesson topics, and their objectives laid out in sequence. The program and its instructional documentation should be subjected to tryouts and pretesting by representatives of the learner population, in order to work through to a final edit and revision of the learning program. Once the pilot programs are conducted and necessary revisions and validations have been completed, the resource person's (instructor's) guides and learner's guides can be prepared for program implementation.

Before a learning program is actually presented in its final form, much has to be done to ensure that everything needed to support the instruction is, in fact, in place and available (see Figure 7.6). Course

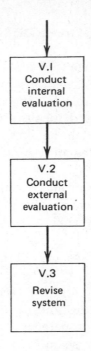

Figure 7.7. Phase V of the ISD Model: Control.

materials, instructional space and facilities, instructional staff, and learners must be ready once the program is scheduled to begin. Program managers and the instructional staff may require training to perform their important roles in the learning process. The instructors, for example, must be trained not only to conduct the instruction but also to collect evaluation data on all aspects of the program. Their evaluation data will be used to improve the program, after completion of each instructional cycle.

Evaluation and revision of the learning program should be an ongoing process, if the program is to remain viable (see Figure 7.7). The internal evaluation most likely will be carried out by the program instructional staff and managers and the instructional designers. The external evaluation should be conducted by those individuals who are not involved in the program design, instruction, or management. The focus of the internal evaluation is on the instructional processes and the measurement of learning that was gained, while the external evaluation focuses on assessment of job task performance on the job, as related to the learning program. All the collected data can be used to ensure quality control over the learning program and serve as a basis for program revision.

A FOCUS ON INSTRUCTIONAL DESIGNER COMPETENCIES

A wise old course designer once told me, "There are only two critical competencies a good course designer must have." The first, he suggested, was "analytical skills, to be able to separate fact from fiction and to specify the 'musts,' 'shoulds,' and 'nice-to's' of course content coverage." The second competency, which he emphasized as being the most important to all designers of learning programs, was "a high tolerance for ambiguity."

There is no question in my mind that my associate was most likely 100% right. There is and always will be a lot of ambiguity to deal with while orchestrating the many variables associated with the design of learning programs. In addition, the designer must have good analytical skills if the learning program is to meet the needs of both the learners and program sponsors.

There have been several attempts, in recent years, to specify the core competencies of instructional designers.[11] Realistically, there will probably never be a "final" list of competencies, because skill and knowledge requirements of the designer seem to be expanding dramatically in recent years, with the advances in instructional technology.

For example, my acquisition of a home computer has led to my learning a vast array of new skills, associated with its use in word processing, accounting/budgeting, and management information retrieval systems. In addition, I am now beginning to transfer many of my previously learned programmed instruction design skills to the design of computer-assisted learning programs, using a computer software package that features authoring and presentation of course material in one easy-to-use program.

The core competencies of an effective learning program designer depend, to some degree, upon where the design work is to be accomplished. In smaller organizations, a designer may be the only person involved in the planning of the learning programs for the organization. Consequently, that designer would be required to have all of the design competencies. In larger organizations, such as the military, for example, teams of designers work exclusively on one of the five phases of the ISD model, often never actually involved in the final learning programs they helped produce. The individuals assigned to do such segmented design work would naturally require far fewer instructional design competencies to perform their jobs.

If you wanted to be a competent designer of learning programs today, just what should you be able to do? The following list, although not in any order of importance, does reflect the majority of competencies needed to successfully design effective and efficient learning programs:[12]

1. Determine Projects Appropriate for Instructional Development

   Analyze information regarding potential projects and decide if instructional development is appropriate.

   Discriminate situations requiring instructional solutions from those requiring other solutions (e.g., job redesign, organizational development, etc.).

   Judge the appropriateness of project selection decisions and provide a rationale for the judgment.

2. Conduct Needs Assessments

   Develop a needs assessment plan including selection of procedures and instruments.

   Conduct a needs assessment and interpret results to suggest appropriate actions.

   Judge the appropriateness, completeness, and accuracy of given needs assessment plans and results.

3. Assess Learner Characteristics

   Distinguish among entry skills assessment, prerequisite assessment, and aptitude assessment.

   Identify a range of relevant learner/trainee characteristics and determine methods for assessing them.

   Develop and implement a plan for assessing learner/trainee characteristics.

   Judge the appropriateness, comprehensiveness, and adequacy of a given assessment of learner/trainee characteristics.

4. Analyze the Structural Characteristics of Jobs, Tasks, and Content

   Select and use a procedure for analyzing the structural characteristics of a job, task, or content that is appropriate to that job, task, or content and state a rationale for the selection.

5. Write Statements of Learner Outcomes

   Distinguish objectives stated in performance/behavioral terms from instructional goals, organizational goals, learner activities, teacher activities, and objectives written in other styles.

   State an outcome in performance terms that reflects the intent of instruction.

Judge the accuracy, comprehensiveness, and appropriateness of statements of learner outcomes in terms of the job, task, or content analysis, and/or judgment/opinions of the client (e.g., subject matter expert, faculty, etc.).

6. Analyze the Characteristics of a Setting (Learning Environment)

Analyze setting characteristics and determine relevant resources and constraints.

Judge the accuracy, comprehensiveness, and appropriateness of a setting analysis.

7. Sequence Learner Outcomes

Select a procedure for sequencing learner outcomes appropriate to a given situation, sequence the outcomes and state a rationale for the sequence.

Judge the accuracy, completeness, and appropriateness of a given sequence of learner outcomes.

8. Specify Instructional Strategies

Select a strategy that is appropriate to information about the learner characteristics, resources and constraints, desired learner outcomes, and other pertinent information and state a rationale for the selection.

Judge the appropriateness of a specified instructional strategy for a given situation.

9. Sequence Learner Activities

Specify a sequence of learner activities appropriate to the achievement of specified learner outcomes and state a rationale for the sequence.

Judge the appropriateness and completeness of a given sequence of learner activities.

10. Determine Instructional Resources (Media) Appropriate to Instructional Activities

Develop specifications for instructional resources required for explicit instructional strategies and learner outcomes.

Evaluate existing instructional resources to determine appropriateness for specific instructional strategies and learner outcomes.

Adapt existing instructional resources.

Prepare specifications for the production of materials where required (e.g., storyboards, lesson plans, script outlines, etc.).

11. Evaluate Instruction

Plan and conduct a formative evaluation (e.g., trials with subjects, expert review, analysis of implementation considerations, etc.).

Develop a range of information-gathering techniques (e.g., questionnaires, interviews, tests, simulations, observations, etc.).

Generate specifications for revision based on evaluation feedback.

Judge the appropriateness, comprehensiveness, and adequacy of given formative evaluation plans, information-gathering techniques, and revision specifications.

12. Create Course, Learning Package, and Workshop Management Systems

Determine the components of a course/learning package/ workshop management system and state a rationale for the selection.

Judge the appropriateness, comprehensiveness, and adequacy of a given management system.

13. Plan and Monitor Instructional Development Projects

Develop and monitor an instructional development project plan (including timelines, budgets, staffing, etc.) that is appropriate to the nature of the project and the setting.

Judge the appropriateness and comprehensiveness of a given instructional development project plan.

14. Communicate Effectively in Visual, Oral, and Written Form

15. Demonstrate Appropriate Interpersonal, Group Process, and Consulting Behaviors

Demonstrate interpersonal behaviors with individuals and groups and state a rationale for using the behaviors in given situations.

Demonstrate group process behaviors and state a rationale for using the behaviors in given situations.

Demonstrate consulting behaviors with individuals and groups and state a rationale for the behaviors in given situations.

Judge the appropriateness of interpersonal, group process, and consulting behaviors in given situations.

CONCLUSION

It can be estimated that the largest part of the HRD learning design activity by HRD practitioners is focused on developing job-oriented training programs. The focus of this chapter and the discussion of both the CEM and the ISD model reflect that reality.

However, it should be emphasized that the other HRD activities of education and development may also be designed, using identical or similar design models. Yet, their similarity ends there.

Human resource development must be viewed, by management and designers alike, as a system operating within organizations that can ensure that employees, supervisors, managers, and the organization's clients and customers can grow with the organization, as it evolves and improves or expands its services and/or products.

An effective HRD system includes not only its formal vicarious learning programs and systematic on-the-job training but also a variety of planned, sequential experiential learnings: job cross education, temporary project assignments, acting supervisor-manager appointments, community and professional organization memberships, committee leadership activities, and product/service workshops and seminars.

The planning and implementation of such a wide range of HRD activities requires the integration of HRD planning efforts into the organization's strategic planning of its mission. The designer of learning programs must play an important part in helping to make it all happen.

NOTES

1. Robert F. Mager, *Preparing Instructional Objectives*, 2d ed. (Belmont Cal.: Pitman Learning, Inc., 1975).
2. Leslie J. Briggs and Walter W. Wager, *Handbook of Procedures for the Design of Instruction*, 2d ed. (Englewood Cliffs, N.J.: Educational Technology Publications, 1981).
3. Leonard Silvern, *Systems Engineering Applied to Training* (Houston: Gulf Publishing Company, 1972).
4. Leonard Nadler, *Design of Training* (Reading Mass.: Addison-Wesley, 1982).
5. F. Coit Butler, *Instructional Systems Development for Vocational and Technical Training* (Englewood Cliffs, N.J.: Educational Technology Publications, Inc., 1972).
6. Ivor K. Davies, *Competency Based Learning: Technology, Management, and Design* (New York: McGraw-Hill, 1973).
7. Silvern, *Systems Engineering Applied to Training*, p. 5.
8. William R. Tracey, *Designing Training and Development Systems* (New York: American Management Association, 1971).

9. United States Government Department of Defense Training Document pamphlet 350-30, August, 1975.
10. United States Navy Education and Training Document 110.
11. American Society for Training and Development. *Models for Excellence: The Conclusions and Recommendations of the ASTD Training and Development Competency Study* (Washington, D.C.: ASTD), 1983.
12. "Competencies for the Instructional Development Professional," *Journal of Instructional Development*, 5(1):51–52.

BIBLIOGRAPHY

Briggs, Leslie J., and Walter W. Wager. *Handbook of Procedures for the Design of Instruction*. 2d ed. Englewood Cliffs, N.J.: Educational Technology Publications, Inc., 1981.

Butler, F. Coit. *Instructional Systems Development for Vocational and Technical Training*. Englewood Cliffs, N.J.: Educational Technology Publications, Inc., 1972.

"Competencies for the Instructional AECT Division of Instructional Development/Training Development Progressional." *Journal of Instructional Development*, Fall 1981. Vol. 5, No. 1.

Davies, Ivor K. *Competency Based Learning: Technology, Management, and Design*. New York: McGraw-Hill, Inc., 1973.

Davies, Ivor K. *Instructional Technique*. New York: McGraw-Hill, Inc., 1981.

Kirkpatrick, Donald L., ed. *Evaluating Training Programs*. Washington, D.C.: American Society for Training and Development, 1974.

Knox, Alan B. and associates. *Developing, Administering and Evaluating Adult Education*. San Francisco, Cal.: Jossey-Bass, 1980.

Mager, Robert F. *Preparing Instructional Objectives*. 2d ed. Belmont, Cal.: Pitman Learning, Inc., 1975.

Nadler, Leonard. *Design of Training*. Reading, Mass.: Addison-Wesley, 1982.

Silvern, Leonard. *Systems Engineering Applied to Training*. Houston: Gulf Publishing Company, 1972.

Tracey, William R. *Designing Training and Development Systems*. New York: American Management Association, 1971.

Wentling, Tim L., and Tom E. Lawson. *Evaluating Occupational Education and Training Programs*. Boston, Mass.: Allyn and Bacon, 1975.

United States Government Department of Defense Training Document pamphlet 350-30, August 1975.

United States Navy Education and Training Document 110, September 18, 1981.

CHAPTER EIGHT

Instructing

DANIEL GULIANO

Not all HRD practitioners instruct, but unless there has been some form of instruction, no learning has taken place. In this chapter and this handbook, instruction is meant to cover any phase of the process whereby learning is provided to the learner. As will be noted in another chapter, the broad designation is facilitator.

Before instruction takes place, a great deal of work must be done in the areas of management of HRD and the design of learning programs. These, and related items, are covered in other chapters in this handbook. In this chapter, the emphasis is on delivery in the most common mode—often called the "stand-up instructor."

Of course, instructing is a skill, and it is not anticipated that such skill will develop just by reading this chapter. However, Guliano provides an insight into what an instructor does and makes suggestions for relating to the learners.

Daniel F. Guliano (Ed.D.) is an instructional development specialist for the Field Engineering Division of IBM. He is also a part-time assistant professor in the School of Education and Human Development, The George Washington University. He has served in the technical part of the HRD field in a variety of capacities, including course design, development, and evaluation. He consults within IBM and is responsible for the development of staff in instructional system design and instructional techniques.

In the process of teaching a class, an instructor has a variety of responsibilities. In addition to being skillful in communicating thoughts so that learners understand the meaning and intent of the experience, the instructor must be aware of learners' needs and sensitive to their problems. The role of the instructor will vary many times during a session—from lecturer and presenter of knowledge, to demonstrator and guide of the learning experience. At times, the instructor will be an administrator, handling all the functions required to run a class smoothly. Instructors will use all the teaching techniques ever learned to ensure that learning will take place.

ROLES OF THE INSTRUCTOR

The instructor plays many roles during the process of teaching a class. To be more precise, roles are pieces of a person's behavior that have been turned into daily routines. During the process of conducting a class, an effective instructor can be described as: one who has the ability to teach others (instructional role), one who can keep records of student progress (administrative role), and one who has the proper skills to interact on a personal level with students (interpersonal role). These roles tend to merge and overlap so that instructors are usually functioning as a composite of the three.

Instructional Role

The most prominent role performed by instructors is instructional, as they initiate and guide the learning process. The instructional strategy selected for the learning process will affect the learning environment and the attitude of the learner. If the lecture method is used to present material, the instructor is the dispenser of knowledge, disseminating information that is difficult to understand, presenting knowledge that cannot be found anywhere else, or gathering and organizing material in a specific format before presenting it to the students to learn. The lecture allows material to be repeated in different words and format, to ensure the students understand it. It allows the instructor to communicate enthusiasm and arouse student interest in the material being presented.

If the discussion method is chosen, the instructor now becomes a facilitator, directing and guiding students toward finding the correct answers to their questions, rather than being an answering service. The discussion method provides for more learner participation, which, in turn, will generate greater learner interest and more enthusiasm in learning the subject matter.

Interpersonal Role

The responsibility of an instructor is to establish the best learning environment for the learner. The interpersonal relationship developed with the learner will go a long way in establishing a positive atmosphere. Being natural in this relationship will help the learner see the instructor in a nonthreatening role.

The instructor should never lose sight of the fact that students are adult human beings and, as such, have certain needs. They want to be recognized when they are doing a good job. The instructor should make every effort to commend learners on their efforts; praising their ability will usually provide the incentive to do better. Remember, praise must be justified. If it has no basis, it will prove to be very detrimental.

Showing empathy for a learner's feelings and problems is a key step in developing interpersonal relationships. One of the best ways of becoming aware of learner's needs is by listening. Unfortunately, instructors sometimes have the wrong interpretation of listening. Listening does not mean waiting for a turn to speak. It does mean having a genuine concern for what is being said and trying to understand the learner's point of view and concerns.

Another important factor that will be helpful in developing an interpersonal relationship with the class is flexibility. Can an instructor accept a change of opinion if new evidence casts some doubt on the original opinion? Without this ability, it is questionable whether a person can grow in the role of instructor. If one cannot grow, one will have difficulty in stimulating others.

Administrative Role

Most professional activities require a certain amount of clerical work, and instructing is no exception. Receiving a roster marks the beginning of an administrative experience. Instructors obtain the necessary documentation to be used in teaching the program, along with supplies for each learner's needs. The day before the session begins, the instructor must check the classroom to make sure it is large enough to accommodate all the students. If there is a need for any audiovisual equipment, the instructor must arrange to have it in the classroom. Throughout the duration of the session, the instructor must keep class records and fill out the forms at the end of the session. Administrative tasks are an ongoing activity throughout every session.

We have discussed the roles that instructors play in their attempt to serve the needs of others. On the other hand, many of the activities instructors perform are also attempts to meet their own personal needs— the need to be recognized, the need for self-actualization. If the role of instructor satisfies these needs, then instructors will grow and enhance their position.

CLASSROOM TECHNIQUES

After completing all the preparations for the class, the instructor usually experiences some anxiety while anticipating the arrival of the learners. Keep in mind that the adult learner who is attending this session will also experience some anxiety. As the learners arrive, the instructor should greet them and make appropriate introductions. This will add a personal touch and help to relieve their anxieties. The events that follow determine whether the learners will have a pleasant or unpleasant association with you.

Class Opening

After all the students have arrived, the instructor should reintroduce himself/herself and welcome them to this session. One thing should be kept in mind; you never get a second chance to make a good first impression. The learners are observing the instructor's actions, emotions, and attitude. Whatever takes place from this point on will be reflected in the learners.

Now, the instructor begins to establish rapport with the learners. This can be a mutual feeling of confidence, respect, and understanding. It begins to take place the moment the instructor steps in front of the class. The first sentence that is completed, the way it is said, and the instructor's expressions, all have an immediate impact on students. These first few minutes will greatly affect whether the instructor will be accepted or not. Remarks, good or bad, will be heard and retained. How instructors say something is just as important as what they say. There is no such thing as "Do as I say but not as I do," when dealing with adult learners, and there is no recipe for developing rapport. A combination of authenticity, enthusiasm, and attitude will help develop a rapport with the class.

What is authenticity? The instructor must be real, not a phony. The instructor cannot be two different people, one in front of the class and someone else when leaving the classroom. If instructors are not themselves, they are constantly anxious that they might make a slip, that someone might see through them. The behavior of instructors who enjoy their work and are dedicated to their profession is simple, natural, and real. In front of a class, instructors should be themselves. They should be natural in giving their presentation, and they will evoke a good response from their learners.

One of the primary elements that will affect instructors' teaching acceptability is their attitude. Therefore, as an instructor, it is important to become aware of the attitude displayed toward the learner, the subject, and the course material. Instructors should be constantly aware of their comments toward the subject or course material. If instructors are negative, this attitude will transfer to the students. Comments, both positive and negative, will be carried away from the classroom. Unfortunately, negative comments receive more emphasis than positive ones. If there is a problem with the subject matter, the instructor should try to present it in a positive manner. This will implant the idea that although it is not the way it should be, work is being done to improve it.

The instructor should be especially aware of the attitude displayed toward the learners. Although instructors may be the subject matter experts, they should not talk down to the adult learners. If instructors do, the class will turn them off, and their teaching will fall on deaf ears.

Enthusiasm is one of the important qualities an instructor should have or develop toward the subject he is teaching. A class is as interesting as an instructor makes it. When an instructor thinks that a topic is exciting to discuss, the learners will also find that topic exciting. The instructor's interest in the subject, eagerness to present it, and the zest with which it is presented will combine to present an image of an enthusiastic instructor. This enthusiasm will be visible through facial expressions, manner of speaking, and mannerisms. Enthusiasm of the instructor does not change goals of the course. Therefore, instructors must like what they are doing and the material they are teaching in order to show real enthusiasm for their work.

After completing the introduction, there are a few things that can be done to help set the learner at ease. Learners should write their names on a tent card. At the same time, instructors should put their name, phone number, and course name on the board. This establishes the instructor as a person of authority who is available if important needs arise. Then the instructor should check the roster to make sure everyone is present. This can be done by asking the learners to respond with their name, where they are from, and what they do. This adds another personal touch and demonstrates the instructor's interest in the learners.

After describing the learning center to the class, indicating the location of the lunchroom, rest rooms, elevators, and other areas of interest, the instructor should ask if anyone has been to the learning center before. Those who have may be used as a resource for recommending places to eat or places of interest to the class. Allowing students to take an active part will encourage freedom of expression and more active class participation later.

Consider using overhead transparencies to describe the location of restaurants, banks, drug stores, and medical facilities. Discuss places of interest learners can visit. Be prepared to discuss outside entertainment, because learners will ask. Keep in mind that a learner's attitude toward learning is greatly affected by his leisure activities.

Smoking in a classroom must be addressed during the class opening. Do not treat this subject lightly. Smoking offends many people. Putting yourself in the position of making all the rules is dangerous. Instead, consider soliciting learner ideas or comments on establishing the guidelines for the class.

After welcoming the learner to the session, it is time to introduce the program. The learners will want to know what the program is all about. Take time to give them a brief overview. Explain to the learners what is expected of them and offer them the opportunity to say what they expect of the instructor. Don't be surprised at their answers. Minimizing what is expected from the learner and what the learner expects from the instructor is dangerous. Learners are greatly interested in knowing how the instructor is going to evaluate them. If there is going to be a formal test, discuss the type of test, how it will be administered, and the topics it will cover. Discuss what other kinds of feedback on performance the learners can expect.

Ongoing Class Activities

The instructor started to establish rapport with the learner during class opening and must continue to develop this rapport as teaching begins. There should not be a breakdown in the atmosphere that was created; it should be an ever-growing rapport until the last day of class.

In preparation for the class, the instructor has probably developed a lesson plan and selected the instructional strategy that will be used. At times, instructors begin their lecture feeling confident that they are doing a good job. But as they look around, they see some students who look confused. The instructors begin to wonder where they went astray when developing their lesson plan. A common pitfall is that instructors fail to take into consideration the individual differences in learners and the fact that learners have different cognitive learning styles. For example, some learners need a very structured and detailed approach to what is to be learned. This learner is interested in outlines and in the sequence of events that are going to take place. There are other learners who are very visual. They prefer pictures, diagrams, and overhead transparencies indicating what is to be learned. Presentations should take into consideration both types of learners. While verbalizing what is to be learned, the instructor should have available diagrams and pictures for the visual learner and a detailed outline for the structured learner to follow.

Another element in ongoing class activities is providing feedback to the learner. An instructor who expects high performance from the learners must provide feedback on their performance. Learners want and expect feedback on both good and poor performance. It lets them know that instructors are interested in their learning and are willing to help them improve their skills. Learners should not be afraid to make mistakes, because an instructor will be there to help them. Learners often become defensive when they are being evaluated, because they have a strong emotional investment in their learning.

Consequently, when instructors provide feedback, they should make sure it is nonpunishing, and will not hurt the learner's feelings or discourage future participation. If the learners realize that the instructor's purposes in providing feedback is to help them learn, more than likely, they will accept it.

Commending a learner for good performance is one way of extending recognition to a learner and setting standards of performance. The instructor is letting the learner know what is considered good performance. Commenting favorably is one method of feedback, since the instructor is referring to something the learner has done well and using the learner's past performance as a measure of what is expected from him or her in the future.

COMMUNICATION PROCESS

Have you ever attended a presentation that you felt was particularly well done? What made it so? Was it the overhead transparencies, the flipcharts, the chalkboard work, or was it the speaker? Perhaps it was all of these, but, most likely it was the speaker. The successful speaker ties everything together and is enthusiastic in conveying the message to the audience. Visual aids are important, but the speaker controls the attitude of the audience. This must also be true of the instructor. The instructor does not have to be an orator who can hold the audience in his hand but should be capable of communicating effectively with the learner.

Communication is the transmission of thoughts from one person to another. These thoughts can be facts, ideas, or attitudes. The transmission of these thoughts can be either verbal or nonverbal. In fact, nonverbal messages or body language have often overshadowed the verbal cues we give and receive. Timing, silences, eye movements, tone of voice, and facial expressions all carry nonverbal messages. These messages reflect our likes, dislikes, attitudes, emotions, and sometimes our responsiveness to another person.

The effectiveness of the communication of ideas rests with two people—the sender and the receiver. A man stranded on a lonely road calling for help is not communicating unless there is someone there who can hear him. The communication process, therefore, is made up of three basic components: the person sending the message (the source), the person for whom the message is intended (the receiver), and the symbol (how the message is transmitted). The symbol can be expressed verbally or visually. The total communication process depends on the interrelationship of these three elements. Words and actions can present different messages simultaneously, but actions usually speak louder than words.

The instructor (the source) communicates with learners by selecting the proper words and putting them together to get ideas across. To successfully communicate, the instructor should select words that fit the learners' vocabulary. Instructors should not try to impress students by selecting complex terms or unfamiliar words or expressions, when presenting ideas. Sometimes instructors may not realize this is happening because the material is so familiar to them that they assume it is also familiar to the learner. If it is necessary to use unfamiliar words, give an adequate explanation of those words.

Instructors must believe the material they are presenting is important enough to learn, or why present it? If instructors have doubts about it, they may unconsciously reveal that attitude to the learner.

Above all, as the senders, instructors should be very knowledgeable about the material they are presenting.

The basic symbols used in the communication of ideas or thoughts are either verbal, nonverbal (visual), or a combination of both. Selecting and assembling the words to form a sentence in one's mind and then verbalizing them is one method of sending ideas to the learner. However, this is only part of the process of communicating. How instructors express themselves is just as important as what they are saying. One of the symbols instructors can use to present ideas is their voice. Enthusiasm, sincerity, self-confidence, and attitude can all be conveyed by a person's voice.

Three voice characteristics that affect the quality of presentation are pitch (sometimes referred to as tone), intensity (loudness), and rate (how fast one talks). Varying the pitch and inflections of the voice will make a presentation more pleasant to the ear. Speaking in a constant monotone is very unpleasant and may put the audience to sleep. Voice inflections are one way to emphasize certain points in a presentation. Instructors should also be concerned with the speed or tempo of their speech pattern. If they talk too fast, learners will have difficulty keeping up with them and may ask the instructor to repeat something a little slower.

On the other hand, if instructors drag their feet, they may bore their learners. While the instructor finishes the presentation, the learner's attention has shifted to something else. Instructors should remember to alter their voice tone and speed to fit the demands of their presentation (i.e., raise the pitch and pick up speed to get the learner's attention to a particular area of a presentation).

There are always people in the back of the room who want to hear what the instructor has to say. To accommodate these learners, instructors should adjust the intensity of their voice, taking into account the size of the room and the number of learners present. The instructor's voice should be loud enough for everyone to hear but not so loud as to overpower the learners. With practice, instructors can develop a speaking voice that is easily heard and accentuated by a variety in tone and rate of speech.

Communication is not based on words alone; gestures, facial expressions, and posture are elements of body language that will either add to or detract from the effectiveness of a presentation. People have a marvelous sensing mechanism; we ofen hear the words but do not believe what was said because the body language (the nonverbal communication) cannot confirm what was said in words. Body language is the visual, nonverbal symbol that one uses to communicate. Visual symbols should occur spontaneously and naturally while one is talking. If they are forced, they become rigid, look insincere, and are easily detected. Facial expressions will unintentionally convey enthusiasm, whether the instructor is relaxed, tense, or confused. The instructor may try to look confident and enthusiastic, but a slumping posture and an expressionless face will convey the instructor's real feelings. Ideas are only communicated when the proper symbols are brought together in concert during the delivery of ideas.

The last element in the communication process is the receiver (the learner)—the one who is going to listen to the instructor's thoughts or ideas. Learners in a class will vary in ability, knowledge, skill, and attitude. These factors should be taken into consideration when developing a presentation, or meaningful communication will not take place. Learners want to understand what is being presented, so the presentation must start at their level and build upon their prior learning and experience. Instructors must also provide for learner participation in their presentation. This can be done by asking questions of the learners and providing time for them to ask questions, in order to clarify points they do not understand. Through the use of questions, the instructor can learn whether the material is understood, and the learners can obtain feedback on whether their responses were correct.

Eye Contact

Another vital dimension of communication is making effective eye contact with the learner. Here, the instructor becomes the listener in the silent communication process. As instructors make eye contact with a learner, they should look for two things—a response to the eye contact and the learner's reaction to the presentation.

What kind of nonverbal responses can an instructor get by looking at someone? The responses are usually a variety of involuntary movements similar to reflexes, facial expressions, head position, or a nod of the head, for example. If the instructor cannot see any response, one can usually be forced by the instructor by nodding, raising the eyebrows in a slight questioning look, or other such movement. The instructor will usually be repaid with an answering smile, shrug, or nod of the head. This response only means that the learner is aware that the instructor has made eye contact; it is an act of recognition. The instructor can also assume that the learner is paying attention and is alert at that moment. On the other hand, if the instructor detects no signs of recognition or attention, even after trying to force it, this might be a clue that the learner is tuned out at the moment. A direct question may be needed to check out this assumption and bring the learner back to the classroom.

Instructors can tell very little about a learner's relationship with the subject matter just by looking around the room, but the learner's body language can tell instructors how they feel about the presentation. Does any learner have a bored or confused expression? Do any of the learners show lack of interest by doodling on their pads? If these things are occurring, the instructor should stop and try to determine the problem by asking the learners where they got lost and why. Instructors should ask themselves: "Were the learners actively participating in the class session?" If the answer is no, the learners are a passive audience and can very easily lose interest. At this point, the instructor should change 'he presentation technique by calling on the learners for greater involvement.

In the final analysis, eye contact is a good way of obtaining information about the class. This will not tell the instructor how well the class is learning, but it will be a good indicator of whether the class is keeping up with the instructor's presentation.

Platform Techniques

Until now we have discussed the individual elements that go into making up the platform techniques needed for a good presentation. Now, let us put them to use.

When instructors enter the room and head for the lectern, they are on center stage. Everyone will be looking at the instructor for the first opening comment. One of the instructor's goals will be to establish a feeling of direct comunication with the learners. This can be done by using the direct pronoun "we," and by recognizing the learners by name. As the opening activities begin, the instructor should attempt to build a rapport with the learners, by frequently moving away from the lectern while talking to the class. This movement will help in the transition from one point to another (i.e., moving to the board to do some boardwork or to use the flipchart), will draw the learners' attention to the instructor, and will keep their attention. There must be a purpose for the movements, however, because too much will be distracting and too little becomes boring.

The instructor's voice is another factor that has a direct impact on the effectiveness of a presentation. Instructors should not speak in a monotone or speak too fast; instead, they should vary the loudness and tone of their voice. This makes a presentation pleasant to the ear. Making gestures a natural part of the presentation is useful as well. Gestures can be used to emphasize a point, show emotions, or describe shape, size, or movement.

A friendly smile by the instructor during direct eye contact with the learner will go a long way in the development of learner/instructor rapport. If the instructor looks directly at the learners while making a presentation, they will feel they are being talked to and will pay attention. The instructor should not look and talk to a big spot located on the wall in the back of the room, because many people have a tendency to distrust a person who does not look another person in the eye when talking to them.

When presenting material, the instructor should never read from a prepared script, or the audience will lose interest. Such a presentation shows that the instructor does not know the material, and it is very irritating to the learner. They can read it just as well as the instructor. The effective instructor has constant communication with the learner by using body language and eye contact; a reader has none.

There are some instructors who are constantly afraid of making a mistake, and this is reflected in the way they speak and in their mannerisms. No one expects instructors to know all there is to know about a subject. There is always room for improvement. So there is no harm in making a mistake as long as the instructor admits it and corrects it. If the instructor does not know or is not sure of the answer to a question, he or she should admit this to the learners and explain that they will get an answer as soon as possible.

The lectern should hold the lesson plan or reference material, as the instructor talks to the learners. It should not be held on to throughout the entire lecture. Instructors should avoid being so engrossed in the presentation that they bury their heads in the lectern and forget to let go or walk around to the front or side. Leaving the lectern will give the instructor a chance to relax and give the learner a chance to take a breather. This will also provide the instructor with an opportunity to view the class and ask questions. It allows the students to ask questions as well.

Instructors should constantly be aware of any mannerisms that may distract the class (i.e., juggling coins, scratching your head, tapping the pointer on the table, or pacing from one end of the room to the other). These will draw attention away from what is being said, to the mannerism that is taking place. These mannerisms are usually caused by tension, but these habits can be broken if the instructor is aware of them.

Trying to eliminate all mannerisms is unwise, because it can detract from a person's individuality. The instructor's personality is partially made up of those individual mannerisms, and they add color and interest to a presentation. Therefore, the instructor should try to eliminate only those mannerisms that are distracting to the learner.

LEARNING/TEACHING

Learning is a basic process in the development of an individual. Through learning, we change our behavior to adapt to various life situations. It is an internal process that involves knowledge, skills, and attitude—the knowledge of what to do, the attitude to apply what has been learned, and the skills to put to use the knowledge that has been learned.

There can be many and various reasons for an adult's decision to enter a learning situation. It could be from a decision to enhance a present job or, perhaps, a desire to change careers. A desire to learn may occur because of a new interest, a hobby, or curiosity about a subject matter. The greatest desire for learning will occur when adults experience a problem that needs solving or recognize a gap between where they are and where they want to be. They will be most receptive to learning when they are confronted with the fact that they do not know something they feel they should know. It is at this point that adults will use any resource they can to obtain the necessary learning. From this, it is easy to see that an adult's readiness to learn is derived from his or her needs.

How can the instructor take advantage of this readiness to learn? Learners are aware that learning will enhance their development and help them advance in their careers. Therefore, when presenting new material, try to associate it with the learner's job or how it can be applied to the work situation. Give problems to solve, early in the class sessions, to illustrate the knowledge and skills needed to solve problems. Then, present the material that has to be learned. Help the adult learners determine the gap between what they know and what they need to know. Then, develop a mutual partnership, with both of you working together to close that gap.

Adults are most interested in seeing immediate application of their new learning. They want to put their new knowledge to work to solve a problem or to resolve a concern that is confronting them now. They want to get an answer to the question: "What will this new learning do for me?" They want to know the practical on-the-job application of what is to be learned. If adult learners fail to see how this new learning will help them reach their goals, they may lose interest.

The instructor should be aware that adults want to try their new learning immediately to see if it works. The problem or concern they are trying to alleviate could be either at home or at work. The instructor should determine what the learner's problem is and make adjustments to the material being presented to show relationship to that immediate problem. This will add relevancy to the material to be learned.

Adults tend to be autonomous and self-directing. As learners, they are made to feel uncomfortable when placed in a dependent role. They are individuals who have accepted the responsibility for themselves and for the families they are raising. Adult learners resent, and will have a tendency to avoid, any situation that makes them feel like children (i.e., a classroom where they are told what to do, what not to do, and where they are talked down to). In such situations, they change from autonomous and self-directed individuals, who are spouses and parents, to children. They have been put into positions that are incongruent with their self-concept.

Obviously, a learning environment of mutual respect must be created. Treat the learners with respect, avoid talking down to them, do not preach, and do not create embarrassing situations. Be friendly, supportive and avoid being judgmental. Encourage the adult learners to be more self-directed by letting them shape part of their own learning. Give the learner the responsibility for working out solutions to problems and then act as a resource person. Guide the learners into evaluating their own progress toward their learning goals. They will see these activities as guiding them to be more responsible for their own learning.

Adults bring to a learning situation many experiences accumulated over a period of years. Some experiences come from various jobs they have had, while others may be the result of being the head of a household where they may have had experience as a car mechanic, plumber, electrician, appliance repair person, or counselor, to meet the needs of their growing family. They have learned to perform these functions through the informal learning process of building experiences by trial and error. As adults, we have a tendency to define ourselves by our experiences, because of the investment we have in them.

The instructor should take advantage of the adult learners' experiences by having them take part in the class activities. Using group discussions or problem-solving techniques allows them to contribute to the learning process. The instructor should not forget that many adults may have a foundation of past experiences that can give meaning to new learning in the classroom. If the instructor fails to use these experiences, adult learners can feel personally rejected and may not take part in the class.

A problem that many adult learners have, and one that is difficult to contend with, is fear of failure. Adults are proud individuals, and they think of themselves as competent people. If they should fail during a learning activity, it could have a crippling effect on their self-concept and their ego. This could prevent the adult from entering any other formal learning activity. The instructor should attempt to establish a nonthreatening learning climate that will help adult learners overcome their resistance to learning. This can be done by being warm, helpful, and understanding of each individual's situation.

Motivation

Motivation varies from one person to another and from time to time in the same person's life. If there are learners in the class who are not motivated to learn, the instructor will have a considerable problem teaching them. Although instructors cannot motivate learners, understanding some of the factors of motivation may be helpful in creating an atmosphere that will be encouraging to the student.

Learners' needs in a classroom fall into two areas, physical and social. Meeting the physical needs will make students comfortable while they are in the classroom. Physical needs include having comfortable chairs, decent lighting, and proper heating or cooling when needed. Although these fall under the instructors' jurisdiction, at times, they may have very little control over them.

The instructor has greater control over the social needs of the learner. Although needs are individualistic, some, such as security, recognition, and self-esteem, are common to all learners.

At times, when presenting new and difficult material to the learners, some experience a feeling of insecurity. The first reaction will be, "I'll never understand this," or "It's too difficult for me to understand." Adults may begin to wonder why they are in the class and ask themselves, "Whatever made me sign up for this course?" What can instructors do to insure that this does not happen? They can give preliminary assignments so that learners have a chance to build a background, in gradual steps. Then, they should begin to present the difficult material at the students' level, establishing a learning set of where everybody should be before beginning. The material being presented should progress in a logical sequence, from simple to more complex, and provide activities that will allow application of what has been learned. As learners begin to understand the material, self-confidence increases and so will their feelings of security.

Adults want recognition and approval from their friends and their manager when a project is completed and is done well. The classroom should be no different. Instructors should respond to this need for recognition and approval by calling each member by name. They should make sure that all successful accomplishments by any member of the class are brought to the attention of the whole class. Learners who have finished a project that was done well feel they have earned the approval of the class and the instructor. This recognition will create a challenge among members of the class and will provide an incentive and motivate them to do better.

Learners have to feel confident in their ability to deal with their problems in a satisfactory way. This is *self-esteem*, the need to view ourselves as being okay. Instructors can build the learner's self-esteem by planning activities whereby the learner experiences success early in the program. If learners have too many failures, they are likely to lose their confidence. Instructors must be very cautious when attempting to build a learner's self-esteem. They must not praise a learner to the point of establishing a false sense of accomplishment. If a failure should subsequently occur, it would be extremely damaging to the learner's self-esteem.

Other learners' needs may come to light while teaching a class. It is the instructor's responsibility to recognize these needs and find ways to satisfy them. This will make the learning environment a place of achievement, not frustration.

EVALUATION OF ADULT LEARNERS

The purpose of evaluation is to determine whether a course is delivering the skills it should or whether there is a learner problem. Before an instructor can make an evaluation, there must be a measurement system, since evaluation describes the process of interpreting the data obtained during the measurement process.

The two measurement systems in use today are the criterion-referenced and normative-referenced systems. The normative approach to measurement is designed to compare individuals with one another; learner ranking or selection is its primary objective. This type of measurement system is not suitable for adult learners, especially if an instructor wants to build a learning environment that is free of anxiety and frustrations. Criterion-referenced measurement is designed to compare an individual with a given performance standard, regardless of how other individuals perform on the same test.

Adult learners enter a learning environment with various abilities and learning speeds. This does not mean that they cannot learn but only that they require a different time span for learning. If a normative system is used, it would compare slower learners against those who can grasp the material more readily. Some of the slower learners could be rated fairly low or could be eliminated from the program completely. The advantage of using a criterion-referenced system is that it compares each individual learner to the skills delivered by the course. This enables you to determine whether a learner can perform the skills and at what level of proficiency. The criterion-reference system takes into account the slow learner who can master the skills but needs more practice to become proficient at them. Criterion testing should be an essential part of any adult training program.

Usually, the designer of the training program determines its minimum criteria. The designer defines what tasks are critical and to what level of proficiency the learner must perform in order to qualify as satisfactorily completing the program. The next step is to define the different levels of proficiency. This can be done by establishing a rating system of 1–5, where 1 would be extremely proficient and 5 would be inadequate. The 2, 3, 4 would indicate different levels that could be achieved.

There are two types of criterion test items that are very effective, one is a performance problem that tests a psychomotor skill and the other is finding a solution to a given problem. In each case, the testing is carried out to determine if learners can apply the skills they have learned.

It is important to keep in mind that adult learners need feedback. They want to know how they are doing. To provide only one measurement device at the end of the course would be an injustice to the learner. There should be criterion-type formative evaluation throughout every program. This will help students during the learning process and serve as a guide to tell the instructor where a student needs remedial work. If the instructor has a good formative evaluation system at the critical learning areas, it will point to those who need help and raise the learning curve for the class. It will also eliminate frustration.

USE OF TECHNOLOGY IN LEARNING

Two of the fastest growing uses of technology in the teaching process are in the areas of computers and videodiscs. Computer-based learning (CBL) is not new, and in the past few years the application of CBL has increased rapidly. One advantage is its ability to allow learners to go through the program at their own optimum learning speed. CBL allows the individualization of instruction through the course structure. It also provides for student control options that allow learners to skip material already learned and concentrate on new concepts. If properly developed, CBL is a very interactive and adaptive learning method. The student could be asked to solve a problem and give the solution to the computer or be asked to look up specific information and respond with the correct answer. Solving the problem could be a step-by-step procedure, with help available and immediate feedback at each step, or it could be a one-step process followed by a positive reinforcement or remedial instructions.

A more sophisticated use of computer-based learning is the area of simulation, which can create most of the actual conditions for a given problem situation that a learner must resolve. Simulation is especially useful when a learner must be aware of the consequences of alternative actions. Other methods of training may be too costly, dangerous, or simply less effective. Computer technology is paving the way for the nonprogrammer educator to create and deliver complex simulation exercises.

The "intelligent" videodisc (or disc programming) has changed video learning from a passive to an interactive learning process. The videodisc, with its self-contained program, combines the power of a microprocessor with the high density storage of a videodisc to provide student-controlled video learning. Videodisc technology permits the student to access and immediately display specific information at any time within a training session. A more recent enhancement to CBL is a computer-controlled videodisc. This computer-controlled, multimedia learning environment allows the student to view an actual activity, a still frame, or an audio of relevant material within a CBL course. By combining the computer and videodisc technologies, the student is exposed to a unified, integrated learning system. Acting as a storage retrieval device for video and audio, the videodisc complements CBL teaching strategies, especially in the creation of sophisticated simulation.

With the advent of personal computers, CBL is no longer confined to learning centers. Each home can be a learning center. There will be libraries of diskettes containing all types of training programs. Learners will be able to sign out diskettes for whatever subject they want to learn and use them on their own computer. They will be able to learn a complete subject at home and come to the classroom only to take a final examination. In the future, personal computers will be able to access data banks for all kinds of information.

Some of this technology will be used in the classroom of the future. The instructor may use a videodisc to support a lecture by making use of its fast, random access and interactive capabilities to show any frame from a video sequence. Use of case studies, role play episodes, and behavior modeling are just a few situations in which a videodisc could prove very useful. As an educational tool, the computer, which can control media selection and use, offers the instructor unprecedented flexibility in selecting an appropriate teaching strategy for students in a class.

Instructional Strategies: Nonmedia

ELLEN WEISBERG MALASKY

In delivering learning, the HRD designer of learning programs must be familiar with the wide variety of instructional strategies that are available. In this chapter, Malasky provides us with information essential to the designer. By no means is it suggested that these are all the nonmedia strategies. In addition, each of the strategies included has many variations, but the material essential to the designer and a bibliography for further assistance are provided.

The HRD instructor-facilitator must know these instructional strategies but must also build skill in using them. It is not suggested that this chapter, or any written material, will enable the instructor-facilitator to reach an acceptable level of competency. Such competency requires experience, coaching, and feedback. This chapter, however, is important to the instructor-facilitator in that it provides an idea of what is available.

The HRD manager and HRD consultant should also be familiar with these strategies to be aware of what is contemplated and used in the various learning programs provided through HRD programs.

Ellen Weisberg Malasky works with a variety of clients in designing, developing, conducting, and evaluating professional presentations and learning programs. She was formerly director of education methods for Arthur Young & Company and was responsible for both internal and external consultation on HRD. She is active in ASTD, having served on several national and local committees. She is the author of the Arthur Young publication, *Guide to Developing an Education Program*, and coauthor of *Discussion Leader Workshop* (American Institute of Certified Public Accountants).

This chapter is intended to be a practical primer on instructional strategies for course developers. I have concentrated on factors relating to selection and use of each strategy, as opposed to techniques for instructors.

In selecting appropriate strategies for each learning situation, you should consider a number of factors, including the learning objectives, characteristics of the participants, competencies of the instructors, and any constraints (i.e., time or physical limitations). Vary the strategies you use to maintain participant interest. Remember, a learning experience will consist of a number of strategies coupled together to make up the overall flow of the experience. The developer is, in essence, an orchestrator, selecting and using the strategies that will create the desired tempo and climate for the experience.

I have compiled the information from a variety of sources, including my own experience. At the conclusion of the chapter is a bibliography of additional available resources.

ACTION MAZE

A printed description of an incident, for analysis, followed by a list of alternative actions is called an *action maze*. Each action choice directs the participant to a new page, which gives the results of that action and a new set of alternatives from which to choose. The results the participant receives after each step may give more information, as well as a reaction to the action taken. The selection may also lead to a dead end, sending the participant back to the original situation to make another choice.

When to use:
 To develop decision-making skills
 To develop problem-solving skills
Requirements:
 Written instructional materials
 Pens, pencils, etc.
Advantages:
 Develops an awareness of alternatives and consequences of decisions
 Intense skill development
 Self-paced

Considerations:

Is costly to construct

Difficult to update. Need to use information that will not change

No opportunity for discussion or interaction with others

Related strategies:

Case study, programmed instruction, computer-assisted instruction, delphi technique

BRAINSTORMING

Brainstorming is a problem-solving situation in which participants are given a problem and asked to bring into the discussion any ideas that come to mind, no matter how outlandish. All ideas are gathered and recorded, without evaluation, before any are discussed. Idea gathering is usually limited to 5–15 minutes.

When to use:

To develop novel or creative solutions to problems

To develop creativity

To stimulate participation by group members

Requirements:

Board or flipchart for recording ideas

Chalk or pens

Tape for posting flipchart pages

Advantages:

Encourages unusual suggestions

Breaks mind sets and allows for new approaches

Although only a small number of the ideas produced are usable, surfaces a significant number of valuable ideas

Maintains interest because of fast moving pace of session

Encourages participation by all group members

Considerations:

Requires skill on the part of the leader to keep the session moving and the ideas coming, as well as to refrain from judging ideas generated

Productivity of the group depends upon the abilities of the participants and their understanding of the process

Requires a nonthreatening environment

Related strategies:

Creative thinking, problem solving

BUZZ GROUP

A large group divided into several small groups of four to six people discuss a topic or perform a task, usually in less than 10 minutes. Originally called the "6 by 6" technique, which meant six people for six minutes, such a strategy has come to be known as a *buzz group*. Although there is no finished product, provision must be made for some feedback.

When to use:

To stimulate thinking to open or start a discussion

To get reaction to a speaker, film, etc.

Requirements:

Space, for groups to talk without interference

Advantages:

Stimulates discussion and generates group interest

Allows participation by those reticent to speak in a large group

Focuses subsequent discussion on participants' interest

Considerations:

Requires instructor who is able to introduce the activity and stop the discussion at the determined time

Sometimes results in domination of the small group by one or two people

Related strategies:

Group discussion, work group, workshop

CASE STUDY

A *case study* is an oral or written account of a realistic situation, including sufficient detail to make it possible for the participants to analyze the problems involved and to determine possible solutions. In many cases, there is no one correct answer. Case studies should, as much as possible, replicate the real world, both in the nature of the content and in the method in which they are presented and completed. While work on the cases may be done either individually or in groups, this method should always conclude with a discussion of the outcomes.

When to use:

To develop critical-thinking, problem-solving, and decision-making skills

To provide realistic and practical experience

To evaluate learning and/or test analytical knowledge or abilities

To learn to separate facts from inferences

Requirements:

The case (written, film, video, or other form of presentation)

Pencils, pens, paper--whatever is necessary to complete case requirements

Board and/or flipchart for case study discussion

Advantages:

Actively involves participants

Keeps interest levels high because of participant activity and relevancy to real world situations

Blends well with other methods (e.g., lecture or readings)

Considerations:

Takes time to work and to discuss

Cases can become outdated by such things as changes in laws, language used, social mores, dates, etc. Periodic revision is essential

Good case studies can be difficult to write. They need to contain enough facts to be completed without making up information. Yet, the information should be organized in such a way that the solution is not obvious. Incomplete or incorrect information, too much extraneous or confusing information, and cute or funny names often detract from the effectiveness of a case. This can cause the participants to become frustrated and direct their energies toward attacking the case, rather than working it

To effectively discuss a case, the instructor, if not the developer, must work the case and be thoroughly prepared to answer any questions that may arise

The instructor must be able to link the case study situation to the "real world," thereby adding credibility to the case

Related strategies:

Action maze, exercises, incident process, in-basket exercises, role play

DELPHI TECHNIQUE

The strategy that employs a number of experts who independently offer judgments on specific questions on two or more successive occasions is referred to as the *delphi technique*. At each iteration after the first, the material to be evaluated is accompanied by information showing the amount of group agreement on the previous iteration. A list of reasons for the judgments of the group can also be provided. Each expert is free to consider this information in reevaluating the items. The purpose of this method is to promote maximum convergence of opinion, without the biasing influences of face-to-face confrontation.

When to use:

To assist in establishing learning objectives (e.g., to elicit information from practitioners in a given career field as to what the "real life" work expectations are)

To project learning needs for the future, as a basis for long-range curriculum planning

To assist groups of learners in establishing collective priorities for learning or problem-solving activities

Requirements:

Paper, envelopes, stamps, pens, etc. for correspondence

A calculator for tabulations or, if a larger study, perhaps a computer

Advantages:

Provides freedom from conformity pressures because of anonymity and isolation of respondents

Simple pooling of independent ideas and judgments facilitates equality of participants

Valuable for obtaining judgments from experts who are geographically isolated

The process of writing responses forces respondents to think through the complexity of the problem and submit specific, high quality ideas

The strategy can be used with large numbers of participants

Relatively low material cost, unless a computer is used for tabulation

Considerations:

Technique can be very time consuming

The lack of opportunity for verbal clarification can create interpretation difficulties among participants

The lack of opportunity for social and emotional rewards can lead to a feeling of detachment from the problem-solving effort. The quality of response is very much influenced by the interest and commitment of the participants

Conflicts are not resolved, since conflicting ideas are handled simply by pooling and are added to the votes of group participants

Strategy limited to participants who have skill in expressing themselves in written communication

Related strategies:

Group process

DEMONSTRATION

A technique that shows how something works or gets done is called a *demonstration*. It is intended to illustrate or clarify an idea, process, or relationship. The participant's role is one of observing, rather than directly participating. Often, this strategy is coupled with participant practicing and receiving feedback on performance.

When to use:

To show how a piece of equipment works

To demonstrate a skill or technique

To show how a technique can be used

Requirements:

Equipment being demonstrated, if applicable

Space requirements as needed

Advantages:

Provides clear, direct example of how something works or is to be done

Is realistic. Can be linked to hands-on application

Is inexpensive to develop

Can use expert to demonstrate and instructor to facilitate learning

Considerations:

Learner not active, so interest may wane, especially at low learning times of day

Need to ensure that all can see the demonstration clearly

Learners may see but not be able to do

Related strategies:

Skit, simulation game, interactive modeling

DISCUSSION

A *discussion* is an exploration of a specific topic by a group. Discussions are most effective in groups of 10–25 participants. They are often coupled with a lecture or other nonparticipative strategy or may serve as a review of individual or group work (e.g., case study). In a discussion, the instructor begins by asking stimulating, usually predetermined questions. During the discussion, the instructor acts as a catalyst and moderator, asking additional questions, recording and/or restating participant responses, and generally guiding the participants in the right direction.

When to use:

To determine learners' knowledge and/or attitude concerning a specific topic

To review case studies or other work assignments

To assist learners to learn deductively

To encourage group participation

Requirements:

Seating so most group members can see each other during the discussion

Flipchart or board to gather ideas

Advantages:

Actively involves participants

Pools knowledge and experience of group

Allows unclear areas to be identified and discussed

Considerations:

Instructor requires good facilitation skills. Must be patient and allow the discussion to evolve

One or two vocal members may dominate

Takes more time than some other strategies (e.g., lecture)

May be difficult to control and can stray from intended topic

Related strategies:

Buzz group, brainstorming, work group

EXERCISE

Similar to a case study, the *exercise* is a short problem focusing on a specific learning point. Most exercises have one correct solution. A group of exercises may be used as a test.

When to use:

To demonstrate newly learned procedures and principles, prior to attempting to apply the knowledge to more difficult and complex case studies

Requirements:

Paper, pens, pencils, etc.

Advantages:

Quickly identifies whether learning has occurred and pinpoints problem areas

Participants actively involved

Helps make transition between conceptualization and application

Considerations:

Should be limited to a single concept or procedure

Takes some time to do and discuss

Need to avoid tendency to make exercise too long or complex

Should be tested to assure it will produce the desired result

Related strategies:

Case studies, incident process

FISHBOWL

A *fishbowl* is a discussion group that is divided in two parts: the inner circle, consisting of four or five people who discuss a topic, and the outer group, consisting of up to 20 people who observe (usually standing). Variations include: (1) members of the outer group may "tap in" or exchange places with members of the inner group; (2) the inner group (half the total group) discusses something for a specific period of time and then rotates with the outer group, who then discusses for a specific period of time; (3) each member of the inner group has an alterego in the outer group to advise and provide guidance. A fishbowl usually runs 20–30 minutes, enough time to let all interested people express their thoughts but not so long as to drag; it should end on a high note.

When to use:
    To open a discussion or stimulate thinking by allowing individuals to present different points of view
    To foster group participation
    To view group process
    To provide formative evaluation
Requirements:
    Physical space for inner and outer circles
    Chairs
Advantages:
    Encourages group participation by all members
    Maintains group interest
    Surfaces ideas and attitudes concerning a topic area
Considerations:
    As the purpose is to stimulate thinking, choice of topic is important. Should be an open-ended topic and one familiar to all the participants
    This strategy should be coupled with a follow-up strategy which allows for a more in-depth examination of the topic (e.g., work group)
    It is wise to have a fail-safe device in the form of a "plant" (a person to help get the discussion started). The role of such an individual would only be to give some direction and ask questions if the group does not appear to be getting involved. The identity of such an individual should not be made known to the group
    The role of the instructor in this strategy is merely to set it up and to listen. Participation in the discussion should be only as a "tap-in"
Related strategies:
    Brainstorming, creative thinking

GAME

An activity characterized by structured competition between two or more participants is a *game*. Each game has its own unique set of rules and learning outcomes. Some games are simple, others are extremely complex. Their primary focus is on participant actions and reactions.

Although it is not always necessary, simulation games can be similar to work situations, but with carefully arranged competitive elements. The game provides a framework, within which participants can be involved in an exciting game mood. This mood allows participants to examine systems of interactive decision-making procedures and to approach problems from the perspective of learning at the same time. The distinguishing features of a game are that it includes a set of structured decision-making tasks typical of a real-life situation and that it provides a systematic means of observing and evaluating participants' decisions. These, then, are fed back to the participants so they can judge their appropriateness. Most games are played by one or more teams, each composed of from one to 20 participants.

When to use:
   To develop leadership skills
   To improve technical performance
   To foster cooperation and teamwork
   To improve decision-making ability
   To evaluate learning

Requirements:
   As needed for game, procedures, written material, or game equipment
   Facilities for groups to work

Advantages:
   Games motivate participants to be highly involved
   They are fun
   Since long periods of time can be compressed into relatively short learning periods, it is possible to provide in weeks the experience that would take years to gain on the job
   Participants become deeply involved in the game and undergo the stresses associated with real situations

Can be used in an infinite variety of ways for all types of learning from orientation to detailed instruction

Can often be used more than once with the same group with additional gains

Takes the positive features of group dynamics and focuses a group's energies on a particular task or a specific concept of change

Considerations:

Participants may be totally involved only in "win/lose" competition if games are not properly constructed and administered

Usually designed to produce a certain set of predetermined learning outcomes and must be carefully adapted if used apart from the original intention

Require sound skills and understanding from the instructor/facilitator

Require a great deal of time and are costly if purchased commercially. Usually cost more in terms of personnel, equipment, and money than other approaches to learning

When a computer is involved, the cost is even greater—for programming, time on the equipment, and operating personnel

Little research has been done on the effectiveness of the game as a learning strategy; therefore its validity has not been proved

Related strategies:

Simulation, exercise, role play, computer-assisted instruction (CAI)

IN-BASKET

The *in-basket* strategy is a timed variation of a case study. Each participant is provided with an in-basket, including correspondence, reports, memos, and phone messages, some of which may be important to the case or process under study, and some of which may be extraneous. The participants examine the materials and take the appropriate actions. Each participant works for a set period of time on his or her own material. Every other participant handles the same material. At the conclusion of the processing time, participants record how they handled each item and, based on the actions taken, assess their abilities in the areas on which the case study focused. Usually, there is a group discussion (small group or entire class) of selected items and of approaches taken.

When to use:

To analyze participants' decision-making abilities so that needed training can be provided

To evaluate managerial skills (e.g., supervisory, communications, time management, etc.)

To provide practice in decision making

To improve participants' understanding of management theories

Requirements:

In-basket exercise package of materials for each participant

Paper, pens, paper clips, erasers for participants to use

Ample physical space for each participant to work

Advantages:

Actively involves all participants

Interesting because of real world nature of materials

Provides for some competition among participants, if that is needed

Provides a way for participants to assess their skills in the areas on which the exercise focuses

Can be constructed to reflect the problems that a particular group is having

Can be built to fit the time period available to the exercise

Provides immediate feedback as to the possible consequences of actions taken

Easy to conduct, although for discussion, instructor requires good facilitation skills

Considerations:

Takes time, usually three to four hours, to conduct and process

Difficult to develop in-house

Can be costly. Costs for in-basket exercise vary greatly, depending on the types of materials being used. The major cost element is the preparation of the materials themselves, particularly if large quantities are required. Some commercial vendors sell in-basket programs. Costs usually range from $40–$80 per participant

May seem unreal in the sense that the participants are put into a situation with no past relationships with the people they must work through. In reality, actions would probably depend on these relationships

May be difficult for those who have not had experience handling job problems through correspondence (e.g., manufacturing foremen who tend to handle forms and get oral reports rather than notes and letters)

Related strategies:

Case study, exercise, action maze, incident process, simulation game

INCIDENT PROCESS

The *incident process* is a variation of the case method. Participants are presented with an incident that is short and lacking in detail. Participants then question the instructor to determine the data needed to complete the assignment. The instructor gives out pertinent facts only as the participants ask for them, forcing the participants to reconstruct the entire situation. Often, an observer-reporter records group interaction. This method provides the participants with the opportunity to examine the present, unravel the past events leading up to the incident, and identify future implications resulting from the incident. This strategy emphasizes the process involved in gathering pertinent information in order to arrive at a decision.

When to use:

To develop problem analysis and problem-solving skills

To develop decision-making skills

To develop observation skills

To develop questioning and listening skills

Requirements:

Physical space for participants to work, at times in small groups

Written incident and additional fact sheets, as needed

Pens, pencils, paper, etc.

Advantages:

Actively involves participants

Has a "living quality," as opposed to a case which is all in writing

Provides an opportunity to reconstruct a case from start to finish

Emphasizes fact-finding process more than the solution

Promotes public speaking and development of summaries

Promotes "openness" of ideas and expression

Incident can be modified to suit the level of the participants

Provides an opportunity to examine consequences of a decision
Considerations:
More time consuming than traditional case studies
Difficult to evaluate transfer of process and utilization on the job
Best suited to groups of fewer than 20–25 participants
Extroverted participants tend to monopolize discussion
Instructor must have all the information needed to respond to the participants' questions. Information may be given orally or on data sheets
Instructor must have good facilitation skills
Related strategies:
Case study, action maze, exercise, simulation game

INTERACTIVE MODELING

Interactive modeling is a means of learning new behaviors by observing model or ideal behavior, trying new behavior, and receiving feedback. This cycle is repeated until the new behavior is learned. The following sequence of four types of behavioral learning activities is involved:

1. *Modeling*—groups of participants watch filmed or acted supervisor and employee model the desired behavior
2. *Role playing*—participants take part in extensive practice and rehearsal of the specific behaviors demonstrated by the models
3. *Social reinforcement*—players receive praise, reward, and constructive feedback from instructor and other participants
4. *Transfer of training*—participants apply learning by being able to model behavior back on the job

When to use:
To orient new employee to procedures
To learn methods of interviewing, counseling, and other similar tasks
Requirements:
Video, film equipment, or script
Space large enough for viewing and for role plays
Flipchart and board

Advantages:

Provides a step-by-step approach for handling difficult interaction situations

Provides a positive model, demonstrating how difficult situations can be handled successfully

Provides practice for each participant in handling difficult situations

Provides on-the-job environment, which facilitates learning

Considerations:

May be difficult to isolate step-by-step procedures for each behavior

Very difficult to find suitable off-the-shelf models

Usually each organization must develop its own film or video. This is costly and requires developers who are able to create realistic demonstration

Purely behaviorist, does not take into account attitudes or feelings

Is time consuming, since cycle is usually repeated several times for each participant

Related strategies:

Role play, demonstration

INTERVIEW

An *interview* is a means of using a resource person who does not make a prepared speech. The resource person is asked questions by participants. Questions can be spontaneous or developed in advance and given to the resource person to allow time for preparation.

When to use:

To obtain from a resource person the information that most interests the participants

To create a relaxed and open environment when dealing with a resource person

Requirements:

A comfortable setting in which the group can meet

Advantages:

Resource person will discuss items of most interest to participants

Allows for give and take among participants and resource person

Often enjoyable for resource person, who need not prepare a formal
lecture

Considerations:

Resource person must be flexible and comfortable in such an
unstructured situation

Discussion can go off on a tangent that may be interesting but may
not focus on learning objectives

It is best to prepare some questions in advance to alert the resource
person to participant interests and to begin the discussion

Some verbal participants may monopolize questioning. The instructor may need to be a moderator and keep discussion open and
moving

Best if used with groups of under 20 participants

An alternative is a dialogue, in which two people have a conversation in front of the group. That may best be used in a larger group.
Conversation may be between the resource person and one or more
participants or between two resource people

Related strategies:

Lecture, panel

LEARNING CONTRACTS

The *learning contract* is a document, drawn up by a participant in
consultation with the instructor, specifying: (1) the learning goals for the
particular learning experience, (2) the methods by which the participant
intends to accomplish those goals, and (3) the method of evaluation.
During the course of the learning, the instructor must be available to
provide counsel, direction, and resources. The contract can be renego-
tiated, if circumstances warrant.

When to use:

For almost all learning situations

Requirements:

Paper

Advantages:

Fosters self-reliance and self-understanding

Individuals can learn in the styles to which they are best suited

Learning can be individualized/personalized

Participant is involved in active evaluation of own progress

Fosters a great measure of personal pride and a high level of commitment

Relatively inexpensive (in terms of time and money) to implement

Places major responsibility for learning on the participant

Considerations:

Demands strong motivation by participant

Requires role reorientation for both the participant and the instructor

May foster a feeling of undue pressure on the participant that may heighten the anxiety level during the learning process

Contract is time consuming to develop

Contracts are in effect over a period of time, usually two to three months, however they can be modified and used in shorter time frames

Related strategies:

Self-study, correspondence courses

LECTURE

A prepared, oral presentation delivered by a resource person to a group of participants is called a *lecture*. Since it is a one-way presentation in which the participants are essentially passive, it should be enhanced with visual aids and be coupled with a more active strategy (e.g., discussion or exercise). A lecture can be delivered to any size group and can be of any duration; however, briefer lectures (15–30 minutes) are the most effective.

When to use:

To inform group of policies and practices

To relay factual information

To introduce and/or explain a concept or theory

Requirements:

Podium and amplification equipment, if necessary

Sufficient space for all participants to see and hear

Advantages:

Covers a large body of information in a short period of time

Relatively easy to prepare and deliver

Inexpensive

Allows many people to hear the same message

Considerations:

Lectures must be well planned and concise

Many instructors lack the presentation skills necessary to be a good lecturer

Difficult to maintain interest

Retention of information is lower than with more participative strategies

Often effective to supplement with listening groups. Divide the participants into general groups, each of which is assigned the task of listening to and observing an assigned part of the lecture or speech and asked to do something (e.g., develop questions, critique research points, etc.)

Related strategies:

Panel, interview, film or video, demonstration

PANEL

The *panel* strategy is a conversation, by several persons, in front of an audience. A group of three to five experts presents short prepared statements. The statements are discussed by the panel members, and questions from the audience are answered. A moderator introduces, coordinates, and often participates in the discussion.

When to use:

To open or conclude the study of a topic

To expose participants to the ideas and opinions of several resource people

To surface differing points of view on a topic, similar to but not as structured as a debate

Requirements:

Chairs for panel members placed to face the participants

Sufficient space for all the participants to see and hear

Amplification equipment, if needed

Advantages:

Can develop an awareness of the complexity of various issues

Exposes participants to several resource people in the same session

Often enjoyable for resource people. Requires little formal preparation beyond the opening statement

A lively panel discussion can be very enlightening and, at times, entertaining

Questioning by participants increases participation and ensures that panel members will discuss points that interest the group

Considerations:

A group of experts can be expensive to assemble, although the cost could be reduced through the use of technology (e.g., teleconference)

Panel members must be at ease and willing to be challenged on issues

A good moderator is essential, in order to prevent one or two panel members from dominating the discussion

Participants are relatively passive

Participants may be hesitant to ask questions. One technique would be to have the participants write questions on pieces of paper and submit them to the moderator to ask to the panelists

Related strategies:

Interview, lecture

PROGRAMMED INSTRUCTION

Programmed instruction is a highly structured form of self-study. Material to be learned is presented to the participant in a series of carefully planned, sequential steps. The steps progress from simple to more complex levels of instruction. At each step, the participant must make a response that tests comprehension. The participant immediately receives feedback as to the correctness or incorrectness of a response. The learner proceeds through the course at his or her own pace.

When to use:

To learn detailed, factual material

To learn policies or procedures

As prework for a formal seminar

Requirements:

Programmed text, pencils, erasers, etc.

Advantages:

Orderly development of skills/knowledge

In-depth learning, especially of factual material

Provides reinforcement without an instructor

Self-paced

High learner involvement by constantly answering questions

Easy to administer

Some are reusable. Tend to have a long shelf life

Relatively inexpensive to purchase and use. Permits decentralized training

Considerations:

Development costs are high. It is extremely time consuming to write and test such materials. Considerations for deciding whether to use include:

Nature of material—should be for stable body of knowledge, so that frequent revision is unnecessary

Shelf life—three to five years is best

Usage—not for "one shot" program, rather for a continuous program with many potential learners

By their very nature, self-instructional programs are designed to be complete unto themselves, requiring no instructor intervention. This should be primary in the minds of those who develop and evaluate such programs. If instructions and/or content is unclear, programs lose effectiveness

The personality of a learner affects the success of the learning. People with high social needs tend to learn best in groups. People with low social needs tend to learn best alone and, therefore, learn well with this type of strategy

Good for knowledge acquisition but not for dealing with attitudes and feelings

Can be used in a group; however, there will be a need to account for different learning rates

Variations of programmed instruction can allow for different levels of knowledge. For example, in a scatter book the material is presented in a scrambled manner. Participants read portions of the text and are presented with several possible actions. They make the preferred choice and proceed to another situation, often skipping through the sequence of pages. If an incorrect choice is made, they are led to additional information or remedial exercises to help in arriving at the correct decision. In the workbook, a book of questions or written exercises provides spaces for the participants to write answers. The questions may be related to readings, to previous learning, or included content material

Related strategies:

Computer-assisted instruction (CAI), action maze, readings

QUESTIONING

The *questioning* strategy consists of developing and asking a variety of questions, designed to test learning and stimulate discussion. The questioning technique helps participants learn to use different modes of thinking, such as inquiry, analytical thinking, discovery, intuitive thinking, and problem solving.

When to use:

To test knowledge learned

To open and maintain discussion

To actively involve participants

Requirements:

None

Advantages:

Determines learning without a written test

Economical

Encourages participation

Shifts focus of learning from instructor to participants

Stimulates alternative ways of looking at problems and solutions

Maintains interest

Considerations:

Questions should be developed in advance. There is the need to develop appropriate questions (e.g., closed questions for testing, open for discussion)

Instructor requires skills in developing and delivering questions

Instructor requires good listening skills

One or two people may want to provide all the answers

The instructor may have to call on people to get maximum participation

Some participants may be hesitant to speak and may need to be drawn out

Related strategies:

Discussion

READINGS

Readings are the printed matter assigned to individuals in the form of articles, books, or pamphlets. All the participants can read the same material, or the readings can be individualized. Readings are often coupled with a study guide or discussion questions for use during a class session.

When to use:

To present factual material

To present policies and procedures

For preseminar assignments or homework

For postseminar materials

Requirements:

Printed matter

Advantages:

Economical, if materials are readily available

Self-paced. The time needed depends on participant's reading skill and comprehension ability. Can be done at participant's convenience

Ensures that all participants will have a common body of knowledge available to them

If used as prework, does not take seminar time that could be used for a discussion of the readings

Considerations:

Selection of relevant articles. Each reading should be carefully chosen and edited to meet the program's needs. Often, published materials include information that is not directly related to the topic. Select only the portions of such materials that are germane. Assigning too much material without proper guidance will often result in a low participant completion rate

Retention of information is lower than more participative methods

While the participants are active, the focus of their attention may or may not be on the relevant subject matter. This is especially true if the readings have not been written specifically for the program. If possible, readings should be organized into a self-study package. These help to ensure that participants will focus on the important issues. The guidance provided in such a package could be in the form of outlines for notetaking, specific study questions related to the important issues, or exercises and/or case studies for application of the learning

It is often effective to have participants read material and make a report to the group, especially if different participants in a class are assigned different readings

Also related to an annotated reading list, in which participants research available literature on a subject matter, read or review materials, describe the contents in a short paragraph, and provide bibliographical information. This is especially useful for post-cominar readings

Related strategies:

Programmed instruction

ROLE PLAY

A strategy of human interaction involving realistic behavior in nonjob settings is called *role playing*. Two or more role players are presented with a hypothetical problem or conflict with which they must attempt to deal. Only a basic description of the role and setting is provided. The role players must improvise and respond spontaneously to each other. Observers critically view the interaction. Following the enactment, role players and observers analyze what has taken place. Through role playing, participants experience their own behavior and emotions and how they affect others in an interactive situation.

When to use:

To practice skills learned in such areas as problem solving, counseling, and interviewing

To promote understanding of the viewpoints and feelings of other persons

To encourage insight into attitudes and behavior

If videotaped and replayed, to gain awareness of one's own style and the reactions of others

Requirements:

Role situation sheets for each player. Guidelines for critiquing and copies of both roles for the observers

Sufficient space for players, far enough from observers to allow free flow of conversation but close enough for good observation

Videotaping equipment, if used

Advantages:

Allows participants to experience and try out new learning and receive immediate feedback

Totally involves participants

Is relatively easy to develop

Provides some realism

Economical, unless video equipment is rented for taping

Can be enjoyed

Considerations:

Can be difficult to use. The instructor must be able to set a climate in which the participants are comfortable enough to role play and do not feel threatened

Must be introduced carefully, because confusing or misunderstood instructions can detract from the effectiveness of the strategy. Care must be taken to ensure that the word "play" is not misinterpreted. The aim is to present a realistic situation and to discourage participants from unrealistic "clowning" or from deliberately presenting confusing facts or giving misleading information

Instructor must ensure that the discussion that follows a role play is objective and constructive and does not become a personal attack on the players

Can be administered in a number of different ways: multiple role playing, in which the entire class is grouped into dyads and play without an observer; triads, with an observer; single group in which two people role play in front of a large group; or teams in which teams prepare, select representative players, and coach their players. Can also include role reversal, in which case players play their roles to a conclusion and then switch roles and "replay" the situation

Somewhat time consuming. Most role plays are 7–10 minutes in duration, and the participants may need 10 minutes to prepare

The critique session, including video replay, usually lasts 15–20 minutes or longer

Care must be taken in developing roles to ensure that the roles are consistent. There should be differences in the perceptions of the two roles but not in the facts of the situation. Avoid using funny or weird names or including too much extraneous information

Related strategies:

Interactive modeling, simulation, game, case study

SIMULATION

Simulation is a representation of a real-life situation—usually a situation requiring appropriate actions and reactions or a situation requiring the demonstration of technical expertise. For some, learning simulations often involve the use of computers or other machinery. Simulations may be relatively simple or quite complex. Some of the most complex are the simulators used to instruct astronauts and pilots. Depending upon the type of learning, simulations may be used by one person or by a group. The number of participants will be determined in part by how many would perform the activity in the "real world."

When to use:

To assess previous learning

To demonstrate technical ability

To bridge between learning and real life

Requirements:

Equipment as needed for simulation

Ample facilities

Advantages:

Presents a situation as close to real life as any learning experience can be. Participants feel real-life stresses associated with the activity.

Activity involves the participant through hands-on experience

Provides individual activity and assessment

Motivates interest

Considerations:

Usually very expensive to develop and maintain. There are high equipment costs and a long development time

Must be specifically developed for each situation, consequently few commercial products are available. Developers must have both technical and educational expertise

Instructors often play role of job supervisor as well as facilitator/evaluator role

Related strategies:

Games, computer-assisted instruction (CAI), role play

SKIT

The *skit* is a short, rehearsed, dramatic presentation, acted from a prepared script. It dramatizes an incident that illustrates a problem or a situation. "Actors" can either be instructors and/or participants. Skits can be an effective way to create situations similar to those created by role plays. While the lack of participant involvement may make them less effective learning experiences than role plays, they are less threatening and easier to use.

When to use:

To demonstrate a procedure or technique

To present a situation, usually an interpersonal problem situation, for the group to discuss

To surface issues

Requirements:

Script and props

Space for "stage" and audience

Advantages:

Roles are rehearsed so that expected action will take place as designed

Members involved in a skit have more responsibility to the purpose of learning than those in role play

A good attention getter, often used to initiate a learning experience

Creates interest in a subject

Usually inexpensive to construct and produce

Entertaining as well as informative

Good way to demonstrate a process

Considerations:

"Actors" may not be totally secure and confident about performing in front of others. Rehearsals take time but are essential

Difficult to find a skit that specifically meets the goals and objectives of a learning experience and a facilitator. It may require special writing

Difficult to include important points of learning experience in a short skit

Difficult to locate skits already prepared for the educational purposes of adults, since most available materials in skits are related to children or social groups

More time consuming to construct, rehearse, and produce than more traditional learning strategies

Requires imagination and creativity on the part of the facilitator

At times, more attention may be focused on the behavior of the players than on the issues for which the skit is being performed

Instructor must be able to lead the group in discussing the issues that surface in the skit

Related strategies:

Role play, interactive modeling, videotape presentations, demonstration

WORK GROUP

Three to eight individuals working together on a specific task to produce some specific output (e.g., suggestions, solutions to a problem, etc.) is called a *work group*. Its purpose is usually to apply learning to solve a problem. It should not be used to introduce new material.

When to use:

To demonstrate and apply learning

To gather questions and/or concerns from the group

To practice making decisions in groups

To encourage teamwork

For case studies, games, or simulations

Requirements:

Ample space for each group to work, perhaps separate break-out rooms

Flipcharts and markers

Advantages:

Active participation by all the participants

Encourages participation by those who are hesitant to speak in a large group

Allows participants to help each other, fosters teamwork

Group answers and/or ideas are often more effective than those of individuals

Considerations:

Time consuming. A work group should last a minimum of 30 minutes, often much longer. Time should be built in for moving to and from break-out rooms, if used. Ample time is needed to discuss the results

Groups may need to choose a spokesperson to record results and report the results back to the whole group. The format of these reports should be understood before the group begins work

Instructor's role is to be sure the assignment and the instruction are clearly understood. The instructor should arrange logistics, materials, and keep group aware of time limitation, and he or she should be available, as needed

Results of work groups should be communicated to the total group. This can be done by spokespersons reporting, by posting all the results and reviewing them, by groups exchanging results and critiquing each other, or by having a general discussion

Related strategies:

Buzz group, discussion

BIBLIOGRAPHY

Craig, Robert L., and Lester R. Bittel, eds. *Training and Development Handbook.* New York: McGraw-Hill, 1967.

Davis, Larry Nolan, and Earl McCallon. *Planning, Conducting, Evaluating Workshops.* Austin, Tex.: Learning Concepts, 1974.

Eisenberg, Helen, and Larry Eisenberg. *The Handbook of Skits and Stunts.* New York: Association Press, 1954.

Engel, Herbert M. *Handbook of Creative Learning Exercises.* Houston: Gulf Publishing Company, 1973.

Espick, James E., and Bill Williams. *Developing Programmed Instructional Materials: A Handbook for Program Writers.* Belmont, Cal.: Fearon, 1967.

Gillispie, Phillip H. *Learning Through Simulation Games.* New York: Paulist Press, 1973.

Graham, Robert G., and Clifford F. Gray. *Business Games Handbook.* New York: American Management, 1969.

Gueulette, David, ed. *Microcomputers for Adult Learning*. Chicago, Ill.: Follet, 1983.

Horn, Robert C., and Anne Cleaves, eds. *The Guide to Simulations/Games for Education and Training*. Beverly Hills, Cal.: Sage Publications, 1980.

Johnson, Kenneth G., John J. Senatore, Mark C. Liebig, and Gene Menor. *Nothing Never Happens*. Beverly Hills, Cal.: Glencoe Press, 1974.

Kearsley, Greg. *Computer Based Training*. New York: Addison-Wesley, 1983.

Klein, Alan F. *How to Use Role Playing Effectively*. New York: Association Press, 1959.

Knowles, Malcolm. *Self-Directed Learning*. New York: Association Press, 1975.

Linstone, Harold A., and Murray Turloff, eds. *The Delphi Method: Techniques and Applications*. Reading, Mass.: Addison-Wesley, 1975.

Maier, Norman R.F., Ayesha, A., and Allen R. Solem. *The Role Play Technique: A Handbook for Management and Leadership Practice*. La Jolla, Cal.: University Associates Press, 1975.

Morris, Kenneth T., and Kenneth M. Cinnamoi. *A Handbook of Non-Verbal Group Exercises*. Kansas City, Mo.: Applied Skills, Press, 1975.

————. *A Handbook of Verbal Group Exercises*. Kansas City, Mo.: Applied Skills Press, 1974.

Morris, Kenneth T., Ph.D. and Kenneth M. Cinnamoi. *A Handbook of Non-Verbal Group Exercises*. Kansas City: Applied Skills Press, 1975.

————. *A Handbook of Verbal Group Exercises*. Kansas City: Applied Skills Press, 1974.

Nadler, Leonard, *Designing Training Programs: The Critical Events Model*. Reading, Mass.: Addison-Wesley, 1982.

Newstrom, John W., and Edward E. Scannell. *Games Trainees Play*. New York: McGraw-Hill, 1980.

Pfeiffer, William, and John Jones. *The Annual Handbooks for Group Facilitation*. 11 vols. Iowa City: University Associates Press, 1982.

Pfeiffer, William, and John Jones. *A Handbook of Structured Experiences for Human Relations Training*. 8 vols. Iowa City: University Associates Press, 1981.

Pigors, Paul, and Faith Pigors. *Case Method in Human Relations: The Incident Process*. New York: McGraw-Hill, 1961.

Potter, David, and Martin P. Anderson. *Discussion: A Guide to Effective Practice*. Belmont, Cal.: Wadsworth Publishing Company, 1970.

Stenzel, Anna K., and Helen M. Feeney. *Learning by the Case Method*. New York: Seabury Press, 1970.

Tracy, William R. *Designing Training and Development Systems*. New York: American Management Association, 1971.

Zoll, Allen A. *Dynamic Management Education*. 2d ed. Reading, Mass.: Addison-Wesley, 1969.

Instructional Strategies: Media

AUGUST K. SPECTOR

In Chapter 9 you found a discussion of instructional strategies that do not use media. In this chapter, however, Spector shares with us some history, pertinent factors, and descriptions of some of the most commonly used media.

Technology of various sorts has had a decided and important impact on the use of media in learning. It has been so pervasive that we sometimes hear of "instructional technology." The term has too many definitions to be generally accepted, but it does reflect the blending of technology with instruction.

This chapter provides only knowledge related to the use of media. Competency in using media can come only from specific learning experiences and the opportunity to apply that learning. For instructional strategists, designers, and facilitators, this information is a must, as these subroles require competency in either designing or using media. Others in HRD may not need to devote as much time to media, as technology is constantly changing. For those people, this chapter provides the essentials regarding the use of media for learning.

August K. Spector is a supervisory and management development specialist with the U.S. Nuclear Regulatory Commission. He has served as director, employee training and development, Bureau of Land Management, Department of the Interior; education technologist, U.S. Civil Service Commission; and director, educational communications, Fort Lee Schools. He was founder and president of the Federal Educational Technology Association.

Throughout the history of human resource development, change and experimentation have been important. This is as it should be. Practitioners in any dynamic area of endeavor are never complacent but are always restless, in search of something better. In recent years, however, there has been an unprecedented upsurge of change. This rapid change has been most evident in the application of technology to the learning process. The use of educational television, teaching machines, learning laboratories, computers, and myriad other devices and techniques has become increasingly popular. In the 1920s and 1930s, the expanding technology in communications sparked the notion of "visual instruction," that is, the use of still photography and motion pictures to add realism to the traditional instructor's lecture. When sound films and other media that used both sound and images became feasible, this movement became known as "audiovisual instruction." As instructors became more experienced in the use of technology and as technological devices became more sophisticated, a new philosophy and mode of operation in the field developed and became known as "instructional technology."

Instructional technology has evolved into a much broader field than the earlier audiovisual instruction. Audiovisual instruction is merely one aspect of instructional technology, for instructional technology is involved with the "facilitation of human learning through the systematic identification, development, organization, and utilization of a full range of learning resources and through the management of these processes."[1] Instructional technology concerns itself with three broad interest areas: (1) the use of a varied range of resources for learning, of which audiovisual resources are only one, (2) the investigation of individualized and personalized learning, and (3) the use of a systems approach to facilitate the learning process. This chapter will consider only one small part of instructional technology—that of audiovisual media. Other chapters consider the systems approach and various learning methods and techniques that encourage individualization.

In 1964, Marshall McLuhan wrote the important and controversial book *Understanding Media*. McLuhan postulated that while messages in themselves have meaning, the medium by which they are transmitted is also of importance in understanding their meaning. In other words, the medium also is a message. When one views or hears a message, different meanings can be interpreted from it, depending upon the medium by which this message is communicated. For example, Moses communicated an important message, the Ten Commandments. The ten statutes he communicated were simple, direct, and on surface easily understood. But imagine the impact of Moses' message on the people when he came down from the mountain holding two huge stone tablets with the ten commandments finely inscribed. The medium—the stone tablets—certainly made an impact, but it also conveyed additional messages, such as authority, permanence, importance. The stones represented a powerful medium, one that not only communicated the important message but delivered it in a way that had its own significance.

The human resource developer, acting in the role of a learning specialist, utilizes various forms of media to deliver the message to the learners. Whether in a formal classroom learning situation where the instructor enhances the lesson by utilizing a motion picture film to clarify a particular principle, or in a completely automated learning environment in which the learners interact with a computer, or in an informal, on-the-job training situation where the supervisor uses a lathe to teach a new employee the rudiments of machining, the instructor will use one or a combination of media to deliver a message.

Prior to World War II, the human resource developer did not generally have available a wide assortment of instructional media from which to choose. There had been the recognition in the armed services, prior to World War II, that instructional technology held important implications for military instruction. During World War I, the military had introduced instructional films, but after the war this effort was continued only on a limited basis. In the 1920s, visual and audio media did emerge, but these were rather limited in scope. Learning specialists utilized the 35mm and 16mm movie films and sometimes filmstrips and lantern slides to emphasize teaching points. These instructional media were generally difficult to create as well as expensive to produce. Still photographs and hand-drawn charts were often utilized to indicate, for example, location of tools and parts or to illustrate the flow of industrial processes, but for the most part, the wide-scale use of audio and visual instructional media was nonexistent prior to the war.

As the United States and its allies began to ready themselves for the war effort, a tremendous learning need occurred. To provide sound, economical, and consistent instruction for industrial and governmental employees, as well as for military personnel, large-scale use of audio and visual aids was developed.

It was during this period that audio and visual media had its first great influence upon industry and military instruction. This was brought about by four important developments:

1. The establishment of training programs (e.g., learning) in industry and in the military that produced unprecedented demands for an effective technology of instruction.

2. The application of a technology of instruction based on prewar scientific research.

3. The emergence of an official governmental policy that encouraged the production of a wide variety of instructional materials and a broad use of instructional media.

4. The allocation of financial resources for the implementation of this technology of instruction.[2]

The early days were difficult indeed for those human resource developers charged with pioneering this new form of instructional technology, since not everyone concerned was convinced that audio and visual media could answer the complex problems of the period.

Floyde E. Brooker was appointed the director of the Division of Visual Aids for War Training, a section of the U.S. Office of Education. One of his first concerns was to promote instructional films by informing congressmen, government officials, HRD practitioners, and laymen of their virtues. In June, 1941, the first instructional film by his division was completed. A small group of persons was invited to learn, firsthand, how film could make instruction more effective. Brooker recounts the following insight into those early days.

The projection was in a huge auditorium with a projector in the last stages of usefulness. The curtains at the windows, billowing open with every puff of air, admitted beams of bright sunlight. The sound drizzled through a sound system that provided its own static. The room was far too light—when the curtains billowed, the dim picture disappeared. No audience ever sat more tensely than the four individuals who were almost lost in the middle of the auditorium. The picture ended...and almost at once the argument started. It's confusing...it goes too fast...it's a step by step explanation...the picture would be clear if the curtains would not billow open...the film is made for trainees who have already seen the machine.

The suggestion was made that the film be shown again. There was no rewind equipment so two of the individuals improvised by putting the 35mm reels on pencils to do the job of rewinding. The second showing was started. Brief splashes of light continued to wash the picture off the screen...and usually at key points of explanation. This time it became clear that the individuals experienced in shop work viewed the picture in one way, and those inexperienced in shop work viewed it another. Some thought it too elementary while the others thought it too technical; some thought it went too slowly, the others were certain it went too fast. Finally, it was decided to await the coming of the second and third pictures before arriving at any decision. It was also decided that vocational shop instructors were really the ones to make the decision.[3]

During this period, military and industrial human resource developers used many forms of instructional media, including projected, graphic, sound, three-dimensional, supplementary manuals and guidebooks, handbooks, and job performance aids. Motion picture film, filmstrips, and photographic slides were used to a great extent. Instructional "kits" were developed that contained complete written lesson plans, a 16mm film, and a set of filmstrips. These kits were distributed worldwide to instructors. The "vu-graph," or overhead projector, was perfected. This device enabled the instructor to project an image, which was hand drawn or printed on a plastic sheet, onto a screen. The vu-graph provided the instructor with added flexibility, since the projected "wall chart" was portable, easily stored, and easily produced. Crude audiotape recordings were made, utilizing an audiotape recorder that played tape made from paper. The thin paper tape was impregnated with ferro oxide material, which, when passed by an electromagnet, would realign the ferro oxide material so a representation of the original sound could be heard when played back. Of course, the audiodisc, or phonograph record, was utilized. One machine combined a phonograph record with a 35mm filmstrip, so learners could not only view still pictures but also hear a narration. Because the early attempts at mediation of instruction seem "old," they should not be considered "out of date." All of these forms of media are still in wide use today. The overhead projector, audio tape recorder, 16mm motion picture projector, and 35mm slide projector are considered by many to be the prime workhorses of audiovisual equipment today.

By and large, these media devices and the images and sounds they projected were considered aids to the prime "medium"—the instructor. Audiovisual aids, as they became known, were designed to supplement the "real" teaching done by the instructor. They were considered useful in providing "motivation" for learning and/or providing a certain amount of realism to the classroom learning environment.

As the war effort grew more intense, military and industrial human resource developers realized they needed more motivating, effective, and efficient instructional techniques. Films, filmstrips, and slides were useful in bringing the outside environment to the classroom-bound learner, but these were found to be limiting. There was great interest in making the learning setting as close to the actual real job situation as possible. A method of simulating an actual work environment was needed. It was found that simplified versions of a real-life situation could be simulated. When a learner was exposed to such an activity, it was possible to learn the characteristics of the real-life situation and eventually, through practice, become proficient in performing the required task. After gaining more proficiency in the simulated environment, the learner would be more apt to transfer that performance to the actual real-life situation.

The Army Corps of Engineers at Ft. Belvoir, Va. instructed mechanical engineers in a realistically simulated "tropic" environment by building a room where men working in a high temperature, high humidity environment were taught installation and maintenance of air-conditioning equipment. Models, mockups, and other devices became popular instructional aids, used to simulate real job-related conditions. Probably the most famous simulator was the *link flight trainer*. The link flight trainer provided a cadet pilot with a moving view of the earth over which he was "flying," accompanied by the realistic sound of aircraft engines on recordings. By using the link trainer, the cadet pilot would learn how to fly an airplane. The link trainer, or *flight simulator* as it is called today, was used by pilots before actually flying a real airplane. This obviously saved many lives, as well as airplanes, from disaster, but it also required the flight school to have fewer instructional airplanes at its disposal, thus reducing costs.

Learning simulators, though, were not the first attempt at integrating the machine and the human learner into some instructional system. Out of the interest of a small group of behavioral psychologists working in the 1920s and 1930s grew the forerunner of the modern approach to machine-mediated instruction. In 1926, Sidney L. Pressey of Ohio State University designed a machine originally conceived as a testing device. He soon found that this device had potential for instructional purposes. The Pressey machine provided a readout of student test scores that was completely visual and became the forerunner of the present day mechanical teaching machine. J.C. Peterson, one of Pressey's students, devised "chemosheets" in which the learner checked answers to multiple-choice questions with a swab. When the wrong answer was selected, it instantly turned red, and the correct ones just as quickly turned blue. In the early 1950s, Norman A. Crowder developed a programmed teaching device for the U.S. Air Force. This device utilized a "scrambled textbook" for teaching the learner to troubleshoot electronic equipment.

However, B.F. Skinner can be attributed with commonly popularizing "teaching machines." In 1954, Skinner, adding to the pioneering efforts of Pressey, began to publish his theories of human learning. In an experiment, he taught pigeons how to play table tennis by using the methods of reward and punishment. This same principle, according to Skinner, was at the root of learning and teaching machines. The difference was that instead of receiving a kernel of corn for the correct response, the learner got the satisfaction of knowing that the answer was correct. Skinner's "operant conditioning theory" holds that for every stimulus there is a response that brings about a new stimulus. This principle of stimulus-response is basic to our more sophisticated computerized "teaching machines" of today.

Out of these early experiments and the resulting philosophy toward learning, the technology of programmed instruction developed. Programmed instruction may or may not require the use of mechanical presentation devices or a "teaching machine." Programmed instruction may be presented utilizing various media, such as printed text materials, live instructor-student interaction, simple mechanical machines, or sophisticated computers. The audiovisual device is used merely as a vehicle for presenting the instructional materials.

Essentially, programmed instruction has these basic characteristics:

1. One relatively small unit of information, known as a *stimulus*, is presented at a time. A stimulus may consist of either a statement and/or question posed to the learner.

2. A *response* to the stimulus is then required of the learner. This may consist of the completion of a statement, an answer to a question, or the performance of some task in response to the stimulus.

3. The learner immediately receives *feedback* about the response. That is, the learner finds out immediately whether the answer is correct or not.

4. The feature of immediate feedback provides *reinforcement*— either positive or negative—to the learner. The program may be designed to explain why a response was incorrect, or it may provide another stimulus-response sequence for the learner to respond to, to clarify the incorrect answer. Of course, if the answer was correct, the learner would be directed to new information.

The newly found interest in programmed learning was misdirected at first. Unfortunately, as with many innovations in learning, there was a tendency to overuse and even abuse the machines to the extent where their value was questioned. Some effort went into promoting "gadgets" instead of the instructional materials so necessary for learning. Experience eventually taught learning specialists that the quality of the instructional materials was more important than the devices used to display that material. The human resource developer learned that, if kept in the proper perspective, technology can contribute much to the development of a well-rounded learning program.

From 1941–1955, the first significant changes in audiovisual instructional technology, as applied to industrial and military learning, occurred. Thousands of human resource developers and millions of adult learners were "exposed" to the new instructional technology. This resulted in an increased sensitivity to the applicability of technology to solve instructional problems. There evolved an increased sophistication concerning the function and role of instructional media and the personnel involved with implementing this media within the total context of the learning program. Thus, following World War II, a period of expansion began in the use of audiovisual materials in the learning arena.

During the early 1950s, programmed instruction was developed, and the more traditional audiovisual aids, as well as the flight simulator, were perfected. However, from 1955 to the 1970s, television began to take on some importance in the teaching-learning process. The early days of television were, by our standards, quite crude and amateurish. Large companies and governmental organizations such as General Electric, Westinghouse, Ford Motor Company, Texas Instruments, the U.S. Army, and many others began to utilize television in their HRD operations.

The early efforts of TV were concerned with broadcast television; in other words, the learning program was distributed over the airwaves. Sophisticated educational television broadcast facilities were established in the late 1950s and early 1960s by government, industry, and universities. These educational television stations broadcast training, education, and development programs within a local area.

Learners were scheduled to attend the learning session at specified times, in some instances, causing disruption to the normal workflow. Some programs were broadcast during the early morning hours, in order to provide an opportunity for the individual to learn before going to work. Examples of these early broadcasts were "Sunrise Semester," "Continental Classroom," and "College of the Air." Television programs were either broadcast "live" or were crudely prerecorded on kinescopes (16mm film of the TV screen). Hence, one of the drawbacks of early television was the lack of a convenient method of recording and distributing the video image. In 1959 the first magnetic videotape recorders were put into commercial use. The videotape recorder then made it possible to record the video and audio signal on a plastic tape for later playback. For the first time, learning specialists could create their own television instructional materials and easily distribute them to the instructional site.

As TV became more sophisticated in the early 1960s and more accessible, due to cost reductions and wide distribution of equipment, new uses were found for it in learning situations. At first, videotape programs were used in much the same way as 16mm film—as an aid to the classroom instructor—but other uses were developed. Dual-track audio was available for producing programs in two languages for audiences of mixed cultures; interactive TV was developed in which the learners responded to the program material, and the program material "responded" to the learners in a fashion similar to the "old" teaching machines. Recordings of learners' performances were made, played back, and evaluated with the learner, in order to improve performance. Television was also used in simulators of various types.

One problem with early TV was the scarcity of professionally produced instructional materials that were available commercially. During the 1960s, most industrial applications of TV consisted of in-house-produced programs, primarily concerned with technical subjects. Today this is no longer true. As television became more popular and the demand for learning programs grew, commercial enterprises began to develop programs specifically designed for learning purposes. Today commercially designed TV programs are available in many content areas, such as management and supervision, electronics, auto assembly and mechanics, computer programming and operation, safety, etc.

During the past several years, we have experienced another change in audiovisual instructional technology. This change has been brought about by the computer. Utilizing the computer's ability to process information rapidly and the programmed instructional technology developed from 1950–1970, learning specialists have at their disposal a device that can act very much as Plato did in his dialogue with Meno. The computer can act as an electronic tutor, providing not only feedback and reinforcement but also a means of practicing what was learned.

Currently, the computer-aided instructional medium is beginning to take on more importance in industrial and governmental human resources development activities as well as in the schools, particularly postsecondary educational institutions. This is evident by the proliferation of small microcomputers found in many HRD programs, as well as within employees' homes. In the future, one can anticipate that the use of computers, as media, will proliferate. Developments in the area of computers are occurring very rapidly, and the reader is referred to a more detailed discussion in Chapter 11 on computer-based learning.

The technological developments of the past few decades have affected the role of the traditional classroom instructor. These decades have been a transition period from the traditional, instructor-controlled teaching environment, primarily verbally orientated, to a learning environment in which audio and visual media supplement the instructor's face-to-face learner contact. In the past, the successful instructor was the one who managed learners. Today, due to the rapid change in information technology, the successful instructor is not only a manager of learners but a manager of information. The instructor attempts to perform in such a way that participants can learn more in less time. The management of information to promote effective and efficient learning is vastly different from the traditional functions of instruction. The new role of the instructor emerges as that of a learning facilitator who works not only with learners but with subject matter specialists, audiovisual specialists, computer specialists, and other technical and nontechnical specialists. These specialists conduct preliminary studies to decide on the specific content to be learned; they design and develop audiovisual instructional materials and other sophisticated techniques that will help the learner to learn. The instructor, in a sense, becomes responsible for managing the instructional process, for performing the various maneuvers, for designing and administering tests to ensure that the learners can perform the actual tasks, and for providing guidance to learners in order to help them acquire the necessary skill and knowledge. To some, these changes have been unsettling and have caused much anxiety. To others, these changes have been a challenge to develop themselves and their profession.

Our technological advancements have provided us with computer-assisted and computer-managed instruction/learning systems; sophisticated telecommunication network interface capability through satellite, cable, and microwave technology; advanced visual and audiotechnology, consisting of machine-simulated speech; holography; three-dimensional visual systems; and simulated human movement. These advancements in technology place an emphasis on new forms of learning in nontraditional environments. Emphasis is placed upon individualized instruction, self-directed inquiry, selection of learning methods according to the learner's cognitive style, participation in learning programs in non–work-related sites, such as the home, automobile, or specialized individualized learning centers, as well as during flexible hours of the day or night. Now is a time when the traditional roles of the human resource developer are influenced by the advancements in technology, a time when the skills, knowledge, and attitude of the human resources developer require reevaluation and redirection. This is an exciting period for the developer of human resources.

TERMINOLOGY

If one reviews the professional literature in the field of instructional media, it will become evident that not all authorities agree on common definitions. At times, it becomes difficult to communicate properly if definitions are not universally accepted. In the space of this short chapter, one cannot solve this problem, but one can shed some light on the issue so that the human resource developer may begin to work toward clarification.

Media

The terms medium and media (plural) are generally used interchangeably. Objects such as motion picture film or a slide-tape presentation, including the necessary devices for projecting them, become instructional media when their function is to provide instruction. Instructional media can be considered part of an open system. Such open systems actively interact with their environment, influencing and being influenced by the environment. Communications theory considers the medium as the channel or network of channels connecting the sender and the receiver. Messages may reach the receiver through various media. These media, in fact, act upon the message by shaping it or altering it according to the characteristics of the medium. Thus, the information conveyed through two different media may not convey the same message.

For example, a story verbally told to a group by an instructor may not convey the same meaning as the same story presented through the medium of film. The two media differ in their characteristics. The difference lies in what happens to information when it is communicated by one or the other medium. Every medium exerts its own influence on the message and, in this sense, becomes a part of the message. Thus, the medium and the message are inseparable. Prior to McLuhan's work, many instructors generally accepted that only the content of the instructional material (i.e., textbook, film, audiotape, etc.) was important to the learners' understanding. Today, it is generally recognized that the medium itself (i.e., textbook, film, audiotape, etc.) influences the learners' understanding of the content. The medium, in fact, can exhibit certain characteristics that may introduce new meaning to the message.

Properties

Instructional media are created and produced by people. Because of this, they are open to human modification and manipulation. The application of media to human resource development and their usage by the learning specialist to carry on the teaching-learning function, become important factors when considering the properties of media. By understanding these properties, the learning specialist will be better able to incorporate media into the teaching-learning process. According to Don Ely of Syracuse University, instructional media exhibit three major properties. These are the fixative property, the manipulative property, and the distributive property.

The Fixative Property.   This property permits the capture, preservation, and reconstitution of an object or event. Photographic film, audiotape, and videotape are raw materials for fixing objects and events in time. Once a photograph is made or a voice recorded, the information has been "saved" and is then available for reproduction at any time. This property enables the record of an event to be transported through time.

The Manipulative Property.   This permits the transformation of an object or event in many ways. The event can be speeded up, as in the opening of a flower bud that is recorded by time-lapse photography with a motion picture camera. Or an event may be slowed down by replaying a motion picture film or videotape at a slower speed than that at which it was recorded. For example, the reaction of chemicals can be observed through this manipulative approach. Action can be arrested, as in a still photograph. It can be reversed, as in a motion picture that is run backwards. Media can be edited. Audiotape may be used to present excerpts of a speech by cutting out irrelevant parts. Events occurring over a period of time may, for example, be sequenced and selected to create a film document. There is, of course, a danger of misinterpretation when audio and visual data are juxtaposed in such a fashion, because the record of the original event is altered in the process.

The Distributive Property.   "While the fixative property of the media allows us to transport an event through time, the distributive property permits us to transport an event through space, simultaneously presenting each of potentially millions of viewers with a virtually identical experience of an event." Once an object or event is recorded on film, tape, or the printed page, it can be reproduced in almost any location at any time. Further, with mass distribution systems, such as television and radio, the potential number of viewers and listeners is dramatically increased.[4]

Methods

The terms methods and media are often used interchangeably, but they are not synonymous (see Figure 10.1). A *method* is the procedure or process for attaining an instructional objective. *Media* are means by which the procedure or process is expressed. An example may help to clarify these differences. Travel by sea is a method of getting from one place to another. Some of the means by which this method of travel is realized are sailboat, cruise ship, oil tanker, and outboard motor boat. These means may be thought of as the media by which the method of sea travel is expressed. Instructional media serve the purpose of vehicles of transportation for helping learners acquire skill, attitudes, and knowledge, and for the instructor to deliver information.

The media utilized in the teaching-learning process involve the learner interacting with the medium, to varying degrees, on a continuum extending from learner controlled to instructor controlled. At one end of the continuum there is total active involvement with the medium by the

Method	Media
A procedure or process for attaining an objective	A channel of communication
Same method may be expressed by several different media	Includes hardware, such as projectors, screens, tape recorders, etc.
Includes methods such as lecture, demonstration, assigned reading, seminar, discussion, programmed instruction, etc.	Includes software, such as films, tapes, computer programs
	Same medium may be used to convey several methods
Examples: The demonstration method may be conveyed on videotape, film, or audiotape	
Programmed self-instructional method may be conveyed by various media, ranging from motion pictures to textbooks	Example: A single motion picture may present various methods, such as a demonstration, a lecture, or programmed self-instructional material

Figure 10.1. Comparison of method and media.

learner. This is due to the great amount of interaction required between the learner, for example, and the instructional medium.

This form is often referred to as *individualized instruction*. It presents instruction-utilizing media designed to treat learners, who learn at their own pace and are motivated by having the opportunity to match their individual needs to learning objectives, according to their individual needs. Learner-controlled media commonly present instruction by way of a programmed instructional format and utilize a mediated device (e.g., teaching machine, computer) to display lesson material and responses, maintain records of learner responses, and allow the learner to control the pace of instruction. Through the computer, for example, the learner is able to interact with the courseware on a one-to-one basis, "totally" interacting with the medium. The "live" instructor is not used except to originally design and/or program the computer with the courseware.

At the other extreme of the continuum, learner involvement is rather passive, while there is a high degree of "live" instructor control in the use of the medium. With instructor-controlled media, the learner merely hears and/or observes the message presented by the "live" instructor, for example, as in a classroom lecture where the instructor utilizes an overhead projector to present a diagram to a group of learners.

One can look upon this continuum as affecting the role of the human resource developer. As more and more learner-controlled learning occurs through mediated instruction, the role of the learning specialist will change from that of manager of instruction to that of manager of learning resources and media for the learner. More and more, in industry and government, we are finding that the successful human resource developers do not manage learners; they manage the media that learners utilize in their learning. This widening of emphasis to manager of instructional media allows the human resource developer to become more efficient as to the number of learners who can be influenced, as well as more effective in terms of the amount and quality of skills and knowledge gained by the learner. Therefore, the human resource developer, must be aware of the various methods and media available for the modern learner. The human resource developer must feel comfortable with less classroom-dependent, instructor-controlled instruction and with more individualized learner-controlled instruction.

Audiovisual Aids

Audiovisual aids may be considered one category of instructional media. *Audiovisual aids* consist of the various audio and/or visual media utilized by an instructor to enhance the lesson. Hence, AV aids are generally considered instructor-controlled media. AV aids come in various forms, such as mockups, models, demonstrations, exhibits, motion and still pictures, television, radio, audio recordings, etc. Aids can be highly complex or simple and mundane. AV aids are a means to an end, not ends in themselves. Instructors may use aids because they help them realize a lesson's objectives. AV aids may be used to motivate the learner, to supplement the instructor's lecture, or for a variety of purposes that help the instructor in the teaching process. When aids are used sensitively, they attract and hold attention, supplement the instructor's classroom presentation with verbal and visual information, and reduce the number of words that must be spoken by the instructor. Aids reinforce classroom activities and illustrate relationships in a way that is simply not possible with words. Aids must be used properly, however, or they will reduce rather than increase instructional effectiveness and efficiency.

GENERAL DESIGN CHARACTERISTICS OF AUDIOVISUAL INSTRUCTIONAL MATERIALS

Audiovisual instructional materials come in various formats, each designed for a particular purpose. Each specific media form (e.g., 35mm slides, overhead transparencies, motion picture film, and audio recordings) has its peculiar characteristics. There are, however, several general characteristics that may be considered when designing, developing, and producing such instructional materials.

Legibility

It may seem obvious that visual media should be legible to the learners, but all too often instructors do not utilize legible material. To be legible, visual material must be able to be seen and deciphered. Legibility is concerned with overall design, size of images, and proper contrast between images and colors. Legible images are not necessarily extremely large, but one must consider how far the learner will be from the projected material. Instructional visuals, viewed at close range (e.g., individualized instructional courseware) only have to be large enough to be seen clearly. If such materials are too large, viewer reading speed may be reduced. Furthermore, it will be less economical, as fewer items can be shown on each frame. One question comes to mind when designing a visual, "Can it be legible to the learner who will be farthest from the visual?"

Audio materials have their own form of legibility. Legible audio materials have clarity of sound, can be easily deciphered by the learner, and have the proper pitch, tone, and volume for the learners.

Often, the audio and visual courseware are quite legible, but the instructional hardware utilized to project them are not adequate. The equipment may be dirty or their motors improperly adjusted and oiled, causing unnecessary distracting noise. At other times, equipment being utilized has too limited a capacity for the room size. This is especially true when conducting a session in a large room with audiotape cassette players that have an undersized loudspeaker. Equipment that will enhance legibility must be utilized and is appropriate for the instructional situation.

Simplicity

It is often said, "There is beauty in simplicity." This is true of both visual and audio media. AV instructional material should be designed so that it is simple and to the point. If the material is simple, it will appeal to a broader audience; whereas, if it is complicated, it may meet with varying degrees of resistance. Furthermore, AV materials that are too complicated will not help the learner comprehend the instructional objective.

Because instructional material is simple in design does not mean it is unsophisticated (see Figure 10.2). We have learned from experience that an overhead projection, for example, generally should have no more than eight lines of information; it should have a title, usually in a different color than other art or lettering; and only relevant, essential information should be depicted. If more information is needed, additional visuals can be made. Eliminating nonessential information will cause less distraction for the learner and promote the effectiveness of the visual. Following these general guidelines will result in better legibility and less confusion for the learner.

Audio materials should certainly be simple and to the point. Audio distraction usually occurs in the form of loud or popular background music. Background music should be chosen carefully so as not to distract from the main verbal message, or, in multimedia presentations, from the visual message. Some instructors feel that a voice, popular with the learner, is necessary on an audiotape. This, too, can be distracting, since the learner may be more interested in the famous voice than in the message being communicated.

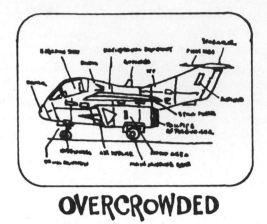

OVERCROWDED

SIMPLIFIED

Figure 10.2.   Simplifying overhead transparencies.

Accuracy

The difference between accuracy and realism is not always distinct.
Generally, *accuracy* means precision. Accurate audio and visual media
must depict information correctly. Statistical formulas, spelling, and
pronunciation of words must be correct.

This does not mean that sentence structure of an audio narration must
be the same as in written language, but it should be accurate spoken
language. We speak and hear language much differently than we read it.

The most important consideration in writing a script is to remember that it will be heard not read. Accuracy serves only to enhance the explanation and add to the realism of the media.

Realism means to depict real objects or events. The visual or audio material does not necessarily have to be "real," for quite often the message is depicted through cartoons or other symbolic illustrations. If the learning task requires actual objects or situations, then, obviously, realism becomes an important consideration.

Color

Color is an integral part of vision; therefore, exploiting the human ability to sense color can help the learner by enabling increased retention of what is learned. A predominant color, for example, can help focus learner attention on a particular part of the visual. Color coding letters, objects, or background is a technique to help the learner retain visual information. This can help the learner associate the color with the information to be learned.

The overuse of color can increase the complexity of the information to be transmitted beyond the information handling capacity of the learner. There can be too much color or the wrong combinations of colors in a visual. The use of incompatible color combinations can also create eye strain for the learner. For example, dark blue and red are such contrasting colors that eye strain can occur if these are used adjacent to each other in the same visual. Some colors produce feelings of excitement, hostility, or passiveness, or may affect the learner in other ways. The learning specialist should always think first of the learning objectives, considering how color or color combinations will affect the learner, and then design the visual accordingly.

Audio media has its "color" too. Often background sound effects are included with a narration to add "local color." The background sounds of actual operating machines, as the narrator explains their operation, can add a dimension of realism.

Durability

Often, much time and money is put into the design, development, and production of audio and visual instructional materials, so it is reasonable to expect them to be durable. Unfortunately, materials used for producing audio and visual materials are not durable by nature, for they are made of plastic, glass, and paper. Plastic materials can melt, glass materials can break, and paper materials can burn. Thus the need for careful storage and handling of these materials cannot be over emphasized. All 35 mm slides should be kept in plastic slide trays (glass mounts are not often used today, as it was found that mold can grow between the glass and the film) away from dust and stored in a dark, cool, dry location. Audiotape and videotape materials usually come prepackaged in their own cassette cases. These should be kept away from magnetic fields and stored in cool, dry locations. Overhead transparencies should be properly mounted in plastic or cardboard frames and stored in three-ring binder notebooks or boxes, again in a cool, dry, dark location. Audiovisual materials should not be stored in a pile, one item on top of another, as heavy weight, over a long period of time, may deform the soft materials and their cases. There are special treatments and chemicals on the market that can be used to prolong the life of audiovisual materials. While no materials will last forever, care in use and storage can considerably extend their useful life.

Manageability

To be useful, audiovisual materials must not only be instructionally sound but must be easily usable by the organization, the instructor, and the learner. Audiovisual materials must be designed so that the instructor will not have a difficult time using them in a teaching-learning situation. Instructional materials should save time and effort in the teaching-learning process and be cost effective in their production and use. If the instructor is required to travel, the material should be portable. The human resources developer will have to determine the need for standardization of the audiovisual equipment for these materials. The type of equipment chosen must be appropriate to the instructional objectives and courseware configuration. Careful attention should be given to choice, as the wrong decision may cause many wasted dollars and probably ineffective instruction. The proper management of standardization of equipment and courseware is based on several factors.

1. Compatibility and availability of courseware. Quite often particular courseware may work only in a specific manufacturer's device. The choice of such materials should be given careful consideration as to their long-term instructional value as well as cost effectiveness.
2. The ability to produce courseware on the local level. Courseware produced locally should have a configuration suitable to the hardware available.

3. Maintenance of courseware and equipment. Standardization will facilitate repair and the purchase of spare parts (i.e., bulbs, belts, etc.).

4. Compatibility with industry and government standards. Equipment and courseware that conform to such standards can be used interchangeably with all machines conforming to that standard. The prime consideration should be compatibility between multi-location instructional sites and among courseware manufacturers.

HARDWARE AND SOFTWARE

Confusion sometimes arises when distinguishing between audiovisual devices (hardware) and audiovisual instructional material (software or courseware). Audiovisual *hardware* refers to the equipment used to project, amplify, or otherwise display the instructional material. As indicated earlier, hardware can influence the message. Today, human resource developers are becoming more concerned with these influences and are beginning to study the relationship between human and machine.

For example, the configuration of a computer keyboard is of some concern to the human resource developer. Studies indicate that different configurations of the standard keyboard can either speed up or slow down the time it takes a learner to interact with the computer and can affect the level of errors in responding to questions. The elapse time—the time it takes for the computer to display new information after it receives a command—can affect attention span of the learner as well as the cost and efficiency of the session. Other concerns are color of the characters on the display screen, height and placement of equipment, environmental factors (e.g., room and furnishing color, background noise, and ventilation). The study of these relationships is known as *ergonomics*. Ergonomics will undoubtedly become more important as work progresses in understanding the relationship between humans and machines.

The variety of hardware is great. Hardware comes in all shapes and sizes. Each type serves a different purpose. Hardware can project images, magnify or demagnify, speed up or slow down motion and sound, amplify or deamplify sound, provide direct learner-machine interaction, carry out a didactic lesson with a learner by utilizing printed words and pictures, or even simulate voice communication. When planning the purchase of AV hardware, the human resource developer should consider the following:

1. Compatibility with existing and planned future courseware materials
2. Effectiveness in communicating the message
3. Availability of repair facility and replacement parts
4. Cost of both the initial purchase and long-term upkeep
5. Ease of utilization by the learner and/or instructor
6. Potential for modification and/or interface with other instructional hardware items
7. Compatibility with other hardware already being utilized or planned for purchase within the organizational system
8. Availability of commercial courseware materials and/or ease in producing in-house materials
9. Distribution and portability of equipment in multilocation organizations
10. Distribution of software in multilocation organizations. This may include transmission via telephone, microwave, or satellite
11. Vendor and manufacturer reliability or ability to "stand-behind-the-product"
12. Potential for obsolescence due to a newer technology or discontinuance of the product by the manufacturer
13. Electrical and power considerations of equipment. This is especially important if equipment will be used in various countries that may have different electrical capacities.

The instructional content materials that the learner is expected to master are known as *software* or *courseware*. The term software is derived from computer terminology and is generally considered synonymous with courseware. Courseware may consist of such diverse media as a 16mm film of some industrial operation, a job performance aid illustrating an administrative procedure, or programmed textbook material that is used to teach English grammar. The variety of courseware materials is limited only by the imagination of the instructional designer. Courseware generally requires hardware for display, but the human resource developer should not be dissuaded from utilizing the large variety of courseware formats because of the limitations of audiovisual hardware available. Quite often, courseware designed to be used in one format may be altered to be used in another. For example, videotape materials can be converted to the motion picture format and vice versa, or an instructional program utilizing a computer may be converted to programmed material in a textbook format. Quite often, a combination of formats can be utilized, such as a computer and videotape or videodisc. Although two or more formats may be combined, the combined material is still considered courseware. Generally, when two or more types of media are combined in a presentation, the term *multimedia* is used.

Selection

As we have learned, the trend toward increased use of audiovisual technology for training, education, and development began in the late 1950s and early 1960s with the increased use of language laboratories, television, audiotape recorders, and various types of "teaching machines." Some of the learning activities that resulted from these devices were successful, but most failed for a variety of reasons (e.g., poor instructor response, poor planning, breakdown of equipment, and poor design and selection of instructional materials). At that time, the interest in instructional technology was misdirected, as most efforts went into gadgetry instead of into design and selection of courseware materials. Although much attention was paid to the equipment used to display the instructional media, it was the courseware that contained the content. Instructional media, whatever the form, serve only one purpose—they are vehicles of transmission of material to be learned.

The human resource developer who must deal with the problem of selecting suitable instructional materials must be concerned with a variety of factors, such as the learners' background, their previous school experience, the instructor's background and style, and the learning objectives to be achieved. Instruction can be considered suitable when instructional objectives (the skill, knowledge, and attitudes to be learned) are matched with instructional methods. The question of matching is not a simple issue; rather, it is a question of degree. While perfect suitability is rare, the less suitable the materials, the less the learner will achieve. The HRD practitioner should carefully study the major factors involved in designing instruction. These factors include:

1. An assessment of the learners' knowledge, abilities, and deficiencies
2. The determination of learning objectives for the learners
3. A determination of types of learning experiences (i.e., methods to be used). Which are best suited to the trainees?

4.   An evaluation process to measure the learners' progress
5.   Feedback evaluation designed for the improvement of the system

Much attention is given, in the courseware selection process, to clearly defining instructional objectives. It cannot be overemphasized that clearly defined objectives are critical to the selection of suitable instructional materials. In terms of media selection for learning purposes, instructional objectives may be grouped into the three categories that Benjamin Bloom indicated in his *Taxonomy of Instructional Objectives*.[5] These three categories are the *psychomotor domain*, represented by skills and performance of some task; the *cognitive domain*, which includes knowledge and information about some point; and the *affective domain*, which includes attitudes and appreciations. Each learning requirement will consider these specific areas.

The primary concern of the human resource developer is to design learning experiences that enable the learner's behavior to change in either one, two, or all three of these domains. Each media form affects the way the learner will relate to each domain. When deciding upon the most suitable media for a specific learning objective, the learning specialist must consider how the media applies to the appropriate domain. For example, video and motion pictures are extremely useful for creating attitudes and emotions by the use of various visual and audio techniques and effects; thus it is an excellent medium for dealing with affective information. The "real thing" or physical object media (e.g., tools and equipment) are especially useful in developing psychomotor objectives, as they provide the learner with the opportunity to practice and test performance by manipulating the object in an actual job situation. The learning specialist would not want to utilize print media exclusively to teach a psychomotor objective related to the operation of a planing machine, although certain cognitive information about the machine's operation can be taught through print media. Quite often, the course designer will utilize a variety of media, capitalizing on the strengths and weaknesses of each to implement specific learning objectives.

After instructional objectives are determined and the method for attaining these objectives decided upon, a decision must be made as to the instructional materials best suited to carry out the objective. Before making a selection of courseware, the human resource developer may wish to consider the following factors:

1.   Learner entry levels and sophistication
2.   Time limitations in which instruction must be accomplished

3. The manner in which the courseware will be used (i.e., as an aid to the instructor [instructor-controlled media] or in a self-instructional mode [learner-controlled media])
4. Appropriateness of the courseware in relation to the learning task to be performed (cognitive, psychomotor, affective domain)
5. Cost to produce and to implement versus the benefit to be gained
6. Technical quality required to meet the instructional/learning objective

There is no easy way to decide on the best selection of courseware development. The HRD practitioner will be able to take several courses of action in the overall selection process:

1. Purchase ready-made courseware produced by commercial firms (commonly called "off-the-shelf" materials)
2. Contract with an outside firm to design and/or produce the courseware
3. Design and/or produce the courseware using in-house staff and facilities

Generally, one has most control over the design and content of instructional materials when they are produced in-house, but the costs and time delays of in-house production can be very high, as compared to off-the-shelf selection or contracting with an outside firm to design and produce. It is recommended that organizations first thoroughly review the many excellent commercial instructional materials already available before attempting to contract for materials and/or produce materials in-house. Those organizations that have a small HRD operation should certainly consider the purchase of ready-made courseware or of contracting with an outside production company. There is a host of available learning materials in such diverse areas as shorthand skills, typing, management, supervision, problem solving, reading, grammar, mathematics, statistics, safety, electronics, machining, etc. These materials generally have a common application for most organizations; therefore, many will be found suitable for specific training, education, or development needs.

The human resource developer should consider the following factors in making a decision to purchase or prepare materials in-house:

1. *Design of Instructional Materials.*   Organizations producing their own materials or contracting specifically for them are generally able to

specify exactly what they need to meet identified objectives. Often, these materials are either designed for the general audience or for a particular group not necessarily resembling the organizations or learners.

2. *Available Equipment.* Here the HRD practitioner must consider the organization's equipment capability, since many off-the-shelf materials utilize audiovisual equipment. Consideration must also be given to the learning environment and its possible physical limitations. Each of these considerations may require specialized equipment.

3. *Availability of Materials.* Available materials will be dependent upon items located in commercial catalogues and upon the supply of items already in inventory. Local production of instructional materials may depend upon the available in-house staff experience, their workload, or private contractor delivery schedules.

4. *Cost.* The cost of in-house or contractor-supplied materials generally is high, if used on a small scale and if staff time and equipment are at a premium. Off-the-shelf materials are generally inexpensive by comparison.

5. *Validity of Instructional Materials.* Here, local in-house or private contractor purchase gives the organization the most control over valid and consistent courseware. Many private off-the-shelf vendor materials have been validated, although the HRD practitioner should consider these validation claims carefully in light of specific needs.

Validation of Courseware

An important function sometimes overlooked by human resource developers is the validation of courseware. *Validation* is a process of testing and revising instructional strategies and materials to be certain that the instructional intent is achieved. Validation is a separate step in the instructional design process and should not be confused with evaluation. Evaluation is discussed in another chapter of this handbook.

The process of courseware validation is usually time consuming, but it is critically important. The effort made will yield significant dividends in terms of more efficient and effective instruction. The validation process basically consists of five steps:

1. Instruction is designed and delivered to a representative sample group of learners.
2. Instruction is tested against performance objectives.
3. Problems arising from the test are analyzed.

4.   Courseware deficiencies are corrected, and courseware is revised.
5.   The process is repeated until the courseware is validated according to the performance objectives, learner population, and other criteria involved.

Is the courseware doing what it was designed to do? Can the learners who have passed through the system perform the tasks that were identified? These are key questions of validation. When the answers to these basic questions are "no," revision and retesting of the courseware is necessary. Validation is specific in its direction, systematic in its method, quantifiably measurable, and can be documented for future reference and adjustment.

Ideally, courseware should be validated using a learner population for which the materials were designed, although this may not always be feasible. When off-the-shelf courseware is considered, producers should be able to supply validation data on their product. This data should be reviewed with consideration given to application within the particular organization. Many off-the-shelf materials may be previewed prior to purchase. This will give the human resource developer time for self-validation before costly purchases are made. If the materials are found unsuitable, they can be returned.

The job of selecting instructional materials is complex. The goal of selection must be the enhancement of learning through the use of the best possible instructional materials. Reaching this goal requires a systematic, scientific approach to the appraisal of materials to determine whether and with whom they work. It becomes clear that the important impact of courseware upon the learner is far greater than dollars spent on the materials. This will be realized when we consider that the improved effectiveness of employees, once back on the job, results in even larger cost savings. The human resource developer must also remember that the ultimate "consumer," the learner, has a right to expect no less than the most effective and suitable instructional materials for the learning tasks to be undertaken.

Effective Utilization

Effective utilization of audiovisual instructional media should not make the teaching-learning process more complex, rather it should enhance the process so that more learning takes place. No universally acceptable guidelines for media utilization have, as yet, been formulated and adopted, but a few broad principles may be helpful for the human resource developer to gain a better understanding of effective utilization of instructional media.

1. Selection of media should be based upon valid learning objectives and the unique characteristics of the learner and of the media.

2. Advanced preparation for use of the media is essential. This can be accomplished by previewing the materials, reviewing any prepared study guides or manuals, and integrating the material into the instructor's lesson plans by considering sequence, timing, and proper conditions for learning.

3. Physical facilities and conditions for using the media should be arranged in advance, in a manner that provides for economy of time and optimum learner attention and participation. All equipment and materials should be ordered and ready before the learners assemble, and these should be in operating condition. Proper environmental conditions should be provided, including arrangement of seating according to the requirements of the media involved, proper lighting, ventilation, and noise control.

4. When using media, effective learner orientation should be encouraged by developing adequate learner readiness. Learner readiness or orientation can be accomplished in various ways, mainly by discussing questions and identifying the problems to be covered. The learner should be alerted to observe specific things (e.g., unusual words, phrases, and symbols), to define specialized vocabulary, and to indicate negative features that may be found in the media (e.g., out-of-date clothing, use of black and white images, etc.).

5. Effective learner participation should be encouraged either before, during, or after a presentation. Follow-up activities that facilitate the learner's ability to form associations to real-life situations and the practice of skill and knowledge gained through the media are ways to provide learner participation.

6. The media and the instructor's own utilization techniques should be subjected to continual evaluation. Did the materials accomplish the intended instructional task? Are there other materials or techniques that might have been more appropriate? Was there positive learner response to the materials and the techniques utilized? These are some questions that might be raised in the evaluation process.

AUDIOVISUAL INSTRUCTIONAL MEDIA COMPARISON

In general, learning programs should be designed so that they result in more effective performance by the learner once back on the job. The selection of audiovisual instructional media should be based on this principle. Since no one technique or aid serves all purposes, a variety of materials is available to the learning specialist. It is important to remember the following when selecting audiovisual instructional media.

1. Use only audiovisual materials that contribute to specific learning tasks. Analyze the content area to determine what aspects of it may be presented more effectively with use of the material.
2. Use audiovisual materials singularly or in combination to achieve desired results.
3. Use audiovisual materials only as an integral part of the learning activity. Coordinate the use of the material with the total presentation of the subject.
4. Use audiovisual materials in a manner most likely to accomplish specific learning objectives. If the materials being used are commercially produced, use only the portion that contributes to the learning objective at hand.

It is not possible to outline the merits of each type of individual instructional media in a single chapter. In order to familiarize the reader with a few of the more common types of audiovisual instructional media, a summary of their advantages and limitations is set forth. The reader is referred to the bibliography for additional sources of information.

Overhead Transparencies

Probably one of the most common audiovisual aids is the overhead transparency (see Figure 10.3). The *overhead transparency* is an image printed on a piece of clear plastic or acetate, specially prepared for use with an overhead projector. The overhead transparency is placed on the projector's clear glass stage. A bright light is shone through the transparency, projecting the image onto a screen. The projected image is extremely large and well lit; thus, this form of media is often utilized in large rooms since the image may be seen clearly by everyone.

Effective utilization of the overhead projector can lead to dynamic and exciting presentations, while improper utilization can lead to learner fatigue and confusion. The instructor normally stands or sits next to the projector, facing the learner, in a lighted room. In this way, the instructor can maintain eye contact with the group, permitting maximum opportunity for interpersonal exchange and encouraging questions and discussion. Next to the instructor are the prepared overhead transparencies, prearranged in the sequence outlined in the instructor's lesson plan. The instructor places the transparency on the clear glass stage and turns on the projector lamp. When the transparency has been shown, the instructor should shut off the lamp and then remove the transparency. In this way, learners do not experience the annoying flash of white light on a blank screen as old transparencies are replaced with new ones. By turning the lamp on and off between each successive projection, the instructor adds a dramatic effect to the presentation.

Overhead transparencies may be made professionally, either by vendors or by an organization's graphic arts department. Professionally made transparencies are produced by a photographic process or by a diazo printing process. These offer the instructor brilliant colors, proper size, and placement of the visual image. Properly made transparencies lend a "professional" air to the presentation, although they can be costly.

Some human resource developers have limited funds, or they may consider the professionally made transparency too costly. If the learning specialist has the artistic ability and the time, transparencies can be made in-house. A variety of methods may be used, singularly or in combination, such as:

1. Write or draw directly on the plastic transparency film with a felt tip pen or grease pencil. Felt tip pens may utilize either permanent or nonpermanent ink.
2. Write or draw on plain bond paper with a pencil, then utilize either a thermoprocess or photocopy process to transfer the information onto the plastic transparency material.
3. Use various direct transfer letters and/or color plastic glued directly onto the transparency film.

The large format of the transparency (8½ × 11) makes the production of instructor-made transparencies relatively easy. The ability of the instructor to write or draw directly on the transparency film makes this medium an excellent replacement for the chalkboard or, in some cases, newsprint. The learning specialist should note that sometimes the less sophisticated overhead transparency can have the same or an even better effect on the learner than the professionally made transparency. The

Figure 10.3. The overhead transparency.

material must match the needs of the learner and the ability of the instructor to be considered effective.

The instructor should be aware of the various techniques when utilizing the overhead projector. These techniques add to the dynamics of the lesson.

1. The plastic transparency material is available in various colors. When projected, either the background, the drawing, or the lettering appear in color. Some instructors utilize combinations of colors on one transparency to dramatize a particular concept. Other instructors use the color to "color key" similar information, so the learner may associate a particular color with the material being taught, thereby increasing ability to recall that information.

2. The instructor can use an opaque pointer, such as a pencil, directly on the transparency to bring attention to a particular detail. The silhouette of the pointer, showing on the screen, will help direct the eyes of the audience and add a dramatic detail to the presentation.

3. Another way to direct attention to information projected on the screen is to use a felt tip pen or grease pencil. Similar to writing on

newsprint or a chalkboard, the instructor writes on the plastic transparency, highlighting details or specific points.

4. The instructor can regulate the degree of the presentation by covering a transparency with paper or cardboard and then exposing the data as he or she is ready to discuss each point. This reveal or "strip tease" technique is often used when the instructor does not want the learners to read ahead as lists of information are projected.

5. The instructor may overlay or superimpose additional transparencies on a base transparency, in order to separate processes or ideas into elements and present them sequentially (see Figure 10.4).

6. Motion can even be simulated by utilizing the effects of polarized light. A special plastic is glued to the transparency. Then a polarized filter is placed above the transparency image. If the filter is attached to a special spinner device, the polarized image appears to move on the screen. This technique is especially useful when illustrating an industrial process, such as the current in an electric circuit.

7. The instructor can illustrate three-dimensional objects utilizing the overhead projector. By placing an object on the glass stage of the projector, a silhouette of the object appears on the screen. Many technical instructors, for example, use this technique when illustrating the motion relationship of gears.

8. Some instructors use the overhead projector in combination with other audiovisual media. For example, a 35mm photographic slide may project a photograph of the real object while the overhead transparency may project a schematic diagram of the object's primary function.

9. Instructors have found the overhead transparency useful in facilitating learner notetaking. Instructors duplicate the transparency image onto paper and distribute these to the class. By doing this, the learner is relieved of the mechanics of copying complex diagrams or outlines.

Equipment placement is an important factor. The overhead projector is usually in the front of a room, relatively close to the screen, and the projection angle can cause distortion of the image. As depicted in Figure 10.5, the image appears in a trapezoid form or in the shape of a keystone. The "keystone effect" may be corrected by tilting the screen to an angle corresponding to the lens of the projector. If the screen cannot be tilted,

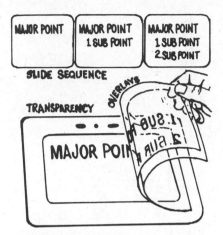

Figure 10.4.   The use of overlays.

the instructor may want to move the projector further away from the screen. When this is done, the image will become larger and may become too large for the size of screen being used. Keystoning distortion can become bothersome to the audience, but there may be little the instructor can do about it.

The placement of the overhead projector is rather important for another reason. The projector should be placed as low as possible (often a low standing overhead projector cart is used for this purpose) and the lens aimed so that the image is projected to a corner of the room. This placement is ideal because the body of the projector does not interfere with the line of vision between the learner and the screen. Proper placement of the projector is extremely important for successful use because, usually, projected materials are on the screen for long periods of time; improper placement can add to viewer fatigue.

There are several advantages to using overhead transparencies.

1.   The equipment can be used in the front of a well-lit room, allowing the instructor to maintain eye contact with the learners. The instructor can observe reactions and adjust the presentation accordingly. This position also promotes discussion and inter-action.

2.   Large images can be projected so everyone can see the instructor's illustrations.

3.   Inexpensive visual aids made by the instructor can be used. These aids can be easily and quickly modified prior to presentation or as

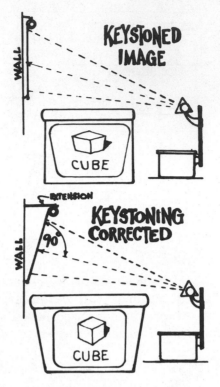

Figure 10.5.   The keystone effect.

a part of the class presentation. The rudimentary art skills of the instructor can produce dramatic transparencies.

4. The instructor can organize and pace the presentation to the needs of the instructional situation.

5. The equipment is simple to operate and requires little maintenance. Generally, the only maintenance is keeping the glass stage clean and replacing the projector light bulb when necessary.

6. Color can be used effectively and economically. Overhead transparency film comes in a wide range of colors. This makes it possible to prepare multicolor transparencies at a relatively low cost.

7. A separate projectionist is not needed to operate the equipment. The overhead projector complements the instructor but is not a replacement. The instructor controls the projector and can integrate visual and verbal comments easily.

8. Projectors are available in models that fit into an attaché case, thus making them portable, especially for air travel.

There are also limitations in the use of overhead transparencies.

1. Equipment must be properly positioned in the room to eliminate the keystone effect and to allow all learners to view the image. Often, a special screen is required to eliminate the keystone effect.
2. Overhead transparencies are used primarily as an instructor-controlled audiovisual aid, not as a learner-controlled medium.

Motion Pictures

A motion picture is a series of still pictures, taken in rapid succession, which, when projected through a motion picture projector, give the viewers an illusion of motion. Learners are generally familiar with instructional films, both silent and sound.

Instructional films commonly come in two formats—16mm or super 8mm. These merely indicate the film width. The 16mm format is most often used in large class presentations, because the image projected is clearer than the smaller super 8mm. Super 8mm film is commonly used for learner-controlled situations in which the learner can view short segments of a film in an individual or small group situation. Most super 8mm films are stored in sealed cartridges, which the learner inserts into a special projector.

Both 16mm and super 8mm can be projected with or without an audio portion. Commonly, audio is added to the 16mm film through optical methods at the time of processing. The super 8mm audio "track" consists of a thin strip of magnetic audiotape attached to the film. This audio track can easily be modified by the instructor, directly on the film, therefore, narration directly applicable to a particular learning situation can easily be made. The super 8mm sound track can also be added at the time the film is processed.

Motion picture film can be a dynamic learning tool. Instructors utilize films to motivate learners or to illustrate an important aspect of a technical process, especially where motion is important. Films may be used to change learner attitudes, notably in sales training programs. Films may speed up a slow process, such as the growth of a plant, or slow down a rapid process, such as a chemical reaction. Films can magnify or minify; they can create a mood.

There is a wide assortment of commercially prepared films, covering a large variety of subjects applicable to learning. Several good sources of these films are indicated in the bibliography, although there are virtually hundreds of organizations that produce and distribute motion picture films suitable for learning situations.

The design of an instructional film is not the same as the design of a film primarily used as entertainment. Several specific suggestions can be made to help the learning specialist in designing and/or choosing an instructional motion picture.

1. Shoot task performance scenes from the learner's point of view. The viewpoint of the camera should always be that of the operator's own eyes. Learners should see the operation as if they were actually performing the task. Scenes that teach the learner how to perform a task should be designed so that the camera angle is over the learner's shoulder—focused on the hands performing the activity.

2. Control the pace of the film to allow the learner to receive the message at a rate slow enough for good comprehension. Too rapid introduction of new facts or ideas, whether visual or audio, will impede learning.

3. Introduce new names and terms only as necessary so as not to confuse the learner. Provide a printed study guide before or after viewing the film. This guide should contain vocabulary and a summary of the important information in the film.

4. Sequence the film so that the important concepts are introduced in a logical order and are repeated or summarized, since repeating and summarizing increases learning. An effective technique for teaching skills is to utilize short film segments (usually placed in a film loop cartridge) that can be viewed repeatedly, as needed by the individual learner.

5. The use of titles or an outline, sequenced between scenes, can help orient the learner while viewing the film.

6. The film presentation can be more effective if it uses the second person ("you") in communications; that is, speak directly to the learner and use the active voice in sentences.

The advantages of using motion pictures are:

1. Motion pictures allow the learner and the instructor to observe processes they otherwise would be unable to experience. Special-

ized motion picture techniques, such as microphotography, telephotography, animation, slow motion, and fast motion permit the viewing of actions that the unaided eye would be incapable of perceiving.

2. Motion pictures are useful in compensating for individual and cultural differences among learners within a group. By presenting a common experience through the film, a basis for discussion can be established. This can lead to a more productive exchange of ideas or a better understanding of particular points of view.

3. Special effects can be produced that may enhance learning. Some of these effects are split screen or multiple images on one screen, visual distortions and/or illusions, compression or extension of time, or the illusion of various activities occurring simultaneously. These effects are especially useful in presenting effective materials and can increase learner involvement in the presentation.

4. Filmed programs can be designed in conjunction with learner workbooks, job performance aids, or even actual hands-on experiences. For example, the film may direct the learner to stop the projector and work with a tool directly. Once this exercise is completed the projector is turned on and the lesson continues.

5. Motion pictures, once produced and edited, lock in content and sequencing of instruction, thus maintaining uniformity of information transfer. This is an important feature in those situations in which it is critical that each learner is "exposed" to the same content.

6. Generally, equipment is conveniently available in most learning facilities and can be easily operated by the instructor or the learner.

There are also limitations to utilizing motion pictures.

1. Well-produced motion picture films are generally expensive. Most organizations do not have in-house capability to produce films, although there are numerous film production companies available for contract work.

2. Film material is fragile and is susceptible to scratches, therefore, great care must be taken in handling films. Film material must be cleaned and repaired frequently.

3. Film processing requires extended time, thus the medium cannot be used for instant feedback of learner or instructor performance.

4. "Locking in" content and sequencing of instruction can also have disadvantages. At times, a portion of the instructional content or sequencing may need to be revised. Since the content and sequencing are "locked" into the motion picture, it may be difficult and costly to update the film with new material.

5. Although modern motion picture projectors are relatively easy to operate in particular instructional environments, a special projectionist may be required to operate the equipment. This disadvantage may pose problems for an instructor not familiar with the specific projector provided or with the requirements imposed by the organization sponsoring the learning activity.

6. Environment may pose another problem. Since motion pictures generally project images onto a screen, the room should be dark to enhance the brightness of the image. Window curtains that block out all distracting light should be provided, and the room's overhead lights should be turned off. If these precautions are not followed, the learner may become distracted, thus reducing the amount of learning that takes place.

Video Media

Television is probably the most familiar medium, yet its use as an instructional medium is often misunderstood. In the 1960s and early 1970s, film producers and television producers were at odds as to the merits of their two media. There was great debate regarding such factors as the quality of image and sound, availability and comparability of video equipment, flexibility of producing and editing movies versus videotape, cost effectiveness of the two media, and so on. Some of those who debated were competing for their market share of the huge HRD budget allocated for "films."

Technology has progressed to the point where movie films are also distributed in the form of videotape for viewing in the TV format, while videotape programs are being converted to film for viewing as movies.

When designing learning materials, the human resource developer should consider both motion pictures and video in a broad perspective, rather than as media used primarily to enhance a lecture presentation. The motion picture and video media have tremendous flexibility and may be used in various situations.

The human resource developer should consider the following elements of these media:

1. Visualizing static subjects, as well as moving objects. Photographs of still objects may be introduced into the film or videotape in combination with the moving subject.

2. Length of a videotape is totally flexible, ranging from a few seconds to several hours. The designer should consider using only a short segment of a videotape in a particular learning situation.

3. Incorporate programming techniques into the videotape to require the learner to interact with the medium and to respond to questions posed through the courseware.

4. Utilization of special techniques, such as animation, slow motion, split screen.

The advantages outlined under the film category are also characteristic of television, although television does have some additional advantages of which the human resource developer should be aware. These advantages are:

1. Live or broadcast television can bring an event directly to the learner as it happens. Live TV adds the dimension of immediacy to events anywhere in the world. Live video reports from the field or from instructors in remote locations can be brought directly to the learner in a classroom thousands of miles away.

2. Events, lessons, demonstrations, etc. can easily be recorded on videotape and shown to learners within minutes of their occurrence. Videotape, for example, is often used in presentation technique courses. A videotape is made of the learner's presentation, and the instructor then plays back the presentation, providing constructive and specific criticism to the learner.

3. Video equipment is easily available, as many learning facilities have the necessary equipment. If the equipment is not available, it can be purchased or rented at relatively low cost.

4. The videotape recorder or videodisc can be connected to a computer, providing for "interactive video" learning materials. Interactive, computer-based video has the advantages of providing for simulation, learner self-pacing, immediate feedback of results to the learner, and standardization of instruction.

There are limitations to the video media. These are:

1. The advantage of live or broadcast television can also be a limitation. Broadcast or live television can cause a scheduling problem. If the human resource developer does not schedule the learner at the time the program is broadcast, the program cannot be seen. To overcome this limitation, some learning specialists videotape the broadcast television program for later playback. Learning specialists should be cautioned that this practice may be in violation of copyright laws.

2. Learners in large group facilities may have difficulty viewing the small image on a television monitor. If this difficulty exists, additional monitors can be connected.

3. The costs of reproducing and distributing videotape materials are low, but production costs for program origination are generally high.

Slides and Filmstrips

Another method of projecting still pictures is through the use of a 35mm slide projector (see Figure 10.6). A slide is a film transparency mounted in a cardboard or plastic frame. The 35mm slide, familiar to the amateur photographer, is the most common slide used for learning programs. This slide, when placed in its mount, is $2'' \times 2''$, although other size film and mounts are sometimes used ($2\frac{1}{4} \times 2\frac{1}{2}$ or $3\frac{1}{4} \times 4$) for special special purpose projection. Slide projectors come in numerous configurations. Some project the image on a large classroom screen, others utilize a rear-view screen fixed on a wall of the classroom. Other slide projectors are self-contained units projecting the slide image on a small rear-view screen built into the projector and used for individualized or small group instruction. The slide is usually placed in a special tray that not only protects the slide but helps organize slides for different presentations. Unfortunately, not all projector manufacturers utilize the same tray configuration or size, therefore, when ordering slide projectors for an organization, the HRD practitioner should specify that only one type of tray be used in all equipment. This will facilitate distribution of instructional materials within the organization.

Often, an audiotape is used in conjunction with the slide projector. In this configuration, the audiotape recorder is connected directly to the slide projector. Audible or inaudible signals are recorded on the tape, which, when played back, automatically signal the projector to change the slide. Utilizing this method, multiple projectors can be "programmed" to simultaneously and automatically project images on

Figure 10.6. The slide projector.

multiple screens. This technique is often used for large sales meetings, stockholder meetings, or public affairs presentations. Of course, narration and music can be added to the audiotape, thus enhancing the message.

Motion can be added to the individual slide, using the polarizing filter spinner in a fashion similar to that of the overhead projector. Again, this technique is useful, for example, when illustrating the flow of fluid in a chemical process.

Slides can also be made by the instructor, using a method called *U-film*. This special 35mm film allows the instructor to draw, write, or even type a message directly onto the film. Although the slides do not usually look "professional," this technique is useful in specific situations.

Specialized electronic equipment can be connected to the projector, causing the slides to appear to fade one image into the next. This technique, known as *dissolve*, eliminates the "blackout" during the time it takes one slide to replace another in the projector. When used effectively, this dissolve technique can give the audience the illusion of motion. I once created an extremely effective lesson, teaching the hand hewing of a log, through the dissolve technique. Each progressive slide depicted another step in the process. When the slides were dissolved one into the next, the motion of hewing a log was animated, thus giving the appearance of movement.

Slides are one of the most versatile media available to the learning specialist. Not only can slides be used by the instructor as an instructional aid, but they can be a learner-controlled medium when used in combination with audio, print, or computer media. Programmed instructional materials can be sequenced with slides (as well as with other audiovisual equipment and real objects) to provide the learner with a complete learner-controlled instructional package. Such programmed instructional materials have been used successfully by the military and in industry for many years. The U.S. Air Force and several major airlines combine slide, audiotape, and print techniques in a programmed instructional format to teach basic flight control principles. Not only is the instruction consistent, but learners have the opportunity to review sections of the material they have not clearly understood. One advantage of presenting instruction in this fashion is the better utilization of instructors for other activities.

The advantages of slides are:

1. Slides can be produced one at a time and reproduced in large quantities economically and quickly.
2. The small size of the individual slide and the relatively compact size of the tray facilitate easy distribution through the mail system and storage of material.
3. Slides produce a high quality image, in color and black and white, that permits the viewing of fine detail. Since individual slides can be held on the screen for long periods of time, class discussion can be enhanced with large photographic visuals.

There are relatively few limitations to slide media. Although preparation of photographic materials is not difficult, adequate time must be provided prior to the instructional activity to develop and arrange the slide material.

Filmstrips

A filmstrip is a long length of 35mm film containing a series of still pictures (see Figure 10.7). These pictures are projected one at a time, in sequence, using a filmstrip projector. Today, the filmstrip is not

Figure 10.7.   The filmstrip projector.

commonly used in learning situations for adults, as slide equipment generally is more available and more flexible. Most of the advantages of using slides also apply to filmstrips (e.g., low cost to produce and distribute, efficient packaging, storage, and distribution). The filmstrip does, however, have disadvantages that make it a less widely used medium. Among these limitations are:

1. The sequence of pictures is always the same, thus eliminating flexibility for easy modification of individual pictures.
2. Lead times to produce filmstrips are longer than for slide production due to the specific graphic and laboratory processes required in their manufacture.

Audio Media

Audio media come in a variety of forms, offering the learning specialist a number of effective, fairly inexpensive instructional techniques. These include audio cassette tapes and compressed speech.

AUDIO CASSETTE TAPES

Audiotape recorders have become commonplace equipment in homes, cars, offices, and in the training environment. The availability of this equipment is extensive and a large number of commercially produced materials are available. However, too often, the human resource practitioner does not consider the audiotape recorder an important training tool, possibly due to the familiarity with the medium.

Audiotape is a long strip of acetate that has been coated on one side with a layer of iron oxide particles. When the tape is passed by the "recording head" in the tape recorder, the iron oxide particles are magnetized. Upon playback, the "playback head" interprets the magnetized pattern of iron oxides and, in turn, produces sound, which is amplified by the built-in amplifier in the machine.

Audiotape is reuseable. The tape can be erased and new information recorded "over" the old, by remagnetizing the iron oxides into a different pattern. The iron oxide surface of tapes lasts such a long time they generally do not wear out. Tapes stored in a cool, dry room will last for many years. Tapes do break when they are mishandled, are too dry, or are used with faulty equipment. Repairing tape is a simple process. Care must be taken to use special magnetic repair materials, not ordinary cellophane tape, which may ruin the cassette and the recording and playback heads of the recorder.

Audiotape recorders can be classified as either reel-to-reel or cassette. The reel-to-reel tape recorder generally produces better tonal qualities than the cassette unit. It is used most often only for original tape production or as a vehicle for "driving" the complex synchronization signals for large, multiscreen, multimedia presentations, therefore discussion of the reel-to-reel equipment will be minimal.

Today most training programs use audiotape in the form of a cassette.[6] The audiocassette is an enclosed case that contains two small reels of magnetic audiotape. When the cassette is placed in its recorder, the machine turns the reels. This passes the tape by the recording heads, which reproduce the sound. Complicated threading of the recorder is eliminated, thus operation is simplified. Cassette recorders and playback units run at $1\frac{7}{8}$ ips. Commercially available cassettes come in lengths of 30 minutes to two hours playing time.

For special applications, cassettes can be custom ordered to hold enough tape for a specific time requirement. Special, endless loop cassettes can also be ordered. These will replay a recorded program without the instructor having to rewind the tape. Endless loop cassettes

are used for automated sales demonstrations where it would be impractical for the salesperson to rewind the tape.

Audiotapes are used for many learning applications, either alone or in
combination with other media. The following are some ways audiotape
materials are being used today:

1. Because audiotapes can assure consistency in repetitive activities,
    they are used to drill students, administer tests, and give instruc-
    tions. These techniques are commonly used in typing and short-
    hand learning activities.

2. Another application of cassette tapes is found in public speaking
    and diction training. Learners are given opportunities to evaluate
    their own speech—tone, pronunciation, enunciation, speed—by
    recording their voice. Upon playback, the instructor provides
    constructive feedback to the learner, who can listen to the errors
    made.

3. The U.S. State Department and many international corporations
    use audiotape to give learners foreign language instruction prior
    to international assignments. The audio medium is used for
    teaching recognition of dialects and accents, as well as for drill
    and practice.

4. Audio-tutorial, self-instructional materials are commonly used in
    technical learning activities. The audio-tutorial technique has the
    instructor program information and directions on the audio
    cassette tape. The learner performs the required activities,
    utilizing various media (e.g., print, slides, videotape, microfiche,
    real objects, etc.). Upon successful completion, the learner is
    certified and returns to the job situation. After learning tasks, the
    trainee applies the learning in an actual job situation, under the
    guidance of the instructor. Various companies have developed
    entire audio-tutorial packages for maintenance workers, machine
    operators, etc. and have found them extremely reliable and cost
    effective.

5. Audio materials are found in individualized learning center
    activities.

6. Since audiotapes are extremely lightweight and inexpensive, and
    the recorders/players generally are abundantly available to the
    learner, they make an excellent addition to correspondence
    courses. The medical and legal professions have been using audio
    cassette tapes to inform doctors and lawyers of the latest develop-

ments in their respective fields. Participants in these programs receive a subscription to a series of audiotapes by direct mail. Participants listen to the tapes in their automobile, traveling to and from work, in the office or at home, thereby allowing the learners to study at their own convenience, in the environment most suitable to them.

Compressed Speech

Among recent innovations in educational technology is the concept of time-compressed speech. *Time-compressed speech* is a method of reducing the actual listening time for a prerecorded audiotape. The technique permits the listener to hear normal speech sounds at a much faster rate. This is accomplished by utilizing a digital computer signal processing technique that allows the learner to play back a recording at one-half to two and one-half times the speed of the original recording. The speaker's original pitch and tonal qualities remain unaltered. Time-compressed speech cassette players allow the user to listen at speeds that can be continuously adjusted to suit his or her own level of interest or under-standing. For example, a recorded, hour-long speech or lecture can be heard, without "Donald Duck"-like pitch distortion, in just 24 minutes, using a time-compressed speech cassette tape player. On the other hand, a tape can be slowed down as much as 50% to permit the learner to take notes, study particularly "meaty" sections, or even understand fast or garbled speech without pitch distortion or loss of speaker identity.

Most learners read from 250–500 words per minute, depending on the material—proof that people can absorb information at a rapid rate. Yet, most individuals speak at the rate of 100 words per minute—a much slower rate. Prerecorded information, played back on a conventional tape recorder, plays at a "real" recording rate. Time-compressed speech equipment allows the learner to adjust the rate of speech to equal his or her reading and comprehension rate. The learner will be able to "speed listen" with improved comprehension, thus reducing learning time. For example, an individualized learning center may utilize the time-com-pressed speech machine to reduce learning time, thus making the center available to more learners.

Time-compressed speech creates a new level of utility for recorded materials, encouraging their wider use. For example, the correspondence school instructor will be able to listen to answer tapes recorded by learners in reduced time, enabling him or her to evaluate and provide feedback more quickly. Although time-compressed speech machines on the market cost $250–$500, the future outlook for less expensive devices is excellent.

Another dimension of time-compressed speech that has been relatively untapped is the utilization of compressed speech in conjunction with slides. I have developed several pilot programs in which the audio portion of a slide-tape presentation was compressed. This, in turn, required that each slide be viewed in a "compressed" mode. Not only was learning time reduced, but there was evidence of higher learning comprehension, not only of the audio material but also of the visual information. A variation of this technique is to selectively compress sections of the slide-tape presentation to emphasize particular portions of the material. This technique was found to be extremely successful in directing the learners' attention to the most significant learning points of the program. Compressed speech equipment holds great promise for providing learning materials designed to consider individual learning needs.

Audio media have certain advantages.

1. Audio cassette tape recorders and players generally are readily available to most learners and instructors. The equipment used for instructional purposes is relatively inexpensive and easy to use; cartridge and cassette tape recorders require no threading.

2. Most small tape recorders utilize battery power, therefore, they are portable. The cassette tapes or cartridges used by these machines are small enough to be distributed through the postal system; this, coupled with their low reproduction cost, make cassette tapes an economical means of distributing audio learning materials.

3. Audio cassette tapes provide versatility in application. They can be combined with other forms of instructional materials, such as workbooks, films, or slides to enrich the instruction. Audio media are often designed to be used in an interactive or a participative learning mode that provides for self-pacing by the learner.

4. Since recordings can be utilized immediately after creation, the medium is often used as a diagnostic tool for helping to improve speech or musical learning efforts. Of course, recordings of events can be saved for later use.

While audio media are versatile, they do have certain limitations.

1. Most audio tape recorders and players have a digital tape counter designed so the user will know how much tape has been recorded

or played. Despite these tape counters, it is often difficult to locate specific recorded sections on the tape. This feature may pose difficulty for the learner.

2. Faulty equipment maintenance of cassette tapes causes the tape to "jam" in the machine, possibly damaging the cassette tape.

3. Audiotape equipment works on a variety of tape speeds (1⅞, 3¾, 7½ ips) and has a number of different "track" configurations (half, quarter, stereo, etc.), which may cause some difficulty if the machines are not compatible.

4. One of the most significant limitations is the use of audio cassette tape recorders in large group learning environments. Because the normal built-in sound amplification system is not designed for large group instruction (sound may be unintelligible), the equipment should be connected to a proper amplification source.

Today the human resource developer has access to a growing array of proven audiovisual instructional materials and techniques. The value of instructional materials, as enhancing the learning process, is generally recognized by adult educators. Human resource developers have a long tradition of effectively utilizing instructional materials.

GLOSSARY

Carrel (Learning).   A study cubicle designed for use by one student or a small number of students. Carrels usually contain audiovisual media for presentation of programmed audiovisual instruction.

Computer-Assisted Instruction (CAI).   An instructional method whereby students interact, most often individually, to instruction presented through a variety of media, usually computer controlled or computer monitored. The student can respond to the stimuli in a variety of ways, such as with a keyset or pointing device. One is immediately informed as to the accuracy of the response. The computer uses algorithms to diagnose the response, to determine the probable reason for any errors, and to present additional instruction in accordance with the diagnosis.

Computer-Directed Training System (CDTS).   A training system that involves dependent subsystems (functional software and courseware) and related documentation. Functional software enables the course designer to code course material and the student to interact with courseware through the use of hardware. Courseware is the subject matter and instructional data in whatever media required by the student to complete his course through use of a computer terminal. (*See also* Computer-Assisted Instruction and Computer-Managed Instruction.)

Computer-Managed Instruction (CMI). In CAI, students interact directly with instruction presented by computer-controlled or computer-monitored equipment. In CMI, the students do not necessarily interact directly with the equipment, although they may be "on-line" for testing, diagnosis, and prescription. The role of the computer in CMI is to aid the instructor in managing the instructional program.

Courseware. The technical data, textual materials, audiotapes, slides, movies, TV cassettes, and other audiovisual instructional materials. (*See also* Hardware and Software.)

Hardware. The physical components of a system (usually electronic or electrical devices) that are utilized in educational processes, including computers, terminals, audiovisual devices, teaching machines, etc. (*See also* Courseware and Software.)

Instructional Media. The means used to present information to the student.

Job Performance Aid (JPA). A device, book, chart, or other reference that facilitates the job performance by reducing the amount of information the human performer must recall or retain in order to successfully carry out a task. The guidelines on a movie projector, showing the path for threading the film, are a job performance aid for the projectionist.

Learner-Centered Instruction (LCI). An instructional process in which the content is determined by the learners' needs, the instructional materials are geared to the learners' abilities, and the instructional design makes the learners active participants. The instructional system development process produces learner-centered instruction.

Learner-Controlled Instruction. An instructional environment in which the student can choose from a variety of instructional options for achievement of the terminal objectives. Students can vary their rate of learning, the media used, etc.

Learning Center. A learning environment that has been specifically developed to foster individualized instruction and that emphasizes employment of media to augment textbooks and manuals.

Medium (Media). A means of affecting or conveying something. Medium is a general term roughly comparable in many ways to tool, instrument, vehicle, means, etc.

Multimedia Approach. The correlated use of more than one type of instructional medium as a vehicle for presenting the instructional materials. Characteristically, an instructional package that employs a multimedia approach may use textbooks, films, slides, etc. to present various segments of the entire package.

Perception.   The process of information extraction. The process by which a student receives or extracts information from the environment through experiences and assimilates this data as facts (sight, sound, feel, taste, smell).

Programmed Instruction.   A student-centered method of instruction that presents the information on planned steps or increments, with the appropriate response immediately following each step. The student is guided step-by-step to the successful completion of the assigned task or learning exercise.

Programmed Instructional Material.   Instructional material (e.g., texts, tapes, films and filmstrips, slides, scripts for live presentations, etc.) prepared specifically to employ techniques of programming.

Simulation.   A technique whereby "job/world" phenomena are mimicked, costs may be reduced, potential dangers eliminated, and time compressed. The simulation may focus on a small subset of the features of the actual job/world situation.

Simulator.   A generic term that includes full mission simulators, part/task trainers, procedures trainers, etc. Simulator and simulator-training device may be used interchangeably.

Software.   The programs and routines used to extend the capability of automatic data processing equipment. (*See also* Courseware and Hardware.)

Training Aid.   Any item developed and/or procured with the primary intent that it shall assist in the training and learning processes.

NOTES

1. Donald P. Ely, "The Field of Educational Technology: A Statement of Definition," *Audiovisual Instruction*, 17(8):36–43.
2. Paul Saettler, *A History of Instructional Technology* (New York: McGraw-Hill, 1968), p. 160.
3. Floyde E. Brooker, *Training Films for Industry* (Washington, D.C.: U.S. Office of Education, Bulletin no. 13, 1946), pp. 2–3.
4. Donald P. Ely and Vernon S. Gerlach, *Teaching and Media: A Systematic Approach* (Englewood Cliffs, N.J.: Prentice-Hall, 1971), pp. 285–286.
5. Benjamin S. Bloom, ed., *Taxonomy of Educational Objectives* (New York: Longmans, Green and Co., 1956).
6. Consumers may purchase various cassette configurations, such as 8 track cassettes or mini cassettes. These configurations generally are not utilized for training purposes.

BIBLIOGRAPHY

Anderson, Ronald H. *Selecting and Developing Media for Instruction.* New York: Van Nostrand, 1976.

Bloom, Benjamin S., ed. *Taxonomy of Educational Objectives.* New York: Longmans, Green and Co., 1956.

Bretz, Rudy. *A Taxonomy of Communication Media.* Englewood Cliffs, N.J.: Educational Technology Publishing Company, 1970.

Briggs, Leslie. *Handbook of Procedures for the Design of Instruction.* Pittsburgh: American Institute for Research, 1970.

Brooker, Floyde E. *Training Films for Industry.* Washington, D.C.: U.S. Office of Education, Bulletin no. 13, 1946.

Brown, James W., Richard B. Lewis, and Fred F. Harcleroad. *A V Instruction: Technology, Media, and Methods.* New York: McGraw-Hill, 1977.

Costa, Sylvia A. *How to Prepare a Production Budget for Film and Video Tape.* Blue Ridge Summit, Pa.: TAB Books, 1973.

Dale, Edgar. *Audiovisual Methods in Teaching.* New York: Holt, Rinehart, and Winston, 1969.

Davies, Ivor K. *Instructional Techniques.* New York: McGraw-Hill, 1981.

Dwyer, Francis M. *Strategies for Improving Visual Learning: A Handbook for the Effective Selection, Design, and Use of Visualized Materials.* State College, Pa.: Learning Services, 1978.

Eboch, Sidney C. *Operating Audio-Visual Equipment.* 2d. ed. San Francisco, Ca.: Chandler Publishing Company, 1968.

Ely, Donald P. "The Field of Educational Technology: A Statement of Definition." *Audiovisual Instruction,* 17(8): 36–43.

Ely, Donald P., and Vernon S. Gerlach. *Teaching and Media: A Systematic Approach.* Englewood Cliffs, N.J.: Prentice-Hall, 1971.

Gordon, George N. *Classroom Television.* New York: Hastings House, 1970.

Gropper, George L., and Zita Glasgow. *Criteria for the Selection and Use of Visuals in Instruction.* Englewood Cliffs, N.J.: Educational Technology Publishing Company, 1971.

Herman, Lewis. *A Practical Manual of Screen Playwriting for Theater and Television Films.* New York: New American Library, 1974.

Information Technology and Its Impact on American Education. Washington, D.C.: U.S. Office of Technology Assessment, 1982.

Kearsley, Greg. *Cost, Benefit, and Productivity in Training Systems.* Reading, Mass.: Addison-Wesley, 1982.

Kemp, Jerrold E. *Instructional Design: A Plan for Unit and Course Development.* 2d. ed. Belmont, Ca.: Fearon Publishers, 1976.

Kemp, Jerrold E. *Planning and Producing Audiovisual Materials.* New York: Harper and Row, 1980.

Lewis, Colby. *The TV Director/Interpreter.* New York: Hastings House, 1968.

Loughary, John W. *Man-Machine Systems in Education.* New York: Harper and Row, 1966.

McLuhan, Marshall. *Understanding Media: The Extensions of Man.* New York: McGraw-Hill, 1964.

McLuhan, Marshall, and Quentin Fiore. *The Medium Is the Message: An Inventory of Effects.* New York: Bantam Books, 1967.

Millerson, Gerald. *The Techniques of Television Production.* New York: Hastings House, 1968.

Minors, Ed, and Harvey Frye. *Techniques for Producing Visual Instructional Media.* New York: McGraw-Hill, 1977.

Mitchell, Wanda. *Televising Your Message: An Introduction to Television as Communication.* Skokie, Ill.: National Textbook Company, 1974.

National Audio-Visual Association. *Audio-Visual Equipment Directory.* Fairfax, Va., 1982. Published annually.

Quick, John, and Herbert Wolff. *Small Studio Video Tape Production.* 2d. ed. Reading, Mass.: Addison-Wesley, 1976.

Saettler, Paul. *A History of Instructional Technology.* New York: McGraw-Hill, 1968.

Spector, August K. "Compressed Speech Reduces Training Time." *The Federal Trainer,* no. 40 (1976).

Tickton, Sidney G., ed. *To Improve Learning: An Evaluation of Instructional Technology.* New York: R.R. Bowker, 1971.

Tracey, William R. *Human Resource Standards.* New York: American Management Association, 1981.

Williams, Richard L. *Television Production: A Vocational Approach.* Salt Lake City, Utah: Vision T.V. Productions, 1976.

PERIODICALS

Audiovisual Instruction. Association for Educational Communications and Technology, 1201 16th Street, N.W., Washington, D.C. 20036.

E-ITV. Educational and Industrial Television, C.S. Tepfer Publishers, 51 Sugar Hollow Rd., Danbury, Ct. 06810.

Educational Technology. Educational Technology Publishers, Inc., 140 Sylvan Ave., Englewood Cliffs, N.J. 07632.

T.H.E. Journal   Technological Horizons in Education. Information   Synergy, Inc., P.O. Box 992, Acton, Mass. 01720.

Training and Development Journal. American Society for Training and Development, Suite 305, 600 Maryland Ave., S.W., Washington, D.C. 20024.

Training Magazine. Lakewood Publishing, Inc., 731 Hennepin Ave., Minneapolis, Minn. 55403.

Training News. 176 Federal Street, Boston, Mass. 02110.

FILM PRODUCERS

Barr Films, 3490 E. Foothills Rd., Pasadena, Cal. 91107.

BFA Educational Media, 2211 Michigan Ave., Santa Monica, Cal. 90404.

BNA Communications, Inc., 9417 Decoverly Hall Rd., Rockville, Md. 20850.

Bosustow Productions, 1649 11th Street, Santa Monica, Cal. 90405.

Cally Curtis Company, 1111 N. Las Palmas Ave., Hollywood, Cal. 90038.

Churchall Films, 662 N. Robertson Blvd., Los Angeles, Cal. 90069.

CRM/McGraw-Hill, P.O. Box 641, Del Mar, Cal. 92014.

Educulture, Inc., 1 Dubuque Plaza, Suite 150, Dubuque, Iowa 52001.

Learning Corporation of America Video/Films, 1350 Avenue of the Americas, New York, N.Y. 10019.

National Educational Media, Inc., 21601 Devonshire Street, Chatsworth, Cal. 91311.

Ramic Productions, P.O. Box 7530, Newport Beach, Cal. 92660.

Roundtable Films and Video, 113 N. San Vicente Blvd., Beverly Hills, Cal. 90211.

Salenger Educational Media, 1635 12th Street, Santa Monica, Cal. 90404.

Time-Life Video, 1271 Avenue of the Americas, New York, N.Y. 10020.

Xicom Video Arts, Sterling Forest, Tuxedo, N.Y. 10987.

Computer-Based Learning

ANGUS STUART REYNOLDS

There is probably no area of technology that holds more promise for HRD than the computer industry, yet it is still ignored by a significant number of people in the field. There are many reasons for this, and Reynolds touches on some of these in his chapter.

One reason not mentioned is that many HRD practitioners went to school when computers were unknown and certainly were not a required area of study. It is very different today, and this change should be reflected in the learners as well as in the younger HRD practitioners.

For all concerned, Reynolds presents an overview of the terminology and concepts involved in using computers for learning. An important aspect of this chapter is the recognition of the adult as a learner, not merely peripheral to the computer.

Angus Stuart Reynolds is a senior human resource development consultant with Control Data Education Technology Center. His principal clients include major multinational companies, governmental organizations, and the United Nations. He is prominent in the field of computer-based learning. He has held several national and local positions in ASTD (president of Washington, D.C. chapter). He has published many articles on the computer and on technology in relation to HRD and has contributed chapters in books on those subjects.

This chapter will examine a *trend* in the true sense of the word. Computer-based learning (CBL) is a growing phenomenon used by increasing numbers of HRD people each year. This trend can be expected to become even more pronounced by the mid-1980s.

Computer-based learning is a technological tool, although not an overly sophisticated one. One does not have to be a "senior" HRD practitioner to employ CBL. It is necessary only to understand how it is used. This chapter will examine four major areas of importance to HRD practitioners: what CBL is about, how it can be implemented in an organization, what the CBL courseware development process is like, and some ideas about what the future holds.

THE NEW HRD ENVIRONMENT

HRD is far from a static field, but one phenomenon is certain to have a major impact. That is the practical use of computer technology for learning. Termed *computer-based learning*, the technology itself has existed for more than two decades. What is new is that we are finally beginning to make both significant and practical use of computers in the HRD field. Today, the number of organizations using computers for learning is still relatively small, clustered around a nucleus that has been using computer-based learning for some time, but the use of CBL is growing at a surprisingly fast rate. A great number of HRD professionals are involved. Those who are not yet involved will be soon.

First, we will examine what CBL is about. We will look at the important terminology currently in use, how CBL fits the "tool kit" of techniques useful in adult learning, and its impact on learning specialists and the HRD organization.

SPEAKING THE LANGUAGE

The use of computers for learning was pioneered through university research. This origin led to use of the term *computer-based education*, or CBE. When industrial organizations began the use of computer-based learning, they substituted *training* for *education*. The result was CBT. Other organizations decided to use *instruction*, producing the term CBI. Confusion does not occur among early users. Examining the meaning of CBL and its related terms will help us to see why.

Preferred Terminology

While beginning to use computers for learning, we are also beginning to use some of the necessary jargon and terminology. Terminology that was well established by early CBL users is becoming muddled. Current, experienced users of CBL are destined to become only a tiny fraction of those eventually using the terminology. As HRD professionals, we must be as careful in the use of CBL terms as we are in other areas.

There are only four basic terms, and one of them is rarely encountered. The terms are:

Computer-based learning (CBL)

Computer-assisted instruction (CAI)

Computer-managed instruction (CMI)

Computer-supported learning resources (CSLR)

The differences between each of these terms will be examined in the following sections.

Computer-Based Learning.   This is the umbrella term (see Figure 11.1). It includes the activities described by the other terms. A personal favorite is the definition given by a man who has been called the "father of CBE," Donald Bitzer of the University of Illinois. Bitzer says that *CBE* can be described as "anytime a person and a computer get together and one of them learns something." As mentioned earlier, CBE, CBT, CBI, CBL, and even CBHRD are really synonyms.

All these variations are commonly used by very knowledgeable people. They are comfortable with this lack of precision, and it does not cause a problem, because practitioners realize that these terms are interchangeable. For reasons of clarity, the term *CBL* will be used throughout this chapter.

It is variations in meaning that can render terms confusing. Some HRD practitioners use *CAI* rather than *CBL* as the general descriptive term. Usually, the person using *CAI* is unaware that such casual use can cause confusion. The main reason for the overly broad use of *CAI* is that many HRD people think that CAI is the whole field. Usually, they are completely unaware of the existence of CMI.

The term *computer-based learning* is becoming increasingly popular, reflecting today's emphasis on learner-centered thinking. It is also appropriate to all settings: academic, business, industrial, and even residential.

Computer-Assisted Instruction.   This term is the main source of difficulty. *CAI* is the use of a computer in the actual instructional process. The various forms that CAI can take are called *modes*. The six modes of CAI are:

Tutorial
Drill and practice
Instructional game
Modeling
Simulation
Problem solving

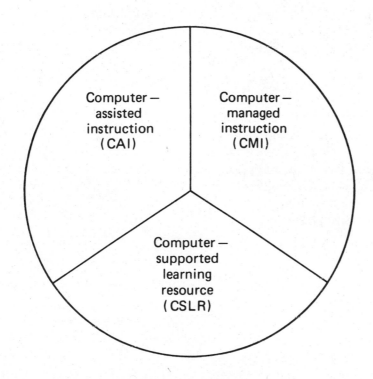

Figure 11.1.   Computer-based learning.

Tutorial

This is the most familiar type of CAI. The learner interacts, one-on-one, with the terminal (technically, it may not always be a *terminal*, but that is beyond the scope of this chapter). Ideally, the process advances just as the best tutor might personally conduct the process. The lesson typically presents some information and then checks the learner's understanding. Based on the learner's understanding or lack of it, the instruction will continue to another point or will repeat the first point in a new way.

Drill and practice

This is also a very commonly encountered mode of CAI. It involves another concept that was well developed prior to the advent of CBL. *Drill and practice* is the repetitive presentation of problems to the learner for solution. For example, the learner is presented with a problem such as, "How much is 2 + 2?" When the learner answers the question, another is presented, such as "How much is 3 + 4?" After a given number of problems have been presented, the learner is usually informed of the total presented, number right, and number wrong.

The common addition series is a simple example of the drill and practice technique. In HRD, the drill and practice mode of CAI may be used effectively in situations where the actual subject matter is much more complex. Drill and practice is a good choice for learning terminology or steps in a procedure.

Instructional game

An instructional game is not necessarily recognizable as a "game" at all. Nevertheless, instructional games are the problem child of CAI. Most instructional games contain an element of entertainment. The experience has been programmed so that the computer "throws the dice" as well as any similar chores, such as looking up a table or keeping score. The dividing line between amusement and learning is not always discernible and is probably not needed anyway. Learning while "playing" is still learning.

Instructional games are a completely valid way to stimulate learning. Some individuals have difficulty believing that learners who enjoy the learning can be having a worthwhile experience. This belief is similar to the idea that "If the medicine tastes bad, it must be good for us." Because of that prejudice, this mode of CAI is not readily accepted by all levels in all organizations. In fact, games have cast a stigma on some projects. At present, HRD practitioners should use instructional games with discretion. There exists a real danger that a CBL project could be characterized as a "frivolous" use of the organization's resources and, therefore, be cancelled.

Modeling

Modeling is the use of the CBL system to represent a system or process. This permits the learner to change values and to observe the effects of the change on the operation of the system. Usually, a realistic representation of the system being modeled is impossible or not attempted. For example, demographic variables such as birth rate, infant mortality, or death rate can be changed in the population model. The results of such changes can be observed as effects on the population over a period of time. Many systems, such as the population example just given, although accurate, do not lend themselves to realistic representation.

Simulation

Simulation involves a representation, with a degree of realism, of an item of equipment, device, system or subsystem by a CBL system. A simulation enables the learner to experience the operation of the target equipment without the possibility of destruction of the equipment, harm to the learner, or harm to others. CBL simulation contrasts with the most familiar examples of simulation—simulators. Simulators are usually very expensive, special, single-purpose (computerized) instructional devices (e.g., aircraft or nuclear simulators). Many learning specialists never stop to consider that simulation can be done on a number of different levels. Simulation can be conducted without a computer, however, the speed and complexity inherent in some simulations require the power of a computer. In fact, simulations are so difficult to do that the power of this strategy is not readily available to most HRD practitioners.

A technique that has proven useful for HRD is implementation of a "part task" simulation on a CBL terminal. For example, a CBL terminal cannot represent the entire cockpit of a modern aircraft. By using the CBL terminal to simulate the systems in the aircraft, one at a time, the learner masters all of the systems. When the learner enters the big simulator, it is not to learn but to demonstrate mastery and to gain experience operating the entire system.

Problem solving

Problem solving is a mode of CAI that is not regularly seen in HRD, although it has good application in math and science instruction. In problem solving, the learner uses the computer itself as a tool in solving a problem. The CAI program monitors these efforts and may carry out steps in a process specified by the learner.

Lessons developed using any of the six modes of CAI form learning resources. A great strength of CBL, compared with conventional instruction, is the ability to assign a learner only those resources that will fulfill the learning need. This is accomplished by CMI.

Computer-managed instruction. CMI is appropriately named. It is indeed the management of instruction by computer. Although *CMI* is not as familiar as *CAI*, this is not a reflection of its inherent worth or frequency of use. Rather, it probably reflects the fact that there is less excitement in managing instruction well than in teaching with an exotic technology. The important distinction is that CAI *always* directly involves learning; CMI does not. The three modes of CMI are:

Testing
Prescription generation
Record keeping

Testing

The CMI testing function should not be confused with quizzes that are sometimes included in CAI lessons. The quizzes in CAI evaluate learning and move the learner depending on the answer given. CMI testing evaluates the learner's mastery of the learning objectives. This determination is the foundation of the power of CMI, since it separates the instructional needs of individual learners. The CMI test makes it possible to prescribe, for an individual learner, precisely those learning activities needed by that individual.

Prescription generation

The CMI system generates an instructional prescription for each unmastered learning objective for each separate learner. All of the prescriptions will have been determined during the design of the instruction. Each individual learner is directed to only those learning resources that support the unmastered objective(s). Since each individual may be expected to master different objectives, each will study only the materials needed. This selectivity results in reduced time spent on instruction (see Figure 11.2).

Record keeping

Records of individual and group progress are generated and stored continuously by the typical CMI system. These records are available to the learning specialist as needed. Certain records, such as the grade book, are often made accessible to the learner.

CMI is a powerful technique. Compared with CAI, a smaller investment of financial and human resources will often suffice to produce equal or even more satisfactory overall results for the HRD organization. In many cases, CMI may be the best way for an organization to initiate use of CBL. In the practical world of HRD, the use of CMI, compared to the use of conventional methods, can often be money saving. A specific problem, whether it be organization, project, or performance, can often be successfully approached using an exclusively CMI solution.

Computer-Supported Learning Resources. This component of CBL is seen least often. For those readers who are comfortable with the term, *CSLR* is usually a "data base." This means that CSLR is a pool of information. It can be used, but it does not teach. Instead, it provides information that we can use to learn. For example, a library is a noncomputer learning resource. Learners use a CSLR in the same way as a library, although a CSLR is supported by a computer program. The CSLR program facilitates the retrieval, examination, and manipulation of the data.

We have examined the essential components that constitute CBL. Other frequently used terms are hardware, software, and courseware.

Hardware, software, and courseware.   These terms are heard frequently during a discussion of CBL. *Hardware* is a straightforward term. It is used to describe the actual physical items involved in the CBL process, including the CBL terminal, disk drives, printers, keyboards, and any other physical items.

Some confusion could arise between the terms *software* and *courseware*. The reason is that, in technical terms, some courseware is software. For learning specialists, there is no need for technical (data processing) precision. *Software* is what makes the computer components of a CBL system work as they should. The system's HRD users may never actually see the software. The computer and noncomputer elements that support learning are called *courseware*. Courseware includes the computer-delivered lessons and tests, the video, audio, texts, and other learning resources.

Now that we have examined some characteristics of the inside of CBL, we need to look at the human side. HRD is concerned with adults, therefore, it is important to know how well CBL fits the adult learning situation.

Adult Learners

The impact on students in HRD situations is generally positive. The CBL system functions effectively in the learning situation. The highly individualized way it handles instruction is a good match for what we know about adult learners.

Some characteristics of adults in learning situations are:

1.   The rate of learning varies between individuals.
2.   Adults enter the learning situation with considerable previous experience and learning.
3.   Individuals have different learning styles and preferences.

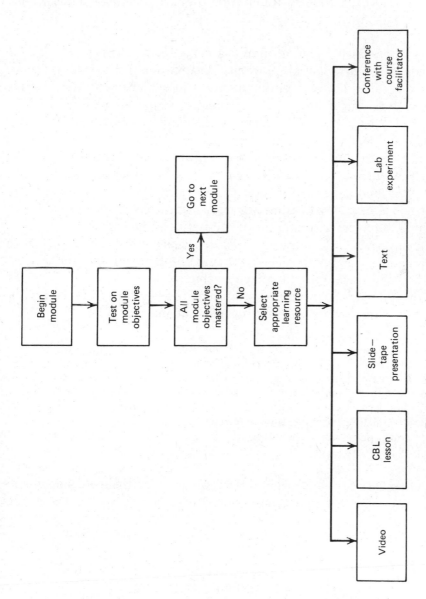

Figure 11.2. Prescription generation in computer-managed instruction.

11.11

4. Individuals may have a variety of goals for learning.
5. Adults need to feel confident that they are learning what is needed to meet their own goals.[1]

Computer-based learning matches very well with these characteristics. Most important of all, it works. An analysis of the results of more than 75 studies showed significant gains in achievement and positive attitude. Most important, learning time was reduced by 25–50%![2]

CBL also has an impact on learning specialists. CBL is an inherently individual form of learning. The obvious implication for learning specialists is that presentations to a group are unlikely to mesh well with CBL. The learning specialist will continue to be important but in a new way. As a facilitator of learning, the learning specialist will perform more enjoyable tasks. Facilitators work with learners as individuals—coaching, tutoring, and guiding the activities of the learner.

The impact of CBL on the organization is an extension of the effect on the learning specialist. To derive the maximum benefits from CBL, it is best employed in an individualized setting.

Although it was not necessarily intended to describe a CBL project, the following is an excellent description of what one should be.

> In short, state-of-the-art instruction derives its objectives from a real need (a job), creates instruction that is tightly related to the accomplishment of those objectives, and removes obstacles between the learners and the learning. It encourages and assists students to progress as rapidly as their growing competence will allow and makes their world a little brighter, rather than dimmer, when they demonstrate progress. It provides instruction and practice until each student can perform as desired, and then it stops.[3]

Adding CBL to a conventional HRD program, without considering its strengths, will only add to the program's cost. We will look at these costs and the benefits that can outweigh them, but first, we will examine the source of the hardware and courseware—the new technology.

WHY THE NEW TECHNOLOGY?

Background

In the year 2000, HRD practitioners may well wonder why CBL was a trend in the 1980s instead of in the 1960s or 1970s. Why are we now calling it a *new* technology when it is older than some of the learning specialists who are using it? The early decades of CBL provided the proof of its basic worth as a tool in learning. Yet, those were really the developmental years. Suddenly, in the 1980s, CBL has arrived. We can credit two major factors for the blossoming and amazing growth of CBL. These factors were sequential and cumulative in effect. The first was the ever-decreasing cost of computer technology in general, from which CBL has benefited. The second factor (made possible by the first) was the wide attention and acceptance accorded personal computers.

The decrease in cost that enabled the increasing use of computer technology was made possible by miniaturization. The ability to increase the number of components on a single microchip translates directly to a proportional growth in power without the corresponding increase in price. This is the fundamental concept behind the CBL trend.

Cost decreases made the university-proven CBL commercially possible. But its advent into the HRD field was assisted considerably by a public consciousness of computers. In the first two years of the 1980s, CBL went from an unknown abbreviation to something that nearly every organization's HRD department felt was worthy of consideration.

Micros, Minis, and Mainframes

The traditional size system had no special name in the beginning. The minicomputer resulted from a conscious effort to provide a computer with less power, at less cost, for applications where that was appropriate. *Mini* was used to indicate the smaller of two types. *Macro*, or large, was sometimes used to describe the larger size, but the much more frequently heard *mainframe* is the term we will use. The situation was further complicated by the advent of *"super"* computers (which have processing power far in excess of currently foreseen HRD application needs) and *micro* computers.

Following the general trend, electronic calculators and microcomputer technology may be combined. It is not clear, as this is being written, whether hand-held (pocket) computers will receive a special name. If they do, *pico* may be used but *puny* will never be appropriate.

Microcomputers are a special case. It was only after the development of personal and home computers that the attention of the general public was drawn to computers as something other than machines used by organizations for various kinds of data processing. This led to confusion as *microcomputer* was used as a synonym for *good*. The term had become meaningless. Terms that are much more useful for use in the HRD field are *desktop computer* and *stand-alone system*. These terms ignore the technical identity, or size, of the hardware, focusing instead on characteristics.

Unlike the terms covered earlier (e.g., CMI and courseware), the learning specialist really does not have to understand the differences in system size. It is increasingly difficult to generate enthusiasm for helping HRD professionals differentiate between different size systems. In the past, each of the size systems represented distinctions worth remembering. Each represented separate levels of cost, physical size, and speed, as well as differences in other technical aspects. There is a trend in computer hardware toward each type moving in the direction of the others. The distinctions have become blurred and, at the same time, relatively unimportant.

HRD professionals need not focus on sizes nor need they start by considering a system based on size. That would be a fundamental error, indicative of a backward approach. One should first determine total requirements, including expansion needs. A complete process of needs analysis will result in definition of CBL system requirements. The requirements are almost certain to focus more on system capabilities, that is, characteristics. This is where the HRD person can use a CBL consultant.

LEARNING SYSTEM CHARACTERISTICS

The characteristics of a practical learning system required to meet the needs of an organization will vary with the particular application selected. The complete system for human resource development would have the following capabilities:

1. A powerful authoring (see glossary) system, preferably with a high level, user-oriented, HRD-specific author language, powerful authoring utilities, and "programmerless" authoring
2. Flexibility in instructional strategy
3. Powerful instructional management system
4. High resolution graphics
5. Learner input through tactile screen interaction (see glossary)
6. Stand-alone delivery capability
7. Auxiliary device control, including random access audio, random access videotape and videodisc, and electronic voice synthesis
8. Transportability of courseware to other systems[4]

Many of these characteristics pertain to the development of courseware. These characteristics, other trends, and future developments in learning systems will be examined later in this chapter. Others, such as tactile input, relate to the use of the system by people. This leads to the consideration of human factors.

Human Factors

Any new technology generates some doubts and very legitimate questions from new users. In the case of CBL, these center on the use of the terminal. There is some concern among new users regarding exposure to the cathode ray tube (CRT). Considerable research has examined the effects of exposure to CRTs. These studies have not identified any harmful effects from working or studying at terminals.[5] The application of ergonomics (human factor engineering) has, and will continue to, improve the physical aspects of CBL.

There is another side of human factors—the courseware itself. There is a wide variation in the "learner friendliness" of courseware. Courseware that is well designed has built-in consistency. The learner will have planned support available, in terms of the use of certain keys. Help will be available to provide planned instructions. By using a help function, the learner will be provided with a predetermined message with information on how to proceed. As CBL becomes more widely used, courseware design that promotes ease of use will be expected and standard.

The desirability of high resolution graphics has been supported since the early years of CBL. Graphics aid learner understanding of complex items or processes, and that can speed the learning process. A number of studies show the power of graphics to improve learning.[6]

Animation is the movement of items on the screen. It is related to graphics. Characters can be drawn, selectively erased, and repositioned to produce animation. In HRD, animation is used to aid understanding through illustration. It also seems to aid recall by highlighting steps in progress.

Computer Learning Environments

There is more involved in CBL systems than the hardware, used for storage and delivery, and the author language or programming utilities (see glossary). There exist entire environments in which CBL development and delivery activities are carried out. In the past, these have centered around hardware. The environment may include: on-line or bulletin board type communications between industry or development groups, and utilities for the creation of portions or types of courseware. Not the least important element of an environment is the group of individuals and organizations using the same system. A considerable amount of sharing is common. We will look at this sharing in greater detail as we look at courseware development.

STRATEGIES FOR THE ENTRY LEVEL ORGANIZATION

There are several basic ways to get started, and there are numerous variations on each.[7] At least some of these possibilities will be examined briefly.

Learning Center Delivery

In certain subject areas, delivery of courseware may be possible in a commercial CBL learning center. Learning centers offer complete CBL courses or curricula for a fee. The subjects available through a learning center are those most commonly used by many organizations. Such courseware is referred to as *canned*.

Learning centers exist in a surprising number of metropolitan areas. By using a learning center, where that method can fit a need, an organization can operate a computer-based learning project and avoid the cost of both hardware and software. That makes it possible, in those cases, to evolve a CBL capability from a very modest start.

Learning centers may also be used for the remote delivery of proprietary courseware. In this situation, the cost of hardware to deliver instruction to employees, distributed widely, can achieve considerable savings. The costs of transportation and lodging for central delivery of the same program may favor learning center delivery.

Another possibility is to obtain canned courseware, ready for internal delivery.

Canned Courseware

In comparison to conventional instruction, CBL development costs are high while delivery costs are low. These development costs have decreased and will continue to do so. However, because of the comparatively high cost of development, quality CBL courseware in all subjects cannot be as readily available as seminars. On the other hand, once developed, courseware remains available nearly indefinitely. These facts explain why the supply of CBL courseware is relatively limited and why, over time, it can be expected to become much more widely distributed.

There may be little or no courseware already developed in very technical and specialized areas. In other areas, there is considerable courseware already developed and suitable for delivery in organizational HRD programs. One leading vendor in the CBL field has thousands of hours of courseware available, and more under development. In general, courseware is more likely to be available in those subject areas where there is a common need by all organizations. Subjects in this category include management, basic math, language, and data processing subjects.

In many cases, the project at hand will require instruction in a subject for which no canned courseware exists. There are still a number of possibilities, one of which is custom courseware.

Custom Courseware

The obvious, although not necessarily best, solution for an entry level organization, is to write its own CBL courseware. This possibility is covered in more detail later in this chapter under "development."

It may be possible to identify another company in the same industry, where competitive factors are not paramount, that will share or sell courseware it has already developed. This may strike some readers as unlikely, but both sharing and selling of courseware do occur within the same industry. If development of courseware is required, an obvious source is the vendor of the organization's CBL system. Most system vendors do provide courseware development services. This source is especially desirable when an organization enters the CBL world. The vendor has a major stake in the success of your CBL efforts and, generally, has more problem-solving resources.

The custom courseware house is a phenomenon of the 1980s. Although not entirely unknown in the past, the economic customer base needed to support CBL consulting did not exist until the 1980s. The CBL consultant house has since become a regular part of the HRD scene.

Consortium Membership

One way to initiate use of CBL is as a part of a group interested in similar courseware. The sharing of expertise and resources can permit development of courseware that a single organization would find too expensive to develop on its own. The early 1980s were characterized by a burst of consortium activity. Examples of consortia are increasingly common as the use of CBL spreads. Excellent consortia concepts exist in the areas of petroleum, nuclear power, and engineering education.

Petroleum companies require employees with special skills. For example, in the area of petroleum geophysics, many petroleum companies need a course to educate petroleum geophysicists. CBL is an excellent vehicle for such education, yet no single company requires the number of personnel necessary to make the CBL approach cost-beneficial. Therefore, a common endeavor makes sense. More than one dozen petroleum companies have formed a consortium to develop the needed course.

A similar situation existed in the area of nuclear power reactor operator training and education. CBL offers many important advantages for power company programs. One especially significant advantage is that the learning can be delivered on-site and at a time most convenient to the learner and the organization. This is especially important, since most reactors are located far from cities, where human resources for programs might be most readily found. When a great need was identified in this area, a group of power companies joined to design and develop a complete curriculum to meet this instructional need.

In the early 1980s, the demand for engineers was greater than the number of engineering school graduates. This condition was exaggerated by the recruiting of faculty members, as well as graduates, to positions in industry. A group of universities joined together to resolve the problem of faculty attrition by reevaluating the requirements for the first two years of undergraduate engineering education. In this case, the CBL component was designed to present the most basic material—those courses least likely to excite university faculty members—leaving the more enjoyable portion of the interaction to those faculty members.

Examples of Applications

There are some excellent examples of the application of CBL in a broad number of subject areas and industries.[8] The examples found in Figure 11.3 represent only a partial list of industries and applications. They show the broad variety of learners and uses for which CBL has been successful.

Industry	HRD Application
Aerospace	Microprocessors for engineers
Automobile	Electronics theory for maintenance
Aviation	Flight crew Aircraft maintenance
Chemical	Product familiarization (technical)
Computer	Computer maintenance Product familiarization (technical) Management training Sales training
Electric utility	System controller Nuclear reactor operator Safety Security
Food	Process operator
Machine tool	Distributor familiarization
Military	Sophisticated weapons system maintenance Basic math, language
Petroleum	Equipment, process applications Seismic data processing Petroleum training (technical)
Pharmaceutical	Product familiarization (technical) Salesperson qualification testing Salesperson refresher
Securities	Certification testing
Telecommunications	Basic math, language Electronic equipment maintenance Equipment operator training Technical training
Tobacco	Microprocessors for engineers Microprocessors for maintenance personnel
Transportation	Subway car maintenance

Figure 11.3. HRD applications.

MATCHING APPLICATIONS TO NEEDS AND GOALS

One guideline that applies to any HRD effort is even more important for the success of CBL. That is, the application that is selected for the initial project should be central to the activity of the organization. It should solve a problem. Ideally, it should apply the greatest strengths of CBL to that problem. It would not be sound, for example, to initiate a CBL project to find a solution for a problem that can be solved conventionally with complete satisfaction. The CBL solution should produce the needed learning faster, better, or cheaper.

Small Project

In general, a prudent approach is to use CBL in a pilot project, in order to gain experience with the technology and acquaint the organization with a new way of doing business. A good way to organize a small start is outlined later in this chapter.

Large Project

Although starting small may be wise in many cases, there is also a rationale in CBL for larger projects. The reason for this relates to the initial costs associated with CBL. A large project offers the possibilities that come with economies of scale. Fixed equipment and development costs can be divided among a greater number of learners or lessons in determining the total project costs. Once an organization has an established CBL capability, delivery costs are reduced and small cost-effective projects can be more readily implemented.

A CMI Approach

The preceding examination of various possibilities has ignored the difference in possible CBL strategies. A unique possibility is offered by CMI. It is possible to use CMI in conjunction with preexisting conventional learning resources. Unlike CAI, CMI can be used with existing programs in small quantities, producing an immediate positive advantage. This method adds the structure of computer management to delivery of existing course materials. All of the attendant advantages of individualization and mastery are almost a bonus.

Certification and Qualification Testing

The needs of certain organizations have been well served by use of a CBL testing, certification, or qualification project. These projects use the obvious strengths of the computer. They do not involve learning but are a part of the organization's overall HRD effort. For example, one pharmaceutical company devised tests for their sales force. The tests insure that the salespersons have a satisfactory knowledge of the company's products. In the securities field, certification examinations are routinely administered using a CBL testing system.

COST BENEFIT ANALYSIS

There are a number of possible ways to justify a situation. In this case, we are addressing only financial justification. The basis for such justification is simple. If the costs of a project are less than the benefits to the organization, the organization is justified in proceeding with the project. This process, called *cost benefit analysis*, is used frequently when introducing a new technology, such as CBL.

What About the Costs of HRD?

The first step in analyzing whether a situation is cost-beneficial is to determine the current or usual costs. For our potential CBL project, these costs may include travel, time lost to HRD, and a performance gap between where learners should be after learning and where they were before.

There are factors that affect the cost of any instruction we may deliver. Such factors include instructional strategy, whether a course already exists or is new, the amount of existing information on the subject (e.g., a new piece of equipment), the amount of individualization desired, and the media used.

Reducing the Costs of HRD

The cost of HRD to the organization can be reduced in a number of ways. Costs or expenses may be directly reduced by scaling down or eliminating certain courses or programs. However, there usually is some penalty for this. Costs may be controlled, rather than directly reduced. This can be severe in its impact, in some cases. More beneficial ways to reduce costs are to improve the effectiveness of learners, to increase the total number of learners with the same resources, to achieve consistency among those finishing the program, and to simplify administration of the program. CBL can be used to reduce costs in all of these ways.

Costs of CBL

The costs of CBL are different for organizations just starting than for those that have a CBL capability. This is due to the necessity of acquiring equipment. The equipment expense makes it more difficult to cost-justify an initial project than a "follow-on" one. The cost of good CBL development is also higher than that of good conventional development, due to the additional programming effort. Naturally, CBL development costs will affect new and follow-on projects equally.

Benefits of CBL

Just as there are typical costs associated with CBL, there are typical benefits. One benefit, reduced delivery costs, balances out the high cost of CBL development and establishes the basis for justifying projects over time. The cost of designing and developing a lecture-based course is relatively low, but the cost of the instructor is repeated each time the course is delivered. The total costs mount steadily due to delivery costs. The developmental cost of a CBL course is higher than a conventional course (see Figure 11.4). As the CBL version is delivered, the costs do increase, but at a much slower rate. By comparing the two possibilities in advance, it can be determined whether the CBL version, with higher start-up costs, will be cheaper over the life of the course.

Another benefit of CBL delivery is the possibility of increased learning. This could result in more accurate job performance by learners, with benefits to productivity. As mentioned earlier, there is evidence to indicate that the individualization (especially CMI) results in

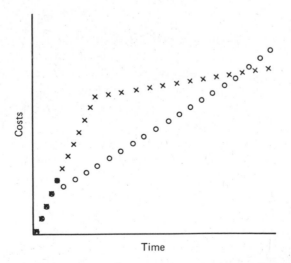

Figure 11.4. Development and delivery costs. (o) Conventional; (x) CBL.

reduced learning time. Reduced learning time can produce considerable savings in the form of reducing HRD costs per learner, reduced per diem costs, reduced loss of productive time away from the job, or earlier readiness for a new job. All of these can be quantified. This is not an impractical theory. Cost benefit analysis is used by successful organizations with good results.[8]

Once a project has passed the selection phases, a new series of processes and decisions come into play. These will be examined as we consider development.

COURSEWARE DEVELOPMENT

One of the main concerns of organizations and individuals getting started in CBL is courseware development. As mentioned earlier, developed courseware and courseware development services are available. The same development procedures are or should be followed, regardless of where the courseware is developed.

The Development Process

The courseware development process frequently used for CBL is the instructional systems development (ISD) model or "systems approach." ISD is also used extensively for development of courseware for conventional delivery. Other development models are not being used extensively for CBL at present. They could be, if they presented an organized approach and were compatible with the use of objectives and mastery learning. ISD is used because the phased approach, instructional objectives, and concept of mastery that characterize it match perfectly with CBL.

The use of a model results in the division of an instructional development project into distinct phases or steps. The steps of a typical model that could be used for CBL development include:

1. Analysis
2. Design
3. Development
4. Implementation
5. Evaluation

CBL Development

ivities in a particular step are the same, regardless of the delivery method used. However, the steps include some items that reflect a CBL orientation or are unique. We will look briefly at each of the steps to identify which activities are unique to a CBL project.

During the analysis phase, one of the tasks typically carried out is defining the needs and the constraints. Identifying the constraints may help in determining possible solutions in a particular case. The availability of funds and the delivery environment are two factors that could either suggest or restrict the use of CBL in an HRD project.

During the analysis of the target population, factors such as geographic location of learners and present qualifications are identified and will have an important impact on the use of CBL. Geographic distribution of learners can favor various CBL strategies. Present qualifications can be important, too. A specific example for CBL in HRD is that without audio capabilities CBL is inappropriate for illiterate learners.

Regular tasks included in the design phase include: specification of learning activities, assessment, and evaluation systems. These tasks are also a part of a non-CBL design, but here, they define the extent of the role CBL will play in a given project. Learning activities may include CAI lessons. The assessment system may be a CMI system. CBL may also be used as a part of the evaluation, or it may be done conventionally.

The development phase is unique for a CBL project, since it includes the development and production of the CBL materials. The CAI, CMI, and CSLR materials are produced by programming or other means.

The implementation phase of a CBL project obviously has CBL components. An implementation item that is different for CBL is related to support. Any course requires certain efforts to support and maintain it. The support and maintenance for a CBL course are quite different from those usually encountered for conventional instruction. Support may include a course telephone hotline that offers help to remote learners. Maintenance includes upkeep of the computer files that contain the CBL materials.

Evaluation comes in two parts, formative and summative. The formative evaluation, conducted while the course is under development, is a means of testing and revising the course materials. The revisions made at this point make the materials better when they are put into general use. The actual production of the final materials is not begun until the formative evaluation is completed. Unfortunately, formative evaluation is often omitted from conventional development. In a CBL course, this is done at great peril. Individual and small group trials of the course materials are very important.

The summative evaluation measures the effectiveness of the course in solving the HRD problem for which it was created. This phase is conducted as the course is in regular use. In CBL, further corrections can be made using the same procedures as course maintenance, usually without interruption in course delivery. The relative ease of revising courseware already in use makes the summative evaluation a powerful technique, rather than an empty exercise.

All of these phases of courseware development produce planning documents. These are used in later phases and are important records as well. These records are called *documentation*.

Documentation

Unfortunately, learning specialists sometimes do not retain documentation of the process used to develop their instructional materials. This can make future revisions difficult. Since the ability to update materials is an advantage of CBL, the importance of documentation is indeed great. This problem is widely recognized, resulting in a very good record of documentation among HRD professionals.

Documents that are used may include: course specifications, learning maps, grouped and sequenced instructional objectives, test items, learning activity descriptions, CAI lesson designs, assessment plans, and evaluation plans.

Among the most important documents are those that will guide the programming. When correctly done, these are called *programmer-ready materials*.

Programmer-Ready Materials

Many organizations have a well-developed conventional courseware production capability. The essential difference between conventional and CBL courseware is the computer program. What is necessary, then, is to be able to produce programmer-ready instructional materials. It is certainly an achievable step for an organization or individual already capable of producing quality conventional courseware.

The organization should establish certain standards that will lend uniformity to the courseware developed and will reduce confusion. For example, specific portions of the screen may be reserved for a certain use, or certain information may always be displayed in the same location or way.

Basically, what is required resembles in form and philosophy the more familiar storyboard used in video development. A page representing the CRT, with exact text and general or specific graphic indications, must be accompanied by notations as to the outcomes of the learner's key-press selections. Such outcomes may replot the screen, provide a "help" display, cause an answer to be judged, or cause some other action to take place. Provided with complete materials, as described, and standards to follow, the authoring system is used to produce the courseware. Basically, a programmer or a clerical staff member can produce the courseware using a courseware generator. A high-level authoring language permits a programmer to achieve just about anything the author intends. The "programmerless" authoring system is generally menu driven. The person using it need not learn a programming language; instead, the person deals with packaged functions that are offered on the menus. The program is produced as a result of menu choices. The lesson generators already exist. The power and flexibility they offer will continue to grow.

How courseware is developed can be expected to change little in the near future. How the courseware is delivered and what it is like will change greatly. Let's examine where the trend of CBL is going.

GETTING READY FOR THE FUTURE

HRD is and ought to be a reflection of the society in which it exists. Our society has been and will continue to be powerfully impacted on by technology. This is simply not the level of impact felt when cassette tape recorders became widely available. A clear signal of the tremendous impact computers have already made was the *Time* magazine selection of the computer as the "man of the year" for 1982. John Naisbitt, writing in his book *Megatrends*, says that "To be really successful, you will have to be trilingual: fluent in English, Spanish, and computer."[9] It seems apparent that HRD will be carried out within a much more technological society than ever before. It will reflect that society in the use of technology for learning.

The Coming Technologies

The impact of computers on society in the early 1980s was entirely predictable. The evolution of technology and the development of each level of miniaturization in microchips led to an increase in the degree of impact. This trend is not over. Laboratories have achieved further miniaturization and other advances that will place more computer power in the hands of the individual. This cycle of practical implementation of successive levels of technology will not run its full course during this century.

The general trend in computers is quite clear. It has been constant for years. There will be ever-increasing power and capacity available to a given level of user. And the unit cost of a given level of capability will decrease. Speech generation and recognition, which have not been widely used in the past, will join the regularly available technologies. Increasingly, available memory will make possible digital storage of video images directly in the computer. The resulting video will make photographic quality graphics available for direct use and manipulation in a learning program, without use of today's video equipment.

One advance that can be expected is greater ergonomics in CBL hardware. A related advance, and one to which HRD practitioners can make a significant contribution not a moment too soon, is greater friendliness in the software.

There is little doubt that our grandchildren will call the systems we use the "Model Ts" of CBL. Some changes are nearly upon us, while others are possibilities.

In the past, instructional television has been a powerful tool for some uses, and now videodiscs and digital video are increasing that power. The CBL course can identify specific segments of information a learner lacks. Video can be immediately delivered to cover the learning items for that point. *Random access*, the ability of videodiscs to play a segment directly without playing any other segment first, makes it suitable for this connection. (Videotape can do the same thing in concept but must travel past all the tape between the present point and the needed information.) This computer and videodisc strategy is generally called *interactive video*.

One of the predictable CBL advances is in this area. The increased memory available will permit an image to be stored in digital form directly in the computer. The similar interactive video delivery will then be possible without the videodisc.

Another area of great potential for HRD is voice recognition and voice synthesis, whereby the CBL system will speak to the learner and understand the reply.

The cost of telecommunications also influences the cost of central system CBL. Micro-based, stand-alone delivery provides an alternative. Progress in communications and the spread of data bases may lead to a new desire for outside links. Advances in communications, including telecommunications, networks, data transfer, and data display TV, offer big power and potential. Any such system with user control offers the possibility of use for CBL. Just what use will be made of this potential remains to be seen.

THE FUTURE WORKPLACE

In the future, more workers will have CRTs at their desks or will use one in the course of their work. These CRTs are potential delivery devices for CBL courseware; however, at some point, these work stations may not be simple CRTs. The work station may include a far more integrated work area. The work surface itself may become active, permitting input and providing output for graphic images as well as text. There will be more data bases with broader access. These powerful and plentiful resources will allow greater learner involvement in the design of the learning.

More workers may work at home with the commercial-grade equipment that can be used for HRD at hours of their convenience. Those whose work involves creation of courseware will have very sophisticated courseware generators. When participating in HRD activities themselves, the direction of their study may be more a result of their own interest and initiative. The possibilities will be greater in the future, just as those of the present are greater than the past.

Universities can exist in concept as well as in buildings. Powerful learning tools linked to the university's resources offer the same options for personal development at home as a part of the organization's HRD. The common access to these knowledge-based systems may contribute to greater cooperation and sharing of resources between them.

CBL SUCCESS

It should be clear that CBL offers great opportunities for most organizations. What is needed are a few simple ideas that offer potential success for many HRD organizations. The strategies that meet such criteria and an idealized start-up scenario follow.

High-Payoff Planning Strategies

One method of planning successful and cost-beneficial CBL projects is to select high payoff strategies. Such strategies with potential for success include: selection of a project with good economy of scale, selection of a project that is impossible without the computer, or selection of a project with a high risk/reward ratio.

An ideal strategy may not be ideal at every time and place, but a sound strategy can be identified. The organization can select a good initial project—one that is cost effective. The HRD department contracts for the design and development of the courseware with a vendor or custom courseware house, while encouraging HRD staff participation. The staff can participate in CBL seminars or even on-line CBL courseware that provides instruction to develop the organization's CBL capability.

The vendor will be glad to involve the organization's HRD staff in the project. The first project may produce sufficient learning for the organization to carry on alone on the next project, or the same arrangement may be repeated with continually increasing participation by the organization. The result will be a proven organizational CBL capability.

CONCLUSION

CBL is a trend, not a fad. Some practitioners and managers who examined CBL at some time during the past two decades remember only what CBL was and what its capabilities and manner of application were. It should be clear that CBL capabilities have been growing and will continue to grow. Those who haven't seen CBL lately haven't seen CBL at all.

GLOSSARY

Authoring. This is the process of creating computer-based learning course material. The author is the person who originates the program ideas. Authoring is distinct from *programming*, which is the task of writing program code for courseware already authored.

Author Utilities. See Utility.

CRT (cathode ray tube). The cathode ray tube refers to the screen used in oscilloscopes, television sets, and computer terminals.

Computer-Based Learning (CBL). *CBL* is the umbrella term that includes all uses of computers in support of learning. The components of CBL are CAI, CMI, and CSLR. The meaning is identical to CBE, CBI, or

CBT, which are based on education, instruction, or training. *CBL* is preferred by those who focus on the learner, rather than the instructor.

Computer-Assisted Instruction (CAI). CAI is the use of a computer to deliver instruction. Modes of CAI are drill and practice, problem solving, instructional games, modeling, tutorial, and simulation. This is the preferred term, although CAT and CAL are sometimes used. CAI, CMI, and CSLR are the components of CBE.

Computer-Managed Instruction (CMI). CMI is that aspect of CBE that includes testing, prescription generation, and record keeping. CMI, CAI, and CSLR are the components of CBE.

Computer-Supported Learning Resources (CSLR). A computer-supported learning resource is any form of computer support or function that supports learning, other than those which teach (CAI) or test, prescribe, or keep records (CMI). A CSLR is often a data base, similar in purpose to a traditional noncomputer learning resource, the library. CSLR, CAI, and CMI are the components of CBE.

Courseware. *Courseware* is the term used to describe those computer application programs, as well as other media (e.g., texts and video), that support educational objectives. Computer courseware is a special form of *software*, a term reserved in this field for the programs that simply make the computer run.

Hardware. This is the category of computer components that involves physical equipment. Hardware includes the instructions to the equipment, which are called *software*, and the instructional software and supporting physical materials, which are called *courseware*.

Software. In computer-based learning, *software* includes those programs that instruct the hardware and run the computer. A special software use by the instructors and students is called *courseware*. Software simply makes the computer work.

Tactile Input (also Tactile Screen Interactions). *Tactile input* is interaction with the computer program by touching the screen, rather than using the keyboard. Tactile screen interaction may be achieved by use of a light pen or touch panel screen. Experience shows that certain categories of users, including doctors and pilots, strongly prefer tactile input.

Utility. *Utility* is a special program that handles repetitive tasks without human interaction. An *authoring utility* is a special program that facilitates courseware production by enabling a content expert to interact with the computer and perform the programming automatically. Such a utility does not require programming knowledge or skill.

NOTES

1. For a more complete treatment of these ideas, see M. Knowles, *The Adult Learner: A Neglected Species*, 2d. ed. (Houston: Gulf Publishing Company, 1979).
2. J. Kulik, C. Kulik, and P. Cohen, "Effectiveness of Computer-based College Teaching: A Meta-analysis of Findings," *Review of Educational Research, 1980,* 50:525–44.
3. R. Mager, *Troubleshooting the Troubleshooting Course* (Belmont, Cal.: Pitman Learning, Inc., 1982), p. 136.
4. This list of capabilities is based on one given in A. Reynolds, "Developing Human Resources with 'State of the Art' Computer-based Learning" (Paper presented at EDINFO-82 International Symposium on Education in Informatics, Madras, India, 1982).
5. The information regarding health hazards is contained in a National Institute for Occupational Safety and Health (NIOSH) report. The contents of the NIOSH report are summarized in very readable form in E. Jones, "Is Your Computer Terminal Hazardous to Your Health?" *Popular Computing* (1982):131–32.
6. A representative study regarding the importance of graphics is M. Szabo, F. Dwyer, and H. DeMelo, "Visual Testing—Visual Literacy's Second Dimension," *Education and Communications Technology Journal,* 29 (1981):177–87.
7. Three good examples of quite different organizational approaches to CBL with different applications are: J. Buck, and P. Beardsley, "How Computer-based Instruction Was Cost Justified in the FAA," *ADCIS Proceedings, 1980.*

   J. Cain, "Computer-based Training at United Airlines," *Training and Development Journal,* 35 (1981):76–78.

   R. Davis, "Approaches to CBI Effectiveness: Activity in the Bell System," *T.H.E. Journal,* 9 (1981):43–45.
8. Descriptions of successful application cases in several industries, universities, and government are given in A. Reynolds, "Computer-based Learning: The Key 'Technological Multiplier' for Technology Transfer," *Training and Development Journal,* 36 (1982):64–67.
9. J. Naisbitt, *Megatrends* (New York: Warner Books, 1982).

BIBLIOGRAPHY

Buck, J., and P. Beardsley. "How Computer-based Instruction Was Cost Justified in the FAA." *ADCIS Proceedings, 1980.*

Cain, J. "Computer-based Training at United Airlines." *Training and Development Journal* (1981):76–78.

Davis, R. "Approaches to CBI Effectiveness: Activity in the Bell System." *T.H.E. Journal* (1981):43–45.

Jones, E. "Is Your Computer Terminal Hazardous to Your Health?" *Popular Computing* (1982):131–32.

Knowles, M. *The Adult Learner: A Neglected Species.* 2d. ed. Houston: Gulf Publishing Company, 1979.

Kulik, J., C. Kulik, and P. Cohen. "Effectiveness of Computer-based College Teaching: A Meta-analysis of Findings." *Review of Educational Research, 1980,* 60:525–44.

Mager, R. *Troubleshooting the Troubleshooting Course.* Belmont, Cal.: Pitman Learning, Inc., 1982.

Reynolds, A. "Computer-based Learning: The Key 'Technological Multiplier' for Technology Transfer." *Training and Development Journal,* 34 (1980):64–67.

Reynolds, A. "Developing Human Resources with 'State of the Art' Computer-based Learning." Paper presented at EDINFO-82 International Symposium on Education in Informatics, Madras, India, 1982.

Szabo, M., F. Dwyer, and H. DeMelo. "Visual Testing—Visual Literacy's Second Dimension." *Education and Communications Technology Journal,* 29 (1981):117–87.

Evaluation of HRD Programs: Quantitative

JACK J. PHILLIPS

Everyone associated with HRD must be concerned about evaluation. In this chapter, Phillips sets forth some clear and distinct ways to design quantitative evaluation.

As most readers will acknowledge there is also *qualitative* evaluation. This should not be confused with *soft* evaluation. The tendency has been to evaluate those things that can be counted, or quantified. Even though we discuss quality of work life, little has been done to find methods of measuring that significant aspect. I had hoped to include a chapter on qualitative evaluation, in this handbook, but could not identify those who would or could write such a chapter. It is certainly an area that needs further investigation.

Meanwhile, we are fortunate to have a good chapter from Phillips on quantitative evaluation.

When economic conditions are poor, quantitative evaluation, which emphasizes dollar results, is especially important to HRD practitioners. During bad times, management looks very closely at every expenditure, and it is only natural that HRD should be an item for managerial scrutiny. If the HRD practitioner waits until that time to design the evaluation, it will be too late. Evaluation should be part of the initial design of every HRD program.

In good economic times, quantitative evaluation is still essential, even though management may not demand it. If the HRD practitioner constantly designs evaluation into every program, it is possible to indicate to management the specific contribution that has been made to the organization through the HRD effort.

The material presented in this chapter should enable all HRD practitioners to build quantitative evaluation into their programs.

Jack J. Phillips is manager of administration, Vulcan Material Company, southern division, Alabama. He is responsible for human resource functions. He has been training and development manager at Stockham Valves and Fittings, training director for the American Enka Company, and involved in training and production at Lockheed-Georgia. He has published over 40 articles in professional and business publications and is the author of *Handbook of Training Evaluation and Measurement Methods* (1983).

PREPARATION FOR EVALUATION

Developing an Evaluation Philosophy

Before presenting specific methods of program evaluation, the proper foundation must be laid. A major part of this foundation is the development of an evaluation philosophy in the organization, a philosophy that emphasizes results and is characterized in the following ways:

1. *HRD Programs Are Not Usually Undertaken Unless Tangible Results Can Be Obtained.* If the effect of the program cannot be measured, then perhaps the program should not be implemented. This approach may be too impractical or unrealistic for some HRD departments. Should a program that represents a significant effort or cost be conducted if its effectiveness cannot be determined? Maybe there are other reasons for proceeding with a program.

2. *At Least One Method to Measure the Results of an HRD Program Is Included in the Program Design.* The evaluation strategy is usually determined when program objectives are established. With this philosophy, evaluation strategy is placed on a level of equal importance with the content of the program, the objectives, the delivery system, and the instructor or program director.

3. *Each Member of the HRD Staff Should Be Committed to Measuring the Results of His or Her Efforts.* Each member of the HRD staff must see the importance of evaluation and the necessity for including it as an integral part of the HRD process. If possible, each staff member should participate in measuring the results of his or her programs.

Purposes and Uses of Evaluation

Evaluation is undertaken for several reasons. Generally, they fall into two categories: (1) to improve the HRD process, or (2) to decide whether or not to continue it. The following list presents in more detail each specific reason:

1. *To Determine Whether a Program Is Accomplishing Its Objectives.* Every properly designed program should have objectives. A very important purpose of the evaluation process is to determine whether or not objectives are being or have been met.

2. *To Identify the Strengths and Weaknesses in the HRD Process.* An evaluation can help to determine the effectiveness of the various compo-

nents of an HRD program. This is probably the most common purpose of evaluation. These include, but are not limited to, methods of presentation, learning environment, program content, instructional aids, facility, schedule, and even the instructor. These variables do make a difference in the HRD effort and need to be evaluated to make improvements in the program.

   3. *To Determine the Cost/Benefit Ratio of an HRD Program.* An increasingly common reason for evaluation is to determine whether or not the program justified the cost. This aspect of evaluation compares the cost of a program to its usefulness or value. It provides management with data to eliminate an unproductive program, to increase support for programs that yield a high payoff, or to make adjustments in a program to increase the benefits.

   4. *To Decide Who Should Participate in Future Programs.* Sometimes a follow-up evaluation simply determines the benefits of the program. Communicating these benefits to prospective learners can help them decide whether or not they need to be involved in the program.

   5. *To Reinforce Major Points Made to the Learner.* A follow-up evaluation can reinforce the information covered in a program by attempting to measure the results accomplished by learners. It reminds them of what they should have accomplished or should be accomplishing.

   6. *To Gather Data to Assist in Marketing Future Programs.* In many situations, HRD departments or organizations delivering learning experiences are interested in why learners attend a specific program. This is particularly true for larger organizations where many programs are offered and the sponsoring organization does not always know why someone is selected to attend. An evaluation can yield information to assist the marketing strategy for future programs. Questions which become relevant are:

   Why did you attend this program?
   Who made the decision for you to attend?
   How did you find out about the program?
   Would you recommend it to others?

These and other questions can give some interesting insight into determining why the learner was there in the first place. This information can easily be obtained as part of the evaluation at the end of the program.

Levels of Evaluation

Evaluation is a systematic process that determines the worth, value, or meaning of something. The question of what to evaluate is crucial to the evaluation strategy and depends on the type of HRD program, the organization, and the purposes of evaluation. The information collected and used for evaluation can usually be grouped into different categories. Some methods of evaluation are more appropriate for the different categories. The types of groupings vary slightly with the different experts in the HRD field.

Probably the most well-known and widely used framework for classifying areas of evaluation comes from Donald Kirkpatrick.[1] In his model, he developed a conceptual framework to assist in determining what data are to be collected. His concept as shown in Figure 12.1 calls for four levels of evaluation and answers four very important questions.

Level	Questions
Reaction	Were the learners pleased with the program?
Learning	What was learned from the program?
Behavior	Did the learners change their behavior based on what was learned?
Results	Did the change in behavior positively affect the organization?

Reaction is defined as what the learners thought of the particular program, including materials, instructors, facilities, methodology, content, etc. It does not include a measure of the learning that took place. The reaction is often a critical factor in the continuance of HRD programs. Responses on reaction questionnaires help to ensure against decisions based on the comments of a few very satisfied or disgruntled learners. Most HRD practitioners believe that initial receptivity provides a good atmosphere for learning the material in the program but does not necessarily lead to high levels of learning.

The *learning* level of evaluation measures the learning of principles, facts, techniques, and skills presented in a program. It is more difficult than measuring reaction. The measures must be objective and quantifiable indicators of how the learners understood and absorbed the material, but they are not necessarily measures of performance on the job. There are many different measures of learning, including paper and pencil tests, learning curves, skill practices, and job simulation.

The term *behavior* is used in reference to the measurement of job performance. Just as favorable reaction does not necessarily mean that learning will occur, superior achievement in a program does not always result in improved behavior on the job. There are many factors, other than the training program, that can affect on-the-job performance.

Evaluations can be used to relate the *results* of the program to organizational improvement. Some of the results that can be examined include cost savings, work output improvement, and quality changes. This involves collecting data before and after the program and analyzing the improvement.

There have been several assumptions made about Kirkpatrick's approach to evaluating reaction, learning, behavior, and results. First, as shown in Figure 12.1, the value of the information becomes greater as you go from measuring reaction to measuring results. In other words, the evaluation of results has the highest value to the organization.

Second, the measurement of reaction is the most frequently used evaluation method, while the measurement of results is the least frequently used method. Many studies support this assumption. Apparently, not enough HRD practitioners are evaluating the results of their efforts.

Finally, another assumption is that measuring reactions is easier than measuring results. This is easily verified when you examine the methods of evaluation presented later. It is a relatively simple process to gather the reactions to a learning program, but it can be extremely difficult to determine an effective way to accurately measure the economic impact of that program on the organization (i.e., the results).

Establishing a Proper Attitude

Developing a strong evaluation philosophy depends, to a large extent, on a proper attitude among the HRD staff. Evaluation goes beyond reaction

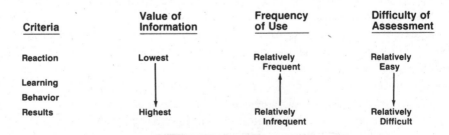

Figure 12.1. Characteristics of the four evaluation criteria.

forms, measuring output data, and presenting statistical analyses of improved performance. It involves:

How they think about evaluation

How they plan for it, implement it, and use it

How much time they are willing to spend on it

How they feel about its relative priority

The HRD staff member who asks the question, "Do we really have to develop evaluation procedures before the program is conducted?" does not have the proper orientation for an effective evaluation. HRD personnel who are not committed to the process will not make the most of an evaluation.

Responsibility for Results

Achieving results from HRD programs is a multiple responsibility. The primary responsibility must lie with the learners, since they must understand the material, put it into practice, and get the desired results.

Others play a very important part in making this process work effectively and smoothly. The reinforcement (or lack of reinforcement) from the learner's supervisor can have a significant effect on the results. The supervisor must show support for the HRD effort and make a commitment to help get the expected results.

The HRD practitioners play a significant role in achieving results. They must conduct programs in an effective manner so that the content is understood. The program designers and subject matter experts share the responsibility, since they must develop a program relevant to the needs of the learners.

Last, but not least, top management shares the responsibility for results. When top management demands results-oriented programs, requires evaluation of all the programs, and communicates their expectations to all parties involved, then the subsequent results will be enhanced. It is only through a shared responsibility for results, with each party accepting his or her respective roles, that maximum results will be obtained.

Types of Data

For convenience, a distinction is made in two general categories of data: (1) hard data and (2) soft data. *Hard data* are the primary measurement

of improvement, presented as rational, undisputed facts, easily accumulated. They are the most desired type of data to collect. *Soft data*, on the
other hand, are more difficult to collect and analyze. They are used when
hard data are not available. The characteristics of the two types of data
are easily identified.

Hard data are:
Easy to measure and quantify
Relatively easy to assign dollar values
Objectively based
A common measure of organizational performance
Very credible in the eyes of management
Soft data are:
Difficult to measure or quantify directly
Difficult to assign dollar values
Subjectively based in many cases
Less credible as a performance measurement
Usually behaviorally oriented

Hard data can usually be grouped in four categories (or subdivisions)
as shown in Figure 12.2. These categories of output, quality, cost, and
time are typical performance measures in almost every organization.
When they are not available, the basic approach is to convert soft data to
one of these four basic measurements. This figure presents several
examples of hard data performance measurements grouped into the four
categories.

The distinction among these four groups of hard data is sometimes
unclear, since there is some overlap. For example, accident costs may be
listed under the cost category, the number of accidents listed under
quality, and the lost time days due to an accident listed under the time
category. The rationale? Accidents represent a cost that can easily be
determined. They are usually caused by someone making a mistake and
are a reflection of the quality of their efforts. The days lost from the job
represent time lost to the organization. In another example, an incentive
bonus may be listed as output, since the amount of bonus is usually tied
directly to the output of an employee or group of employees. On the other
hand, the bonus is usually presented in cash, which represents a cost to
the organization. The distinction between the different subdivisions is
not as important as awareness of the vast number of measurements in
these four areas.

HARD DATA

OUTPUT
Units Produced
Tons Manufactured
Items Assembled
Money Collected
Items Sold
Forms Processed
Loans Approved
Inventory Turnover
Patients Visited
Applications Processed
Students Graduated
Tasks Completed
Output Per Man Hour
Productivity
Work Backlog
Incentive Bonus
Shipments

COSTS
Budget Variances
Unit Costs
Cost By Account
Variable Costs
Fixed Costs
Overhead Cost
Operating Costs
Number of Cost Reductions
Project Cost Savings
Accident Costs
Program Costs
Sales Expense

TIME
Equipment Downtime
Overtime
On Time Shipments
Time to Project Completion
Processing Time
Supervisory Time
Break-in Time for New Employees
Training Time
Meeting Schedules
Repair Time
Efficiency
Work Stoppages
Order Response
Late Reporting
Lost Time Days

QUALITY
Scrap
Waste
Rejects
Error Rates
Rework
Shortages
Product Defects
Deviation From Standard
Product Failures
Inventory Adjustments
Time Card Corrections
Percent of Tasks Completed Properly
Number of Accidents

Figure 12.2. Types of hard data.

There is no good substitute for hard data. However, there are times when hard, rational numbers just do not exist. When this is the case, it may be more meaningful to use soft data in evaluating HRD programs. Figure 12.3 shows typical kinds of soft data. Soft data are behaviorally based; it is difficult to measure them accurately or to assign them dollar values. Soft data have been categorized or subdivided into six areas: work habits, new skills, work climate, development/advancement, feelings/attitudes, and initiative. There may be other ways to divide soft data into categories because there are so many types of soft data. The possibilities are almost limitless. As with the hard data, these subdivisions have some overlap. Some items listed under one category could just as appropriately be listed in another.

SOFT DATA

WORK HABITS
Absenteeism
Tardiness
Visits to the Dispensary
First Aid Treatments
Violations of Safety Rules
Number of Communication Breakdowns
Excessive Breaks

WORK CLIMATE
Number of Grievances
Number of Discrimination Charges
Employee Complaints
Job Satisfaction
Unionization Avoidance
Employee Turnover

FEELINGS/ATTITUDES
Favorable Reactions
Attitude Changes
Perceptions of Job Responsibilities
Perceived Changes in Performance
Employee Loyalty

NEW SKILLS
Decisions Made
Problems Solved
Conflicts Avoided
Grievances Resolved
Counseling Problems Solved
Listening Skills
Reading Speed
Discrimination Charges Resolved
Intention to Use New Skills
Frequency of Use of New Skills

DEVELOPMENT/ADVANCEMENT
Number of Promotions
Number of Pay Increases
Number of Training Programs Attended
Requests for Transfer
Performance Appraisal Ratings
Increases in Job Effectiveness

INITIATIVE
Implementation of New Ideas
Successful Completion of Projects
Number of Suggestions Submitted
Number of Suggestions Implemented

Figure 12.3.   Types of soft data.

EVALUATION METHODS

Testing

Testing is important to many program evaluations. Precourse and postcourse comparisons using tests are very common. An improvement in test scores shows the change in skill, knowledge, or ability of the learner and should be attributed to the program.

There are several types of tests used in the HRD field. The most common are oral examinations, essay tests, objective tests, norm-referenced tests, criterion-referenced tests, performance tests, and attitude surveys.

Oral examinations and essay tests have limited use in HRD program evaluation. They are probably more useful in academic settings. Objective tests have answers that are specific and precise, based on the objectives of a program. Attitudes, feelings, creativity, problem-solving processes, and other intangible skills and abilities cannot be measured accurately with objective tests. A more useful form of objective testing is the criterion-referenced test discussed later. The last four types of tests listed are more common in HRD evaluation efforts. They are described here in more detail.

Norm-referenced tests compare learners with each other or to other groups, rather than to specific instructional objectives. They are characterized by using data to compare the learners to the "norm" or average. Although norm-referenced tests have limited use in most HRD evaluations, they may be useful in programs involving large numbers of learners where average scores and relative rankings are important. In some situations, learners scoring highest on the exams are given special recognition or awards or made eligible for other special activities. The criterion-referenced test (CRT) is an objective test with a predetermined cut-off score. The CRT measures against carefully written objectives for the HRD program. In a CRT, the interest lies in whether or not learners meet the desired minimum standards, not how one learner ranks with another. The primary concern is to measure, report, and analyze learner performance as it relates to the instructional objectives.

Performance testing allows the learner to exhibit a skill (and occasionally knowledge or attitudes) that has been learned in an HRD program. The skill can be manual, verbal, or analytical, or a combination of the three. Performance testing is used frequently in job-related training, where the learners demonstrate what they have learned. In supervisory and management training, performance testing comes in the form of skill practices or role plays. Learners are asked to demonstrate discussion of problem-solving skills they have acquired.

Attitude surveys represent a specific type of test with several applications for measuring the results of HRD progams. A program may be designed to change employee attitudes toward work, policies, procedures, the organization, and even the immediate supervisor. Before and after program measurements are required to show changes in attitude. Occasionally, an organization will conduct an attitude survey to assess employee attitude toward one of the areas listed previously. Then, based on these results, HRD programs are undertaken to change attitudes where improvement is needed.

The following guidelines are recommended for the design and administration of an effective test.

1. *The Appropriate Type of Question(s) Must Be Selected.* Basically, there are five types of questions. A test may contain any or all of these types of questions:

Open-ended question.   This is a question with an unlimited answer. The question is followed by an ample blank space for the response.

Checklist.   This type of question lists items and directs the learner to check those that apply to the situation.

Two-way question.   This type of question has alternate responses, a yes/no or other possibilities.

Multiple-choice question.   This type of question gives several choices, and the learner is asked to select the most correct one.

Ranking scales.   This type of question requires the learner to rank a list of items.

2.   *The Test Should Be a Representative Example of the HRD Program.*   The test should allow the learner to demonstrate the skills and knowledge gained from the program. This increases the validity of the test and makes it more meaningful to the learner.

3.   *The Test Should Be Thoroughly Planned.*   Every phase of the test should be planned—the timing, the preparation of the learner, the administration of the test, and the evaluation of the results.

4.   *Thorough and Consistent Instructions Are Necessary.*   The quality of the instructions can influence the outcome of a test. All learners should be given the same instructions. They should be clear and concise. Charts, diagrams, blueprints, and other supporting information should be provided, if normally provided in the work setting. If appropriate and feasible, the test should be demonstrated by the instructor so that the learners see how the skill is practiced.

5.   *Procedures Should Be Developed for Objective Evaluation.*   Acceptable standards must be developed. For some tests, standards are sometimes difficult to develop because there can be varying degrees of speed, skill, and quality associated with test outcomes for performance tests. Predetermined standards must be developed so that the learners know in advance what must be accomplished for satisfactory and acceptable completion of the test.

6.   *The Test Should Not Include Information That Will Lead Learners Astray.*   The program is conducted to learn a particular skill. The learners should not be led astray or tricked into obvious wrong answers, unless they face the same obstacles in the real-world environment.

Learner Feedback

Feedback from learners is the most frequently used and least reliable method of collecting data for evaluation.[2] The popularity of this form of data collection is astounding. Ratings from reaction questionnaires can be so critical that a person's job may be at stake, as in the case of instructor ratings in school systems.

While learner feedback is popular, it is also subject to misuse. Sometimes referred to as a *happiness rating*, it has come under fire from many HRD practitioners because it is considered worthless. The primary criticism concerns the subjectivity of the data. Possibly the criticism is unjustified.

Research shows a direct correlation between positive comments at the end of a program and the actual improved performance on the job.[3] Elkins' research was based on 90 government supervisors and managers who completed a basic management course. In all the variables examined, learner reaction was the strongest determinant of on-the-job application of the new management principles. The learners who enjoyed the program most were the ones who achieved the most on the job. Those who did not like it apparently did not bother to do too much of anything with it.

Armed with these data, HRD managers could logically assume that if learners enjoyed the course and said they planned to use the materials, they probably would.

A word of caution is in order. This research might be measuring the effect of the self-fulfilling prophecy. There is no substitute for hard data in evaluating programs. But a carefully designed, properly used feedback questionnaire at the end of an HRD program might suffice for a more sophisticated evaluation method. There is a definite place for feedback questionnaires in HRD evaluation.

The areas of feedback used on reaction forms depend, to a large extent, on the organization and the purpose of the evaluation. Some forms are very simple, while others are very detailed and require a considerable amount of time to complete. The feedback questionnaire should be designed to supply the proper information. The following areas represent a listing of the most common types of feedback solicited:

Program content
Instructional materials
Out of class assignments
Method of presentation
Instructor/speaker
Facilities
General evaluation
Planned improvements

Objective questions covering each of these areas will provide very thorough feedback from the learners. This feedback can be extremely useful for making adjustments in a program and/or assist in predicting performance after the program. The area of instructor evaluation (including guest speakers) is very important. In some organizations, the primary evaluation centers on the instructor, and a separate form, covering a variety of areas, may be used for each instructor.

There are a number of useful tips that can improve the effectiveness of this data collection method.

1. *Consider an Ongoing Evaluation.* For lengthy programs, evaluation at the end of the program may leave the learners unable to remember what was covered at what time. To help improve the situation, an ongoing evaluation can be implemented. This evaluation form is distributed at the beginning of the program, and the learners are instructed how and when to supply the information. After each topic is presented, learners are asked to evaluate the topic and speaker.

2. *Try Quantifying Course Ratings.* Some organizations attempt to solicit feedback in terms of numerical ratings. Although very subjective, these can be useful to program evaluators.

3. *Collect Information Related to Cost Savings.* It is difficult to get realistic input on a feedback form related to cost reductions or savings, but it is worth a try. The response may be surprising. Just a simple question will sometimes cause learners to concentrate on cost savings. A possible statement might be:

As a result of this program, please estimate the savings in dollars that will be realized (i.e., increased productivity, improved methods, reduced costs, etc.) over a period of one year. $_____ Please explain the basis of your estimate.

_____

_____

Express the confidence you place on your estimate as a percent (0% = no confidence, 100% = certainty). _____

4. *Allow Ample Time for Completing the Form.* A time crunch can cause problems when learners are asked to complete a feedback form at the end of a program, particularly if they are in a hurry to leave. Consequently, the information will be cut short in an effort to finish and leave. A possible alternative is to allow ample time for evaluation at a scheduled session before the end of the program. This could possibly be followed by a wrap-up of the program and the last speaker. Another

alternative is to allow learners to mail the evaluation later. With this approach, a reminder may be necessary to secure all of the forms.

Feedback from Others

Another useful evaluation method involves soliciting feedback from other individuals closely identified with the learners in the program. Typically, these groups fall into five categories: (1) supervisors of the learners, (2) subordinates of the learners, (3) peers, (4) members of the HRD staff, and (5) specially trained observers.

The most common group solicited for feedback is the supervisors of those attending HRD programs. This feedback provides detailed information on performance improvement as a result of the program. Possibly the best person to evaluate performance is the supervisor, particularly if he or she has been instructed to observe the learner. This "feedback from the boss" is usually obtained during a follow-up evaluation using an instrument such as a questionnaire or an interview. This method can develop very reliable feedback data.

Probably the next most commonly used feedback group is the subordinates of the learners. This information may not be as reliable as that obtained from the supervisor; nevertheless, it can be valuable in the evaluation process. The information will be subjective and may be biased or opinionated, depending on the employee's attitude toward the learner. Generally, with this type of data collection method, employees are asked about changes or improvements in their supervisor's behavior since attending a specific HRD program.

Probably the least used feedback group is the peer group. This involves soliciting feedback from peers to see how learners have performed after an HRD program. This technique is rare, since it is highly subjective and may be unreliable because of the loose ties between the evaluator and the learner. The other two groups have a closer identification. The techniques of data gathering for this type of feedback are questionnaires or interviews.

Another group used for feedback purposes is the HRD staff. In these situations, staff members, properly trained in observation techniques, observe learners and provide feedback on their performance. This evaluation can be very helpful and can represent a very professional and unbiased method of data collection.

The final method of data collection, involving feedback from others, is a formal procedure called the *assessment center method*. The feedback is provided by a group of specially trained observers (called *assessors*), not usually HRD staff members, as in the previous method. For years, the assessment center approach has been a very effective tool for employee selection. Recently, it has also shown great promise as a tool for evaluating the effectiveness of an HRD program.[4]

Assessment centers are not actually *centers*, (i.e., a location or building). The term refers to a procedure that can be used for evaluating the performance of individuals. In a typical assessment center, the individuals being assessed participate in a variety of exercises that enable them to demonstrate a particular skill, knowledge, or ability, usually called *job dimensions*. These dimensions are important to on-the-job success for individuals for whom the program was developed. The learners are evaluated or assessed by the assessors, and the evaluation is in the form of a rating for each dimension. It takes anywhere from four hours to three days to complete all the exercises. The assessors then combine individual ratings and remove subjectivity to reach a final rating for each learner.

Although the popularity of the assessment center seems to be growing, it still may not be feasible in some organizations. The use of an assessment center is quite involved and time consuming for the learners and the assessors. The assessors have to be carefully trained to be objective and reliable. However, for programs that represent large expenditures aimed at making improvements in the soft data area, the assessment center approach may be the most promising way to measure the impact of the program. This is particularly true for an organization where the assessment center process is already in use for selection purposes.

Follow-up Evaluation

Another common evaluation method is the learner follow-up, conducted at a predetermined time after the program completion. The follow-up evaluation should follow an end-of-the-program evaluation. In fact, in many situations the follow-up relates back to a previous evaluation. This follow-up normally involves the use of a feedback questionnaire, although other variations include interviews and observations. The primary purposes of the follow-up are:

To help measure the lasting results of the program

To isolate the areas where learners show the most improvement

To compare the responses at follow-up time with those provided at the end of the program

Here are a few useful guidelines that will enhance the effectiveness of a follow-up evaluation.

1. *Determine Progress Made since the Program.* This is an excellent time to determine what the learner has accomplished with the material presented in the HRD program. Ideally, there will be additional data that reflect the success of the program. Each item that required an action at the end of the program should be checked at the follow-up to see what was accomplished.

2. *Ask Many of the Same or Similar Questions.* To provide the continuity for data comparison, the questions asked on the end-of-program questionnaire should be repeated on the follow-up, if appropriate. If the learner was asked to estimate a dollar savings as a result of the program, then a follow-up question should ask what dollar savings actually materialized as a result of the program.

3. *Solicit Reasons for Lack of Results.* Not all follow-ups will generate positive results. Some will indicate no improvement or will contain negative comments. A good follow-up will try to determine why the learner did not get results. There can be many obstacles to performance improvement, and identifying these obstacles can be almost as valuable as identifying the reasons for success.

4. *The Learners Should Expect a Follow-Up.* There should be no surprises at follow-up time. The intention to administer a follow-up instrument should be clearly communicated during the program, preferably at the end. Also, learners should know what information is expected from them in the follow-up.

5. *Follow-Up Information Should Be Shared with the Learner's Supervisor.* Ideally, the learner's immediate supervisor should be involved in the application of what was learned in the HRD program. At a very minimum, the supervisor should know what results have been achieved and receive the information on the follow-up evaluation.

6. *Completing the Follow-Up Should Be Required.* The follow-up evaluation should not be optional. Learners are expecting it, and the HRD department must see that it is accomplished. This input is essential to determine the impact of the program. Obtaining a good response from the follow-up evaluations is not difficult.

7. *Consider a Follow-Up Assignment.* In some cases, follow-up assignments can enhance the evaluation process. In a typical follow-up assignment, the learner is instructed to meet a goal or complete a particular task or project by the follow-up date.

Action Plan Audit

An action plan audit is an extension of the follow-up assignment described in the previous section. In this approach, learners are required to develop action plans as part of the program. These action plans contain detailed steps to accomplish specific objectives related to the program. The action plan shows what is to be done, by whom, and when, in order to accomplish the objectives. The action plan approach is a straightforward, simple method for determining how learners will change their behavior back on the job.

The development of the action plan requires two tasks: (1) determining the areas for action, and (2) writing the action items. Both tasks should be completed during the HRD program.

The areas for action should come from the material presented in the HRD program and, at the same time, be related to on-the-job activities. A list of potential areas for action can be developed; a list may be generated by the learners in a group discussion; or possibly, a learner may identify an area needing improvement in the particular situation.

The following questions should be asked when developing the areas for action:

How much time will this action take?
Are the skills for accomplishing this action item available?
Who has the authority to implement the action plan?
Will this action have an effect on other individuals?
Are there any organizational constraints for accomplishing this action item?

The specific action items are usually more difficult to write than the identification of the action areas. The most important characteristic of an action item is that it is in writing and specific so that everyone involved will know when it occurs. Some examples of action items are:

Learn how to operate the new RC-105 drill press machine in the adjacent department
Identify and secure a new customer account
Talk with my employers directly about a problem even though this can result in a confrontation

If appropriate, each action item should have a date for completion and should indicate which other individuals or resources will be required for completion. Also, planned behavior changes should be observable. It should be obvious to the learner and others when it happns.

Action plans, as used in this context, do not require prior approval or input from the learner's supervisor, although it may be helpful. Learners may not have prior knowledge of the action plan requirement for the program. Frequently, introducing and describing the process are integral parts of the program.

The action plans should be reviewed before the end of the HRD program to check for accuracy, feasibility, and completeness. At that time, it should be made clear that the plan will be audited.

To tabulate the results achieved from the action plans, an audit (or follow-up) is conducted, usually four to six months after the program is completed. This audit will reveal and document what progress has been made toward the planned objectives and will review the detailed steps that were planned. It can be accomplished by a questionnaire or interview.

In the questionnaire method, the questionnaire is mailed to learners at the specified follow-up time. The questionnaire has a cover letter followed by a detailed list of questions about the action plan, much like any other audit. The questionnaire has ample space for the learner to describe, for each action time, what was done, how it was done, who was involved, and how often it was tried. The detailed results are documented. If the items were not accomplished, information is gathered to explain why. Problems encountered or obstacles to success are listed.

Using the previous approach, questionnaires are gathered directly from every learner. Other effective options are:

Contacting only a sample for a follow-up
Reconvening the class to complete the follow-up questionnaires
Obtaining input from both the learner and supervisor

The interview method begins with a letter reminding learners about the follow-up. This letter focuses on the action items before the interviews take place. Learners are contacted for an appointment. The learner should be interviewed at a convenient time and place, to minimize distractions on the job. Basically, the same information is obtained in the interview that is obtained in the questionnaire, but the information is gathered face-to-face or over the telephone.

Performance Contract

The performance contract is another effective evaluation method. Essentially, it is a slight variation of the action plan process described in the previous section. It is based on the principle of mutual goal setting, which has become a well-established process. It is a written agreement between the learner and the supervisor. The learner agrees to improve performance in an area of mutual concern related to the subject material in the HRD program. The agreement is in the form of a project to be completed or goal to be accomplished soon after the learning program is completed. The agreement spells out what is to be accomplished, at what time, and with what results.

Although the steps can vary according to the specific kind of contract and the organization, a common sequence of events is as follows:

1. The learner and supervisor mutually agree on a subject for improvement.
2. A specific, measurable goal(s) is set.
3. The learner attends the HRD program. Here the contract is discussed, and plans are developed to accomplish the goals.
4. After the program, the learner works on the contract against a specific deadline.
5. The learner reports the results of the effort to his supervisor.
6. The supervisor and learner document the results and forward a copy to the HRD department along with appropriate comments.

The mutually selected subject or topic for improvement can cover one or more of the following areas:

Routine performance
Problem solving
Innovative or creative applications
Personal development

The topic selected should be stated in terms of one or more objectives. The objectives should state what is to be accomplished when the contract is complete. The details to accomplish the objectives of the contract are developed following the guidelines under action plans presented earlier.

If the contract extends more than one month from the end of the HRD program, learners should, if possible, submit progress reports, outlining what has been accomplished. Upon completion of the contract, a summary report should be submitted to the learner's supervisor. The report outlines the initial objectives and the standards by which the objectives were measured. It reviews the problems encountered and how they were solved, along with specific activities, costs, and benefits. A detailed statement of the results achieved is a significant part of the progress report. In addition, the learner's supervisor, after reviewing the report, makes appropriate comments, outlining the degree of satisfaction with the activity. Then, the progress report is forwarded to the HRD department and becomes additional data on which to evaluate the program. Several variations are possible on the follow-up of the performance contract. The methods outlined in the previous section may be helpful to assure that this final report is accomplished and is ultimately received by the HRD department.

Simulation

Another method of evaluation is the use of job simulations. This method involves the construction and application of a procedure or task that simulates or models the activity for which the HRD program is being conducted. The simulation is designed to represent, as closely as possible, the actual job situation. Simulation may be used as an integral part of the HRD program, as well as for evaluation. In evaluation, learners are provided with an opportunity to try out their performance in the simulated activity and to have it evaluated, based on how well the task was accomplished. The assessment center method, discussed earlier, is actually a simulation. Each exercise is designed to reproduce a work situation where learners exhibit behavior related to one or more job dimensions. Simulations may be used during the program, at the end of the program, or as part of the follow-up evaluation.

A more detailed explanation of each of these methods of evaluation is found in Phillips.[5]

MEASURING THE RETURN

Data Analysis

The evaluation methods in the previous section yield numerical data that must be analyzed and interpreted to be meaningful. The type of analysis necessary is usually determined when the evaluation is designed. Data analysis is a complex but important subject.

Before approaching the use of statistics, let us review a few basic guidelines for analyzing evaluation data.

1. *Review for Consistency and Accuracy.*   While this guideline may be obvious, additional checks are desirable to ensure the accuracy and consistency of the data. Incorrect or insufficient data items should be eliminated. A simple scan of data will usually reveal extreme data points or values that may seem impossible to obtain. The analysis and interpretation will only be as reliable as the data itself.

2. *Use All Relevant Data.*   In most evaluations, improvement is desired by the person conducting the evaluation. This may provide a built-in bias. Improvement will not always materialize. Some data will be both positive and negative. It may be tempting to eliminate data that does not support the desired outcome. For a valid analysis, all relevant data should be used. If not, there should be an explanation of why they were deleted.

3. *Treat Individual Data Confidentially.*   Frequently, data collected will be the result of individual performances. In analyzing and interpreting the data and reporting results, the confidentiality of the individuals should be an important concern unless there are conditions that warrant their exposure.

4. *Use the Simplest Statistics Possible.*   There are many ways to analyze data. A variety of different statistical manipulators can be used to compare changes in performance. Additional analyses, which may serve no further benefit, should be avoided. The analysis should be kept as simple as possible and confined to what is necessary to draw the proper conclusions from the data.

This chapter is not intended to make a statistician of the reader. Many other books serve that purpose, some of which are identified in the bibliography. The use of statistics in evaluation has three primary purposes:

1. *Statistics Enable Large Amounts of Information to Be Summarized.*   Probably the most practical use of statistics is the summary of information, for which there are two basic measures. One is the measure of central tendency, the mean, median and mode. This measure presents, in a single number, a summary of the characteristics of the entire group,

such as the average absenteeism rate for a group of employees. The second is the measure of dispersion, or variance, which is the standard deviation. This reveals how much the individual items in the group are dispersed. For example, a large standard deviation for an average attendance means that there is a wide variation among the absenteeism records for the group of employees.

2. *Statistics Allow for the Determination of the Relationship between Two or More Items.* In analyzing data, the relationship between one or more items may be important. The term used for this relationship is *correlation*, which represents the degree to which the items are related and is expressed as a coefficient. A positive correlation between two items means that as one item increases, the other increases. For example, a high achievement score on an examination in an HRD program might correlate with a high level of performance on the job. There can also be a negative correlation between items. In this case, the correlation coefficient is negative, and as one item increases, the other decreases.

3. *Statistics Show How to Compare the Differences in Performance between Two Groups.* When performance improves after an HRD program, there is a question that is likely to be asked: "Did the improvement occur because of the program, or could it have occurred by chance?" In other words, without the HRD program, would the same results have been achieved? How accurately can the conclusions be drawn? Statistics enable a confidence level to be placed on conclusions about differences in groups of data.

Assigning Values to Data

Before either type of data can be used to compare benefits versus costs, the data must be converted to a dollar value. Except for actual cost savings, the easiest program measurement to convert to a dollar value is a change in output. An increase in output can appear in a variety of forms, such as increased production, sales, or productivity. Savings in time and improvements in quality are a little more difficult to convert to a dollar value, while the greatest difficulty is encountered when attempting to convert soft data, such as changes in attitudes, a reduction in complaints, or the implementation of new ideas.

Changes in output are the goal of many HRD programs. In most situations, the value of increased output can be calculated easily, although in a few instances, it may be difficult. For example, in a sales training program, the changes in sales output can be measured easily.

The average sales figures before the program are compared to the average sales figures after the program. The average profit per sale is usually easy to obtain. Therefore, the increased earnings, as a result of increased sales, are the increase in sales multiplied by the average profit per sale.

Assigning a value to cost savings appears to be redundant. An HRD program that produces a cost savings usually has a value equal to the cost savings. However, one item should be considered when assigning these values—the time value of money. A savings realized at one point in time, may be worth more than a savings at another time. A cost savings, experienced by an employee or a group of employees over a long period, might have a greater value than the actual savings, since costs normally increase during that period.

Many programs are aimed at reducing the time for learners to perform a function or task. Time savings are important because employee time is money, in the form of wages, salaries, and benefits paid directly to the employee. There are several economic benefits derived from time savings:

1. *Wages/Salaries.* The most obvious time savings result in reduced costs of labor involved in performing a task. The dollar savings are the hours saved multiplied by the labor cost per hour. The labor cost per hour can be an illusive figure. Generally, the average wage, with a percent added for benefits, will suffice for most calculations. However, time may be worth more than that. More elaborate purchases can be considered to determine how much time is worth, such as secretarial support, office space, and general overhead.

2. *Better Service.* Another potential benefit of time savings is better service. This is particularly true when production time, implementation time, construction time, or processing time is reduced, so that a product or service is delivered to the client or customer in a shorter period of time.

3. *Penalty Avoidance.* In some situations, reductions in time can avoid penalties. For example, in processing invoices for accounts payable, a reduction in processing time can avoid late payment penalties and possibly earn a discount for the organization.

4. *Learning Time.* Frequently, HRD programs will be improved to reduce the previous time alloted for learning. With new instructional technology and refinements, as a result of program evaluations, a new program can possibly accomplish the same objectives in a shorter period of time.

An important and frequently used target of HRD programs is quality improvement. Programs are developed to overcome employees' deficiencies made evident by low quality output or an excessively high error rate. The cost of poor quality to an organization can be staggering. The measurable impact of a program for quality improvement can usually be calculated without difficulty. The value of this improvement may have several components:

1. *Scrap/Waste.* The most obvious cost of poor quality is the scrap or waste generated by mistakes. Defective products, spoiled raw materials, and discarded paperwork are all the results of poor quality. This scrap and waste translates into a dollar value that can be used to calculate the impact of an improvement in quality.

2. *Rework.* Mistakes and errors may result in costly rework to correct the problem. The most costly rework occurs when a product is delivered to a customer and must be returned for correction or when an expensive program has been implemented with serious errors.

3. *Customer/Client Dissatisfaction.* When errors or mistakes are made, the organization suffers a tremendous loss in the form of customer or client dissatisfaction In some cases, serious mistakes can result in lost business. Customer dissatisfaction is difficult to quantify, and attempts to arrive at a dollar value may be impossible. Usually, the judgment and expertise of sales and marketing management are the best sources for measuring the impact of dissatisfaction. It may be more realistic to list this loss of satisfaction as an advantage of improved quality without trying to quantify it.

4. *Product Liability.* In recent years, premiums for product liability insurance have soared, due to an increase in the number of lawsuits brought against businesses. An organization that experiences more than average product defects will usually experience a greater product liability insurance premium. Therefore, better quality can result in fewer customer complaints and, consequently, fewer lawsuits and lower premiums.

5. *Internal Losses.* There is still another type of loss that is not covered in the categories mentioned previously. These are internal losses caused by employee mistakes. For example, an overpayment to a supplier can represent a loss that cannot be recovered. It does not result in rework or produce any waste, but it costs the organization.

While soft data are not as desirable as hard data, nevertheless, they are important. The difficulty arises in collecting the data reliably and in assigning values to the data. Almost any assignment of value is subjective and must be used with that in mind. There are four basic approaches used to convert the soft data to dollar values:

1. *Existing Data/Historical Costs.* Frequently, tangible items or historical costs will be intertwined with the soft data. For example, the cost of tardiness by employees can be calculated by making a number of assumptions about what happens when an employee is absent for a short period of time. Another example is the cost of grievances. Although an extremely variable item, historical costs are usually available, and they can form a basis for estimating the cost savings for a reduction in grievances.

2. *Expert Opinion.* Expert opinions are sometimes available to estimate the value of the soft data. The experts may be in the organization, within the industry, or specialists in a particular field. Extensive analyses of similar data may be extrapolated to fit the data at hand. For example, many experts have attempted to calculate the cost of absenteeism. These estimates can vary considerably, nevertheless, they may serve as a rough estimate for other calculations, making adjustments for the specific organization.

3. *Learner Estimation.* The learners in an HRD program may be in the best position to estimate the value of an improvement. Either at the end of a program or in a follow-up, learners should be asked to estimate the value of the improvements. They should also be asked to furnish the basis for that estimate and the confidence placed on it. The estimations by learners may be quite realistic, since they are usually directly involved in the improvement.

4. *Management Estimation.* Another technique for assigning a value to soft data is to ask the management concerned with the evaluation of the program. This management group may be the superiors or the learners, top management (who are approving the expenditures), or the members of the program review committee, whose function is to evaluate the program. This approach solicits an estimate of what it is worth to improve on a particular soft data item, such as the implementation of new ideas, resolving conflicts, or increasing personal effectiveness. When management develops an estimate, it then becomes their figure. Even if it is extremely conservative, it can be very helpful in the final analysis of the HRD program.

One word of caution is in order. Whenever a monetary value is assigned to subjective information, it needs to be fully explained to the audience receiving the information. By all means, when there is a range of possible values, use the most conservative one. It will improve credibility.

Cost Classification Systems

There are two basic ways to classify HRD costs. One is by using a description of the expenditure, such as labor, materials, supplies, travel, etc. These are expense account classifications. The other is by using the categories in the HRD process or function, such as program development, delivery, and evaluation. An effective system will monitor costs by account categories, according to the description of those accounts, but it also includes a method for accumulating costs by the HRD process/functional category. Many systems stop short of this second step. While the first grouping is sufficient to give the total cost of the program, it does not allow for a useful comparison with other programs nor does it indicate areas where costs might be excessive by relative comparisons. Therefore, two basic classifications are recommended to develop a complete costing system.

Figure 12.4 shows the process/functional categories for costs in four different examples. In column A, there are only two categories: (1) support costs, and (2) operating costs. Operating costs include all expenses involved in conducting the HRD program; whereas, support costs include all administrative, overhead, development, analysis, or any other expenditures not directly related to conducting the program. While it is simple to separate the two, it does not provide enough detail to analyze the cost on a functional basis. Column B gives a little more detail, since costs are divided into three categories. This is more useful than column A but does not give any information on program development costs, a useful item to have. Column C provides for development costs as a separate item. It still falls short of the ideal situation. There is no way to track evaluation costs, which are becoming a more significant part of the total HRD process. Column D represents a more appropriate HRD process cost breakdown: analysis, development, delivery, and evaluation. The administrative costs are allocated to one of these areas.

An extremely significant step in developing an HRD cost system is defining and classifying the various HRD expenses. Many of the expense accounts, such as office supplies and travel expenses, are already a part of the existing accounting system. However, there will be expenses unique to the HRD department that must be added to the system. The system

SUPPORT COSTS	CLASSROOM COSTS	PROGRAM DEVELOPMENT COSTS	ANALYSIS COSTS
OPERATING COSTS	ADMINISTRATIVE COSTS	ADMINISTRATIVE COSTS	DEVELOPMENT COSTS
	PARTICIPANT COMPENSATION	CLASSROOM COSTS	DELIVERY COSTS
		PARTICIPANT COSTS	EVALUATION COSTS
A	B	C	D

Figure 12.4.   Examples of cost categories.

design will depend on the organization, the type of programs developed and conducted, and the limits imposed on the current cost accounting system, if any. Also, to a certain extent, the expense account classifications will depend on how the HRD process/functional categories have been developed.

Calculating the Return

The return on investment is an important calculation for the HRD professional. Yet, it is a figure that must be used with caution and care. There are many ways it can be interpreted or misinterpreted. This section presents some general guidelines to help calculate a return and interpret its meaning.

Return on investment (ROI) may appear to be improper terminology for the HRD field. The expression originates from the finance and accounting field and usually refers to the pretax contribution measured against controllable assets. In formula form:

$$ROI = \frac{\text{pretax earnings}}{\text{average investment}}$$

It measures the anticipated profitability of an investment and is used as a standard measure of the performance of divisions or profit centers within a business. For HRD program evaluation, the return may be expressed in the following way:

$$ROI = \frac{\text{net program benefits (or savings)}}{\text{program costs (or program investment)}}$$

The investment portion of the formula represents capital expenditures, such as a learning facility or equipment, plus initial development or production costs. The original investment figure can be used, or the present book value can be expressed as the average investment over a period of time. If an HRD program is a one-time offering, then the figure is the entire original investment. However, if the initial costs are spread over a period of time, then the average book value is usually more appropriate. This value is essentially part of the initial costs since, through depreciation, a certain fixed part of the investment is written off each year over the life of the investment.

In many situations, a group of employees are to be trained at one time, so the investment figure, represented at the bottom of the equation, is the total cost of analysis, development, delivery, and evaluation. Assuming that all the learners attend the program or have attended the program, the benefits then are calculated based on whether the return is a prediction or a reflection of what has happened.

To keep calculations simple, it is recommended that the return be based on pretax conditions. This avoids the issue of investment tax credits, depreciation, tax shields, and other related items.

Return on investment is sometimes used loosely to represent the return on assets (ROA) or the return on equity (ROE). *Equity* usually refers to the net worth of a company. The *assets* represent the total assets employed to generate the earnings, including debt. The ROA and ROE are more meaningful when evaluating the entire company or a division of the company. ROI is usually sufficient for evaluating expenditures related to an HRD program.

Finance and accounting personnel may actually take issue with calculations involving the return on investment for efforts such as an HRD program. Nevertheless, the expression is fairly common and conveys an adequate meaning of financial evaluation. Some people avoid the work *return* and just calculate the dollar savings as a result of the program, which is basically the benefits minus costs. These figures may be more meaningful to managers, so the ROI calculation is not confused with similar calculations for capital expenditures.

For a calculated return to be meaningful, it must be compared with a predetermined standard. A 30% ROI is unsatisfactory when a 40% ROI is expected. There are two basic approaches to setting targets. First, the normally accepted return on any investment may be appropriate for the HRD program. Second, since the ROI calculation is more subjective than the ROI for capital expenditures, the company may expect a higher target. This figure should be established in review meetings where top management personnel are asked to specify the acceptable ROI for the program. It is not uncommon for an organization to expect an ROI for an HRD program to be twice that of the ROI for capital expenditures.

The calculation of the return on an HRD program is not feasible or realistic in all cases. Even if the perceived benefits have been converted to dollar savings, the mere calculation of the return communicates to a perceptive manager more preciseness in the evaluation than may be there. Usually, the ROI calculation should be used when the program benefits can be clearly documented and substantiated, even if they are subjective. If management believes in the method of calculating the benefits, then they will have confidence in the value of the return. The nature of the program can also have a bearing on whether or not it makes sense to calculate a return. Management may believe, without question, in an ROI calculation for sales training programs. They can easily see how an improvement can be documented and a value tied to it. On the other hand, a training program that teaches managers the principles of transactional analysis is difficult to swallow—even for the most understanding manager. Therefore, the key considerations are how reliable are the data, and how believable are the conclusions based on subjective data.

NOTES

1. D.L. Kirkpatrick, "Evaluation of Training," in *Training and Development Handbook*, ed. Robert L. Craig (New York: McGraw-Hill, 1976), p. 18.
2. R. Catalanello and D.L. Kirkpatrick, "Evaluating Training Programs—The State of the Art," *Training and Development Journal* (1968): 2–9.
3. A. Elkins, "Some Views on Management Training," *Personnel Journal* (1977): 305–311.
4. W.C. Byham, "How Assessment Centers Are Used to Evaluate Training's Effectiveness." *Training, The Magazine of Human Resource Development* (1982): 32.
5. Jack J. Phillips, *Handbook of Training Evaluation and Measurement Methods* (Houston: Gulf Publishing Company, 1983).

REFERENCES

Byham, W.C. "How Assessment Centers Are Used to Evaluate Training's Effectiveness." *Training, The Magazine of Human Resource Development* (1982): 32.

Catalanello, R., and D.L. Kirkpatrick. "Evaluating Training Programs—The State of the Art." *Training and Development Journal* (1968): 2–9.

Elkins, A. "Some Views on Management Training." *Personnel Journal* (1977): 305–311.

Kirkpatrick, D.L. "Evaluation of Training." *Training and Development Handbook*, 2d ed., edited by Robert L. Craig. New York: McGraw-Hill, 1976, p. 18–20.

Phillips, Jack J. *Handbook of Training Evaluation and Measurement Methods.* Houston: Gulf Publishing Company, 1983.

BIBLIOGRAPHY

Evaluation and Measurement

Davis, L.N., and E. McCallon. *Planning, Conducting and Evaluating Workshops*. Austin, Tex.: Learning Concepts, 1974.

Deming, B.S. *Evaluating Job-Related Training*. Englewood Cliffs, N.J.: Prentice-Hall, 1982.

Denova, C.C. *Test Construction for Training Evaluation*. New York: Van Nostrand Reinhold, 1979.

Fitz-Gibbon, C.T., and L.L. Morris. *How to Design a Program Evaluation*. Beverly Hills, Cal.: Sage Publications, 1978.

Goldstein, I.I. *Training: Program Development and Evaluation*. Monterey, Cal.: Brooks/Cole Co., 1974.

Hakel, M.D., M. Sorcher, M. Beer, and J.L. Moses. *Making it Happen: Designing Research with Implementation in Mind*. Beverly Hills, Cal.: Sage Publications, 1982.

Henerson, M.E., L.L. Morris, and C.T. Fitz-Gibbon. *How to Measure Attitudes*. Beverly Hills, Cal.: Sage Publications, 1978.

Katzer, J., K.H. Cook, and W.W. Crouch. *Evaluating Information*. Reading, Mass.: Addison-Wesley, 1978.

Kearsley, G. *Costs, Benefits and Productivity in Training Systems*. Reading, Mass.: Addison-Wesley, 1982.

Kirkpatrick, D.L. *Evaluating Training Programs*. Washington, D.C.: American Society for Training and Development, 1975.

Mager, R.F. *Measuring Instructional Intent*. Belmont, Cal.: Fearon, 1973.

Morris, L.L. and C.T. Fitz-Gibbon. *Evaluator's Handbook*. Beverly Hills, Cal.: Sage Publications, 1978.

Morris, L.L. and C.T. Fitz-Gibbon. *How to Measure Achievement*. Beverly Hills, Cal.: Sage Publications, 1978.

Morris, L.L. and C.T. Fitz-Gibbon. *How to Measure Implementation*. Beverly Hills, Cal.: Sage Publications, 1978.

Odiorne, G.S. *Training by Objectives: An Economic Approach to Management Training*. New York: Macmillan, 1970.

Patton, M.Q. *Practical Evaluation*. Beverly Hills, Cal.: Sage Publications, 1982.

Peterson, R.O., ed. *Determining the Payoff of Management Training*. Washington, D.C.: American Society for Training and Development, 1979.

Phillips, J.J. *Handbook of Training Evaluation and Measurement Methods*. Houston: Gulf Publishing Co., 1983.

Sax, G. *Principles of Educational and Psychological Measurement and Evaluation*. 2d ed. Belmont, Cal.: Wadsworth, 1980.

Spector, P.E. *Research Designs*. In *Quantative Applications in the Social Sciences*, vol. 23, ed. J.L. Sullivan. Beverly Hills, Cal.: Sage Publications, 1981.

Stone, E.F. *Research Methods in Organizational Behavior*. Santa Monica, Cal.: Goodyear, 1978.

Thompson, M.S. *Benefit-Cost Analysis for Program Evaluation*. Beverly Hills, Cal.: Sage Publications, 1980.

Tracey, W.R. *Evaluating Training and Development Systems*. New York: AMACOM, 1968.

Tracey, W.R. *Human Resource Development Standards*. New York: AMACOM, 1981.

Warr, P., Bird, M., and N. Rackham. *Evaluation of Management Training*. London: Gower Press, 1970.

Data Analysis

Anderson, R.A., D.J. Sweeney, and Williams. *Introduction to Statistics: An Applications Approach*. St. Paul, Minn.: West Publishing Co., 1981.

Ben-Horim, M., and H. Levy. *Statistics: Decisions and Applications in Business and Economics*. New York: Random House, 1981.

Hinkle, D.E., W. Wiersma, and S.G. Jurs. *Applied Statistics for the Behavioral Sciences*. Boston: Houghton Mifflin, 1979.

Levin, R.I. *Statistics for Management*. 2d ed. Englewood Cliffs, N.J.: Prentice-Hall, 1981.

Render, B., and R.M. Stair, Jr. *Quantitative Analysis for Management*. Boston: Allyn and Bacon, 1982.

Professional Growth for HRD Staff

NEAL CHALOFSKY

Often, we have heard that, "The shoemaker's child goes barefoot and the baker's child goes hungry." In our field, such a statement tells us that people in HRD devote their efforts to the growth of others in the organization. But who provides for the HRD staff's professional growth?

There is no foolproof way to achieve this growth, but Chalofsky lists some of the various possibilities. Some are obvious, perhaps, but others may come as a surprise.

It is recognized that there are different categories of HRD practitioners, as discussed in Chapter 1. In this chapter, Chalofsky focuses essentially on category 1—those who are or want to be professionally identified. This chapter emphasizes that professional growth has many dimensions. As the HRD practitioner becomes involved in this professional growth, the organizations and individuals involved in this process will also grow.

Neal Chalofsky (Ed.D.) is an assistant professor of education at Virginia Polytechnic Institute and State University. He is responsible for the human resource development graduate concentration. Dr. Chalofsky formerly was employed in the Office of Productivity Programs of the U.S. Office of Personnel Management. He also served as director of the Executive Development Institute of the Department of Health, Education, and Welfare and as a training specialist with the National Aeronautics and Space Administration. He has provided HRD services to a variety of organizations and has held numerous offices in ASTD, including: national vice president for professional development (1983–84), and chair of the HRD futures task force. He has published in the *Training and Development Journal* and is coauthor of *Up the HRD Ladder: A Guide to Professional Growth* (1982).

INTRODUCTION

Do Unto You As You Would Do Unto Others

The training, education, and development of HRD specialists have a special significance for our profession; we cannot advocate and provide HRD services for others unless we believe in it for ourselves. If we do not "practice what we preach," we will fail as role models to our organizations and, more important, we will fail to provide the most effective HRD services and products possible because we will not be as competent as we could be.

Professionals in all occupations have an ethical responsibility to strive to be as competent and effective as possible. We who are dedicated to the development of human potential can do no less.

PROFESSIONAL DEVELOPMENT

Definition/Description

"Professional development is a process of keeping current in the state of the art, keeping competent in the state of practice, and keeping open to new theories, techniques, and values."[1] It is related to present and near future positions and usually is based on work objectives.

To achieve professional development, an individual must be able to anticipate potential problems in the organization and identify the resources that will help the organization deal with those potential problems before they become crises. You must be prepared to proactively support your organization as it develops, changes, and grows. Most successful HRD specialists have internalized the need for professional development so that it becomes a constant process of self-renewal and growth.

Professional development for ourselves involves nothing more sophisticated or complicated than what we do for the rest of the organization. There are two key ingredients to this process: assessment and development planning.

Assessment is the use of one or more measuring techniques to ascertain the level of proficiency, compared to a given objective or competency. Knowles[2] uses the following typology for objectives or competencies:

Knowledge

Understanding

Skill

Attitude

Values

For example, one competency can be "to have an understanding of adult learning theory." Another might be "to have a skill in setting objectives." A value competency could be "to respect the uniqueness of all human beings." Furthermore, a hierarchy of standards you can use to evaluate yourself is:

Competent. Satisfactory, able to perform the competency, professional

Proficient. Above average, able to perform the competency well, expert

Excellent. Extraordinary, able to perform the competency superbly, guru

This last level is what Richard Bolles, in his keynote address to the 1981 ASTD National Conference, called "being a magician."

Development planning means preparing a plan of action to train, educate, and develop yourself, based on a set of learning objectives drawn from your self-assessment. The action plan could be as simple as planning to read a book on a particular subject that you want to know more about, or it could be as extensive as planning to complete a doctoral degree in HRD.

Our field has almost reached a point where we have available the knowledge and lists of roles and competencies necessary to guide us in our professional development efforts. The ASTD Competency Study will contribute significantly to that body of knowledge, and we are beginning to see some agreement and standardization of both academic and nonacademic program content and competency assessment.

Keeping up with the state of the art and practice of HRD for the sake of being competent is only half the picture—the other half is change. The demands on our profession and the appropriate responses to those demands are changing more and more frequently. We must stay on the cutting edge if we are to proactively help people and organizations solve problems, change, and grow.

Self-Development

Whether you are an external HRD practitioner or a member of an HRD staff within a corporation, a large part of the responsibility for your professional development will fall on your own shoulders. If you are employed in an organization, it is hoped that your manager will take on the responsibility for developing the HRD staff. However, as this does not always occur, it may be necessary for you to initiate your own self-development process.

Such a process is represented in Figure 13.1. It is a fairly simple process, but it does require work and commitment. It is based on the premise that HRD professionals can have a great measure of control over their own growth. If you choose, this process can involve your supervisor, peers, subordinates, or friends.

Briefly, the first step is to identify what you do. You already have a detailed position description that spells out the tasks you are expected to perform, although such descriptions do not always represent reality. On the other hand, you may need to construct a list of your tasks. It would be a good idea to involve others, in order to validate your lists. Make sure your list is proactive and takes into account what you should be doing now and what you would like to be doing in the near future, carefully delineating each. This will not only help you establish the parameters of your present job, but it can assist you in determining the job changes necessary to improve your effectiveness and provide increasing challenges.

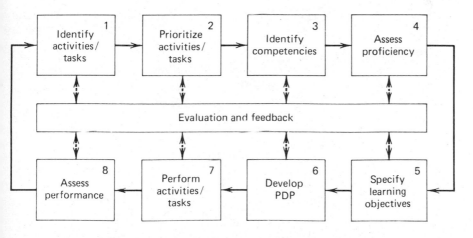

Figure 13.1. Professional self-development model.

Step 2 involves prioritizing your list, because you probably will not be able to work on everything at once. You need to ask yourself questions like:

What accomplishments have I been rewarded for in the past, and what do I want to be rewarded for in the future?

What are the least important activities of my job, and can I eliminate them?

Can I get management support for what I should or would like to do?

Who are my clients, and am I providing what they need?

Are my work activities in line with my life values and career objectives?

Once you have the answers to these questions (and again at this time you may want to explore these questions with peers or friends) and have prioritized your list, you are ready to identify the competencies needed to perform each activity. This is step 3. Ask yourself what knowledge, understanding, skills, attitudes, and values you need to perform a particular task. Do not get too detailed, but do not lose sight of important elements either. Think about what the results of an activity should be, and then, think about what you need to know to reach that goal. If you want to develop a role play, is it enough to know how to design a role play or how role plays are used? Or do you also need to know something about the psychology of learning and human behavior, so that you will develop the right role play to accomplish the learning objective of the session? In addition, do not forget the conditions under which you will perform the activity.

Step 4 includes assessing your level of proficiency against your list of competencies, identifying the gaps, and specifying your learning objectives, based on the assessment.

To develop your professional development plan, start with a prioritization of your learning needs (step 5). Then conduct an exploration of the best learning strategies to meet those needs (step 6). Include an evaluation plan to determine if those needs were met.

Steps 7 and 8 involve actually performing the tasks and then assessing your performance to determine your level of proficiency on the job.

Evaluation and feedback occur at every step to ensure consistency and organizational support. At each point, you should be validating your process with others and building support and commitment from your organization for your continued professional development.

Professional development is a continuing process, especially in our field where new theories, techniques, and approaches emerge almost daily.

FORMAL HRD RESOURCES

Introduction

It used to be extremely difficult to find a selection of formal resources to improve one's competence in HRD. Sharing and learning informally from others was usually discouraged because it meant admitting to a lack of knowledge or skill. In fact, academic degrees were perceived by many as a negative credential; you were expected to develop your own learning programs, no matter how many other versions of the same program existed, so that you could demonstrate proficiency.

Fortunately, things have changed. Now a significant number of HRD professionals have graduate degrees, numerous nondegree alternatives are available, and self-directed learning and networking are commonplace.

This does not mean that the resource you need or want exists right in your own backyard. To find the program(s) that will best suit your needs, a certain amount of initiative is required. A convenient resource will not always be available to assist you in finding what you want. In fact, you may have to make a number of phone calls, write several letters, and make more than one trip around your local area. During this period, a high level of commitment will be needed to maintain the initiative necessary to find what you want.

Furthermore, you may have to be creative, imaginative, and flexible in order to complete a program you have planned. The courses, seminars, workshops, books, films, and cassettes that are available are only pieces of the whole. A local university may not offer an HRD program, per se, but as you examine the total curriculum you might discover that courses related to HRD are available through several colleges within the same university. Pick one of the colleges, talk to the dean, and find out whether you can design your own program. Most universities are willing to help meet the needs of persistent students.

Degree-Granting Programs

In the last several years, colleges and universities have been rushing to include HRD programs in their curricula.[3] The George Washington

University put its current program in place in the 1960s and is recognized as the HRD academic pioneer in this country.

In October, 1982, ASTD held its Third Invitational Conference on the Academic Preparation of Practitioners in Training and Development/ Human Resource Development in Kansas City. An outcome of that meeting was the decision to update the 1981 edition of the *ASTD Directory of Academic Programs in Training and Development/Human Resource Development.* Later editions will probably list more than 200 programs offered by more than 100 U.S. colleges and universities at the certificate level through the doctorate level.

If you live in a city where there is a formal academic program in place, your task is easy. Visit the school, examine the curriculum against your objectives, and enroll. If there is no HRD program available in your community, seek out the "University-Without-Walls" programs (UWW) available around the country. Most UWW programs will accept courses taken at local universities/colleges, thereby allowing you to take advantage of local courses that meet your objectives. In that way, you will be able to move toward a degree, if that is part of your overall goal.

Whether you plan to enroll in a campus-based or UWW academic program, you should ask several questions:

> What is the overall philosophy of the HRD program you are considering?
>
> In which department or school is the program based, and is the program interdisciplinary?
>
> How flexible is the program? How tailored is each student's plan of study?
>
> Is it a subject-centered or competency-centered program?
>
> Does the program encourage internships, practicums, or other field experiences?
>
> Can you transfer credits from other programs? Does the university give credit for experience?
>
> Does the university provide job placement assistance for graduates?
>
> What are the professors' individual teaching styles?
>
> What previous experience (if any) has the faculty had as HRD practitioners?
>
> How relevant are the courses to the real world of work?
>
> Can I get the names of present students and graduates to obtain their opinions?

Non-Credit Academic Programs

Colleges and universities (and some adult education programs) offer a rich supply of noncredit courses and workshops. These programs may be more appropriate to your objectives than credit programs. However, all these programs may not be listed in one booklet. Your task will be to determine what programs are offered, which departments are offering them, and when they are offered. The director of continuing education would be the logical person to contact. You will want to find out who is offering what courses, so that you can decide if the courses are what you need and want. A good example is the well-known University of Michigan's Programmed Learning Workshop. Another is the "Training the Trainer Workshop" conducted by the University of Maryland.

You may find a number of courses/seminars available in your city. There are several series of HRD seminars offered by universities such as University of Mid-America and Georgetown University. Through an investigation of the courses, their objectives, and the methodology used to instruct, you may be able to acquire some or all of the competencies you want.

OTHER FORMAL LEARNING OFFERINGS

Every year, there are thousands of formal programs offered by professional societies and private consultants/vendors. A description of some of these programs follows. It includes a discussion of what is available, by whom, and how you can access more information about each.

Professional Societies

A primary activity that professional societies can provide to promote their members' professional growth is learning programs. Most professional societies offer formal learning programs to their members. Usually the programs are available to nonmembers as well, at a slightly higher cost.

The American Society for Training and Development (ASTD) is the predominant association for HRD professionals. It offers a variety of activities on several levels.

Local chapters of the society exist in more than 125 cities in the United States. They provide learning experiences in a wide range of HRD areas at their monthly meetings. The chapter's mission includes development of its members and leaders. You can talk to the chapter's program vice president/chair to find out what the annual program schedule includes. Your local telephone book may have an ASTD listing, or you can call ASTD in Washington, D.C., (202) 484-2390, for the name of the nearest ASTD person to call.

ASTD regional conferences are held every fall in eight or nine locations throughout the country. These conferences are two or three days long and may include as many as 40–60 learning activities in the program. The ASTD office in Washington, D.C. has the dates, locations, and contacts for each regional conference.

ASTD professional practice area networks consist of people who have identified a common interest area. At the present time, there are six such practice areas: career development, organization development, sales and marketing, technical skills training, media, and international. There are also two networks—a network of women and a minority network. These subunits of the society publish books, articles, papers, and newsletters for their special membership. Also, they are responsible for a portion of the learning offerings in the chapters, the regional and national conferences, and the national workshops.

ASTD national professional development workshops are conducted all over the United States and are three-day or four-day programs that focus on specific HRD topics in depth. A workshop booklet is published semiannually, listing the dates and locations of all workshops. The booklet is available free of charge from the ASTD office in Washington, D.C.

ASTD national conferences are held annually in May or June of each year in a large city with adequate conference facilities to accommodate the more than 6000 attendees. At the week-long national conferences, there are hundreds of HRD programs/workshops available. In addition, there is an exposition of hardware and software, and vendors who service the HRD community are present. Attendees find the national conference an intense learning, informational, and networking experience. The ASTD office in Washington, D.C. has brochures and other information available about the national conference.

The American Society of Personnel Administrators (ASPA) includes HRD professionals in its membership. The society has a certification program for "trainers." In addition, it has a catalog of programs/institutes offered each year. These programs are conducted all over the country and vary in length from one to three days. The programs include courses in compensation and benefits, employee and labor relations, employment, placement and personnel planning, health, safety and security, management practices, training and development. The catalog and information about membership are available by calling ASPA at (216) 826-4790.

The National Society of Performance and Instruction (NSPI) includes HRD people who specialize in the design of training programs. This society holds an annual conference in a different U.S. or Canadian city, and has an active chapter network. You can obtain more information from the NSPI office in Washington, D.C., (202) 861-0777.

The International Federation of Training and Development Organizations (IFTDO) holds a conference once a year in a different country. The five-day conference includes concurrent sessions designed specifically for HRD people. Information about the IFTDO conference can be obtained by calling ASTD and asking for the field service representative for the international division.

Other associations that provide material, services, and activities for HRD professionals include: The American Association for Adult and Continuing Education (which has an HRD practitioner subgroup), the Organizational Development Network, the Association for Humanistic Psychology, the Association for Educational Communications and Technology, and the Human Resource Planning Society.

Professional societies can promote the growth of the HRD practitioner by furthering the development of leadership skills and by providing an opportunity for members to contribute to the field. Most societies have a volunteer governing structure that enables their members to make professional contributions to the society.

For example, in ASTD, at the chapter, regional, division, and national levels, there are leadership roles available for members. You can be elected to serve as a chapter officer, a member of a division executive committee, a member of the board of directors, or you can be appointed as a committee chairperson. Through these experiences, you can improve your management skills or acquire knowledge and understanding of volunteer training and education. You can chair a committee and improve your problem-solving or group facilitation skills, develop learning programs for chapters, design instructional strategies for presentation at conferences, and interact with experts in the field who are on national committees. You can become the president of a large chapter (more than 1000 members) or the whole association, which offers a good opportunity to practice your management skills. Using your objectives, you can shop around until you find exactly the right program and/or leadership role to meet your needs.

Consultants/Vendors

These organizations provide the software/hardware that HRD people need to accomplish their jobs. You may hear about their products if you are seeking programs already developed to meet your organization's needs. If you are expanding your HRD facility to include up-to-date technology (i.e., computer-assisted instruction), you might ask vendors to submit proposals or bids for your review.

If you are currently a member of a professional HRD society, you are probably receiving hundreds of brochures each year from consultants/vendors which offer programs in a range of HRD topics. One example is the American Management Association (AMA). AMA lists more than 300 courses in its human resources catalog. These courses are given throughout the year in major metropolitan areas. Some of the courses are designed to train you; some are designed to train your customers or clients. Other well-known professional program organizations include: National Training Laboratories (NTL), University Associates, and Practical Management Associates.

A major advantage of offerings by consultants/vendors is that they are extremely flexible. Objectives do not have to be set a year in advance. The consultants/vendors can change course content as new material is developed, print up new brochures, and offer the redesigned program in just six to eight weeks. You have an opportunity to obtain the latest information via this vehicle.

A major disadvantage of courses offered by consultants/vendors is that no quality control is available to assist you in separating the professional people from the "dog and pony show" people. Theoretically, the professional people earn credibility, and their programs survive over time. Unfortunately, some of the "dog and pony show" people have learned how to mass merchandise effectively, and they, too, have survived over time.

You can become your own quality control person. When you find a program that appears to be what you want, call or write the consulting firm offering it. Ask the firm to give you the names of three satisfied customers and three dissatisfied customers. Call or write those six people and find out why the program succeeded or failed. If the consulting firm refuses to give you the names, ask yourself if you want to risk the time and money to discover firsthand what the quality will be. Professional consultant/vendor organizations are usually more than willing to help you evaluate their programs.

If you do not know what consultant/vendor programs are available, both ASTD and *Training: The Magazine of Human Resource Development* offer consultant buyer's guides for little or no cost. These directories give you the names, addresses, listing of programs, etc. that member consultants/vendors offer.

In-House Courses

If you are currently working for a large organization, there may be in-house programs available that will meet your needs. The federal government, for example, through the Office of Personnel Management, has programs available for federal HRD professionals. Xerox, IBM, General Motors and others offer "train the trainer" programs for their HRD staffs. Some corporations have even started to market their in-house programs to the public HRD community.

These in-house programs have advantages and disadvantages. Perhaps the major advantage is that the content of the program is designed to meet your needs within your organization. Consequently, as you learn, you can easily apply the knowledge to what you are being asked to do.

A major disadvantage is that the course may have been designed by people who have the same perspective and knowledge base as yourself. If their knowledge, skills, and attitudes are limited to how HRD is practiced in your organization, the courses may lead to an "exchange of ignorances." You have a responsibility to yourself to find out about the background and qualifications of the people who lead these programs. If the programs are not up to date and the designers are not professionally oriented, go outside to meet your objectives.

SELF-DIRECTED LEARNING

Introduction

According to Allen Tough, the learning experiences that are the most meaningful and beneficial to the adult learner are those that are self-designed and implemented.[4] Knowles calls this type of do-it-yourself learning "self-directed learning."[5]

Self-directed learning should probably be the first option you consider in your professional development plans for several reasons:

1. It is usually very inexpensive or frequently free (except for the

time spent in learning on the job). When little or no training money is available, this may be your only option. At the least, it will make a favorable impression on your management.

2. You can tailor each learning experience to your own specific needs and match those needs with specific resources.

3. You can schedule your learning experiences to be congruent with your work/life activities.

4. You can work with a group or on your own.

Networking

This is probably the most recent and most important type of self-development option. Networking is the sharing of information, ideas, and theories through a confederation of people with similar interests and/or needs. (Not to be confused with an information network, which is a method of tapping into various automated and manually organized data sources.) A professional society is a network in a very formal sense. A support group might be considered a network in its least formal sense.

National Networks.   A good example of a nationally organized professional network is the career planning and adult development network. (Unfortunately, there is no national network devoted specifically to training or HRD.) This network consists of at least one contact in every state, as well as one contact in four other countries. These volunteer contacts are people who have an expertise in career development and act as brokers, matching requests for information and assistance with appropriate resources. You can join the network for $24 a year, which covers the cost of a monthly newsletter that includes articles, book reviews, and notices about reports, meetings, new ideas, conferences, periodicals, research materials, directories, workshops, and academic programs. The network also publishes a quarterly journal for its members.

Special Interest Groups.   Another type of network is the special interest group (SIG). This is a group of people that meets to focus on a particular subject or issue. Many special interest groups are sponsored by local or national professional societies, while some are self-initiated and self-maintained. One rather unique group that can appropriately be called a special interest group is also the oldest HRD group in the United States— the Training Officers Conference. The Training Officers Conference was started by a group of government training (HRD) officers in 1938 in Washington, D.C. and still meets monthly.[6] It has no dues, no constitution, and no governing structure. Every year, several people volunteer to coordinate the activities of the group. The group has a monthly meeting with a program or workshop and a day-long institute each year. Also, it maintains a mailing list to which anyone's name can be added.

Most special interest groups meet because of a specific focus. It might be an HRD role, such as consulting; a type of instructional activity, such as computer learning; an issue, such as women in HRD; a program area, such as career development; a geographic base, such as HRD specialists in Fairfax County, Virginia; or an organizational base, such as government HRD specialists.

Support Groups. A third type of network is a support group. This is a group of professionals who meet periodically to share ideas, test out new theories, strategies, and techniques, and maintain their friendships. Many independent consultants belong to a support group in order to maintain a collegiate base; other HRD specialists belong to one because it offers a safe environment to test out ideas; and for some it is a place where personal growth and experimentation are encouraged. Again, it is a highly informal structure. Some groups, such as the Woodlands Group, have regularly scheduled meetings, and the members come from all over the country. Most groups decide at each meeting when to meet again, with the host of the meeting responsible for the topic (if it is not a free discussion type of group).

The significance of networking, in whatever form, is sharing. Since so many new theories and techniques are being developed in our profession and so much information is being disseminated, it is impossible to single-handedly keep up with all of it.

If there are no networks in your community that meet your needs, start one. Get four or five people together and ask each to bring one or two others. Decide on the focus and scope of the group, and include people who would be responsible for bringing resources and sharing experiences.

Sharing is the key to effectiveness and growth. "It's not what you know but who you know," applies very aptly to our field—not just in terms of career and career movement, but in terms of professional development.

Learning Projects. These projects may be done inside or outside your organization, depending on your needs and resources. Once you have determined what you want to learn, ask yourself, "Can I arrange a special project that will allow me to meet my objectives?" Your organization may already have some special assignments pending that may require people interested in professional growth.

Your first option should be to talk with your manager and find out if he or she can direct you to a special assignment or at least give you the names of people to call.

If that is not an option, lay out a proposed project for your organization that will benefit both your employer and yourself. Then talk with your manager and find out how you can sell this idea to the organization. If your ideas is a good one, you may reap a double reward—the opportunity to get your learning needs met and some positive regard from the management people who accept your proposal.

Another option is to think about the organizations in your community. Is there some place where you can set up a learning project on a volunteer basis? For example, you may find an organization that wants to do some research in the community. In such a learning project, you can acquire the skills to design instruments, identify a target population, survey the population, collect and analyze data, and so on. A small organization might be willing to let you do the research, since it probably will not have the resources, money, or people to handle the project on its own. This option is a long shot, but with creative thinking, you may find exactly what you want.

There are many volunteer organizations that have training needs. For example, the United Way trains thousands of people to collect funds in its annual drive. In a learning project of that size, you may be able to select a staff, train them, design and develop the training program for the fund collectors, and implement it. Once again, you may reap a double reward—meeting your own learning objectives and assisting an organization that you support philosophically.

Mentors.   Working for or with a master is an excellent and exciting way to learn. Ask an expert in your field whether you can help with a project or whether you can work with him or her in a voluntary setting, such as a professional society or community social service activity. If you can, try to get involved in a long-term HRD effort, so you can experience the whole process of that effort.

A quick and easy way to learn from experts is to "pick their brains." This simply means questioning the experts. Most big names are very accessible to other professionals. Just pick up the phone and call or make an appointment. Most experts have learned from others and will encourage and support people who want to learn from them.

Reading List. In the field of HRD, there is a constant supply of new books, articles, and papers being published. Develop a reading list that supports your objectives. Include journals and newsletters that are published regularly, books that examine new aspects of the field, and research reports that break new ground. Make the reading list a habit that you acquire, use, and share with others. It is a good idea to ask others to recommend new reading materials.

TAKE THE INITIATIVE

These alternatives are presented to you with no priority ranking in mind. Select the best alternative for yourself, based on your available time, money, and resources. If you are working full time and must continue to do so, you will not be able to consider becoming a full-time student in a traditional school. If you live in a small community or in a remote geographical area, you may have to select the self-development approach.

If you start with a clear set of objectives that are designed to move you toward a concrete goal, then selecting the best alternative to achieve those objectives can be done logically and easily. All it takes is initiative.

CONCLUSION

Being a Professional

Keeping up with the state of the art and practice of HRD is only one aspect of professionalism. There are other points to consider:

Have a philosophical and theoretical foundation.

Understand why you do things a certain way.

Develop a personal belief and value system for your practice of HRD. Know why you do things a certain way.

Have a career/life plan. Know where you are going and how you are going to get there.

Seek feedback. Know who you are and how people perceive you.

Be open to change. Desire to grow both personally and professionally.

We should strive not to be merely competent, but to be excellent—to be professional.

NOTES

1. N. Chalofsky and C.I. Lincoln, *Up the HRD Ladder: A Guide for Professional Growth* (Reading, Mass.: Addison-Wesley, 1983).
2. M. Knowles, *Self-Directed Learning* (New York: Association Press, 1975).
3. Chalofsky and Lincoln, *Up the HRD Ladder: A Guide for Professional Growth.*
4. A. Tough, *The Adult's Learning Projects*, 2d. ed. (San Diego: Learning Concepts, 1979).
5. Knowles, *Self-Directed Learning.*
6. L. Nadler, *Developing Human Resources*, 2d. ed. (San Diego: Learning Concepts, 1979).

PROGRAM AREAS OF HRD

CHAPTER FOURTEEN

Sales Programs

H. STANLEY CONNELL III

It has been said that sales are essential to any industrial system. Without sales, very little happens.

As Connell points out in this chapter, the training and education of salespeople has been woefully neglected until recently. Even now, there are still those who insist that salespeople are born and that formal learning programs are irrelevant. In the words of "Music Man" Harold Hill, "You've got to know the territory." Few in the sales field would challenge that statement, particularly in the technological world of today, where knowing the territory is not enough.

Connell had difficulty finding education programs in the sales field. This is certainly worthy of more exploration by others. The absence of development (as defined in the glossary and earlier chapters) should also be noted.

H. Stanley Connell III is president of Productive Concepts Systems, Inc., a sales and sales management consulting firm. He has been in the sales field, including the HRD side, for more than 25 years. He has been a field sales manager and has provided training and education in sales and sales management. He will serve as director of the Sales and Marketing Division of ASTD during 1984–85.

DEFINITIONS OF SALES AND SALES MANAGEMENT TRAINING

Sales and sales management training and educational programs are those programs that provide the learner with the skills and knowledge necessary to perform those functions assigned to salespeople and their managers and which are not generally taught with the same emphasis to other employees. The functions include such tasks as organizing and operating a sales territory, meeting sales quotas, and performing reporting activities for the salesperson. A sales manager's tasks include managing a sales district or region, field coaching and counseling, recruiting and selecting sales personnel, office management, and sales planning. The skills necessary to perform these functions are often learning topics.

SALES TRAINING AND ITS PLACE IN HRD

Similarities Between Sales and Other HRD Program Areas

The core human relations skills for salespeople and sales managers are the same as for others in an organization. Sales personnel, like everyone else, need coaching and counseling by their manager, and the methods for doing this are the same. Although performance factors may vary, the way salespersons' performance and the performance of others in an organization are appraised does not differ. The principles of time control and basic organizational skills apply to everyone, including salespeople. Furthermore, all employees need to understand the corporate structure and philosophy of their company. Although company policies may differ, most of them apply to all employees, including those in sales. It is just as useful for salespeople, when practical, to attend the same new employee orientation as others in order to help them gain a broader overview of their company and how it operates.

How Sales HRD Programs Are Different
from Other HRD Program Areas

Specialized skills are needed to sell and manage a sales district. Unlike most other employees in an organization, salespeople perform almost all of their tasks alone and generally without much supervision. Consequently, it is critical that they receive more training on organization, time management, and self-assessment than other employees. Creating a motivational climate for salespeople is also different than for other workers because usually salespeople have a greater need to achieve than to be liked or to have power. They also must be self-motivated since they work alone. Therefore, motivation is usually of greater concern to sales managers than their counterparts in other departments.

Selling skills are specialized communication skills that successful salespeople must acquire and perfect. In one form or another, these skills are emphasized in sales HRD programs more than any other skills, because the correlation between sales and selling skills is so direct and so obviously affects corporate profits.

Finally, the knowledge of company products required of salespeople varies from that which other departments need to know, since for salespeople the emphasis must be on the benefits of the product and how it differs from those of the competition.

THE EVOLUTION OF SALES HRD PROGRAMS

For almost any company, their own products and markets are, to some extent, unique. Therefore, it is necessary to provide some sort of training for newly hired salespeople and newly appointed sales managers. For this reason, formal learning in sales is provided more often by companies than learning in any other area. On the other hand, accountants, secretaries, machine operators, managers, and many others can often be productive after very little formal training, since they can apply past learning (education) more readily.

Before and during the 1930s, very little training of any kind was provided for salespeople. Selling skills were unheard of, and the popular myth "Salespeople are born, not made" was universally accepted. Products at that time were not nearly as sophisticated as they are today, and neither were those responsible for their purchase. In this setting, sales managers recruited and hired men and women who were "good talkers." The task of the sales manager who trained these people was to show them around the territory and give them a price book. Very little formal training took place. Since a large percentage of the salespeople were paid strictly on commission, their tenure depended upon learning the job quickly. It is not surprising that turnover was very high for new salespeople. Learning programs were not yet considered a means for improving productivity.

Job Instruction Training (JIT) was introduced to sales managers in the 1940s. At that time, few people were actually assigned sales training responsibilities, since the little training that was offered was conducted by the salesperson's immediate supervisor. These managers were often given the JIT steps to be followed in both formal and on-the-job training (OJT). Probably the first job aids for sales managers were cards listing the steps in training: (1) prepare, (2) tell, (3) show, (4) have him do it, and (5) check, with a brief explanation of each step. In spite of the first attempts at formalized learning programs for salespeople, the myths of previous decades persisted throughout the 1940s. Most management still accepted such statements as "Selling is a mystery," and "Selling is something you can't tell a person how to do—they either have it or they don't."

Formal sales learning programs came into their own in the 1950s. That was a period of time when most salespeople were taught canned sales presentations. Learners often spent hours memorizing these presentations and reciting them to a manager. The primary method used for learning was lecturing. Since someone had to do the lecturing and insure that the memory work was perfected, a person was assigned to this task. He (with rare exceptions both learners and managers were male) was most often an experienced and successful salesman and most frequently was called a sales training manager. His selection was based on sales success rather than on managerial or HRD skills.

Two audiovisual tools were introduced and used in the 1950s, films and phonograph records. The Borden and Busse film series was the first sales learning tool of this type. Although rather crudely done, with salesmen as actors, the films depicted salespeople and provided "how to" in various selling situations (behavioral modeling in the 1950s?).

Sales managers of this era had a lot of concern for motivating their salespeople, and they have ever since. Phonograph records by the sales gurus of that period flourished. Frank Bettger and Elmer Wheeler were listened to and revered. Their inspirational messages were assumed to be the answer to the question of how to motivate a sales force.

Sales management training in the 1950s was limited. "Motivate them and make them do it" was the underlying theme of most of the learning programs provided to sales managers. The learning programs for salespeople were conducted almost exclusively by sales departments. It was generally accepted that they were the only ones that knew how to do it.

Many of the theories used by other HRD people were adapted for use in sales and sales management training in the 1960s. This reactive rather than proactive stance continues today, though to a much lesser extent. Off-the-shelf programs became widely used in the 1960s. The most popular of these included programmed learning. It became widely accepted that the sales process consisted of several logical steps that could be learned. Films became more sophisticated and continued to present and model selling skills and techniques (persuasion skills). Maslow's Hierarchy of Needs, The Managerial Grid, and other new theories became part of many sales management learning programs. They also made their way into some learning programs for salespeople; however, this application was much more crudely done, probably due to insufficient understanding by managers.

In the 1970s, sales managers and those conducting sales HRD programs reacted to and adopted new behavioral science theories in rapid succession. The sales process was much clearer then, and the application of many theories became more obvious.

Since earlier myths about selling were no longer accepted, the need to recruit top salespeople to conduct sales learning programs became much less important. It was discovered that midrange sales performers often made the best sales HRD managers. Also, the notion that perhaps HRD skills were more important than sales experience for sales HRD managers was considered, since it now was generally accepted that selling skills were learned behaviors.

Unquestionably, sales skills received a great deal of emphasis in the 1970s. Unfortunately, the problem was that in many instances sales skills seemed to be separated from product knowledge and were over-emphasized.

Then, women and minorities entered the selling field. After some experimentation and quite a few mistakes, sales managers found that using the same criteria for hiring, regardless of race or sex, and providing training to meet learners' needs produced positive results. The problems sales HRD managers thought they would face with minorities and women rarely occurred, and those that did develop were manageable.

More new audiovisual equipment, especially videotape, became sales HRD tools. Role playing, which had been an important part of sales HRD programs since the 1940s, was enhanced by videotaping and the playback of sales demonstrations. It is still one of the most valuable learning tools today. Films for salespeople flourished in the 1970s, most of them a new type—the so-called "sales motivation" film. They featured sports stars or other well-known figures, who readily shared their success stories and discussed how their techniques could easily be applied by others to achieve greater sales success. Today's sales HRD professional questions some of these analogies.

A variety of new types of programs were also introduced. Assertiveness, negotiation skills, listening skills, time management skills, and a host of other topics quickly gained popularity. Numerous psychological theories were adapted to fit selling and sales management with varying success. This was also a period of fads—some things worked well, others not so well. For salespeople and their managers this endless stream of "the very latest thing" often missed the mark in providing meaningful learning.

The 1980s showed a solidification and refinement of those techniques and theories that produced results. Sales HRD managers no longer could attend a three- to five-day course on the latest fad and become self-proclaimed experts. A balance seems to have been struck between sales skills and product learning. Companies are more aware of the competencies required of sales HRD professionals and are selecting them more on the basis of those skills. Management has also shown a greater concern for learning related to performance results. In response, sales HRD people have moved to the forefront by linking their learning programs to increased sales productivity. Better program design and an increased use of behavior modeling have contributed to this linkage. The 1980s should be noted as a period when sales fully integrated itself into the HRD field.

THE RESPONSIBILITIES OF SALES HRD PRACTITIONERS

For sales HRD practitioners the usual scope of responsibilities is limited to providing learning programs for those people who have a direct effect on sales. This includes salespeople, sales managers, and customer service and marketing personnel. In fact, some sales HRD managers are responsible for conducting learning programs for almost everyone in the sales department.

The specific responsibilities of sales HRD practitioners vary according to whom they report. A primary difference, at least at this time, between sales HRD people and other HRD people is that the former are much less likely to be in a human resource unit. Tradition has it that sales organizations and sales departments conduct their own sales learning programs. Consequently, sales HRD practitioners often report to people with titles such as vice president of sales, vice president of sales and marketing, or general sales manager. There are also examples of sales HRD practitioners reporting to the presidents of a very large corporation or to a district sales manager. It should be noted that there is a trend toward moving sales learning program responsibilities into the human resource domain.

Although sales HRD learning programs cover a wide variety of topics, selling skills learning is most universally provided by sales HRD managers. These learning programs include the traditional skills of opening and closing a sale, plus listening, nonverbal communication, motivation, negotiation, and a host of others.

Sales HRD managers must perform tasks such as analyzing needs, making recommendations, designing programs, planning meetings, assessing currently available packaged programs and seminars, implementing and conducting sales programs, conducting field OJT, keeping abreast of the latest technological advances, and maintaining membership in a professional association.

EDUCATION PROGRAMS TO PREPARE PEOPLE FOR THE SELLING PROFESSION

Despite the large number of high school, and two-year and four-year college graduates who enter the sales field each year, it is almost impossible to get the appropriate preparatory education. In fact, I know of only one college that offers a degree (associate) in sales, although a number of colleges offer sales courses as a part of their marketing programs. There are also several colleges that offer sales management courses as a part of their marketing programs.

These marketing and sales management courses do not provide the education needed by salespeople. The reason is simple; no companies hire people right out of a college or university as sales managers, and very few of them will hire graduates for marketing positions. Perhaps the lack of responsiveness to the students' needs by educational institutions is due to the fact that few of the students entering these institutions are planning for a sales career. Why is this, when so many sales jobs are available each year? High schools may not adequately describe selling and the scope of the sales field, or higher learning institutions may not know what education is required. Why? Most likely, it is a lack of communication on the part of the business community, accepting the status quo rather than confronting educators with the problem.

Whatever the reason for this lack of proper education for people entering the sales field, the result is that the student desiring a sales career suffers. Many of the companies having the most desirable sales jobs will hire only experienced salespeople for these positions. This means that most students starting a sales career must begin with jobs that accept entry level people. *Entry level* in sales is almost synonymous with a lack of selling experience and a lack of understanding about how to sell. Education can help shorten the time a person needs to gain this experience, and educators could play the largest part in helping to lessen this time.

Organizations, then, hire people for a sales career who frequently know little about the sales profession. The organization's most pressing need is to teach new salespeople how to sell, so that they will be productive as soon as possible. Some organizations do a good job in preparing people through education, while others do not. Therefore, it usually cannot be assumed that an experienced salesperson has sufficient knowledge to perform successfully. This is why most companies put everyone through the same initial training course, teaching the same basic skills.

In-house programs to educate employees from other units for sales are rare, although some companies educate and prepare customer service people to move into sales. Even in this case, the initiative usually lies with the customer service person who expresses an interest in and asks for the education. It seems strange that, considering the high cost of selecting, hiring, and training salespeople, the idea of internal sales education programs has not been more popular.

Most sales managers, including top sales management, move up "through the sales ranks." Therefore, companies usually have a program for spotting potential sales managers from among their salespeople. This begins with field coaching visits and continues as the sales personnel participate in sales meetings and learning programs. Many companies offer special courses on sales management and on conducting sales training to these potential managers. Frequently, these prospective managers are asked to assist in the field training of other salespeople or to accept short-term sales HRD assignments. As a rule, salespeople must have two to three years experience before they are considered for management. Larger companies often develop a career path for likely sales managers that includes both internal HRD programs and outside programs conducted by universities or vendors. It is far less common than it was in the past to have a salesperson placed in a management position without any formal education for that position.

Having discussed the role of sales HRD, the evolution of sales HRD learning, and education programs that prepare people for selling, we will spend most of the balance of this chapter considering learning programs provided to salespeople and their managers and some special concerns facing sales HRD practitioners.

LEARNING PROGRAMS FOR SALESPEOPLE

Salespeople and their managers, like most others in an organization, participate in four basic types of learning programs:

1. Those designed and conducted in-house
2. Off-the-shelf programs, either conducted in-house or by a vendor
3. Conferences and seminars, either in-house or public, conducted by vendors
4. Programs developed and perhaps conducted by consultants

The type of program or combination of these programs is dependent upon a number of factors, including the size of the organization, the size of the sales force, and the number of people on the sales HRD staff. A small company that uses a sales manager or someone else in the organization to handle sales training as a part-time responsibility is more likely to use off-the-shelf programs that are not instructor dependent. Organizations that are a little larger, with one person handling sales HRD programs, probably will have a combination of in-house and off-the-shelf programs. They may also use independent consultants to design and conduct programs. Large companies will do more of their own program design; however, in most instances, they also utilize off-the-shelf programs. They also use vendors and independent consultants in roles that range from needs analysis to design and implementation of programs. Conferences and seminars are attended by people from companies of all sizes. Films and videotapes are often used by all three groups.

The programs for salespeople generally fall into four categories:

Selling skills
Product knowledge
Organizing
Company policy and procedures

Selling Skills

Selling skills are those skills that a salesperson uses with a sales prospect. They are usually thought of as being used in face-to-face selling situations; however, many of these skills work equally well on the telephone. Selling skills can include: the approach or opening, needs gathering, the asking of questions, presentation, management of objections, and the closing. Other communication skills such as negotiation, oral and nonverbal communication, and motivation are also considered selling skills.

Many medium-sized and large companies provide multi-level selling skills programs. The sophistication of the skills learning program is dependent upon the experience of the salesperson and the type of product being sold. Some companies hire relatively inexperienced (entry level) salespeople who need to learn the basic core selling skills. Other companies hire experienced salespeople and provide them with more sophisticated programs that include advanced communication theories and techniques.

In-House Designed Programs. These programs are almost always tied to the organization's particular markets and products. There is usually a heavy emphasis on content rather than process, since skills are being taught only so the product can be presented and sold.

The most frequently employed methods for providing this learning are self-study and formal classroom work. Self-study can take the form of programmed learning in workbooks or written materials (e.g., product specification sheets and brochures). Occasionally, companies prepare their own complete selling skills programs, but seldom has this practice proven to be cost effective. The vendor can spread design costs among many clients over a long period of time.

Formal classroom selling skills learning programs that include role play are the most common. This role play often utilizes videotaping and feedback. Films are also used when only one or two skills are to be learned at a time.

A combination of videotapes, used to model desired behavior using company products, followed by the videotaping of role plays that are critiqued by peers, provides the greatest opportunity for transferring learning to the sales territory. These videotapes use company products and are usually produced in-house.

Off-the-Shelf Skills Programs. Off-the-shelf selling skills programs flourish. They vary from strictly programmed learning to multimedia with high participant involvement. These programs are normally two and a half to five days long. Some of them require up to 25 hours of prior work, while others do not ask for any advance preparation. Overhead transparencies, 35mm slides, and videotapes that model both desirable and undesirable behaviors are frequently a part of these programs. Often, the programs make supportive audiovisual material optional.

Many off-the-shelf programs are designed to be conducted by field managers with limited experience in formal instructing, rather than by sales HRD practitioners. The programs simply require a good administrator and the proper equipment. These programs are, by design, either totally or heavily process oriented, and any linking of the skills to company products must be done by the program administrator. When this link is not made and an opportunity to practice using the skills with company products or services is not provided, these off-the-shelf programs usually do not produce the desired results.

Another kind of off-the-shelf program requires the instructor to be proficient in working with groups and in the skills being taught in the program. Practice in conducting the program is usually also required. These are called *instructor-dependent programs*, since they require the administrator to take an active role in assuring the success of the program.

Organizations that have full-time sales HRD practitioners on their staff, especially the larger ones, generally prefer instructor-dependent programs since they offer more flexibility and often the ability to incorporate company products or services into the learning. Instructor-dependent programs usually require certification of the instructor, since more skill is required. Unfortunately, there is a trend in the design of off-the-shelf programs toward less instructor dependency. This may be advantageous to the vendor who is marketing these programs, but it is not to the benefit of the learner, since there is less opportunity for interchange and exploration of ideas, which are principles of adult learning.

A few off-the-shelf selling skills programs are designed for specific industries (e.g., retail sales) and range from self-administered to instructor-dependent programs.

Many film producers and distributors offer their films in learning packages that sometimes include workbooks, 35mm slides, and audiotapes. Generally they do not provide the flexibility or completeness available in off-the-shelf programs. Firms that offer off-the-shelf selling skills programs determine what skills need to be learned and then develop learning objectives that meet these requirements. Once this has been done, they select the most appropriate media from the full range available. Film companies, on the other hand, have already determined the media to be used (e.g., film or videotape) and build a program around that media. Any other materials they develop appear to be an attempt to provide a packaging or multimedia effect. Films, however, can be very useful for learning or reinforcing a single skill.

Most vendors of off-the-shelf programs, as well as sales HRD consultants, conduct selling skills programs for clients both in-house and in public seminars. As a rule, only larger companies can afford vendor-conducted, in-house programs. Both in-house and public seminars are generally geared toward salespeople with at least some knowledge of selling.

Selling skills training and practice are widely used by most firms. In fact, some small and medium organizations only provide on-the-job selling skills training. This approach can limit the salesperson's understanding of selling skills to those modeled by the trainer. The success of the training is directly related to the sales and HRD experience of the trainer and the variety of selling situations that are faced during the training. The more well-rounded and successful approach is a combination of formal training followed by field training. The positive behavioral change that selling skills programs have as goals are unlikely to be achieved without field follow-up training, practice and coaching. The skill of the field manager is, therefore, the determining factor in the success or failure of a program.

Product Knowledge

In most industries, product knowledge is conducted in-house. Companies usually prefer not to use outside vendors or even associations for product learning, since they believe they better understand their own products and their benefits over the competition. The way product learning is provided and the time needed to teach it varies widely according to the complexity of the product.

Since the widespread application of programmed learning, HRD managers have discovered that many products can readily be learned using this media. Among the benefits of programmed learning are time and location flexibility. Thus a salesperson can work on the job and study products at night or on the weekend.

The methods most frequently employed in product learning continues to be a combination of studying specification sheets and formal classroom lectures and discussion. Perhaps one reason for this is that marketing people, such as product managers who are commonly involved in product training, often prefer these methods.

In addition to these methods, sales HRD practitioners also use videotapes, sound-slide programs, computer-assisted instruction, and audiotapes to assist in product learning. If these programs are not prepared in-house, they are prepared under the direction of in-house personnel.

No discussion of product learning would be complete without mentioning when the majority of substantive product learning takes place—while interacting with customers in selling or servicing situations. Users of a product or service can best describe its benefits to the inquiring salesperson. Prospective customers will ask questions that can help the salesperson learn the product better. The sales HRD practitioner can serve salespeople well by training them on how to gain product or service information from the customer. Field managers also teach product knowledge to new salespeople while making product demonstrations to customers. This kind of guided field experience can also serve to inform the salesperson as to how much and what product knowledge is necessary.

Company Policy and Products

Learning company policy and procedures is necessary in a company of almost any size. In the simplest of terms, a salesperson must know how to write an order, what the product prices are, and where to send the order. Most companies have reporting, accounting, and other forms that must be completed and policies and procedures that must be followed. Almost all training programs for policies and procedures are internally designed and conducted.

No doubt, lecture and discussion are the learning methods used most often; however, they are not always the best. Programmed instruction, for example, lends itself very well to learning how to complete forms or read a price book. It is self-paced, can be done independently, reinforces the learner, and can be reviewed at any time. Computer-assisted instruction can help the trainee to learn policy and how to complete forms, again providing the specific learning an individual needs, rather than what various members of a group may need. Sound-slide programs are used to teach policy and to explain why it is important.

Merchandising and Market Penetration

Merchandising and market penetration training is usually designed and conducted in-house for new sales employees. Experienced salespeople are sometimes sent to outside seminars or attend advanced company-designed programs.

The most accepted method of learning merchandising and market penetration is by actually doing it in field situations. A field manager (e.g., a district manager or field trainer) demonstrates the necessary skills, techniques, and procedures, allows the salesperson to try them, and then coaches the person as needed. Companies that provide limited training usually employ only this method.

In-house, formal learning programs most frequently utilize workbooks or self-study material and lecture/discussion sessions with the HRD practitioner citing examples.

A few public programs for salespeople are held on market penetration; however, most of them are for specialized fields, such as insurance and securities sales.

Time Management and Effective Organization

Time management and how to organize for effectiveness are topics that are integrated into most programs for new salespeople.

In recent years, greatly increased sales costs have increased the need for sales personnel to manage their time better. This topic has probably become more important to those in field sales than to other parts of the organization, since these salespeople are relatively unsupervised. For some entry-level salespeople, this lack of supervision must be replaced by procedures and techniques for organization and time control. Time management workshops are also offered to experienced sales personnel. These workshops are usually only one day in length. Films, sound-slide programs, books, and packaged programs conducted by vendors and external consultants on time management are readily available. Most sales HRD practitioners prefer to develop their own time management programs, using the resources available from vendors. This in-house design links technique and theory with the real-world situations that sales personnel are facing.

How to organize and operate a sales territory are topics almost exclusively learned through in-house programs. This is necessary, due to the variety of products, markets, and organizational makeup. Varied media are used to assist learning; however, lecture and sound-slide programs reinforced with written materials seem to be most prevalent.

Learning how to organize and work in a sales territory is essential in most instances. Again, it is up to a field district manager or field sales trainer to provide field training and reinforcement. Most sales territories are sufficiently different from one another to require this kind of training. Ideally, the new salesperson receives a combination of formal and field learning.

Telephone Selling

The increasingly high cost of making a sale today requires that salespeople lower the ratio of calls per sale, while maintaining a sufficient number of sales. Telephone selling, or telemarketing, plays an important part in helping sales personnel maintain acceptable productivity levels.

The most popular and widely quoted telephone sales program is the Phone Power program developed by AT&T. The steps presented in this program appear frequently in other packaged programs. In addition to the AT&T program, numerous other vendor-produced programs are available that include films, videotapes, audio cassettes, and programmed instruction. Almost all of these programs include role play as a key ingredient. Telephones and a tape recorder capture the conversations, which are then played back and critiqued.

Programs developed in-house which incorporate one or more of the films or sound-slide programs available allow the salesperson to work on situations similar to those encountered on the job, although several vendor off-the-shelf programs also allow for this. Without question, the key to insuring that the learning is applied on the job is the role play of real situations encountered on the job.

Communication and Self-Awareness Programs

The area of communications and self-awareness includes most of the other kinds of learning programs in which a salesperson is likely to participate, including:

Negotiation skills
Listening skills
Stressless selling
Nonverbal communication
Public speaking
Speed reading
Interpersonal skills
Motivation
Interviewing skills
Assertiveness skills

Most of these programs are conducted by either vendors, independent consultants, or in-house HRD managers who have gone through a certification program conducted by a vendor. Off-the-shelf programs are also available on most of these topics. These kinds of programs provide the opportunity for a field manager to send salespeople to workshops that relate to their specific needs. Sometimes, a workshop dealing in one of the areas listed will do more to influence a salesperson's productivity than one of a more generalized nature. A primary role of sales HRD practitioners is to be aware of what programs are available and to inform field management about them.

LEARNING PROGRAMS FOR SALES MANAGERS

Programs for sales managers may vary somewhat from one company to another; however, there are some that are common to almost all of them.

Coaching and counseling
Recruiting and selection
Office management
Motivation
Instructing and conducting meetings

There are also programs for the development of sales management skills. These are the core skills of planning, controlling, organizing, and directing, as they apply to a sales manager.

There seems to be less urgency to train sales managers than to train salespeople. This is probably part of the "I have appointed you a manager, therefore, you are one" syndrome. The learning programs provided for sales managers are often in reaction to problems that actually occurred, rather than a desire to provide an education and lay a foundation for future development and growth.

Some companies offer a learning program to every newly appointed sales manager. Usually it is designed in-house and includes sales management skills and policy and procedure matters. The length of time for these courses can vary from one day to two weeks with four days being average. Films, videotapes, and manuals are often used to assist learning.

The first problems a new sales manager faces most likely center around recruiting, hiring, selecting, coaching, counseling, or motivation.

Therefore, these are often the topics for workshops that new sales managers attend. In-house programs are often developed based on these topics and utilize some of the films and videotapes available from vendors, but, frequently, off-the-shelf programs or public seminars are used.

Targeting sales managers for specific learning programs, to meet their needs, is much more prevalent than it is for salespeople. Many companies budget specifically to send managers to these courses. Public speaking, assertiveness, and marketing are among the many public courses attended by field sales managers.

A few universities and associations hold courses lasting for several weeks at a time. However, most sales HRD managers claim that the content of these programs is too generalized to warrant the time or expense of sending their managers. They prefer to respond to each manager's specific needs, in-depth, through programs not lasting more than a week.

Many of the learning programs that are offered to managers in other departments are also offered to sales managers. Courses on budgeting, forecasting, or introduction to data processing can be as helpful to the sales manager as to other managers. These other management programs can usually be enhanced by the participation of sales managers, because of the different perspective they can offer.

Each organization has its own particular sets of learning programs. These programs can include technical product data, team building, communication skills, writing skills, budgeting, and so forth. Sales managers, like other managers in the company, need to participate in them.

LEARNING PROGRAMS FOR DISTRIBUTORS
AND DEALER SALES PERSONNEL

Some companies sell their products through wholesale distributors or retail stores, rather than through their own sales force. This necessitates providing learning programs that teach product knowledge and in many cases selling skills. This adds an additional dimension to the sales HRD manager's responsibilities. Not only do their field personnel have to learn how to train others and how to conduct meetings, but learning programs must be developed for these outside people.

Learning programs developed by manufacturers for distributors and retailers fall into two categories: those that are prepared and packaged so that these outside people can conduct them without company assistance and those that are designed to be conducted by company field personnel.

The programs packaged for outside people most often consist of programmed learning booklets, audio cassette tapes, or reading material that can be studied at the convenience of the learner. More frequently, videotaped programs are being made available to them. Programs developed for people outside a company are designed to be used by as wide a variety of salespeople as will be involved in selling the product or products. Therefore, the subject matter and the situations depicted are general rather than specific, and questions unique to a different business may not be answered.

The learning programs conducted by a company's own field personnel are usually not more than an hour long. This is because more time is seldom available. In retail stores, they are conducted before or after business hours. Audiovisual support materials (e.g., videotapes, films, or slides) are often a part of these programs. Many of these learning programs also include the introduction and use of point of sales material.

The emphasis of programs provided to dealers and wholesalers is to help them know the products and how to sell them. Most manufacturers believe that if salespeople are more comfortable with their product line and have ideas for selling it, they will present those products to their customers.

When the salesperson knows a product well and uses good sales techniques, product returns are usually greatly reduced.

LEARNING PROGRAMS FOR OTHER CUSTOMER CONTACT PERSONNEL

Since the organization of HRD functions varies so widely from one company to another it is difficult to describe exactly what responsibilities the sales HRD manager has in providing programs for other customer contact personnel. The important point is that all customer contact people need to have product knowledge, and most of them need some understanding of sales skills.

Besides their sales personnel, most companies' customer service or customer relations people also have contact with customers, and some manufacturers have employees who service products in the field. Both of these groups must have some understanding of the company's products. They are not only asked about the product the customer has already purchased but about other company products as well. This requires some product knowledge learning and, in many cases, sales skills.

Customer relations personnel normally are not trained by sales HRD personnel, although occasionally HRD personnel provide them with learning in selling skills. An understanding of the salesperson's task helps the customer relations personnel do a better job of supporting their efforts. Some organizations consider customer relations the stepping stone to a sales representative's job. In those instances, learning programs in both products and skills are at least partly the responsibility of the sales HRD manager.

Service personnel are also not usually trained by the sales HRD manager. There is one exception to this. Some service personnel do actually sell products or get sales leads for products. In those instances, they are trained in selling skills and sometimes in product knowledge by sales HRD managers.

SPECIAL CONCERNS FOR SALES HRD PRACTITIONERS

Sales HRD people encounter some special problems that are less likely to be faced by those in other HRD fields. These problems should be considered by those who are thinking of entering this specialized area.

The people participating in sales and sales management learning programs are likely to be dispersed throughout the selling area. This means that learning programs are often conducted in field locations where the organization's salespeople are based. Therefore, sales HRD people generally do a lot of traveling. Granted, other HRD practitioners often travel a great deal, but usually not to the extent that those in sales do. Since various locations are used for programs, this must be taken into consideration when selecting, designing, and scheduling such programs.

There is much less opportunity for on-the-job learning reinforcement in sales than for people working in offices or plants. Sales managers can only work with one salesperson at a time, and some only spend 50% of their time (perhaps even less) doing this. Most salespeople do not see their manager more than four or five times a year. This means that learning programs must be designed so that the learner will receive reinforcement and guidance through correspondence or the telephone. Sales managers need to have a high level of coaching and counseling skill. They should also understand how to establish positive motivational climates for their salespeople. The implication here is that a sales manager needs more training than the average manager to obtain satisfactory subordinate performance.

Those sales HRD practitioners who have not had one or two years of successful field sales experience are often criticized by both field managers and salespeople as having only "school book" knowledge. Other HRD managers may face this problem, but not to the same degree. Sales managers have almost always worked as salespersons in their companies before being promoted to management, and many of them believe this experience is the only practical way to learn how to sell and, in turn, to teach others how to sell. They frequently subscribe to the notion that a sales HRD person is not credible without successful field sales experience.

Linked to this same problem is the idea that some field sales managers have that formal learning programs are a waste of time, since the only way to learn how to sell is by doing it. Lingering myths about selling lead to the notion that selling skills are not really learned behaviors.

One additional concern that sales HRD practitioners have is that most of them do not report to the same person as other HRD people. For many, this issue is a two-edged sword. They can work independently of other HRD people and perhaps maintain an aura of mystique around sales learning programs, but, at the same time, they do not have the opportunities to share and develop ideas with their peers. This is changing, however, as more and more sales HRD people are reporting to a manager with company-wide HRD responsibilities. While many believe this to be beneficial, others are insecure with this new relationship.

There are, of course, many other concerns and problems a sales HRD practitioner faces, but most of them are shared with other HRD people.

PROGRAMS TO MEET THE FUTURE NEEDS OF SALESPEOPLE AND SALES MANAGERS

The sales HRD field is changing as the complexion of U.S. business changes. Learning programs for people in sales will be responsive to these needs. It is hoped that educational institutions will also be sensitive to the need business has for students prepared to enter the sales world.

As the United States continues to grow as a worldwide supplier of information, educating salespeople about selling and marketing internationally will be a more important part of the responsibilities of sales HRD practitioners. They may also be called upon to develop or purchase materials to train and educate people in other countries. The need to understand other cultures and customs will be a necessary requirement.

Communication skills will remain a key ingredient of programs to assist sales personnel in improving productivity. As theories such as right brain–left brain are applied to selling and as future theories are developed, the sales HRD practitioner will have to integrate these into learning programs as a way of increasing productivity. In recent years, sales HRD has come a long way in providing communication skill learning and application. This will continue in coming decades.

Learning the use and application of electronic data transmission and the computer will be a necessity for most salespeople and their managers. The use of this equipment seems to affect almost every salesperson's job. Salespeople, calling on retail stores, on wholesalers, and on people in other fields must have an understanding of how a computer works, and, even more, of what can be done with the computer. Communicating with company headquarters on matters such as orders, sales activities, and services for customers are only some of the data that will be handled routinely by electronic transmission. Computers, from mainframe to micro, will impact on the way salespeople and sales managers perform their jobs in the future.

Salespeople will continue to play a vital role in the future of world business.

THE FUTURE FOR SALES HRD

For sales HRD practitioners, the future depends greatly upon the proactive stance they take. It is no longer sufficient for organizations to appoint a person to handle sales training just for a short period of time, in order to help them prepare for other sales management responsibilities. People in the sales HRD function require education and skill practice, so that the organization can assist in developing people. Sales learning programs need to be based on accurate needs analysis and linked to the company's marketing plans. Furthermore, a direct connection must be made between the sales HRD function and the sales results, in order that the value and credibility of the sales HRD manager is assured. The sales HRD practitioners need to move forward, along with their counterparts in other HRD areas, learning the innovations and new theories in productivity improvement and then applying them.

BIBLIOGRAPHY

Dubinsky, Alan J. *Sales Training: An Analysis of Field Sales Techniques.* Edited by Gunter Dufey. Ann Arbor, Mich.: University Microfilm International, 1981.

Harrison, Jared, ed. *Management of Sales Training.* Reading, Mass.: Addison-Wesley, 1977.

Hopkins, David S. *Training the Sales Force: A Progress Report.* New York: The Conference Board, Inc., 1978.

McLaughlin, Ian E. *Successful Sales Training: How to Build a Program that Works.* Boston: CBI Publishing, 1981.

Stroh, Thomas E. *Training and Developing the Professional Salesman.* New York: AMACOM, 1973.

SOME MAJOR SUPPLIERS OF
OFF-THE-SHELF SALES PROGRAMS

Dimensional Training Systems, 8201 Maryland Avenue, St. Louis, MO 63105

Mohr Development Inc., 30 Oak Street, Stamford, CT 06905

Systema Corporation, 150 North Wacker Drive, Chicago, IL 60606

Xerox Learning Systems, 1600 Summer Street, Stamford, CT 06904

Executive, Management, and Supervisory Programs

LEONARD B. POULIOT

It is generally agreed that the majority of HRD programs are in the areas covered by this chapter. Therefore, the reader should pay particular attention to the concepts and processes that Pouliot describes here.

Frequently, there are debates about whether an organization should devote so many of its resources to executives, managers, and supervisors. It is even suggested that HRD practitioners prefer to deal with upper management, as it provides an oportunity to associate with the higher levels of the organization.

Whatever the reaction, and there are many, it is unlikely that we will see any significant decrease in HRD programs for those levels of employees. Actually, there is an increased interest in productivity. It has been recognized that productivity and other operational improvements must start with the top levels of the organization if they are to be successful.

Leonard B. Pouliot is president of International Consulting Associates. Prior to this position, he was vice president for personnel for a multinational company, a presidential appointee as administrator for management and administration of the Federal Energy Administration, and held other similar positions. He has served as president of the Washington, D.C. chapter of ASTD and as chairman of the executive management and supervisory development program of the USDA Graduate School.

INTRODUCTION

The development of executives, managers, and supervisors has taken on new meaning. This is partly due to heightened international competition, the world economy, and the acceleration of technological, social, and other changes that are causing corporations, government organizations, and other businesses to look inward for answers.

There is also a growing realization that organizational complacency and yesteryear management may have contributed to technical and management obsolescence, the underdevelopment of human assets, and other business difficulties. While scientific and technological advances continue to propel the forces of change in an astonishing manner, it has been the application of new technology that has radically altered traditional management strategy and leadership.

There are basically three kinds of managers: those that make things happen, those that watch things happen, and those that wonder what happened.

Those nations, industries, and businesses that thrive on change are on the forefront of organization and management excellence and seem to be exercising visionary leadership and a finely tuned understanding of the development process.

What does this mean to the HRD practitioner? Management HRD programs cost billions of dollars annually and will probably increase in cost considerably in the near future, as a result of the magnitude of changes taking place in electronic and computer technology. Organizations that hope to stay on the cutting edge of excellence must look to the HRD practitioner to help forge an HRD strategy that will ensure a cadre of leaders—executives, managers, and supervisors who can adapt to and cope with change, whatever its forms, intensity, or direction. This will require greater visibility and the acknowledgement of HRD as a vital process in the influence of individual, team, and organizational behavior.

Executives, managers, and supervisors from both the private and public sectors have indicated that the urgency to produce is greater than ever. Productivity, quality of products and service, and increased cost effectiveness are emphasized. With the exception of highly automated operations, people costs make up a large part of the budget, and these managers say this is the area where they will have to demonstrate a greater return on investment. Perhaps a new term is needed, such as *ROD* (return on development) or *ROL* (return on learning).

In terms of their own development, managers feel that few people, other than their own managerial colleagues, truly understand their job and its diverse pressures. Figure 15.1 represents a composite of these external and internal influences and forces taken from my interviews and discussions with many managers. HRD practitioners need to consider these influences in executive, management, and supervisory development programs. The internalized value system of each manager (e.g., pride, challenge, recognition, etc.), shown in Figure 15.1, must also be addressed.

Effective HRD programs do not necessarily come easily. The persistent dilemma is determining the competencies needed in the present and future and developing a continuum of learning experiences to build or sharpen these competencies. The process of identifying these competencies and of enhancing executive, managerial, and supervisory effectiveness is addressed in this chapter. Also, the role of the human brain in management learning is considered to be of major importance to HRD practitioner to help forge an HRD strategy that will ensure a cadre of leaders—executives, managers, and supervisors who can adapt to and

MANAGEMENT COMPETENCIES

Competence is one of the most cherished of all ambitions. Organizations strive to achieve it for a wide variety of reasons, including:

Their image
Return on investment
Attractiveness as an employer
A model for the work force
Survival

Individuals generally perceive competence as a self-realization achievement, a hallmark of excellence, and a vehicle to success. While this rationale may not always be valid, there is usually an intrinsic feeling of high self-esteem and motivational drive accompanying opportunities to demonstrate competence. Recognition of true competence by others, especially by supervisors, managers, or executives, can have important psychological rewards that far exceed the tangible rewards normally available in organizational systems.

What do we mean by management competencies? A review of the literature does not reveal a facile definition. For purposes of this chapter, the following definition is offered as useful:

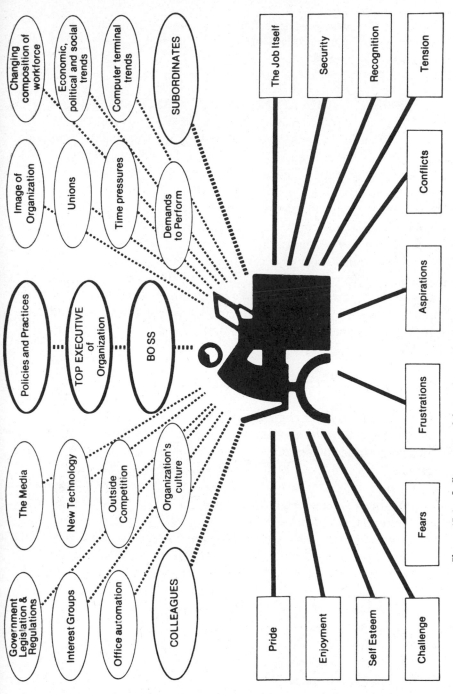

Figure 15.1. Influences and forces impacting on executives, managers and supervisors.

Changing composition of workforce

Economic, political and social trends

Computer terminal trends

SUBORDINATES

Image of Organization

Unions

Time pressures

Demands to Perform

Policies and Practices

TOP EXECUTIVE of Organization

BO SS

The Media

New Technology

Outside Competition

Organization's culture

Government Legislation & Regulations

Interest Groups

Office automation

COLLEAGUES

The Job Itself

Security

Recognition

Tension

Conflicts

Aspirations

Frustrations

Fears

Pride

Enjoyment

Self Esteem

Challenge

15.5

A composite of capabilities embodying knowledge, skills, abilities, and those personal attributes (values, traits, and motives) that enable a person to excel in performance.

COMPETENCIES AND EFFECTIVE PERFORMANCE

A number of studies have been done to determine the specific management competencies that seem to make a difference between effective and noneffective performance. There is an extraordinary wave of interest in competency models, and it is quite likely that current and future HRD programs will highlight competency models as the cornerstone of management HRD programs. Competency-based career development models, seminars, workshops, and performance appraisal systems are beginning to flourish everywhere, especially in the computer field.

According to James L. Hayes, chairman of the board, American Management Association, "There are underlying characteristics which distinguish superior performance from average or poor ones, and that specific types of managerial behaviors are causally linked to superior performance."[1]

The AMA/McBer Study

J.L. Hayes's comments were derived from a joint AMA/McBer and Company study to develop a competency model for managers. This study, encompassing some 2000 managers and 41 different managerial jobs in 12 organizations, represents a decade of research. The study was published in 1982 by Richard E. Boyatzis.[2] The American Management Association incorporated the findings of this study into its unique master's in management program.

The study identified 19 managerial competencies under five broad, cluster headings. These competencies were considered to be directly related to effective on-the-job performance:

1. Goal and action management
   Efficiency orientation
   Proactivity
   Diagnostic use of concepts
   Concern with impact
2. Leadership
   Self-confidence

Use of oral presentation
Logical thought
Conceptualization

3. Human resource management

Use of socialized power
Positive regard
Managing group process
Accurate self-assessment

4. Directing subordinates

Developing others
Use of unilateral power
Spontaneity

5. Others

Self-control
Perceptual objectivity
Stamina and adaptability
Concern with close relationships

"Goal and action management" represents the entrepreneurial way of making things happen, that is, according to plans and efficiency. It suggests that leadership is inspirational and insightful, both inside and outside the organizations; able to make stimulating presentations; able to organize thoughts and activities in a systematic manner and to use conceptual skills in seeing patterns and themes impacting the organizational setting. "Human resource management" involves an understanding of the human system and the ability to coordinate the varied interests of groups of people while having a keen knowledge of self. "Directing subordinates" indicates those activities that influence subordinates to follow directions and policies, that are involved with improving performance through feedback and development, that are generally good for the overall organization. It represents a balanced view with real objectivity as a goal, and it suggests durability and flexibility for performance under stress and a caring attitude toward others.

The Hughes Aircraft Company Study

Another impressive study is the five-year effort by the Hughes Aircraft Company[3] (from 1973 through 1977) of 2350 research and development managers and senior technical personnel and 59 organizations. The study utilized the expertise of 28 leading organization, management, and behavioral science authorities, an extensive literature review, and information from 23 seminars.

While the thrust of this serious study was to determine those factors contributing to research and development productivity, the findings are considered applicable to a broad spectrum of multilevel managers in all types of organizations. HRD practitioners can make use of this milestone study in the planning, development, and management of HRD programs in general. Highlighted from this study are the findings on organizational climate and effective supervisory techniques.

Organizational climate

The finding that organizational climate directly affects employee attitudes, motivation, development, and performance is not new to HRD practitioners. Executives, managers, and supervisors generally set the climate in organizations through their enlightened management actions or their lack of them. The Hughes Aircraft study, which involved 33 major U.S. corporations, 13 top-ranked universities, and 12 federal government agencies, identified seven characteristics that a successful organizational environment should exemplify:[4]

A professional atmosphere where high standards prevail

A clearly understood set of organizational objectives and performance goals

An open climate where people can be themselves

An opportunity to make a meaningful contribution

An objective climate in which politics and gamesmanship are minimized

A climate favorable to career planning

A stable job climate

The characteristics depicted above present a formidable challenge for most enterprises. In most of the organizations studied, similar findings have been encountered. Why should such a desirable environment be so elusive? Where are the million plus alumni of management development seminars and workshops? Most experienced executives, managers, and supervisors can cite the rules of leadership behavior as fast as most HRD specialists. Notably, the characteristics all seem to involve the human system—a system of infinite complexity that seems to defy general principles, where the sum of the whole does not equal the disparate parts.

Effective supervisory techniques

Supervisors provide the most direct leadership over the work force. In effect, they are on the firing line: making spontaneous decisions; facing myriad human and other resource situations, problems, and complexities; and responding to upper levels of management, the unions, and in many cases, to clients of the organization. Supervisors must comprehend, interpret, and apply the policies, rules, regulations, and procedures directly to the work force. In most cases, supervisors do not have the flexibility of consulting staff resources before they have to respond. Generally, their decisions have to be immediate.

The Hughes Aircraft study identified 20 supervisory competencies that should be addressed in supervisory HRD programs:[5]

1. Make a genuine effort to understand subordinates; know their strengths and weaknesses, their primary sources of motivation, their career goals, etc.
2. Effectively integrate the abilities of all individuals within the organization.
3. Match individuals to the jobs for which they are best suited.
4. Involve subordinates in planning, goal setting, and decisions that affect them.
5. Let employees demonstrate their capabilities and grow professionally; help subordinates prepare themselves for jobs to which they aspire.
6. Set high standards and high expectations, and encourage subordinates to achieve them.
7. Keep subordinates fully, but not excessively, loaded with work.
8. Maintain light pressure on subordinates to produce. (This must be done skillfully—mild pressure properly applied can stimulate productivity, but excessive pressure can easily become counterproductive.)

9. Avoid treating all tasks as maximum efforts or special cases; avoid rush and overtime followed by delay; and avoid surprises and unexplained changes.

10. Be available to subordinates through an open-door policy.

11. Provide subordinates with feedback on their performance; recognize and reward achievement; cite mistakes fairly and tactfully.

12. Make a special effort to help subordinates who are deficient in certain aspects of their jobs.

13. Represent all subordinates and their work equitably to higher management; whenever possible, allow the worker who originated a unique idea or did an outstanding job to brief management.

14. Be sensitive to factors that cause employee dissatisfaction and frustration; get to the root of such factors; and resolve conflicts in a timely manner.

15. Serve as a buffer to protect subordinates from many of the daily administrative and operational frustrations.

16. Maintain an effective flow of two-way communication.

17. Serve as a catalyst to insure effective technology exchange within the organization.

18. Keep employees informed of the broader aspects of company operations.

19. Encourage team building, but be careful not to create provincialism.

20. Avoid imposing personal standards on subordinates and "oversupervising."

THE FORCES OF CHANGE

What will the forces of change mean to competencies as we have come to know them? The process of discovering and categorizing managerial competencies has been more or less evolutionary, with the most significant findings occurring during the last two decades. Many conventional and some innovative HRD programs seemed to have grasped the full meaning of human resources development and instituted truly credible programs. The evolutionary aspects of the change process allowed HRD practitioners a comfortable margin of time to build upon research, experience, and individual effort.

The situation has now been altered dramatically. The late 1970s and the early 1980s demonstrated that we are all on an inescapable path of revolutionary change. Those changes have affected and will continue to affect the lives and careers of people inside and outside of organizations. The HRD practitioner is in a unique role to help executives, managers, and supervisors with the learning implications of these changes.

Information technology is one of the most noticeable changes in today's society. The office of the future is here now. Word processors are replacing typewriters; microprocessors are providing graphics as well as text for budgets, projects, research, and many other functions; computers are replacing most manual methods of filing, record keeping, and transmission of business information and letters; and personnel records are being formatted on discs, with interactive display terminals handling the changes.

Computer usage is now found in just about every professional discipline, and managers are becoming more involved as they see the benefits of having operational information readily available. Modeling with graphics is being used as decision support systems. As pads and pencils are replaced by computer terminals managers have more time for tasks other than paperwork. Managers are finding desk-top computers easier to use than originally anticipated and are authoring their own management information systems, customized to their unique operations.

Computer-based courses and instruction are available in an increasingly wide range of programs, giving managers a new flexibility. As the desire for learning increases, small "learning" rooms may be springing up in both line and staff offices.

The process of change must be managed just like any other program. Some people accept change as inevitable. For others, change is threatening and makes them insecure. Some people relish change because they find it exhilarating; and, in effect, they become change enthusiasts. Today, as the intensity of these changes increases and we consider the host of emotions tied to them, HRD practitioners may find it necessary to include the "management of change" in most developmental programs, in order to overcome resistance to change and to accelerate the learning cycle.

While teleconferencing, videotext, satellite communications, and information-processing technology are overshadowing many of the changes taking place, there are other changes of significant HRD interest, such as the demographics of the work force. New workers entering organizations have a higher level of schooling than previous work forces. These new workers have higher expectations, more of a willingness to challenge supervisory actions, and a desire to move faster through the career or promotional system.

In contrast, life expectancies are generally longer, indicating a possible tendency to remain more active, even in the labor market. The idea of multiple careers has become a reality. Also, women are entering the work force at a rapid pace and are currently occupying approximately 20% of the management positions.

The Potential for Obsolescence

Change has many attributes, and progress is inextricably linked to it. However, a casualty of change is obsolescence. Change may literally leave people, organizations, and whole enterprises behind in skills, knowledge, abilities, technical competence, or even spirit. It may exhaust those who are unwilling or unable to cope with it. Change is often met with an equal force of resistance, and management history is replete with the failures of those who tried to implement change for change's sake.

Management HRD programs have a vital role to play in helping executives, managers, and supervisors maintain their leadership competence in the face of change. According to Peter Drucker, "We need management development and manager development precisely because tomorrow's jobs and tomorrow's organization can be assumed, with high probability, to be different from today's jobs and today's organization."[6]

THE BRAIN AND HUMAN RESOURCE DEVELOPMENT

One of the most important advances in science during the past decade has been the unprecedented research on how the human brain functions. Of profound significance is the mounting evidence that there are different roles for the right and left cerebral hemispheres—each having preferred learning and thinking styles and specialized functions that cope with and respond to an infinite array of external stimuli. The human brain plays the central role in governing all individual behavior and developmental phenomena, and HRD practitioners must incorporate this phenomenon into HRD programs.

Our increased knowledge and understanding of the impressive synergistic system of the brain provides boundless opportunities on which the HRD practitioners can capitalize. They are in a position of making pivotal contributions that could materially influence the concepts, techniques, and methodologies of executive, management, and supervisory learning programs—indeed, the entire field of HRD.

The Left Hemisphere

The left cerebral hemisphere appears to be the analytical half of the brain and is responsible for:

Sequential tasks	Speech
Language comprehension	Writing
Logical deduction	Verbal tasks
Structured thinking	Calculations
Handling details	Reading

Traditional education, training, and developmental programs seem to cater to left brain strengths. Textbooks, reading requirements, exercises, and most lectures are examples of this orientation. Organizational programs that emphasize written policies, rules, regulations, and procedures are another example.

The Right Hemisphere

The right cerebral hemisphere appears to be the intuitive, creative, and artistic half of the brain and specializes in:

Conceptualization	Spatial/musical activities
Nonverbal activities	Visualization
Pattern simulation	Holistic perception
Synthesizing	Insight
Comprehension of abstract situations	Emotional response

The Brain and Memory Formation

Memory is undoubtedly one of the most important links to every facet of life. It determines the effectiveness of individuals, groups, and organizations. Memory is fundamental to human development and provides a point of reference upon which learning is based. Without memory, where would we be? How could we relate our experiences, learnings, likes and dislikes, or formulate a basis for development without memory?

The process of memory is sensory—allowing us to remember faces, emotional events, or smells—and verbal—allowing us to store and express words and ideas. The process of memory may also be either short term or long term. Memory storage is highly selective, with much of the information rapidly forgotten. The way information is stored is related to the way it was learned.

Short-term memory involves things that are not considered important enough for lifetime storage. Generally, this temporary storage system tends to hold seven to eight items at a time while deciding what to do with the information.

Long-term memory is a much more deliberate process of storing perceived meaningful thoughts and experiences. It seems to relate to emotional experiences and to the associations made with faces, behavior, events, and any other circumstances that tell the brain, in effect, to "print it." The information is then logged into any number of neural sets available for recall.

Implications for the HRD Practitioner

Nedd Herrmann, former manager of General Electric's Management Development Institute and now a brain researcher and instructor, recently concluded:

> If an individual's brain dominance did not match the way the learning point was designed and delivered, he or she would perceive it in a different way or not perceive it at all.[7]

He suggests that those involved in learning programs have to rethink the traditional approaches to the delivery of learning to include the new knowledge of the brain's learning styles.

Important considerations for HRD practitioners in the design and conduct of HRD programs suggest that:

The organizing and presenting of materials in segments or chunks enhances learning and retention.

Imagery is a valuable technique in memory storage and serves as a link to recall and application.

The more associations one makes with information or activities, the greater the recall.

A specific meaning connected to programs, work, or experiences is essential to memory storage and learning.

Each individual has a unique way of organizing information.

Retention of information improves when a similar task or exercise follows a preceding one.

Visualization surpasses verbalization in learning.

There is no question that individualized learning programs will be the new wave of HRD efforts. HRD practitioners are expected to play a major role in this new wave by directly applying new and tested techniques that demonstrate an understanding of the functions of the brain and the uniqueness of each individual.

When asked by a manager what the brain has to do with management learning, Nedd Herrmann replied: "Everything."[8]

DESIGNING A DEVELOPMENTAL PROGRAM

Only a small fraction of an individual's management techniques is learned in the classroom.[9]

Honeywell, Inc. arrived at this conclusion during an in-depth search for a comprehensive corporate management development strategy for the 1980s. David Dotlick, Honeywell's HRd manager, working with a managerial task force, surveyed some 300 Honeywell managers at five different levels, ranging from premanagement to top-level executives, to determine:[10]

What managers learned at different levels and phases of their careers

What the process of learning was, and from whom it came

What factors helped them to acquire needed knowledge, skills, and abilities

What barriers stood in the way of learning

In addition to the findings that management techniques are not generally acquired in classrooms, Honeywell found that learning generally takes place from two vantage points—contacts with other managerial staff who serve as mentors and from actual job experience.

Now in the fourth year of the program, Honeywell feels that the corporation has produced a learning environment. Honeywell has some 500 quality circles, a management training center, and a variety of developmental sources, including an in-house HRD consulting and research service.

Dotlick, in a conversation regarding this chapter, indicated that Honeywell has definitely deemphasized classroom training as a developmental tool. In its place is a continuing analysis of the learning processes involved in actual job assignments and relationships with other managers. Specific learning programs based on this analysis are continuously being developed.

WHAT APPROACH IS RIGHT FOR YOUR ORGANIZATION?

"Our organization is unique." How often do you hear or identify with this phrase? It must be one of the most universal perceptions in organizational society. This message is conveyed repeatedly during the conduct of organizational needs assessments and program designs. This perception of uniqueness by managers or anyone else is generally not an illusion, since organizations are, in a very real sense, quite unique. From the moment organizations are formed or transformed, the phenomenon of uniqueness begins and evolves throughout the life of that organization, much like any other organism. Additionally, the perceptions of being unique do not belong solely to the organization—individuals also see themselves as being unique.

Perceptions guide decision making, provide the motivation behind thought and action, and influence the way people cope with the challenges of their environment. From an HRD standpoint, these perceptions have to be included in the total equation of the learning program.

The Prescriptive Approach

The prescriptive approach to executive, managerial, and supervisory development is built upon the premise of someone knowing what is best for others. A number of programs are modeled on this approach. Usually, a central staff (in some cases, a single person) exerts a considerable amount of effort in the planning, organization, and preparation of a formal developmental plan and then announces it.

There are instances when a program or elements of a program are "directed" by a higher-level authority in the organization. For example, an authority figure might say, "I think our supervisors should all be run through a course on ethics," or "Our managers don't know anything about computers, get them up-to-date." This imposed situation may or may not be relevant to the work actually being performed and usually is resented by the managerial target group.

Many of you are probably aware of elaborately constructed management HRD programs generated almost totally from the prescriptive approach. This does not imply that some brilliance has not been shown in the design; however, it does imply that the management group in the organization was not a party to something that involves their destiny and, perhaps, success. A prescriptive program is one with built-in risks. It is much like a patient going to a physician and being told before the examination: "Take two aspirins and call me if you don't feel better."

The Resource Market Approach

The human resource market is a commercial enterprise of gigantic proportions internationally. This multibillion dollar business can provide HRD practitioners with everything they want to know in any field of human resource development. The professional consulting services, prepackaged programs, equipment, films, instruments, exercises, meeting sites, media, books, and manuals are limitless.

This market, which consists of varying qualities of products and services, supplies an insatiable group of customers—managers from every type of organization, faculties of academic and other professional institutions, and the HRD practitioners themselves. Very few groups of professionals seem to have the same thirst for other people's products and services as those in the HRD business. It is a continuous search for new products or methods, tested or untested.

In designing or attempting to refine a management program, HRD practitioners can, from their own offices, call on any number of outside firms to request that the firms demonstrate their competence in selected areas of management development. HRD personnel may even request complete *turn-key* programs (process of design through total conduct of the program). In fact, this is what a fairly large number of organizations do and is why the market keeps expanding. The majority of the products and services are generic in nature, and HRD practitioners must use their expertise and be well disciplined to ensure that the products and services are directly related to the desired objectives and to ensure those products can or should be modified to accommodate the needs of managers.

If this system is combined with the prescriptive model, rather than a diagnostic approach, the programs may not be specific enough to the organization to produce successful management learners. On the other hand, careful selection of outside resources can mean the difference between failure and success. The use of external resources to complement internally designed programs is generally viewed as the best of both worlds.

The Diagnostic Approach

The philosophy behind this approach is that the managers in any organization are in the best position to know the requirements of their job, the environment in which they have to work, and the internal and external factors that influence their effectiveness. They also have a fairly good idea of what they need to learn and how to obtain that additional learning.

"Diagnosis before prescription" is the methodology involved in carrying out this approach. It is a synergistic team effort of the HRD and managerial staff to identify the real-world ingredients necessary for a more dynamic executive, management, and supervisory program. The task force technique used in the Honeywell model to conduct a diagnostic assessment typifies the approach that helps to establish a degree of ownership on the part of the managers. When managers feel this sense of ownership in shaping their program, there is a much higher level of commitment to make it work.

The heart of the diagnostic approach is the EMS (executive, management, or supervisory) individual and organizational needs assessment. There are many kinds of assessments, and it is important to determine precisely what information is needed and what will be done with the information. The assessment must:

Be well organized

Have a clear definition or purpose

Include a strategy for informing the managers of the progress and outcome of the effort

Result in a constructive action plan acceptable to the managers

While this may appear to be fundamental, too many managers are frustrated and resentful at the conclusion of these studies because not enough homework was done before the assessment was launched.

Involvement of the EMS Hierarchy.   As previously mentioned, the feeling of ownership in planning, developing, and controlling programs that ultimately affect personal and organizational careers is important from many aspects and is clearly an emotional issue with behavioral implications. Positive modification of behavior is a definite objective of the learning programs; therefore, it is logical that a strategy to include the EMS hierarchy be incorporated into the management of any assessment and follow-on program.

Involving the EMS group requires an understanding of the existing organizational culture. For example, there may be certain executives, managers, or supervisors who have shown specific interest, knowledge, or skill in management development. Some might be more interested in training, others in education or development. Some may already be serving as mentors for one or more managers and have hands-on experience as developers of others and possibly themselves.

An EMS Resource Board.   An EMS resource board or committee, composed of a representative sample of different levels and experience in the organization, adds substantially to the credibility of the HRD program. The role of the board can be defined in any way that helps promote, clarify, organize, or review EMS development programs. In some firms, it serves as a policy-making body and sounding board. In others, it serves as a screening device to monitor and provide guidance. In the U.S. federal government, such boards are required of every agency and have specific functions relating to the careers of federal executives.

The Assessment Process.   The model depicted in Figure 15.2 represents an assessment process for conducting individual and organizational needs assessments. It is an experience-based model and has proven to be workable in a variety of management studies. The EMS resource board is usually composed of five to nine members with representatives from the executive, managerial, and supervisory levels. In some organizations there are separate boards—one for executives, another for managers, and a third for supervisors. They may also be called *planning* or *development committees.*

The needs assessment task group carries out the assessment and is represented by a combination of executives, managers, and supervisors, along with members of the HRD staff. Some organizations may prefer separate task forces (e.g., one for executives, one for managers and one for supervisors), but both line and staff managers should be involved. Whatever the combination of task groups established, all members should meet regularly to review and share their findings and to plan the next steps. A functional approach has, at times, proven useful. In a functional approach, certain members of the task group concentrate on items such as task analysis, career development, program design, or organizational issues, versus a holistic approach by one or all members.

The HRD staff has a central role in the entire assessment process. The relationship of the HRD practitioner to the EMS board, to the top executive of the organization, and to the task group, usually influences the

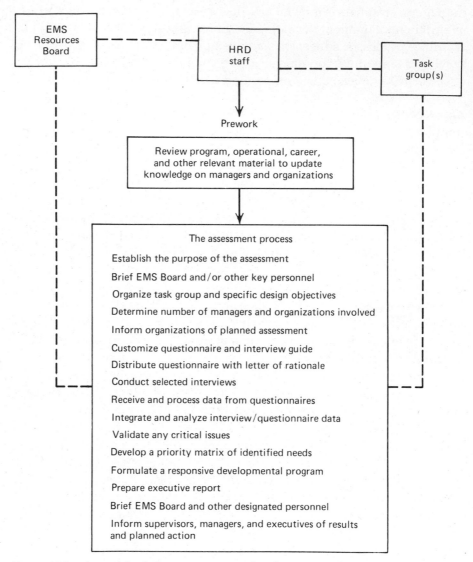

Figure 15.2. A model of the management development and organizational needs assessment process.

outcome and acceptance of the assessment. This relationship also influences the subsequent design and implementation of the program itself.

Upon establishment of the EMS board or a similar group, it is wise to brief the members and keep them advised before, during, and upon completion of the assessment. Avoid taking for granted that every member is fully informed. An informed group member is in a position to effectively deal with and report any comments, negative or otherwise, about the way the assessment is being conducted. The value of such a group is not to be underestimated. If such a group does not exist, HRD practitioners should attempt to have one formed, even on an ad hoc basis.

Once the purpose of the assessment has been clearly defined, key executives briefed, and each task group member's roles identified, the next step is to determine the number of executives, managers, and supervisors involved and the best method of advising them of the upcoming study. Presumably, the HRD practitioner has asked members of the board and task group to inform their own staff or colleagues as part of the design strategy. If not, there needs to be some sort of advance conditioning with the management target group. Their understanding and acceptance of the assessment is just as important as the study itself.

Interview Guides and the Questionnaire.   There are scores of questionnaires available commercially, and most HRD practitioners generally have a variety on file. New ones are being developed and tested continuously in public and private organizations. Custom-tailored questionnaires, however, still appear to be the most dynamic. They allow the IIRD practitioner to incorporate the latest thinking in the field of management HRD, while addressing current issues in the environment of the organization. A useful technique in designing a questionnaire is first to conduct a limited number of interviews with members of the management group. The interviews should address:

Competencies needed to perform effectively

Performance indicators of those competencies

Ways of staying current in the field of expertise

Sources for on-the-job learning

Organizational situations that help or hinder the application of managerial competencies

Opportunities for growth

Relationships that foster individual development

Extent of self-directed learning

How the HRD or any other program can or has helped enhance individual/organizational competencies

Projected needs for the future

When the information on the areas listed above is obtained and analyzed, HRD practitioners have a nucleus for the design of a useful questionnaire or survey instrument. Such predesign interviews have proven useful and generally make the difference between organization-specific and manager-specific assessments and the more general and broad surveys. An additional step to assure the quality of the questionnaires is to test a final draft with three to five managers. These managers actually complete a questionnaire that is then analyzed to make sure it is doing what it was designed to do. Once these preliminaries have been accomplished, HRD practitioners can feel confident that the foundation for obtaining the right kind of information needed to design a management HRD program has been established and that they may have begun the process of ownership by the managers.

Should questionnaires be sent to all or to a statistically defined number of supervisors, managers, and executives? Historically, there has been a tendency to use the sampling technique, and most researchers still feel comfortable with the results obtained. With the increased emphasis on individualized learning, HRD practitioners will have to determine how long they will be satisfied with merely representative information, even when statistically justified.

In some recent studies of small, medium-sized, and large technical and nontechnical organizations, questionnaires or survey instruments were sent to all executives, managers, and supervisors. Computer-assisted analysis of the results is, of course, one reason why a sampling technique may not be necessary or desired. There are a number of other reasons to include the total managerial society in any organizational assessment:

Opportunity for direct feedback by the respondents to an audience beyond their local jurisdiction,

Personal satisfaction of being able to express internalized feelings, knowledge and convictions,

Avoidance of the psychological phenomenon of inclusion/exclusion,

A vehicle for potential interactive discussions between the respondents with attendant generation of other relevant information,

Just plain good politics

Interviews.   How many supervisors, managers, and executives should be interviewed? This depends on the objectives of the assessment, but it is generally a good idea to have a representative cross section of managerial levels, years of experience in the position, and different technical/professional support functions.

One method is to interview the head of the total organization; the majority of, if not all, office, division, or similar level chiefs; and a 10–15% sample of varying managerial and supervisory levels below them. Senior executives or managers are excellent sources of determining which managers, supervisors, or other people under their jurisdiction might make good candidates for interviews.

Interviews help to provide the rationale behind some of the perceptions and information rendered in questionnaires. Selective interviews with different levels of line versus staff managers also give a perspective that is difficult to acquire from questionnaires. Additionally, the interaction between the respondent and the interviewer usually produces valuable information not previously contemplated.

While interviews are generally conducted with one person, there are times when group interviews may be particularly useful. Group interviews can be designed to focus on a specific organizational area, designated managerial positions or levels, or to gather information on critical learning requirements tied to new organizational priorities or objectives.

The culture of the organization at the time the interviews are being conducted may also be a factor in determining the extent of interview coverage. It is important to take the pulse of the organizational culture at the time the overall assessment is being made. If major changes in policies, programs, or other situations have influenced either organization, the particular groups, or the individuals, there will probably be a halo effect to the information acquired.

Redundancy of information is a clue in deciding how many more people need to be interviewed. If, during the course of interviews, the information becomes redundant, an option is to change direction and schedule a different organization or group of individuals for the remaining interviews. However, there may be circumstances when it would be unwise to change the schedule, and it might be more prudent to simply increase the number and variety of people to be interviewed.

ASSESSMENT TO DESIGN

There are many variations and approaches to executive, management, and supervisory HRD programs, and perhaps this is as it should be.

Although there are universal objectives in HRD programs (e.g., improved organizational effectiveness, enhanced leadership, application of new quality performance, or application of productivity goals and policies), each organization needs to shape and mold a program to its own distinctive environment and requirements.

A key to the success of any HRD program, however, is the extent to which the program is customized to current and long-term needs of its executives, managers, and supervisors. Customizing a responsive program implies that a foundation of substantive knowledge has been established upon which to design, implement, and institutionalize a relevant program that is organization-specific and manager-specific.

BEYOND THE GENERICS

Generic management HRD programs are the most common of all HRD programs. Most programs (e.g., training) are provided to enable managers to improve their competencies in their current assignment, although some (e.g., education) are also provided to enable managers to move into other positions in the future. This is not to negate the need for some generic programs. It is, however, the responsibility of skillful instructors to modify the classic concepts and to enable the managers to use them in applied situations on the job or in anticipation of the future job.

Whether or not they truly understand or know how to apply the concepts, practicing managers who have participated in a number of generic or off-the-shelf seminars over the years are beginning to ask, "How many times do I have to go through:

Maslow's hierarchy of needs
Theory X, Y, . . . Z
Motivation-Hygiene theory
The Johari window
1/1 to 9/9
Systems 4
One-way, two-way communication
History and principles of management?"

Most HRD practitioners would probably acknowledge that these concepts still seem to be popular in some settings. However, relating the concepts of most generic programs to the actual work environment is difficult, and the answer must be beyond the generics.

DESIGNING AN ORGANIZATION-SPECIFIC LEARNING PROGRAM

How do you design an organization-specific program that integrates the immediate, mid-term and long-term needs of the organization with those of the executives, managers, and supervisors? If the program is to be organization-specific rather than generic, it will be necessary to customize the priority of identified needs through a design model or models. The model should address a spectrum of learning activities responsive to the executives, managers, and supervisors as discrete groups, as individual learners, and as developers of others. Additionally, the model should encompass a sequence of learning activities relevant to the management learners' experience in the organization. For example, new employees require a different course of learning than those with one to five years of experience and those with more extensive experience. There are different requirements for management learners making career moves from functional to more general management career positions. General Electric has a customized program for this group because the transition is considered to be a difficult one. HRD practitioners might have to establish other customized programs for similar situations.

Which models should be selected for the design of a customized program? While most HRD managers continue to use or experiment with a number of models, the critical events model (CEM) developed by Leonard Nadler[9] may prove reliable for most program design processes. Although Nadler suggests that this CEM open model (see Figure 15.3) is essentially for training, the model, with minor modification, has proven useful for education as well as overall developmental programs.

A Model for Organizational Excellence

During the past few years, I have initiated a number of custom-designed organizational models to enhance executive, management, and supervisory programs. The model in Figure 15.4 was recently developed for a technology-based organization and originated from a comprehensive needs assessment. It represents an open, interactive system of individual, team, and organizational learning and performance improvement.

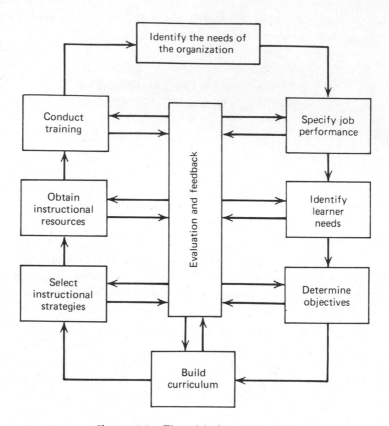

Figure 15.3. The critical events model.

The model, in its early stages of implementation, was presented to the entire staff in an open forum by the chief executive. Additional briefings were held with the senior managers in terms of stewardship of the model. The interrelated variables include an organic curriculum designed to be responsive to changing priorities. The performance task groups have an ongoing responsibility to improve individual, team, and organizational effectiveness in five major areas—communication systems, program management, technology development, human resource management, and financial management. The task groups are composed of multilevel managers, engineers, and a crosssection of support personnel. These task groups have access to resources throughout the organization in a matrix concept. An outside consultant works with each as a coordinator/ facilitator and is available for coaching and counseling on an individual or team basis.

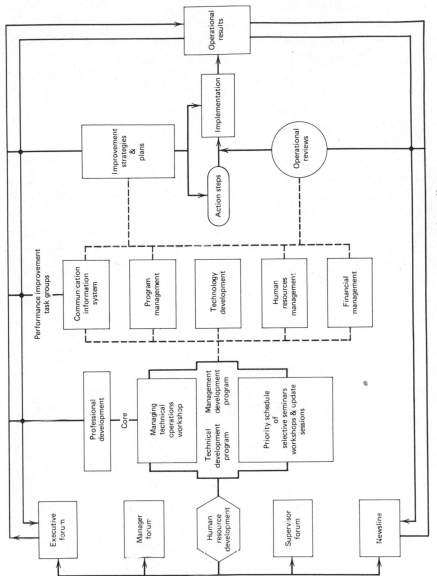

Figure 15.4. Model for organizational excellence.

15.27

An integral part of the model is the professional development program that includes a core workshop for all management and technical professionals entitled "Managing Technical Operations." It is an organization-specific 40-hour activity conducted four hours each day (the remainder of the day is spent on the job). It addresses actual problems, issues, concerns, and plans confronting the organization.

There is also a dual-track curriculum focusing on technical and management development and consisting of a series of multidisciplinary seminars and workshops to be designed and conducted according to organizational priorities and individual or group needs on a short, mid-term, and long-term basis.

The HRD director has a central role in the model, initiating resources whenever necessary, participating as a member of the chief executive's steering group, and helping to monitor the operational results. The HRD staff and the steering group receive consultative assistance in assuring that the interactive systems in the model are functioning in a constructive manner.

External technical and management authorities are invited periodically to address planned forums for the executive, management, and supervisory groups. These forums are designed to initiate a dialogue between the internal management professionals and selected outstanding authorities on a wide range of subjects that influence the organization.

A common goal in the model is for the task groups, forums, and the HRD staff to keep the momentum for performance improvement on a continuum and to keep the work force informed of progress toward the goals. The task groups accomplish this through briefings and by disseminating a periodic "Newsline" report.

CONCLUSION

HRD is on the threshold of becoming a dynamic force in the formulation of new work environments and the institutionalization of computer and electronic technology for executive, management, and supervisory programs as well as the work force in general.

The accelerating forces of change will continue to create demands and challenges for the HRD practitioner to respond in innovative ways and to design programs that are visibly results oriented.

The identification and relationship of management competencies to current and projected operational requirements will play a major role in the planning of HRD programs. Emphasis will be on developing individualized learning models based upon specific needs assessments.

HRD practitioners will have to become familiar with the developing knowledge of how the brain functions, particularly in terms of learning styles, memory formation, and decision making.

The opportunities for HRD practitioners to demonstrate their role in helping executives, managers, and supervisors meet new leadership direction are unprecedented.

NOTES

1. James L. Hayes, "What Is a Manager," *The Bureaucrat*, Journal for Public Managers, 1982, Vol. 11, no. 3, p. 12.
2. Richard E. Boyatzis, *The Competent Manager* (New York: Wiley, 1982), pp. 61–160.
3. Hughes Aircraft Company, *R and D Productivity: An Investigation of Ways to Improve Productivity in Technology-Based Organizations*, 2d ed, (Culver City, CA: Hughes Aircraft Co., 1978).
4. Ibid., pp. 6–7.
5. Ibid., pp. 54–55.
6. Peter F. Drucker, *Management: Tasks, Responsibilities, Practices* (New York: Harper & Row, 1974), p. 424.
7. Ned Herrmann, "The Creative Brain II," *Training and Development Journal*, ASTD, December 1982, Vol. 36, no. 12, p. 80.
8. Ned Herrmann, "The Brain and Management Learning," *The Journal for Public Managers—The Bureaucrat* Fall 1982, Vol. 11, no. 3, p. 17.
9. Richard Broderick, "How Honeywell Teaches Its Managers to Manage," *Training* 1983, Vol. 20, no. 1, pp. 18–20.
10. Ibid., pp. 18–20.
11. Leonard Nadler, *Designing Training Programs: The Critical Events Model* (Reading, Mass.: Addison-Wesley, 1982).

BIBLIOGRAPHY

Boyatzis, Richard E. *The Competent Manager.* New York: Wiley, 1982.

Broderick, Richard, "How Honeywell Teaches Its Managers to Manage." *Training* (1982): Vol. 20, no. 1, p. 18.

Drucker, Peter F. *Management: Tasks, Responsibilities, Practices.* New York: Harper & Row, 1974.

Hayes, James L. "What Is a Manager." *The Bureaucrat, Journal for Public Managers* (1982): Vol. 11, no. 3, pp. 11–13.

Herrmann, Ned. "The Brain and Management Learning." *The Bureaucrat, Journal for Public Managers* (1982): Vol. 11, no. 3, pp. 17–21.

Herrmann, Ned. "The Creative Brain II." *Training and Development Journal* ASTD (1982): Vol. 30, no. 12.

Hughes Aircraft Company. *Research and Development Productivity, An Investigation Ways to Improve Productivity in Technology-Based Organizations*, 2d ed. Culver Ci CA: Hughes Aircraft Company, 1982.

Nadler, Leonard. *Designing Training Programs: The Critical Events Model*. Readi Mass.: Addison-Wesley, 1982.

Technical Programs

DOUGLAS J. BARNEY

There is some difficulty in finding the correct term for this particular area. It is frequently called *technical training,* but that does not clearly define the field. *Technical* has generally been thought of as low level and manual, but the inclusion of the high-technology area certainly makes that perception inappropriate. The term *training* is likewise incorrect, as technical programs certainly require a great amount of education.

Once we get over the confusion in terminology, we can focus more directly on what the field has been, what it is, and what it may become. Barney provides some insight into the field in this chapter.

As we appear to be moving from a manufacturing-oriented country to a service-oriented one, the question might well be raised as to the significance of the technical area. To respond to that change, it is important to note that the technical area includes activities that are relevant to the service areas.

Douglas J. Barney is a staff HRD consultant for the Link Simulation Systems Division, The Singer Company. He is also director of performance consultants. He has previously been employed in related areas by Newport News Shipbuilding and Dry Dock Company. He retired from the U.S. Air Force, where he served in a wide variety of programs related to HRD, including those for aircrews.

Technical HRD is as old as humanity and as new as tomorrow. Those conducting technical HRD are from as diverse backgrounds and positions as are the learners with whom they interact. This diversity extends to the types of skills and knowledge learners obtain and to the methods of designing, developing, and delivering the learning activities. While other human resource development activities are usually relatively consistent in the types of skills and knowledge they are concerned with, those encompassed by the technical areas often change very rapidly. This change must keep pace with and often precede technological advances. The objectives of this chapter are to provide an overview of the history of technical HRD, to review technical HRD today (in terms of the personnel and delivery methods), and to present a glimpse into technical HRD in the future.

HISTORY

The history of the teaching of skills goes back a very long way. The cave man passed on his skills of spear and arrow making to his sons, while the cave woman taught her daughters the skills required to turn rough animal hides into soft, warm garments. This form of close instruction and supervision has continued throughout time and is still prevalent today. Originally, the skills needed were those required for survival, for obtaining food, and for protection from marauding animals. As the early bands of wanderers began to settle in one place, new skills were developed and then passed on from father and mother to their offspring.

As the agricultural age came into being, there was also a great need for new skills that would provide goods and services to others (e.g., the shoemaker and baker). This period marked the beginning of the apprenticeship approach to technical transfer. Apprenticeship is often classified as the major educational institution for the middle class of that period, since schooling was not normally available to them. The farmer would send his son to live and study with the shoemaker. When the child reached his teens, he would move on to work for another shoemaker as a journeyman. Then he would go to study with other shoemakers, prior to becoming a master craftsman. The basic survival skills evolved into the skills required to live in a civilized world.

The apprenticeship system continued into the nineteenth century. The Industrial Revolution, which came to the United States in the middle 1800s, was the primary method of learning specific job skills. The apprenticeship system, which provided education in highly developed skills, gave way, as early factory requirements were only for very simple skills. These new skills did not require any education. The supervisor or a more experienced worker would show the new worker what was required and then watch as the new worker performed the task. This simple on-the-job training was the responsibility of the first-line supervisor. Today, the supervisor still has the responsibility for on-the-job training. These early skills were generally simple psychomotor tasks. However, as the industry became more complex, these skills developed into complex clusters and hierarchies of skills and knowledge that began to require more formal technical and skills training and education.

The Industrial Revolution also resulted in a revolution in education and training. During the early nineteenth century, traditional education became available to an ever-increasing number of people. Formal schools for manual education were introduced to provide the skills required by the new industries. In Europe, John Henry Pestalozzi, often called the "father of manual education," started his school of manual education to teach the required skills for a variety of trades. This movement did not continue as trade schools but was soon modified into reformed schools. These institutions were not for the middle class or for workers. They were for orphans, pauper children, and children guilty of criminal acts.

Social conditions in the United States were no different than in Europe as became obvious with the opening in 1814 of the Farm and Trade School in Boston and in 1824 of the Industrial Reformed School. These taught basic skills, but often the skills were not those required by the fledgling industries.

Since there was a need for new skills and the schools of the fledgling industries were not filling that need, workers often started their own schools. The Mechanics Institute Movement saw schools started for the purpose of providing instruction to the laboring class. The first one in the United States was established in New York City in 1820 by the General Society of Mechanics and Tradesmen, and others soon followed. The movement subsided, however, as state schools began to respond, prompted by the financial assistance of the Land Grant Act of 1862.

Machines became more complex and the number of workers that were needed increased. New methods were needed to provide workers with the required skills. Cooperative systems and technical skills were learned on the job, and it became quite common for science and other basic knowledge to be taught at night in local schools. Trade and professional schools sprang up. Some U.S. companies started their own schools, and in-house HRD systems were started during the 1870s. These efforts were the exceptions, however, as most employees still learned their skills on the job and not through formal training or education programs.

Mass production became a reality at the turn of the century. The rapid expansion of the labor force was typified by those in Cleveland machine shops, where the work force increased by 33 percent from 1910 to 1915. Operators of these new machines learned their skills on the job in a few days or weeks. The apprentice program, often depicted as expensive and unnecessary, was all but dead. The movement was from skilled machinist to unskilled operators. This move was due, primarily, to the simplification of work, which was the result of improved and more complex machine tools. These operators learned their skills on the job in two weeks. Public schools had little to offer in the way of skills education. The majority of these workers were self-taught in that they learned by performing as helpers on the job.

After the turn of the century, a new kind of worker emerged, though very slowly. The college-educated engineers were frequently very knowledgeable but were unable to perform until trained by their new employers. Many new industries and the increased automation of old industries began to require workers with more sophisticated skills. Cooperative education programs between universities and companies began to evolve, in an effort to ensure that engineers and technicians would be able to perform as soon as they started their careers. Company schools also flourished, as evidenced by the formation in 1913 of the National Association of Corporation Schools. Public and private schools moved from providing specific job skills to almost exclusively filling the general education void.

The great prosperity of the 1920s was followed by the great Depression of the 1930s. There was little interest in or innovation of HRD efforts during this period. Employers had little need to ensure efficient production when times were good; and when times were bad, there was no money and no reason to provide HRD, as skilled workers were in great supply. The establishment of the American Management Association in 1923 was of considerable significance, as were the Hawthorne Studies, which still have an impact on HRD and management today. This almost tranquil period for HRD heralded the most hectic period in technical and skill HRD, which began with the advent of World War II.

The need to change, overnight, from a nation of civilians and homemakers into one of efficient factory workers and military personnel was unparalleled in history. (This requirement, more than anything else, forced technical and skill HRD to evolve into a profession with a strong research base and identified practitioners in the field of technical and skill HRD). Government and military communities provided millions of dollars to research the best methods of determining training and education requirements, selecting qualified learners, and conducting technical programs.

The field of instructional research came into its own during this period of great strife. The effectiveness of the research base and the huge and multifaceted delivery system was evidenced by the success of the American military supported by the civilian industrial worker. The foundation was laid during World War II, and there were many who started in HRD then and continued in the field in research and instructional design and delivery. The popularity of technical and skill HRD faded after the conflict.

The movement from the industrial era into an advanced age of high technology has pushed technical and skill HRD programs back into the limelight. The development of the systems theory of engineering has also moved into the field of HRD with the development of Instructional Systems Development (ISD). The system, now mandated by the armed forces, is an engineering one, a very systematic and often very detailed approach to the determination of learning requirements and the most opportune and effective means of delivering the program. The professional organizations, National Society for Performance Instruction, Society for Applied Learning Technology, American Society for Training and Development (Technical and Skills Division), have all seen a dramatic growth in membership in recent decades.

The passing on of skills from one to another began in the caves of early man. It is the oldest form of training and education. Learning methods have varied from apprenticeship to learning the required skills while on the job. Skills have also undergone tremendous changes, from the making of an arrow head to the design and repair of advanced computers that speak to us. The field has remained in the forefront of the application of new instructional methods and techniques. The future will require more technical HRD programs at an ever-increasing rate of change.

WHAT IS HRD IN THE TECHNICAL AREA?

There is no commonly accepted definition of technical HRD. The common term is *technical training*, but this also includes education and even some development. We find some very restrictive definitions that allow only for the acquisition of highly technical skills and knowledge. Other definitions include any learning of skills required in the workplace, in apprenticeship programs, in vocational courses, and for professional growth, often leading to advanced engineering degrees. Between these extremes, there is an acceptable definition of technical and skill HRD.

There are some similarities in these definitions. The activity for which the knowledge or skill is required is always a specific, job-related, hands-on activity. These newly acquired skills and knowledges are desired because they will further the goals and objectives of the organization (i.e., workers can perform their assigned task, and do so in a more efficient manner). The definition that I find most acceptable today is that technical HRD consists of those learning systems that provide job-related knowledge and skills specifically required by employees to design, operate, and maintain modern technology.

The variety of jobs encompassed by this definition is almost endless. The engineer who designs advanced computer technology must stay abreast of the latest research advancement and does so through technical training. The secretary who will soon have a word processor must learn the operation through technical training. Those who become robot mothers and are responsible for the programming and maintenance of these new marvels of automation do so through technical education. Those who conduct research into the most efficient and effective methods of determining learning requirements and meeting those requirements are also members of the technical HRD community. The rapidly increasing use of technology to create and deliver technical learning has also created a new breed of technical HRD people. Technical HRD provides skills and knowledge to all members of our society who must deal with technology in the performance of their occupations.

TECHNICAL HRD TODAY

The majority of technical HRD today is concerned with programs for operators. The rapid invasion of technology into what were previously manual skills occupations has pushed operator programs to the forefront of the technical HRD world. The most prevalent type of operator program provides the knowledge and skills to enable workers to operate in the new world of computer technology in a variety of work stations. These work stations provide word processing and data storage for the secretary; accounting and budgetary manipulations for the administrative assistant; computer-aided design for the engineer; and even authoring or lesson design systems for the instructional designer who develops computer-aided learning materials. Because the computer has extended its tentacles into all aspects of our society, operator learning associated with the computer now encompasses a large segment of the technical training world. The operation of new pieces of technology in our industrial organizations is a never-ending task for those in technical HRD. Other operator learning activities involve the operation of automated processes in manufacturing and the production of electricity.

For example, the nuclear incident at the Three Mile Island nuclear reactor in Pennsylvania resulted in federal requirements for complex replications of the nuclear power sites control room in the form of control room simulators. These replicas, exact both in appearance and in the observable operation, provide highly regulated technical training, not only for the licensed power plant operators, but for those who must maintain the power plant instruments and equipment as well.

Operator training and education has also always constituted a large part of the military's HRD budget. Learning to operate the nation's newest military weapon systems also makes use of advanced electronic simulators, and like the learning activities for the power generation industry and industries that utilize automated processes, the learning is often team oriented, not geared toward the individual as more traditional operational and other technical learning generally is.

As automation replaces manual methods of creating products, the number of workers producing these products decreases. On the other hand, the number required to service the new automated processing equipment is ever-increasing. Rapid advances in the technology used in these new systems places an additional burden on both learners and HRD staff, that is, keeping pace with the job requirements. Those responsible for the maintenance of these systems cover a continuum. There are those who require little knowledge but considerable manual skills, as the electronic systems will diagnose their own malfunctioning components. There are those who require few manual skills but extensive knowledge of system theory, allowing them to troubleshoot complex systems to identify malfunctioning components. Those responsible for the maintenance of these new technical wonders require extensive operator education in the systems they are going to maintain and in the new world of diagnostic and maintenance equipment, which is often extremely complex. There seems to be an endless cycle of needs—first maintenance training, then operator training, then maintenance training again, and so on.

The demand for engineers and technicians to design and develop new and more advanced technology is great, as new research developments multiply at an ever-increasing rate. These engineers and technicians need technical training at very advanced levels, in order to apply recently developed research advancements.

The military community has mandated use of Instructional Systems Development (ISD) by both the military community and civilian contractors to determine learning requirements, the design of learning materials, delivery methods, and evaluation methods. This systems approach to technical learning matured in the late 1970s. The civilian community has developed several modifications of the more detailed military ISD process. But what is ISD? ISD is a systematic learning system that is based upon the systems engineering concept and is behaviorally oriented. It identifies specific required and performed employee skills through a job/task analysis. This analysis is then reviewed and learner-oriented behavioral objectives are developed for those skills that require learning activities. Objective methods of testing and evaluating the possession of such skills and knowledge are then developed. An analysis of various learning methods and media is then conducted, in relationship to the previously developed behavioral objectives. This is the initial step in the development of actual instructional materials. Methods to determine the effectiveness of the learning system are developed in conjunction with a feedback system to ensure the modification of the instructional system when required.

The ISD process can be a very complex, detailed, and time-consuming effort. The military community utilizes ISD because of the size of their weapon system procurements and the number of personnel required to operate and maintain the systems. The civilian world often utilizes less detailed and less time-consuming models in determining, designing, and delivering required technical learning. The systematic application is the crucial element in ensuring that skills crucial to the job are learned.

The studies of the brain and cognition have also had a great impact on the concept of instructional design. The design of the instructional material that the learner receives or interacts with is the target of this new emphasis. The right and left lateralization provides techniques for the delivery of instruction that allow for effective absorption of the material. Some organizations are pretesting learners to determine their dominant hemisphere and then placing them in an appropriate learning tract, where the materials are designed for their dominant hemisphere.

Many programs are now designed to increase the use of the less dominant hemisphere of the learners. Many programs are also designed to account for the normal hemispheric orientation of the typical learner. These designs are generally very systematic for the left hemisphere, with many rules and logical progressions. For the right hemisphere, the designs are very abstract and visual. Technical learning is generally designed for the logical, systematic individual, or the left hemisphere. The work of Ned Herrmann[1] and others is calling attention to the design of learning for specific hemispheres and for whole brain learning designs. Though some work has been done in this area, it will increase as research provides more information.

TECHNICAL HRD PERSONNEL

There are three general categories of personnel directly associated with technical HRD programs: (1) employees who are responsible for providing the learning, (2) outside consultants and vendors, and (3) learners. Within each of these categories are several different types of people whom we shall investigate. Traditionally, there have been two types of personnel assigned to the technical HRD function.

The HRD function has always been considered a career step in the upward mobility ladder for professional personnel. They are often initially assigned as instructors or designers and after they have returned to their primary jobs for several years and advancement, they return as supervisors or managers. Again, this change is only for a few years before they return as a supervisor or manager in their primary field. The resumés of a large percentage of the senior managers in many organizations include experience in HRD positions. (See discussion of Category II personnel in Chapter 1.)

The other traditional group is composed of people who are placed in the HRD function because they are unable to perform elsewhere, are injured, or have been with the organization for a long time, but their positions have been eliminated. These people are technically competent and often exceptional managers; however, they generally lack an HRD background. This lack of competency in instructional development and delivery often results in the perpetuation of the same instructional strategies under which they learned their skills. Many of these types of people move into HRD function actively seeking out learning that will allow them to become HRD professionals.

A new movement is rapidly gaining in popularity. There is a new kind of HRD practitioner appearing on the scene. These people often have advanced degrees in some aspect of HRD, along with an undergraduate or a second advanced degree in their original technical or engineering profession. These HRD professionals are often subject matter specialists. They possess the ability to identify a need and then to develop and deliver effective and efficient learning. There are some HRD positions for which this dual specialty is a minimum requirement.

Medical institutions are increasingly requiring that those responsible for providing HRD for the nursing staff be experienced nurses and have a graduate degree in some form of learning. For many employees, such as data processing personnel, nuclear power plant operators, and aircraft pilots, professional standing in the field is demanded, but experience and formal education in HRD or a similar program of study are minimum requirements. These are highly paid HRD professionals who are often responsible for skills programs that are critical to the health and well being of those whom the learners serve.

Organizations sometimes have a very small full-time HRD staff. These organizations utilize other employees to conduct the actual training and education. The HRD professionals determine the need for learning and design learning programs in conjunction with subject matter specialists and supervisory personnel. They then teach selected managers, supervisors, or skilled line personnel the tasks and required knowledge, as well as how to effectively conduct the learning activities. The actual delivery of learning is then provided by these non-HRD personnel. This method is efficient and effective. The learning often receives greater acceptance, because it is being provided by those who are accepted as being experts and as having "been there in the real world." The cost of the learning effort is generally lower than if provided by full-time HRD personnel, particularly if the learners are dispersed over a large geographic area.

Learning is often designed, developed, and sometimes delivered by those outside of the organization. This includes consultants, HRD organizations, and organizations that develop learning materials for general distribution. Consultants perform a wide range of services, as do HRD organizations. They may only assist in the analysis and assessment of performance problems, or they may contract for a complete learning program, including delivery. These outside technical HRD professionals have increased in number in recent years. Often they are able to provide HRD services to other organizations far more efficiently than a full-time in-house HRD staff. The learning may be of a better quality due to the ability of an HRD manager to shop around for the best and most efficient method of meeting learning requirements. This allows the HRD manager to select a different set of experts for each learning effort. Though these third party HRD organizations often provide many types of learning programs, the individuals assigned to specific types of programs are often highly specialized. They may have competencies far in excess of most in-house staffs. They often have a staff of highly competent instructional specialists who oversee the instructional qualities of the learning packages. Many organizations have also allowed their HRD departments to openly market their programs, which were previously only offered to employees or customers.

Continuing education departments of colleges and universities have also moved into providing learning activities, on contract, to organizations as well as to the general public. The advent of self-study packages, both in written format and in visual and electronic media, has allowed the growth of HRD organizations that develop general technical-learning packages, which vendors then sell on the open market. These organizations also tailor their packages to the specific needs of organizations.

The learners in the world of technical HRD fall into three general categories: (1) employees and their families, (2) customers who purchase the organization's products, and (3) learners who receive training through general sales or as the general public.

Employees often receive initial orientation to the organization and its procedures. This orientation for newly graduated engineers may consist of 80 to 120 hours of instruction. It includes tours and laboratory exercises that allow new junior engineers to be productive far earlier than when more traditional on-the-job orientation programs were used. New equipment requires the updating of the skills of maintenance and service personnel. New technologies require that design engineers have training to update their knowledge base. This allows them to utilize the new technology in the design of new products, which in turn requires the updating of the skills and knowledge of service personnel. Organizations are rapidly obtaining large numbers of computers for use in many jobs that previously utilized only manual machines. Most significant in this group are the secretaries, office administrators, and managers. They utilize word processors and small computer systems to generate documents and reports, to store information and reports, and to instantly obtain information from a variety of sources. These occupations require training and education in the use of these new technologies and the specifics of their particular systems and operations.

Customers who purchase products often spend large sums of money to obtain maintenance and operator learning. This learning can be conducted at the manufacturer's facility or at the purchaser's own site.

Many organizations are also taking advantage of HRD programs that are offered to various sectors of the industrial and organizational communities or to the general public. These are often in areas already in large demand, such as computer technology, telecommunications, or micro processing. These are typically offered at local motels, hotels, and college or university campuses.

THE HOW OF TECHNICAL PROGRAMS

There are a variety of delivery systems for these HRD programs. Many of these are very traditional, and some are very innovative. The rapid advancement in technology used for electronic instructional delivery also has many advocates. Traditional delivery methods primarily encompass the classroom, lecture, laboratory, and "on-equipment" instructional delivery methods. These are the methods by which most people have learned their skills and knowledge, and, therefore, many consider that these are the best ways to pass on one's skills and knowledge.

Those who rely on these methods are often those who do not know of the existence of the variety of instructional designs and strategies. Previously, these approaches may have been effective and efficient, but they should not be considered the only methods of delivery. Generally, traditional classroom activities only involve a few learners. The lecture method, with little if any learner involvement, is often the principal method of delivery in the classroom. The laboratory provides practice on the equipment or at least practice on a replica of the actual piece of equipment. The above methods have been used for many years and, in general, allow an instructor who has had little if any preparation in instructing to provide what is often very effective training.

The use of on-the-job training has moved from a very informal effort to a new dimension of structure. For many years, the supervisor has been providing training while the learner is actually on the job. There has generally been little if any structure to this training effort, with the supervisor/trainer providing what was felt to be the most appropriate learning strategy in what was often a haphazard effort. This is changing. There is a movement toward designing well-structured, on-the-job training and toward providing training for the supervisors who will be responsible for conducting the training. These new programs include materials for the learner and the supervisor/trainer that direct the learner in the study of technical documents and provide evaluations to ensure that a minimum level of learning has taken place. The supervisors/trainers receive training on how to conduct OJT and how to interact with learners. They also receive instruction for the on-the-job training packages.

Other more traditional methods of learning include the use of programmed text. Organizations that are dispersed over a large geographical area are using correspondence packages to conduct technical learning. These may be combined with other media, such as sound slide or video. The use of sound slide has received a boost with the advent of computer control for the audio and video, including multiple projectors with faders and other electronic controls. The uses of sound slide vary from a small portable unit that is designed for self-study to large, highly automated classroom units under the control of a computer. These can be extremely effective when used properly. There is, however, the danger of being carried away with the novelty and the tremendous "Hollywood" type capabilities.

The videotape machine has been used in technical learning for many years. The reduction in cost of equipment, for both studio and location taping, allows for an extremely effective method of delivering technical learning. The videotape is used as a stand-alone medium or is used in combination with other delivery methods. Often the videotape is designed to be used by an instructor to augment more traditional classroom learning. Videotapes designed for self-study are also utilized as stand-alone presentations or in combination with other media, particularly programmed texts. More recently, the use of random access videotape units has allowed for computer controlled interactive video. This method allows for the incorporation of previously recorded actions into what was previously only text or graphic computer-based learning. The new random access allows the instructional designer to design the computer-based learning lesson so that it can present any piece of video in any sequence, based upon learner actions.

Electronic learning devices have been used since World War II with aircraft pilots and crew. Learning devices for other operation and maintenance personnel have generally been mockups of the actual equipment, pieces of the actual equipment, or instructional devices with limited functions. Rapid advances in electronic technology have recently opened new vistas. These new devices are computer based and, in general, fall into one of two categories.

Learning devices that are a complete duplication of the operational environment have been very popular in military and aircrew learning activities. These devices often create such realism, that once the session begins the learners often forget they are in an artificial environment. These complete re-creations are now mandated in the nuclear power industry, and their use in industrial automation is rapidly increasing. Complete re-creations are also utilized extensively in pilot and aircrew programs as well as with other military occupations (e.g., engine room operators aboard ships and submarines). Many of these devices are specifically for team learning, which focuses on the interactions between the various team members. Research has been conducted on individual learning, but learning for technical teams has not received sufficient attention.

Another mode for instructional devices is the use of an electronic learning device for maintenance or equipment operation. These new devices are often very elaborate deliverers of computer-based learning. There is increased use of a computer-based learning system to provide initial tutorial learning in equipment operation or maintenance activities. The computer prompts the correct learner activities and is commonly found in simple tabletop devices and elaborate full-scale replicas. These systems also often provide competency-based evaluations for the learners, schedule the learner through the curriculum, and maintain learner and curriculum records.

Early learning systems were engineering devices designed with little thought to learning value, other than the re-creation of an environment. The capabilities of existing systems are often determined in the early stages of the instructional systems development process, and the devices are well integrated into the classroom, into traditional laboratory exercises, and into operations in the real world environment. These fully integrated instructional systems are proving extremely effective and efficient. They focus on those capabilities required to learn specific skills. They are designed to complement the real world environment and to provide for the rapid acquisition of the critical and required skills and knowledge.

COORDINATION WITH HIGHER EDUCATION

Higher education institutions have provided several generations with education related to some technical areas. This education may be for a known local need or for specific vocations. There is also a movement that joins local industry with the training and education capabilities of the local colleges. Community colleges have often been in the forefront of providing technical learning activities in response to specific requirements of local organizations. This often takes the form of educating the initial cadre of employees for new industries. These employees are hired conditionally and paid by the new organization while they attend classes at the local community college. When the factory is ready to start production, they have an educated work force that has been prepared by the local community college and is ready to begin producing. Those who do not successfully complete the required education are provided education for other positions. Their permanent employment is conditional upon successful completion of that second education program.

Local colleges provide a variety of services to local industries and organizations. These can include both consultation on problem analysis and the delivery of learning to meet specific technical learning requirements. These activities are conducted both on the campus and at sites selected by the contracting organization. Recently, electronic media has been used in videoconferencing. Colleges and universities often form consortia to provide technical learning activities that can include advanced degree requirements. These programs are often directed to the engineering and scientific disciplines. Technical learning activities designed to meet the needs of large sectors of specific industries are generally provided through the auspices of the continuing education department of the college or university. These again are generally directed to the engineering and scientific disciplines, although some computer learning is designed for nontechnical occupations.

The close cooperation between higher education and those in need of technical learning is a welcome addition, as it not only provides needed skills, but brings the world of academia and the world of industry together. A corollary movement is that of industry and business providing instructors and professors to higher education institutions. These people are paid their normal salaries by their sponsoring organization and, generally, serve part time or, occasionally, full time at the educational institution for up to one year. Occasionally, professors from the local higher education institution also work in local organizations for varying periods of time. This exchange of personnel between these two worlds, as well as the expansion of experiences for personnel of both worlds, is a much welcomed movement and one that has the possibility of providing great benefits.

TRENDS

Technology is advancing so quickly that tomorrow very rapidly becomes yesterday. As technology moves rapidly ahead, the skills and knowledge required by those in the workplace and those in the military must also remain in a constant state of transition in an attempt to meet tomorrow's needs. Other societal and demographic factors are exerting great pressure on technical learning activities. The movement from smokestack industries to service and information industries has resulted in new trends and problems. Labor's awareness of the transitional nature of many jobs and skills has resulted in labor contracts that include transition learning for labor. Labor hopes, as does industry, to minimize the number of workers displaced by technological advancements. These same technological advancements often provide new tools for instructional designers. They, in turn, use them in the delivery of technical programs to meet new and complex learning requirements.

Demographic changes are having an increased impact on those who deliver learning. The average age of the work force is increasing at a rather rapid rate. This increase has resulted in a smaller percentage of workers filling supervisory and management positions. Those workers not moving into supervisory positions provide new challenges for HRD practitioners. These workers generally have performed well in their jobs for many years, only to find that they are no longer able to function in another position. These workers often need education, since they lack the skills required to move from an essentially manual occupation to one requiring considerable cognitive abilities based on knowledge they do not possess. This challenge is often complicated by the large-scale layoffs in many of the traditional smokestack industries (e.g., steel and auto industries). Delivering adequate transitional education is a major and critical problem and will increase in severity as we further reduce employment in traditional smokestack industries.

Organizations are increasingly seeing the need for and the value of technical learning and are recognizing that there is a large need outside of the more traditional target group (i.e., employees or customers). These programs are often provided by those in high technology and information areas. Programs and courses are generally centered around technological advancements or the use of computer-related products. Members of this technical learning distribution community include the university and local community colleges.

The rapid advancements in technology have provided the instructional designer with new methods of meeting technical learning requirements. The innovation with the most promise is the videodisc. This disc is similar to an audio record, but it digitally records up to 54,000 images, each of which is directly accessible in fewer than two seconds. This ability to rapidly access any of a great number of images or to run them sequentially, as in a movie, provides the computer-based instructional designer with one of the most powerful tools ever possessed. The combining of videodiscs, computers, videotape, high quality color graphics, and interactive learner-machine interfaces (e.g., touch screens and voice control and synthesis) moves technical learning forward. There is an inadequate research base on which to rest the design of the learning environment. This technological movement has resulted in the ability to electronically join several geographically isolated learning sites together to form a single electronic classroom. This classroom allows each learner to see and converse with all the others, including the instructor. This technology, when coupled with videodisc and computer technology, provides almost limitless possibilities for effective and efficient delivery of learning activities.

As more and more products include microcomputers as their brains, the instructional designers will work more closely with the engineers who are designing the products. These instructional designers will be designing learning that is embedded into the device itself. It becomes a self-contained, computer-based learning program that will provide initial familiarization and operator or maintenance learning activities.

As electronic technology increasingly provides us with newer and cheaper tools, the instructional designer will look toward electronic learning devices as solutions to an ever-increasing number of problems. These devices include a computer-based learning device that not only allows practice of skills, but provides instruction, tutorials, and testing of these skills. The use of the interactive videodisc and high quality color computer graphics provides the instructional designer with the capacity to provide extremely high quality, efficient learning environments. The full simulator, which duplicates an environment such as an aircraft or nuclear power plant, also provides for increasing use of computer-based learning activities. The instructional designer often performs work equal to the engineer and will probably move to a significant level of importance.

The use of electronics and the computer will increase and assist in more traditional delivery methods. In the classroom, the large screen projection system under the control of a small computer will become commonplace. This system allows instructional designers and deliverers to provide action, to combine illustrations with computations, and to highlight various pieces of information. In short, it provides untold possibilities and increases the ability of the instructor to interact with the learners. These electronic classrooms will often have a terminal for each of the learners, sometimes with a large screen projection system. Learners will be able to interact with the instructor and then on their own system. This will enable them to progress and perform as best meets their individual requirements and desires.

A word of caution must be provided as we move rapidly into an age of electronic learning. There is little, if any, research base available to us for the design or use of these electronic marvels of the twenty-first century. How do we design learning materials that will utilize the capabilities of these marvels? What learning theories are used most appropriately as the bases for instructional design? Must new theories be developed? What are the competencies required of the new electronic instructional designer? What instruction must be designed for groups, and how should it be designed? There are many questions that must be answered.

Technical HRD has been around as long as there have been people. Methods have changed, as technology has become more advanced (beginning with the innovation of fire and continuing through the industrial age and into the new information and service age). Technical learning is perhaps one of the most important of the human resource development areas of concentration. It is the basis for all production, design, manufacture, operation, and repair.

The HRD practitioner with a technical background has become an increasingly important member of the organization and will continue to increase in importance. We must continue the systematic and efficient development of employee skills and knowledge, using the most advantageous technologies for design and delivery. We must also realize that our activities must be based on solid research, which may often only confirm what is known.

The challenges to the HRD technical practitioner are to provide widely divergent programs for new employees and for those currently employed. There is also the need to educate those who have been displaced by technology. They must find ways to work closely with management and the research and development units to anticipate the HRD needs of the future.

NOTE

1. Elizabeth Shey Gorovitz, "The Creative Brain II: A Revisit with Ned Herrmann," *Training and Development Journal* 36 (1982): pp. 74–88.

BIBLIOGRAPHY

Butler, F. Coit. *Instructional Systems Development for Vocational and Technical Training.* Englewood Cliffs, N.J.: Educational Technology Publications, 1972.
Davies, Ivor K. *Instructional Techniques.* New York: McGraw-Hill, 1981.
———. *Objectives in Curriculum Design.* New York: McGraw-Hill, 1976.

Davies, Ivor K. *Competency Based Learning: Technology, Management, and Design.* New York: McGraw-Hill, 1973.

Gagne, R.M. and Briggs, L.J. *Principles of Instructional Design.* New York: Holt, Rinehart and Winston, 1974.

Mager, Robert F. *Troubleshooting the Troubleshooting Course.* Belmont, Cal.: Pitman Learning, 1982.

Mager, R.F., and P. Pipe. *Analyzing Performance Problems.* Belmont, Cal.: Fearon Publishers, 1970.

Nadler, Leonard. *Designing Training Programs: The Critical Events Model.* Reading, Mass.: Addison-Wesley, 1982.

O'Neil, Harold F. Jr., ed. *Computer-Based-Instruction: A State-of-the-Art Assessment.* New York: Academic Press, 1981.

_____. *Issues in Instructional Systems Development.* New York: Academic Press, 1979.

_____. *Procedures for Instructional Systems Development.* New York: Academic Press, 1979.

CHAPTER SEVENTEEN

The Federal Government

EDWARD A. SCHROER

The U.S. federal government, like any other major employer, provides HRD experiences for its vast numbers of employees. Given the wide range of activities in the government, it can be expected that its HRD is quite diverse.

In this chapter, Schroer provides us with insight on and specifics about this gigantic HRD operation. It is possible to identify the operating factors and the legal basis for providing HRD. Statistics have been limited, as they are constantly changing, but up-to-date information is readily available to interested parties. This is not generally the case in the private sector.

Edward A. Schroer is the assistant director for training of the U.S. Office of Personnel

Management (OPM). He has held a variety of posts at OPM including: director of the Division of Planning and Development, director of the Office of Management, and director of planning and evaluation. Before moving to OPM, he worked in the office of assistant secretary of defense for systems analysis on a variety of projects related to HRD, and he served as education advisor to the U.S. Army Quartermaster School.

This chapter describes the human resources development program of the federal government for its own 1.8 million civilian employees, including the civilian employees of the defense agencies. The government does not generally use the term, *human resources development*. However, here, *HRD* or *development* is used in lieu of *training*, except where a government document is quoted or paraphrased.

The chapter does not examine the HRD programs of the uniformed members of the defense agencies or those of the U.S. Postal Service. Nor does the chapter examine the human resource development programs run by federal agencies for nonemployees. Such programs are inherent in the missions of the agencies and operate within special charters and unique rules. Examples of such programs include: the Comprehensive Employment and Training Administration (CETA) programs funded by the Department of Labor, and emergency management programs provided to public, state, and local government employees by the Federal Emergency Agency.

This chapter is divided into eight sections:

Philosophy, policies, and organization
Demographics
Planning for human resource development
Supervisory, management, and executive programs
Education
Use of learning technology
The HRD community
The employee's perspective

PHILOSOPHY, POLICIES, AND ORGANIZATION

The personnel system of the federal government is based on the premise that when employees are hired by the government they are able to perform the tasks of the job for which they are hired. It is the exception that employees are hired and then educated to perform the duties of a job. Thus, for the most part, HRD for federal employees is aimed at teaching governmental processes and procedures, introducing new technology, and preparing employees for higher-level jobs.

The Congress has established the program in law, and it is supplemented by presidential executive order, Office of Personnel Management (OPM) regulations, and several chapters of the *Federal Personnel*

Manual (FPM). In these laws and regulations, we find the philosophy, policies, and responsibilities under which the federal government operates its human resource development program for its own employees.

It should be recognized that HRD in the federal government is well established and systematized. It has been more than 25 years since the passage of the Government Employees Training Act (GETA). The systems used by most of the agencies—especially the larger and older agencies—are well established. Most of the issues associated with HRD systems have been confronted and satisfactorily solved. The agencies have documented systems for planning HRD and for operating HRD programs.

Because of the decentralized responsibility and authority for HRD, there is great diversity in the details of these programs. Agencies tailor their programs to accommodate the cultures of the agency.

Legal Basis for Federal Employee Training— Statute and Executive Order

Chapter 41 of Title 5, United States Code, is the basic statute authorizing HRD throughout most of the government. It codifies most of the provisions of the basic law of July 7, 1958, the Government Employees Training Act (GETA). Executive Order 11348 of April 20, 1967, provides agency heads with additional presidential direction on the manner in which the general statute is to be used. Both the law and the executive order authorize OPM to issue regulations governing various aspects of the law.

GETA declares the following to be the policy of Congress:

1. In order to promote efficiency and economy in the operation of the government and provide means for the development of maximum proficiency in the performance of official duties, to establish and maintain the highest standards of performance in the transaction of the public business, and to install and utilize effectively the best modern practices and techniques which have been developed, tested, and proved within or outside of the government, it is necessary and desirable in the public interest that self-education, self-improvement, and self-training be supplemented and extended by government-sponsored programs for training in the performance of duties and the development of skills, knowledge, and abilities which will best qualify employees for performance of official duties.

2. These programs are to be continuous in nature, subject to super-

vision and control by the President and review by Congress, and established so as to be readily expansible in time of national emergency.

3. The programs shall be designed to lead to (1) improved public service, (b) dollar savings, (c) the building and retention of a permanent cadre of skilled and efficient government employees well abreast of scientific, professional, technical, and management developments both in and out of government, (d) lower turnover of personnel, (e) reasonably uniform administration of training, consistent with the missions of the government, and (f) fair and equitable treatment of employees with respect to training.

Chapter 41 makes available to practically every federal agency a very flexible management tool with which to increase efficiency and effectiveness of operations and to decrease adverse effects of and the necessity for reorganization or reductions in work force. Chapter 41 places responsibility for HRD specifically with the head of each agency, who is authorized and directed to establish needed programs.

In general, authority granted by the law is sufficiently broad and flexible to enable an agency to provide whatever HRD is necessary to develop the skills, knowledge, and abilities that will best qualify employees for the performance of official duties. An agency covered by the law is authorized to:

Establish or strengthen needed HRD programs

Send agency employees to programs conducted by other governmental agencies, to the extent that those agencies are able to accept them; admit employees from other agencies to its own program—with or without reimbursement

Send agency employees to nongovernmental facilities for needed learning not reasonably available within government; pay all or any part of the expenses of such learning

Pay expenses of employees attending meetings that will contribute to better supervision and management of the agency's substantive functions, as well as meetings concerned with the substantive functions themselves

Permit agency employees to accept HRD contributions and awards from nongovernmental sources

Permit agency employees to accept payment from nongovernmental sources for expenses connected with meetings they attend

Provide HRD for agency employees for positions in other agencies if the employees would otherwise suffer a no-fault separation from service

Under the law, HRD may be conducted full time or part time, on duty or off duty, day or evening, or any necessary combination of these. It may be provided by the agency itself, by another government agency, by a school, by a manufacturer, by a professional association, or by other competent persons or groups, in or out of government. It may be accomplished through correspondence, classroom work, conferences, workshops, supervised practice, or combinations of such methods. Agencies may pay all or part of the expenses of authorized HRD. Payment may be made directly to the facility (in advance, if need be), or the employee may be reimbursed.

Oversight, Control, and Guidance Structures

Government-wide oversight and central management of federal training is accomplished through the interrelated and mutually supporting functions of the central federal management agencies: Office of Personnel Management (OPM), Office of Management and Budget (OMB), General Services Administration (GSA), General Accounting Office (GAO), and the Congress.

The Office of Personnel Management.   OPM is responsible for establishing regulations needed to implement the law and its prescribed leadership responsibilities for HRD. Principal areas of coverage include: establishment of HRD programs, program administration, agency review of training needs and annual program reports, use of governmental and nongovernmental facilities.

Federal HRD purposes set forth by OPM are:

1. Developing among agency employees skills unavailable through existing recruitment sources.
2. Improving employee performance of current duties.
3. Assisting the upward mobility of lower-level employees.
4. Providing employees with the skills, knowledge, and abilities necessary to accommodate changing policies, technology, equipment, or mission assignment.
5. Keeping employees abreast of the "state of the art" and maintaining specialized proficiencies.

6. Providing for the agency's future labor requirements through the systematic development of high potential employees.

In addition to providing interagency or special, single-agency classroom programs, OPM furnishes special instructional technology services vital to the development of cost effective, competency-based learning. OPM also provides an important quality control service for agencies by monitoring HRD work done by contractors. They see to it that vendors participate in a wide range of fair competition and assure agencies that vendors assign qualified professionals to the development of HRD products.

The OPM's evaluation function is accomplished through compliance reviews that determine whether agencies are meeting the requirements in the law (FPM). Agencies are also responsible for internal HRD program reviews that complement the selected OPM evaluations.

The Office of Management and Budget. OMB impacts directly on federal development through funding and financial control mechanisms. Agency budget reviews frequently identify HRD resource shortfalls or excesses that must be resolved in the budget review process. OMB also issues various directives that influence agency HRD functions. Nearly all OMB directives on staffing, finances, travel, and outside contracting will directly or indirectly affect agency management decisions on HRD functions.

General Services Administration. GSA activities influence HRD by the direction and control exercised on the management of items necessary to accomplish HRD. These items include procurement, travel, space, and forms of technology (e.g., computers and related devices).

General Accounting Office (legislative branch). GAO's congressional oversight role on the behalf of Congress complements the functions of the other lead management agencies and provides a mechanism for objective review and strategic intervention. These reviews lead to policy and procedure changes that make HRD more effective and efficient.

The Congress. Congress directly reviews HRD programs during hearings on enabling legislation and during oversight hearings. Appropriation subcommittees review the larger HRD programs during annual appropriation hearings. The governmental operations committees and the civil service subcommittees have reviewed HRD as well. The civil service subcommittees receive an annual report from the Office of Personnel Management and have directed a number of special studies of HRD.

Development Proponents:
Lead Agencies and Interest Groups

Most HRD needs are inherent in the dynamic nature of modern governmental operations, in which constant change calls for skills development in both new and experienced employees. This pressure is augmented by pressures from various central management agencies (frequently via task forces and special committees) and by special interest groups that recommend learning as a way of solving problems of interest to the group, or in the case of government agencies, as a way of carrying out their responsibilities. In all of these situations, the assumption is that a more highly skilled staff increases productivity and effectiveness or leads to direct savings (e.g., training to improve the skills of procurement officers).

No comprehensive list of all such pressures exists; many are within agencies or agency-specific. The categories that follow are neither comprehensive nor mutually exclusive. However, a general awareness of such forces will help us to understand the diverse and decentralized nature of HRD decision making.

1. A number of agencies and groups encourage training and education to improve the skills of particular occupational groups:

    The President's Council on Integrity and Efficiency upgrades the skill of Inspector General staffs.

    OMB, through the Federal Acquisition Institute of the Office of Federal Procurement Policy, upgrades the skills of procurement specialists of all types.

    GSA, through its "Contracting Officers Warrant Program," assures minimum skill levels for contracting officers.

    Federal Aviation Administration develops performance certification requirements for air traffic controllers.

    GAO, OMB, the Department of the Treasury, and OPM (members of the Joint Financial Management Improvement Group) provide direction and impetus for refining the skills of those in the financial management occupations.

2. In other instances, advocacy for training to solve organizational problems does not focus as directly on particular occupations as it does on particular functions:

>OPM task forces on cash management and debt collection upgrade skills of staff performing these functions.

>OPM increases the ability of agencies to handle Reductions-in-Force (RIFs) and performance appraisals.

3. As an enlightened employer interested in having employees make a career of civil service, the government uses various mechanisms to sponsor HRD for career enhancement.

>HRD is typically an integral part of agency career programs. For example, the FAA, the Internal Revenue Service, the National Park Service, and the Army have built formal education programs for air traffic controllers, revenue officers, park rangers, financial managers, and education specialists.

>HRD programs have become standard features of upward-mobility programs for the agencies.

4. Management and unions have negotiated many agreements regarding HRD.

>In a recent survey of labor relations agreements, 50% of the contracts surveyed stressed the need for HRD as a means of enhancing efficiency and effectiveness. Of the remaining 50%, 30% (15% of the total) guaranteed employees access to particular programs. In all the contracts surveyed, HRD was emphasized as a means of: cross-training to ensure a more competent work force; minimizing personal impacts of Reductions-in-Force; ensuring upward mobility; allowing employees to keep abreast of changing policies and technologies; and leading to higher levels of productivity.

5. In recent years, both OPM and the agencies have emphasized programs to develop supervisors, managers, and executives.

>The result has been an emphasis on HRD programs for those groups that stress use of on-the-job learning and rotational job assignments, supplemented by formal instruction.

>The government-wide guidance for these programs is in Chapter 412 of the *Federal Personnel Manual*. This does not make HRD mandatory (except for participants in the formal "Senior Executive Service Candidate" programs). In turn, agencies have applied this guidance to their individual situations in a

variety of ways, sometimes making minimal levels of HRD mandatory.

It is important to remember, however, that the principal factors in the federal HRD programs are the agencies. The head of each agency is responsible to the president, within law and regulation, for:

1. Determining the HRD needs of the agency.
2. Establishing and òperating programs to meet these needs.
3. Determining the kinds of training and education to be provided and the facilities to be used.
4. Establishing and making full use of the agency's facilities for providing HRD.
5. Extending agency programs to employees of other agencies.
6. Establishing interagency learning facilities in areas of substantive competence.
7. Establishing criteria for the selection of employees for HRD programs.
8. Selecting and assigning employees to programs.
9. Determining the method and extent to which the agency will finance HRD.
10. Evaluating the results of HRD.
11. Establishing appropriate administrative controls.
12. Reporting to OPM on HRD activities.
13. Encouraging the self-education, self-improvement, and self-training of employees of the agency.
14. Providing on-the-job training at all levels in the agency.
15. Conducting research related to learning objectives, as needed, to improve the effectiveness of the agency's programs.
16. Conducting research into instructional technology, when assigned by OPM.

As was noted, the laws and regulations place the responsibility for HRD with the agencies (about 80 different agencies have such authority). The heads of these agencies delegate authority and responsibility to subagencies, the subagencies delegate it to lower organizations and regional sites, and so on. The result is an extremely decentralized program in which most of the decisions about who gets which HRD programs are made by individual supervisors (the approximate number of supervisors is 240,000). Of course, each level in the chain of organization may also determine which HRD programs are required for employees in that organization. Thus you might have a chain of decentralized authority going from the Department of the Treasury, to the IRS, to regional commissioners, to supervisors. The IRS may decide that all newly appointed supervisors are required to have a basic supervisory course, and an individual supervisor may direct an employee (or approve his or her request) for training in a new computer programming language. Under such arrangements, if you are an HRD vendor, it is not possible to think of the government as a client. Minimally, the government is dozens of clients or even hundreds or thousands of clients.

The federal HRD mosaic includes a large number of different actors. While there are many *employee development specialists* (the job designation of the HRD practitioner) who play a major role in providing HRD to the federal work force, their principal role is as expeditors. They perform a variety of staff functions, including needs assessment, planning, acquisition, and evaluation. However, the mission program managers make almost all of the decisions on who, what, how much, and when. For the most part, the money used for HRD is part of the program manager's budget. It is not in an HRD budget managed by the HRD practitioners. There are some exceptions, primarily for the money spent for career development of managers and executives, which frequently is centralized.

DEMOGRAPHICS

It is not known exactly how much HRD programming is actually provided to or received by federal employees. The record-keeping systems have a number of weaknesses, and funds have simply not been available to make them more comprehensive and accurate. However, what is known presents a fairly good picture of the magnitude of HRD and the trends. Figure 17.1 presents the basic data on the characteristics used by the government to measure the amount of HRD programming. These data measure formal programs, but not the other aspects of HRD.

Employee Training in the Federal Service, the government publication that documents the above data, points out that the data, particularly the cost data, are not accurate and are probably understated. In addition to the data systems not capturing all the instances of HRD, there is the problem of determining the appropriate elements of cost. The data in Figure 17.1 do not include salary costs of those attending HRD sessions.

Students' salaries are not a cost of HRD programming in the same sense as the other costs. If HRD programming is not done, most of the

	1980	1981
Occurrences	828,000	781,000
Individuals	522,000	492,000
Program hours used	33,500,000	29,844,000
Total expenditures	$400,000,000	$371,000,000
Average length of occurrence	40 hours	38 hours
Average cost per occurrence	$396	$370
Average cost per program hour	$9.76	$9.61

Figure 17.1. HRD program measures used by government. Source: Office of Personnel Management in the federal government.

costs would be saved, at least eventually, but the students' salaries would continue. This is especially true for most federal "students" who typically attend only very short courses (under a week, on the average) and are not replaced on the job by another employee. Although agencies do spend extra funds to improve the work of employees, using more overtime for example, at present the government does not have a way of determining those costs throughout the federal government.

Governmental HRD, as defined in the law, is

> the process of providing for and making available to an employee, and placing or enrolling such employee in, a planned, prepared, and coordinated program, course, curriculum, subject, system or routine of instruction or education, in scientific, professional, technical, mechanical, trade, clerical, fiscal, administrative, or other fields which are (i.e., training) or will be (i.e., education) directly related to the performance by such employee of official duties for the government, in order to increase the knowledge, proficiency, ability, skill, and qualifications of such employee in the performance of official duties.

The extent to which government and nongovernment sources are used to provide HRD for employees is a popular way to look at the federal HRD picture. The sources of HRD are:

Government agency HRD provided by the employee's agency and conducted by agency staff

Government interagency HRD provided by an agency other than the employee's agency or interagency

Nongovernment HRD provided and given expressly for the agency by an individual company, school, professional association, or consultant under contract to the agency or a standard HRD experience offered

Agency	Total instances of training (in thousands)	% In-House	% Interagency	% Nongovernment
Total government	825	62	13	25
Air Force	67	69	10	21
Agriculture	56	67	13	12
Army	144	54	20	26
Commerce	13	35	14	51
Department of Defense	32	47	25	28
Justice	30	80	7	13
Labor	13	63	15	22
GSA	13	46	32	22
Interior	29	38	23	39
NASA	16	18	10	72
Navy	109	56	13	31
Treasury	97	88	5	7
Veterans Administration	74	69	7	24
All Other	135	56	15	29

Figure 17.2. A comparison of the sources of HRD for various federal agencies. Source: Office of Personnel Management in the Federal Government.

by a company, professional association, school, or other source (e.g., university courses, professional symposia).

Figure 17.2 details the amount of training for each source.

PLANNING FOR HRD

Both the government-wide guidance of OPM and the internal agency guidance recognize the need to plan for HRD. Historically, the process is called *determining training needs*. More recently, it has been referred to as *training needs assessment*. Both are attempts to project how many employees need to acquire some particular knowledge, skills, or abilities.

It is useful to recognize that planning goes on at two principal levels: at the *aggregate level*, where an attempt is made to estimate how many employees need a particular learning experience; and at the *individual level*, where an attempt is made to plan the HRD activities for each individual employee. Both the individual employee and the supervisor agree in writing to an individual development plan.

The quality of the aggregate level planning is extremely varied among agencies and occupations. Often it is not done at all. Sometimes, agencies make estimates of long-term and short-term staffing needs (by projecting staff buildups, cutbacks, and turnover) and then try to determine which of those staffing needs can and should be met by HRD programs. While there are exceptions, aggregate planning of this type is not done often or well by the government.

Another kind of aggregate planning focuses on providing minimum levels of learning for certain populations to meet specific needs. An agency may determine that all of its newly appointed supervisors should receive a two-week course on supervisory skills. The agency then projects, for the year or longer, how many programs it must provide to meet the requirement. For example, when the performance appraisal system was initiated in 1980, it was determined that all supervisors needed a minimum amount of training on how to use such a management tool. Most agencies made projections of the courses, sessions, and trainees necessary to meet such a requirement. This kind of planning is done extensively and repeatedly throughout the government.

Typically, the results of both individual and aggregate planning are pulled together into an annual HRD program or plan. In small agencies, such programs exist for the agency as a whole; in larger agencies, they exist at much lower levels in the agency (e.g., regional office).

In recent years, agencies have more frequently employed sophisticated methods for assessing learning needs. (Frequently one or more survey techniques aimed at supervisors are used.) Agencies often use specialists (in-house and others) for assistance in this process. The guidance provided by the *Federal Personnel Manual* on this subject indicates that the government does appreciate the importance and sophistication of planning. It says,

> Agencies will get best results when reviews of training needs:
> — Are conducted in a planned and systematic manner;
> — Are conducted both at local levels to identify specific, local needs and at agency levels to identify general, overall needs;
> — Are based on realistic assessment of organizational conditions and operating problems as well as an overall assessment of the performance of the agency's workforce;
> — Take into consideration future program and staffing needs, and potential for meeting those needs, including the potential of employees of the agency for advancement within their present occupations or for assignment and advancement within other occupations in the agency;
> — Provide reasonable opportunity for employees and employee organizations to express their views on training, especially any which management determines that employees shall take;
> — Identify all significant needs, regardless of whether they can be met with available resources; and
> — Represent the conclusions of line management as well as the views of personnel and training staffs.

Budgeting and Financing

Budgeting for HRD is done in a variety of ways. Agencies have considerable leeway in determining the HRD programs they will provide and how they will be managed and funded. This procedure is consistent with the decentralized, government-wide approach to HRD, but it does not diminish the responsibility of agency heads to ensure that HRD is adequately planned and funded, in accordance with OMB/OPM policy and guidance.

Agencies approach the planning and funding process in different ways depending upon their agency mission, occupational composition of the work force, internal development capability, and availability of facilities and funds.

Operating Budgets. The monies budgeted for development are typically included in the line operating budgets of the various agency programs. The government supervisor or manager who wants to provide HRD spends operating money to pay for the program, whether that program is provided in-house, interagency, or by nongovernmental organizations. Typically, the money budgeted for such HRD activities is not specifically identified in program budgets.

Direct Funding. There are many significant exceptions to the operating budget approach. Some agencies have small HRD management staffs that are directly funded. These staffs provide overall general direction, assistance to line managers, and ensure that record keeping and reporting requirements are met. The specific dollar amounts and staff authorizations budgeted for these functions are well documented in internal agency budgets, even though they may not show up specifically in the president's budget.

Some learning delivery is also directly funded; that is, the school or HRD center gets the money to deliver the program (and house and feed the learners, if it is a residential course). In such situations, the line manager pays only for travel of the learner, if necessary. Most often, this approach is used when an agency has a large number of employees, or when turnover, growth, or new technology create a continuing HRD requirement. The IRS, the FBI, the FAA, and a number of Department of Defense agencies use this approach.

Direct budgeting is also often used by agencies to finance management and executive HRD programs. Since these programs are centrally managed in agencies (decisions are made centrally, usually under the supervision of an executive resource board, on the nature of the program and who gets what learning, when and where) the budgets for these programs are also centralized. Line managers do not budget for such HRD programs.

Reimbursable Funding. In-house HRD programs can be paid for on a reimbursable basis; that is, the HRD center is financed by the fees paid by the learner's operating agency.

Reimbursable HRD represents a classic example of the free marketplace. Line managers choose the program they want, at the best price available, and send employees only as long as they think the program is a good one.

Interagency HRD is a small portion of total HRD, and is financed on a reimbursable basis. An exception here is the Federal Law Enforcement

Training Center (FLETC) run by the Treasury Department. Several agencies budget the necessary funds, which are transferred to the FLETC. Learners are then sent to FLETC by the contributing agencies. Individual students are not charged a fee.

Contracting. Most HRD programming outside of the government is paid for by the operating program managers on a per learner basis, but there are instances where an agency contracts with a university or private vendor to develop and deliver a course. When this is done, it is typically for a fixed fee, and individual learners are not charged. The budgets for the contracts may be shown in the HRD management budget, in an account for centrally funded services, or in the budget of a line program where the learners are employed.

OMB Circular A-76, together with OPM policies and guidance in FPM Chapter 410, requires agencies to use nongovernmental service sources for HRD services when this is cost effective. Agencies frequently use contracts for all types of HRD support (e.g., courseware development, whole course development, delivery, and instructor/speaker augmentation) even when a similar program is offered by a government facility.

Thus, when we talk about HRD budgets in an agency, the most visible ones are for the HRD management staffs, the directly funded HRD delivery center, and the centrally funded management and executive HRD programs. Beyond these, research is required to know what additional funds are budgeted for HRD.

SUPERVISOR, MANAGER, AND EXECUTIVE DEVELOPMENT (SME)

The government has long had a special concern for the development of its supervisors, managers, and executives. After 1978, with the passage of the Civil Service Reform Act, an even greater emphasis was placed on the development of what are presumed to be the generic skills of executives and managers and, by implication, of supervisors. Since the passage of the act, OPM has been very active in promoting supervisory, managerial, and executive (SME) HRD programs, and the agencies have actively responded.

As with all development activities in the federal government, the authorities and repsonsibilities for SME development programs rest with the agencies. However, with these programs, the tendency within agencies has been to centrally manage them (and often to fund them), rather than to delegate the decisions to lower levels. One reason for this is that OPM has been more aggressive in prescribing guidance for such programs and for requiring the submission of plans for approval. In addition, of course, SME programs lend themselves to long-term planning and central management.

The government-wide guidance and the individual agency programs generally distinguish among supervisors (first-line managers), managers (mid-level managers at the GS-13, GS-14, and GS-15 levels), and executives (members of the senior executive service). At the same time, the government has tried to foster the philosophy that these three groups form a management team that has to function well at all three levels for the government to be effective and efficient. Thus the government has emphasized the development of generic knowledge, skills, and abilities at each level and stresses a whole career approach, where the development at the manager level builds on first-level supervisory skills, and development at the executive level builds on managerial skills. Some agencies have excellent programs judged by any criteria. In general, however, the government has a long way to go to build a cohesive management team development program.

The SME development programs have usually been thought of as serving two main purposes: (1) Provide incumbents (particularly newly appointed incumbents who go through a one-year probationary period) with the KSAs they need to manage the programs and staffs they head (i.e., training), and (2) Provide for the systematic replacement of any agencies' supervisors, managers, and executives as they retire or otherwise leave the work force (i.e., education).

EDUCATION

While the government does not make the distinction between *training* and *education* in the sense that the private sector does, it does support developmental activities that, in the conventional sense, are education activities. Two examples illustrate the type of educational activities supported: long-term training (120 days or more) and tuition assistance programs.

Long-Term Training

GETA authorizes heads of agencies to "make agreements or other arrangements for the training of employees through non-government facilities." It requires employees who are sponsored for training outside of government facilities to agree to continue in the service of their agencies after the training is completed for a period at least three times the length of the training. If the employee leaves his or her agency voluntarily before that time is up, he or she must pay the agency for the training. The head of the agency may waive recovery of costs in the interest of equity or the public interest.

The law also places certain limitations on the use of nongovernmental training (these apply to all nongovernmental training programs, not just long-term training):

1. The number of staff years of training for an agency in a fiscal year may not exceed one percent of the total staff years of civilian employment in the agency.

2. An employee having less than one year of civilian service is not eligible for training, unless specifically excepted by the head of his or her agency in the public interest.

3. The time spent by an employee in training may not exceed one year of service for each 10 years of civilian service. (This limitation, however, may be waived in individual cases by the head of the agency to allow up to two years of training in a decade of service.)

4. Agencies may not sponsor employee training that is provided solely for the purpose of obtaining a degree or for the purpose of providing the employee a degree in order to qualify for a particular position for which the degree is a requirement.

Year	Participants
FY 1961	189
FY 1964	509
FY 1968	2,004
FY 1972	1,411
FY 1976	970
FY 1980	548
FY 1981	599

Figure 17.3. Long-term government trainees. Source: Office of Personnel Management in the Federal Government.

Agency heads have authority to determine the necessary training expenses and to pay such expenses. In general, these include salary, travel and per diem, tuition, fees, and books.

The number of long-term trainees grew rapidly after passage of the Government Employees Training Act in 1958, reached its zenith in FY-1968, and has been declining since, although the decline has slowed in the last few years (see Figure 17.3).

College Courses

Government employees attend many college courses at government expense. It is estimated that in 1981, 95,000 employees attended 146,000 courses at a total cost of about $46 million.

Certainly these courses contribute to the education of the employees. However, it is not the intention of the government to further the general education of its employees, but rather to provide the knowledge, skills, and abilities that employees need to perform their official duties. Duties include the employee's presently authorized duties or those he or she can reasonably be expected to do in the future.

Considerable caution is exercised by the agencies to preclude authorizing courses that are not related to the present or future jobs. Agencies cannot sponsor students for the sole purpose of obtaining degrees. However, the receipt of an academic degree can be an incidental by-product of job-related courses.

Agencies are also authorized to allow attendance at college courses during duty time. Government-wide data on how much of such development is off duty and how much is on duty is not available, but a recent study by GAO indicates that it varies widely by agency and activity. Of four activities surveyed, one used 18% off-duty time, and one used 91%.

The expenses of college courses can also be paid by the government. Practices here also vary widely. In general, agencies tend to pay fewer expenses and require the employee to use off-duty time when the courses are not directly applicable to current jobs but are related to future employment or career development.

LEARNING TECHNOLOGY

The government's employee development specialists, be they course designers, instructors, or HRD program managers, have been very conscious of the value of multiple approaches to learning. They are andragogists who emphasize the participative techniques implied by that approach. They are especially open-minded about audio and visual aids of every kind. They have a diversified, eclectic approach to the use of methodology, media, courseware, hardware, location, resident/ nonresident, as programming techniques. They make or manufacture many of their own materials, buy others on the open market, and contract with specialists for special purpose materials.

Most of the courses are during the work day. Some are located at the work site, others are in centrally located training centers, including national centers and regional centers. These facilities are fully equipped to support any kind of medium or activity required by a particular learning experience.

While the government operates few resident learning facilities, those they have are fully equipped to support all types of learning experiences.

Independent study systems (correspondence courses, self-paced instruction, home study) are not widely used in government HRD, but their use is growing. In 1982, the Office of Personnel Management enrolled 20,000 students in its independent study courses—up from 13,700 in 1980. Further, as the costs of transportation rapidly rise along with the cost of food and lodging, agencies are looking for more economic training delivery methods and are turning to independent study.

On-the-job training (OJT) is probably the most widely used method for employee development in the government. In a number of agencies, OJT is highly organized, formalized, and evaluated. In most places, however, OJT just happens. It is ad hoc, probably very inefficient, and unappreciated. The high potential of formal OJT is slowly being recognized, and agencies are beginning to incorporate it into their HRD programs. There is very little written guidance available on this subject.

High Technology

When a new technology that has HRD applications surfaces, it takes no time at all for some employee development specialist to try it out. Government HRD people are eager experimenters. There is extensive use of video in a great variety of situations. There are experiments with the very latest variations: videodiscs, laser-read discs, and at least one combination of computers and videodiscs. Many attempts are being made to capitalize on the characteristics of the teleconference, including the use of satellites.

In recent years, the government trainer has cautiously experimented with incorporating the computer into learning. It is used extensively to support the administration of learning, and more recently, actual learning is done on the computer. The computer presents the information, questions the learner, requires the learner to apply the information and practice skills, and finally, evaluates the learning. The government does not do a lot of this, but the use of the computer is growing.

Evaluation

Evaluation is one of the least developed aspects of the federal government's HRD program. While there are examples of very good practices, in general, good evaluation is not widespread. To many in the field, evaluation seems too complicated, too risky, too costly, or deserving of only limited commitment. The federal government's attitude parallels the situation in other sectors.

The pressures to perform more evaluation and to make what we do more effective are increasing. One reason is the rising cost of development and the need for managers to justify to themselves and others the investments they make in development. The Congress, through the General Accounting Office, has frequently called for better evaluation. Other groups that have studied federal HRD have done the same.

The government has responded by increasing the amount of evaluation, by inventing new and simpler methods, and by making a concerted effort to share methodology among the agencies. As a result of the highly decentralized authority and responsibility for development, there are many approaches to evaluation. The following are four specific examples that are highly valued by the federal community:

1. IRS Level II Evaluation Process is a process used by the Internal Revenue Service that links on-the-job tasks, training objectives, and measurement items that evaluate learning achievement.

2. Participant Action Plan Approach (PAPA) is an OPM-developed approach intended to gauge trainee performance and application and lead to course refinement and redesign.

3. Training Value Model I (TVM-I) is an OPM-developed process intended to forecast the extent to which training can lower organizational costs or increase organizational output.

4. "Toward an Effective Evaluation Methodology" is a methodological approach developed by Dr. Carolyn Bassin of the Nuclear Regulatory Commission.

Personnel	Agency Instructors		Other Agency HRD Personnel (GS-235 or Equivalent)		Administrative and Clerical Support Personnel	
	Staff Years	Total Salary Costs*	Staff Years	Total Salary Costs	Staff Years	Total Salary Costs
Full-time personnel	2703	$61	3225	$ 90	2196	$34
Part-time personnel	261	6	948	22	631	8
Total	2964	$68	4173	$112	2827	$42

*In millions of dollars

Figure 17.4.   Staff years devoted to HRD activities.

THE HRD COMMUNITY

The HRD community of the federal government, while large in total numbers, represents a relatively small percentage (0.6%) of the total work force. The job classification systems used by the government identify four occupational series directly related to human resource development. The community also includes a fifth group made up of the administrative and clerical support people who directly support HRD. The last group may be members of any number of classification series.

The latest data available on the number of staff years devoted to HRD activities are from FY 1981 (see Figure 17.4).

The four occupational series used by the government are:

1. *Employee Development Specialist Series (GS-235).* This job classification series covers positions involving planning, administering, supervising, or evaluating a program designed to train and develop employees. It also includes positions involving guidance, consultation, and staff assistance to management concerning employee and development matters.

2. *General Education and Training Series (GS-1701).* This series includes positions that primarily involve research or other professional work in the field of education and training when the work is of a generalized nature.

3. *Education and Vocational Series (GS-1710).* This series covers positions requiring application of full professional knowledge of the theories, principles, and techniques of education and vocational training in such areas as instruction, guidance, counseling, administration, development or evaluation of curricula instructional materials and aids, and learning tests and measurements.

4. *Training Instruction Series (GS-1712).* This series covers positions concerned with administration, supervision, or instruction in a program of learning in an occupation, trade, craft, or subject where the essential qualifications for the work of the positions are a mastery of the knowledge and skills characteristic of the occupational or subject field and a practical knowledge of the methods and techniques of instruction.

In 1976, the OPM published the results of a major study on the roles of HRD specialists in the government and a curriculum plan for providing the learning experiences needed. The five roles follow.

1. A *career counselor* facilitates the selection of training and development alternatives concerning career progression, utilizing knowledge of training and counseling skills, tools, and resources.

2. The *consultant* is concerned with research and development of tools, methods, and so forth to improve training and with providing management and employees with advice and assistance on a variety of organizational problems.

3. The *learning specialist* designs, develops, conducts, and evaluates learning experiences. Learning specialist activities are the base of the training job. Reasons for further development in the role are: (1) more agency in-house training is needed; and (2) a systematic approach to training design should be implemented.

4. The *program manager* sets policy; plans, controls, and manages the various training and employee development functions, curricula, programs or courses; and interacts with all management levels in an organization. This role is not restricted to a director of training, but is carried out by anyone performing a management-related activity.

5. The *training administrator* arranges, coordinates, and maintains the support services of the various training and development programs.

FROM THE INDIVIDUAL EMPLOYEE'S PERSPECTIVE

While the government's human resource development program emphasizes the responsibilities and authorities of the government's managers as an employer, it also emphasizes the responsibilities of the individual employee. Moreover, in actual practice, much HRD programming results from the initiatives taken by the employee, such as personal career planning, individual development planning, requests for specific learning experiences, pursuit of college and graduate degrees, meeting certification requirements, and so forth.

The words *self-education, self-improvement,* and *self-training* clearly place responsibility and authority with the employee. The government's programs supplement and extend the employee's initiatives. In actual practice, the HRD programs are combinations of individual and employer activities. The more knowledgeable and ambitious employees understand this and act accordingly.

The merit system concept is important to the individual's development in two ways. First, only employees with basic knowledge, skills, and abilities for a job are hired. For example, the government generally will not provide basic accounting education to develop its accountants. It hires educated accountants and then provides them with training on the government's accounting systems. Entry-level technical and professional education or training is not provided to employees. Second, employees have equal opportunity for HRD experiences. This means they have the same rights to development as others but may have to compete with others for those opportunities.

Thus HRD opportunities are associated with the processes of applications, tests, reviews, panels, and finally selection of a few from among the many. Particularly, most management and executive HRD programs include this competitive feature.

There is widespread use of career programs within the government, but the comprehensiveness and effectiveness of such programs varies widely. The civil service itself is often called the career service, implying that one works for the government throughout a career. That is true for many occupations, and much of the process associated with the civil service personnel systems is to assure promotion from within the service in a fair and equitable way.

Usually when we speak of career programs from an HRD point of view, however, we have a more narrow concept in mind. We are referring to occupational careers within departments or agencies. For example, there are personnel specialist career programs in the navy, the revenue agent career program in the IRS, the forest ranger career program in the National Park Service, and the procurement career program in the army.

These career programs typically have the following characteristics: a personnel information data base of all the people in such jobs, central management of assignments and promotions above certain grades, geographic mobility for participants, and fairly elaborate development patterns for the members. The latter becomes a model for the members to follow so that employees have some idea of what kinds of experiences they should seek at various stages of their careers. The individual employees must take the initiative to obtain the necessary experiences.

While there has long been a performance appraisal process in the government, the Civil Service Reform Act of 1978 added great emphasis to the practice. Now, every employee has performance standards and annually must have his or her performance appraised against those standards. It is important for each employee to understand the process, actively participate in setting his own standards, and develop confidence and skill in participating in the performance reviews.

An integral part of the standard setting and review process is the individual development plans for each employee. One result of the performance review process is the individual development plan. Supervisors and subordinates together negotiate a plan for the employee's development over the ensuing year. The plan may be devised to correct deficiencies noted in the review, to enhance the employee's ability to perform his or her job, or to prepare the employee for greater responsibility. While the individual development plan is a supervisory responsibility, it is also an important opportunity and tool for the employee. The development activities called for in the individual development plan may be anything that could help in the employee's development, such as task force assignments, details to other jobs, HRD experiences, writing or publishing assignments, and so forth.

The government also takes the position that, as an employer, it should provide certain services to support the employee's self-development activities. Therefore, employees are provided with:

1. Professional developmental counseling.
2. Information about the various developmental activities available to them.
3. Specific assistance, such as the purchase of self-study materials, financial assistance for tuition and books, adjusted work schedules, leave without pay to attend school.
4. A record of all activities in the official personnel file of the employee for consideration at time of promotion or assignment.
5. Monetary and nonmonetary recognition for job performance improvement resulting from self-development activities.

The government is authorized to, and generally does, pay the salaries of employees while they participate in an HRD activity. It also may pay travel expenses, extra food and lodging costs, costs of books, tuition, lab and library fees, and so forth. For long-term HRD located at nongovernmental facilities (e.g., a university), the government may require the employee to agree to remain as an employee of the government for a specified period ("continue-in-service" agreements).

The employee needs to recognize that the policy of the government is that the individual employees are primarily responsible for their own development. Further, the government sees that it has two supporting responsibilities. First, it should help the employees in their self-help HRD programs, and second, it should supplement the self-help programs with programs of its own to which it assigns employees. In all cases, the employees should take the initiative for their own HRD activities.

CHAPTER EIGHTEEN

Schools

RALPH R. GLAZER

To avoid confusion, the reader should recognize that in this chapter Glazer is focusing not on the students, but on the teachers and administrators in the school system (K–12). It is not that the students are unimportant. Quite the contrary—the purpose of providing HRD for school systems is to continually improve the teachers' and administrators' performance for the benefit of the students.

As Glazer notes, HRD is new to school systems. It is not that learning experiences have not been provided in the past, but that they tended to be classes for teachers and administrators with little or no relation to their needs.

Glazer discusses some of the concepts and practices that are evolving as HRD is being introduced into an increasing number of school systems.

Ralph R. Glazer (Ed.D.) is an administrator in the Fairfax County Public School system in Fairfax, Virginia and is responsible for HRD for school staff. He has worked with various school districts as a consultant and workshop leader in HRD. His doctoral dissertation focused on staff developers (HRD practitioners) in school systems.

INTRODUCTION

One of the most challenging tasks for schools in the 1980s will be how they as organizations manage to develop the human resources they possess. In the face of increasing budget constraints, declining enrollments, a changing employee work ethic, and other seemingly insurmountable pressures, educational leaders will be hard-pressed to find solutions or alternatives for coping with these and other complex problems. Human resource development in schools is a field of endeavor that has great potential for the future effectiveness of schools and, in fact, may already be found as part of the organization pattern in several innovative school districts.

Several years ago, Leonard Nadler[1] envisioned the contributions that HRD could make to staff development and made the following recommendations:

1. Learning should be based on identified needs.
2. The HRD unit should have obvious and concrete managerial support.
3. There should be an HRD unit or person (with HRD as a major responsibility).
4. Objectives should be clarified: Is it training, education, or development that is needed?
5. Content should be related to the needs of the learner, not to the availability of outside resources.
6. Classroom learning is only one strategy. Others are readily available.

These and other observations form the basis for our exploration of human resources development in schools.

HRD and Staff Development Defined

Nadler defines HRD as organized learning experiences for a specified period of time, designed to bring about the possibility of behavioral change.[2] Given this conceptual base, it should be easy to see why staff development in schools is also the focus for HRD in schools. That is not to say that the ramifications do not extend beyond the boundaries of what is considered to be the domain of staff development operations in a school system. Human resource development implies, as Nadler's definition indicates, a change in both the organization and the individual. A brief examination of what several staff development leaders say about the definition will help to demonstrate the relationship between the two fields.

According to Betty Dillon-Peterson, staff development coordinator in the Omaha, Nebraska school system, and one of the founders of the National Staff Development Council, staff development is "a process designed to foster personal and professional growth for individuals within a respectful, supportive, positive organizational climate, having as its ultimate aim better learning for students and continuous, responsible self-renewal for educators and schools."[3] Ideally, *staff development* is a process used to provide learning opportunities for all people working in schools or responsible for them.

Three Approaches to Staff Development

In defining the mission of staff development, one can identify three approaches: the deficiency model, the developmental model, and the curriculum development and implementation model.

The deficiency model requires teachers to become students in order to bring their initial education up to an acceptable level. With this model, teachers are perceived as not having all the necessary skills required to perform their duties. Therefore, the overall aim of this approach is to correct the deficiency by providing a set of appropriate ideas, skills, and methods (which need developing).

The developmental model emerged as teachers became better educated and more skilled upon entry into the profession. This model focuses on further development of the individual's professional skills and knowledge. A similar goal is seen in staff development related to the curriculum development and implementation model.

T.L. Sergiovanni and D.L. Elliot describe a most prevalent philosophy of staff development in schools: "Staff development is not something the school does to the teacher, rather it is something the teacher does for himself.... Staff development does not assume a deficiency in the teacher but rather assumes a need for people at work to grow and develop on the job."[4]

Rationale for School District Support of Staff Development

In a study conducted by S.J. Yarger, K.R. Howey, and B.R. Joyce,[5] it was discovered that the rationale for school district support of staff development rested on one fundamental premise—the student-teacher relation ship. Instructional quality, it is argued, is largely dependent on the personal and professional competence of those who provide the instruction. School personnel who continue to grow are more likely to continue meeting the needs of students in a constantly changing society.

Beyond this basic premise, three additional factors are commonly cited:

1. *Declining Enrollments and Stable Staffs.* Declining enrollments in K–12 schools have stabilized school staffs. Often, it is no longer possible to hire new staff who have had special preparation to deal with new needs. Instead, existing staff must be prepared, through in-service education and staff development programs, to handle those needs.

2. *New Expectations for Schools.* Changing values and societal conditions have continued to alter the expectations of what schools should do. Recent examples include the education of the handicapped, bilingual education, and multicultural education. Whether the new expectations have come from the courts, legislatures, local communities, or school personnel themselves, all have emphasized the importance of staff development for effective implementation.

3. *Insights into the Change Process.* School personnel, with the help of researchers, have come to realize that change is a process, not an event, and that before schools can change, the individuals within them must change.[6] Through staff development programs, the concerns of individuals can be appropriately addressed to allow effective implementation of change to occur.[7]

Best Practices of Staff Development

In a survey of staff development best practices focusing upon major studies of educational change, Harry M. Hutson, Jr. identified "fifteen best practices in in-service education," as follows:

1. Decision making should proceed as an authentic collaboration of in-service clients, providers, and constituencies.

   Corollary: Decision making should involve those affected by in-service decisions and be as close to their situations as possible.

   Corollary: Decision making should represent the shared interests of agencies and major interest groups.

2. The incentives for participating in in-service programs should emphasize intrinsic professional rewards.

   Corollary: There should not be disincentives (e.g., inconvenient times or locations, etc.) that would penalize participation.

3. In-service programs should be explicitly supported at the outset by district and building administrators.

4. Outside agencies or consultants may be helpful in supportive roles.

   Corollary: Outside agencies or consultants should offer neither too much nor too little help.

5. The implementation strategy should include continual professional growth activities and the local development of materials within a framework of collaborative planning by participants.

6. The design of in-service programs should be complex and ambitious.

   Corollary: In-service goals should be clear and specific.

7. In-service programs should be planned in response to assessed needs.

   Corollary: The interests and strengths of participants should also be assessed.

8. In-service trainers should be competent.

   Corollary: Each person is often his or her own most competent trainer.

9. The school site should be the locus of in-service activities.

10. In-service evaluation should be a collaborative venture whose primary purpose is to assist with planning and implementing programs.

11. In-service content should be derived from assessed needs.

    Corollary: Problem-solving skills are likely to be a needed content dimension of in-service.

12. In-service content should be directed toward changing teaching behavior, not student behavior.

13. The process of in-service education should model good teaching.

14. In-service education should follow a developmental model, not a deficit model.

15. In-service should be an integral part of the total school program.[8]

EVOLVING CONCEPTS

Over the past several years, staff development has been severely maligned for many reasons, not the least of which is due to significant disagreements as to the meaning of the word. For instance, many terms are used interchangeably with *staff development,* among them:

In-service education	Continuing education
Renewal	Professional growth
On-the-job-training	Professional development

As Ben M. Harris points out, distinctions in meanings can and should be made among these terms.[9] However, the interchangeable use of these terms serves to perpetuate the uncertainty and confusion that already exists. Nadler, a recognized authority in the field of human resource development, has already provided a framework for delineating the various functions of training and development that are directly applicable to the staff development field.[10] HRD focuses on learning experiences provided by an organization to achieve the goals of the organization. Three different types of learning experiences represent the major activity areas in HRD. They are *training, education,* and *development.*

Training

Training focuses on the employee's present job. Such learning experiences are concerned with actual job performance. Furthermore, it is expected that the learners will use the training immediately, on-the-job, and that the organization can reasonably expect some return on the job now being done by the trainee. Training is considered a low-risk activity, and the expenditure is minimal.

A time management workshop for administrators or a writing skills workshop for English teachers are examples of training activities that form a staff development program. In both instances, the learning experiences focus on actual on-the-job behaviors. The school system could reasonably expect to see some direct evidence, on the job, of skills acquired. There is a low-level risk involved since there is a close correlation between the training experience and the observation of results.

Education

The emphasis of education is on the individual preparing for a different job. The most common use of education is to prepare an individual for a promotion. Time frame or utilization for education is the future, but a not too distant future, perhaps a few months to a year. Two possibilities exist for education in this regard: (1) a definite job to be filled at a definite time, and (2) a definite job to be filled at an indefinite time.

Education is an investment, though generally a short-term one. However, it is possible that an investment will not provide a return to the organization. For example, an employee may be educated for a job that does not become available. In this regard, education is a medium-risk activity. It is expected to pay off, and an organization provides education with a high expectation of return. Still, it is an investment with all the risks attendant on an investment.

Education in staff development programs can be demonstrated in activities such as administrative seminars or academies that prepare prospective candidates for management positions. The Des Moines (Iowa) Public School System has an administrative academy that provides ongoing education for school administrators. The director of staff development is responsible, in this case, for the training of staff development leaders, for program planning, for scheduling, for budgeting, and for the day-to-day operations of the academy.

Development

The focus of development is on the organization. It is based on experience that has shown that organizations must grow and change in order to remain viable. Development provides learning experiences to employees so they may be ready to move in the new directions that organizational change may require. The time utilization for development exists in the distant future, and is, therefore, a long-term investment. Development is also a high-risk activity.

The most obvious example of development activities in staff development programs today are those involved with computer technology. This area is a wave of the future, and providing the necessary skills in computer literacy, computer programming, and other applications to staff development is in tune with preparing for future developments in a school system. Today, due to severe budget cutbacks, very little emphasis or funding can be found in school systems for this area of development. However, it is a dimension that is vital to staff development planning if the pitfalls of reactive programming are to be avoided.

HRD AND ORGANIZATIONAL PATTERNS IN SCHOOLS

Evidence of an organization's commitment to developing its human resources can be traced directly to how close that function, in an organization, is located to the top, decision-making apparatus. In the case of a school system, that would imply proximity to the office of the superintendent. It may simply depend on whether or not there is a separate unit designated with such responsibility and whether or not that unit's purposes are haphazard and sporadic. Staff development units have this responsibility and, in many cases, are only remotely accessible to the superintendent or assistant superintendent.

Isolation of Staff Development

What is the typical picture? According to Robert W. Houston,

> The isolation of staff development is a major reason for its impotence. With few exceptions, staff development programs are designed to fulfill state requirements or local school board regulations. These requirements and regulations are backed financially by less than one percent of most school district budgets. The director of staff development typically reports to an assistant superintendent who reports to the superintendent. Sometimes the chain of command reaches even lower into the district hierarchy before a responsible person is found.[11]

According to Donald R. Moore and Arthur A. Hyde in a report to the Ford Foundation,

> We found that major decision making about the shape of staff development was carried out primarily by individual specialists and administrators in the school district, including central office department directors, coordinators, curriculum specialists, supervisors, and principals. These individuals make decisions and take the initiative concerning staff development largely on their own.[12]

There is usually little coordination and communication among the leaders of staff development efforts.

Limited Access and Little Power

In a study of staff development personnel in six different school districts, Jo Anne L. Vacca discovered the following perceptions from staff developers themselves.

> A commonly held perspective among key personnel involves their linkage to district decision making. While some staff development personnel cite direct and open channels of communication to top level administration, most experience only indirect contact with "higher-ups."[13]

No one identifying primarily with staff development claimed to experience intimate involvement in the decision-making process. Staff developers perceive themselves as middle managers with limited access and little power. Nevertheless, they are virtually unanimous in their view of the potential importance of staff development in the implementation of district goals.

The "Consumer" Model

What, then, are the organizational patterns in school districts, and how do they reflect staff development responsibility? Swenson[14] describes three organizational patterns that emerge for organizing staff development programs in schools. The first such pattern is what can be called the *consumer model*. This model involves the *consumers* of the staff development (those for whom it is intended, usually teachers) in planning, decision making, and evaluation of the program. Yarger, Howey, and Joyce report that "teachers perceive themselves to be quite involved in developing in-service programs," to the extent that the data would seem to counter the common perception that in-service programs provided by school districts are controlled by administrators who are totally removed from the concerns of the classroom teacher."[15] Roy A. Edelfelt agrees: "Increasingly, teachers are more involved in decisions about in-service education as a result of teacher demands (in some cases negotiated into collective bargaining contracts) and in response to research showing the advantages of involving teachers."[16]

In-Service Councils and Policy Boards

Applications of the consumer model frequently take the form of in-service councils or policy boards, with classroom teachers comprising the majority of the membership. Other members are usually principals, central office administrators, support staff (curriculum coordinators), and, in some instances, board of education members and parents. Districts using in-service councils or policy boards typically make these bodies entirely responsible for organizing the district's in-service program. Members are responsible for conducting needs assessments, determining program activities, identifying in-service instructors, evaluating the activities, and allocating the available in-service funds. In addition to planning in-service activities throughout the district, within a school building, or within a department, in-service councils or boards will often manage the district's procedures for attendance at conferences, conventions, or workshops outside the district. Some are also given responsibility for determining salary schedule advancements by teachers for their professional improvement efforts.

The Office and Director of Staff Development

Larger school districts tend to have an office of staff development headed by a director who administers the staff development program for the entire district. This program usually works closely with subgroups within the district to organize activities at a variety of levels (e.g., building, department, grade levels). Because of their size, larger districts are able to organize programs of voluntary, after-school courses and workshops for their own personnel. The director of staff development will typically be responsible for organizing these voluntary programs.

The Hierarchical Pattern

A third common pattern for organizing training and staff development is the traditional "top-down planning and decision-making arrangement." The district administrator or a designated administrative assistant autonomously plans and conducts the district's in-service programming. School personnel may be consulted for their staff development ideas, but they are seldom invited to participate in the decision making.[17]

NEEDS ASSESSMENT IN STAFF DEVELOPMENT

Another key component of HRD in an organization is the process and method by which needs are assessed. HRD programs are based on a needs assessment. For example, training programs arise when there is a variation between what the employee is expected to do on the job and the actual job performance.[18] Since HRD, by definition, is concerned with changes created via learning experiences, the content for a program will always arise from the needs of the learner, whether it focuses on training, education, or development. How do school districts typically approach this important aspect of staff development?

Methodologies and Guidelines

The most common needs assessment methodology is a topical survey in which respondents indicate their preferred in-service topics. This is usually done in the spring for the forthcoming school year. While these surveys can provice some useful information, they often measure interests rather than needs and ignore the question of how respondents best learn. School districts that do a thorough and effective job of assessing needs tend to conform to the following guidelines:

1. *Use of Multiple Methods.*   Several measures are employed, including the analysis of existing data (budget documents, goal statements, test scores), interviews, observations, surveys and questionnaires, group discussions, and evaluations conferences.

2. *Attention to Process as well as Content.*   Information is gathered on how participants best learn in addition to on what they wish to learn.

3. *Consideration of Timing.*   The context within which data are gathered is carefully planned and structured, the goal being to provide respondents with the opportunity to thoughtfully consider their needs, at a time when they are ready and willing to do so.

4. *Provision for Feedback.*   When needs assessment data are gathered, respondents are told how the data will be used, and, later, they are given feedback on the results.

5. *Use of Evaluation as Further Assessment.*   The evaluation data gathered to judge the results of in-service activities are used as assessment information for future programming.

The critical factors in school districts' organizational patterns for training and staff development appear to be (1) the extent to which school personnel are involved in the decision making and planning for their in-service programs and (2) the quality of the needs assessment methods employed.[19]

THE GROWING EDGE: CURRENT PROGRAM APPLICATIONS

Adult Learning Theory

Staff developers now regard adult learning theory as a crucial element in the planning, designing, and implementing of in-service activities. Malcolm Knowles has contributed an andragogical model of learning that is based on the following "foundation stones of adult learning theory":[20]

1. Adults are motivated to learn as they experience needs and interests they want satisfied; therefore, these needs and interests are appropriate starting points for organizing adult learning activities.

2. Adult orientation to learning is life centered; therefore, the appropriate organization of adult learning consists of life situations, not subjects.

3. Experience is the richest resource for adult learning; therefore, the core methodology of adult education is the analysis of experience.

4. Adults have a deep need to be self-directing; therefore, the role of the teacher is to engage in a process of mutual inquiry, rather than to transmit knowledge to adults and allow them to evaluate their conformity to it.

5. Individual differences among people increase with age; therefore, adult education must make optimal provisions for differences in style, time, place, and pace of learning.

Adult Learning and Staff Development Practices

Over the past seven years in the Denver Public School system, staff development specialists have depended on adult learning theory in conducting such programs as Project CARE, Instructional Improvement, and Mastery Learning in Basic Skills. Four assumptions constitute the guidelines for these successful, on-going programs: adult learners are products of experience; adult learners are products of perceptions; adult learners are products of time; and adult learners are products of emotions. The overall result of such an approach is to invite teacher participation in less threatening and more creative ways.

Adult Learning and Change

In the Lincoln (Nebraska) Public School system, a decision was made to implement a new program based on the "Concerns Based Adoption Model." The staff development personnel and others involved in the change effort participated in a series of seminars entitled "Adult Learning and Change." The purpose of the seminars was to provide a base for staff members to become more knowledgeable about and competent in applying principles of adult learning to their staff development work.

Staff Development: An Andragogical Dilemma

A staff developer committed to an andragogical or adult learning orientation is often faced with learners conditioned to learn by a pedagogical approach. They want to sit and be told what they need to know, to be given insights, and to be told how to apply them on their jobs. The staff developer, expecting participant involvement, is headed for frustration. How does the staff developer resolve the dilemma? Burton Wood, staff development coordinator for the Milwaukee (Wisconsin) Public School system, suggests there is only one choice: a development role for adult educators.

> A key step in assuming an andragogical role is in making a commitment to that role. The next step involves the establishment of an underlying orientation to andragogy in all of your work. Finally, I believe it is necessary to develop a repertoire of developmental approaches to use as subject matter, learners, circumstances, and other variables permit.[21]

Adult education influences the behavior of adults. Persuading adult learners of the advantages of self-renewal, guiding them toward discovery of how to do this, and providing opportunities to practice new skills in a reinforcing atmosphere are the important tasks staff developers face if they are to adopt an andragogical approach to learning.

Management Concepts

Traditionally, the responsibility for professional growth and development of school administrators has been left with the individuals themselves. Although some school districts have had isolated training activities for their administrators for a number of years, most do not offer on-going programs to improve managerial skills. Staff development initiatives and programming in the Des Moines School system are good examples of how to provide a support system for the decision makers that will reflect more commitment to the development and maintenance of good leadership. The administrative academy model includes five basic operational criteria that are fundamental to its existence—collaboration, peer leadership, a sound cognitive base, experiential activities, and an on-going support system.

In addition, staff development programs are emphasizing systems four, theory X/theory Y, management by objective (MBO), organizational renewal, time management, situational leadership, grid management, and other concepts.

THE EMERGING ROLE OF THE STAFF DEVELOPER

The role of the staff developer has changed dramatically over the past decade. Once primarily considered a resource teacher, the staff developer has emerged into a coordinator of training programs, a team leader, a consultant, a counselor, a public relations expert, a budget analyst, and an instructor. Staff developers are critical to the success or failure of staff development programs. Their role is one of complex leadership that requires them to possess a diversity of skills, ranging from knowledge of adult learning theory to current management practices.

Recently, increased attention has been focused on the background and preparation necessary for the role of staff developer in schools. Vacca noted in a study of six school districts that how staff development is delivered is as important as what is delivered. Four major criteria for successful staff developer performance cited by Vacca include content delivery, personal influence, professional competence, and arrangements. Teachers responding to Vacca's critical incident interview cited *content* as most important to the measure of successful performance, followed in order by professional competence, personal influence, and the arrangements for the session. An important finding from her study was that at present time there do not exist any formal mechanisms through which professionals can be prepared for the challenges and responsibilities of the role of the staff developer.[22]

The National Staff Development Council conducted a study of 300 of their members selected at random. These staff developers expressed their own needs and concerns in 10 categories, which can be classified under four training areas broadly labeled: *politics* (in the general society, in the organization, in collaborative relationships); *implementation* (management skills, evaluation skills, staff development technology, pedagogical knowledge, understanding adult clients); *keeping current;* and the *state of the field.*[23] Three significant recommendations were offered as a result of the study:

1.   The characteristics of effective staff development and practices of the effective staff developer should be more clearly defined. Until agreement is reached, staff developers will continue to express concern and frustration over the ambiguity and confusion that surrounds their role.

2.   Staff developers, at this point in the evolution of their roles, must take responsibility for their own growth. Staff developers appear to want for themselves what they promote for their clients—meaningful oppor-

tunities to learn an array of contexts, times, and styles from various people. Until more training programs become formalized, staff development for staff developers will continue to be self-development.

3. The continuing education of staff developers should be a priority. Consideration should be given to the fact that the career paths of staff developers might lead to positions out of staff development. These persons should not be forgotten. They will continue to be strong sources of support, if communication is maintained. Efforts should be made to continually provide challenges for those who choose to remain in the field.

It is in this arena of continuing education and professional development for staff developers that human resource development may make another significant contribution to the field of staff development. Based on the Nadler model of the three major roles and 11 subroles for the human resource developer, I have designed a questionnaire and conducted a role perception study of regular members of the National Staff Development Council. Preliminary returns from the study indicate that staff developers find the Nadler model to be descriptive of their roles. Results from the study may provide a conceptual basis for the future training, education, and development of staff developers.

THE FUTURE OF HRD IN SCHOOLS

The future of HRD in schools is vast and significant. Schools in the United States are being forced to turn to their most valuable asset— human resources—in order to survive. HRD is already contributing to schools in many areas of application, knowledge, skills, and research and it has the potential to make greater contributions in the future. Several organizations supporting the growing movement of HRD in schools should be noted:

National Staff Development Council. A national organization of professional staff developers dedicated to providing a network of support, research, skill development, and communication. The council is currently exploring the many applications of HRD to the professional development of staff developers.

Association for Supervision and Curriculum Development. A national organization that publishes a monthly magazine, *Educational Leadership,* concerned with the most current trends in HRD in schools, especially in the area of administrative leadership.

National Institute of Education. A federal agency that funds R & D centers, laboratories, teacher centers, and so forth, operates current staff development programs in the field of education, and provides the framework for state-of-the-art research.

Human resource development in the school setting, and in staff development in particular, is a concept that will continue to gain prominence throughout the 1980s. Leonard Nadler is quoted as saying, "HRD is first and foremost concerned with change. There is no justification for the expenditure of energy and resources if there is no intent of producing change."[24] Educational leadership must make the intelligent decisions to help school systems move forward in the 1980s and come to grips with the realization that HRD in schools is only a beginning. HRD as a total concept, concerned with the growth of the institution and the individual, is important for the entire mission of schools in America and for the future.

NOTES

1. Leonard Nadler, "Learning from non-school staff development activities," *Educational Leadership*, 34 (1976): 201–204.
2. Leonard Nadler, *Developing Human Resources*, 2d ed. (Austin, Tex.: Learning Concepts, 1979), p. 3.
3. Betty Dillon-Peterson, "Staff Development/Organization Development—Perspective 1981," *1981 ASCD Yearbook* (Alexandria, Va.: Association for Supervision and Curriculum Development, 1981), pp. 1–10.
4. T.L. Sergiovanni and D.L. Elliot, *Educational and Organizational Leadership in Elementary Schools* (Englewood Cliffs, N.J.: Prentice-Hall, 1975), p. 152.
5. S.J. Yarger, K.R. Howey, and B.R. Joyce, *Inservice Teacher Education*, (Palo Alto, Cal.: Booksend Laboratory, 1980), p. 35.
6. G.E. Hall and S.F. Loucks, "Teacher concerns as a basis for facilitating and personalizing staff development," *Teachers College Record* 80 (1978): 36–53.
7. See Thomas L. Swenson, "The state-of-the-art in in-service education and staff development in K–12 schools," *Journal of Research and Development in Education* 15 (1981): 2–7.
8. Harry M. Hutson, Jr., "Inservice best practices: The learnings of general education," *Journal of Research and Development in Education* 14 (1981): 1–9.
9. See Ben M. Harris, *Improving Staff Performance Through In-Service Education* (Boston: Allyn and Bacon, 1980), p. 20.
10. Leonard Nadler, "Implications of the HRD Concept," *Training and Development Journal*, May 1974.
11. Robert W. Houston, "The nature of change in schools and universities," in *Staff Development and Educational Change*, eds. Robert W. Houston and Roger Pankratz (Reston, Va.: Association of Teacher Educators, 1980), p. 6.
12. Donald R. Moore and Arthur A. Hyde, "Making sense of staff development: An

analysis of staff development programs and their costs in three urban school districts," report prepared for NIE and Ford Foundation (Chicago: Designs for Change, 1981).

13. Jo Anne L. Vacca, "Establishing criteria for staff development personnel," report prepared for NIE (Troy, N.Y.: Russell Sage College, 1980), p. 51.

14. Swenson, *Journal of Research and Development in Education*, pp. 2–7.

15. Yarger, Howey, and Joyce, *Inservice Teacher Education*, p. 14.

16. Roy A. Edelfelt, "Six years of progress in inservice education," *Journal of Research and Development in Education* 14 (1981): 112–119.

17. Swenson, *Journal of Research and Development in Education*, pp. 2–7.

18. Charles H. Kepner and Benjamin B. Tregoe, *The Rational Manager*, (New York: McGraw-Hill, 1965).

19. Swenson, *Journal of Research and Development in Education*, pp. 2–7.

20. Malcolm S. Knowles, *The Modern Practice of Adult Education* (Chicago: Follett, 1980), p. 38.

21. Burton Wood, "You're the teacher: Tell us what we're supposed to know: An andragogical dilemma," *The Journal of Staff Development*, Vol. 1, no. 2 (October 1980), pp. 119–125.

22. Vacca, report prepared for NIE, p. 51.

23. V. Randall Flora and Jane Applegate, "Concerns and Continuing Education Interests of Staff Developers," *The Journal of Staff Development*, Vol. 3, no. 2 (November 1982), pp. 29–37.

24. Nadler, *Developing Human Resources*, p. 5.

BIBLIOGRAPHY

Blake, Robert R., and Jane S. Mouton. *The Managerial Grid*. Houston, Tex.: Gulf Publishing, 1964.

Dillon-Peterson, Betty, ed. Staff Development/Organization Development—Perspective 1981. *1981 ASCD Yearbook*. Alexandria, Va.: Association for Supervision and Curriculum Development, 1981, 1–10.

Drucker, Peter F. *Managing for Results*. New York: Harper & Row, Publishers, 1964.

Edelfelt, Roy A. "Six years of progress in inservice education." *Journal of Research and Development in Education* 14 (1981): 112–119.

Flora, V. Randall, and Jane Applegate. "Concerns and continuing education interests of staff developers." *The Journal of Staff Development* 3 (1982): 26–37.

Hall, G.E., and S.F. Loucks. "Teacher concerns as a basis for facilitating and personalizing staff development." *Teachers College Record* 80 (1978): 36–53.

Harris, Ben M. *Improving Staff Performance Through In-Service Education*. Boston: Allyn and Bacon, 1980.

Houston, W. Robert. "The nature of change in schools and universities." In *Staff Development and Educational Change*, edited by W. Robert Houston and Roger Pankratz. Reston, Va.: Association of Teacher Educators, 1980.

Hutson, Harry M., Jr. "Inservice best practices: The learnings of general education." *Journal of Research and Development in Education* 14 (1981): 1–9.

Kepner, Charles H., and Benjamin B. Tregoe. *The Rational Manager*. New York: McGraw-Hill, 1965.

Knowles, Malcolm S. *The Modern Practice of Adult Education.* Chicago: Follett, 1980.

Koll, Patricia and Jim Anderson. "Cooking and staff development: A blend of training and experience." *The Journal of Staff Development* 3 (1982): 45–53.

Laekin, Alan. *How to Get Control of Your Time and Your Life.* P.H. Wyden Publishers, 1973.

Likert, Rensis, and Jane Gibson Likert. *New Ways of Managing Conflict.* New York: McGraw-Hill Book Company, 1976.

Lippitt, Gordon. *Organizational Renewal.* New York: Appleton-Crofts, 1969.

McGregor, Douglas. *The Human Side of Enterprise.* New York: McGraw-Hill Book Company, 1960.

Moore, Donald R., and Arthur A. Hyde. "Making sense of staff development: An analysis of staff development programs and their costs in three urban school districts." Report prepared for NIE and Ford Foundation. Chicago: Designs for Change, 1981.

Nadler, Leonard. *Developing Human Resources.* 2d ed. Austin, Tex.: Learning Concepts, 1979.

Nadler, Leonard. "Learning from non-school staff development activities." *Educational Leadership* 34 (1976): 201–204.

Sergiovanni, T.L., and D.L. Elliot. *Educational and Organizational Leadership in Elementary Schools.* Englewood Cliffs, N.J.: Prentice-Hall, 1975.

Swenson, Thomas L. "The state of-the-art in in-service education and staff development in K–12 schools." *Journal of Research and Development in Education* 15 (1981): 2–7.

Vacca, Jo Anne L. "Establishing criteria for staff development personnel." Report prepared for NIE, Troy, N.Y.: Russell Sage College, 1930.

Wood, Burton. "You're the teacher: Tell us what we're supposed to know: An andragogical dilemma." *The Journal of Staff Development*, Vol. 1, no. 2 (October 1980), pp. 119–125.

Yarger, S.J., K.R. Howey, and B.R. Joyce. *Inservice Teacher Education.* Palo Alto, Cal.: Booksend Laboratory, 1980.

CHAPTER NINETEEN

Special Populations

LAWRENCE G. BROWN, LANNIE J. BROWN, AND VIRGIL E. COLLINS

Most of this book deals with those who are regularly in the work force. We all know, however, that there are many of our citizens who have never held regular jobs or are woefully unemployed. Since the recognition of that condition over 25 years ago, many different labels have been used. Today, the term *special populations* has begun to replace the former designations that were generally based on race or ethnic background.

The authors help us understand some of the past legislation and bring us up to date as best they can. They cannot foretell the political future of these programs, since such programs change with different administrations and philosophies. However, the common denominator of all the programs is concern for those citizens who cannot fully enter the work force.

So far, no political party, economist, or social scientist has been able to provide a satisfactory response to the problem. This does not mean that it cannot be solved—only that we have not yet been able to identify the necessary actions.

Those actions require the cooperation of both the public and private sector. Neither can do it alone. It is essential for all HRD people to be familiar with the history and programs presented in this chapter and for them to keep current as programs change.

Lawrence G. Brown is administrator of Co-operative Education and engineering personnel liaison for the Advanced Technology Group of the Sundstrand Corporation. Prior to obtaining the Sundstrand position, he had experience as an officer in the U.S. Navy and served as leadership management education and training course director at the Navy's human resource management school. He is also currently active in community activities related to HRD.

Lannie J. Brown has a wide background in working with special populations and projects. She has been an instructor of psychology at the University of Guam; instructor at the State Technological Institute, Memphis, Tennessee; and assistant to the director for program planning and development at the Janet Wattles Mental Health Center, Rockford, Illinois.

Virgil E. Collins is director of human resource development for the Akron City Hospital. Prior to this position, he held various HRD positions in manufacturing, local government, and healthcare. He has served in many capacities in ASTD, including director of the Minority Network.

DEFINING SPECIAL POPULATIONS

Several programs have been designed in the past to compensate for socioeconomic factors that have contributed to the broadening chasm between the "haves and have nots," the rich and the poor, the supporters and the supported, the contributors to society and those to whom society must contribute. The demographics, while remaining fairly constant for some special groups, change in defining qualities with each succeeding decade. The 1960s gave birth to the term *disadvantaged* to identify those groups not having the advantages of mainstream Americans (i.e., people living in the U.S.). Included in these groups were those who had been disadvantaged because of race, creed, color, religion, national origin, sex, and so forth. Legislation dictated defining and redefining these groups, in an attempt to keep pace with the changing populations of these groups at a given time. Various arguments have been made to support the view that the newest and/or fastest growing groups of disadvantaged in this country are people over 70 years old, women, Hispanics and other nonwhites. Granted, identification and classification of this segment of the population is important for a number of reasons. However, it is a moot point, because regardless of how the groups are defined or who does the defining, there remains a substantial portion of the population that has a history of unemployment and remains underemployed or increasingly unemployed.

Traditionally, the composition of the economically disadvantaged groups has been as previously stated. However, the recession and/or depression of the early 1980s contributed to the emergence of yet another new (and very large) group of unemployed—a group that in the past enjoyed the pleasures and indulgences of the mainstream. To appalled observers, who believed in the rituals to achieve the American dream, they were seen as secure—even as insulated from the plight that they faced. Later in the chapter we will examine this newest group of the unemployed and their comparability to the traditional, less empowered special populations.

HUMAN RESOURCE DEVELOPMENT PRACTITIONERS

The term *human resource development* was defined by Leonard Nadler in *Corporate Human Resource Development; A Management Tool* as meaning "those learning experiences that are organized, for a specified time, and designed to bring about the possibility of behavioral change."[1] These learning experiences are of a nonincidental, purposeful, criteria-focused nature. While the term is currently employed in a much broader context, during the 1960s it was used in conjunction with efforts undertaken by the U.S. Department of Labor involving the disadvantaged, and implied that training was needed. Human Resource Development practitioners are those individuals engaged in the design, management, implementation, and delivery of those learning experiences.

Do individuals who manage and work in programs for the disadvantaged consider themselvles Human Resource Development practitioners? The answer, in far too many cases, is no. No, because of unfamiliarity with, misunderstanding of, and disassociation from those who consider themselves professional practitioners of human resource development. Human resource development practitioners in academia, industry, and the public sector have a responsibility to those whose profession it is to work with the disadvantaged, as evidenced by the results of a survey conducted by the American Society for Training and Development.[2] The survey population consisted of a small group of senior managers of Human Resource Development in the private sector. The results follow:

1. What role(s) do you believe would be most appropriate and effective for the federal government in job training?
   a. Operating federal job training programs such as CETA... 17%
   b. Providing incentives (e.g., tax credits) to employers to invest more in job training (either through in-house programs or through outside services) 78%
   c. Using federal funds to improve existing public education systems 29%
   d. Providing incentives to both employers and educators to work together more effectively 69%
2. Do you believe that employers should play a role in retraining workers for new jobs?   Yes-83%

(See American Society for Training and Development National Report, February 19, 1983.)

In question 2, we also asked, "If so, how?" The responses ranged from "Only if they plan to hire them (the trainees)" to "In-house resources or shared programs with other companies."

It is true that "the poor we will have with us always." It is not true, however, that we as a nation can afford to continually accept double-digit unemployment as a way of life. It defies reason that we can put a man on the moon but cannot put people back to work.

The theories and technologies found throughout this chapter deal with the full development of human potential. People and productivity go hand in hand with the economic health and well being of the nation. Is it not true that the HRD practitioners, who so capably consult with and instruct the corporate staff of American industry, can apply those learning experiences to the task of putting all of America back to work? Partisan politics and misguided ideologies have no place. The urgency of the situation is as critical as a strong national defense.

Through the efforts of the American Society for Training and Development governmental affairs office, HRD practitioners are engaged in tackling the problem. Proactive efforts, designed to continue the learning process for our legislators and practitioners in the field, are ongoing.

LEGISLATION

In 1921, a presidential commission was formed under the chairmanship of the secretary of commerce, Herbert Hoover. It was the first significant attempt at manpower planning made by the federal government. For a detailed description of programs and policies the interested reader should see *Manpower Policies and Programs: A Review, 1935–75* by Joan Claque and Leo Kramer.[3] Programs for the last two decades have been influenced most by the 1962 Manpower Development and Training Act (MDTA). The legislation and its amendments embodied two concepts:

1. The need to retrain skilled workers who had been displaced by automation
2. The need for education and training of the unskilled unemployed to enable them to obtain and hold jobs

The act's most important feature was the making available of federal assistance to any geographic area in the nation.

Sar Levitan and Garth Mangum in their work, "Federal Training and Work Programs in the Sixties" stated the basic objectives of the Manpower Development and Training Act:

1. To meet labor shortage needs in specific industries
2. To provide employment opportunities for the unemployed
3. To upgrade the labor force
4. To provide an escape from poverty[4]

There were problems inherent in the achievement of these objectives. Among the difficulties were restrictions designed into the program. MDTA was mainly an education program for those already in the work force. Eligibility for admission was restricted to unemployed heads of households who had at least three years of work experience.

These difficulties were further compounded by job placement agencies, whose goals were to provide the most qualified men and women for each opening. Those workers who were inexperienced or hard to employ were not included. A rule, stating that one-third of the job placements had to come from the least qualified, had to be enacted in an attempt to correct this problem. This stop-gap measure emphasized the magnitude of the problem but failed to sufficiently address the critical, long-term problem of the hard to employ. Subsequent programs and legislation enacted throughout the 1960s and early 1970s were designed to further correct the problem. In 1964 the Economic Opportunity Act (EOA) was passed. Amendments to EOA followed in 1966 and 1967. The identification of distinct target populations and specially designed problems was begun as a result of this legislation. It was during this time that the older workers became grouped with other protected classes. "Operation Mainstream" was the most notable of the programs designed for older workers during this period.

The efforts of the Department of Health, Education, and Welfare (HEW) and the Department of Labor (DQL) resulted in the Work Incentive Program (WIN). All aspects of home management and skills for improved job performance were emphasized. By the end of the 1960s, programs for the disadvantaged had become big business.

Dozens of federal agencies were involved, many with differing and overlapping functions and objectives. The Concentrated Employment Program (CEP) was designed to overcome this problem by integrating the various delivery systems and providing a full range of services. Still, the job was not being done adequately. The National Alliance of Business was formed to increase the involvement of industry. By the beginning of the 1970s, millions of dollars were being spent to recruit, to educate for jobs, and generally to upgrade the skills necessary to gain and maintain employment. One lesson that could be learned from the 1960s and 1970s was that no single approach could be applied. A total social effort was not only needed, but required, to make substantial progress towards eradicating poverty and improving the plight of the disadvantaged in our society.

According to Levitan,

The experience of the 1970s offers little hope that poverty will be eliminated in the United States in the near future. However, major strides have been made in that direction. Poverty as defined by government statistics has been sharply reduced and, as was pointed out, actual progress has been far greater than the official government data indicated because the official poverty count fails to take account of in-kind assistance which has expanded much more rapidly than cash assistance....Even if the media does not publicize the continued expansion of aid to the poor and political leaders in the 1970s have failed to take credit for the major accomplishments, the fact is that the price tag of programs in aid of the poor has grown.[5]

What specifically is the progress that Levitan speaks of, and how has it come about? There were two major pieces of legislation that provided the framework for special programs and enabled significant progress to be made—the Comprehensive Employment and Training Acts of 1973 and 1978 (CETA). The Manpower Development and Training Act, The Economic Opportunity Act, and the Emergency Employment Act were all forerunners of the Comprehensive Employment and Training Acts. (The Job Training Partnership Act of 1982 will be discussed later in the chapter.) A review of the successes and difficulties experienced by CETA and its major component, the Opportunities Industrialization Center (OIC), deserves mention.[6]

CETA 1973-1981

Some major components include:

Title I. Provides guidelines for grants to states and localities (446 in FY 1977) that serve as prime sponsors for employment and training programs offering such services as recruiting, testing and placement, classroom and on-the-job training, work experience, transitional public service employment, and supportive services.
Eligible. The unemployed, underemployed, and economically disadvantaged.
Title III. Part A covers special target groups such as native Americans, migrant and seasonal farm workers, and other national emphasis groups (e.g., ex-offenders, older workers, people with limited English-speaking ability), and summer programs for economically disadvantaged youths. Part B covers research and technical assistance

and training and labor market information. Part C covers youth programs added by the Youth Employment and Demonstration Projects Act of August, 1977.

Title IV.   Details the Job Corps, which is a residential program of intensive education, training, and counseling for the disadvantaged youths, with operations at 60 centers across the country. The Economic Stimulus Disappropriations Act (May 13, 1977) funded an extension of capacity from 22,000 to 44,000 openings.

Title V.   Established a National Commission for Manpower Policy, appointed by the president, comprised of federal, state, and local employment and training officials; people served by these programs; and members of the general public.

Purpose.   To identify the nation's employment and training needs, to research and evaluate the effectiveness of federal programs, and to report annually to the president and the Congress.

Title VIII.   Details the Young Adult Conservation Corps, which was added by the Youth Employment and Demonstration Projects Act and provides jobs and training for disadvantaged youth from all economic backgrounds. It is operated by the Department of Agriculture and the Department of the Interior, through an interagency agreement with the Department of Labor, in both residential and nonresidential settings. It offers work on conservation, wildlife, and recreation projects for 22,000 youth.[7]

Giving Credit Where Due

In assessing the utility and impact of CETA, many may argue that it was a nine-year $53 billion failure. Such conclusions are frequently drawn in the absence of supporting, objective analysis. Comprehensive research data exist that extend beyond the essentially distinctive aspects of the programs. The data encompass an integration of the multiple factors that are viable and those that are ill-conceived, nonfunctional, or not to the advantage of those whom they are intended to benefit. In spite of the difficulties experienced and the tremendous obstacles faced, the accomplishments of CETA, OIC, Private Industry Councils (PICS) and the National Alliance of Business (NAB), taken together, have been noteworthy. There are many who may take exception to this statement. The following success stories, provided by the National Alliance of Business Clearinghouse, are presented to illluminate the scope, diversity, and outcome of HRD programs for special populations.

SMALL BUSINESS INTERNSHIP PROGRAM

Type of Program. Combined preemployment education and work experience designed to lead to on-the-job level employment

Program Operator. Central Ohio Rural Consortium Employment and Training Administration

Major Program Goals and Distinctive Features. The program gives CETA-eligible clients basic preparation for the world of work and then places them in four-week internships with small firms that have entry-level openings. If the employer is satisfied with the intern's performance, the employer is encouraged to hire that worker under an on-the-job training agreement. Some employers choose to hire the person directly at the end of the internship.

Number of People Trained/Enrolled. In the first cycle, 27 enrolled; 21 completed preemployment training; and 19 entered internships or employment. In the second cycle, 24 enrolled, 19 completed preemployment training; and 15 entered internships or employment.

Cost Per Person. $2500 per person completing the program

Funding Level of Program. $100,000

The Learners. Twelve women and nine men completed the first cycle. The average age for men was 26.4 and for women was 28.7. The participants had an average of 11.7 years of schooling. One black was included in the first group (fewer than 4% of the county's population are black). Eighteen women and one man completed the second cycle. Two blacks were included in this second group, which was slightly older than the first.[8]

INROADS, INC.

Type of Program. Academic education and summer internships for minority youth of college age

Name of Operating Company/Organization. Inroads, Inc. headquartered in Chicago, Illinois

Unique Program Features. Inroads, Inc. is a nonprofit agency that operates a unique program in nine U.S. cities. The program is designed to prepare talented minority youth for highly competitive management positions in business and engineering. Funded by more than 300 major corporations, Inroads, Inc. recruits top graduates from inner-city high schools and offers them a four-year package of counseling, tutoring, and summer internships with sponsoring firms while they attend a local university. The program helps minorities overcome academic and cultural barriers so that they can enter the mainstream of corporate America.

Number of People Trained/Enrolled.   630 enrolled in nine cities in 1983

Cost Per Person. $1650-$1900 per year

Major Program Goals and Objectives.   The purpose of the program is to help minority students strengthen their academic and business-related skills to prepare them for leadership programs in America's corporations.

The Inroads, Inc. program began in Chicago in 1970 with 25 students. Since that time, it has spread to eight more cities throughout the United States. In 1983, major corporations sponsored 634 students.

The program is aimed exclusively at minorities. Approximately 85% are black and most of the remaining 15% are Hispanic. Thus far, participants have been almost evenly divided between men and women. Although the program is not funded by the government and does not need to select low-income students, approximately three-quarters of the students come from economically disadvantaged families.

Problems/Progress.   Inroads, Inc. defines *successful graduates* as those who complete the program and take jobs with Inroads, Inc. companies. Out of these graduates, 60% accepted positions in the corporations that sponsored them. The remaining 40% took jobs with other Inroads, Inc. firms.[9]

THE INSTITUTE FOR BUSINESS AND INDUSTRIAL TECHNOLOGY AND THE BUSINESS AND INDUSTRY MULTI-PURPOSE CENTER COLORADO SPRINGS, COLORADO

Type of Program.   A dual-purpose, one-stop center for skills training and education and business development

Program Operators.   City of Colorado Springs/El Paso County Industrial Training and Human Resource Development Administration (CETA prime sponsor), Colorado Springs Chamber of Commerce,

Colorado Springs Private Industry Council, and the city of Colorado Springs.

Major Goals and Distinctive Features. The major goals of the Institute for Business and Industrial Technology are to provide skilled workers to fill industry's employment needs and to prepare economically disadvantaged and other unemployed workers to fill those needs, particularly in high-technology fields. In addition, the center provides facilities and equipment to educate and train current employees.

The major goals of the Business and Industry Multipurpose Center are to provide, at cost, space for business activities: workshops, seminars, conferences, industrial shows, and business social occasions (e.g., chamber of commerce luncheons) and to provide a place for businesses to display their products.

A distinguishing feature of the program was the amicable working relationship among the local Comprehensive Employment and Training Act (CETA) administration, the city of Colorado Springs, and the business community. Business groups identified their training and education needs and developed the curricula; the CETA administrator implemented the needed learning programs; and the city acted as a landlord, providing space for training facilities. The Colorado Springs Private Industry Council (PIC) and the CETA planning council met as one body, pooled their resources, and made all program and funding decisions as a group.

Since the institute was not classified as a school, it was not subjected to regulation by the Colorado Department of Education. Thus, at an employer's request, its flexible programs could be used to deliver short, intensive courses in highly specialized subjects or, by contractual agreement with a college, to provide more general courses for which trainees received college credit.

Participating Companies. TRW, Inc., Texas Instruments Incorporated, Honeywell, Inc., Ampex Corporation, Rolm Corporation, Litton Data Systems, NCR Corp., Digital Equipment Corporation, United Technologies Corp., Inmos Corporation, and Hewlett-Packard Corporation participated in the project.

Because the local community and technical colleges took two years to train electronics technicians or machine operators—too slowly for business needs—the Local Industry Council revived the 1976 curriculum group to develop a purely technical curriculum for CETA trainees at Pike's Peak Community College and Colorado Technical College. The curriculum required no humanities, social sciences, or

other general education courses. This fast-track curriculum, instituted in 1977, gave trainees 30 hours per week of technical training
and enabled the colleges to train an electronics technician in 10 months
and a machine operator in six months.

The director, who was the city's CETA administrator, acted as a
broker to bring businesses that needed trained workers together with
training providers. On the other hand, the administrator could also
contract with a community-based organization or a private individual
to teach a noncredit course in a highly specialized subject like Equal
Employment Opportunity (EEO) regulations, a course tailored to the
needs of a particular firm.[10]

INSURANCE SERVICE TRAINING PROGRAM

Type of Program.   Classroom training in the insurance field

Program Operators.   Private Industry Council–National Alliance of
Business (PIC–NAB) of Atlanta and the Opportunities Industrialization Center (OIC) of Atlanta, Inc.

Major Program Goals and Distinctive Features.   The goal of the
Insurance Service Training Program is to prepare CETA-eligible
people for professional careers in the insurance field, a service
industry that is thriving in Atlanta. The intensive training course—
funded by the Atlanta PIC–NAB and operated by the Opportunities
Industrialization Center of Atlanta—is specifically designed to prepare trainees for national-certifying exams administered by the
Insurance Institute of America and the Life Officers Management
Association.

The specific training and placement objectives, set by the program
operators, are that 80% of the enrollees complete the training and be
placed in private sector insurance jobs. Upon graduation, participants
are qualified for entry-level positions as insurance underwriters,
claims adjustors, loss control experts, or field representatives—
professional jobs paying an average of $13,000–$17,000 a year to start.

Program Description.   Atlanta's Insurance Service Training Program is an eight-month course that offers economically disadvantaged
people an opportunity for professional careers in the casualty, property, or life insurance fields. The program is especially suited to the
city's needs, since Atlanta has a service-based economy and a strong
insurance industry.

The course began in 1978 as a demonstration project under CETA's Skill Training Improvement Program (STIP I). The curriculum was developed by the OIC of Atlanta, a branch of a national nonprofit organization offering employment and training services in approximately 150 cities. In designing the curriculum, OIC was assisted by a technical advisory committee composed of insurance industry representatives.

Three cycles of training were completed under the demonstration program, with 84% of the graduates finding jobs in the private sector.[11]

INTERNATIONAL BUSINESS MACHINES (IBM)
ARMONK, NEW YORK

Types of Projects.   Education, employment, community service, support to enterprises, and accommodation of the handicapped

Community Action Goals.   IBM is involved in an extensive range of community-based programs that give economically disadvantaged, minority, and handicapped people opportunities to obtain employment. The corporation's goal is to make these community programs self-sufficient.

Major Community Activities Affecting the Local Labor Force.   IBM supports two major entry-level job training projects: job training for the economically disadvantaged and computer programmer training for the severely disabled. In addition, it runs a work experience program (within the company) for deaf college students.

IBM also purchases products and services from minority-owned, female-owned, and handicapped-owned companies and participates in the National Minority Supplier Development Council.

Program Funding.   IBM has spent approximately $12.8 million since 1968 for job training and education programs for the economically disadvantaged, primarily for equipment and HRD staff. In addition, since 1973, IBM has provided approximately $1.7 million to support the computer programmer learning program for the severely physically disabled, mostly for transportation costs for IBM employees involved in start-up operations.

Job Training Programs for the Disadvantaged.   Under this program, IBM lends equipment, training materials, supplies, and IBM personnel to community-based organizations, for major job training and education centers, where disadvantaged students can learn data and word processing skills. Since the program began in 1968, more than 6000 participants have graduated, 80% of whom have been placed in jobs.

The first center opened in 1968 in Los Angeles, where IBM, in partnership with the Bank of America and the Urban League, founded a program that has graduated nearly 1900 formerly unemployed or underemployed people and placed almost 1600.

In December, 1978, the Urban League Word Processing Training Center was established in Washington, D.C. It has enrolled 234 students, most of whom are black females, and 163 have graduated. The entry-level salaries of graduates averaged $13,000 in 1981.

The school's success resulted from the Urban League's experience in tailoring programs for the economically disadvantaged and from IBM's business and management expertise, HRD staff, and equipment. The Washington, D.C. Private Industry Council assisted by providing funds and recruiting learners for the program. The District of Columbia government contributed the school building, and the Urban League provided administrative staff, counseling, and job development.

Students learned to operate such equipment as IBM's memory selectric typewriters, mag-cards, IBM dictation and transcription equipment, and word processors. They also studied business skills and academic subjects (including grammar, punctuation, spelling, and proofreading) and learned to prepare employment applications, write résumés, and interview for jobs.

In 1982, IBM expanded the number of major data and word processing job training and education centers from eight to nineteen. In addition to these major projects, there were more than 200 smaller HRD operations, for which IBM provided typewriters and data-entry machines that were used to instruct the disadvantaged in office skills. In total, approximately 160,000 people have graduated from IBM-supported job training and education centers.[12]

THE OPPORTUNITIES INDUSTRIALIZATION CENTER (OIC)[13]

A Case Study

The Opportunities Industrialization Center (OIC) is the survivor of many legislative changes over the past decade. It has a long history of successive victories. In its 14-year history, the program has grown from the confines of an abandoned jail to approximately 140 operating OICs in every state and in several foreign countries. The philosophies, strategies, and models for success of the OIC enhance the program's ability to meet its unique mission. The OIC epitomized the concept and ideals contained in the Job Training Partnership Act (JTPA). The language of the JTPA recognized the contributions of OIC and its unique qualifications in meeting the needs of special populations.

With the passage of the JTPA, the OIC has the opportunity to build the type of citizens that our country and the world must have to peacefully cohabit on this planet Earth in a progressive, growth-oriented atmosphere.

OIC was originally developed to serve the needs of disadvantaged, poor, unskilled, and unemployed minority people in Philadelphia. It has expanded into communities nationwide—city by city, town by town, state after state. Now there are operating OICs or developing OIC interest groups in every state.

This is how OIC operates:

1. *Recruiting Outreach.* OIC recruitment/outreach workers move out into the community to contact potential OIC enrollees in person, where they live or habitually gather. They contact young people, women with dependent children, and people who have given up hope of ever finding jobs and getting off welfare.

2. *Intake.* OIC counselors interview prospective enrollees and explain details of the program and outcomes to be expected. They review enrollees' job histories, experience, and school achievement. The beginnings of an employability plan are shaped through a mutual assessment process.

3. *Vocational and Personal Counseling.* Counseling is given to OIC enrollees at regular intervals throughout their OIC experience and even afterwards if needed.

4. *Orientation Assessment.* OIC counselors introduce small groups of learners to the OIC concepts of self-help, self-improvement, and ethnic pride. Building a sense of self-worth is the foundation for motivating helpless people to try, to work, to learn, to achieve, and to succeed.

5. *Feeder.* The OIC feeder program is designed to prepare enrollees for skills learning. OIC developed this diagnostic, learning, and motivational program phase, and it has been adopted by other employment and HRD professionals under the term *prevocational training.* Individual assessments, including identification of needs for computational and

communications skills, English language proficiency, and general functional competence, are made in the feeder program. Individual learning and program services to meet learners' needs are planned and instruction follows in areas matching such needs.

6. *Vocational Skills Training.* Over 100 specific skills areas are offered in OICs throughout the country. Curriculum planning is done by OIC job developers and local employers to better assure OIC learners of job placement upon completion of the learning. Local business and industry provides support to OIC affiliates.

7. *Job Development.* This phase is essential and a unique strength of OIC. Knowing employers' needs assists OIC to develop HRD efforts that match work force needs. Well before OIC enrollees complete the program, job developers work to arrange suitable job placement for them.

8. *Job Placement.* The goal for OIC enrollees is placement in employment that is related to their learning. All previous developmental steps in the comprehensive OIC service program are designed to lead to the matching of an OIC enrollee with a permanent employment opportunity that has growth potential.

9. *After Graduation Follow-Up.* Following the placement of an OIC enrollee, OIC counselors call on the new employee and the employer at regular intervals to determine whether either is having problems. Assistance is given in solving such problems.

10. *Supportive Services.* Service for the whole person means extensive counseling support. Counselors deal with the peripheral problems and concerns of an OIC trainee as well as employment and learning needs. OIC counselors help solve the problems that can deter eligible people from enrolling in OIC job services and from becoming economically independent. Family problems, transportation problems, housing problems, and work-related problems are dealt with so that the trainee can enter into the program without the worries that would detract from learning.

11. *Special Needs Programs.* OICs have developed specialized programs to meet the unique needs of such groups as ex-offenders, former drug users, seasonal and migrant farm workers, non-English–speaking people, women desiring to enter nontraditional occupations, youth, the handicapped, and veterans. OICs have entered into constructive working relationships with employee unions, economic and community development projects, youth diversionary programs, and housing renovation and rehabilitation programs. For employers, OIC has developed programs to

meet the special needs of industry, such as developing the skills of minority workers, operating in-plant HRD programs, solving onsite problems, conducting awareness training for supervisors, and providing specialized recruitment to bring minorities and women into new occupations. Some OICs have contracts with private industry to provide special readiness and occupational training.

FINDINGS

The most significant, but not surprising finding is that those programs that have been the most effective are the ones in which the private sector, industry, and the local community have collaborated in problem-solving efforts to operate programs that were tailored to meet specific needs.

THE JOB TRAINING PARTNERSHIP ACT
PUBLIC LAW 97-300 (S.2036)

History will be the ultimate judge of how successful or unsuccessful the programs of the past really were. In an attempt to build on the lessons of the past, on October 13, 1982, President Ronald Reagan signed into law the Job Training Partnership Act, Public Law 97-300 (JTPA). It became effective in October, 1983. President Reagan stated that it "beseeches business to do what it does best." William Kolberg, president of the National Alliance of Business, termed the act "A social experiment of tremendous significance." Pennsylvania Governor Richard Thornburgh called the act "Our moment of truth." James B. Campbell, president of Mississippi School Supply in Jackson, remarked that "Most jobs in the future will be in small- and medium-sized businesses, and each community knows best what these jobs are. Each area has the flexibility to gear its job training and retraining needs to its own market...and many of our institutions, such as the area voc-tech and junior colleges are already in place to help do the job." The Job Training Partnership Act not only served as a bridge from CETA to the present, but it provided a launching pad from which the future of special populations could be launched.

Assistant Labor Secretary Albert Ingrisam's statement denotes the gravity of the situation. He told the National Alliance of Business convention delegates, "We cannot afford to fail. You have your destiny in your hands."[14] The reality is that the destiny of the nation is at stake. The price of failure is too high to be considered negotiable. The details of the Job Training Partnership Act (JTPA) are of far-reaching significance.

The Specifics of the Job Training Partnership Act[15]

Introduction

The Job Training Partnership Act of 1982 marshals federal, state, and local resources to help prepare economically disadvantaged and long-term unemployed people to become productive labor force members.

For the first time, the private sector has equal responsibility with the government in shaping federally funded job-training programs. Through their chief elected officials and Private Industry Councils (PICs), localities have considerable flexibility to decide how funds are administered and how programs are managed.

The status of business as an equal partner is demonstrated by the fact that the PICs and the chief, locally elected official have joint policy-making responsibilities. Through the Job Training Partnership Act, the private sector has unprecedented latitude to shape local job-training programs.

The Job Training Partnership Act has five sections:

Title I.   Sets up the state and local delivery systems and addresses general program and administrative issues, delineating the public/private partnership

Title II.   Authorizes funding and sets requirements for local training services for disadvantaged youth and adults. It outlines population groups eligible for Title II assistance and the variety and limitations on Title II programs and services. Title IIA funds are for adult and year-round youth programs, and Title IIB money is for summer youth activities

Title III.   Establishes a program for dislocated workers

Title IV.   Establishes funding and requirements for federally administered programs

Title V.   Amends the Wagner-Peyser Act, the Social Security Act, and other laws to foster coordination with the job-training system

State and local delivery systems

Funding to the states began in October, 1983 for programs to train economically disadvantaged youth and adults.

Service delivery areas (SDAs) are the districts within a state through which direct job-training services are delivered. SDAs include more than one general purpose local government but do not split local political jurisdictions. Each SDA has a PIC. States have passed on 78% of their allocations to SDAs in the first fiscal year of operation.

The PIC shares overall policy and supervisory responsibility for local programs with chief, locally elected officials. The PIC represents local business leaders, who make up a majority of its members. Whenever possible, half of that business majority represents small businesses. Other PIC members represent education, organized labor, rehabilitation agencies, community-based organizations, economic development agencies, and the local employment service.

The State Job Training Coordinating Council shares decision-making authority for many state functions with the governor, who serves in an advisory capacity. The council, appointed by the governor, must have a nongovernmental chairperson and draw one-third of its membership from business and industry (including business representatives from local councils); at least one-fifth from state legislatures and state agencies; and at least one-fifth from other relevant interests. The state council plans, coordinates, and monitors state employment and training programs and services. It is not allowed to operate programs, to provide direct service programs, or to provide direct services.

Local public/private partnership

The Job Training Partnership Act sets up a new and unique public/private partnership. PICs and chief locally elected officials have balanced roles in program planning and management, with agreement between the public and private lenders required on most major policy issues. PICs and locally elected officials can choose who receives funds directly from the state, who administers the funds, and who operates the programs. PICs can exercise program supervision independently.

A two-year planning cycle is mandated by law, in order to encourage long-range planning and continuity of programs. Plans must be agreed upon by both the PIC and the chief, locally elected official. In labor markets with more than one SDA, plans for job development and placement activities must be coordinated.

Most PIC structure and management decisions are reserved for the PIC. Thus a PIC elected its own chair, decided whether or not to incorporate, and determined its own procedures for removing PIC members.

Activities and use of funds

The Job Training Partnership Act forces radical changes from past legislation regarding the design and content of training and education programs.

Client eligibility criteria specifies that 90% of all Title II participants be economically disadvantaged. At least 40% of the Title IIA funds are to be spent on year-round youth programs, with Aid to Families with Dependent Children (AFDC) recipients and school dropouts being served on an equitable basis.

Up to 10% of participants in all regular youth and adult programs (Title IIA) can qualify, regardless of income, if they face other employment barriers (e.g., displaced homemakers, handicapped people, older workers, etc.). Title IIA funds must be spent in the following ways: 70% on training and the remaining 30% divided between a maximum of 15% for administrative costs and 15% for wages, allowances, and support services. Significantly, the law mandates no specific types of programs. Local option is the determinant in this critical area.

All of a state's Title IIB summer youth funds must pass from states to local SDAs, with none of the 70/30 requirements that are applicable to Title IIA funds. The local plan should address youth, from ages 14 through 21.

The use of funds for Employment Generating Services (EGS) is unlimited as a percent of total funds, but EGS activities must contribute to increasing employment opportunities for eligible participants.

Performance standards

Rather than measuring compliance to process, performance standards are used to assess program effectiveness. Federally developed performance standards emphasize return on investment, quality (not just quantity) of training and placements, and reduction of welfare dependency.

Exemplary performance, as measured by the performance standards, is rewarded, and poor performance is penalized. Specifically, the governor can use up to 6% of Title IIA funds as incentive grants to reward superior performance in an SDA and must initiate a variety of strong corrective actions in response to poor performance.

Auditing, monitoring, and reporting

States establish fiscal controls and accounting procedures, and independent audits of each fund recipient must be conducted at least biennially under federal guidelines. Misspent funds must be repaid. While state and local agencies have program-monitoring responsibility, the Department of Labor (DOL) monitors certain aspects regarding use of federal funds. DOL also sets record keeping and management system standards.

Employment service

The legislation amends the Wagner-Peyser Act, which governs the U.S. Employment Service (ES), to forge a stronger link between the Employment Service's labor exchange function and local job-training programs for disadvantaged people. In particular, there are joint planning requirements for the local ES office, PICs, and locally elected officials. The law also revises ES funding formulas.

State roles

The governor, with assistance from the state job-training council, is responsible for coordinating state and local job-training programs with all other related activities administered through state agencies. (The 22% of Title IIA funds set aside is used for coordinating job-training services with state education and training agencies (8%) that provoide training for older workers (3%) and other program efforts.)

The law also authorizes a state dislocated workers program (Title III) to fund a wide variety of public and private activities that assist workers facing permanent job loss. A 50% nonfederal match is required.

Federal roles

Federally administered job-training and education activities include programs for native Americans, migrant and seasonal farm labor, and veterans. This is accomplished through the Job Corps; multi-state programs, research and demonstration, establishment of a comprehensive labor market information program, and a computerized job bank. The Department of Labor also funds the National Commission on Employment Policy, which advises the secretary on performance standards.[16]

THE PRESENT AND THE FUTURE

For the past several decades, U.S. workers have enjoyed the benefits of being employed by the highest paying industries in the world. They had two cars parked in their garages, a boat on the side, and a camper out back. The American dream was healthy. Any steel worker, auto assembler, or other related industry employee in the country would have agreed. No one dreamed that the "middle" would fall out. Then came the 1980s. Double-digit inflation coupled with double-digit unemployment brought back haunting memories of the Great Depression. Once proud, middle-class citizens who had felt that welfare should be abolished, that able-bodied people should work or starve, and that CETA and other such programs were a bad joke found themselves eagerly awaiting the next welfare check. Some stood in line all night with 2000 others waiting to apply for 200 jobs. The dream had taken a nasty, nightmarish turn. Why? What went wrong? The system had failed. The factory had closed, and daytime television was back in vogue. The city of Rockford, Illinois was front page news because it led the nation with 22% unemployment. Across the nation, record-breaking unemployment continued unabated for blacks, Hispanics, and several other minorities. Emergency legislation helped keep the wolf at bay but did not render long-term solutions. It defied reason to apply old solutions to new problems. JTPA and its accompanying emergency actions were a step in the right direction. Title II of the JTPA addressed this need specifically. Again, history will judge.

HRD practitioners must become involved in interdisciplinary and collaborative efforts and must look more closely and think more realistically of ways to solve problems of the present and coming decades.

At ASTD's request, Stanley T. Schrager, vice president of the Chase Manhattan Bank, testified before the House Subcommittee on Labor Standards and alerted Chairman George Miller, a Democrat from California, and his colleagues to the growing issues of a trained work force in the exploding data processing field. According to Schrager, "By 1990, the $100,000 non-managerial technicians will not be considered extraordinary."[17] The hearing was one of a series that focused on the impact of automation on employment in the work force. Schrager's statement underscores the philosophies put forth in *Megatrends*.[18]

CONCLUSION

We no longer live in an industrial society. We are, in fact, transforming into an information society or, as John Naisbitt called it, "the time of parenthesis."[19] The implications are staggering. The reality is that we are still focusing our HRD efforts and dollars on physical skills. All of the technologies at our disposal must be increasingly utilized to prepare employees to enhance their mental powers. There must be a balance achieved between the two. High-technology skill vacancies go wanting, with the need outdistancing the supply. (By applying a positive Pygmalion effect, rather than the misguided stereotypes that never had any usefulness and were much too costly, we can, and must, turn things around.)

The untapped capacities of the so-called disadvantaged and/or special populations can no longer go unnurtured and underutilized. Everybody loses. Special populations have special gifts, talents, and perspectives they can bring to a special situation. This necessitates a holistic approach to HRD. HRD mechanisms are needed to integrate the psychological, physical, and social skills necessary for meaningful existence in our society. These skills, coupled with a healthy self-concept, will ensure that all Americans can participate in the dream and make it a reality. The cooperation and collaboration of all parties involved is the key.

NOTES

1. Nadler, L. *Corporate Human Resources Development: A Management Tool*. New York: Van Nostrand Reinhold Co., 1980.

2. *American Society for Training and Development, National Report,* Vol. 9, No. 3. Washington, D.C.: ASTD, 1983.

3. Claque, E., and Kramer, L. *Manpower Policies and Programs: A Review, 1973-75.* Kalamazoo, Mich.: W.E. Upjohn Institute for Employment Research, 1976.

4. Levitan, Sar A., and Mangum, Garth L. *Federal Training and Work Programs in the Sixties.* Ann Arbor, Michigan: Institute of Labor and Industrial Relations, University of Michigan and Wayne State University, 1969.

5. Levitan, Sar. *Programs in Aid of the Poor for the 1980's.* 4th ed. Baltimore, Maryland: John Hopkins University Press, 1980.

6. Some of the data in this section is taken from Anderson, B.E., and Sawhill, I.V. *Youth Employment and Public Policy.* New Jersey: Prentice-Hall, Inc., 1980.

7. U.S. Department of Labor, Region V CETA Letter No. 83-3, November 10, 1982.

8. National Alliance of Business Clearing House Bulletin: #N383, July 1982.

9. Ibid., #N116, July 1980.

10. Ibid., #N394, October 1982.

11. Ibid., #N88, March 1981.

12. Ibid., #N344, March 1982.

13. The information provided in this section has been excerpted from the original OIC philosophy statement and other printed material presented by Dr. Leon H. Sullivan.

14. All the quotations cited above are found in Marth, D. "A Victory for Business and a Challenge." *Nation's Business,* January 1983, pp. 59–61.

15. The information provided in this section has been gathered from the National Alliance of Business. *Summary and Explanation of the Job Training Partnership of 1982,* October 6, 1982.

16. *Phase Down/Close Out of CETA Activities,* United States Conference of Mayors, Office of Urban Employment and Education, Washington, D.C., January 7, 1983; The National Alliance of Business. *Business Currents,* Vol. 3 (1), January 24, 1983, Supplement No. 1, January 4, 1983, Technical Bulletin, No. 6.

17. *American Society for Training and Development, National Report,* Vol. 8, No. 11. Washington, D.C.: ASTD, 1982.

18. Naisbitt, John. *Megatrends: Ten New Directions Transforming Our Lives.* New York: Warner Books, Inc., 1982.

19. Ibid.

CHAPTER TWENTY

Organized Labor

STEPHEN H. CONFER

Some of you may be very surprised to find a chapter about unions in a book devoted to human resource development. In part, this is due to the dichotomous approach that too often puts unions at one end of the continuum and employers at the other. This need not be the case. Although there are areas of conflict, there are many more areas of agreement. HRD is one such area.

This is the only chapter of this handbook in which the terms *training* and *education* are used differently. This is due to several unique factors in the history of the union movement in the United States. To minimize confusion, Confer's terms are being used, but they will always appear in italics so the reader will be able to differentiate between their use in the chapter and their use in the rest of the handbook. As Confer points out, there is not total agreement in the union movement on these terms, but they are the ones most commonly used.

Aside from terminology, you will find many areas of overlap

between what unions offer and what employers want. The gap that has existed between them in the HRD area is rapidly closing.

Stephen H. Confer is director of the Communication Workers of America (CWA) National Training Fund for the communications industry. He is also an administrative assistant to the president of the CWA. Previously, he was the CWA's director of education. He has authored numerous articles in areas related to labor and HRD.

INTRODUCTION

The history of organized labor is the history of men and women working collectively to improve their condition through education and training. While the popular picture of labor union activity is that of confrontation and, at times, violence, the long-term commitment to improving their members' skills as workers and citizens is more pervasive and central to labor unions. While education and training are normally the first casualties of economic downturn and restrictive budgets in other organizations, union policy-making bodies have traditionally chosen other areas of their activities for reduction, when such steps have been necessary.

This chapter will discuss the extent of human resource development activities within organized labor and those sponsored by unions alone or jointly by labor and management. It will not attempt to analyze individual programs or to provide a "how to" guide to establishing labor union HRD programs. For these reasons, much of this chapter will consist of historical recitation and comparisons. Obviously, there is a need to provide a context within which this group of providers of HRD activities can be better understood.

A MODEL OF HRD ACTIVITIES IN THE LABOR MOVEMENT

These activities in organized labor have been known by several names over the years. *Labor education, labor studies*, and *workers' education* are the labels that have been attached to training and education activities sponsored by unions. Indeed, the number of varied labels have prompted a number of articles by practitioners in the field. They have attempted to bring order to both the labels and to the wide range of activities associated with them. It has been helpful to me to consolidate this work of others into a simple model that serves as a framework for classifying a diverse field. It might be useful to point out that practitioners in one area of the field, using a term to describe what they are doing, do not necessarily agree that others, using the same term to describe what they are doing, are entitled to do so, due to the differing natures of their work. Furthermore, some organizations are successfully active in more than one area of the field.

The model I use for describing human resource development activities within organized labor ascribes different sets of activities to *workers' education, labor studies*, and *labor education*.[1] All of the activities included in the three terms have a common intellectual bias. It is this bias that marks the difference between the HRD activities sponsored by business, industrial, and governmental organizations and those sponsored by organized labor. Indeed, all too often, there are practitioners whose skills might well fill a useful purpose within union programs, but they are not acceptable, due to their misperception of the bias upon which these programs are built.

Labor education is a set of activities with the objective of improving the effectiveness of the union representative doing his or her union job. Grievance handling is normally the most basic activity undertaken by these persons. On a day-to-day basis, most union representatives spend the majority of their time and energy processing grievances. Interviewing grievants, researching precedents, interpreting contracts, and making skillful presentations are all inherent to the effective processing of grievances. So, too, are the skills that make it possible to refuse to process a grievance when it does not have merit. Recently, court decisions have made these decisions increasingly more critical under the "failure to represent" principle.

In addition, most unions, through their own HRD departments, provide a series of programs designed to improve the immediately needed skills of their local and national representatives. Local officers must learn to manage offices, staff, and budgets. They must improve their platform skills and their understanding of the nature of groups. Full-time staff members of national unions normally undergo some training as an introduction to the nature of their jobs. While the extent and depth of these programs vary, unions have a deep and abiding commitment to the concept of developing their human resources, as a way of improving the effectiveness of the union.

While most unions have their own mechanisms for the delivery of these training activities, in those cases for which they do not, they make use of university *labor education* centers. Delivery through these centers may be sponsored jointly by the center and the individual union whose representatives are attending, or they may be made available by the center alone and open to a number of unions in the immediate geographical area.

In comparison to *labor education, labor studies* is characterized by its more theoretical content and less direct application. It is directed at those with more than a passing interest in the labor movement and with a possibility of deeper, longer-term involvement in its activities. It is more than the study of the labor movement and its environment. Many times, it is associated with some university-sponsored, credit program and is more traditionally academic.

Subject areas covered by a *labor studies* curriculum include, but are not limited to, sociology and social psychology applications to workers' organizations; practical politics, comparative political systems, and the American political structure; the application of psychology to effective leadership; and the American economic system and its implications for the labor movement. In addition, university *labor studies* programs and many individual unions sponsor short programs to provide their leaders and interested members with information about laws currently under consideration by Congress and the state legislatures. They also acquire information about collective bargaining issues, directions in labor-management relations, and the current economic conditions.

The third term used as a descriptor in the model is *workers' education*. Activities included under this term are those designed to contribute to the awareness and effectiveness of workers as participants in the economic, political, cultural, and social systems. There are any number of activities that may be described under this label. It is, essentially, where the labor movement meets the system in the providing of activities for its members. *Workers' education* programs can include cultural and workers' rights activities, presentations on labor history, and vocational and apprenticeship training. Unions have sponsored panel discussions on the major events in our economic and political life. The Communications Workers of America has sponsored a series of panels, through public television, on the changing nature of communications and its impact on our working and political lives. Unions have contributed to the writing and producing of plays that depict episodes in labor history. They were instrumental in producing a series of filmed documentaries that was made available to the public through public television. The leaders of the American labor movement were most active in the establishment of the public communications network in the United States and are most supportive of its continued existence.

While individual unions and university centers have sponsored many of the programs of this type, there are a number of joint labor-management programs as well. Most apprenticeship programs are jointly administered and fall into the category of *workers' education*. Further, while the potential growth and applicability of apprenticeship may be questioned, other joint HRD ventures have been created for the purpose of addressing the massive training and education dilemma that has recently faced our nation's businesses. There is a genuine commitment on the part of many of our business and labor leaders to solve this dilemma through joint action.

While practitioners of HRD may, and often do, argue about the extent, relevance, and nature of their activities inside the labor movement, there are, in fact, substantial collaborative efforts to train and educate union members and their leaders. Many of the complaints uttered by these practitioners sound very much like those of their colleagues in business, industry, and government. Those shared complaints seem to center on their perception that if more people take part in the programs offered and make greater use of the available skills of the HRD practitioner, the skills of the leader and the organization would improve. "One of the reasons for the limitations of labor education is the reluctance of the union movement to utilize it as an integral part of its existence."[2] Just as in other parts of our socioeconomic system, some labor organizations have a deeper and longer-term commitment to training and education than others. On the other hand, some practitioners have been more successful in making their cases than have others. In this sense, there is little difference between HRD activities inside the labor movement and those that occur elsewhere.

One difference is the bias, referred to earlier, that directs the activities within the labor movement. While HRD practitioners in the business and industrial world are encouraged to direct their attention to their organization's profitability and to how their efforts contribute or detract from it, there is no equivalent, measurable result to which HRD practitioners in the labor movement can be directed. Their activities are directed toward social change, with training and education as the media. Even where there is disagreement over the nature and goals of human resource development activities in the labor movement, the primary orientation is toward change. One author, while discussing these disagreements, makes this point: "Is the primary purpose of labor education or labor studies to socialize and indoctrinate participants to the goals, values, and actions of the labor movement, or should it be an instrument for changing goals, values, and traditions?"[3]

HISTORICAL PERSPECTIVES

Early on, unions recognized that education and training were important to the economic development of their members and to the integration of immigrants into the general society.

From the 1840s up to the 1880s, education was viewed by many organized workers as an instrument for changing the social system. The Knights of Labor, perhaps the last major federation of labor to share this belief, saw education as a means by which labor would abolish the wage system and replace it with a cooperative commonwealth.[4]

This interest took many forms. Some of them were uncoordinated efforts that seemed to have the almost mystic vision of a society of loyal, effective workers well schooled and devoted to intellectual development, working within a "cooperative commonwealth." Perhaps this vision is recognizable, due to shared characteristics with the Japanese system as it has been presented to us in the popular literature. For example, in some work locations, people were at times sponsored to read the classics aloud while workers were at their jobs, laboring in spiritually and physically crushing environments. Other efforts were more pragmatic and included citizenship and English language classes for immigrants.

Early in their history, unions included education and training activities as a part of their formal structure. The International Ladies Garment Workers' Union established an internal "education" department in 1900. This was closely followed by similar department formations by the American Federation of Hosiery Workers in 1913 and the Amalgamated Clothing Workers in 1914. The activities of these new departments were oriented more toward what we are here calling *labor studies* and *workers' education* than to *labor education*.[5] What these early organizations did, however, established the standard against which later efforts have been measured.

Labor education specifically directed at women workers was a significant fixture early in the development of these programs. The Young Women's Christian Association was an early leader in these developments when it passed resolutions concerning learning for women in industry at its 1910, 1919, and 1920 conventions. The YWCA also established an industrial department to provide learning opportunities for women in industry—an effort that the YWCA still continues. At the 1916 convention of the National Women's Trade Union League, women's colleges were urged to open their doors to working women during the summer months. In 1921, the Bryn Mawr Summer School for Women Workers in Industry held its first session.[6]

The year 1921 was important in other ways for *labor education* efforts. A group of *labor educators* and union leaders determined a need for an organization to promote the growth of *labor education* efforts, particularly those under the administrative control of unions. The organization that was founded, the Workers' Education Bureau, was the forerunner of other organizations created to promote *labor education*, including the Affiliated Summer Schools and Local 189 (originally a local union of the American Federation of Teachers).

Following World War II, *labor education* programs were developed at several universities in highly unionized industrial states through the universities' extension services.

Programs that came to be known as "labor studies" grew out of the efforts of colleges and universities to extend services to organized labor. At least four factors contributed to this transition: (1) the demand for "relevance" in higher education and the concomitant growth of "area" studies programs; (2) the awareness that the "tool course" approach of labor education, however necessary, was insufficient to cope with social problems that transcend employment relationships and collective bargaining; (3) the pressure for credentialing; and (4) working-class insistence on the right to receive a liberal education in a supportive atmosphere.[7]

While universities were actively establishing departments to provide support to labor organizations, unions were arguing that land grant institutions had the obligation, under the terms of their charters, to provide services to working men and women as well as the organizations that represented them. Whether the universities or the labor organizations were more effective in exerting pressure for the growth of these programs, it remained that by 1976 there were 6000 students in *labor studies* credit programs. The majority of these were union members who studied part time and were over 25 years old.[8]

From time to time, the federal government has also taken steps to promote the growth of HRD programs oriented toward organized labor. This support was based on the premise that productivity growth and labor peace were appropriate goals for the government to pursue. Pursuit of these goals has, at times, been centered on the assumption that the more prepared (through training) the leaders of the various unions are as they conduct their daily business, the greater the possibility that industrial conflict will be resolved through means other than confrontation.

In 1943, the Division of Labor Standards of the U.S. Department of Labor published *Preparing a Stewards' Manual* and *Settling Plant Grievances*. These pamphlets were designed to be used in the training of labor leaders, and in 1944, the division used them in various *labor education* classes. In 1946, Congress established the Labor Education Service, which conducted a number of activities during its one-year life. From time to time, labor representatives have argued for the further development of these programs on the basis of an access to resources equal to that enjoyed by the business and industrial community.

Government attention to what we have previously identified as *workers' education* has been more continuous, although such support has indeed varied from administration to administration. Although a survey of locally run apprenticeship programs indicated that only a small minority made use of any government funds for the support of their operations, a number of national and regional programs have done so, and it has resulted in making great contributions to their overall effectiveness. For example, the Operating Engineers used funds from a Department of Labor program to develop a set of job-related competencies. This work has since been developed into a competency-based apprenticeship program. Thus the union, in this case, was not only willing to address the issue of time versus competency-based apprenticeship, they found that many of their members who had previously experienced the time-based apprenticeship preferred the newer system, as it assured the continued, highly skilled stature the craft had enjoyed in the past.

During the late 1970s, the Bureau of Apprenticeship and Training of the Department of Labor solicited unions to establish apprenticeship standards and programs in occupations that had not had them previously. An extensive promotional effort was conducted, with teams of bureau representatives meeting with union and employer representatives to determine potentials and levels of interest. From that effort grew the New Initiatives program, which provided start-up funds for organizations interested in further developing the apprenticeship concept for other job titles. New career areas promoted under this program varied from a number in the performing arts to those in the communications and electronics industries. Some still continue, in spite of the lack of administrative support in the early 1980s.

In addition, the current upsurge of interest within joint labor-management committees to address areas such as safety and health, productivity, technological change, and the quality of working life, has resulted in a range of government programs to promote and assist these efforts. Of special note is the program of technical assistance established by the Federal Mediation and Conciliation Service (FMCS). The FMCS provides a wide range of learning and consulting services to labor and management groups wishing to establish mechanisms for the improvement of their long-range relationship. They have also sponsored national conferences to facilitate information flow about new and particularly interesting efforts in this field.

CURRENT ACTIVITIES

The current scope and range of HRD activities in the labor movement is growing in some respects and changing in others. Unions and universities continue to develop and sponsor programs for their leadership and members. In some respects, however, reports from those programs indicate a change in the way the participants and their sponsors view them. In the past, these programs contained a strong element of indoctrination that was designed to develop: (1) loyalty to the union and its leaders; (2) knowledge of the ideals and principles of the labor movement; and (3) the skills and knowledge necessary to carry out the union jobs of the participants. Recently, HRD practitioners in the labor movement have remarked that participants are making stronger demands for more professional programs that are more specifically directed to their needs.

Naturally, the ups and downs of the economy, together with the growth and demise of some of its segments, resulted in some very innovative programs being endangered or reduced in scope. Over the years, several unions developed residential learning centers designed to provide a range of services to their members and leaders. One of the most innovative of these was built by the United Auto Workers in Black Lake, Michigan. This well-designed facility was constructed to operate year round, supplying training and education to improve the union-related skills of its leaders and members. One of the center's early programs provided for the families of the persons attending. The families were allowed to attend and to take part in seminars and discussions about the union, the labor movement, their spouses' roles, and the impact of their spouses' union involvement on the family and marriage.

The most extensive of the residential HRD programs sponsored by the labor movement is the George Meany Center for Labor Studies. Established by action of the AFL-CIO Executive Council in 1969, the Meany Center has developed into the major force guiding union-related HRD activities in this country. Since the Meany Center is the creation of multiple unions and involves itself in a wide range of activities, it has an impact on the labor movement's HRD that is disproportionate with its size and budget. Clearly, this can only be attributed to the vsion of the executive council who established the structure of the center and the efforts of its staff to assure quality and learner-centeredness.

As an example of the extent of the programs conducted at the center, the 1982 trustees' report shows that 3284 labor leaders attended programs there. Some attended one of the 44 multiunion programs, others attended one of the 12 programs sponsored by individual unions using center staff, and others attended one of the 33 programs conducted by 12 unions using their own staff. These programs varied and included the basics of collective bargaining, organizing, arbitration, psychology for the union leader, union administration, and labor law. In addition, the more trendy subjects, such as computers, the automated office, issues in the economy, dealing with the news media, stress, unions in the year 2000, international affairs and technological change were also included.

In addition, the center conducts a four-year *labor studies* degree program in cooperation with Antioch College. This program permits labor leaders who never had the opportunity to obtain what they normally consider precious credentials to expand their knowledge of the larger world within which labor relations are conducted. There are approximately 300 persons taking part in this program, and approximately 100 have graduated.

The center also has an active arts program and an artist in residence. Participants in the various programs are exposed to sculpture, painting, photography, music, and theater. For an extended period, a collection of the works of the center's namesake, George Meany, was exhibited on the lobby walls.

A program that is conducted at the Meany Center, but with a separate staff, is that of the American Insitute for Free Labor Development (AIFLD). The AIFLD programs provide opportunities for hundreds of labor leaders from South and Central America to receive basic training in the skills needed for effective union leadership. In 1982, approximately 300 people attended extended programs in their native language at the center. These efforts were started and continue because of the American labor movement's conviction that a free labor movement is a necessary precondition for a free political system. Not only is the AIFLD supported by contributions from labor, but the business, industrial, and government sectors of our society also make contributions.

FORCES FROM THE FUTURE

As the situation changes, new approaches and new relationships are required to address the changing work force. There is a significant movement away from U.S. dominance of economics and technology to international interdependence. D. Quinn Mills[9] pointed to a number of significant demographic trends in our work force during the 1980s. He suggests that these trends will be important to human resource planners.

The labor force will increase 12% during the 1980s compared to 21% during the 1970s.

The percentage of women in the work force will increase slowly from 41%.

Women entering the work force will be better schooled. In 1950, enrollment was 68% male and 32% female. By 1978, the number of women enrolled in higher education equaled that of men.

Workers over 55 years old will decrease from 17.5% of the work force to 11.2%.

Our work force will continue to be supplemented substantially by 3 to 12 million illegal aliens.

The greatest employment growth will occur in the South and West, where there is a concentration of illegal aliens.

Black unemployment will increase, due to concentration of that part of the work force in the North and East.

In addition, our school system is coming under increasing attack by writers and politicians for not delivering graduates with the levels of skills and knowledge necessary for success in an increasingly complex world. Science and mathematics teachers are increasingly attracted to the high salaries offered by private industry. In a statement before the House Committee on Science and Technology, George A. Keyworth[10] pointed out the nationwide trend toward reduction of high school graduation requirements in mathematics and science. As a result of this trend, colleges have reduced their math and science requirements for admission. Only 9% of our high school students take physics, 15% take chemistry, and only 3% take calculus. Seven states require no high school math at all.[11]

While the nature of the work force is changing, so too are the jobs to be filled by that work force, due to increased automation in the factory and the office. Automation will directly affect 45 million jobs. Surprisingly, as a *Business Week* article pointed out, 38 million of those jobs are in the office environment rather than in the factory environment where automation is normally pictured.[12]

Yet, even those jobs in factories are increasingly scheduled for major change. The introduction of increasingly sophisticated components in manufactured items has already significantly reduced the numbers of persons directly involved in the manufacturing process. As an example, NCR reported in 1975 that the electronic products they were manufacturing at that time were produced using only 25% of the labor required by their predecessors.[13]

More important, however, is the change in the composition of the work force associated with the manufacture of communications equipment as it becomes increasingly electronic in nature. For crossbar, or mechanical switching, 92.3% of the manufacturing work force was directly involved in materials fabrication, assembly, and wiring. Only 7.7% were involved in testing and quality control. However, for the more sophisticated digital switching equipment, those figures become 58.3% and 41.7%, respectively.[14]

The greatest impact will be felt in the office and similar environments. It has been estimated by *U.S. News and World Report* that 70% of the employees at General Motors are involved in the creation or manipulation of information, as opposed to direct manufacture.[15] It is clear that the pressure to improve productivity has resulted in a change of focus from the factory floor to the carpeted office.

Naturally, a great deal has been written regarding the nature of the changes that face our society. All of these writings claim to be the accurate description of the new age into which we are supposed to be moving. One group of writers praises high technology as the salvation of a lagging economy. Another group tells us that the future success of our nation depends upon our ability and commitment to reindustrialization. A third group tells us that the high technology promise has failed, and as proof of that failure, they point to Atari's decision, as reported in an issue of *The Wall Street Journal*, to move their manufacturing facilities outside the United States.[16] These conflicting points of view raise questions about the descriptions of the future that are being presented.

Most authors writing about the future describe it as moving from a current, recognizable situation to one that is not so recognizable. Some describe it as a change from dependence upon basic industry to a dependence upon electronics and computers. Others describe it in terms of geographical shifts from the traditionally industrialized North and East to the less-developed South and West. Still others describe the future as the shift from industry to service, from large organizations to small, and from centralization to distribution. It is my contention that while all of these are legitimate observations of the current situation, they are symptoms of a more basic change that has significant meaning for the human resource development professional.

A group of persons employed in the communications industry were faced with a list of inputs and outputs and the request to determine which of the inputs and outputs would increase or decrease in demand over time (see Figure 20.1). After considerable discussion, they concurred that the demand for capital, entrepreneurship, and knowledge would increase, while the demand for labor and natural resources would decrease. Further discussion provided some clarification of their definition of the term *labor* as observed, physical effort toward a goal.

In the same manner, this group was asked to identify which of the outputs would increase and which would decrease. There was agreement that products would decrease and that knowledge and service would

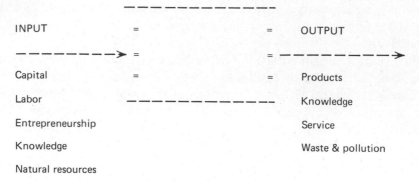

Figure 20.1. A simple input-output model of the economic system.

increase. Again, some discussion clarified their definition of the term *product* as something physical and tangible.

Some patterns began to emerge as a result of these discussions. It became clear that knowledge was taking on dimensions in the economic system that it had not had before. In the first place, knowledge was identified as both an input and an output. Second, it was anticipated that the demand for knowledge and the amount of knowledge generated would increase. Knowledge was apparently acquiring greater economic value. Third, tangible and observable inputs and outputs were on the decrease, while those not so readily observable (and measurable) were on the increase.

From this examination emerges the contention that our economy has moved from a production orientation to a knowledge orientation. In other words, when it is suggested that the electronic, computer, or biotechnology industries are examples of the new kind of industry, which will typify the new economic system toward which we are supposed to be moving, a point has been missed. What, indeed, is truly different between the production of an automobile and a computer? Production lines all look pretty much alike. The work that people do on production lines is pretty much the same. Certainly, there are differences, but those differences are mostly a function of the end product and not the essential work being done. Production is still broken down into small units with different people performing highly segmented portions of the total production.

It is the possession, generation, and application of knowledge that is the difference. By the time a product has reached the point where mass production is possible, it is old technology that is being applied. The knowledge that was used to generate that product has already been changed and increased as the result of the development of that product and toward the end of generating new ones. The knowledge is growing and vital, while products made possible by its past application are becoming obsolete and shopworn.

If it is true that knowledge will constitute greater and greater proportions of both input and output in our economic system, then that fact should also be reflected in the skills and knowledge requirements of the jobs in the economic system. The same group of workers in the communications industry, described previously, were asked to respond to a survey in an attempt to determine whether the complexity of the skills and knowledge required to perform work has been changing over the past few years. They were asked to think back to when they first went to work in the industry and to reflect on the job to which they aspired at that time. They were asked to list as many of the skills and knowledge areas as they could remember that were required to perform that job— even if those skills have since disappeared. For each skill, each person applied a ranking scale, assigning the number 1 if the skill was relatively simple, contained few steps, and no decisions on the part of the worker. A ranking of 2 was assigned if the skill was moderately difficult, with many steps, and very few decisions. If the skill was difficult, with several steps and many decisions for the worker to make, a ranking of 3 was assigned. In the same manner, for each of the knowledge areas identified, a ranking of 1 was assigned if the worker had only to memorize information and supply it upon demand. A ranking of 2 meant the worker was required to find and then to apply information to varying situations. If the worker was required to make comparisons, to analyze information, and to act upon that analysis and comparisons, a ranking of 3 was indicated. The analysis of this data indicated that the hypothesis of increasing complexity in the work to be performed is indeed true.

The respondents were divided into two groups depending upon the length of time they had been working in the communications industry. As Figures 20.2 and 20.3 illustrate, those with fewer years in the industry viewed the desired job as requiring skills and knowledge of much greater complexity.

The data used to develop Figures 20.2 and 20.3 are not in a form that permits an accurate examination of the comparative skill and knowledge content of the jobs as they were viewed by the two age groups. Therefore, it cannot be said that there is conclusive proof that one job contains more skills or knowledge than another. It is the relative shape of the curves that is intended to demonstrate the points being made here.

While these data (see Figures 20.2 and 20.3) cannot be regarded as definitive, they are suggestive of some trends. While work is becoming

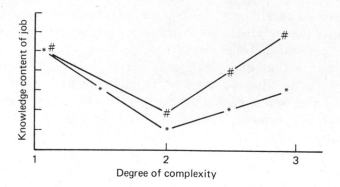

Figure 20.2.   Comparisons of degree of complexity of the knowledge required to perform work.

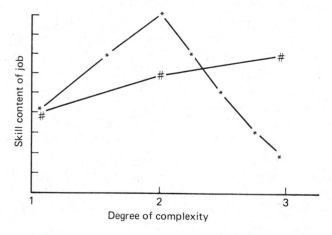

Figure 20.3.   Comparisons of the degree of complexity of the skill required to perform work. (*) Respondents with 14 to 35 years of experience in the communications industry; (#) respondents with 6 to 11 years of experience in the communications industry.

increasingly complex, the worker is coming to the work situation with decreased preparation. The employer has two possible responses to this situation.

The first is to engineer out the human element where possible and to depend upon a few "super techs" to deal with the equipment situations where engineering and technology cannot bypass human decision making. With this approach, jobs will be fractured, as those tasks with automation potential are submitted to analysis. This will result in a reduction in the need for the numbers of highly skilled individuals, who will be replaced by low skilled attendants of computer terminals, carrying out the equivalent tasks with lower deviations from standards and at lower costs. A small task force would be sent in to deal with those tasks that could not be automated or could be automated only at major costs.

The second response is to establish a mechanism to provide continual learning for personnel. This approach assumes that the basic math and science skills have already been learned. If they have not, then the employer must be willing to undertake this task at what will probably be considerable expense.

Clearly, the problem is of such significance that no one segment of society can be expected to undertake the solution alone. The school system is already overburdened and underfinanced. Some employers do not feel it is their responsibility to address the problem of the lack of basic skills with which their new employees are coming to work. The workers are frustrated as they attempt to carry out their work and to make progress in their careers in an environment where they understand less and less. The situation does call for the development of new ways of doing things and a reassessment of the appropriateness of the traditional adversary approach to dealing with differences.

THE RESPONSE TO CHANGE: SOME DIRECT APPROACHES

The labor movement's most widely known approach to human resource development is apprenticeship. *Apprenticeship* is an age-old form of skill development. As it is implemented today under the minimum standards of the Bureau of Apprenticeship and Training, it consists of two distinct components.

1. Planned on-the-job training under the supervision of skilled journeyworkers and following a set of predefined work processes essential to the craft.
2. Related education and instruction in the theory and knowledge of the craft.

Apprenticeship is voluntary in nature, since in most cases where it exists it is a matter of negotiated agreement between an employer or a group of employers and an organization representing the employees. It is usually administered by a joint committee of employer and employee representatives. Financial support is a negotiated item, and while that support may be looked upon as an employer contribution, it may also be considered the result of an employee decision to divert some portion of their total compensation to the support of learning activities. Also, apprentices generally attend classes and complete the related classroom instruction portion on their own time and without pay.

Since the educational component of apprenticeship provides for planned on-the-job training and does not generally result in a loss of productivity that could have been caused by time off the job, apprenticeship is probably an extremely cost effective method of skill development. Thomas Gilbert estimated that for the typical U.S. company sponsoring the standard classroom-oriented learning activity, learner costs constituted 90% of the total cost of the activity.[17] Because apprentices are not normally paid for their classroom time, this portion of their learning costs does not accrue to the participating employer. Further, the costs of curriculum and materials development are shared, in many cases, among several employers, lowering the cost of learning even more. Some recent data from the American Vocational Association provide an indication of the return on an investment in learning. Classroom instruction returns $1.14 for every dollar invested, while on-the-job training returns $2.28 for every dollar invested.[18] As apprenticeship incorporates both components, there is some indication of the cost effectiveness of that approach.

A worker's total compensation consists of wages plus the costs of various benefits and payments to funds and plans on his or her behalf; required contributions that the worker must make are subtracted. This is often made very clear to the worker when the results of bargaining are discussed and voted upon. It might be expected that there would be some opposition on the part of workers to diverting some of their total compensation to their own learning, particularly in industries where HRD has traditionally been the responsibility of the employer. However, there is some indication that the resistance may not be as great as expected. A survey of 400 technicians in the communications and electronics fields indicated that after a distribution of total compensation to wages, pension, and health plans was completed, they felt that the next most important area to which money should be distributed was HRD. Indeed, the data indicated that 10% of total compensation should be distributed to HRD.

The current interest in the establishment of joint labor-management committees to address a wide range of issues, including productivity, safety and health, and quality of working life, would suggest a similar interest in the growth and resurgence of joint apprenticeship and HRD committees. That is not so, however. The facts do not support a growing interest. While the Bureau of Apprenticeship and Training estimates that there are 50,000 programs in the nation, the most extensive list of active programs has only 1400 entries. In addition, information reported in 1983 by the bureau in the *Employment and Training Report of the Secretary* indicated that there were 300,000 apprentices in each of the past three years.[19]

A survey of the directors of 18 joint apprenticeship programs indicated that only three had made any changes in their curriculum during a year and only six had any plans to do so in the future. The kinds of changes that did take place or were planned to take place are of interest. One added a solar-heating component to their program, another added supervision, and the third added office skills. One respondent indicated that they had added numerically controlled manufacturing to their curriculum but removed it at a later date.

In general, the joint labor-management approach, in its application to HRD, has taken some interesting turns. The United Auto Workers negotiated an agreement with Ford Motor Company that established a jointly administered Employee Career Development Plan (ECDR). The Ford/UAW ECDR provided for employer contributions to a fund that would be used to maintain workers' technological currency. Of particular import was the fact that the developments need not be in the automobile industry, but might be elsewhere as the industry changed. It also provided for the education of laid-off workers for jobs outside the automobile industry, permitting up to $3000 per laid-off Ford worker. The UAW and General Motors have negotiated a similar agreement.

The Communications Workers of America (CWA) has announced its intention to establish similar programs in their agreements with their employers. Its Committee on the Future has established specific goals for a "strategy-driven" union with training and education as a major strategy. They have also established a joint National Training Fund for the communications industry. It is designed as a self-supporting, entrepreneurial organization that will provide learning for CWA members through tuition-refund programs, access to state vocational funds, and other sources of funds and programs.

The Sheet Metal Workers Union has established a curriculum through its national joint committee for the installation of solar-heating systems. The Department for Professional Employees of the AFL-CIO, working with the entertainment unions and employers, has written standards for apprenticeship programs in the performing arts. The Operating Engineers have developed competency-based apprenticeship, as opposed to time-based apprenticeship, and have successfully implemented this approach with the approval and encouragement of their journeyworkers and participating employers. While the list is not endless, it is substantial and suggestive of the kinds of opportunities that are currently being pursued.

There is no question but that the labor movement in the United States has been a significant factor in developing human resources. Unions have had a long history of providing HRD for their members under a variety of labels.

We have now entered a new era in which there is closer cooperation between unions and employers in their efforts to provide HRD for the workers. Additional opportunities for cooperation are being created and will contribute to productivity, labor peace, and the general welfare of the American worker, so long as neither management nor labor approach them with narrow, short-term objectives. Some of this is due to the pressure of unemployment, regardless of the cause. The new approaches are also a manifestation of unions' intent to contribute to increased productivity (and to receive a fair share of its benefits) but to avoid the negative practices that some employers have used in the past.

All parties recognize that union-management strife is detrimental to the interests of individuals and their country. By becoming more involved in HRD programs, unions seek an opportunity to make positive contributions to the economic and social health of our country.

NOTES

1. Stephen H. Confer, "HRD Activities and Organized Labor," in *Critical Research Issues Facing HRD*, ed. Jay Alden (Washington, D.C.: American Society for Training and Development, 1981), p. 144.
2. Al Nash, "Labor Education, Labor Studies, and the Knowledge Factor," *Labor Studies Journal* 3 (1978): 9.
3. Dieter Schachhuber, "The Missing Link in Labor Education," *Labor Studies Journal* 4 (1979): 149.
4. Nash, *Labor Studies Journal*, pp. 7–8.
5. Florence Henley Schneider, *Patterns of Workers' Education* (Washington, D.C.: American Council on Public Affairs, 1941).
6. Richard E. Dwyer, "Evolution of the Affiliated Schools in Workers' Education from Coordination to Educational Service," *Labor Studies Journal* 2 (1977): 38–39.
7. Richard E. Dwyer, Miles E. Salvin, and Simeon Larson, "Labor Studies in Quest of Industrial Justice," *Labor Studies Journal* 2 (1977): 118.
8. Lois Gray, "Labor Studies Credit and Degree Programs: A Growth Sector of Higher Education," *Labor Studies Journal* 1 (1976): 115–22.
9. D. Quinn Mills, "Human Resources in the 1980's," *Labor Studies Journal* (1978): 156.

10. George A. Keyworth, Statement before the Committee on Science and Technology, U.S. House of Representatives (Washington, D.C.: Executive Office of Science and Technology Policy, 1981).

11. General Robert T. Marsh, Speech before the Armed Forces Communications and Electronics Association (Washington, D.C.: November, 1981).

12. "Changing 45 Million Jobs," *Business Week*, August 3, 1981, pp. 62–67.

13. Confer, *Critical Research Issues Facing HRD*, p. 144.

14. Confer, *Technology—Its Impact on CWA—Today and Tomorrow* (Washington, D.C.: Communications Workers of America, 1980).

15. "Where Hot New Careers Will Open in the '80s," *U.S. News and World Report*, December 7, 1981, pp. 70–71.

16. "Warner Plans Layoff of 1,000 at Its Atari Unit," *The Wall Street Journal*, June 27, 1983, p. 5.

17. Thomas F. Gilbert, *Human Competence* (New York: McGraw-Hill, 1978), p. 221.

18. "Classroom Training Pays Off," *AVA Update*, November/December, 1981, p. 3.

19. U.S. Department of Labor, "The National Apprenticeship Program," *Employment and Training Report of the Secretary, 1983* (Washington, D.C.: U.S. Department of Labor, 1983).

BIBLIOGRAPHY

"Changing 45 Million Jobs." *Business Week*, August 3, 1981, pp. 62–67.

"Classroom Training Pays Off." *AVA Update*, November/December, 1981, p. 3.

Confer, Stephen H. *Technology—Its Impact on CWA—Today and Tomorrow*. Washington, D.C.: Communications Workers of America, 1980.

_____. "HRD Activities and Organized Labor." In *Critical Research Issues Facing HRD*, edited by Jay Alden. Washington, D.C.: American Society for Training and Development, 1981.

Dwyer, Richard E. "Evolution of the Affiliated Schools in Workers' Education from Coordination to Educational Service." *Labor Studies Journal* 2 (1977): 37–49.

Dwyer, Richard E., Miles E. Salvin, and Simeon Larson. "Labor Studies in Quest of Industrial Justice." *Labor Studies Journal* 2 (1977): 95–131.

Gilbert, Thomas F. *Human Competence*. New York: McGraw-Hill, 1978.

Gray, Lois. "Labor Studies Credit and Degree Programs: A Growth Sector of Higher Education." *Labor Studies Journal* 1 (1976): 115–122.

Keyworth, George A. Statement before the Committee on Science and Technology, U.S. House of Representatives. Washington, D.C.: Executive Office of Science and Technology Policy, 1981.

Marsh, General Robert T. Speech before the Armed Forces Communications and Electronics Association. Washington, D.C., November, 1981.

Mills, D. Quinn. "Human Resources in the 1980's." *Harvard Business Review* (1978): 156.

Nash, Al. "Labor Education, Labor Studies, and the Knowledge Factor." *Labor Studies Journal* 3 (1978): 5–18.

Schachhuber, Dieter. "The Missing Link in Labor Education." *Labor Studies Journal* 4 (1979): 148–158.

Schneider, Florence Henley. *Patterns of Workers' Education*. Washington, D.C.: American
    Council on Public Affairs, 1941.

U.S. Department of Labor. "The National Apprenticeship Program." *Employment and
    Training Report of the Secretary, 1983.*

"Warner Plans Layoff of 1,000 at Its Atari Unit." *The Wall Street Journal*, June 27, 1983, p.
    5.

"Where Hot New Careers Will Open in the '80's." *U.S. News and World Report*, December 7,
    1981, pp. 70–71.

CHAPTER TWENTY-ONE

National Voluntary Organizations

ELIZABETH A. OLSON

The United States is often referred to as a nation of volunteers. Indeed, we do have a long history of such activity. What may be less recognized is the tremendous commitment of resources by voluntary organizations to HRD programs for their volunteers and to the paid staff who support them and contribute to the services authorized by the volunteers.

In this chapter, Olson sets forth some of the factors that must be considered in establishing and providing HRD services and programs. In many ways, the HRD programs are similar to those offered by many organizations in both the public and private sectors. However, there are many significant differences, and Olson directs our attention to these.

Those who are unfamiliar with the HRD programs of the national voluntary organizations will find this chapter valuable to their understanding of the program development process for HRD in national organizations. Those who know of the programs will find that Olson has put them into an organizational perspective that underlines the necessity for sound planning and administration of HRD programs.

Elizabeth A. Olson retired as national director of training and development for the American Red Cross and now works with a variety of clients in the international field, providing management and volunteer HRD programs and the design and delivery of HRD systems. She is active in several professional associations and has written articles for the *ASTD* and *Lifelong Learning*, the journal of the American Association for Adult and Continuing Education.

INTRODUCTION

Human resource development in voluntary organizations plays a vital role in identifying, developing, and achieving organizational goals. In this respect, the role of HRD does not differ from that of other organizations, public or private. However, the performance of any key role or function within a voluntary organization presents the worker with values and conditions related to volunteering that create unique expectations from both volunteer and paid staff. Because both values and conditions are an integral part of the organization's existence and behavior, it is easiest to look at the organization in general terms, before considering those factors significantly related to volunteerism. The same judgment may be applied to HRD as a key organizational function. Therefore, throughout this chapter, both in relation to the organization as a whole and to HRD, the approach will be to examine what is going on or emerging in general, before identifying special, volunteer-related issues.

Characteristics of Today's Voluntary Organizations

National voluntary organizations that are large, complex, and highly decentralized are common in the United States. The YMCA and YWCA, the Boy Scouts and Girl Scouts, the American Red Cross, the Salvation Army, and the Family Service Association are some that have been part of American life for three generations or more. Since World War II, a wide range of large, national voluntary organizations has developed, many of them umbrella organizations that relate to and coordinate the common interests of their affiliates. In the past 25 years, health organizations, originally small and centralized, have added regional, state, and local units that have greatly expanded their total structure and work. Specialists of almost every profession or technical field have developed national associations or societies, from the National Rifle Association to Public Citizen. All of these have programs tailored to the needs of certain segments of society. As they have grown, they have developed highly sophisticated management systems with professional staff to support and guide volunteers at both national and local levels. Volunteer leaders share a partnership with managers and increasingly pride themselves on the businesslike character of their operations.

Relationships and division of responsibilities between volunteers and paid staff vary among voluntary organizations, affected by the stages of growth of the organizations, the degree of public support, and the status of the professional and technical fields related to their work. At times, the volunteers possess the power and prestige; at other times, greater power accrues to paid staff. Recently, there has been growing recognition of the necessary and actual interdependence of volunteers and paid staff; therefore, teamwork between volunteers and paid staff has become a central issue. The status and role of all volunteers have been influenced by corporate policy statements mandating the importance of volunteers to organizational mission and operations. These statements are reinforced by periodic directives from governing boards and management that reiterate the need for and importance of volunteers and that mandate support for them as a key responsibility of paid staff. At the same time, clarification and stronger recognition have been given by organizational leaders to the contributions of paid staff (warranted by the nature of the organization's work, as well as by the scope and level of its operations). As both volunteers and paid staff are recognized as being essential to successful and growing organizations, collaboration between the two groups has become more efficient and effective.

In addition to businesslike practices and increasing interdependence between volunteers and paid staff, many national voluntary organizations have made great strides in applying the principles of participative management to their relationships with regional and local units. With more frequent opportunities to share in organizational decision making and planning and more opportunities to extend the field of their influence and activity through helping other units or participating in task forces, conferences, or HRD activities, individual units have tended to become stronger and to build sound relationships with both headquarters and peer units.

One other characteristic of national voluntary organizations is noteworthy. The financial situation of many national voluntary organizations has become a gigantic and endless headache. A number of factors have contributed to the growing problem, including the proliferation of voluntary organizations; the rising costs of operating them; the competition for contributions, grants, and other sources of funds; the problems of the economy; and the continued rising needs and expectations of constituencies and the public for service. Annual appeals for funds have given way to year-long, varied strategies and tactics that not only solicit financial contributions but also initiate changes in programs, structure, staffing, and all aspects of organizational operations, in order to effect economies or cost recovery. However impressive the results in terms of income or savings, they seem rarely sufficient to meet current and anticipated needs.

These are but a few examples of emerging characteristics of national voluntary organizations. Voluntary organizations are changing rapidly because of internal and external forces. The purpose of the general statements is to illustrate the approach taken in this chapter. There will be no attempt to discuss the many differences among specific organizations. Rather, this chapter presents some general observations and conclusions about what is happening in national voluntary organizations, based on personal experience. It is impossible to present such a view except in the context of organizational change.

Within the HRD function of national voluntary organizations, one finds many effects of the general organizational patterns just cited. There is growing use of business practices, such as a marketing approach to planning HRD programs. There is interdependence of volunteers and paid staff, as illustrated by the increasing frequency with which volunteer leaders are included in management HRD programs previously reserved for paid staff. Participative decision making abounds, within and between levels of the organization, (e.g., the spreading utilization of HRD advisory councils). Serious financial limitations must be accommodated as we move away from major dependence on centralized training events that necessitate expensive travel, lodging, and meals for both participants and instructors.

An essential step in laying the groundwork for determining effective HRD in voluntary organizations is to look at relationships between top leadership/management and the HRD personnel. At this point, it is not necessary to differentiate between volunteer and paid personnel in either group.

THE GENERAL MANAGEMENT OF VOLUNTARY ORGANIZATIONS

By definition, management at all levels has responsibility for resource management and development, whether human, physical, or financial. As each of these fields has become "professionalized," "systematized," and "technologized," to use a rough shorthand for changes of the past quarter of a century, general managers have tended to assign responsibility to specialists for the administration of human, physical, and financial systems. The more technical or professional the specialists' functions became, the greater the physical and psychological distance between the general managers and the specialists. Delegations of responsibility and authority became broader. Separate offices for personnel, for finance and budgeting, and for property management were established. In some instances, the HRD function was assigned to the personnel office; in others, it was set up separately, with a structure parallel to the other resource administration specialties.

How did general management relate to each of these offices? In what kinds of situations did it become directly involved? To what extent were specialists allowed largely to manage their own offices? In general, the answers to those questions are covered by the response: "Top management is directly involved in problem solving and the initiation of change in which the external community is significantly involved or the public image or standing of the organization is at stake, for better or worse."

Fund raising and budgeting processes became the core of all organizational planning, as well as the first item on every meeting agenda. Special committees, as well as governing boards, kept management attention focused on financial dilemmas and decisions, and finance-related staff seemed to spend most of their time in the offices of top management. The prevailing attitude was, "We will do whatever the money we get will permit us to do." This seemed to push all other criteria for setting objectives into a secondary role.

Close behind the subject of funds has been personnel administration, predominantly with respect to paid staff but periodically involving volunteer matters as well. In the early 1960s, the "involving and serving" movement encouraged voluntary organizations to greatly broaden their base for recruitment and for the placement of volunteer and paid personnel. That was done to assure greater community involvement in decision making related to programming. However, almost immediately, the movement toward affirmative action, in the broadest sense, began. New federal laws and regulations and new national and community expectations strongly urged organizational leaders and management to institute changes in personnel policies and practices for both paid staff and volunteers.

The Civil Rights Act of 1964, its supplements and amendments, the Equal Pay Act of 1963, the Service Contracts Act (1965), amendments to the Labor-Management Relations Act (1935, 1947, 1959), the Occupational Health and Safety Act (1970), the Comprehensive Employment and Training Act (1973), the Employee Retirement Income Security Act (1974), the Privacy Act (1974), and the Veterans' Readjustment Act (1974)—these were some of the laws that brought boards, personnel committees, and management together with their personnel specialists and attorneys to study, ponder, and to deal with individual problems and court cases, and to plan to change specific policies and personnel practices.

With all of these demands for direct management involvement, keeping up with new information and experience data from their own and similar organizations became the most important learning commitment of top management, and they joined their personnel specialists in almost daily conferences on how best to apply what they had learned. Specialized offices charged with providing HRD for volunteers and paid staff were often perceived as fairly tranquil oases, whose problems and proposals or needs for change could be postponed or left, administratively, to specialists or lower levels of management. Specific needs assessments and proposals for innovations in HRD programs or in delivery systems were usually examined by management from the standpoint of what would constitute reasonable and timely support, rather than deep involvement in or commitment to the change process itself. This approach had both positive and negative implications for the HRD specialists, as well as for the organization's ability to benefit from the HRD programs.

From the mid-1960s through the 1970s, two major HRD themes tended to have the strongest and most active support from the leaders and managers of voluntary organizations:

Standardization and decentralization of organizational HRD programs for volunteer and paid staff, through fairly superficial needs assessments, very careful course design, and the establishment of delivery systems that utilized organizational instructors, both volunteer and paid.

Management HRD programs, utilizing internal and external resources, covering a broad spectrum of behavioral skills, systems administration, fiscal management, and strategic and operational planning.

BUILDING EFFECTIVE HRD IN VOLUNTARY ORGANIZATIONS IN THE 1980s

It is in the context of emerging strategic planning and management that one must identify effective HRD systems and programs in voluntary organizations today. The management of human resources is an integral part of organizational management, whatever its theoretical base or style. Volunteers and paid staff combine their competence, energy, and motivation to plan and perform the organization's work and to assess the results and consequences in relation to organizational goals and objectives. Setting and achieving development objectives for work performance, personal competence, and career advancement are part of the planning cycle of the organization.

Every individual, volunteer or paid, carries part of the responsibility for planning his or her own development and for assessing its results. Individuals with supervisory responsibility at any level share with their subordinates the responsibility for the subordinates' development planning and assessment.

If an organization addressed the subject of human resource development no further than through the foregoing statements, the very nature of people and the changing goals, tasks, and conditions of the organization would guarantee the existence of much learning and teaching. However, in most voluntary organizations HRD has a much stronger foundation. Corporate goals usually contain at least one statement related to human resource management, including development. Further, most organizations have corporate policy statements mandating HRD in broad terms. In addition to a corporate commitment, both functional and jurisdictional units usually have specific objectives, policies, and systems for personnel or member development.

In addition to planning for individual development, units at all levels of the organization plan for unit (group) training and education in response to needs such as:

Organizational changes that affect the units.   For example, a new organizational accounting system may necessitate changes in financial reporting that require new skills on the part of all units and staff.
Changes within specific units.   For example, a social service unit may reach a formal agreement with a public agency that entails change in information needed from workers for referral services.
Changes within professional or technical fields related to an organizational unit's work.   For example, a publicly aired problem involving a health services' procedure may lead a number of organizations to schedule seminars for their units whose work is affected by the procedure.

Obviously, managers must not only see and understand the needs, they must also plan and take action internally or in cooperation with other units to ensure appropriate unit development.

Traditionally, the largest part of an organization's HRD effort has been directed to the needs of individuals, whether volunteer or paid staff. All larger voluntary organizations pay continuing attention to job-related (training) needs. Again, much of the response to job-related needs is given informally, on the job, through interaction between supervisors and staff or between more experienced and knowledgeable workers and those with less experience and knowledge. These interactions usually increase the competence and productivity of individuals or groups. The aim is for staff and volunteers to do their work, to achieve their objectives at higher levels of quality, quantity, timeliness, and to impact on other tasks, objectives, or people.

However, voluntary organizations, like most large organizations of the public, private, and nonprofit sectors, do not rely solely on informal interactions or even on coaching or monitoring to be sure that the necessary job-related learning takes place. Structured and scheduled events, to which staff are invited or assigned, are planned at unit or organizational levels. There are instructors, facilitators, or resource persons "in charge." They make presentations, produce materials, lead discussions, and provide practice opportunities designed to bring about increased awareness, knowledge, understanding, or skill.

Most voluntary organizations are especially careful to make group learning experiences available to new workers, volunteer and paid, and to introduce them to their jobs, to the work of their unit or group (e.g., health services, the board of directors, the finance committee), and to the organization itself. Development needs of individuals are often assessed in connection with periodic performance reviews, and data concerning the needs are then compiled and analyzed. Group learning needs related to specific positions (e.g., those of caseworkers, supervisors, secretaries, managers, troop leaders, committee chairpersons) are most frequently used as the basis for planning HRD. Workshops may be designed on an ad hoc basis or for continuing use, for local aplication or for use throughout the nation. The designs, with or without guidelines for instructors, may be published and distributed for anyone to present, or they may be put into a carefully planned, organizational delivery system.

It is a predominant practice to respond to the individual's job-related learning needs by offering group learning experiences planned and conducted by organizational personnel. As a result of this practice, HRD units emerged in voluntary organizations. Two factors were especially important in the establishing of centralized HRD units for the organizations. The first was the awareness, when each unit planned and implemented its own HRD programs, that there were some duplications, some major gaps, and some contradictions in the assumptions, philosophies, and theories that were being utilized. The second factor dealt with the size, scope, and cost of HRD when scattered throughout the organization without coordination in planning and without overall, planned assessment. People moving from one unit to another raised questions about their experiences, and organizational management began to seek ways to resolve the problems.

The establishing of a centralized, organizational HRD unit has frequently had as its initial purpose the coordinating of HRD activities already in existence, rather than the planning and implementing of new HRD programs. Acceptance of the HRD unit by operational units has often been based on what the organizational unit will gain through the coordination of logistics and schedules, rather than what they might lose by turning over the HRD responsibility for their own people. In these circumstances, HRD units are most effective when they begin their services to the organization at the level of understanding and acceptance of management and other units and then gradually work with them toward more substantive HRD objectives, in which needs assessments, resources, and efforts are shared.

On the other hand, the initial intention of management may be to install professional HRD leadership that will plan and provide organization-wide programs and resources for volunteer and paid staff development. If that is the situation, then a primary task of the HRD manager may be to negotiate collaboration with other units in a marketing approach to needs assessment and resources identification. This will be followed by the establishment of priorities for programming that may involve significant changes in the nature and delivery of existing HRD programs. In this kind of situation, it is extremely important for management to work with all unit heads in setting a climate of mutual understanding, in establishing priority needs, and in reaching agreement on human and material resources to be used. Human resource development then becomes a central organizational concern, and the core leadership person for the effort must be a part of the top management team.

The advent of organizational strategic planning is often a major factor in helping top management to visualize professional HRD leadership as part of the management team. However, some organizations elect to identify a management member as the primary overseer of the total HRD effort and establish a professional director for the unit. An advisory chairperson or committee may be placed at the same level. Other organizations may decentralize all operational aspects of HRD and retain a management-level, staff office for HRD. Still others may unify human resources at the top management level and place professional specialists at the top of each "branch" of human resource management.

Specific structuring decisions, whatever they may be, seldom make or break the effectiveness of HRD. But many HRD professionals seem to agree that the human development goal and key strategies for approaching it must be an integral part of management concern and action— requiring at least as serious an effort as for financial development. In both cases, development planning greatly reduces the time needed for solving problems of deficiencies.

If the organizational executive develops, with broad assistance, some major HRD objectives and strategies, then he or she can begin to define specific competencies for HRD leadership. In a systems approach, with intended outcomes in mind, the competencies can be clarified without having to finalize every function to be performed. One manager of a large urban unit described his vision of an HRD director in these terms:

> If our personnel offices for volunteer and paid staff can be counted on to get the right people into the right jobs and situations at the right times, then I want my HRD director to be my right arm in seeing that all these people understand why we are in business, and why this is a great organization, and what some of our problems are, internally and externally....I expect the (HRD) director to be a part of my team and to help to build it, and to lead us in setting development goals and plans that will get results in staff performance and motivation that we can all see. I want the director to be a model for us all in continuing to grow on the job, and to take on increasing responsibilities—or different ones—that will help us become an even greater organization. And I hope that he or she will find so much to challenge him or her, and to enjoy, in our organization and this community, that he or she will stay with us for years!

Such a charge provides a foundation for envisioning and building effective HRD unit leadership in a number of ways:

Establishing role relationships with management and other offices that will include flexibility, teamwork, and development

Becoming an integral part of organizational strategic planning

Defining functions and programs that will complement and enhance other HRD efforts already in place

Setting standards of excellence

Recognizing and sharing models of HRD competence

Planning and implementing delivery systems, making use of all possible internal resources, including management

Functioning as part of organizational management in relation to overall organizational needs and problem solving, not only HRD

Continuing as an HRD professional with an individual development plan, networking and making work-related and profession-related contacts in the field

The key strategy for accomplishing these tasks in a large voluntary organization is use of a participatory process, one that involves ad hoc or continuing representation from management and other offices throughout the organization. A core HRD council may serve best with a rotating membership (volunteer and paid, functional and jurisdictional) and varied levels of job responsibility. An HRD council will need people with expertise in a range of fields (e.g., management, HRD, systems administration, audiovisual production, computer usage, Organizational Development (OD), planning, finance, and the professional and technical areas that form the base for organizational service programs). If a matrix approach is used, specific activities, functions, or objectives may be handled through ad hoc task forces or subcommittees. In such groups, the activities will develop from the responsibilities or concerns of the council, rather than from delegation in the HRD office itself.

Several factors are crucial to the effectiveness of this kind of group. First, an agreement must be reached between the HRD office and top management regarding the responsibilities of the group, its administrative relationship to the HRD director, and its chairperson. Second, the relationships between the group and management, the group and services, and especially the group and other human resource management offices must be defined. Third, the role of the council in organizational strategic planning and its performance standards, accountability, and provision for performance review must be defined. There is probably no best way of constituting this kind of council. Although the HRD office must have a key role in its governance, management and the participating offices should certainly be able to have input into the initial design, into subsequent changes, and into the assessment of its effectiveness. Keeping it an open system is essential; extending the openness to include representatives of the larger or professional community on an ad hoc or continuing basis, inevitably necessitates making a role decision. Will community representatives be kept to the "outsider" perspective or allowed to become volunteer "insiders," by virtue of their membership in the group? If the former consideration is preferred, rotation is usually in order, since voluntary organizations have a way of quickly redrawing "circles" to include people (see Figure 21.1).

SOME KEY FUNCTIONS OF AN HRD UNIT'S ADMINISTRATIVE STAFF

Earlier statements indicated belief that human resource development, in any organization, must be concerned with development of the individual, the group or unit, and the organization as a whole. Contacts with national voluntary organizations in the field of community service indicate a trend toward upgrading the functions and positions in the HRD office,

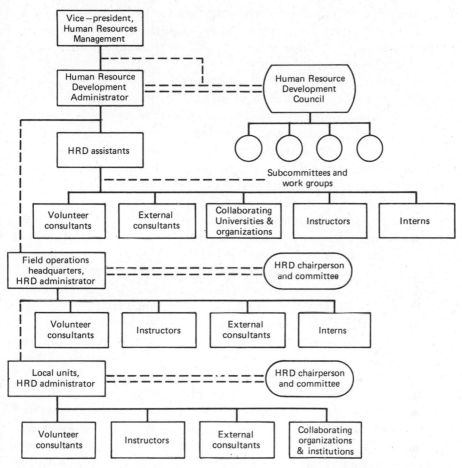

Figure 21.1.   An approach to organizing HRD in a voluntary organization.

from a general role of supporting HRD in various offices to coordination of HRD planning and programming. Most recently, the trend has been toward consultation with management, concerning the needs, problems, change efforts, and direction of the organization that may have implications for HRD. This includes participating in data gathering and analysis and then providing leadership, resource assistance, or collaboration for selected HRD priorities. The trend in this direction has been hastened by the continuing decentralization from national to regional or local units of operational management responsibilities. Expansion and growing sophistication of information and communications systems, along with rising costs and tighter budgets, encourage the national HRD units of voluntary organizations to focus on organizational problem and issue analysis, survey and research design, and data analysis. The HRD units must also focus on the selection of key target groups for attention, on the identification of intended outcomes, and on relevant action and programming to meet priority needs.

In more specific terms, the HRD manager should serve as an internal consultant to management, able to discuss problems related to the organization's mission, as well as strategic plans and probable progress. The HRD manager must have the knowledge and skill needed to define and diagnose problems, to identify and help to select targets for change, and to understand the purpose and nature of theories, strategies, technologies, and interventions that might be useful to bring about the changes needed. Armed with that kind of understanding and with personal knowledge of resource persons inside the organization (e.g., members of boards, committees, or special staff) or outside the organization (e.g., from universities, consulting firms, professional societies, or companies with specialized OD staff), the HRD administrator can assist management in making a sound decision as to why, when, and where to seek appropriate assistance on critical organizational concerns.

Second, the HRD manager should serve as a consultant to management regarding the development planning of key volunteer leadership and executives. At this point, the availability of data concerning performance results is critical. Program development and effectiveness, human and financial resource management, intraorganizational and interorganizational relationships and accomplishments, feedback of community and public relationships, and evidences of collaborative effort and problem solving may all be indicators for development needs. Planning to meet these needs cannot be the sole responsibility of HRD, even with top management support. People who have experience in the jobs represented and internal and external volunteers and staff who are extremely knowledgeable about the subject and the learning strategies can join the HRD administrator in identifying creative responses to specific needs.

A third area for consultation with management lies in reviewing the nature and scope of the organization's linkages with outside resources for HRD purposes. Again, a participative approach might be used through an ad hoc task force. Who is called upon to assist with HRD programs or activities? Why? What kind of feedback is received from the participants? What kind of feedback is received from the resource persons? What are the results for individual, group, or organizational practices? Are external resources, such as independent consultants from government, industry, labor, professional societies, and voluntary organizations, helping to build skills and to instill creativity, an experimental attitude, confidence, independence, and interdependence? What have the results of these HRD experiences taught the organization about the resources themselves? What has been learned about the process of working with such resources? What has been learned about when and why to use external resources rather than internal ones?

A very important function in which the HRD manager and top management need to collaborate is the planning and implementation of operational management programs. Not only are data available to top managers concerning the accomplishments, problems, and future direction of the organization's operations, but top management's judgments also exist concerning operational managers that will affect placements, careers, and future relationships. Therefore, it is crucial that middle managers have an opportunity for self-assessment, for feedback from colleagues, and for learning to plan their own change efforts and growth. Whether internal or external resources are used for these purposes, the critical decision that the HRD administrator and top management must make is to select the approach and resources that will work and that can continue to work over a substantial period of time. Operational managers hold the keys to the reality of all HRD programming for volunteers and paid staff. If they understand how to use the keys and use them for themselves, they will authorize, facilitate, support, and reinforce their use for others.

Volunteer managers and administrators have learned that unless they participate in the same kinds of growth experiences, their acceptance and usefulness as partners in operational management will be sharply limited. HRD managers must also work with operational managers as ongoing participants in the self-assessment/professional growth planning process, if they are to become effective consultants to others who learn or use the process.

Although not always seen as a functional responsibility of HRD managers since much of the attendant activity may seem to take place off the job, the responsibility for active involvement in professional organizations and in informal networks in HRD belongs near the top of the job description. Every organization that uses professionals from any field needs a two-way relationship with the professions concerned, and that is most readily available through professional societies or organizations. For organizations in the fields of human services, the performance of life-and-death or quality-of-life functions often depends on continual updating of research findings, better theory, and more highly skilled practice. For all organizations that are labor intensive, as are all voluntary service organizations, the quality of human resource development activities, philosophy, and approaches depends greatly on the factors of research, theory, and practice. Competence brought by the HRD manager to the organization is derived not only from previous learning, volunteering, and work experience, but also from professional reading and contacts in the field. In turn, the organization's experiences with human resource development activities provide valuable input into the HRD profession.

When meeting with other professionals in the field, the HRD administrator discusses the organization's experiences; reflects on them with others; tests them against new research, theory, and practice; exchanges new insights with others; and returns to his or her own job, a better professional. These professional linkages produce other kinds of benefits for the organization and for the profession. Interorganizational relationships are strengthened, making it easier to collaborate in addressing shared problems of organizations or the community. Awareness of and support for both the organization and the profession increase. Opportunities for involving new, professional volunteers or paid consultants in organizational work are identified, and in turn, organizational representatives, other than HRD staff, may contribute to the profession through such activities as speaking at a professional society's meeting, offering the use of facilities or resources for professional groups, supporting a university-sponsored project, and so forth. As networking professionals know, one open door frequently reveals another.

CRITICAL TARGETS AND PROGRAMS FOR TODAY'S HRD OFFICES IN VOLUNTARY ORGANIZATIONS

A typical corporate goal statement, related to human resources, calls for an effective organization-wide system for recruitment, development, and deployment of people that will lead toward the achievement of organizational goals. In national voluntary organizations, the duties of all supervisors and managers include the responsibility for human resource management and development. As HRD offices are established and grow, their basic role remains, fundamentally, to assist organizational management in carrying out their responsibilities for human resource development.

As might be expected, the activities of HRD offices at various levels of the organization's structure are specifically related to the nature and scope of the management jobs at those levels. Unity and consistency among HRD offices are maintained, as they are for managers and other offices, by the need to observe priorities established by corporate goals and by the organizational definitions of each office's basic functions and level of authority. Within that framework, there is still much room for flexibility. HRD staff are limited in number, so another good reason for unity and consistency among these specialists is to concentrate on agreed-upon priorities, to facilitate vertical and horizontal cooperation, and to strengthen the total HRD influence on organizational standards, direction, and growth.

If the table of organization has structurally divided HRD responsibility for volunteers from HRD responsibility for paid staff and if the two offices have a peer relationship, then continuing attention and effort must be made by the two offices to join forces, to work for specific objectives, to cooperate in almost every function, and insofar as possible, to develop unified programs, systems, and materials. The case for unity in HRD planning increases every year, as shared responsibility and accountability of a volunteer/paid staff management team are defined in more organizational units and at more organizational levels.

A number of approaches are possible for organizing a presentation of the program and activities of HRD offices for paid and volunteer personnel in relation to organizational goals and HRD functions most frequently found in national voluntary organizations. The approach used here is built around the three major target groups within the organization that must always command HRD concentration, namely the individual, the group, and the organization. Although voluntary organizations differ in purpose, scope, size, and staffing patterns, it is possible to illustrate the meaning of each category, as frequently dealt with by HRD personnel. Individuals, both volunteer and paid, encounter a wide range of job-related situations for which training, education, and development may be useful. Groups tend to be identified either as *family groups* (i.e., people forming part of a unit) or *cross-sectional groups* (i.e., a group identified in terms of specific positions, levels of authority, or functional commonalities). Organization is most often thought of as the total entity, but from the HRD viewpoint, those large segments or units perceived by many people as fairly autonomous operating entities may be dealt with in a fashion parallel to the appproach to the total organization (see Figure 21.2).

It would be impossible to present any inclusive list of HRD programs typically designed and used within national voluntary organizations. Workshops and courses proliferate and vanish, changing with the needs of individuals, groups, and the total organization. However, there are some kinds of HRD programs frequently found in voluntary organiza-

INDIVIDUALS: National, regional, and local; headquarters and field

All volunteers	All paid staff
Chairpersons, officers and members of the board and volunteer offices	President, vice presidents, chief executive officer
Chairpersons, officers and members of committees, standing and ad hoc	Managers, deputies and assistants
Consulting generalists or specialists	Heads of services and offices and their assistants
Instructors and instructors of instructors	Project directors
	Administrators and assistants
Direct service volunteers	Professional consultants, internal and external
Support service volunteers	
Special purpose volunteers (e.g., advocates, research)	Providers of direct services
	Providers of administrative support services or technical services
Interns and student volunteers	
	Providers of clerical services
	Providers of maintenance services (professional, technical, labor)

GROUPS: National, regional, and local; headquarters and field; volunteer and paid

A. All categories of personnel in a given umbrella unit

   National headquarters' personnel
   Field or regional offices' personnel
   Local unit or affiliate group
   Field station unit

B. Functional unit or grouping (by nature of service provided)

   Volunteer groupings (e.g., national board of governors, local board of directors, advisory committee on personnel, ad hoc task force on planned financial giving)

   Age groupings (e.g., youth group, senior citizens' group)

   Community connections groupings (e.g., labor relations group, military wives' group, community college group, chamber of commerce group)

   Professionally related groupings (e.g., medical advisory group, nurses instructors' group)

   Job-related or position-related groups (e.g., clerical staff, blood technologists' group, field representatives' group, chapter chairperson's group, field volunteer consultants' group)

Figure 21.2. The human targets of HRD planning and programs.

ORGANIZATIONS:

The total national voluntary organization

A local autonomous unit or affiliate

A crosscut of the total organization with highly interdependent units within it that have most of their own resources

A section of the organization that functions largely through affiliation with comparable segments of other organizations (e.g., the international arm of the organization)

Figure 21.2. The human targets of HRD planning and programs. (continued)

tions. Some of these relate to supervisory, management, and volunteer leadership skills. In most large organizations, designs abound for the development of skills related to specific program functions performed by many of an organization's volunteers and paid staff. Guidelines are often prepared for planning and implementing nonclassroom HRD programs. A small sample of these three kinds of HRD programs is presented in Figure 21.3.

Courses for Group Instruction

    One-day Workshops
        Orientation to the organization
        Assessing community needs
        Volunteer and paid staff working together
        Planning and conducting effective meetings
        Preparing proposals for financial grants
    Multiday Courses
        Preparation of instructors
        Effective writing (series)
        Essentials of supervision
        Consulting skills
        The art of helping (series)

Courses for Individual Study

    Using audiovisual resources
    Developing and maintaining HRD records
    Preparing objectives and action plans

Figure 21.3. Some typical kinds of internal HRD programs found in national voluntary organizations.

Courses for Peer-Assisted Learning

Team-building techniques
Developing performance standards
"I Can" (a tool for career development of volunteers)
Effective management of an organizational unit (series)

Videotapes with Discussion Guides

Introduction to serving on the board of directors
How to chair a committee effectively
Planned giving

Mini Designs for Incorporation into a Conference Program

Computer literacy
Making an effective presentation
Becoming acquainted with the personal computer

Designs/Outlines of Learning Programs

Guidelines for establishing a college or graduate student internship
Planning and conducting work performance reviews
Planning and conducting a youth leadership center

Resources for Tuition and Accrediting Learning

Academic tuition program
Obtaining college credit
Awarding CEUs for organizational HRD

Work/Learning Assignments

Loaned executive program with the United Way of America
Working on a disaster emergency operation
Interorganizational project for a small group (e.g., planning a joint project)

Figure 21.3. Some typical kinds of internal HRD programs found in national voluntary organizations. (continued)

THE HUMAN RESOURCES FOR THE HRD EFFORT IN A VOLUNTARY ORGANIZATION

As previously stated, HRD offices tend to be small in voluntary organizations, but management and representatives of all offices that have a stake in providing HRD for their people take part in needs assessment, planning, and design activities. It has also been stated that all persons with supervisory responsibility must take an active part in the development of their staff, both volunteer and paid. Each individual throughout the organization, regardless of position, has final responsibility for his or her own growth and certainly controls his or her own learning.

If these statements are accurate, then one might conclude that everyone in the organization is part of the HRD staff, and that is somewhat the situation.

A first reaction to the statement that "everyone is a part of the training/education/development effort" might be to assume that the main task of a central HRD office would be to organize the overall involvement. This would seldom be a feasible or desirable task in any large organization, except in the broadest sense. One practical approach to facilitating planning and communication about HRD throughout an organization lies in helping to define and clarify the kinds of contributions to HRD that might be expected from persons in specific roles. The tentative formulation that follows is presented more to stimulate thinking than to serve as a model.

Learners

Everyone should assess their own needs for learning at different intervals and in new situations. They should decide on major goals (intended outcomes) and priorities for learning and try to understand the kind and amount of effort necessary to achieve those goals. Learners identify resources, inside or outside the organization, and assess their own commitment to learning in relation to the apparent requirements of the resources. They reach decisions as to the best courses of action; request approval or support, if needed for use of the specific resources; and embark on the programs or activities. They test or apply the learning in accordance with the intended outcomes, solve learning problems that arise, report completion of the learning experience, and seek whatever reinforcement or support is appropriate.

Supervisors

Supervisors at every level, whether volunteer or paid, periodically review their people's performance and development records, assess the individual's contribution to total unit performance, and examine the unit's commitments and action plans for the year ahead. They confer with each person to assure the appropriate input into the individual's assessment and goal-setting processes. They help to identify internal and external resources for needed learning and development, and they participate in testing the feasibility of various resources from the standpoint of the individual and the organization. They relate proposed development plans to those of other staff and to the unit's work schedule, and they grant or obtain approval for the time, the finances, or the other organizational contributions involved. They help individuals to make advance preparations and help them to follow through after the learning experience. They offer needed support and reinforcement for learning applied in the work environment. They report learning activities of staff and respond to requests from management or the HRD office for assessment of the meaning and usefulness of the activities to the individual and the unit.

Managers

Earlier, some suggestions were made for management inputs that establish an effective working relationship with the HRD administrator. In addition, management can make some vital contributions to the total HRD program, namely, offering suggestions, advice, and support, engaging in collaborative planning, and providing the necessary coordination and controls. Representatives from volunteer management or the board of directors may be involved at various stages of strategic HRD planning for volunteers and paid staff. If there is an office of volunteer personnel administration, both the leadership volunteers and the paid administrators must contribute to HRD planning.

The management representative who supervises the HRD staff responsible for volunteers and paid personnel ties the HRD office into all aspects of organizational strategic planning and helps to integrate HRD contributions with all major organizational change efforts. The same person suggests or arranges professional "stretch" activities for HRD staff through special assignments, involvement in board or management projects, or temporary placements in varied settings or situations.

HRD Councils, Other Offices, and Operating Units

Organization-wide representation of other functional offices is necessary in at least two of the core responsibilities of the HRD office—program design and the development of delivery systems. Earlier discussion indicated that strategic HRD planning involves environmental analysis, analysis of previous accomplishments, assessment of strengths and weaknesses, identification of current issues and needs, selection of priority targets for future application of programs and delivery systems, and development of objectives and action plans. It was indicated that all national strategic planning is collaborative and is a part of the framework of the organization's total planning process. If one then pursues the earlier approach of using work groups in HRD, with a core HRD council responsible for each main stage of planning, there is an immediate base for interoffice and interlevel involvement.

In addition to sharing in the planning, other offices are involved in the implementation of whatever programs and delivery systems are developed. In fact, programs and delivery systems become resources to operating units (optional or mandated), to the extent that they are essential to the accomplishment of specific performance standards or objectives adopted throughout the organization. The resulting data from the operating units must be part of the input for changed or new elements used in HRD planning.

An example of how this process works may be useful. Suppose the centerpiece of an HRD program for middle managers involves a series of learning experiences that includes: individual assessment based on solicited feedback from colleagues, a one-week residential learning experience, work/learning experiences tailored to individual needs, independent study, and two short workshops made available periodically by the national organization. If, over a period of two or three years, data show that the programs initiated by middle managers who have completed the series are of short duration or outright failures, these managers are deemed to be deficient in program development skills. Obviously, one of the elements that would warrant very serious review would be the HRD series for middle managers. Only the national HRD council would have the data, the access to a range of people and services, and the combined expertise to do a sound analysis and projection of change in the HRD series.

Figure 21.4 provides an overview of some of the competencies most likely to be addressed frequently by an HRD council and the HRD office. The list includes the cross-sectional kinds of knowledge and skills needed by individuals in most services, offices, and general management as they move up their career ladders.

Offices Having Highly Technical Positions

Not included in Figure 21.4 are high-level technical or professional competencies. The major responsibility for planning HRD experiences for such persons lies with the jurisdictional office. These offices often

For Job Performance and Career Advancement

Undertaking new roles/responsibilities
Self-assessment and planning for career choices
Meeting performance standards for specific roles

For Being a Part of the Organization's Work Force

Decision making/problem solving
Interpersonal skills in conferring, coaching, counseling, consulting
Group work skills for meetings, teamwork, staff groups, participative leadership skills
Using a systems approach; working with computerized information systems
Skills in establishing relationships with volunteers and paid staff

For Developing External Relationships

Marketing/public relations
Understanding elements and dynamics of the community, the society, the world
Skills in working within a profession; developing personal, external involvement

For Leadership/Management Roles

Working in the field of voluntarism; understanding voluntary organizations
Skills in financial management and development
Skills in program development
Skills in human resource areas
Skills in organization of a unit's work
Skills in planning and using the resources of boards, committees, task forces
Skills in working with community organizations, power groups, governmental agencies, legislatures
Skills in participatory management; team building
Skills in effecting change, resolving conflict, negotiating
Knowledge of adult learning philosophy and principles
Skills in strategic planning and management.

Figure 21.4. Areas of competency for continuing development of the effective volunteer or paid staff member.

request asistance from universities or peer organizations known for exceptionally good performance in a particular field. Because of the numbers of persons in any specific, highly technical, or professional position, the jurisdictional office consults with the HRD office about matters of delivery and scheduling when planning internal seminars or workshops. Collaboration is also essential between the offices or with the HRD council to avoid needless overlap or contradictions in core values or principles promulgated in the learning designs. Collaboration is also essential to assure the availability and use of organizational HRD resources related to aspects of the technical/professional positions that are also common to other positions (e.g., management responsibilities, financial administration or marketing functions, etc.).

External Resources

External resources are used for the design or delivery of HRD programs in areas other than highly specialized offices. HRD councils and HRD offices have good reasons for considering external resources to assist with:

Updating of national and local board members (e.g., in community fund raising, public relations problems, legal challenges, etc.)

Programs dealing with advanced management skills for executives

Middle management programs involving changes in feedback and disclosure practices

Course or workshop designs for which research, theory, or skill input needs a broader base than is available internally

Conferences for specific position groups, territorial staff, or other groups in which a learning component will benefit from a change in leadership or point of view

Any participatory workshop or institute in which competent external resources can and should challenge internal perceptions, practices, or philosophy

As previously suggested, patterns of relationships and experiences with external HRD resources need to be reviewed periodically. However, if purposefully selected and carefully negotiated and planned, external resources can be a valued and essential part of organizational HRD resources.

Supervisors of Work/Learning Experiences

In addition to their developmental work with their own staffs, some supervisors are selected to provide special work/learning experiences, for a period of time, for individuals from other units. A volunteer or paid staff member may be placed on a work/learning assignment for one or more of a variety of purposes: to have an intensive exposure to a different kind of work setting; to begin to learn a new kind of job; to concentrate on the development of some specific skills; to have access to some resources not available back home; to face a more complex or demanding work situation; and so forth. With the assistance of the work/learning supervisor, the individual works out specific knowledge, skill, or performance objectives related to his or her current job, to an intended career change, or even to testing specific potential abilities. The objectives of the learner's performance during the temporary assignment must fit in with the current objectives of the host unit. The supervisor must have great skill in designing and administering the special program as an integral part of the host office's operations.

Process models for designing and administering these experiences are often prepared by HRD staff. In some situations, detailed content or specific assignments are outlined to assure the development of certain competencies. If needed, the HRD resources (e.g., workshops, tuition for outside study, etc.) may also be built into the work/learning assignment. HRD staff and the host supervisor may be used as mentors or monitors of the work/learning experiences. However, the genius of the supervisor lies in two areas and warrants the supervisor's being included among the respected HRD resources of the organization. First, the supervisor works to keep the learner in the driver's seat as much as possible. This enables the learner to get the most out of all of the learning experiences planned, including self-assessment before and after the specific assignment is undertaken. Second, the supervisor works to take impromptu advantage of any situation to reinforce, synthesize, deepen, expand, or stimulate the learning process, without capriciously shifting from or diluting the basic progressive plan. Organizational crises often permit individuals to engage in unanticipated and demanding tasks that test competencies and confidence differently than daily routines. Skilled supervisors can also find challenges in the ordinary course of events.

Work/learning supervisors are also frequently drawn into supervision of student interns. Increasingly, universities and their students are seeking internships in the voluntary sector. The HRD unit may reach agreements with specific universities about periodic placement of interns in offices related to their major studies, undergraduate or graduate. An internal system for collecting information about various offices' needs for interns, as well as tentative plans for their use, may be developed by the HRD office and a subcommittee of the HRD council. As students undertake more of their own curriculum planning, there are more three-way conferences involving student and university representatives and the voluntary organization's supervisor. These conferences plan, monitor, and assess the effectiveness of intern programs.

Instructors

A final HRD resource to be considered is the organizational instructor system that is designed nationally for delivery of HRD programs. Large voluntary organizations that do continuing needs assessments and plan for periodic updating and replacements of course materials and instructors need to keep careful control of the number and nature of organizationally sponsored courses and workshops, as well as of by whom, where, and how often they are used. Management approval of completed materials or of proposals for new or updated courses is based on past experience and new organizational needs. Other procedures related to course development are helpful to the HRD office and the HRD council for quality control and for assuring that courses are currently relevant to the needs of specific target groups.

As HRD councils or informal work groups have been strengthening the organization's learning programs, common concerns have arisen about instruction, especially about the internal instructors for internal HRD of volunteers and paid staff. Course planning and delivery cannot be dealt with unit by unit when operational management of a large organization is increasingly decentralized. Although HRD delivery systems are seldom planned *in toto* but rather gradually emerge as national offices learn to collaborate, the following elements have usually found their way into voluntary organizational delivery plans:

Written guidelines for assessment of learning needs

Listing and description of courses/workshops available to accomplish specific learning objectives, including information about the general focus, intended learners, time involved, method of scheduling, instructors, and how to prepare for the learning experience

Procedures for selecting learners or for learner application; confirmation of participation, time, place, and instructors' names

Suggestions for supervisory involvement, in advance and follow-up

Guidelines for instructor selection, preparation, practice, certification, commitment to instruct, and opportunities for feedback and growth

Costs of learning, including who pays, how much, and for what

Procedures for reporting and record keeping, including why, who, what, where, and when

Evaluation and recognition of instructors and learners

As HRD offices and other national offices have worked within the framework of an HRD council and sometimes outside of it to resolve issues of policy, standards, systems, and procedures related to elements of delivery systems, they have learned that local users of HRD programs and delivery resources greatly appreciate simplicity of administration, consistency in national planning, and mutual support rather than competition. Local managers have urged unified planning.

Decentralized operations have also been a major influence on the emergence of a more unified instructor system as the key to effective delivery of HRD. Many national offices of voluntary organizations accustomed to centralized HRD using primarily national instructors had highly individualized approaches to selection, preparation, and authorization of national instructors for internal HRD. Decentralization and the high cost of centralized HRD encouraged instructors to be readily available in all parts of the country, prepared to use national course materials. Local units urged selection and preparation of instructors from their own volunteer and paid staff. They strongly approved agreements among national offices on standards and procedures for selection, preparation, and support of their local instructors. Local managers favored the designation of these instructors as "national" instructors, because it meant they had ready access to various kinds of national recognition and resources and meant they could, on occasion, fill instructional assignments in other nearby local units with full recognition of their competence to serve as organizational instructors. This approach was aided by the tradition among voluntary organizations of not having full-time instructors for internal HRD. Instead, organizational instructors have been and are volunteer, part-time instructors who ask for and carry that privilege and responsibility along with other duties for whatever office is their home base.

National HRD offices have given much time and effort to their work with other national offices, as well as with field service and local units, to build organizational consensus on various aspects of HRD delivery systems. The HRD council, however formally or informally constituted, is greatly helping that movement. The preparation, monitoring, and upgrading of instructors seems to be the most critical issue related to HRD delivery, but increasing progress is being made. The need for quality control in a widely dispersed system challenges everyone's ingenuity and cooperative spirit. Some thoughts about effective decentralized instructor systems are beginning to emerge:

1. It is important to provide for coverage of organizational jurisdictions by instructors in relation to key target groups for learning for a period of three to five years. Where are the greatest needs for new instructors? Where are needs for current instructor monitoring, support, or updating? Where are currently available instructors of instructors? Where are subject matter experts, who serve as resource persons in course content to instructors, located? Using the information gained in response to such questions, gradually build a decentralized system for preparing and developing instructors by stages and in areas having priority needs.

2. As part of decentralization, make the initial preparation of instructors part of the whole system by selecting and preparing instructors of instructors not only to handle the initial preparation but also to do monitoring, coaching, updating, upgrading, certifying, and terminating of instructor services. In addition, prepare them to help instructors build and implement their own professional development plans, as instructors.

3. Design a number of models for effective networking among instructors (e.g., showing why, with whom, and how) and encourage their use. Help to locate resource persons who can assist others to use networking techniques.

4. Develop and distribute, for use by instructors, a wide range of substantive resource materials relating both to the subject matter of courses and to adult learning and teaching; keep these materials updated. Develop lines of communication among instructors and between local and national units through newsletters, small regional meetings, teleconferences for critical problems or decision making, audio and video cassettes, field testing of new materials, and so forth. Make feedback a high priority and keep as much of it oral as is feasible. Cut down administrative paperwork.

5. Work toward useful computerization of information concerning instructors, schedules, and courses by testing, over a period of time, who really needs to know what. Collaborate with other offices of human resource management.

6. Clarify the career development aspects of serving as organizational

instructors by identifing and recognizing outstanding competencies or results of HRD in personal and organizational performance. Invite competent instructors to apply for positions of greater responsibility within HRD.

7. Devise incentives for this volunteer work (e.g., "instructor of the year" awards, an annual recognition of organizational instructors, etc.). Include instructors not only on HRD committees and task forces, but also in other groups where an HRD perspective might help or where an individual might have a professional development opportunity.

Summary

These key resources for effective human resource development in voluntary organizations—each individual serving the organization, all supervisors, all managers, the HRD council and its work groups, external resource persons, supervisors of work/learning experiences, and instructors—join with the HRD specialists of the HRD offices, both volunteer and paid, to plan and implement the activities most vital to the organization's goals and change efforts. How all of these resources are tied together depends first on the kinds of objectives and delegations for HRD delineated at each level of the organization. Second, the degree of unity is greatly affected by practices of collaboration between volunteers and paid staff, among all offices concerned with their personnel's HRD, and among the administrative levels of the organization. These practices should be continually and realistically analyzed by HRD offices, in order to help establish development goals for HRD as an organizational system. Third, HRD offices need to work toward the development of organizational policies, standards, and research directed toward HRD that are inclusive of all HRD efforts, not only those directly within the jurisdiction of the HRD offices. Fourth, HRD offices need to encourage all organizational information and communications systems to be operated within the philosophy of participatory management. All of these efforts will facilitate the establishment and achievement of organizational priorities in HRD, while also encouraging full attention to individual, unit, or other group needs.

Current emphasis in HRD within national voluntary organizations is on building the strength and availability of HRD resources, as close as possible to the people carrying out the member-directed or community-directed services of the organization. This trend complements the focus on increasing the skills and motivation of individuals to understand their current competencies and readiness to undertake continued learning in relation to their jobs, their careers, and their life planning. Only through an organization-wide effort at the local level to support individual planning for development and to facilitate the identification and involvement of internal and external HRD resources (volunteer and paid, part time and full time), can HRD make a real difference in both the quality of organizational services and of organizational life for its volunteers and paid staff. That kind of nationwide local movement can, in turn, make HRD a more influential instrument of organizational growth and effectiveness in the national sector.

WHAT OF THE FUTURE?

These days, many scenarios for the future are being projected for organizations and institutions, for nations, and for the planet Earth. These scenarios tend to communicate an overall attitude of optimism or pessimism regarding how well the players in their scripts will succeed in the roles and responsibilities they carry. Rather than pursue that kind of model, I will present several statements that are forward-looking for HRD and will reinforce the basic messages of this chapter.

The first message relates to a new emphasis on the role of HRD programs and activities within a national voluntary organization. The most effective HRD units, along with collaborating offices and the HRD council, have tried at all times to be responsive to organizational needs and to requests received from managers and volunteer leaders, whether expressed through needs assessments, statements of objectives, or conference findings. The suggestion for the future is that when an organizational need or deficiency is identified, for which HRD may be a resource, such a situation should not immediately trigger the design of a learning activity. Too often, by the time the activity is implemented throughout the organization, the perception or reality of the organizational situation may have changed sufficiently so that its relationship to the learning is lost. The activity probably will then fall into the category of useful skills development.

If, in their role of assisting management with human resource development, HRD staff remain an integral part of the strategic planning to the entire organizational situation (including comprehensive data collection and analysis), learning interventions can be designed in the light of the findings of the whole process. Learning interventions can also be introduced throughout the organization in the context of the larger situation and with reference to other interventions being made as well. Overall expectations of results from all of the measures help people see the learning as an integral part of organizational improvement, change, problem solving, or renewal. Assessments of results may then be made at the level of the specific desired outcomes for the learning experience and at the level of its contribution to the larger effort.

A special benefit might accrue through this approach, in terms of the perception by leadership volunteers of the value of their participation in the learning event, as well as in other interventions or in decision making. Their motivation for sharing in the learning experience would be influenced by their seeing it as an identifiable part of an organizational change effort.

A second message is a kind of corollary to the first. It is that HRD specialists, volunteer and paid, may be able to play a more useful organizational development role by taking the initiative and the responsibility for highlighting the development process that probably takes place as strategic and operational planning cycles are completed and repeated. In addition to the objectives/action plan/outcomes cycle, an evolutionary continuum might be identified. In spite of obstacles or even some reversals, the use of strategic systems over a five-year period changes the organization in terms of administrative and resource development objectives and in terms of greater organizational competence and strength of character. Each planning cycle builds on the past, and patterns of increasing involvement of people in the planning result in both higher skill and greater acceptance of responsibility for the success of the process.

Since volunteers are usually heavily involved in the planning process, they might take particular satisfaction in sensing that their contributions have greatly aided the development of the organization. It would be a logical role, and one that is within the competencies of experienced HRD administrators, to serve with volunteer colleagues from inside and outside the organization as "trackers" of development for the human resources of the organization and the organization itself that occurs through involvement in strategic planning.

A third message relates to volunteers. From the standpoint of competencies, HRD people have repeatedly recognized that there are no significant patterns of differences based on whether individuals are involved in HRD as volunteers or as paid staff. The more important variables of academic level, experience, motivation, intelligence, and interpersonal skills affect individuals in learner and instructor roles or affect the development or implementation of HRD programs. These variables have little correlation with the volunteer or paid status of HRD personnel. Certainly the total HRD effort is enriched by volunteers and by paid staff volunteering as organizational instructors or HRD coordinators. These efforts are highly prized by paid administrators, who are well aware of economic constraints and who welcome the increased human resources and the multiple ideas, views, and experiences in adult learning programs.

There are two issues regarding volunteers that complicate the HRD situation. One issue relates to a tendency to separate volunteer input from that of paid staff when planning decisions are to be made. Except for those organizational policy decisions clearly defined as volunteer prerogative (paid staff provide advisory input), the volunteer role in many offices is primarily defined as *advisory*, and the role of paid administrators is defined as *decision making*. Attempting to actualize these differences by first inviting volunteer input and then having paid staff decide, tends to lower that quality of the final product. Since volunteers are involved in all levels and echelons of HRD, decisions usually affect volunteers as much as or more than paid staff. So their stake in planning decisions is high. If they shared in the total process as collaborators, they could contribute much to examining possible consequences of various courses of action and to interpreting decisions throughout the organization. For these reasons, HRD people, both volunteer and paid, need to periodically review their practices to determine how collaboration might be improved.

A second issue related to volunteers involves accountability. In an era of growing attention to results assessments, HRD people are also expected to do more than count the courses designed, the learners registered in internal or external learning activities, and the instructors prepared and used. If HRD resources are to help achieve both organizational and individual objectives and to improve the quality of organizational service and of organizational work life, then volunteer and paid HRD people need clearer agreements as to what and how results will be assessed and to what extent and in what ways each group is accountable.

This is not an easy task. One approach reemphasizes collaboration. If volunteers and paid staff make a joint decision or a recommendation about an HRD objective to management, they might pursue the process by looking at intended results in advance and by discussing openly what might be the consequences of failure and of success for both volunteers and paid staff. Together they need to look at how performance and results will be assessed and by whom. Isn't it feasible for volunteers involved in accountability to deal openly with limited success or even failure, if that is done within the supporting climate of a development plan that is part of a performance review event? Too often paid staff expect to bear the accountability alone; but that approach denies to the volunteers the opportunity to follow through, with their paid colleagues, on a developmental approach to improvement. Conversations on this rather sensitive topic are very much in order.

A final message is addressed to the learner, that is, all of us. We are in the middle of a learning revolution of very complex dimensions. To tackle just one aspect from the point of view of national voluntary organizations, I would elect to emphasize the importance of each of us attempting to manage our own learning better by putting it more consciously into a larger framework. Instead of being satisfied with a task-related focus to which certain skill development activities are related, we need to take a "learning to learn" approach. This involves consciously broadening and deepening our understanding of our own organizations and the communities of which they are a part. It also includes periodic assessment of our development in relation to the changes in our organizations and being certain that they are in agreement. We need to understand our own learning practices and how effective they are. Then we can determine how to enhance what we learn, how to learn effectively and efficiently, and how to actually apply our learning. We must see ourselves and our colleagues as part of a learning society, so that we have a sense of what we are trying to contribute, through our organizations, to improving organizational goals and the conditions in which we live and work.

Why, in this chapter, should one urge assessment of ourselves as learners, and try to see opportunities for improving that function in ourselves and our colleagues? One response is that if the essence of a voluntary organization lies in its freedom to determine its own purpose and direction, to seek and select its own resources, and to assess its own results and worth, then a philosophy of self-directed learning best reinforces that pattern. For persons striving toward greater self-direction as learners, effective HRD in an organization means helping to find and develop a wide range of resources for learning, in order to solve problems, to strengthen performance and get better results, to open new doors, to help determine new organizational directions, to build new, human linkages and to deepen the old. In short, HRD plays a critical role in assuring the achievement of organizational and individual goals. In that context, learning provides the best opportunity for the organization to benefit from its human investment.

BIBLIOGRAPHY

American Red Cross. *Listening and Speaking—A Marketing Point of View.* Washington, D.C.: American Red Cross, 1982.

Borst, Diane, and Patrick J. Montana. *Managing Nonprofit Organizations.* New York: AMACOM, 1977.

Chalofsky, Neal, and Carnie Ives Lincoln. *Up the HRD Ladder.* Reading, Pa.: Addison-Wesley, 1983.

Craig, Robert L., ed. *Training and Development Handbook.* New York: McGraw-Hill, 1976.

Cross, K. Patricia. *Adults As Learners.* San Francisco: Jossey-Bass, 1981.

Goodman, Paul S., and associates. *Change in Organizations.* San Francisco: Jossey-Bass, 1982.

Hardy, J.M. "Crystal Gazing; What's Ahead for Nonprofits?" *Nonprofit Management* 1 (1979).

Huse, Edgar F. *Organizational Development and Change.* St. Paul, Minn.: West Publishing Co., 1975.

Naisbitt, John. *Megatrends.* New York: Warner Books, 1982.

O'Connell, Brian. *Voluntary Organizations.* New York: Association Press, 1976.

Pavlock, Ernest J. *OD: Managing Transitions.* Washington, D.C.: ASTD, 1981.

Peters, Thomas J., and Robert H. Waterman, Jr. *In Search of Excellence.* New York: Harper and Row, 1982.

Rubright, Robert, and Dan MacDonald. *Marketing Health and Human Services.* Rockville, MD.: Aspen Publications, Aspen Systems Corps., 1981.

Schindler-Rainman, Eva, and Ronald Lippitt. *The Volunteer Community.* Fairfax, Va.: NTL Learning Resources Corp., 1971.

United Way of America. "What Lies Ahead—A New Look." Alexandria, Va.: United Way of America, 1983.

Yankelovich, Daniel. *New Rules.* New York: Random House, 1981.

SECTION THREE

INTERNATIONAL AREAS OF HRD

An International Perspective

TOM JAAP

Given the interdependency of nations, events in any part of the world tend to have an effect on many other parts of the world. HRD is not and should not be outside of this interdependency. Even more so, HRD in any one country can affect many other countries.

Therefore, it becomes essential that we all develop an understanding of this interdependent world and the place of HRD in it. In this chapter, Jaap helps us understand this. Even if you do not consider yourself involved in the international HRD scene, it is still important to read this chapter and be sensitive to the international forces at work on and with HRD.

Tom Jaap is director of Human Resource Associates (London), an international firm that specializes in helping organizations and individuals to be more effective. He has had extensive international experience and was one of the founders of the International Federation of Training and Development Organizations. During 1984–85, he will serve as director of the International Division of ASTD. He is a chartered engineer and a frequent presenter at international conferences.

As we entered the 1980s, the world faced one of the most challenging periods in its history, due to the impact of the economic recession and the burgeoning of technology. The most visible characteristics of the impact were the number of vacant factories and the increasing number of unemployed people. Although there have been a great many advances in the quality of work life, there is a tendency to focus on the problems. The reality, to most HRD practitioners, is the view that there are many more problems than opportunities. However, throughout the world, there is still the possibility to creatively discover and implement solutions.

In some regions, the term *industrial desert* was accurately used to describe the devastation the recession created. It was fortunate, however, that an increasing number of HRD practitioners began to face the exciting challenge of what HRD could do for individuals and organizations in what will be a very different future.

Terminology is a dangerous area, for semantics are covered with national pride and can get in the way of effective communication. In the 1950s, references were made to the *developed* countries and the *underdeveloped*. By the 1960s, the terminology had changed, and the latter were than referred to as the *lesser developed*. By the end of that decade, the term had changed to *developing* or *emerging* countries. In the 1970s, the references were to the *newly industrializing* or the *preindustrial* countries. These terms emphasized industry as the key determinant. It is probable that during the 1980s another term will emerge.

In this chapter, the term *developing* will be used for those countries generally considered to have not yet reached the point to be called *developed* countries. There are no absolute criteria to make this distinction, but it is generally accepted that most countries fit into one category or the other. National pride may make that determination, but, in this chapter, the distinction will involve factors such as: economic independence (to the degree it is possible in this interdependent world), literacy, and exportable manufactured products or services.

GLOBAL AWARENESS

The massive changes in employment characteristics that have taken place are being perceived as something more than the normal cyclical variations. HRD practitioners are awakening to the significance and challenge of this radical change. In developing a planned response to the challenge, HRD practitioners are beginning to identify and chart the pertinent factors.

Viewing the factors from a purely national perspective is recognized as inadequate and highly dangerous. It is no longer possible to arrive at effective solutions to national problems. They must be constructed within a global framework. We have reached an advanced stage—when one nation catches cold, a host of others sneeze.

This leads to an important reason for being globally aware. Recognition and understanding of how the world has changed can provide an effective backdrop for shaping future solutions. Adopting a "head-in-the-sand" posture results in inappropriate solutions. This can be illustrated by the rising demand for protectionism, which allows a nation's trade to prosper. Protectionism appears to be a simple solution, but it has potentially catastrophic results for a country's export trade.

STRATEGIC PLANNING

The effective manager is aware of the multitude of factors that influence decision making. Active involvement in the strategic planning process of the organization enables a manager to assess both internal and external environments. For many organizations, even those that are considered to be domestic, the strategic planning process must include recognition of the international marketplace and international labor conditions.

HRD FACTORS

Organizations mean people. As change becomes more rapid and international interdependency is achieved, the people dimension becomes more difficult to predict. The strategic planning process requires stretching the mind to take into account factors previously considered unnecessary. The following factors must be included in the thinking of HRD practitioners:

Unemployment tends to have its greatest impact on the young and the old.

Youth unemployment affects those with lower levels of schooling.

The world-wide increase in longevity will increase pressure on public expenditures.

European countries will probably experience a zero or negative growth.

In developing countries, there is a 2% to 3% growth in population (an enormous rate).

There are developing countries where 50% of the population was under 15 years of age at the start of this decade.

Food could become a strategic weapon in shaping future international arrangements.

Conservation of resources and nuclear armaments are becoming major issues throughout the world.

International banking has been shaken by the massive loans to developing nations, some of which have been unable to repay as scheduled.

Labor is becoming internationally mobile.

The HRD practitioner is being confronted with issues that previously would have been considered outside the HRD area. The issues stretch beyond the usual concerns, as it is recognized that what happens anyplace in the world can have a significant impact on HRD in one's own organization. HRD practitioners are faced daily with problems that require urgent solutions. This tends to restrict thinking to specific local issues, rather than to international issues, which are considered esoteric.

Let us look at some of the problems that appear to be local but are, in fact, influenced by other countries.

Declining Industries

Since the middle 1970s, developed countries have experienced an unprecedented rapid decline in many of their traditional industries (e.g., mining, shipbuilding, heavy engineering, and textiles). During the early 1980s, a great deal of analysis and research was undertaken to identify the causes. Much of the change could be attributed to the world recession at the time. There was the belief that those industries would recover as soon as the recession ended. Slowly, it was realized that much of the decline was irreversible, regardless of the state of the world's economy.

Newly Developing Countries

An examination of the global picture shows the impressive industrial growth that has taken place in many countries since 1945. This was primarily funded by the developed countries with their foreign aid and general overseas commitment on either a unilateral basis or a multilateral basis (e.g., United Nations Development Program).

The newly developing countries, sometimes called the *developing* countries, acquired a significant advantage over the developed countries. The former have newer technology, better working methods, lower operating costs, and lower labor costs. These provide them with an edge over most of their competitors in terms of quality, delivery, and price, and developed countries are presented with the phenomenon of unfair competition from newly developing countries.

Investment in Research and Development

Investors appear to be cautious about investing their money in research and development (R & D). Part of the problem are the enormous costs associated with R & D as the organization enters new generations of high technology. R & D is a risk operation with no guarantee of immediate results and that has resulted in some apparently exciting investments failing. It does not take many failures to produce a low-risk attitude that does not encourage R & D. We find an exception in Japan, where it is the practice to increase investments in R & D for the long-range benefits.

Organizations in Europe and in the U.S. need to learn how to make strategic use of R & D activities and need to have adequate funding to do so. In most of Europe, there does not appear to be any real strategy regarding R & D, and funds available for this activity are spread thinly over many activities. This places Europe and the U.S. in a vulnerable position, regarding the development and application of technology. There may be a time when the majority of advanced technology and hardware will have to be purchased from Japan.

Protectionism

Fear is a powerful force, one that can produce harmful reactions when it affects solving problems such as high unemployment. In many countries, the reasons for high unemployment are not fully explored, but the reaction to fear causes many to be strongly in favor of policies that would protect a country's productive capacity.

Dumping products to capture a market, limiting the manufacturing capacity of Country A's organization located in Country B, or other such tactics put pressure on governments to introduce tariff barriers to protect their indigenous products. As manufacturers continue to focus their attention on protection (being reactive), their overseas competitors are creating new solutions and products to improve their competitiveness.

The competition also exists among developed countries; it is not limited to North-South or developed-developing distinctions. To illustrate this, we need only look at how the Japanese were successful in capturing the memory chip market. From a very slow start, the Japanese gained a commanding position in the production and marketing of memory chips, known as 64K RAM bits. While still in control of the market, they forged ahead to develop the 256K RAM chip, even though it appeared to compete with their hold on the market. In a few years, they moved ahead, through vast investments in R & D, to replace the United States as the leader in this technology.

Technology

The microchip has changed the face of the industrial environment by making available inexpensive memory devices that can be used in an increasing range of products.

Information storage and processing can be readily handled by word processors and computers. Software is constantly being developed to enable an increasing number of organizational tasks to be accomplished through the use of computers.

The ability to manufacture computers is limited to only some countries in various parts of the world. The ability to use computers is not restricted to any place or group. As long as they have a reliable source of electrical power (possibly the only limitation), any nation in the world can use computers to handle organizational tasks.

The impact of this technology will have different effects in the various parts of the world. Generally, most countries will see the following factors in their future:

The bulk of information will be handled by some form of technology.

Technological equipment will become increasingly user friendly, no matter what the language or country.

Executives and managers will be released from tedious and time-consuming tasks to devote more time to product development and customer service.

Technology will result in the reality of the global village through rapidly expanding national and international networks.

Changing work patterns will make today's activities seem primitive and dehumanizing.

Technology will provide individuals with time to devote to community and other non-work-related activities.

Communication among all the peoples of the world will be enhanced.

We have moved rapidly into this new world of work, but it is also apparent that many businesses still rely on mechanical and electronic equipment to process paper work or enhance productive capability.

We cannot foretell the future. Will the newly developing countries feel that they must go through the same growth patterns as the developed countries and, therefore, take 100 years to close the gap? Or will these developing countries skip over that century of growth and move directly into the new technological area? This will pose a challenge in the coming decades.

Resistance to Change

The apparent reluctance of large sectors of European and U.S. business, as well as those in developing countries, to adopt new technology needs further examination. This can start with an exploration of the implications of technology for people.

Among the factors are:

Changed work patterns and relationships. This is a problem for developing countries, where the work patterns and relationships can go back many centuries.

Need for rapid response to situations. Rapid response has traditionally been considered a virtue in developed countries. There appears to be less of that behavior today than in the past. Developing countries have generally not had a rapid response mode as part of their cultural norm.

Less socializing and interaction. The pressure in developing countries for improving the quality of work life has encouraged more socialization and interaction just at the time when some new modes of work (e.g., using machines for communication) have been reducing face-to-face interaction. Developing countries, where a high level of socialization and interaction have been common, are being pressured to change that behavior.

Fear of technology. This appears to be present in many countries, regardless of economic state of development.

Less need for middle management. The recession/depression of the early 1980s brought to light the fact that many organizations were overloaded at the middle management level. Also, new technologies require fewer levels of management.

When many of these changes are translated into reality, no one should be surprised to find resistance to change. Some of the reasons are:

People continue to resist change as long as change remains a threatening experience.

People are reluctant to use new technology, as they are uncertain about its capability and uncomfortable with its use.

Unemployment is attributed, in part, to technology, in general, and microtechnology, in particular.

There is a lack of user-friendly technology and reader-friendly instructions.

There is confusion about the use of technology, due to the lack of integration of the various systems.

Information technology represents a hardware and software jungle.

We can also add the following consequences:

Industry is increasing output and raising productivity by reducing the work force. This is particularly hard for those countries with soaring birth rates of 2% to 3%, mentioned earlier.

More groups, traditionally not significant in the work force (e.g., women, some races, religions, castes), are now entering in large numbers.

In many countries, increasing legislation is being passed to safeguard the rights of the individual.

Value systems are rapidly changing, perhaps with less regard for authority and discipline than in the past.

How can change be achieved against such a difficult and apparently depressing background? Solutions may be difficult to discover, unless new perspectives are developed that change the way work is regarded in many parts of the world.

ASSESSING WHAT THE FUTURE OFFERS

Governments, employers, and employee organizations throughout the world are becoming increasingly aware of the long-term nature of people issues. Considerable efforts are being made to discover solutions that can be applied to produce effective results. HRD is part of the solution, but by no means can HRD alone be expected to deal with all the issues raised earlier.

There are some regional, if not global, efforts that can be identified. The countries within the European Economic Community (EEC) are attempting to achieve a coordinated strategy to resolve some of the issues. Their efforts are being hampered by the traditional conservative versus socialist dimensions that have been part of recent European history. The pictures of the future, painted by both extremes, tend to be in conflict with the perception of many who are seeking a more leisure-oriented and cooperative, community-based economic system.

There are some issues that are specifically HRD oriented.

Attitudes Toward Work

Current indications are that a majority of individuals will work fewer hours at a lower wage. Attitudes toward work will need to change, if the practice of being paid for one's labor at the "rate for the job" is replaced by the concept of being paid for one's contribution to society. Acceptance of this concept raises issues that are in conflict with the central belief of the work ethic held by so many, particularly in those countries influenced by the Judeo-Christian approach to work. (This is sometimes referred to as the *Protestant work ethic*, but it does not seem fair to ascribe it only to them.)

In general, HRD is concerned with attitude. The argument is not being made here that we should use HRD to brainwash or indoctrinate. The role of HRD in evolving new attitudes toward work is still to be explored. It will certainly vary from country to country, but there will be experiences and concepts that need to be shared.

The Right to Work

A key paradox in this process is that while a country may desire to provide people with the right to work, they must face the reality of being unable to accomplish that aim. A second paradox facing many countries is that there is more than enough work to keep everyone busy who seeks work. Then, why do we have a problem? Part of the answer lies in the attitudes and practices regarding work.

In many developed countries of the world, the practice has evolved of paying employees for the time spent working. Each person employed offers labor in return for money. Over the years, this process has been refined to arrive at what is considered the "rate for the job". Employers and employees negotiate, often through a very complicated process, to achieve agreed-upon rates for different jobs. This process may involve the use of diagnostic techniques of evaluation to differentiate among the work content of different jobs. In many countries, this has resulted in the cost of labor being priced so high that some entrepreneurs have found work too expensive to undertake. It must be acknowledged that, in some countries, unions have fought hard and long to achieve the best possible benefits for their members.

It is, however, becoming increasingly clear to many that a different approach to the question of work is urgently required. As these new approaches evolve, HRD practitioners throughout the world must be sensitive to the changes and identify the contribution that HRD can make to this change process.

Careers

In general, HRD practitioners are mainly concerned with the growth of individuals in work situations. In some countries, the HRD efforts have been supported by a school system geared to equipping individuals for a career in industry, commerce, or the professions. Acquiring appropriate qualifications assured individuals of a life-long career, if that was what they desired.

The career scene for young people is changing. Having the necessary qualifications (i.e., a diploma or certificate) no longer guarantees a career in the world of work. Many young people are questioning the value of a school system that appears to be out of touch with the real world.

This problem of articulation between school and work occurs in many countries, regardless of the country's stage of economic development. The problem is substantial and requires careful handling to find solutions that meet the needs of the young in a rapidly changing society. In some countries, a unique but necessary approach is to equip young graduates with survival skills that will help them cope with either employment or unemployment.

HRD FOR THE UNEMPLOYED

For purposes of this section, I will include the underemployed with the unemployed. The distinction is that those in the former category are working but usually earning so little as to barely subsist. They are usually part-time or temporary workers and lack the skills needed to move into more permanent and lucrative positions.

Learning Programs for the Unemployed

In many countries, the young unemployed are ill-equipped to cope with life as adults. Their school systems, if they went to school, did not give them the necessary life skills to deal with a world in which they would not be able to get jobs upon leaving or graduating from school.

This has required the development of special programs for young people, including:

Remedial instruction in basic numerical and written skills

Social skills that enable them to be effective in a variety of situations other than those they have known

Basic work skill that is transferable from one work situation to another

Exposure to technology so as to acquire a level of comfort

Building self-esteem has become an important part of many such programs. In developed countries, being unemployed is considered shameful and to be the result of the inadequacy of the individual. When the chances for employment are seriously reduced by economic factors beyond the control of the young person, it is essential that young persons be provided with learning experiences that teach them how to cope with being unemployed.

The United States has developed a comprehensive program for the young unemployed called the Youth Training Scheme. The program is operated by the Manpower Services Commission, a tripartite body with representatives from employers, unions, and the school system. All young people without jobs are offered places in the program. Education can last for a period of up to one year in an employer's establishment. A weakness of this kind of program, as with others like it, is that there are no guarantees of employment after the education.

In developing countries, the impact of unemployed youth has generally not been as significant. In some of those countries, there has always been a limited expectation of full employment. However, the expectations are rising. Through television, movies, and other media, the youth learn of others with jobs and wonder why they are not employed. This provokes unrest. Aside from the political issues, the developing nations are faced with the problem of enormous numbers of young people (it is not uncommon to find almost half the population under the age of 20), and the competition for the limited number of jobs is very intense.

In the efforts to make youth more employable, (e.g., the Youth Training Scheme), there is a significant role for HRD practitioners. They are the important link between the program and the employer. As these programs are all based on learning, the HRD practitioner is the appropriate person from the employers' side to be highly visible. This is a new challenge for many HRD practitioners.

Apprenticeships

West Germany appears to have fewer problems with unemployed youth. Some attribute this to their well-conceived and diligently executed apprentice system. Its aim is to educate and train young people who want to enter the work force, in specific trades and professions. At the beginning of the 1980s, over half of those in the 15–18 age bracket were in some type of apprenticeship program. The program requires three days a week in a learning situation with an employer and two days in a school.

In 1981, about 651,800 of the 1.7 million young people had begun their apprenticeship. Both totals were an all-time record. This process assured the nation's industries of a steady flow of skilled workers.

It is not being suggested that such a vast program is necessary in every country. There are other ways in which a country can meet its needs for a skilled work force. Also, such a program must be kept flexible as the needs of the workplace change.

In the United Kingdom, the number of apprenticeships was reduced by half during the 1970s. The loss was mainly in traditional industries. There are many reasons for this, but the situation has encouraged all sides of industry, government, and labor to reexamine every aspect of apprenticeships to eliminate outdated practices.

HRD FOR THOSE EMPLOYED

Most employers are aware of the need to maintain an effective and efficient workforce at all levels of the organization. The HRD practitioner is a key person in providing learning experiences to make that happen. There are some interesting trends that may have escaped those who are looking at only one country—their own.

Skilled Workers

In Europe, during the early 1980s, there was an increasing trend toward providing more training to enable the work force to cope with rising standards and the need for increased productivity. Increasingly, this training is provided onsite and is paid for by the employer.

In addition, many governments in Europe have adopted a policy of providing training and education for those skilled workers who have been made redundant (laid off). This provision for learning enables the redundant worker to receive training to maintain an appropriate skill level until rehired. It also provides for additional training on new technologies so the worker's skills will not become obsolete. In addition, education is provided if it is apparent that the worker cannot be rehired in the same kind of work.

In developing countries, an interesting practice has begun to emerge. When a foreign country wants to function in a host country, there are usually involved negotiations on finances, taxes, and so forth. Another item that has been added is HRD. Some host countries are telling the foreign countries that for every national who is hired and educated by the foreign company, there must be one national who is not hired but still educated by the foreign company. That is, the foreign company must prepare skilled people to work for national companies that lack the resources to provide their own HRD.

Managers

It is obvious to most observers of the management scene that the ability to cope with change is one of the major competencies required by a manager. The factors regarding change, outlined earlier in this chapter, indicate the pressures being experienced by a majority of managers in developed countries.

There are many similarities in the challenges and problems that face managers in both developed and developing countries. There are, however, some significant differences.

In developed countries, managers are facing new problems of managing with limited resources. For years, in some countries, it was possible to solve all problems by using additional financial resources and being unconcerned about physical resources. With the tightening of budgets and increased concern about the environment, previous alternatives are not as readily available as before.

In developing countries, there was a history of having to work within severe limitations of financial and physical resources. Then, the oil-producing nations raised their prices. For them it seemed to be an adequate response, for it meant increasing financial resources, while conserving physical resources. Management became much easier. The plethora of financial and physical resources made it relatively easy to acquire human resources from outside the country.

The effect was felt in oil-consuming nations. Managers had to learn how to manage with fewer financial resources and even limited physical resources. At the same time, downturns in the economy were heralded by increasing unemployment.

Then, in the early 1980s, the price of oil dropped. Managers in oil-producing nations found that they, in turn, had to cope with managing with reduced financial resources. Projects were halted or disbanded and expatriates were asked to go home. Human resources became limited.

These and other factors caused many countries (and employing organizations in those countries) to take a much closer look at the need for various levels of management. In addition, much more attention was paid to finding ways to evaluate managerial performance. As this movement continues, there will be different and increased demands on the HRD practitioner to provide the appropriate learning experiences for the new kind of manager.

Learning Resources

More organizations are discovering the need for stronger inhouse HRD capability. One advantage is that it enables the organization to have a shorter response time to problems involving performance, where learning can be the appropriate response.

Developing nations have been striving, in many cases, to build in-country competence in HRD. They recognize the gap that can be left when expatriates are asked to leave. In 1975, Venezuela acquired the foreign oil companies and then discovered the HRD capability did not accompany the equipment and machinery. There were some qualified HRD practitioners among the Venezuelans who had been employed by the oil companies, but there were not enough of them. For years after the nationalization, they had to rely on expatriates to meet their HRD needs, until they could build in-country HRD capability.

CONCLUSION

This chapter has been a brief attempt to look at some of the international conditions that influence HRD. There are many more that cannot be fully discussed here.

It is most important that HRD practitioners recognize that it is no longer possible to be isolated. The world is much more interdependent than most people realize. HRD practitioners of today, no matter what their country, will be influenced by events and conditions in other parts of the world.

There is much we can learn about HRD from those in different parts of the world. There was a time when the developed countries could teach the developing countries. Today, both can learn from each other about improving HRD.

Working Internationally

MICHAEL J. MARQUARDT

It has been said that the world is a global village. The truth of this statement is borne out by activities in HRD that transcend political boundaries. Marquardt helps us see the fact of interdependence and then goes on to show us how HRD functions as an international force.

If you are not involved internationally, you may be tempted to pass up this chapter and perhaps this whole section on the international aspects of HRD. All parts of the world influence each other and, therefore, they influence us in our work life and during our nonworking hours. It is important, then, for each of us to learn as much about the international arena as possible.

Michael J. Marquardt (Ed.D.) is deputy director for international programs, USDA Graduate School and a part-time instructor in human resource development in the graduate program at The George Washington University. He has designed, conducted, and evaluated HRD programs in over 30 countries throughout the world. He has provided technical services and cross-cultural learning for many people from the United States preparing to work overseas. He also served as training director for the Overseas Education Fund. He was a member of the executive committee of the International Division of ASTD (1982–83). He has written articles for numerous professional journals.

Alvin Toffler, well-known author of *Future Shock* and other works on the future, writes in his latest book, *Previews and Premises*, that the provision of continuous learning for the work force (HRD) will be one of the fastest growing industries of the 1980s and will soon be one of America's greatest exports.

A quick glance at recent statistics from the U.S. Department of Commerce and other sources confirms Toffler's prediction.

In 1982, the United States imported over $270 billion of goods and services and exported $230 billion.

Over 30,000 U.S. companies are involved in import-export activities, with thousands more entering the international market every year.

Thousands of companies from all over the world—Japan, Germany, Brazil, France, Italy, Nigeria, Saudi Arabia, Venezuela, Singapore— have established operations in the United States.

Nearly 330,000 students and officials from 150 countries of the world studied and were trained or educated in the United States in 1982. This figure is expected to jump to over 1 million by the 1990s.

The international labor pool, which is growing at a rate of over 50 million a year, requires greater and more complex technical skills to work in today's advanced technological and industrial world.

Millions of people in the United States are involved in jobs that are dependent on imports and exports. Hundreds of thousands more work in the U.S. for foreign-owned corporations such as Sony, Michellin, or Volkswagen of America. In addition, there are nearly 1 million Americans (including U.S. military personnel) who live and work abroad. Finally, there are the millions of local nationals working for U.S. firms overseas.

All these figures clearly demonstrate the growing interdependence of today's world and the ever-expanding need for international HRD practitioners, practitioners with unique kinds of international cross-cultural, training, education, language, and consulting skills. These unique skills are needed because working internationally in HRD is more than just transporting the American ways of training, educating, and developing people. The significantly different value systems, organizational structures, school levels, supportive resources, and political realities all dictate that the HRD practitioner must function differently in order to be successful. One must adapt the best of the American HRD technology to the new environment as well as *adopt* the new HRD techniques and ideas of the new cultures.

In spite of (or maybe even because of) the complexities, difficulties, and frustrations encountered when one operates in the international scene, working internationally in HRD is as exciting, fascinating, and enjoyable as any challenge one can ever have in the field of human resource development. It provides tremendous opportunities—opportunities to impact a country's development, to experience a totally new way of doing things, to develop unique cross-cultural HRD skills, and to travel and work in all the exotic parts of the world.

This chapter will attempt to prepare you (if you are new to international HRD) or enhance your capability (if you are an international HRD veteran) to work effectively in international HRD. First, we will examine the values and behavioral differences between U.S. and non-U.S. cultures, and how these differences impact HRD activities, specifically learning and consulting. Then, we will examine the international HRD job opportunities existing in multinational corporations, U.S. government, international organizations, schools and private development institutions, foreign corporations, and consulting firms. Finally, we will examine what it is like to live and work abroad as an HRD practitioner.

CULTURE AND INTERNATIONAL HRD

Simply stated, *culture* is defined as the customs, assumptions, thought processes, values, language, and behavioral patterns of a group of people.

There is a tremendous contrast between the culture and the resulting basic value systems of people from the United States (which are similar, though not identical, to that of Canada and most of Western Europe) and the remaining seven-eighths of the world.[1]

The manner in which we live, work, and learn; how we are motivated; our personal goals; and our ideals—these are all conditioned by cultural values. Successful HRD professionals are very conscious of these values as they design and conduct learning programs.

If a person from the United States were to implement an HRD activity in another culture without making adaptations, disaster would be guaranteed. To be successful, that person must fully understand and carefully consider the new culture.

Although there are numerous cultural values that could be contrasted with American values, there are seven that seem to have the greatest impact on any international HRD activity.

Change Versus Tradition

Americans and Western Europeans generally perceive change to be good, to be synonymous with growth, progress, and improvement. Most other cultures, however, do not view change in such a favorable light. For them, change involves a loss of stability, continuity, and tradition. It is seen as destructive (as compared to the good old days) and should therefore be avoided.

Bringing in new technology and new information results in cultural as well as technological change. It inevitably has sociological effects, such as changes in power structures in the role of men and women, in overall relationships, and in behavioral patterns. The outside stranger is seen as introducing new life styles and material possessions that may not be favored by all the local people. They may feel that their prized and cherished local culture will be destroyed.

In introducing new information or new technology, the HRD practitioner should not assume automatic acceptance without reservation or even resistance. Careful analysis of the local culture, however, might enable the practitioner to identify ways in which this change can relate to and even be compatible with the local rich tradition.

Fate Versus Control

Most of the world believes religiously in the concept of *fate*. From the Arab nomad (who conditioned every plan with an "if Allah wills") to the Latin American peasant or the Bangladesh merchant, this concept literally rules their lives. Fate controls who they are and what they can do. These people are also much more inclined to seek a harmony with and an acceptance of nature.

Americans, on the other hand, feel as if they can totally control the environment around them and the future ahead of them. They do not accept the fact that there may be things that are beyond their control.

People of other cultures may not be so easily convinced that a hydrodam will or should stop future flooding or that a new education program will or should involve lower castes or women. Whereas we see a problem as a challenge to be solved, other peoples see it as an obstacle, willed by God and not to be tampered with. We likewise see a direct, logical link between cause and effect. Other cultures do not accept such a linear sense of history in which one thing follows another.

The international HRD practitioner should recognize that the learners may have these beliefs and should work with some degree of humility, acknowledging that an individual cannot totally control the future.

Equality Versus Status

For Americans, equality is one of the most important values. To them, all people are equal. Americans try to play down inequalities and equalize opportunities.

Most countries of the world, however, including some European countries (e.g., Greece and Spain), perceive the concept of equality quite differently. For them, rank, status, and class delineation are the more desirable conditions. Knowing your status and, therefore, your role in society, provides a great sense of security and certainty. They do not mind showing deference and respect to those of higher class or authority.

Therefore, HRD activities that create change and upset this status may be resisted by the local population, both at the bottom and the top of the socioeconomic scales. U.S. industries that attempted to break the status culture of the U.S. South by involving blacks in their work force know the complexity of introducing such change and the strong resistance it aroused. Another factor to consider is that learners/employees actually may not wish to do better than those of higher status. They may intentionally lessen their efforts and achievements in order to avoid ostracism later from their own kind.

Individual Versus Group

Over an 11-year period (1967–78) Geert Hofstede[2] conducted a study of how different cultures perceive the relationship between the individual and his or her fellow individuals. In the United States and Europe he found societies in which the ties between individuals are very loose. Everyone is concerned with his or her own self-interest and, perhaps, the interests of the immediate family. Throughout most of the rest of the world he found societies in which the ties between individuals are very tight. People are born into collectives or into groups that may be their extended family, tribe, or village. These people are tightly integrated into the group and gain their identity from the group.

This group-oriented or collective-oriented value structure significantly affects HRD efforts. Whereas Americans will study and work for the purpose of doing something well and to master the subject, other peoples may place a priority on a job well recognized, on acquiring status and prestige, or on preserving respect. For them, the relationship comes before the task.

This value system would also affect the motivation of prospective learners/employees. Whereas U.S. companies may reward individual initiative, enterprise, and success, the local people may feel that loyalty to a group or a company should be more highly rewarded. The Japanese, for example, place a very high premium on employees who are loyal and serve the company on a life-long basis.

Action Versus Acceptance

Americans like action and like to be busy doing things—getting things done. In most other cultures, however, there is a greater orientation toward acceptance, of being rather than doing. Instead of controlling the river, one flows with it and follows its current. The authority of the manager or HRD person is followed, not challenged.

We are also practical. What works now, even if it has not been tried before, is the guideline. We are also more inclined to make decisions. We encourage learners/employees to be responsible and to take an active part in the decision-making process. In many cultures, such direct action and initiative is inappropriate for most people. It may even be seen as presumptuous and arrogant on the part of the learner. Hence, it may be difficult for the learner in HRD activities to actively participate. Sometimes learner participation can come only after a period of time, when they perceive such behavior as appropriate.

Informality Versus Formality

In the United States, managers, instructors, and leaders are encouraged to be informal and at ease in formal situations. Our president is seen in shortsleeves and jeans. Instructors and learners are seen as partners in the learning process. Managers work side-by-side with employees in matrix teams or in quality circles.

Formality is the norm in almost every other country in the world (including communist and equalitarian countries). Everyone dresses appropriately and avoids the use of first names until a personal relationship has been established. Instructors lecture formally from behind a podium; they do not sit casually on a desk or table. Informality is disapproved of because it may connote disrespect, and it can be confusing to the learner who is expecting authority and orderliness in the instructor-learner relationship.

Directness Versus Indirectness

We are encouraged to be direct and frank in our actions. We are open in stating our concerns and feelings about our relations with others and about our work or learning situation. If one is unable to do something, one says so. If one is having difficulties with another employee or learner, one is encouraged to deal with that person directly.

This value is very difficult for most other cultures to understand, much less to accept. These other cultures place a high premium on not harming the other person. Conflict is an evil since it causes a person to lose face.

Agreement is indicated even if it is not meant. For example, a *yes* is often not a *yes*. The yes may be said for many reasons, even when the speaker means *no*.

1. The speaker may recognize that you may feel hurt and rejected if you receive a *no* response.
2. The situation may change. For example, the speaker may say *yes* to a request with no intention of completing it. The speaker does so hoping you will forget about it, you will not need it, or he will not be here tomorrow.

A recent example of the indirectness and avoidance of confrontation was shown by the action of an Indonesian manager in one of my training programs who had a personality conflict with one of the instructors. Instead of confronting the instructor, he asked me if he could receive this necessary training from another person or from another institution.

These seven basic contrasts in the values of people in the United States and those of most of the rest of the world profoundly impact the manner in which HRD activities are implemented on the international scene. Unless the HRD practitioner is able to understand and appreciate these value differences, strong HRD skills will be ineffective in a different cultural mileau. On the other hand, incorporating these values into one's own thought processes, and hence into the HRD activities, will result in greater acceptance and success.

In addition to those more universal contrasts, there are many, and some very subtle, cultural uniquenesses in each and every culture. The successful HRD practitioner is able to objectively gather such information, filter out what is important and relevant to HRD activities, and quickly and creatively adapt to these differences.

There are a number of resources to which one can turn to become informed and updated on cultures and how they impact human resource development. The best single source is the Society for Intercultural Education, Training and Research (SIETAR), an international association with local chapters throughout the United States and other parts of the world. SIETAR sponsors numerous conferences and workshops, including a "Training of International Trainers" every July in Washington, D.C. Two publications, *The International Journal of Intercultural Relations* and *Communique*, provide members with information on intercultural activities, position openings, research, and publications. SIETAR has also published several books in the area of intercultural training.[3]

LANGUAGE AND CULTURE

Knowing the language(s) of the learner is very important for the HRD practitioner (for general communication and for HRD purposes), since language has a strong impact on a society's values and is a manifestation of the culture.

Many countries do use English as the official language, and in many other countries the learners will speak English as a second or third language. However, for most peoples of the world, English will not be understood at all. People from most Spanish-speaking and French-speaking countries will expect you to speak their language when you work in their country, even if they themselves can speak English.

Of course, for many of us, it is not impossible to speak the local or national language. Learners will not necessarily be offended if you do not. It is important, however, to remember that learning is hampered if the learner is not being instructed in his or her native language. The learner will obviously function at less than full speed. Likewise, the HRD professional may not be able to instruct as well in a language other than his or her native language.

When the HRD practitioner is not able to carry out HRD functions in the local language, there are two limitations.

1. Translation is required. This slows the learning process and can cause the excitement of the activity to be lost. If there is no translation and the learner is being instructed in other than the native language, there may be misunderstanding of words and ideas.

2. Every language contains implicit cultural elements that affect the thought processes and action orientation of the user.

Here are two examples that show how language affects behavioral patterns in a culture.

1. To describe dropping an object, an American would say, "I dropped it," implying my action, my control, my responsibility. In Spanish, one says "se caho sobre me," "It dropped on me," implying passive receiving and lack of control.
2. English is very informal, with only one form of the second person singular, (i.e., *you*). In a more formal, hierarchical culture (e.g., Vietnamese), there are 12 forms of the second person singular. Accordingly, it is much more natural for Americans to be informal and direct, whereas the Vietnamese must always carefully choose the appropriate form to address someone.

Although the HRD practitioner cannot always speak the local language, a special effort should be made to know the value influences of the particular language and at least to learn some basic phrases of greeting and questioning. The local people will appreciate your demonstration of interest in their language and, thereby, your interest in them. Your understanding of their thought processes and reactions will likewise be tremendously increased.

An excellent resource for obtaining information on culture and language is the Language and Intercultural Research Center of Brigham Young University in Utah.[4]

LEARNING INTERNATIONALLY

When an HRD practitioner is working with learners who are not from the United States (whether the program is in the United States or abroad), it is necessary to make a number of modifications in the design, implementation, and evaluation of the learning program. Figure 23.1 contrasts the American and non-American approaches to various learning activities. The different emphasis of the American learning system (based on American values) and the non-American learning system (based on their values) requires the HRD practitioner to make a significant adjustment while carrying out learning programs in other cultures.

Learning Activities	American Approach	Non-American Approach
Climate setting	Very important; includes environmental, interpersonal, and organizational climate; informal and relaxed	Less important; schoolroom setting; formal relationship with instructor
Planning	Done by instructor and learners; learners are responsible for their own learning	Done solely by instructor who is expert; accepted by learner
Needs assessment	Input sought from learner and other sources; important base for determining objectives	Needs determined by instructor; learners cannot be expected to know what they need to know
Setting objectives	Jointly determined by instructor and learner; negotiable and mutually acceptable	Set by instructor who should tell learners what they must know; clear-cut and nonnegotiable
Design	Use variety of learning methodologies; learners and outside resource people used	Lecture methodology; learning is by listening and remembering
Implementation	Instructors and learners responsible for implementing learning experiences; learning by doing is considered most effective technique; occurs in various settings	By instructor only; instructor tells, models correct way; experimental learning is risky and may expose learner to looking foolish
Evaluation	Done by instructor and learner; includes evaluation of learning content, process, and instructor; variety of evaluation techniques utilized	Done solely by instructor; based upon retention of learning content and skills; written tests

Figure 23.1. Learning: American versus non-American approaches.

We will examine these differences in some detail and see how the practitioner might successfully adapt the different components of learning to a different culture.

Selection of Learners

In the United States, learners are generally (although not always) selected because of their actual need for learning and/or because they are the most qualified to receive such learning.

This may not be true in other countries. Learners may have been chosen because of kinship to the local leader or for other political reasons. As a result, they may not be qualified to receive the learning, or they may not even be interested in it. Motivation may be at minimal level.

Motivation to learn, to acquire skills, and to change behavioral patterns may also differ between learners of different cultures. Generally, Americans are more achievement oriented and success motivated. Other cultures are more affiliation oriented. Learners may be more concerned about their family and community and not seek to excel over others.

The HRD professional should be involved, if possible, in (1) development of selection criteria and (2) the selection process itself. Failing this, the HRD person should at least know what criteria have been used or have some awareness of the background, interests, goals, and aspirations of the learners. Then, the HRD practitioner will be better able to set reasonable targets for the learners and others involved in the learning situation.

Climate Setting

When conducting a learning program in another country, it is important to realize that you are considered a stranger, an outsider, who does not fully understand and appreciate the local culture. You bring with you the "baggage" of being from the United States with all the good and bad preconceptions that being an *American* (a totally incorrect term) implies (e.g., efficient, rushed, insensitive, productive, individualistic, capitalist, etc.).

Hence, it is very important that the HRD practitioner develop a supportive climate and a respectful relationship before the program begins. Try to attend village ceremonies. Demonstrate a caring attitude toward the learners. Show them that you are interested in their country. Get to know the important places and people. Discuss the learning objectives.

As much as possible, attempt to break down the "us versus them" attitude. Show them that you have a desire to learn about them and appreciate their culture.

Determining Needs of the Learner

Whenever possible, international HRD practitioners should involve the learners in determining their learning needs. This, however, may be very difficult. Frequently, the learners will attempt to guess what you are looking for and give you that response. Most cultures are cultures of agreement and politeness. They wait for you to indicate what answer you may be seeking and then give you that response. If you are not sensitive to this cultural fact, you may be instructing people in an area in which they are already knowledgeable.

Another reason for difficulty in deciphering learner needs is their reluctance to admit a need. Such an admission would indicate a weakness, a vulnerability. For them, it is better to say that everything is fine than to lose face identifying limitations.

Finally, people from most cultures would consider it inappropriate for an instructor to ask them what their learning needs might be. The HRD person from the United States is presumably the expert, and as the authority, he should know what is needed. This opinion will obviously be fully accepted by the learner. Anything less than authoritative direction provided by the HRD person can be considered an indication of a lack of ability.

The HRD practitioner must, accordingly, strike a delicate balance between discovering and predetermining the needs. It is probably best to gather information from other sources initially and then to confirm these needs with the learners when stating the objectives.

Setting Objectives

In the United States, HRD people are taught to set clear-cut, performance-based objectives for learning programs. Long-range planning, management by objectives, and weekly targets are all part of the U.S. management culture.

From many other cultural groups, such clearly defined objectives may be seen as either

1. *Presumptuous.* The learners may wonder how the instructor can know beforehand what the learners will be able to do and/or what Allah/God knows.

2. *Threatening.* If the learners are unable to achieve this, they will
   have failed.

The HRD practitioner must be careful so as not to be caught in the trap
of, on the one hand, being the authority who is expected to tell them what
to do and, on the other hand, being the reverent person who respects the
fact that the future cannot be controlled or predetermined.

My experience has taught me that one needs to gradually incorporate
values (e.g., mutual goal setting) into an HRD program; that is, set some
initial general goals that can later be modified by the participants.

Methodology of Learning

HRD people in the United States stress the importance of learning by
doing. They believe experimental learning is the most effective form of
learning. Learners are continually involved and active through use of
case studies, role playing, group discussions, and simulation.

For people of other cultures, such learning methodologies can be truly
foreign. They feel that learning is best done by rote. One learns skills best
by observing the instructor who serves as the model. Learning by doing is
perceived as risky. It can cause a person to look foolish.

The instructor should first demonstrate the correct approach or state
the right answer. The learner should not be forced to work out the right
answer and possibly become embarrassed in the process.

Another factor contrasting U.S. and non-U.S. learners is left-right
brain preference. American learners are accustomed to logical, inductive, left brain learning. Many other cultures are deductive, right brain
oriented. Americans tend to be more specific and practical, whereas
other cultures are more philosophical and generic in their thought
process.

When selecting an instructional methodology for use in other cultures,
the instructor should ask three questions.

1. What methodology is the group expecting?
2. What methodology do I feel would work best?
3. What methodology would work best and could be handled by the
   learners?

In conducting learning programs, the HRD practitioner might need to
begin formally, through lectures and modeling. Only after gaining the

respect and confidence of the group should the HRD practitioner move into more learner-centered methodologies.

Evaluation

A competent U.S. HRD person or project manager seeks feedback on the learning or the project that is being implemented. Learners are encouraged to identify ways in which the learning can be improved. They are asked to identify changes that need to be made.

Although Americans may be comfortable in providing such information, people from most other cultures would be very uncomfortable with such a request. Responding with suggestions and criticisms would imply a lack of confidence and respect for the authority figure. They would feel unsure of how that information would be used. So they generally would respond with only positive comments.

Therefore, evaluation may need to be done by the instructor, by a coinstructor, or by another HRD team member (if they are present and are from a culture that allows evaluation). If the evaluation can focus on improving the learning without critiquing people, greater input of ideas is likely.

Follow-up

Following any international program, one must be conscious of the fact that change has or should have occurred within the learner. The learner must now return home (i.e., to the village or workplace) with information and experience that is quite different from the indigenous culture. These internal as well as external changes will provide potential difficulties and challenges for the learner.

During any learning program that I plan and coordinate, time is set aside to discuss the impact of the new learning and the new technology on the learner and the country. We explore how the learner can best implement what has been learned. We also examine what adjustments the learner will need to make when returning home and to work.

Any HRD practitioner who wishes to remain knowledgeable about the latest developments and key activities of the international HRD field, particularly as it relates to learning, should consider joining the international division of the American Society For Training and Development (ASTD). The international division sponsors international institutes in cities throughout the United States as well as workshops at ASTD's national conferences. The ASTD is a part of the International

Federation of Training and Development Organizations (IFTDO), which encompasses national HRD associations from every part of the world.

Consulting in Another Culture

The international HRD practitioner usually will be working with or through a host country organization or community or will be providing consultative services directly to that organization or community. These institutions function quite differently from U.S. institutions and communities (again, because of the different value systems affecting them). Figure 23.2 provides some general contrasts between how a U.S. organization or community functions, versus a similar institution in many Asian, African, or Latin American countries.

In some communities or organizations, there may be mixtures of these two value systems. Such complexity requires even more creativity and ingenuity on the part of the HRD consultant.

GUATEMALA: A CASE STUDY

An HRD program that I managed in Guatemala demonstrates the complexity and challenge of working in a multicultural community where both U.S. and non-U.S. values are exhibited.

Two basic cultural groups live and work side-by-side in the Guatemalan highlands: the Latinos (who are the cultural and biological descendants of the Spaniards) and the native Indians. They interact with each other across a gulf formed by contrasting cultures, behavioral patterns, thought processes, and organizational mechanisms.

The leadership styles of the two ethnic groups are radically different. Latinos tend to operate well in hierarchical structures. They tend to take little initiative without checking with a superior. Thus Latinos defer decisions to a *jefe*, or boss. External change agents, such as HRD consultants, will find the situation frustrating. Among Latinos, the consultant must work at the top, especially with social contacts. Approval from the top will accomplish more throughout that community.

By contrast, the Indians have a system of community government that is quite equalitarian. At town meetings, change is a slow process, because leadership and authoritarian statements are the Latino culture rather than Indian. An Indian man who may think differently will hang back, hoping to get a hint that his peers think the same way before committing himself. Tactically, in dealing with an Indian community, the consultant

Activities	American Values and Practices	Non-American Values and Practices
Planning and innovating	Future is controllable; planning from throughout; change is good; creativity is rewarded	Future is uncontrollable but subject to fate; planning done by superiors; respect for tradition and what has worked in the past
Organizing, controlling, and leading	Management by objective and results; individual responsible for production; extensive delegation; respect shown for competence	Past patterns and leaders for models for control; top-down approach; based upon personal relationships; no delegation, since that implies loss of control and incompetence
Recruiting and selecting	Based upon qualifications; recruit from outside and within community or organization	According to past patterns; selection by superior only
Motivating and rewarding	Reward competence and production; profits important; rewarded with status, greater job responsibility, and power; motivated by power and money	Reward loyalty and longevity; people important; friendship oriented; patronage; motivated by position and prestige benefits
Problem solving, decision making	Team approach; what works best	Superior does decision making and problem solving; what is least controversial
Conflict resolving	An essential part of good management; handled directly	Avoided; hope conflict passes away or is buried; avoid loss of face

Figure 23.2.   Community or organization functions: American versus non-American.

must circulate from house to house (as many as possible) in the evenings, planting the idea of a change and carefully detailing its rationale to the families in each household. The consultant should not apply pressure to force a decision during the visit. Rather, the consultant should provide sufficient time for the Indians to consider the idea, without the consultant being there, before a community decision is made. Above all, the HRD consultant should never suppose that an Indian respected village elder or *Alcade* (mayor) can dictate. If any Indian does so, he becomes un-Indian and Latinolike and loses his position of respect. Thus the numerous honored men in the community should be contacted as much as a month before the community meeting at which there will be a public discussion and community consensus, it is hoped, in favor of the HRD effort.

In consultation, friendship and social connections should also be considered. Since the Spanish conquest, Latinos have managed their lives by cultivating friendships. Today, extensive networks of friends of friends and interconnections among kin reach across the country. The consultant must recognize this and cultivate social ties, in order to interact effectively within the group and to secure the help of various national institutions. The consultant should have parties, invite guests, be gracious, and perhaps even do chores for counterparts; these actions constitute a bank of favors that build good will.

The consultants can expect Latino peasants to exaggerate their physical resources and intellectual assets. By contrast, Indians will downplay their physical resources and label themselves less capable than they are. No one is lying. Both groups are simply reading the environment with their ethnic cultural perspectives, and as a result, they are seeing the situation differently.

Given the Indian aversion to outsiders, the HRD consultant should not organize Indians into hierarchies to accomplish a task. For Indians, cooperatives would be hard to form or to maintain. By contrast, shallow hierarchies can facilitate Latino cooperation, if accepted leaders are incorporated into that hierarchy.

If we attempt to consult based on our own cultural value systems, we will frustrate both the Indians and Latino peasants. For example, the U.S. notion that all people should be treated as equals may seem cold to a Latino counterpart, for the latter would like to be friends and, therefore, may feel special treatment is due. Once the friendship of a Latino counterpart is alienated, institutional cooperation will become very official, slow, and unresponsive. To counteract this, the U.S. HRD practitioner should make a conscious effort to be gracious and do favors, yet not break the rules.

On the other hand, U.S. assertiveness and individualism are most likely to confound the Indian. The Indian wants to be an individual in the sense of being left alone; there is no need to be different or unique. American individualism will send shivers up the spine of the Indian, who wants to hang back until it is clear that the proposed change conforms with the general movement of the majority.

This example shows clearly the critical necessity for the HRD consultant to know how organizations and/or communities of other cultures function. Being aware of the cultures of the Latinos and Indians and how their values contrast with each other, as well as with U.S. cultural values, can alert the U.S. HRD consultant to the necessity of drastically adapting consulting behaviors in order to be successful in Guatemala.

INTERNATIONAL HRD EMPLOYMENT OPPORTUNITIES

Having discussed the cultural skills, attitudes, and knowledge unique and necessary for international HRD efforts, let us now examine the international HRD job market, in order to gain a glimpse of potential employment opportunities for HRD practitioners.

As noted in the introduction to this chapter, there are thousands of people presently working in international HRD jobs both in the United States and in over 160 countries in the world. In this section, we will explore six categories of the international HRD job market:

1. Multinational corporations
2. U.S. government
3. Public international organizations
4. Private, nonprofit educational organizations
5. Foreign corporations in the United States
6. Consulting firms

Brief descriptions of general HRD opportunities and specific HRD jobs in each category follow.

Multinational Corporations

Over 30,000 U.S. corporations are involved in international activities—exporting and importing of products, drilling oil, building schools, selling tractors, buying coffee, renting hotel rooms, and training and educating technicians. These corporations come in all sizes, from the giants of the Fortune 500 to firms of only a few people.

Although most U.S. international businesses are still in Europe, a progressively greater portion are locating in the OPEC countries and in the countries of Africa, Asia, and Latin America.

Most multinational corporations rely mainly on personnel from the host country to carry out their business activities. The obvious reasons for this are (1) the high costs of having Americans work overseas, (2) the greater understanding of the local culture by host country people, and (3) the requirements of local governments to train, educate, and use the local citizens. A high percentage of human resource development positions, however, are still filled by people from the United States.

Multinational corporations generally assign to overseas positions those employees who have demonstrated familiarity with the company's operations and loyalty to the company itself. An HRD practitioner who wishes to work abroad should join a company that sends many employees abroad. Interest should be expressed in international work and those capabilities and contacts developed that are required for the company's overseas work. The international opportunity will subsequently follow.

Three typical HRD opportunities with multinational corporations include:

1. *Program Manager for Education Services, Xerox Corporation.* The HRD practitioner in this position conducts and markets training programs for employees of regional offices and for customers worldwide.
2. *International HRD Coordinator, Citicorp.* Based in New York City, this person selects and manages instructors and consultants who assist Citicorp employees in countries where Citicorp operates.
3. *Technical Training Specialist, Mobil Oil.* This HRD practitioner trains a local counterpart in a technical area (e.g., equipment repair, finance management) so that the local person will be able to assume that responsibility when the person from the United States leaves.

U.S. Government

The U.S. government employs nearly 50,000 civilians and 500,000 military personnel abroad. In addition, another 50,000 U.S. citizens work on international projects for the U.S. government but are based in the United States. These international workers may be either Foreign Services Officers (FSOs) or General Schedule (GS) employees.

The U.S. government agencies that are most active in international work are the Department of State, U.S. Agency for International Development, Department of Defense, U.S. Information Agency, Department of Commerce, Department of Agriculture (Foreign Agricultural Service and Office of International Cooperation and Development), Export-Import Bank, U.S. Geological Survey, and Peace Corps.

There are large numbers of international HRD opportunities in all these agencies. A high percentage of the over 4000 employees of the U.S. Agency for International Development are involved in HRD, since HRD is a major mission of the agency (i.e., to provide training, education, and technical assistance to the people of the developing countries so that those countries will be able eventually to manage and to develop on their own). The primary learning areas of AID are in the fields of rural development, health, nonformal and formal learning, and nutrition. AID also contracts with hundreds of consultants who assist in developing the human resources of the Third World.

It is very important to have had international work experience if you wish to be employed as an international HRD practitioner. The Peace Corps is an excellent place to acquire such experience and has provided that first international opportunity for over 80,000 Americans since its inception by President Kennedy in 1961. Peace Corps volunteers are involved in training and educating host country people in animal husbandry, road construction, food production, appropriate technology, language learning, primary health care, community development, and a myriad of other areas.

Another way in which U.S. people have gained international HRD experience is with the U.S. military overseas. For example, to service the 500,000 military personnel stationed abroad, hundreds of HRD practitioners provide the technical and managerial skills necessary for a well-prepared military.

Typical examples of international HRD jobs include:

1. *Chief, Training Division, U.S. Information Agency.* This HRD managerial position includes responsibility for training and educating Foreign Service information officers in crosscultural, language, and technical areas.

2. *Curriculum Development Specialist, Department of Navy.* This person designs and develops technical manuals for use in training and educating navy personnel.

3. *Foreign Agricultural Officers, Department of Agriculture.* The HRD specialists in these positions train, educate, and advise ministries of agricultures throughout the world in areas of agricultural research, nutrition, trade, and so forth.

4. *International Education Specialists, Department of Education.*

Working in the Division of International Education, this person plans and administers a variety of learning, institutional development and research programs and services, to expand and improve the international dimensions of U.S. schooling.

Public International Organizations

The various public international organizations employ over 50,000 people, approximately 15% of whom are from the United States. Many of these positions are HRD related, since the primary purpose of these organizations is to provide technical assistance and learning to developing nations.

The United Nations (UN) is composed of specialized agencies with offices all over the world. The largest of the specialized organizations are the UN Development Program (UNDP), Food and Agriculture Organization (FAO), International Labor Office (ILO), UN Education, Scientific and Cultural Organization (UNESCO), World Health Organization (WHO), and UN International Children's Emergency Fund (UNICEF).

Public international organizations also include financial institutions (e.g., World Bank, International Monetary Fund, Inter-American Development Bank) and regional organizations (e.g., Organization of American States, North Atlantic Treaty Organization, Organization for Economic Cooperation and Development).

In these organizations, nearly all the professional staff have advanced degrees, successful international work experience, and facility in two or more languages. Accordingly, people interested in HRD opportunities with public international organizations are advised to obtain a good education and experience elsewhere before applying.

The key fields in which these organizations provide technical assistance are public administration, agriculture, education, statistics, finance, engineering, communications, social services, and transportation. In addition to having full-time employees, each of these agencies utilizes a large number of consultants for assignments of several weeks to a year or more.

A potpourri of HRD jobs in public international organizations include:

1. *Instructor, Economic Development Institute, World Bank.* Instructors at the Economic Development Institute develop and conduct courses in numerous management techniques for high-level officials from Third World countries, both at World Bank headquarters in Washington, D.C. and at regional learning centers in Africa, Asia, and Latin America.

2. *Research Specialist, United Nations Institute for Training and Research.* This person researches and develops reports on the latest learning methodologies and materials utilized in HRD programs all over the world.

3. *Technical Assistance Specialist, UN Development Program.* Located in over 100 developing countries, these experts assist local government personnel in large-scale development projects such as transportation and trade.

Higher Education Institutions and Private Development Organizations

There are over 2000 colleges, universities, and private development organizations in the United States that are involved in international HRD efforts, ranging from highly specialized technical research and instruction to general grass-roots community development.

Higher Education Institutions. These include the many colleges and universities that carry out independent or government-funded training and education programs overseas and for foreign officials in the United States. The University of Massachusetts, for example, has operated large-scale HRD projects in Ecuador and Indonesia over the past decade under contract with the U.S. Agency for International Development. Each year, both in the United States and abroad, the USDA Graduate School trains and educates more than 3000 Third World officials in management, English language, marketing, agriculture, finance, and industrial development.

Exchange institutions such as the Experiment in International Living, Youth for Understanding, and American Field Service provide crosscultural learning for thousands of families who wish to have foreign students live with them for a few months to a year.

Many higher educational institutions also employ HRD staff to serve as foreign student advisors (some U.S. universities have over 5000 foreign students), language instructors, and crosscultural specialists.

Organizations such as the Academy for Education Development, Institute for International Education, and the American-Mideast Educational and Training Services (AMIDEAST) are involved in managing cultural exchange programs between Americans and officials from other countries and in developing the human resources in these countries through vocational training and education, finance, computers, and telecommunications.

Private Development Organizations.   Several hundred private, nonprofit development organizations are active throughout the Third World, training local citizens in basic human needs (i.e., food, water, housing, schooling, and health).

The two largest private development organizations are Cooperative for American Relief Everywhere (CARE) and Catholic Relief Services (CRS). Both agencies have annual budgets of over $200 million and employ several hundred technical advisors in over 60 Third World countries.

Many of these organizations (e.g., Overseas Education Fund, Save The Children Federation, and Agricultural Cooperative Development International) employ HRD specialists who are involved in every aspect of HRD work—developing and designing instructional manuals, arranging learning workshops, evaluating management development programs, and conducting staff orientations.

Foreign Corporations in the United States

As Leonard Nadler stated in the October, 1982 issue of the *Training and Development Journal,* "There are so many foreign companies now in the United States that international is no longer someplace overseas. It is all around us right here!"[5]

The increase of foreign corporate activity in the United States will, no doubt, result in a corresponding increase of HRD opportunities with non-U.S. corporations.

The role of the American HRD practitioner who works for non-U.S. managers but instructs Americans offers a new twist to the HRD role. The practitioner must be able to interact effectively with supervisors of another culture and to develop HRD activities that are acceptable and successful for both U.S. and non-U.S. people.

Examples of the HRD positions in these foreign corporations include:

1. *Manager, Sales and Marketing Training, Volkswagen of America (German).*   This person manages HRD programs for all sales and marketing staff.
2. *Training Coordinator, Ciba-Geigy Corporation (Swiss).*   The HRD practitioner in this position develops and conducts the data processing programs for Ciba-Geigy employees.
3. *National Service Training Manager, Sony Corporation of America (Japanese).*   The training manager coordinates HRD in the areas of service and repair for Sony dealers and employees throughout the United States.

Consulting Firms

The five categories of international HRD employment opportunities described above each employ thousands of consultants to carry out international HRD and technical assistance programs in the United States and overseas. In 1981 alone, AID spent over $2 billion for consultants, while the World Bank contracts for consulting services totalled nearly $1 billion. Some consultants are self-employed while others work for very large international consulting firms. These consultants are generally well-skilled, highly experienced experts, although people with lesser capabilities are also involved as assistant or staff (backstopping) consultants. Consultants are hired to perform contract work in a variety of technical areas.

Among the largest and best known of the international consulting firms are Louis Berger International; Booz, Allen and Hamilton, Inc.; Development Alternatives; Arthur D. Little, Inc.; Bechtel Power Corporation; and McKinsey and Company, Inc.

Typical HRD consulting positions include:

1. *Vice President, Human Resource Development, Transcentury Corporation.*   This senior HRD person is responsible for developing proposals for U.S. governmental organizations that fund technical projects for Third World countries. He or she also manages staff development programs.

2. *Training Specialists, Management Systems International.*   The training specialist conducts management training workshops for government officials of Latin America, Africa, Asia, and the Middle East.

3. *Consultant, Resources for Action, Inc.*   Funded by contracts from AID, the Organization of American States, and private development organizations, this HRD practitioner assists local organizations in the development areas of management, housing, and community development.

WORKING AND LIVING ABROAD

Living and working abroad as an HRD practitioner is an exciting and challenging opportunity. To make it as valuable and as worthwhile as possible, the HRD practitioner should gather basic factual information about the country in which the work will take place. Having such information will provide the practitioner with reference points, case studies, resources, and cultural values—all of which can make the HRD program more relevant and effective.

Robert Kohls,[6] in his book *Survival Kit for Overseas Living*, suggests a checklist as a means of gathering valuable information about the learner's country (see Figure 23.3).

In addition to this general information, the HRD practitioner should begin to identify the spoken and unspoken set of rules and expectations the local culture may have for the foreigner. Find out the problems that you as a person from the United States are likely to encounter. And finally, be sure that you know the basic logistics of the country (e.g., documents needed, innoculation requirements, banking, housing, transportation, communication, etc.). These support services are obviously important as you carry out the HRD activities in the host country.

Although this information will prepare you for overseas living, the HRD practitioner should be aware of the following common problems that affect Americans living abroad:

Language barriers

Lack of mobility (political and/or cultural restrictions)

Slow pace of life

Lack of conveniences

Ambiguity of the new culture

Unrealistic goals

Administrative red tape

In addition, the HRD practitioner may not be fully appreciated by the foreign counterparts with whom the practitioner is working and/or training. The U.S. HRD person may be seen as displaying "U.S. superiority" and "having all the answers."

These factors and others (especially being less successful than you would like to be) will undoubtedly give you and any U.S. person who has lived abroad for a period of time *culture shock*, that is, a psychological disorientation caused by the new culture.

For some people, culture shock is brief and barely noticeable. For most of us, however, it is something that will last for a long time and will be quite painful. But as Kohls says, "Culture shock is the occupational hazard of overseas living through which one has to be willing to go in order to have the pleasures of experiencing other countries and cultures in depth."[7]

Symbols

Symbolism of flag
National anthem
National flower, etc.
Myths and legends of ethnic group(s)
National holidays
Traditional costumes

Human and Natural Resources

Geography and topography
Regional characteristics
Major cities
Natural resources (flora, fauna, minerals)
Climate
Demographic information
Transportation systems
Communication systems
Mass communication media

Family and Social Structure

Family structure and family life
Family roles
Social classes
Social organizations
Social welfare
Customs (re: birth, marriage, death, etc.) and courtesies

Religion and Philosophy

Religious beliefs (indigenous and borrowed)
Philosophy
Proverbs
Superstitions

Fine Arts and Cultural Achievements

Painting   Dance
Sculpture   Drama
Crafts   Literature
Folk arts   Poetry
Architecture   Cinema
Music

Economics and Industry

Principal industries
Exports/Imports
Foreign investment
Cottage industries (if any)
Industrial development
Modernization (if applicable)
Urban and rural conditions
Agriculture (crops and animal husbandry)
Fishing (if it is a major activity)
Marketing systems

Politics and Government

System of government
Political parties
Government organization (national and local)
Current political figures
Police system
Military

Science

Inventions and achievements (throughout history)
Science
Medicine

Figure 23.3.   Host country checklist.

Education	Sports and Games
General approach (e.g., rote memorization versus problem-solving approach)	Native sports (unique to the country) Modern world sports Traditional children's games
School system College and universities Vocational training	National Foods
	National Language
	Local Dialects/Languages

Figure 23.3. Host country checklist. (continued)

There are a number of things that the HRD practitioner who is working internationally can do to overcome culture shock.

1. Continue to learn more about the host country
2. Attempt to find the cultural reason behind everything in the new environment
3. Do not succumb to disparagement of the host culture
4. Identify sympathetic host country people to share confusion and frustration
5. Have faith in yourself and in the positive outcome of the experience

GENERAL SKILLS OF THE SUCCESSFUL HRD PRACTITIONER

Numerous organizations (Control Data, Experiment in International Living, Peace Corps, International Career Consultants) have carefully analyzed their experiences in sending Americans abroad. They have identified the following general (in addition to HRD specific) sets of skills and attributes as being necessary for an HRD professional to function successfully in another culture:

1. Management Skills
    Information gathering and diagnostic skills
    Problem solving and decision making
    Planning capabilities
    Capacity to be nonjudgmental

2. Communications

    Ability to look at the world through others' perspective, empathy

    Ability to transmit sincere interest and respect

    Ability to avoid moralistic, value-laden statements

    Written, verbal, and nonverbal language capabilities

3. Interpersonal/Organizational

    Flexibility to function effectively in other cultures

    Ability to thrive on ambiguity, to accept a degree of frustration

    Patience and tact

    Sense of humor

    Interest in people

4. Commitment/Motivation

    Give one's best

    Committed to the needs of the client

    Self-starter

5. Creativity

    Able to identify new, creative responses to unexpected situations

    Ability to adapt American ways to the local culture

6. Learning/Technical Skills

    Technical competence in field

    Ability to quickly absorb and analyze new information

CONCLUSION

Working internationally in HRD can be one of the most exciting professional adventures to HRD practitioners. The opportunities to significantly impact the economic growth of a country are many and varied, and indeed, the HRD practitioner can have a profound influence on such development. The opportunity to learn and to interact with people of other cultures is likewise a tremendous experience.

For these opportunities to be fruitful and beneficial, however, the HRD practitioner must fully understand and appreciate the value systems of other cultures. The practitioner must be able to adapt the HRD skills and capabilities to the new cultures. It is essential to be able to synergize one's professional competence and own culture with the resources, needs, and culture of the host country, so as to fully develop the human resources that are present there.

NOTES

1. The author is aware that there are many subcultures within the United States and that no single, monolithic value system is practiced throughout the United States. There do exist, however, unique Western values that are very different from those of Asia, Africa, Latin America, and the Middle East. In this section these predominant values are contrasted with the values of the rest of the world.

2. Geert Hofstede, "Cultural Dimensions for Project Management," *Proceedings of 7th World Congress on Project Management*, Copenhagen, September 12–17, 1982, pp. 683–700.

3. For additional information contact, Society for International Education, Training and Research, 1414 22nd Street, N.W., Washington, D.C. 20037.

4. For more information, write to the Language and Intercultural Research Center, Brigham Young University, Provo, Utah.

5. Len Nadler, "International Is Not Someplace Overseas," *Training and Development Journal*, Vol. 36, No. 10, p. 4.

6. Robert Kohls, *Survival Kit for Overseas Living* (Chicago: Intercultural Press, 1979), pp. 78–79.

7. Kohls, p. 62.

CHAPTER TWENTY-FOUR

Latin America

ZEACE NADLER[1]

How should one refer to those countries in the southern part of the American continents? It has been customary to call them South America. In gathering data for this chapter, it became evident that people in those countries prefer to be called *Latin Americans*. That terminology has been adopted for this chapter.

As with any continent, one can expect to find differences among the various countries. This is true of Latin America, though there is one significant similarity. Most of the countries have some kind of government-sponsored or government-directed national HRD activity. This varies from one country to another, but the differences do not relate to the type of political system, the social system, or the level of economic development.

[1] The author wishes to acknowledge the significant input of the following: Aracely Baldizon, Julio C. Casas, Abraham Dantus, and David Getter.

Zeace Nadler is vice president of Nadler Associates, a firm that provides services in HRD to a variety of clients in the United States and throughout the world. She has worked in South America, both in instructing and consulting. She has taught English to Japanese businessmen, preparing them to come to the United States and to do business with English-speaking foreigners in Japan. In 1960, she was featured on Japanese radio and television, conducting a series of programs designed to help the Japanese speak English. She is coauthor of *The Conference Book* (Gulf Publishing, 1979) and serves as a consulting editor to the Human Resource Series of Jossey-Bass, Inc. Publishers and *The Trainer's Resource* (HRD Press, issued biannually).

Aracely Baldizon is an organizational consultant for C.E.N.S.A. (Pepsi Mexico) and also works with Dantus y Asociados, S.C. Her major field is organizational communication, and she conducts in-company communication audits and research for major companies.

Julio C. Casas (Ph.D.) was appointed by the president of Venezuela as president of the National Institute for Educational Cooperation (INCE) in 1979. Prior to that position, Dr. Casas was director general of the Institute for Training in Petroleum and Petrochemicals (INAPET). He came to that position after 26 years with Lagoven S.A. (formerly Creole Petroleum). He is a member of numerous professional associations and has served as the president of AVAD (the national HRD organization in Venezuela, similar to ASTD). In 1981, he was elected as the training personality of the year by AVAD.

Abraham Dantus is a principal with Dantus y Asociados, S.C., an organization that provides HRD services in Mexico as well as other countries in Latin America. Previous to forming his own organization, he worked with various organizations including: Peat Marwick Mitchell & Co, Jusidman y Asociados, S.C., and Bustamente y Asociados, S.C. He has been very active in AMECAP (the Mexican equivalent of ASTD).

David Getter is executive vice president of FACTOR HUMANO, an HRD organization in Venezuela. He first came to Venezuela as a Peace Corps volunteer in 1964. He has been head of HRD for the Ministry of Public Works, assistant manager for HRD at CORPOTURISMO (the tourist development organization), and head of recruiting and development at INTEVEP S.A., the petroleum industry's research and development center. He has served as vice president of AVAD (the Asociacion Venezolan para Adiestramiento y Desarrollo), the professional HRD organization in Venezuela.

Latin America is a vast continent, containing countries ranging from very small (e.g., Costa Rica) to extremely large (e.g., Brazil) and was known essentially for agriculture, cattle breeding, and mining until the early 1940s. Given the diversity, it is difficult to cover all aspects of HRD in all the countries. What is presented here is a synthesis of material provided by the contributors, but the editor of this chapter accepts responsibility for the content.

There has been HRD in Latin America for centuries. For example, the pyramids and other vast structures of the Mayan civilization in Mexico and the Incas in Peru stand as mute testimony to the skills that were taught—those of HRD.

A long-standing problem that still exists today is the lack of adequate schooling. Part of the problem is demographic. In some of the countries, 50 percent of the population is under the age of 20. The population increases more rapidly than the ability of most of the countries to provide the necessary schooling. The end result is an overabundant work force that is not prepared for the technical and managerial jobs required by industrialization. Illiteracy is one of the major obstacles that still faces most of the countries of Latin America.

There was also a conflict at the university level until the end of World War II. On the one hand, industrialization had required adapting the worker to the enterprise. On the other hand, schools in Latin America had traditionally focused on the cultural, spiritual, and social factors. The challenge was to prepare people to enter into an industrialized situation that conflicted with the creative freedom that was part of the culture found in most of Latin America. The problem was not new, but most of the major industrialized countries of the world had faced that dilemma more than a century earlier. At that time, those countries developed political systems and an infrastructure that could support the emerging industrialization.

In Latin America, political turmoil had been pervasive, and it was only quite recently that a measure of political stability emerged in some countries. Without that stability, industrial progress was virtually impossible.

In the late 1940s, there was a significant movement toward HRD as the result of industrialization. Prior to that time, most of Latin America relied on cottage industries, though some isolated industrial complexes did exist. The movement toward industrialization required HRD in order for the emerging industries to compete across borders and outside of Latin America.

Two major events altered the slow progress toward a more systematic and comprehensive approach to using HRD. One was the interest shown by industrialized countries in the opportunities offered by the region, that is, as a market for products, equipment, and the operation of firms in agriculture and industry. The other was the pronounced trend throughout Latin America toward industrialization and overall modernization. In both cases, the situation called for the accelerated development of human resources to meet the needs in many universal-type occupations, required by privately owned as well as state-managed enterprises.

A significant part of the land of Latin America is devoted to agricultural production, but many of the methods are antiquated. Only the largest landholders can afford the equipment and research that can make agriculture profitable. In May 1983, the International Conference on Education and Work was held in Cuernavaca, Mexico. Participants came from Nicaragua, Costa Rica, Chile, Brazil, and Argentina. They emphasized the need for increased HRD in industry and commerce and the need to continue HRD activities that were just beginning in the agricultural sector.

Most of this chapter, however, will focus on the HRD in the industrial sphere, as that is where most of the action has taken place so far.

NATIONAL EFFORTS

As some countries began to recognize the problem, they became pioneers in developing institutions and organizations to facilitate the HRD programs that were needed. The examples that follow are intended to give the reader some idea of the movements that have taken place in Latin America—some of which are very different from anything developed in the United States and Canada.

Beginning with some priority areas of industry, each of the Latin American countries came to regard the need to better qualify its human resources as a cornerstone for all-around development. In response to the concern, the International Labor Office (ILO) established a Human Resource Department and later assisted the countries of Latin America in the creation and/or further development of specialized institutions for HRD.

In most cases, national institutes were created at the initiative of governments. Inspired by the ILO's tripartite principle (i.e., government, major employers, and labor organization), governing bodies were established. In a few cases, the government delegated its HRD function to the private sector, while in others these functions were solely the government's responsibility.

Whatever the system, a crucial point for HRD is funding. In Latin America the financing of national institutes tends to be based on a levy scheme. In most of the countries, this feature calls for an obligatory contribution from the private sector based on a specified percentage of all annual wages and fringe benefits paid for by the employer. There is often also a small percentage deducted from the employees' wages. In addition, the government contributes a set percentage calculated on the basis of all funds collected by the institutes from the other two sources. In several countries, the government pays the entire cost, while in others the private sector funds all expenditures.

The countries discussed here (in alphabetical order) were among the Latin American pioneers in developing national systems to provide learning for those entering the work force or for those already in the work force.

Argentina

Just after the first program of Brazil, Argentina organized The National Commission of Professional Learning and Orientation (CNAOP) in 1944. As in Brazil, the effort was financed by a 1 percent tax on payrolls.

In 1959, Argentina endeavored to integrate its national program into its regular school system through the National Bureau of Technical Education (CONET). The only other Latin American country that has moved in that direction is Uruguay with the Labor University (UTU).

Brazil

In 1941, the government of Brazil saw the necessity for organizing a national plan to create a competent work force. They established a 1 percent tax on private sector payrolls and formed the National Service of Industrial Apprenticeship (SENAI). This pattern of financing a national HRD program set an example for Latin America and for many other parts of the world.

The main purposes of SENAI today are:

To provide, in its own centers, the learning required by those in their area of concern

To help employers in their HRD programs

To offer short courses with scholarships as required

To participate in research in technology and the work force

To act as an advisory body to the federal government of Brazil in the HRD area

SENAI provides learning for a variety of groups:

Young people (14–16 years old) who are preparing to enter the work force

Adults who require either training or education to participate more effectively in the work force

Working managers and technicians who require additional learning

SENAI uses what they call the "Individual Development Method" to provide learning. With this method,

Individuals are encouraged to accept responsibility for their own learning

Students learn how to learn

Students learn according to their own characteristics, taking advantage of previous learning and experience

The student cannot progress to the next lesson until the previous one has been mastered

Cognitive and psychomotor skills are emphasized

Individualized programs are used—students can start at any time and there is no formal graduation

Prospective students are informed about SENAI through formal programs, including the use of films showing different occupations. They are then tested and involved in group sessions to explore their interests in the skill areas being offered.

The focus of SENAI has been to serve the industrial sector. Soon after SENAI was first created in 1941, the government created the National Service of Commercial Apprenticeship (SENAC) to help meet the work force needs of the commercial sector. It operates in areas such as communication, secretarial, sales, advertising, shipping, lodging, tourism, sanitation, and health. Both programs are organized into segments related to the private sector.

In 1975, Brazil passed laws providing financial incentives for private companies that had acceptable HRD programs. Government agencies were established to encourage this. In Brazil, the Labor Federal Board and the Labor Department of the Ministry of Labor have prime responsibility in this area.

Chile

As in Brazil, Chile has also moved in the direction of having the government take an active part in providing HRD. In 1966, the National Institute of Professional Training (INACAP) was formed. It has provided service to those preparing to enter the work force as well as to those who are already employed, with a major emphasis on technicians.

In 1975, Chile passed a law providing financial incentives for private companies that had acceptable HRD programs. In 1976, the National Service of Training and Labor (SENCE) was created by law. SENCE reports to the Labor and Social Security Ministry.

Colombia

In 1957, Colombia established the National Apprenticeship Service (SENA). This was financed by a 2 percent tax on payrolls of enterprises that had a capital stock of at least 50,000 pesos and had more than nine employees. SENA was organized as a separate unit. It has its own budget and is not under the legislative or administrative arms of the government. It nominally reports to the Ministry of Labor.

The SENA program is involved with every sector of the economy.

Mexico

Mexico has passed laws setting forth the obligation of enterprises to provide HRD to all workers. In 1965, that national institute was ARMO. In 1978, the government created the Coordinating Unit of Employment, Training, and Instruction (UCECA), which is actually a branch office in the Labor and Social Welfare Ministry (STPS). Its function is to organize, promote, and supervise HRD programs.

The UCECA is headed by a general coordinator who works with executives from other related government agencies. The direct work is done by mixed commissions, including employer and union representation. They register both internal and external HRD practitioners as well as company programs, and they verify that learning is provided only by authorized persons.

In 1983, Dr. Fernando Arias Galicia and Dr. Victor Heredia Espinoza reported the results of their research on HRD in the federal district (similar to the District of Columbia in the United States). They found that 17 corporations had spent 500 million pesos in three years. Given the fluctuation of the peso, it is not possible to translate this directly into U.S.

dollars. To put it in some understandable dimension, however, that amount would pay the minimum wage for 37,362 people for a month!

About half of the companies did not have any policy or procedure manual regarding HRD. The internal organization of HRD was strongest in banking, finance, and insurance.

Most of those in charge of the HRD function had an M.B.A., although there were others with degrees in engineering, psychology, and industrial relations.

Only about half the respondents indicated that they had specific goals when offering HRD programs. Most of the organizations had internal instructors and learning facilities. Most indicated, however, that they used external sources for HRD on a regular basis. About 75 percent of the supervisors and managers thought they needed to be trained in leadership, administration, communication, and decision making.

In general, it appears that in Mexico HRD is more related to quantity than quality. HRD seems to be aimed at general needs, not the specific needs of organizations. There needs to be more specific planning that relates to organizational goals.

Venezuela

Many of the HRD activities came out of the United States, particularly the use of Training within Industry (JIT, etc.) during World War II. This was the period when the original model for the national institute was created.

The Institute of Cooperative Education (INCE) was created in 1959 under the newly formed democratic government headed by President Romulo Betancourt. From its beginnings, INCE has endeavored to play a responsible social and political role in carrying out its HRD programs.

INCE is a semiautonomous organization, administratively linked to the Ministry of Education. INCE controls, directly or indirectly, a great percentage of all the HRD activity in Venezuela's private sector.

The public sector is generally under the central personnel office (Oficina Central de Personal), which reports directly to the president of the republic. There are a wide variety of state-controlled enterprises, such as the petroleum, iron, steel, and aluminum industries. Roughly, six out of every ten employees in Venezuela works in the public sector.

INCE's budget comes from three sources: (1) a payroll levy of 2 percent paid by firms with over five employees, (2) 0.5 percent of the accrued annual severance pay benefits (the employee's contribution), and (3) an additional 20 percent added by the federal government.

Seventy percent of INCE's activities are related to basic industrial

HRD programs. There are education programs for unemployed young people and training for those employed in areas requiring skills. INCE requires that every organization with more than 20 employees have apprentices equal to at least 5 percent of their work force. In addition, INCE offers various technical, self-improvement, and literacy programs on a large scale through more than 100 centers throughout the country.

INCE also monitors and supports efforts in the private sector. Organizations that contribute the levy described earlier are allowed to deduct the greater part of the cost of privately contracted HRD programs from their overall assessment. Those programs must be presented as part of the annual HRD plan that the firms present to INCE each year.

A unique program is in the petroleum sector. In 1976, Venezuela nationalized that industry. Prior to that time, many of the foreign petroleum companies had excellent HRD units that included many Venezuelans. After nationalization, the Instituto de Adiestramiento Petrolero y Petroquimico (INAPET) was formed as the basic unit providing HRD for the oil industry (although several of the operating affiliates of Petroleos de Venezuela still have their own units).

There are many multinationals operating in Venezuela (e.g., Xerox, Ford, GM, IBM). They utilize both their local HRD personnel as well as those they bring in periodically from the United States and other countries.

Other Efforts

In the Caribbean countries, the focus was on preparing qualified labor through the regular school systems. For example, six Caribbean countries of English and Dutch background adopted a tripartite scheme of employers, employees, and the government.

Other national efforts include:

Peru. SENATI in 1961

Guatemala. CENDAP in 1961 and INTECAP in 1972

Costa Rica. INA in 1965

Ecuador. SECAP in 1966

Nicaragua. INA in 1967

Paraguay. SNPP in 1971

Bolivia. FOMO in 1972

Honduras. INFOP in 1972

Dominican Republic. INFOTEP in 1980

A distinctive feature of national institutes is their growing concern for *horizontal cooperation*, that is, the collaboration among these institutions as well as across national borders. This meets the need to exchange ideas within the Latin American context and to help each other in the adoption and adaptation of locally successful experiences.

The result has been the development of better and more common guidelines for HRD in Latin America and the stimulation of creativity in approaching problems related to HRD. The interchange of materials has already provided less expensive and less dependent transfer of technology.

UNEMPLOYED AND UNDEREMPLOYED

Historically, Latin America has suffered from unemployment and underemployment. With the increasing use of technology, the private sector has tended to become more capital intensive than labor intensive. This has contributed to the continuing crisis in unemployment.

In 1983, there were 120 million unemployed in Latin America. The natural resources are plentiful, but it takes a vast capital investment to utilize these resources effectively. It is estimated that to generate just one job in the private sector requires an investment of $30,000. To solve the problem of unemployment would require about $3.6 trillion! It would also require programs far broader than those described earlier to provide the necessary work force. Given those figures, one can see the seriousness of the problem. It can help us understand how continuing unemployment leads to marginality, social stress, crime, and revolutions.

CONCLUSION

There appears to be an enthusiasm and vitality in Latin America, related to HRD, that holds significant promise for the future. The activities reported in this chapter indicate a new spirit and a willingness to identify and deal with problems in the area of HRD. Such efforts can lead to accelerated social and economic development in Latin America.

CHAPTER TWENTY-FIVE

Africa

CRISPIN GREY-JOHNSON

The continent of Africa presents a broad range of HRD efforts. It includes countries that have been occupied by a foreign power, those that have always been free, those that are new, and many that are constantly undergoing change.

In this chapter, Grey-Johnson has provided us with an overview of what is happening on that continent. It has serious problems related to HRD but a tremendous potential. Indeed, given its vast physical resources, it is imperative that attention be given to the human resources if the countries of that continent are to survive and prosper.

It is difficult to discuss Africa in depth in just one chapter; however, Grey-Johnson provides sufficient insight so that the problems and potential of Africa can be understood.

Crispin Grey-Johnson is an economic affairs officer with the United Nations Economic Commission for Africa in Addis Ababa, Ethiopia. He is Gambian but has worked in many different countries. His specialty is human resource development and manpower planning.

INTRODUCTION

Africa, the least developed of all the world's continents, is reputed to be the best endowed in minerals, energy, land, water, and other natural resources. The abundant concentration of numerous natural and physical resources in this one region makes it possible for Africa to be self-sufficient in food and energy production and to have within the continent all the physical ingredients for the development of technology and industry. However, the socioeconomic situation that prevails within the continent is one of low productivity in agriculture, low industrial output, high illiteracy, high infant mortality, and low life expectancy—in short, a generally low quality of life.

Structural economic imbalances account for a good part of the African socioeconomic problem. From the days of colonialism, African economies have been developed to respond to the needs of markets in the industrialized, developed world. African economies are export oriented, and the natural resource base is exploited for the use of others. It is this situation, more than any other, that accounts for Africa's chronic underdevelopment.

Since the years of independence, however, African governments have shown a growing commitment to economic and social development. They have made and continue to make major investments in public and social services (e.g., schools, hospitals, roads and railways) and in the development of their economies (e.g., rural and agricultural development; the development of industries; strengthening of the services sector through the development of banking, insurance and transport; and the development of the telecommunication infrastructure).

Planning national investments is undertaken periodically by every African government in the national development plans that have proliferated on the continent over the last two decades. Over time, however, and in spite of the efforts to achieve meaningful socioeconomic development targets, development planning seems to have brought about more problems than solutions: wide and growing rural/urban imbalances; large numbers of underemployed and unemployed; the emergence of an underclass, euphemistically referred to as the "informal" sector; accelerated rural exodus; the brain drain; and an alarming rate of crime in urban areas. In crude economic terms, development planning has not achieved miracles for agricultural and industrial development. Africa, an agricultural continent, spent $5 billion for food imports to feed its people in 1982, while industrial output was almost stagnant, at a little over 0.6% of total world output.

Over the years, Africa's development planning balance sheet has not been impressive. This may be because of what is now recognized as a misunderstanding of what inputs go into the planning process. Planning has tended to rely on two factors to stimulate growth and produce development: land and capital. Labor is taken into account only with regard to its quantitative abundance. Its potential qualitative contributions to the development process have, at best, received low priority. Thus the human variable in the development equation has traditionally, in Africa, not received the attention it deserves.

In their pursuit of socioeconomic development, African governments have been concentrating on the provision of capital and physical resources and the exploitation of a large unskilled labor reserve, neglecting in the process the most fundamental ingredient for development: human resources. The capability of an economy to effectively combine capital with physical and natural resource inputs in order to achieve growth and development is determined to a large extent by the way these inputs mix with the quality of available human resources. If that quality is low, the end result will be disappointing, for it is only high quality human resources that can maximize gains in investments in capital and natural and physical resources. Therefore, the lower an economy's quality of human resources, the greater are its chances of being unable to achieve meaningful development. Thus the existing human resource situation—in terms of skill levels and numbers in any given economy—is the principal yardstick for determining that economy's potential to achieve growth and development.

The concept of human resources as inputs into the development process assumes a qualitative consideration in the main. Human resources can be described as the skills, knowledge, attitudes, initiative, and resourcefulness that constitute the human catalysts needed to bring about improvements in production, services, technology, and management. They are the principal agents of development. Inculcating or developing these attributes within a given population or among groups of individuals calls for interventions that can only be sought within education and training systems. Education and training, therefore, are the foundations of socioeconomic development.

HUMAN RESOURCES AND THE NEW AFRICAN DEVELOPMENT STRATEGY

The development strategy adopted by African governments through the 1960s gave undue weight to industrialization. It was only after 10 years of pursuit of this strategy that it became clear that the repercussions on national economies were undesirable. First, it was found that the industrialization strategy placed a heavy burden on foreign exchange reserves for the imports to run the growing numbers of industrial establishments within the continent. In order to do so, greater quantities of primary commodities had to be produced for export to markets of the industrialized world. Second, in the process of concentrating on maintaining if not increasing levels of industrial output and the attendant demands on the production of primary commodities for that purpose, the food production sector of African economies began to suffer neglect. Food production fell to levels so low as to warrant the import of millions of tons of food from industrialized countries; thus worsening the strain on national foreign exchange reserves. Third, the structure of industrialization did not allow for any meaningful backward linkages with primary producing sectors of the economy, such as agriculture and mining, or any forward linkages with other industries. Not enough was being done to develop the basic industries (e.g., the iron and steel industries; agro, food, and forestbased industries; chemicals and petrochemicals industries) that would rely on the exploitation of the existing natural resource base and, at the same time, provide production inputs into other industries (e.g., engineering industries).

In 1979, African heads of state and government met in Monrovia, Liberia to work out a new set of priorities and a strategy for the continent's development.

They decided on the following:

1. The attainment of self-sufficiency in food production within the region

2. The development of the basic industries as the basis for any meaningful industrialization effort

3. The exploitation of Africa's natural resource base for use within the continent, rather than for export

4. The development and integration of transport and communications systems with a view to widening internal markets

5. Inward-looking trade policies that would allow for an appreciable increase in intra-African trade.[1]

The 1979 African summit was followed by another in 1980 in Lagos, Nigeria. That meeting of heads of state and government came out with what is now referred to as the Lagos Plan of Action.[2]

The Lagos Plan of Action prescribes measures for attacking problems constraining the development of all facets of socioeconomic life in Africa. As concerns agricultural development, the Lagos plan identifies measures that will minimize food losses, ensure food security, and boost food production. A plan is also formulated for a substantial increase in fish production and to integrate forestry more closely with agriculture. The plan takes into account the need to develop the relevant institutional support services if the new objectives for agricultural development are to be attained. In this, it identifies scientific, technological, and agricultural research as being indispensable. In addition, it identifies as critical the planning and timely provision of the relevant trained labor power to provide the technical, managerial, research, and extension services without which the plan would most certainly flounder.

With regard to natural resources and industry, the Lagos Plan of Action identifies resources that would successfully link the two and contribute to the effective development of eight priority, basic industries by the year 2000. Here again, the plan recognizes that implementation will only be made possible if the provision to these two sectors of institutional and relevant labor power capabilities is planned and made available in time.

Apart from these two critical sectors, other socioeconomic development areas are considered within the Lagos Plan of Action. They include science and technology, rural development, transportation and communications, housing and urban development, trade and finance. In all these sectors, the need for trained labor is fully recognized as a prerequisite of development.

The plan devotes an entire chapter to measures to be applied to ensure a rational development of Africa's human resources. It describes human resources as "the custodian and mentor of socioeconomic development," and it suggests ways of planning their development so that they could play their "role in ensuring the continent's survival and progress."[3] These suggestions include:

1. The establishment of a training administration and guidance coordinating machinery
2. The establishment of national training funds
3. The creation of national central advisory councils on training
4. The strengthening or establishment of training development programmes, especially those with a high multiplier effect potential (e.g., training of training officers) in the following priority areas: Science and technical teacher training

Training of training/staff development officers

Skills development programmes for the critical production sectors (e.g., industry, agriculture, transportation, and communication, etc.)

Training of producers in agriculture and the urban informal sector

Training of women for their more effective integration in socio-economic development activities

The African heads of state and government decided further that the objectives agreed upon in the Lagos Plan of Action shall be implemented at the national, the subregional, and the continental levels.

THE MAGNITUDE OF THE NEED FOR HUMAN RESOURCE DEVELOPMENT

All African countries are now well aware of the fact that the lack of middle-level and high-level human resources constitutes the single most difficult constraint to their development. The critical skills areas in which great shortages are recorded in Africa are managerial, technical and engineering, scientific, and all occupations within the skilled worker category. To illustrate the magnitude of the need for middle-level and high-level labor, we shall examine three industries for which growth targets for the year 2000 have been set collectively by African governments. These industries are iron and steel, chemicals, and food and agro industries.

The independent countries in eastern and southern Africa decided in 1981 to embark upon a subregional iron and steel project, in conformity with the Lagos Plan of Action, and to increase that subregion's iron and steel production capacity from 500,000 tons in 1980 to 1.6 million tons by 1985, 5 million tons in 1990, and 10 million tons in the year 2000. Figure 25.1 shows the projected needs in high-level and middle-level engineering and technical labor to operate the steel plant.

With the present structure and bias of third-level (i.e., postsecondary) learning facilities, it was determined that it was absolutely necessary that vigorous efforts be embarked upon immediately, in order to institute education and training programs that would consider the needs in labor power for iron and steel development. It became obvious that eastern and southern African countries together would only be able to provide some

Specialization	Numbers (Projections)
Chemical/metallurgical/process	1727
Electrical	1727
Mechanical and plant maintenance	2898
Civil	240
Design, instrumentation, hydraulics	1958
Total	8550

Figure 25.1. High-level engineering and technical labor needs in eastern and southern Africa steel projects. *Source:* UNECA: The Preparation of Manpower for Industrial Development, Table IV, Addis Ababa, 1982.

2110 engineers and technicians to their iron and steel projects. As a result, by the year 2000, there would be a direct shortfall of 6400 professionals in those fields of specialization.

In West Africa, which has been plagued with problems of drought and famine, ministers of economic planning met and decided that among measures to be taken to save that subregion's agricultural production, fertilizer production should be increased from its present capacity of 1.07 million tons to 2 million tons by the year 2000. Figure 25.2 lists the occupational categories and the numbers that would be needed to produce the target output by the year 2000.

The availability of the last three categories was thought not to constitute any problems at all. However, for the first five occupations, educational and training facilities in western Africa would, if the present

Occupational Category	Numbers (Projections)
Managers and supervisors	310
Health personnel	80
Engineers and chemists	360
Draughtsmen	30
Skilled workers, foremen	1302
Secretaries and clerks	420
Operators	1664
Unskilled and service workers	3194
Total	7360

Figure 25.2. Labor requirements in year 2000 for the western African fertilizer project by occupational categories. *Source:* UNECA: The Preparation of Manpower for Industrial Development Table VI.

Category	Numbers (Projections)
Professional occupations	4442
All other engineering	524
Mathematical scientists	6
Chemists	700
All other physical scientists	25
Life scientists	88
Purchasing agent/buyer	574
Accountants/Auditors	1908
All other professionals	617
Technical occupations	1858
Engineering technicians	170
Biological science technicians	1203
All other science technicians	157
All other technicians	327
Total	6300

Figure 25.3. Projected additional demand for professional and technical workers in the food and agro-industries in Africa by 1990.

situation there persists, be unable to meet the need. There would be a shortfall, by the year 2000, of 2082 (Figure 25.2, first five categories) high-level and middle-level professionals in those categories.

As regards planned growth in food and agro industries, a growth target of 30% of present output by the year 1990 was agreed upon. That pace of growth would require professional, scientific, engineering, and technical labor as shown in Figure 25.3.

It can thus be seen that if modest growth should be achieved in only three relatively small industries, at least 17,200 managers and high-level and middle-level engineers and technicians will be needed in the next 15-20 years.[4] The magnitude of demand for general human resource development for socioeconomic transformations to occur in Africa must truly be staggering.

The demand for high quality human resources does not stop at the direct demand induced by growth within one industry, it has a ripple effect within the entire economy. Thus, growth in agro-industrial production will increase demand not only for a certain type of engineer for that industry, but it will also create a demand in commerce, for example, that will create a need for more commercial and business lawyers, managers, accountants, clerks, typists, and so forth.

It is evident that human resource development systems in Africa are faced with a major challenge. Postsecondary institutions will have to assume the responsibility for providing the general knowledge, skills, and attitudes that will act as catalysts for socioeconomic growth and development in Africa. Human resource development systems will have to assume the tasks of refining the skills, knowledge, and attitudes in order to make them relevant to the job needs within African economies. Obviously, if these go unfulfilled, so will the socioeconomic development objectives of African governments.

The foregoing illustrates the future magnitude of demand for skills in Africa. The present sitatuion, with regard to skills availability, shows a shortage of alarming proportions. A study in 1978 showed that shortfalls in high-level technicians all over the continent might be as high as 100,000 people.[5] In addition to this, there are hidden shortfalls in the large and growing numbers of non-African nationals filling in skill gaps in African economies. Their numbers are larger today than they were before independence.

Even among the present work force, there exists a serious problem for human resource developers—the problem of underemployment. The underemployed fall into three broad categories:

1. *Visible underemployment.* This category includes a large number of workers in agricultural activities. The seasonal nature of production allows more time than is desirable for leisure or noneconomically productive activities.

2. *Disguised underemployment.* This category includes those whose labor can be released without affecting production levels, should there be simple changes in methods of production without any additional increases in capital stock.

3. *Hidden unemployment.* This applies to labor engaged in second choice employment activities, because jobs of their preference are not available to them at their level of skill or their desired wage rate.

Visible and disguised underemployment are prevalent in the rural/agricultural sector. They affect an estimated 63.3 million workers in that sector. Hidden unemployment is concentrated more in the urban, informal sector, in government, and in the public services, in the formal sector. Disguised underemployment is now becoming a problem in the public services. In industry, transportation and communications, banking and insurance, the public services, and government, some 20 million workers are underemployed in one form or another.[6]

The task of correcting this undesirable situation lies to a large extent on the shoulders of human resource practitioners.

AFRICAN EFFORTS TO ACCELERATE THE DEVELOPMENT OF HUMAN RESOURCES

African governments have placed a high premium on educating and training their people; facilities and opportunities for the development of human resources have grown significantly over the years. For example, between 1960 and 1976 enrollment in African schools increased by almost 130%, from 21 million to 56 million students. In the eight years between 1965 and 1973, African governments spent $17.7 billion to educate and train their people. Per capita expenditure for that purpose grew from $5 in 1960 to $20 in 1976. During that same 15-year period, the number of Africans who were sent to Europe and the Americas for education and training increased tenfold. Figure 25.4 gives an indication of the numbers of Africans enrolled in education and training courses in selected foreign countries. Most of these are African students in universities and other postsecondary institutions, but a growing number are employees back home who are participating in learning new management and production techniques to meet the job needs of a changing African economy.

Apart from the quantitative growth in opportunities for human resource development, qualitatively, efforts have been made and continue to be made to improve structures, orientation, and practices in HRD. In the past, training for meeting the specific skill needs on the job was, in most African countries, undertaken at the level of the organization. Increasingly, however, with the priorities placed on HRD and the need for large outlays of funds for that purpose, African governments are taking on more responsibility for the training function. This move is rational since the public sector in the formal sector of most African economies is larger than the private and continues to grow, being thus responsible for much of the employment and productivity within that sector. Further, because the public sector sets the pace and the direction for economic growth, provision of the skills input to growth becomes largely its responsibility. Therefore, skill needs of the job as well as the employee's performance on the job and productivity become a big responsibility for the public sector. Increasingly, African governments

Country of Study	No. of African Students	Humanities, Education, Science	Law and Social Science	Natural Science	Medicine	Engineering	Agriculture	Not Specified
France	55747	25.9	32.0	—	—	15.6	—	26.5
United States of America	33990	13.2	31.5	13.1	6.0	19.2	6.1	10.9
Federal Republic of Germany	4196	11.8	14.6	12.8	33.8	9.0	7.4	10.6
Canada	2696	12.3	26.9	9.0	21.6	1.8	5.0	23.4
Saudi Arabia	1479	48.3	33.8	8.8	4.2	3.0	1.5	0.9
Italy	1364	4.8	15.2	7.4	29.4	35.1	6.3	0.4
German Democratic Republic	1129	9.6	7.8	6.3	28.7	9.2	16.5	1.8
Total (% includes other countries)	104127	20.9	31.4	5.9	4.8	16.0	2.6	28.4

Figure 25.4. African students by field of study in some major foreign countries. *Source:* UNESCO: Office of Statistics, Paris, 1981.

have been coming up with labor power plans and projections. Education and training needs fulfillment are, to a large measure, the responsibilty of government, so that the tasks of selecting candidates and providing learning, monitoring, evaluation, and placement are more frequently being assigned to governments.

It can be seen, therefore, that structures, and administrative, management, and staffing capabilities in most governments have to be established or developed to fit governments' emerging role in HRD.

In most African countries, the HRD function has been institutionalized. Some countries, such as Zimbabwe and Tanzania, now have ministries responsible for human resource development; others have departments within the ministry of economic planning that are responsible for labor power planning and HRD. In yet some others, the function is assigned to the ministry responsible for the public service. There is hardly any country in Africa that does not have a government institution or an administrative and management structure set up for HRD. Their functions include:

1. Planning the supply of skills to the economy
2. Organizing and executing training and education programs
3. Providing financial, material, and other resources for HRD
4. Managing HRD
5. Monitoring and evaluating HRD
6. Providing management improvement services
7. Accepting overall responsibility for implementing policies on HRD

Human resource development policies are also being formulated and explicitly stated by governments. These policies articulate the acceptance of the HRD function as a responsibility assigned primarily, though not solely, to government; recognize HRD as an investment and not a waste; and acknowledge that training, education, and development are the lifeblood of a productive work force. Historically, responsibility for the provision of schools for the people has rested with the government; adding HRD to this responsibility is a new recognition of their interrelatedness and the new importance now being accorded to HRD.

Education and training are a costly undertaking, therefore, in order to avoid waste and optimize investments in them, it is important to plan their provision carefully. Accordingly, many African governments now insist on identifying the need for learning before proceeding to provide it.

A scale of priority learning areas is generally set to correspond to priorities within the economy, within sectors of the economy, and within industries and establishments. In all African countries, management is a high priority. Learning for scientific, engineering, and technical fields is next, followed by medical and related occupations, teaching occupations of all types, and a wide variety of middle-level support occupations.

Such an approach to HRD allows for a more rational use of meager resources. As has already been mentioned, large and growing amounts are allocated yearly to HRD programs. These funds have come mainly from government coffers, but with the continuing strain on these funds, it has been necessary to ask the private sector to contribute more to providing the competencies that the government supplies to it to help increase its profits. In Kenya, Nigeria, and Zimbabwe, private firms are required to pay a levy of a certain percentage of their payroll to a national training fund. Other countries have devised other systems, through the normal tax contributions from industry, for extracting a contribution for HRD. Funds are disbursed through the provision of fellowships, the purchase of learning materials, remuneration to staff and resource persons, and so forth. In cases where there is no special tax levied on the private sector for HRD purposes, establishments are required to provide part of the learning at no cost to government, by accepting learners who are not employees into programs such as in-plant attachments, study visits, work/study programs, and industrial breaks. They are also required to provide education for skill upgrading to workers, supervisors, secretaries, bookkeepers, and other middle-level category workers.

Efforts to develop human resources at the national level are supplemented by subregional, multinational, and international programs for HRD, including management improvement, staff development, and the development of HRD practitioners. These groups are favored because the effect of their new skills is felt much more quickly on the national level. Hundreds of African nationals have gone through learning courses and seminars of these types.

There is also a great deal of cooperation between individual governments in providing learning for each other's nationals, in training technical and managerial personnel on the job, and through observation in industry and government.

In addition to national efforts to develop human resources, there are also collective African endeavors to do so. At times, human resource development ventures in certain key economic sectors prove to be too expensive for individual countries to embark on alone. In such cases, a number of countries pool their resources to provide the service. It is in this way that over the years some forty learning and research institutes of a regional character have been set up all over the continent. Their areas of specialization include: agriculture, finance and banking, industry and technology, natural resources, statistics, international trade, transportation and communications, management, and social and economic affairs.

The Regional Training and Fellowships Programme for Africa has also been created. Through this program, African governments hope that training and education of their nationals will be facilitated within a framework of cooperation. They make financial contributions to the program or provide learning facilities that can be used in providing HRD for other nationals. Contributions are also encouraged from sources out of the region. This program, which has been in existence since 1977, is administered by the Economic Commission for Africa and has, since its inception, provided fellowships and HRD to several thousand Africans in the critical areas of management, industry, and science and technology.

The efforts to develop Africa's human resources are indeed laudable, but the results are still far from having the desired impact. Labor shortages are still rife within African economies, at the same time that there are some 2.6 million "educated" (i.e., schooled) unemployed within the continent. Worker productivity is still low, due partly to low capital inputs, partly to management practices, but largely to low or irrelevant work-related skills.

Administrative and management structures, inherited from bygone days to fulfill a colonial purpose, have not yet gone through a transformation to fully serve the needs of socioeconomic development. Curricula in school systems are biased away from objective needs for the development of agriculture, technology, and industry. HRD systems are still in their infancy. Something needs to be done.

TOWARD A NEW STRATEGY FOR THE DEVELOPMENT OF HUMAN RESOURCES IN AFRICA

To create effective measures to mitigate a disastrous human resource situation in the future, African governments, both individually and collectively, will need to consider exactly what needs to be done to rationalize, harmonize, and plan the development of human resources within the continent. There is much room for improvement in planning, in learning practices and content, in the operation of existing human resource development machineries, in providing adequate quantity and quality of HRD staff, in career guidance and counseling, in improved personnel management practices, in financial allocations to HRD programs, and in efforts to optimize efficiency and output of the present work force.

Policy Framework

First, the government should achieve a clear policy on human resources that would have as objectives the following:

1. To ensure that adequate labor of the right skill levels is made available, as needed, to run the entire economy and to assure gains in socioeconomic development ventures
2. To promote efficiency and enhance productivity among the work force through appropriate skills development programs that produce a positive and measurable impact on performance
3. To identify talent within the work force and to develop it for use in accelerating the pace of economic growth
4. To mobilize and organize all available resources, both local and foreign, in order to fulfill identified human resource development needs
5. To provide the required management and administrative support services that would facilitate the attainment of these objectives

Policies should, in addition, reflect the need to expand the concept of human resource development to include the requirements of a large number of workers with low productivity in the rural/agricultural and the informal sectors of African economies. Also to be reflected in these policies is the need for the improvement of working conditions to enhance greater worker productivity.

These policies would, in effect, amount to a set of guidelines that would ensure continuity in human resource development interventions for the further development of the individual, the organization, and the entire economy.

Planning HRD

African needs in human resource development are vast, and the resources for that purpose are meager. Therefore, in order for HRD efforts to address themselves to the most fundamental requirements of the organization and the economy, some kind of planning is necessary. Such planning should be undertaken both at the level of the organization and at the level of the economy. Since it is being argued that because of the high priority accorded to HRD in African countries, governments should now assume primary responsibility for it, we shall confine ourselves to considerations for planning at the level of the economy, that is, macro planning.

The first requirement for effectively planning human resources is to relate them to the economy and its needs for brawn and brains. Human resource planning would thus be integrated into national economic development planning and be acknowledged as much of an input into socioeconomic growth as are capital, technology, and land.

Planning means preparation for some action in the future. Applied to human resources, it suggests identification of what they will be, what they ought to be, and how they will be produced. Thus it will look at the present and project into the future by making forecasts of demand and supply situations. Human resource development cannot produce results overnight. It seeks to bring about behavioral change; it therefore needs time to do so. Depending on the type of intervention being planned, time needed to complete the process might range from 10 years (in the case of education) to a few days (in the case of training). The time perspective for a macro human resource plan should therefore be no less than 10 years.

Implicit in the idea of human resource planning is the assumption that the economy will be in need of their skills and services and that they will be willing and able to provide these. In other words, it is assumed that there will be an economic demand for human resources and that there will be an adequate supply in the employment market.

Essentially, human resource planning will seek to determine:

1. What skills will be rendered obsolete by technology change or different methods of production as well as the nature and depth of human resource intervention needed to produce the new skills required should the supply projections indicate their absence or insufficiency

2. The types and quantities of skills that will be in demand as against the stocks identified within the supply projections, thereby indicating the type and extent of HRD intervention that will be required

3. The areas of future skill over supply or shortage to allow for corrective measures to be undertaken through career and occupational guidance and services and through the setting of HRD priorities

4.   What growth directions education and training institutions should follow as well as what orientation HRD policy should choose
5.   The extent and type of future staff, financial resources, and material resources that should be allocated to HRD
6.   The general ordering of priorities for education, training, and staff and career development

In Africa, human resource planning is still in its infancy. The effort has started with an inventory of skills within national economies as a basis for determining areas of shortage or oversupply. Although a number of countries have conducted labor surveys, none has so far gone beyond that exercise. In the recent past, Zimbabwe, Liberia, Uganda, Sierra Leone, Zambia, and Lesotho have conducted labor surveys. These surveys have been confined to establishments providing wage employment only and have left out workers in the large, agricultural sector as well as the self-employed in the urban, informal sector. The extent to which these surveys will reflect the true skills endowment situation in African economies is not yet known. What is certain is that should they prove to be useful to the planning effort, they would have made human resource planning possible for only the formal sector, which, in Africa, constitutes between 10% and 15% of the economy. A large part of the economy with its own needs in skills would have been left out.

Managing HRD

Government policies on or plans for human resource development will have to be implemented by someone. Similarly, responsibility for monitoring, coordinating, and evaluating the implementation of these plans and policies should be assigned somewhere. In Africa, the effort to carry out this task has been too diffuse. Most ministries and government departments have their own internal arrangement for providing HRD. Ministries of education function as an island in themselves. Invariably, all these different efforts do not converge at a common result. The picture is further complicated by the presence, in the HRD scene, of hundreds of private and voluntary organizations, each doing its own thing, creating more confusion and duplication of efforts.

For example, in Lesotho (population 1.3 million), it was discovered in 1978 that more than 50 private and nongovernmental organizations were involved in nonformal education and training activities, with no one monitoring and evaluating their contributions to the HRD effort. Clearly, something must be done to manage the HRD function more rationally. In some countries, the machinery for managing HRD appears to be more workable than in others. We shall examine two cases: Ghana, where what has been set up is amenable to achieving the objectives; and Nigeria, where a more complex system renders desired results difficult to attain. The former case describes the situation in the smaller countries, whereas the latter illustrates the problems of the larger ones.

Ghana.   In Ghana, a directorate responsible for HRD was created within the civil service in 1976. This move was made in response to the need to coordinate and monitor HRD activities in all government ministries and departments. It is headed by a director who reports to a permanent secretary in the establishment secretariat. The directorate implements government HRD policies and manages several national HRD institutions, among them,

1. The Ghana Institute of Management and Public Administration (GIMPA), which has responsibility for training line managers
2. The Management Development and Productivity Institute, set up for management staff development
3. The Institute for Technical Supervision, which provides HRD to industry supervisors and foremen
4. The Civil Service Training Centre, which provides training for government employees
5. Vocational and technical training institutions, polytechnics and institutes of technology

The directorate works very closely with the Ghana Manpower Board to ensure that the national HRD effort is rational and that the outcomes are used to optimize efficiency in the public service.

The Ghana Manpower Board, in addition to monitoring the supply of competencies into the economy, undertakes periodic reviews of education and training activities within the country. This is done in order to determine their degree of effectiveness and to ascertain whether education and training priorities are consistent with national HRD priorities. Its findings are relayed to the directorate to enrich the HRD needs assessment exercise and to guide future program development.

More specifically, the directorate is charged with responsibility for making curricula more job relevant, improving the quality of HRD programs, and developing HRD staff. It also receives and disseminates information on HRD activities both nationally and abroad if these international HRD activities are thought to be relevant to local needs.

Nigeria.   In Nigeria, coordination of HRD has not been as orderly and clear as is the Ghanaian case. Lola Ajila refers to the situation as a "mixed-bag case" with unlinked "systems that very often do not cohere."[7]

As early as 1960, the Ashby Commission influenced the creation of a Nigerian National Manpower Board. The board's responsibilities included, *inter alia*, the formulation of programs "for manpower development through university expansion and training, scholarships, fellowships and other facilities; and coordinating the policies and activities of the Federal and Regional Ministries primarily concerned with manpower problems."[8]

For more than 10 years after its creation, the National Manpower Board proved unable to handle the task of coordinating HRD in a large country such as Nigeria. The problem was further compounded by the existence within the country of other national and largely autonomous institutions charged with the task of HRD. Among them were:

1. The Federal Ministry of Establishment
2. The Administrative Staff College
3. The Nigerian Council for Management Development
4. The Centre for Management Development
5. The Industrial Training Fund

Each of these institutions operates under a different ministry.

Also, in Nigeria there are scores of public and private institutions engaged in HRD in a most uncoordinated manner. Further, each of the 19 states has its own ministry of establishment with responsibility for HRD in the state public service, and in state public and private institutions engaged in HRD. They cover a wide range of HRD activities, including: induction courses for new job entrants, supervisory management courses, design and implementation of HRD programs, the preparation and execution of career development plans, the monitoring of HRD activities, the organization of management development programs, the funding of HRD, and so forth. The situation thus engendered is one of disarray as was recognized in *The Third National Development Plan*:

> As individual provisions are severally made by the Government, public
> agencies, and private employers for the development of various categories
> of manpower, there is the risk of taking the tree for the bush, of a number of
> areas being neglected or not being adequately covered and of the common
> and global objectives being lost in a welter of solitary and confined efforts.[9]

In view of this undesirable situation, the board had its responsibilities broadened, enabling it to monitor and control the interventions of agencies and institutions in the national HRD effort and to coordinate all activities in order to ensure efficiency and effectiveness in attaining national HRD objectives.

In spite of these efforts, the management of HRD has not undergone significant changes over the years. Much more needs to be done to improve management of the HRD function in Nigeria.

Zambia.   In Zambia, modest results have been achieved over the years in efforts to manage HRD in a rational manner. At the national level, responsibility for HRD is shared between the National Commission for Development Planning (HRD planning) and the Ministry of General Education and Culture (education and training). At the sectoral level, the cabinet office and the personnel division take responsibility for HRD, whereas, in the public sector, efforts in this regard are left to parastatals such as the Industrial Development Corporation, which oversees most activities in private industries. The Zambia Federation of Employees and the Congress of Trade Unions provide feedback to the appropriate authorities on needs in HRD and effectiveness of programs. The situation is not perfect, and Zambian authorities realize it.

In March, 1983, the government of Zambia organized a national seminar to provide guidelines to government that would assist efforts to strengthen management of the HRD function in that country. The seminar report, which considered problems of coordination, is being considered by government for implementation.

Thus, in Africa, there are varying degrees of HRD management effectiveness. The need for coordination and a certain amount of centralization cannot be denied, especially in view of the potential waste that might result if things continued uncontrolled. It is true that most HRD activities are and will continue to be executed at the level of the organization and the institution. An effective management machinery will monitor these activities, provide resources to facilitate their success, and ensure that they all converge toward the fulfillment of national HRD objectives.

Financing HRD

One of the biggest constraints on human resource development is the inadequacy of financial resources for institution building, materials procurement and development, and provision of fellowships for learning and research. Several courses of action can be taken at the national, subregional, and regional levels to improve this situation.

A substantive amount of funds for HRD, particularly for education and training of Africans, is provided from sources outside the continent. Funds come through bilateral and multilateral assistance schemes, grants and fellowships from international organizations, and private institutions. Commendable as these aid schemes may be, they do have some shortcomings. First, they are an accelerator of the brain drain, since a good number of Africans who go to Europe and America for education and training do not bring the new skills and knowledge acquired back to Africa. Second, educating and training Africans abroad provides human resources to the continent but fails to give Africa the capability to produce that resource itself. Africans further complicate this situation by spending an estimated $1.04 billion every year to educate and train their nationals outside the continent. That amount of money, added to the millions of dollars provided through aid sources for education and training, could be used within the continent to provide first-rate human resource development services to Africans.

More vigorous attempts should be made by the entire continent to optimize the utilization of existing HRD facilities. National institutions with recognized competence in a particular area should be developed and placed at the disposal of other African countries. Collectively, groups of African countries should pool their meager resources to make it possible for them to create good education and training institutions in critical areas of need for the use of all countries.

The regional fellowship program that is being administered by the Economic Commission for Africa should be strengthened, and African governments should agree on a formula for making contributions to and deriving benefits from it. They should consider designating a certain percentage of the national HRD budget to the regional program and allocating a certain number of places in their learning institutions to other African nationals. At present, the program's resources are too limited to respond to all the demands from African governments.

At the national level, efforts to obtain funds for HRD should be increased. There are several ways of doing so:

1. A fund for HRD should be established and administered by the minister responsible for human resource development.
2. A levy should be used. Every establishment in the private sector and all parastatals (i.e., quasi government) should be required by

law to pay into the fund, on an annual basis, a certain percentage of the previous year's total payroll or turnover for HRD activities. A fine of a certain additional percentage of the annual payroll or turnover should be levied on all establishments that fail to comply with the law.

3. A tax rebate should be used. Establishments that have provided HRD and whose effectiveness has been verified should be entitled to a tax rebate of a percentage of their annual tax set by a formula to be designed by government. In this way, employers will be encouraged to spend more of their profits on HRD.

4. A selective employment tax should be used. Establishments intending to employ a nonnational should be required to pay a certain percentage of that individual's monthly salary into the fund. This system will act as an incentive for training and education of nationals and will ensure that the search process for skilled nationals is more thorough.

5. All financial aid for education and training should be paid into the fund and administered by the minister responsible for human resource development.

6. A substantial increase in government allocations to HRD should be made and paid into the fund.

7. A ministry responsible for HRD should provide management consultancy or instructional services to organizations and establishments in the public or private sectors or in the parastatals. The cost of such services should be paid into the fund.

A well-conceived system to generate funds, established along these lines, would ensure that the HRD function at the national level is provided with the resources necessary to make HRD effective.

Staff Resources for HRD

As in most skill areas in Africa, HRD suffers from a shortage of personnel. Its first task, therefore, is to provide its own human resources. This can be done in third-level educational (i.e., postsecondary) institutions. Degrees and diplomas would help to establish accreditation and recognition of the profession. At present, only one university in Africa—Lagos University—has a program in human resource development. Most efforts in this regard concentrate on schools in the formal system, or on adult education in the nonformal system. HRD for the work force, the individual, the organization, and the economy is still to be developed within African institutions.

Through cooperative arrangements, it should be possible for countries with more experience in producing HRD staff to assist African countries in developing capabilities to produce their own. In addition, the few local human resource practitioners should establish national associations that would be federated into a regional association for human resource development. Already, there are a number of professional associations, such as the African Adult Education Association and the African Association for Training Development. One regional management association exists—the African Association for Public Administration and Management. These and other HRD-related regional associations should come together to create an African association for human resource development and to develop human resource practitioners by publishing professional journals, holding seminars and workshops, and organizing courses.

CONCLUSION

Without appropriate skills and a high level of efficiency in Africa, African socioeconomic development efforts will be meaningless. With inadequate resources available for HRD in most African countries, rational and judicious use of these resources should be made, in order to avoid waste and to optimize efforts to develop human resources.

Realistic policies on human resource development must be formulated by African governments; appropriate machineries must be created to implement these policies; and plans should be made to ensure that HRD does not turn out to be a wasteful exercise with little or no positive impact on the skills needs of the economy. It is also important that an efficient system be created to manage the HRD function and that the human resource practitioners who will operate this system should practice what they preach by discharging their duties with efficiency and at a high level of productivity.

Human resource development activities produce an output for use as an input to production and services. The users of this input should be made to contribute to the growth of HRD. Industry and establishments should provide funding for HRD, as should individuals and organizations benefitting from the service.

Training and education of HRD practitioners should also command priority, for without the staff resources, human resource development cannot exist. Therefore, governments, institutions, and professional associations should encourage the development of HRD practitioners.

Unless measures are undertaken immediately to solve some of the problems confronting the development of human resources in Africa, the continent will continue to face meager chances of raising the standard of living of its people.

NOTES

1. OAU/ECA: *Strategy for the African Region in the International Development Strategy for the Third Development Decade*; E/CN.14/1F/107, Addis Ababa: Organization of African Unity/Economic Commission for Africa, 1979.

2. OAU/ECA: *Lagos Plan of Action for the Implementation of the Monrovia Strategy for the Economic Development of Africa*, Lagos: Organization of African Unity/Economic Commission for Africa, 1980.

3. Ibid, p. 41.

4. The figure of 17200 represents the labor power needed in the first five categories in Figure 25.2 and the total needs in Figures 25.3 and 25.4.

5. J. Garber and C. Grey-Johnson: "Feasibility of Establishing an African Institute for Higher Technical Training and Research," Addis Ababa: Organization of African Unity/Economic Commission for Africa, 1978.

6. UNECA estimates, 1983.

7. J. Lola Ajila, "Manpower Training Development Status in Nigeria," paper presented to the AATD Conference, Addis Ababa, 1979.

8. *Nigeria Gazette*, Feb. 15, 1963.

9. Federal Republic of Nigeria, *The Third National Development Plan, 1975-1980*, Nigeria: Federal Republic of Nigeria, p. 134, 1975.

Human Resource Development in Asia

ASIA

VANKATRAM K. RAMCHANDRAN

Of all the regions of the world, Asia probably presents the greatest contrasts. It contains one of the most developed countries of the world (i.e., Japan) and many lesser-developed countries.

For those unfamiliar with Asia, the discussion that Ramchandran presents on the national productivity organizations will be of prime interest. There is no similar counterpart in the United States, though remnants of similar organizations can be found in some western European countries.

As Ramchandran points out, the Asian Regional Training and Development Organization (ARTDO) has been instrumental in bringing together the several national organizations. The value of ARTDO to all the nations in the area is becoming obvious. Effective linkages through the International (or World) Federation of Training and Development Organizations are still to be developed to a more effective level.

It is not possible for Ramchandran to present in-depth material on all the activities in the region in one chapter. As interest in international HRD activities increases, perhaps so will the demand for more written material, so we can share in this interdependent world.

Vankatram K. Ramchandran (Ph.D.) is retired from his position as principal of the Air-India Staff College in Bombay. He was also a senior director and chief consultant with the National Productivity Council of India. He has been president of the Indian Society for Training and Development and president of the Asian Regional Training and Development Organization. He is on the expert panels of several United Nations specialized agencies and other bodies, such as the Commonwealth Fund for Technical Cooperation.

Asia covers a vast territory. In a single chapter, it is not possible to adequately cover the myriad of HRD activities in the region. I will limit myself, therefore, to national and significant efforts in various countries, in order to provide the reader with some understanding of what is going on in HRD in Asia.

There is considerable diversity among the countries of Asia, in terms of size of the country, population, structure of the economy, availability of natural resources, per capita income, and so forth. Figure 26.1 provides some such information for 12 countries in Asia.

Two other factors that greatly influence HRD are the literacy level and the age of the population. These data are presented in Figure 26.2. People from developed countries may not fully appreciate what those figures mean. Since a large population percentage below 15 years of age means that there will probably be an increase in the working population within the next 10 years or less, more people will be looking for jobs but will probably not be prepared for them.

The basis for sound economic growth in any country is a highly literate population that can adapt to change. The United Nations (UN) has estimated that a literacy rate of 40% is essential if a country is to be developed. As Figure 26.2 indicates, more than half of the countries in the area surpass that literacy rate. It is interesting to note, however, that these countries exist side by side with other countries that have not yet reached that rate.

In addition to being literate, there is the need to have a work ethic that applies knowledge and skills in a diligent way. In short, schools should prepare people in appropriate work attitudes, apart from giving them knowledge and skills that can be used in work. Societal mores may sometimes get in the way of the attitudes just mentioned. Professor Sadli points out, with reference to Indonesia

Often education consists more of rote learning, and the stimulus or motivation to apply scientific methods and innovation to cope with daily life is still not strong. For the middle class and elite, going to school is often regarded as a means to improve social status. The need for more technical education is recognised rationally, but this is not easily translated into more resources allocated to build technical schools. There is a basic inertia in the society, because many see education as an end in itself, not as an input for industrialisation.[1]

Technical education is paramount for the growth of any economy, whether rural, industrial, or service oriented. Technical skills are

Share of GNP (in percent)

Country	Per Capita GNP[1]	Population[2]	Agr.	Mfg.	Other	Year
Japan	7280	115	5	29	66	1978
Singapore	3290	2	2	26	72	1978
Hong Kong	3040	4.6	2	25	73	1977
Republic of China	1400	17	10	38	52	1978
Republic of Korea	1160	36	24	24	52	1978
Philippines	510	46	27	25	48	1979
Thailand	490	45	27	18	55	1979
Indonesia	360	136	31	9	60	1978
Pakistan	230	77	32	16	52	1979
Sri Lanka	190	14	35	23	42	1978
India	180	640	40	17	43	1978
Nepal	120	14	62	10	28	1977

[1]in U.S. dollars
[2]in millions mid-1978

Figure 26.1. Share of gross national product. *Source:* "A.P.P. Basic Research: Factors Which Hinder or Help Productivity Improvement in the Asian Region." Organization report by Prof. Y. Nayudamma, p. 88.

Country	Claimed Literacy Level	Population Below 15 Years of Age
Australia	100	27
Japan	99	25
Republic of Korea	91	37
Hong Kong	90	30
Philippines	87	46
Vietnam	87	44
Thailand	82	45
Republic of China	82	33
Peoples Republic of China	80	33
Singapore	75	31
Iran	50	46
Malaysia	36	42
India	36	42
Bangladesh	22	46
Pakistan	21	47
Afghanistan	12	45

Figure 26.2. Literacy levels in east Asia (in percent). *Source:* "East Asia's Awkward Corner." *The Economist*, by a special correspondent. November 1981, p. 27.

provided by several institutions in Asia, including the Foreman Training Institute in Bangalore, India; the Advanced Training Institute in Madras, India; the National Manpower and Youth Council in Manila, Philippines; and the Vocational and Industrial Training Board in Singapore. There are other equally important institutions in other parts of Asia.

These various institutions can work cooperatively through the auspices of the Asian and Pacific Skill Development Programme (APSDEP). This program can take on the task of upgrading those technical institutions already operating by providing experts from other countries in Asia and elsewhere. Needless to say, since there are several countries in Asia that are primarily agricultural, technical HRD programs should encompass that area as well. The term *agriculture* includes everything related to the rural economy, such as crop-growing, animal husbandry, and pisciculture, as well as village and small-scale industries. This is what is commonly referred to as *agribusiness*.

IN-HOUSE HRD

In addition to the general efforts of government, of which more will be said later, there is a great deal of HRD being conducted within organizations in the private sector. In the introduction to Larsen and Toubro's yearly calendar of HRD programs, the Vice President of Personnel and Organizational Development points out:

> In our preoccupation with current work and goals, we tend to overlook the need to pause and evaluate what we are doing and find out the scope for stretching our personal strengths. In an age when theoretical and applied knowledge expands at a tremendous pace, there is danger of relative fossilisation, if we do not update ourselves in the relevant area of our concern. The losers in such a situation are both the individual and the organisation, through not realising their full potential. In the case of the individual, it also means stagnation and frustration instead of development and taking on fresh and rewarding challenges.
>
> It is against this background that our corporate management attaches great importance to personnel training and development on a sustained basis. Our HRD department monitors the training needs of employees through performance appraisal forms and responds with a balanced blend of training programmes.[2]

Another example of in-house HRD programs is provided by the Sime Darby Organization in Malaysia. This company has 200 subsidiaries in different parts of the world. According to Tunku Abdul Aziz, Group Director of Personnel, their HRD policy points out the need for a philosophy of management.

> The goals and objectives of any plan are the reflection of the wider philosophical perspectives of an organisation. A company must establish what it considers to be a management philosophy which can give substance and meaning to its legitimate aspirations. The philosophy of any organisation, while nothing more than an organised body of thought based on careful and mature consideration of basic principles, policies and objectives and ways and means of arriving at the solution to some sets of problems, is, nevertheless the starting point of corporate existence.
>
> If top management is to manage in a socially and morally acceptable manner consistent with the new concerns and values, it has to develop a totally new and heightened sensitivity in its approach to public issues because business objectives encompass not only the interests and aspirations of the shareholders, bankers, customers, suppliers and employees but those of the public at large.

The development of top managers of the present and foreseeable future, must be directed not only at the how but more important the what and why of business.[3]

Many other private sector organizations in Asia, particularly the multinationals, place great emphasis on HRD. They maintain HRD units that frequently include people from several different countries, in addition to the particular country in which the organization or its units are functioning.

EXTERNAL HRD

Organizations that do not have full-fledged internal HRD units or are inadequate in certain areas resort to using external programs conducted by academic institutions or HRD (training and development) organizations, management associations, or personnel management associations. There are also numerous companies, frequently called *consulting companies*, that also provide programs. Some of these programs are conducted at the company site for the employees of that particular organization. Other HRD programs are conducted as public seminars, and various companies send their employees to these external programs.

ASIAN PRODUCTIVITY ORGANIZATION

A leading external organization is the Asian Productivity Organization (APO). It has done considerable work in HRD during the past 20 years. APO was created as part of the foreign aid program of the United States, but since the middle 1960s, it has functioned as a self-sustaining organization. The APO is a unique organization; the only similar body is the OECD in western Europe that grew out of the Marshall Plan—the U.S. foreign aid program of the 1950s.

APO is an intergovernmental body with which the national productivity organizations of the following countries are affiliated: Republic of China, Hong Kong, India, Indonesia, Iran, Japan, Republic of Korea, Nepal, Pakistan, Philippines, Singapore, Sri Lanka, Thailand, Bangladesh, and Malaysia. APO is trying to enlarge its membership, particularly among the other countries in the South Pacific.

In the various countries, the national productivity organizations are either part of the government or are organized in what can be termed a *quasi-governmental* organization. In India, for example, the National Productivity Council (NPC) has a governing body that includes representatives from the government, employers, and employees. NPC operates through 48 local productivity councils and its regional directorates.

Since its formation, APO has focused much of its activity on HRD, including: training and education courses; observational study missions; technical and expert services; research, seminars and conferences; publications; and the development of audiovisual materials. The philosophy underlying APO's orientation toward HRD is that

> productivity is an attitude of mind and the key factors influencing productivity are the enthusiasm and creative skills of human beings, which make them productive. This philosophy and stress on human resources development have been the main pillars of APO's growth and to a certain extent that of the National Productivity organisations as well.[4]

In October 1980, the APO celebrated 20 years of operation by holding a seminar in Hong Kong. The theme was "New Dimensions of Productivity and Development Strategies for the 1980s." The seminar placed great emphasis on HRD.

Harumi Takeuchi, then Secretary General of APO, notes in his foreword to the publication *Twenty Years of APO:*

> The new dimensions in productivity as I see them, are in one word the *humanisation* of productivity, because in the final analysis it is not the machine which advances productivity, but the man behind the machine. How to motivate him and his will to work, his will to improve—this, I think, is the crux of the whole programme which we are putting up for the improvement of productivity.

> There could be many ways of humanising productivity. There is much discussion of the quality of working life, and the need to satisfy the workers in their own working environment. Many devices are being tried to improve this quality, and perhaps this is the leading aim which we should follow in our endeavour in the future.[5]

In its retrospective report in 1978, the APO noted that the backbone of its activities was "manpower development with multi-country training courses" whose aim was

> to train individuals who can achieve the multiplier effect afterwards. Hence, trainees are mostly drawn from trainers and consultants working with the national productivity organisations or similar organisations in the member countries who can in turn conduct training courses or serve as consultants after their return to their respective countries.

The APO also holds multicountry *seminars* that are of shorter duration than a training course and planned for participants of a higher level than those in a training course. In a seminar, the discussions are two-way, in order to exchange experiences and to elicit new approaches to upcoming problems.

One other aspect of institution building, which the APO has expanded in recent years, is the joint gathering of data and emerging theories in the Asian socioeconomic context. These will strengthen and support the work of the national productivity organizations. By these varied means, the APO has been seeking to create a group of strong and professionally competent individuals. APO has launched a multiyear survey of technical assimilation and adaptation in APO member countries in an extremely significant area. They are examining the learning process by which high technology, imported from developed countries, is assimilated into the socioeconomic environment of the recipient country. This is an extremely important endeavor in an area where there is too little hard data.

Once a year, the heads of the various NPOs meet in a different country for a workshop. This workshop group serves as the planning body of APO. Their agenda includes a review and evaluation of APO activities for the preceding year, a review of programs conducted, a review of financial estimates for the current year, and the formulation of programs for the coming year. In addition, during this workshop, plans are made for the next two years within the framework of the APO rolling Five-Year Plan.

The workshop group breaks into two committees—one for industry and one for agriculture. This reflects the overwhelming importance of agriculture for the region served by the APO. All workshop recommendations are presented to the Governing Body of APO that has responsibility for policy. That group meets once a year.

In August, 1982, the APO Governing Body set forth its policies for the remainder of the 1980s. Relevant statements from these policies are contained in Appendix A.

NATIONAL PRODUCTIVITY ORGANIZATIONS[6]

It is not possible to discuss the work of each National Productivity Organization in any detail, as most of the NPOs have numerous programs related to HRD. The following presentation should provide an understanding of some of the activities from a variety of countries.

Bangladesh

One objective of the Bangladesh Industrial and Technical Assistance Center (BITAC) is to promote productivity in the economy and to develop the work force through intensive, practice-oriented training and education.

The emphasis is on meeting the requirements of the emerging small industries. Advanced learning is provided for participants in the fields of metal trade and automobiles with emphasis on: electrical maintenance and repair, heat treatment, protection coating (electroplating), foundry work, pattern design, sheet metal, welding, and mechanical maintenance.

External resources are also utilized. BITAC has an agreement with a Swiss company, and they established a joint HRD center in Bangladesh. With this sophisticated machinery and the expert services, BITAC is contributing to upgrading the skills of technicians within their country.

Republic of China

The Republic of China is small, but it contains a significant concentration of multinational companies involved in high technology. Many of these companies provide their own HRD staff or recruit local people, and many have extensive programs.

The NPO is the China Productivity Center. It disseminates information regarding modern management and provides technical assistance to medium-sized and small companies. Among the activities and HRD programs offered by the center are:

Quality control techniques
Low-cost automation
Industrial safety and hygiene
Technology and materials management
Management philosophy and techniques

Hong Kong

In addition to the HRD professionals in Hong Kong, there is also a significant number of expatriates providing HRD services in that country. There are two conditions that are new to Hong Kong and have increased the need for HRD.

For many years, Hong Kong has been an industrial center with many small companies engaged in manufacturing. Most of these have not used modern technology but have based their operations on the vast supply of labor available in Hong Kong. The trend now is away from industrial operations and toward business. Hong Kong is becoming the financial center of the region. This trend is moving Hong Kong from labor intensive to capital intensive companies.

The second factor is political. The British lease on Hong Kong expires in 1997. Although the situation can change, as frequently happens in the political arena, it appears that the People's Republic of China (PRC) will have some kind of control. It is already beginning to happen through PRC banks and companies operating in Hong Kong. Although not openly discussed, the PRC has been sending some of its people to Hong Kong for training and education. This has presented a language problem, since the prevalent language spoken in Hong Kong is Cantonese, while people from the PRC speak Mandarin. Many organizations in Hong Kong have had to organize language training in Mandarin for their employees.

Given these factors, the Hong Kong Productivity Center is in the process of change. It is still providing essential HRD programs, while adding new ones to reflect the changes. Its HRD offerings include microprocessing applications, plastics, heat treatment, metal industry, computer services, and quality control.

India

The National Productivity Council of India is a dynamic organization. The Prime Minister designated 1982 as the *productivity year*. At a meeting of the national council, held early in 1982, special emphasis was placed on the following subjects: energy conservation, materials management, maintenance management, labor-management relations, pollution control, production management and monitoring, and productivity. These programs were to focus mainly on the small organizations including *khadi* and village industries.

As agriculture is an essential part of the Indian economy, the NPC has set up an agricultural production center to strengthen crop and livestock production systems, agro-based industries, and postharvest activities.

NPC conducts two-year courses in industrial engineering, plant engineering, and fuel efficiency. They also offer a diploma program in supervision that is recognized by the government of India. This correspondence program consists of four units:

1. Principles of supervision
2. Personnel management and industrial relations
3. Productivity techniques
4. One of the following subjects as selected by the candidate: work planning and control, storekeeping and stock control, and office supervision

This HRD program has met with good response from employees working in various industries.

Indonesia

Indonesia has a high rate of unemployment and underemployment. Only a small segment of its economy could be called *modern*. There is a significant overpopulation problem, and this pressure varies from one region of the country to another. Attempts have been made by the government to accomplish transmigration of people from one part of the country to another to alleviate some of the population problems.

The HRD needs cover a wide spectrum relating to agriculture and the rural sector, cottage and small industries. The National Productivity Center has been conducting supervisory and middle-management programs and achievement motivation programs to encourage self-reliance. Business management training is provided for cottage and small-scale industries and businesses.

Japan

The Japan Productivity Center (JPC) organizes programs for leaders in business on current and emerging issues (e.g., limited natural resources, aging labor force, etc.). The Center has also been arranging programs on labor management consultation, in addition to programs for trade union leaders.

The JPC has been concerned with how technological innovation, such as the introduction of microcomputers and other electronic devices, and other aspects of technology may affect labor practices in the future.

In its early days, the JPC, in cooperation with the United States, sent many study teams from Japan to the United States. Today, the JPC still does this, but it also arranges for study teams from the United States and other countries to learn about Japanese business and industry.

Korea

The government designated 1982 as the year of "Productivity Enhancement," and the Korean Productivity Center (KPC) was identified as the leadership organization to carry out the program. HRD courses were organized in the fields of personnel management, labor management, planning, business finance, accounting, marketing, and production control. In addition to these programs, KPC implemented HRD programs for productivity instructors and productivity counselors. The KPC also provided productivity enhancement seminars and a lecture series for executives of public corporations.

KPC has also focused attention on assisting small-scale and medium-scale enterprises. In the future, KPC activities will be influenced by the fact that Korean industries are moving from labor-intensive operations to high technology operations.

Malaysia

In Malaysia, the National Productivity Center has embarked on a program to create and develop entrepreneurs in rural and underdeveloped sectors of the economy. This is part of the thrust of the *Bumiputra* movement, which encourages more Malays (the numerically predominant ethnic group in Malaysia) to become small businessmen.

NPC has launched a hotel-restaurant HRD institute as a reflection of the growing tourist trade in Malaysia. Toward the end of 1981, the NPC was given a mandate by the government to launch a productivity-consciousness program throughout the country.

Nepal

The Industrial Services Center (ISC) in Nepal focuses on cottage and small-scale industries as that area of industrial development is still in its infancy.

The ISC conducts studies on the identification of existing managerial manpower and their learning needs in the emerging industrial sector. These data are used to create HRD programs for managers.

Pakistan

The activities of the Pakistan Industrial Technical Assistance Center (PITAC) are primarily in the metal trades industry. The PITAC provides

HRD programs and consulting services in a wide range of topics related to the metal industry. It has introduced the concept and application of low-cost automation and maintains a fully equipped laboratory managed by a competent staff.

Philippines

The Productivity and Development Center (PDC) of the development academy of the Philippines has been working to create an awareness of the significance of increasing productivity in that country. It has been concentrating on small-scale and medium-scale firms, energy management, and prevention of postharvest waste and losses. Furthermore, it is organizing productivity associations to promote consciousness of this concept in the countryside.

In 1981, the PDC was appointed as the secretariat of the National Productivity Commission, which is a tripartite body whose objective is the promotion of the productivity movement and the formulation of supportive policy recommendations.

Singapore

This country has set its economy on a new path in an effort to shift it from labor intensive to capital intensive, from low skill to high technology. A Skills Development Fund has been created through a corporate payroll tax levy of 4% of the salaries of those earning $750 a month or less. Organizations can draw from this fund to defray the cost of HRD programs. In addition, technical training and education centers have been established.

In response to the government's policy to restructure the economy, the National Productivity Board (NPB) has expanded its activities to cater to the need for:

1. Improved labor relations, provided by such programs as quality circles, performance appraisal, and improving human relations at work

2. The adoption of improved top management and functional management practices by providing HRD programs for managers and executives

3. The upgrading of supervisory skills through training for supervisors and Training Within Industry courses in job relations, job instruction, job methods, and job safety

4. The improved application of industrial safety and occupational health practices through courses for managers and supervisors, such as safety instruction and building construction safety

In Singapore, a National Productivity Council has been formed to monitor the promotion of the productivity concept and the awareness of the people at-large concerning productivity.

Sri Lanka

The activities of the National Institute of Management (NIM) are in the areas of management and supervisory programs. The NIM has experimented with the modular supervisory learning program produced by the International Labor Office and has conducted diploma programs in business management, industrial engineering, marketing, and personnel management.

The NIM also conducts two-day seminars for small industrialists. A fairly recent innovation has been the diploma program in business management, conducted in the local language, Simhala.

Thailand

The Management Development and Productivity Center (MDPC) has been conducting HRD programs in marketing management, organization, methods management, personnel management, management accounting, production management, and computers for management.

A growing portion of the MDPC activities focuses on the rural aspects of development, such as production and marketing, farm mechanization, prevention of waste, and water management. Future plans include the promotion of rural, small-scale industries.

Conclusion

The reports presented in this section are an overview of the activities of national productivity organizations. They indicate, however, that there is considerable activity in the HRD field in these various countries. Some put more emphasis on managerial aspects, some on technical, and others on technomanagerial—depending on the current needs of those countries.

To acquire a better grasp of these activities, one must refer to the annual reports of the different national productivity organizations and the other organizations related to them. These reports change yearly, as the plans and needs of the countries change.

HRD ORGANIZATIONS

In addition to the various HRD programs being offered by the national productivity centers, other government and quasi-governmental organizations, and the private sector, there are also membership organizations. These can be found in the areas of HRD (training and development), personnel management, and management associations. All of these, and more, provide a variety of HRD activities in the region.

An extremely important organization is the Asian Regional Training and Development Organization (ARTDO), which is heavily involved in HRD in the Asia-Pacific region. In fact, the brochure published by this organization for its membership drive referred to ARTDO as the "HRD Club."

ARTDO was founded in 1974, and its secretariat is located in the Philippines. Its objective is to link together various professional HRD groups and similar organizations under one umbrella. ARTDO is a private, nonprofit organization with membership representation from most parts of Asia and the Pacific.

ARTDO has three categories of membership:

1. *Regular.* Duly accredited national (HRD) organizations or associations from countries in the Asia-Pacific region.
2. *Associate.* Other professional organizations with objectives similar to ARTDO's. This includes national and international foundations and government organizations committed to HRD.
3. *Affiliate.* Organizations operating outside of the Asia-Pacific region but subscribing to the goals of ARTDO.

At the end of 1982, on the basis of fully paid subscriptions, ARTDO's membership consisted of 51 organizations from 23 different countries. ARTDO is affiliated with the International Federation of Training and Development Organizations.

One of the most important activities of ARTDO is the regional conference conducted annually in a different country in the region. Conferences have been held in: Manila (1974), New Delhi (1975), Canberra (1976), Suva, Fiji (1977), Ranchi, India (1978), Manila (1979), Palmerston North, New Zealand (1980), Kuala Lumpur (1981), Hong Kong (1982), Taipei (1983), and Sydney (1984).

The secretariat issues a quarterly bulletin called the "ARTDO report" to keep in touch with its members. Apart from news about member organizations, the newsletter includes information about what is happening in HRD and what is being written about it.

ARTDO provides an annual award called the "Asia-Pacific Human Resource Development Award" in recognition of the outstanding contribution made by an organization or individual in the HRD field. The award for 1982 was given to the Asian Institute of Management in Manila.

While ARTDO has done well, particularly since 1977, its problems are similar to those of most voluntary organizations—lack of adequate finances and shortfall in effectiveness. The latter arises from the fact that the various executive committee members live in different countries and are not able to meet often enough to guide the organization. As is the case with many such regional organizations, the executive committee only meets once a year, during the annual conference.

National Organizations

As noted earlier, there are 23 countries represented in ARTDO. It would fill a book to describe each of the organizations. The operations of each of the HRD organizations vary from country to country. Some are very active, while others are not. A brief description of the Indian Society for Training and Development (ISTD) follows, as I am most familiar with that.

ISTD held its first annual conference in New Delhi in April, 1970. Since that time, it has grown and has many chapters throughout the country. It currently provides a diploma program in training and development to "professionalize the training and development function in India." The program started in April, 1977. It is a one-year correspondence course followed by an internship of six months. The curriculum consists of the following:

1. Human Resource Development
2. Behavioral Science and Organizational Behavior
3. Planning Manpower and Training
4. Planning of Training
5. Training Methodology
6. Evaluation of Training

After an individual has passed the written tests in the designated areas, there is an internship for six months, supervised by a person designated for this purpose by the ISTD Board of Studies. The internship may be carried out in the candidate's own organization. No leave of absence from work is required, since the intern can do the task after office hours. At the end of the internship, the candidate submits a report for evaluation by the board of studies.

CONCLUSION

The field of HRD is immense in Asia, since the range of activities covers the entire gamut of a nation's economy. This calls for leadership of a high order, leadership that can bring about changes in as smooth a manner as possible to overcome the inertia of the ages.

As far as the industries are concerned, Professor Mendoza was correct when he said:

> The rapid introduction of new ideas and techniques require that all the members of the organization be in a constant state of "learning readiness" to stave off personal and professional obsolescence. Managers have to attend many times during their careers, HRD programs, since knowledge is expanding fast and they have to update themselves, so that they may adopt or adapt the ideas and implement them in their organizations.[7]

NOTES

1. "Development Strategies for the 1980's," report of the Asian Productivity Congress (Hong Kong: October, 1980), p. 75.
2. Larsen and Toubro Ltd., Human Resources Department, "In-Company Training Programme, 1982–1983," (Bombay, India), p. 2.
3. Tunku Abdul Aziz, "Training and Development for Top Management," paper presented at the Eighth ARTDO conference, Kuala Lumpur, November, 1981.
4. Asian Productivity Organization, *Twenty Years of APO*, 1982, p. 35.
5. Asian Productivity Organization, *Twenty Years of APO*.
6. Matter relating to APO and the NPOs has been taken from: *Proceedings of the Governing Body, 24th Session*, held at Medan, Indonesia in August, 1982; *Twenty Years of APO*; and the *APO News*.
7. A. Mendoza, "Challenges for Human Resources Development in Asian Countries in the Eighties," paper presented at the Eighth ARTDO conference, Kuala Lumpur, November, 1981.

APPENDIX A

APO Governing Body—Policy for the Eighties

1.   As a *think tank*, providing leadership, thinking, and foresight into the type of productivity programs most needed by member countries in their efforts to accelerate economic growth and improve the living standard of the people.

2.   As a *catalyst*, promoting greater multilateral cooperation among member countries and encouraging national and regional endeavors to increase and improve productivity.

3.   As a *regional advisor* on productivity matters, bearing in mind the country-specific nature of national economic and development policies and helping member countries obtain the optimal productivity mix under changing conditions.

4.   As a productivity *institution builder*, helping member countries strengthen their professional capability through a human resource development program, with emphasis on software development and product improvement at the micro level.

5.   As a *clearing house of information* on productivity thus stimulating a vigorous exchange of information among member countries and with organizations in other parts of the world.

Regarding item 4 above, the details are:

1.   To train trainers/consultants of NPOs and similar institutions in various managerial and technological subject areas.

2.   To provide technical expert services, organize observational study missions, and supply case studies, manuals, and training aids in printed and audiovisual forms.

3.   To offer help to NPOs when requested to have access to sources of information on management and technical know-how and to encourage them to perform the role of technology transfer catalysts or agents.

4.   To encourage bilateral cooperation between NPOs.

JAPAN

LEONARD NADLER

This is an addition to Chapter 26 written by Ramchandran. Although Japan is in Asia, it has been given special mention in this handbook as it has a unique place in the international arena. It is a highly developed and industrialized country in a region of the world where lesser developed or newly industrializing countries abound.

The culture of Japan also makes it unique. Of course, other countries have their own cultures, but in Japan we find the interface between an old, traditional culture and industrialization.

Japan has recently been the model for industrialized countries, but the Japanese are beginning to question some of their practices over the past 25 years. It will be unfortunate if executives and HRD practitioners continue to rush to Japan to see what they are doing, while, at the same time, Japanese HRD leaders indicate that Japan is changing. Some of the changes, as seen by the Japanese, are noted in this chapter.

Leonard Nadler (Ed.D.) is professor of adult education and human resource development, School of Education and Human Development, The George Washington University. He has been involved in the fields of HRD and adult education since 1983, except for three years working for an accounting company and two years as a cost accountant in an industrial plant. Prior to coming to GWU, he was a training officer with the Agency for International Development in Japan and Ethiopia. He works internationally in HRD and has worked in 31 different countries. He was a national board member of ASTD for five years and has served as president of three chapters. He has published five books and over 125 articles.

As with any complicated and sophisticated industrialized country, it is not possible to cover all of Japan's HRD activities in one article. This brief account is included in this handbook to give the reader some idea of what has happened and is happening in Japan. It is not meant to be comprehensive, but, rather, illustrative.

BACKGROUND

We can begin to draw the picture of HRD in Japan just after World War II. This does not mean that there was no HRD before that period, but significant advances took place after World War II. The occupation forces conducted HRD programs for Japanese employees using U.S. materials that had proven themselves in our economy and society. Among these were Training Within Industry (TWI) programs such as Job Instruction Training and Job Methods Training.

In 1955, the U.S. foreign aid program was extended to include Japan, as the United States endeavored to turn over all operations in the country to the civilian sector. A core element of the program was to establish a counterpart agency, an approach that had worked very well earlier in Europe. The Japan Productivity Center (JPC) was established and is still extremely active today.

A major HRD activity was to send selected Japanese to the United States for study tours that lasted about 12 weeks. Those selected were carefully prepared in Japan prior to departure with the United States Agency for International Development (USAID) training officer spending time with JPC and the team to refine the learning objectives.

During the early 1960s, HRD was conducted mainly in the large companies in Japan through in-house schools. These schools were often quite elaborate and sophisticated, but the curriculum was designed essentially to prepare the individual for lifelong employment with the company. Practicing on company equipment was emphasized and very little theory was included.[1]

Since that time, the HRD systems have changed considerably. In many ways, they are similar to those in the United States, although there are some cultural factors, as one might expect, that produce differences.

Until the late 1970s, the practice in most companies had been to first promote individuals and then provide training. In general, promotions were based on longevity and ability to get along with others. It is becoming apparent that longer service does not necessarily mean a greater knowledge of new technologies. More recently, some companies have begun to provide education for those individuals who are being considered for promotion.

THE JAPANESE EMPLOYMENT SYSTEM

The employment system in Japan has many significant differences from those in the United States. Some examples, although not a comprehensive listing, follow:

Lifelong Employment

It has been traditional in the larger Japanese companies for employees at all levels to stay with the company until retirement or death. In smaller companies, this was the intent, but it was not always possible.

The practice has changed somewhat, but there is still the intent of lifelong employment. In the past, employees tended not to specialize. Instead, most of the work force were generalists—they were expected to move into any job the company requested. New technology forced the use of specialists in some of the technical areas.

The Company as Family

An employee is seen as part of a family—the company. This is not rhetoric, but a cultural norm. As such, they must live as a family—with some tensions but essentially in a cooperative manner. Some companies (e.g., Mitsubishi) have gone so far as to have a special section in the administrative staff that is concerned with arranging marriages. Also, many Japanese from large companies wear the company emblem, in the form of a pin, in the jacket lapel. This signals the family identification. When introducing oneself in Japanese, it is customary to first give the company name and then your own. For example: "I am Mitsubishi. My name is _____."

The Reward System

The Japanese work force has been one of the wonders of the world since 1960. They utilized quality circles[2] and other unique practices. It was generally assumed that the Japanese workers were concerned only with doing their best for their employers.

In fact, the Japanese system had significant rewards and punishments built into the workplace. Of course, part of this was due to Japanese cultural factors. However, other rewards and punishments were similar to those found in any good organization.[3] One factor was the promise of promotion, even though much of the take-home pay was not based on position in the organization. A survey conducted in 1979[4] asked the question, "Do you undertake difficult assignments to increase your promotion chances?" The respondents replied:

16% — Yes, I do.
29% — Yes, I'm afraid that's the only way.
51% — Definitely not.

This is in conflict with the traditional view that some have held of the Japanese work force.

Retirement

In 1945, the retirement age was 55. At that time, the life expectancy of the Japanese male was 45. By 1980, the life expectancy had almost doubled, but the retirement age had only increased by five years. Japan is facing the same problem the United States is, that is, a significantly "older" population. They do not yet face a significant "graying of the work force" because of forced retirement at no later than age 60.

As the numbers of retirees increase, however, so will the problem. The practice in Japan is that most workers do not receive a pension until five years after retiring.[5] In the past, this did not pose too great a problem, as the immediate family provided for the retirees during that period. As the number of retirees increases, at a rapid rate, this can produce some imbalance in the Japanese economy and social system.

It is not only an economic factor, but also one of self-image. Many people who are forced to retire still want to be considered productive members of society. At one time, a man who reached the age of 60 (when very few did) would put on a red suit and take part in a ceremony that proclaimed to the world that he was no longer responsible for himself. It was considered second childhood, as the person over 60 no longer had responsibilities and could expect others to take care of him.

A different way of dealing with the retirement problem has been attempted by reemploying retired workers as temporary workers. They are not considered permanent and, therefore, do not receive many of the benefits they had when they were employed prior to retirement. In some situations, the retired worker returns in a completely different capacity. Some companies have begun to experiment with education programs to prepare employees long before they reach the 55–60 age bracket.

HRD PRACTICES

The following discussion is based on material provided by the Japanese companies indicated. Their HRD systems are actually much more complicated than reported here. The material has been abstracted from much longer documents. These examples are designed to provide some insight into HRD practices in some large companies in Japan.

Canon Company

This is a major camera and optics company. In 1975, the company implemented a six-year "Yuryo Kigyo Plan" (Plan for Corporate Excellence). During this time, they acquired other companies in Japan, increased sales and profits, and were generally successful. This was followed by the "Second Yuryo Kigyo Plan" (1982–1986).

As with many Japanese companies, Canon strives for lifelong employment for all its male work force until the mandatory retirement age of 60. In 1982, they reported that annual turnover, among males, was less than 1% per year.

This company sees HRD as one of its most important activities. This is particularly so when it comes to responding to technological developments and industrial innovations.[6] In 1981, Canon employed 10,742 people and provided 80,000 hours of formal instruction. No breakdown is provided as to learners, but the work force was 60% male. It is probable that most of those training hours were provided to the male employees.

There are two training units:

Ability Development Department. Responsible for HRD for the head office.

Technical Training Center. Responsible for skills and apprenticeship programs.

In addition, about 50% of the HRD program is decentralized into the operating divisions.

In 1958, Canon established a Trade Skill Training Center for new employees who had completed high school. In 1967, they expanded the curriculum to include electronics and lens processing. Every year they train about 80 learners, who they expect will become the leading skilled workers of the future.

Yasuda Fire and Marine Insurance Company

This company was established in 1887 and writes insurance for automobiles, fire, accident, and marine areas. As can be expected, they have two major HRD systems. One is for employees, and the other is for agents who are not employees.

They have an extensive program and, specifically, provide training for employees at all levels who have been promoted within the year.

The program for agents is conducted in conjunction with other companies, and learners must pass examinations given by the Marine and Fire Insurance Association of Japan.

There is a variation of the two-system approach that is apparently characteristic in the insurance business. Yasuda will hire a person as one of their employees. After 18–24 months, with appropriate training and education, they will enable him to become an independent agent working exclusively for Yasuda. In the insurance business, this is seen as a practice of enabling some individuals to have their own agencies.

Yasuda is particularly concerned about their existing systems and whether they will be suitable for the future. They are also questioning their previous practice of instruction, accomplished mainly through lecture, and are exploring alternatives. They are even considering establishing a research institute for HRD.

Takeda Chemical Industries

This company has been in the pharmaceutical business since 1781. Obviously, the exact nature of their business has changed over that 200-year period. Today, the list of their products would take an entire page in this book.

Their HRD program is located in their "Personnel Training Center" that reports directly to the president of the company. At this corporate level, the center is responsible for a variety of activities, including holding a conference, twice a year, with the HRD staffs in divisions, branches, and plants. In addition, the center conducts specified company-wide courses.

The company expects managers and supervisors to have the basic responsibility for providing HRD. There are HRD units in each division of the company.

MAX Precision Products Corporation

This is a new manufacturing company that came into existence in 1976. Perhaps this explains their approach, which is much different from those of the companies cited previously.

The company philosophy is that each individual is responsible for their own learning, and the emphasis is on individualized instruction. Learning outside of Japan is an essential element of the HRD program.

The company offers self-study groups for department managers. A manager can study with a group or independently. Some of the usual formal courses for new managers and foremen are also offered. A course in creativity is available to technical people and to those working in quality circles.

Mitsui Engineering and Shipbuilding Company

This company, known as *MES*, is part of the Mitsui conglomerate. It has extensive works and branch offices throughout Japan and in 11 overseas offices.

The philosophy of the company, expressed in their *In-House Training Manual—Fiscal 1983* is that favorable results can be expected only when the learner is self-motivated. They see the role of the HRD staff as supporting the employee and the supervisor.

Shiseido Company

This company was founded in 1872 as a pharmacy, but it now specializes in toilet articles. The head office is in Tokyo with 72 subsidiary companies and 26 branches in Japan. It also has ten companies and three branches in various foreign countries.

As can be expected, the major part of its HRD programs focuses on salespeople. In addition to HRD programs for their employees, they also conduct nonemployee HRD, particularly for chain store operators, who are their major outlets.

In 1971, they completed their Izu Training Center, which is a residential learning center located in a beautiful section of Japan.

THE CHANGING PICTURE

Employee Motivation

Many studies are being done, and the results show that there are some significant changes in values and attitudes among Japanese workers. For example, one study in 1982 summarized the findings by noting that an apparent increase in complacency among employees had been found. The study concluded that employee motivation will be a major problem in the future.[6] Contrast this with what we have heard about the Japanese worker.

As far back as 1975, there was increasing evidence that the values of some of the work force was changing. A study by the Japanese Labor Ministry uncovered a group labeled *bachelor aristocrats* (dokushin kizoku). Their prime interests are sports and other leisure activities—not their jobs. Given the Japanese salary system, these unmarried workers earn far less than their married counterparts. They do, however, have larger disposable income. They usually have dormitory housing, provided free of charge by the employer.[7]

From Manufacturing to Service

Japan faces many problems, as do many industrialized countries. The major problem is that the future success of enterprises in Japan will depend on how well they can adapt to an economy dominated by the service sector. Another problem is that it will become increasingly difficult for workers to secure managerial posts.

Traditionally, the practice in Japan has been to promote or reassign workers and then provide training. The reassignment of workers at all levels has been generally expected and usually proceeds at a fairly leisurely pace. The feeling among some Japanese leaders is that this practice must change. Lead time is required so that workers at all levels can be adequately educated before they move into the new jobs. One report stated specifically that "It is in this area that human resource development programs will be fundamental to management's plans and strategies."[8]

The aging of the work force in Japan is an allied factor. Some Japanese leaders feel that a reappraisal of past methods of job design is needed. There needs to be a careful examination of redesigning tasks to suit older workers.

CONCLUSION

There is no question that HRD has been a significant part of the Japanese scene. Given the emerging problems, there appears to be an even larger part to be played by HRD.

In the years to come, it will be interesting to see how Japan and the United States, two major industrialized countries, cope with the significant problems that are emerging. It is important, in both countries, that the HRD practitioners become involved in searching for solutions to those problems.

NOTES

1. A discussion of some of the amenities in the workplace can be found in Leonard Nadler, *Employee Training in Japan* (Los Angeles: ETC Publications, 1965). Although this was written many years ago, the list of amenities is still valid today, although there may be some additional ones.
2. There has been a great deal written about Quality Circles. The definition and practice related to that activity keeps changing. One Japanese view can be found in *TOC and Quality Circles, The Cambridge Report #1, 1982* published by the Cambridge Corporation of Japan. It contains the papers and comments from a conference on Total Quality Circles and Quality Circles held by the Japanese.
3. See Tomas J. Peters and Robert H. Waterman, Jr., *In Search of Excellence: Lessons from America's Best-Run Companies* (Harper and Row, 1982). They discuss their research into U.S. companies that are considered among the best, particularly from the viewpoint of employer-employee relationships. All of the companies cited were in existence before 1960, and many were visited by the Japanese during their study tours.
4. *Nihonjin No Shokugyo-Kan (The Japanese View of Work)*, Public Research Institute, NHK (Japan Broadcasting Corporation), 1979.
5. *Koreika Shakai No Koyo To Seikatsu: Shakai No Katsuryoku Iji E Mukete (Work and Life in an Aging Society: Maintaining Social Movement)*, Research Group for Problems of an Aging Society (Koreika Shakai Mondai Kenkyukai), October 1982.
6. The Japanese View of Work, p. 9.
7. "Bachelor Aristocrats of Japan Show Low Motivation Toward Work," *World of Work Report*, December 1976, p. 12.
8. Tadashi Amaya. *Human Resource Development in Industry*. Japanese Industrial Relations Series #10. The Japan Institute of Labor, 1983.

CHAPTER TWENTY-SEVEN

Western Europe

NEAL NADLER

In Western Europe we find the largest concentration of industrialized countries. However, this does not mean they are all the same. In this chapter, Nadler provides an overview of what is happening in some of those countries regarding HRD.

Each of the countries faces a variety of problems. Each has a different economic, social, and political background. Yet, we can find some similar trends. It is interesting to note that governments are moving towards a more concerted effort than in the past. Previously, in some countries, there was a clear division between the private sector and the government.

I would like to thank all of those people who took the time to share their ideas and perceptions with me. In particular, I would like to thank the IFTDO organiation and the following persons: A. Bertelsen (Denmark); C. Carroll (United Kingdom); F. Greig (United Kingdom); L. Maillard (France); E. Mico (United Kingdom); R. Picaud (France); J.B. Senior (United Kingdom); and J. Waldus (The Netherlands).

We also find Western European countries making plans to cope with rapidly changing technologies and with the impact this has on the work force. This is not only a Western European problem, as becomes obvious when reading the other chapters dealing with HRD internationally. Perhaps Western Europe and the United States should have been planning for this situation many years earlier.

This chapter highlights how much we have to learn from each other, internationally, and how much we have to share with each other.

Neal Nadler is president of NNA, an organization that provides HRD services in the United States and in many other countries. He has worked extensively with the World Bank and has been an adjunct faculty member in the fields of HRD and management at four major universities in the United States. He has written articles for professional journals in the United States and other countries, and he has also contributed chapters to several books.

HRD IN WESTERN EUROPE

This chapter is the culmination of a study undertaken in Western Europe and incorporates over 300 data sources encompassing

Public and private sectors
Government organizations
Industry and service organizations
External HRD consultants
Internal HRD managers
Internal HRD learning specialists
Internal HRD consultants

I talked to a great many practitioners, but information about the HRD function within government and the private sector in several Western European countries is sparse.

HRD TRENDS, PRACTICES, AND ISSUES

HRD trends and practices were determined through in-depth interviews with numerous HRD professionals. The data presented here are, with few exceptions, the perceptions of these professionals. As the interviews progressed, trends, practices, and issues began to emerge. These major areas include:

HRD definitions
Learning
Emphasis on training support systems
Skill-building learning activities
Systematic approaches to HRD
Government-supported adult learning

Each of these areas will be discussed, and examples will be given to support these trends.

HRD Definitions

It is interesting that the definitions, which are basic to human resource development (i.e., *training, education,* and *development*), have a variety of meanings in different countries. For example:

Training.   A training director from Denmark referred to *training* as a generic term for any HRD activity. To a British consultant, *training* referred to activities directed at "assisting the individual trainee in doing his or her present job better." To an Italian practitioner, *training* implied the process used in any HRD activity.

Education.   Most HRD professionals referred to *education* as "formal university learning," while one Swiss trainer referred to *education* as synonymous with learning.

Development.   To several Dutch trainers in Holland, *development* referred to what an individual does to better himself or herself, regardless of the time frame. In Germany, on the other hand, *development* referred to an individual who is preparing for the next job.

While there was no general agreement as to the definition of these HRD terms, the context in which they were used always fell into three separate categories:

1. *Learning activities* - designed to help the individual in his or her present job.
2. *Learning activities* - designed to prepare the individual for the next job.
3. *Learning activities* - designed to help the individual to cope with future changes within the organization.

The one HRD concept on which all practitioners agreed was that the basis for all HRD activities was learning.

LEARNING

The general consensus of those interviewed was that learning is the key to all successful HRD activities. It was not surprising that a large portion of every interview dealt directly or indirectly with this concept.

At the 1983 International Federation of Training and Development Organization Conference (IFTDO) held in Amsterdam, Holland, the topic was productivity. Over half of the speakers addressing this topic directly implied that learning on the part of the organization, the managers, and the workers was essential to the successful implementation of any increased productivity plan. Learning how to learn and then applying it is an essential dynamic for the development of civilization (Pat Meade, Director and Cofounder of the International Training Services, Ltd., London, England). Learning is an essential element of productivity (The Director of Training for Bayer Company, Herald Richter - Federal Republic of Germany). A worker can attend many HRD activities but, without learning, it is time wasted. Learning is also the key to all successful HRD activities (John van Sprang, Director of Managerial and Technical Training for Volkswagen, Porsche, Audi of Holland). The learning referred to encompasses both what is learned during a needs assessment review and what the individual learns during a successful HRD activity. The evaluation of an activity is nothing more than learning what worked and what did not during that process. The application of these learnings help the corporation provide training/education that then meets the trainees' needs; provides the trainee with appropriate skills, knowledge, and attitudes; and allows the process to be self-renewing.

A large number of interviewees described a growing trend toward training support systems as a method of maximizing learning.

EMPHASIS ON HRD SUPPORT SYSTEMS

One of the emerging trends in HRD is the emphasis on support systems. While specific countries referred to the support systems in different ways, the general concept remained the same. The *support system* describes those activities performed by those within the organization to ensure that the learnings gained from HRD activities will be supported on the job. These support systems manifest themselves in several different ways.

In Spain, managers are used as facilitators of learning (Julian Mesa, Spanish Consultants, Madrid, Spain). The banking industry, for example, utilizes key managers of banks in this role, and this has been very successful. These managers then provide the appropriate support and encouragement on the job.

Managers in Holland's Volkswagen-Porsche-Audi organization (John van Sprang), have been trained to provide the support systems necessary to ensure that skills and knowledge gained in HRD activities are utilized. Each manager meets with his or her staff before any of them attend an HRD activity. At this time, the manager explains what the course will cover, what will be expected of them when they return to their job, and how the newly gained knowledge and skills will help the company. Each manager then meets with the various staff members upon their return to the workplace to find out what was learned and whether or not the program was effective.

This Dutch organization and several others reported that this type of involvement by managers was far more cost effective than any previously attempted techniques. An important aspect of this approach is that it begins with the managing director and filters through the entire organization. It is believed that this process produces high motivation among participants and long-term retention.

In Sweden, there is a different approach (Sven Johansson Learning Productions, AB, Stockholm, Sweden). In the SARA Corporation, the approach is centered around using internal, non-HRD practitioners as learning facilitators. Each individual is given a "train the trainer" course and then returned to his or her workplace. (These persons may or may not be managers.) Then, HRD (training/education/development) is provided for all levels of the organization, from the managing director on down, with each level supporting the next. According to Johansson, "everyone supports everyone else's learning."

The HRD support systems have been most successful in the skill-building activities area.

SKILL-BUILDING LEARNING ACTIVITIES

The Western European HRD community greatly emphasizes specific skill building. The difficult economic period that was experienced increased the need for specific programs that were cost effective and results oriented.

In Holland, Denmark, and England this type of training is short, one-day or two-day sessions; at most, one or two skills are taught.

Poor economic conditions have forced companies in the United Kingdom (Tom Attwood Cargill, Attwood and Thomas Ltd., London, England) to support shorter training directed to more specific skills (e.g., time management).

In Denmark (Andreas Bertelsen, Dansk Arbejdsgiverforening) employee training is short (one-day or two-day programs), and very specific skills are taught. For example, for a manager, critical interviews or time management topics are covered. For a worker, specific instructions are given for working with a new machine or filling out a new form. After the

HRD program, the individuals return to their workplace to test their newly acquired skills. Two weeks later, these same individuals return to the classroom and are debriefed on problems and successes encountered. In this way, each skill is reinforced before moving on to the next skill training experience.

Technology developed in the United States is used for much of the skill building. However, the material has been adapted to make it more culturally appropriate. This has markedly improved the technique in all cases.

SYSTEMATIC HRD APPROACHES

Not all Western European nations have fully developed professional HRD organizations. England and Holland are the most highly organized, and France, Spain, and Italy are the least organized.

It is generally agreed that HRD for HRD's sake is a waste of money. HRD activities must be preceded by an in-depth needs assessment review that ensures that the learning will be appropriate for the situation or problem. HRD activities must be tied to the individual's needs, as relates to the national and corporate needs. While the types and methodology may differ, it is generally felt that an HRD activity without an evaluation is like a blind housepainter. The painter knows that something was painted but is never quite sure of the results. Some corporations have tended to use HRD as a be-all and end-all, without recognizing that HRD is not the answer to every problem. Increasingly, companies are differentiating between the problems for which HRD could be the solution.

GOVERNMENT-SUPPORTED ADULT LEARNING

One of the dynamics that supports these systematic approaches to HRD is the strong emphasis placed on adult learning by the government. The adult learning activities described here were designed to prepare members of the population to enter the work force.

With few exceptions, each nation in Western Europe has some type of government-supported adult learning program. These programs differ in many ways, but the emphasis is on making each adult a viable member of the country's working population. The following is a description of the approaches used in several countries.

United Kingdom

The British government's initiative has three major components:

1. Youth HRD Program.
2. Adult HRD Program.
3. Technical Distance Learning Program.

This initiative was the culmination of research into many government-supported vocational programs across Europe and was designed to comprise the best elements of each of those programs.

Youth HRD Program. This program is a fundamental redevelopment of existing youth programs (George Webster, Executive Director of the Institute of Training and Development, Beaconsfield, England). The philosophy of this program is that everyone should have an opportunity to learn a skill. Prior to this initiative, many youth left school and were unable to obtain entrance to an apprenticeship program. This program is designed to allow more youth to acquire a marketable skill after dropping out of school. The youth program combines expertise from industry, commerce, and schools. Sixty-five accredited training centers were established across the United Kingdom to educate youth in specific skills over a one-year period. An estimated 460,000 persons participated during the first year. The plan was for industry to provide information concerning the skills that each industry could use and to take a very active role in absorbing many of the newly educated people. The skills taught were identified by a study conducted by the Institute of Manpower Studies. That study identified groups of skills required for industry and commerce. Also included in this program are courses in life skills, such as personal finance and budgeting.

Adult HRD Program. This is the second aspect of the initiative. It was designed for those people who had not attended a university and who were unable to gain entrance into an apprenticeship program. In the United Kingdom, generally, entrance into apprenticeship programs was controlled by the unions. If a person reached adult life without having gained entrance to a skilled profession, it was very difficult to become an apprentice. This initiative proposes that programs be set up to allow adults to attend classes in their own geographic areas in order to be educated in a field where they can be gainfully employed.

Open TEC Program. This is the third aspect of this initiative. *Open TEC* is a distance learning program that gives people easy access to learning in technical areas without mandatory class attendance. It is similar in process to the successful "Open University" but deals more with technically oriented programs. The core element of this approach is a learning package, similar to a correspondence course. Each course varies in length and difficulty. The "distance" student signs up for the course and receives the material by mail. Each package clearly states the objectives and contains all the material needed to complete the course. Students can work at their own pace. A tutor, assigned from the student's local area, meets the student face-to-face, grades homework, and can advise. Some of the topics taught include: telecommunication systems, electrical drawing, and electrical principles.

Germany

In Germany, the government's approach is directed primarily at the youth between the ages of 16 and 17 who leave school after completing only 9–10 years of formal education. Most of these students enter the government-supported apprenticeship programs. They attend part-time vocational school one or two days per week and spend the other three or four days each week at a company that provides on-the-job training. They may also participate in the company's HRD center. These schools are fully government supported. Industry pays for all the on-the-job programs and pays the learner's salary. This salary is negotiated between the unions and employers, but salaries do vary among industries. As an example, the chemical and high technology industries pay higher salaries than the craftshops. Generally, however, the salary is about one-third of the minimum wage of the average worker. Because of the close relationship between industry and government, work force planning for entry-level workers appears to be more accurate in Germany than in other European countries.

France

While the French have several government-supported initiatives designed to stimulate HRD, the most interesting is a law that requires every company to spend a certain percentage of their annual budget on HRD. This requirement is regulated by the National Fund for Employment that works in concert with the Ministry for Professional Training for Adults. The subjects taught by the companies are not legislated, but if the companies do not spend the total amount of money allocated, they must pay that to the government in the form of taxes. Consequently, several companies provide training for training's sake, without relating the training to their needs.

Some of those who participated in this study felt that this government initiative could be successful if several changes took place. First, organizations must become more concerned with the quality of HRD, rather than just with spending the money in the HRD budget. Second, there must be a national society created to provide a forum for sharing what HRD professionals in France are doing.

Denmark

Denmark has adopted a very comprehensive government-supported HRD strategy for helping youth/young adults enter the work force. Although these programs are run by the labor and education ministries, the youth/young adult programs fall under the operating responsibility of local and county authorities. Legislation requires that money be provided from local revenues to support these programs. This means that approximately 60% of the program costs are locally raised.

Two of the more unique strategies offered are part of the government-operated apprenticeship programs. The first is a traditional approach that usually lasts for two and one-half to three and one-half years. The learner entering this program is indentured to the employer for the duration of the program. However, the learner may, within the first three months, withdraw from the contract should he decide not to pursue the program. Approximately 80–85% of this apprenticeship period is spent on the employer's premises, with the remaining 15–20% in a classroom environment. At the completion of the program, the individual is accredited as a skilled worker. There does not appear to be any preapprenticeship counseling to help the learner make the decision to either remain in the program or to withdraw.

The second apprenticeship program is called the Basic Vocational Training Program (EFG). This approach is based on a one-year basic learning period in a government-supported technical or commercial school. Prior to entering, the intended participants are tested, in order to determine their qualifications. There are approximately eight fields to choose from, and the education tends to be broader in scope than the apprenticeship learning program. In addition to selecting a particular field of study, each participant is given a common education that covers such subjects as: Danish, a foreign language, math, sociology, business studies, and sports.

Although the EFG is free, as contrasted with the traditional program, no salary is paid during the first year. Following completion of this year, apprentices may move on to a two and one-half to three-year apprenticeship indentured to an employer. However, after that basic year, there is no guarantee that those newly educated students will be placed in an indentured position. For example, in 1979, only 21,000 of 26,000 successful graduates were placed.

Republic of Ireland

The Republic of Ireland has several government-supported HRD programs. One of the unique features of the Irish system is their industrial HRD programs. While the primary responsibility for industrial HRD falls on the company, the government-supported Industrial Training Authority (AnCO) assists these companies in meeting their varying HRD needs. In many cases, AnCO provides HRD programs for all levels of industry and commerce. This HRD-oriented organization is funded by the Department of Labor, the European Social Fund, and a levy system from industry.

AnCO's governing body is a Council consisting of the Minister for Labor and representatives from the educational sector, trade unions, and employer organizations. This council is advised by industry and commerce committees that represent the seven major industrial and commerce groups in Ireland. They are: textiles, clothing and footwear, drink/food/tobacco, construction, printing and paper, chemical and allied products, and engineering.

AnCO influences HRD by:

1. Regulating all apprenticeship programs.
2. Directing HRD activities at their own and other organizational centers.
3. Organizing in-house, company specific HRD programs.

The in-house HRD is financed through the levy system. Organizations of a specified size pay AnCO a levy of 1–1.25% their total annual wages. Each of these organizations can regain 90% of this levy by applying for grants from AnCO for approved HRD activities. This ensures that the learning programs conducted are based on real needs, are appropriate, and attain the required standard of quality.

The following section will deal with those practices, strategies, and activities that HRD professionals throughout Western Europe felt were unique and those from which others could learn.

HRD INNOVATIONS

During the research for this chapter, each professional interviewed was asked to give an example of a philosophy, a technique, or a program that each felt was unique to their countries and from which HRD professionals from other countries could learn.

"We are not afraid to admit that we can learn from other people and other countries." The organization (Tom Attwood - UK, Cargill and Attwood International) researches various technologies for solving specific HRD problems that exist all over the world. These technologies are combined with existing techniques or altered appropriately and then adapted to the cultural climate. The result is a better product.

Another approach is educating people for multicultural understanding. This makes people aware of their own culture-bound values, so that each person will in turn be able to understand and be sensitive to other cultures. The philosophy here is that when trying to prepare people to deal internationally, it is more important to make them multicultural than it is to make them bicultural or multilingual.

Many countries need cost efficient learning programs, delivered by the Open University concept (George Webster - UK). The idea behind the Open University is to make a free, accredited academic program available to the public. In the United Kingdom, entry into a university is quite difficult and requires high academic standings from secondary school. The Open University allows those people who do not have the qualifications or the time to obtain entrance into a university and to participate in a university-level learning program. It is open to everyone through the use of television. Tutors are provided for "local cells", which are determined by registered student density. The learner must also attend summer school, which provides for laboratory work and covers those subjects that do not lend themselves to television. The individual who participates in the programs builds credits toward a college degree. In the process, there are both compulsory and elective credits for each degree. The degrees bestowed range from Science to Liberal Arts.

The learner may be charged a minimal amount for this type of learning. For example, the cost for a certain course may be higher, due to the need for a specially designed low-cost microscope for use in laboratory work. When an individual registers for a course, a package is sent to the student outlining the needed materials. While some revenues are gained from this tuition, the government provides the majority of financial support.

Many countries use HRD programs to achieve short-term benefits and immediate results. German industry (Herald Richter, FRG) expects long-term benefits. However, long-term results are perhaps 10 years away.

The German approach combines training, education, and sometimes development into one learning period. For example, a German worker is given skills and knowledge that are directed at the present job, but the worker also acquires the skills and knowledge that may be required in a number of years. The participants in these learning activities are given more skills and knowledge than they actually need to accomplish their present job, so that they can advance to a future job. "We give them an input and then let them struggle." Individuals may come out of this learning a bit overqualified for their present job, but it pays off for German industry in the long term. In times of economic hardship, when people are being made redundant, these people can learn new jobs faster because of their initial learnings. German industry has undertaken this type of program because there has been relatively little turnover in industry, and, therefore, it could afford the "long-term payoff programs."

These programs also fit into the corporate philosophy of many of the German companies, since these companies almost always promote from within and recruit from the outside only when seeking highly technical staff or entry-level positions.

In Ireland (Kevin O'Kelly - Computer Aided Manufacturing of Galway), one company developed programs that utilize computer-aided instructions for Irish youth/young adults entering the work force. This approach allows young adults, between the ages of 14 and 18, to orient themselves to future growth in the technical and nontechnical areas. It is designed to give the participants an education that will lead to apprenticeship or similar programs. It gives them enough orientation toward specific jobs so that they can make enlightened decisions before entering the work force.

The Danish approach to HRD (Ben Gjedsted - Consultant-Denmark), emphasizes a hands-on experience. The Danes believe that too often, in countries like England and France, there is too much lecturing. In Denmark, the most widely used learning strategy gives the participants a brief introduction and then immediately immerses them in an experimental learning activity. The chief philosophy is learning by doing. There is an emphasis on ensuring that this approach is culturally appropriate.

In Sweden (Sven Jorgensson - Sweden), they utilize small, self-administered, self-contained HRD packages, designed to introduce skills to be used immediately. For example, a package consists of a book that explains what is to be done and a tape that emphasizes the major points to be learned. This approach, while not utilized for all types of skill building, is particularly effective in commercial areas for new product introduction or customer relations work. They are in the process of researching what the implications of this technique might be for more technical skills.

In Holland (Jan de Jung - President of The Eureopean Society of Training and Development Organizations, Amsterdam, Holland), supervisors are used as instructors. The advantage is that it provides a built-in support system that allows the worker to utilize the learnings attained immediately, on the job. The supervisor is able to coach and counsel appropriately. This approach can also be used with middle managers, so that they, in turn, can instruct their first-line supervisors; and it can be used with executives, so that they will instruct their middle managers. Although this practice is moving slowly, it is spreading and is very successful.

Practitioners from several countries discussed providing HRD within an organization by forming groups made up of representatives from different parts of the company. For example, each group receives instruction in problem solving and communication. Following the learning, the group(s) are given either a real case study or a company problem and asked to review it and develop recommendations on how they would solve it. The participants involved in this action learning approach are debriefed by a facilitator. The facilitator then evaluates each participant in light of the learning they have just participated in. Not only does this technique produce skills and knowledge, but it solves corporate problems as well.

THE FUTURE IMPACT ON WESTERN EUROPEAN HRD PROFESSIONALS

Each HRD professional was asked to identify key issues they thought their countries would face in the next five to ten years and what role the HRD practitioners would have in solving or supporting these issues. Their answers indicated that in many cases strategic planning was being done.

It is very difficult to differentiate between countries when dealing with the future of Western Europe, due to the close ties between most countries in this area. There were several recurring themes that emerged from the research concerning the future and the roles HRD professionals would play in it. The topics mentioned most often were:

New high technology

Dealing with change

High productivity

More efficient use of HRD resources

Doing more with less

More leisure time

Sharing

Interdependence of HRD practitioners

The introduction of new technology was a central theme for the future. The HRD practitioners were especially interested in the area of computers and were concerned with keeping abreast of changes in technology in the workplace, in production-oriented areas, and in the specific area of HRD. How will new technology (e.g., interactive video, computer-assisted instruction, and telecommunication networks) change the practice of HRD in Western Europe? The role of the HRD practitioner mentioned most frequently was that of helping people to deal with change. Most of these practitioners were interested in such topics as stress management and dealing with change, as areas for help in the future.

The new technology being introduced is designed to improve productivity. HRD practitioners will need to be up-to-date in the most advanced techniques for training, educating, and developing people, if new technology is to be used efficiently. Not only will the companies be interested in increasing the productivity of the worker on the floor and of the manager, but they will also be interested in helping the HRD professionals to produce cost effectively and efficiently. As the workplace becomes attuned to doing more with less, so will the HRD departments. This will require every HRD practitioner to keep abreast of the newest and/or most appropriate techniques for training, education, and development. To do this, a massive increase in sharing between HRD professionals around the world will be necessary. This networking will need to be done to reduce the trial and error approaches that are sometimes associated with new or modified HRD techniques.

Many practitioners projected that as Western European nations become more productive and use fewer people, there would be much more leisure time. It was generally felt, that for sociological reasons, people will need to learn how to utilize this leisure time. As a result, more service-oriented companies will be formed, companies that will, in turn, utilize internal and external HRD practitioners. It is interesting that all those interviewed anticipate that the HRD professional will be among the main characters in Western Europe's move to the future.

SUMMARY

This chapter is an overview of HRD in Western Europe in the first half of the 1980s. The exciting aspects of HRD described here are just the tip of an iceberg, but, in these brief pages, an HRD professional can see the innovations that are developing in this area.

The predominant, underlying concept that recurs throughout this work is

> that we, as HRD professionals, need much more international awareness. This awareness should cause us to be more interested in exploring the interdependence between nations. While there are differences in the levels of sophistication among countries, each HRD professional has something to offer, namely, a perspective that is new and unique. It is important, therefore, for us to remember that in HRD, the exchange of ideas, concepts, practices, and strategies is always a two-way street. To negate this idea is to negate the ever-present need to learn, which is the cornerstone of our profession.

HRD in Western Europe is a dynamic and growing profession, much the same as in the United States. It is beginning to attract many more young professionals with new and innovative ideas. As in the United States, there are no generally accepted definitions of HRD, and, for both regions, this must change if the profession is to continue to grow.

HUMAN RESOURCE AREAS RELATED TO HRD

CHAPTER TWENTY-EIGHT

Human Resource Management

FRANCIS X. MAHONEY

The title of Mahoney's chapter can be misleading, for the use of the term *human resource management* (HRM) keeps shifting. At this time, it has two different meanings. One is that *HRM* represents the total human resource picture. The other is that *HRM* is essentially what has been called *personnel* in the past. This chapter uses the former definition.

In that sense, Mahoney sees HRD as part of the HRM function in an organization. This is important, as HRD cannot and should not function as an entity unto itself. It has specific and significant contributions to make to the total human resource picture, as becomes clear in the various chapters in this handbook.

In this chapter, Mahoney helps us understand the relationship that must exist among the various human resource functions.

Francis X. Mahoney (Ed.D.) is vice president of the Institute for Management Improvement and is responsible for the development of HRD software as a modular series on HRD for managers and organization effectiveness. He is also an adjunct professor at Houston Baptist University, teaching graduate courses in human resource management, organization behavior, and HRD. Previously, he worked for Exxon for 17 years in industrial relations, HRD, and organization development. He also served in the U.S. Army for 13 years in command and staff management assignments. After active service, while with the Army Reserve, he was awarded the Legion of Merit for his responsible assignments. He is the author of numerous articles, chapters, and monographs.

INTRODUCTION

Human resource management (HRM) is a pervasive consideration in any organization. Human resources are the major contributors to organizational effectiveness and performance. Managers have been saying for years that people are an organization's most important asset. This is true; there is not a thing that goes on in an organization that is not in some way influenced by its human resources. For this reason, human resource management, although supported by a specialized staff, is truly a general management area. Every manager in an organization, top to bottom, must be concerned and involved in HRM. Management philosophy and behaviors are key issues in how human resources are employed and the extent to which they find satisfaction in working for an organization. Those of us in human resource management frequently say that HRM is simply too important to be left to the specialized personnel or human resource staff. That is not an adverse reflection on the staff or its capability, but, rather, it emphasizes in a dramatic way the necessity of having the line organization heavily involved in HRM.

Human resource management had its origin in the traditional personnel office, which generally came into being in the early twentieth century. The earliest practices of personnel were first to stabilize hiring practices and to improve hiring procedures so that the best possible people would be brought into an organization; and second, these practices were to provide some sort of protection from life's great disasters (e.g., death or disability) in the form of benefit programs. As we moved into the 1930s and the passage of the National Labor Relations Act, personnel people began dealing with unions. When the Fair Labor Standards Act was passed in the late 1930s, they became involved in legal pay issues. As time passed, they continued to design wage and salary systems that were not only legal but were consistent and understandable. As a result of work done in the 1930s in the behavioral sciences, personnel staff had extensive involvement in human relations training for supervisors just prior to World War II. This involvement peaked in the 1950s. Personnel units have often become involved in human resource development (e.g., training) not handled by line operating people. Even when handled by others, personnel people have almost always been involved in HRD planning and design.

Earlier personnel organizations were set up to handle these specialized activities. The various activities typically would have one or more people assigned to cover them. This led, in many ways, to compartmentalized behavior and increased the difficulty of coordination of personnel functions within organizations. Personnel units did and still do see employee representation as a major role. There was slow recognition of the opportunity to contribute directly to organizational performance improvement as part of the management team.

Today, the modern human resource unit deals with many exciting things. There is still the need for consistent and rapid handling of personnel problems and concerns; but, beyond that, there is the need to optimize human resource utilization within a complex legal framework. There are new challenges of updating organizations and individuals to respond to changes in society and technology, especially the impact of the computer. There is the need to provide the people in organizations with a quality employment relationship that includes an appropriate level of involvement, communication, and teamwork. There is the need to find ways to allow human resources to influence and interact with management at all levels, in order to ensure that we have fully utilized all the energy and talent available to the organization. Finally, there is the need to develop human performance systems that will enable individuals and their organizations to do a topnotch job. On an individual basis, this means a renewed focus on objectives, standards, evaluation, and feedback. On an organizational level, it means focus on performance criteria, data gathering, assessment of progress, and organization development. All this is very challenging. In every sense, it is a very long way from whatever stereotype people may have developed about earlier personnel shops and the somewhat clerical nature of the work that was done. These new areas are substantive, exciting, different, and challenging and hold great potential for significant contributions.

The specialized human resource staff mentioned earlier tends to operate in three major areas. System-oriented writers would describe each one as a subsystem of the overall HRM system. The first focuses on external relationships, such as those with governments and unions. The second focuses on the traditional and historical personnel operations, which need to be handled efficiently and effectively. The third focuses directly on impacting organizational performance. While all three areas contribute in some way to organizational effectiveness, the first two do so occasionally and sometimes obliquely, in terms of human resources. The last one deals with it directly, through the organization's human resources. Improved organization performance is the essence of this portion of HRM work.

HRM units are not necessarily set up in terms of the three major activity areas. Some may be, but that would be a coincidence. Depending on mission and organizational size, there will always be units with sections or individual assignments that are combinations of some or all of the functions detailed in this chapter. But it is sensible to proceed from the three activity areas and the functions associated with them, rather than from a traditional organizational chart. After examining the activity areas and their functions, it should be easy to understand where they fit in one's own organization.

EXTERNAL RELATIONSHIPS

The essence of this major system within the HRM unit is the protection of the organization—*protection* in the sense of avoiding interference with or change of management decisions by outside parties. The environment is largely a legal one, with government action having a direct impact on the organization. In a broader sense, it is also influenced by social values, technology, demographics, and the state of the economy. There are four activity areas that we will want to examine:

1. Union/Labor relations
2. Equal employment opportunity (EEO)
3. Safety and health activities
4. Discipline administration

Each of these four functions will be considered in a standard format, and for each we will examine the goals associated with it, typical activities, key players, major issues, and the keys to successful performance. We will also consider how the human resource development staff interacts with each function and how each contributes to organizational effectiveness and performance.

Union/Labor Relations

The major goals for this function include:

Obeying the law
Avoiding a union
Avoiding work stoppages

Having a favorable collective bargaining agreement and relationship with the union

Resolving problems and grievances quickly

Managing arbitrations

Maintaining positive employee relations

Typical activities in this area include: countering union organizing efforts, negotiating the collective bargaining agreement (i.e., contract), administering the agreement, and handling grievances and arbitrations.

The key players include the human resource manager, the labor relations staff, operating and senior managers, and attorneys.

The major HRM issues include the psychology of union organizations and leadership, preventive nonunion policies, effective negotiating skills, and an ability to handle conflict. The keys to success are constructive employee relations, good channels of communication with employees, management philosophy sensitive to HRM, and a reasonable balance of power among the several parties.

What is the significance of HRM *issues*? The most straightforward answer is that they represent areas that deserve close attention to be sure all goes well or, saying that another way, to be sure things do not go awry. Because there are a few partial human resource theories and few or no comprehensive laws, we have to watch a number of activities and events to be sure they mesh well with each other and are implemented so as to successfully achieve our HRM goals. The *keys* are simply broad criteria to consider when dealing with the various issues.

The HRD practitioner can make a direct contribution by training supervisors and managers to avoid unions or to work with them if present. The organizational effectiveness implications of the nonunion shop are very clear. Without a union around, management has the greatest degree of flexibility in establishing and changing work rules. Even with a union, if it is a local independent, the same degree of flexibility usually is available, because the union leadership is focused on local working issues. It is most difficult to work with a large international union, because it may have a number of issues in which its interests go beyond what happens inside the gate of the local plant. A certain amount of inflexibility in work rules and other arrangements is associated with the large international union. To the extent that the HRM organization can avoid outside groups interfering with effective work practices or restricting work output, there is a direct contribution to organizational effectiveness. To the extent that there are positive employee and union relations, legal costs are also reduced.

EEO Activities

The major goals for this function area include:

Obeying the law
Managing compliance reviews
Managing any charges that develop
Maintaining equality of employee treatment, sensitivity, and fairness as organizational values

Typical activities involve working with compliance officers and dealing with discrimination charges. If the organization is a government contractor, there are also major steps involved in taking affirmative action. Affirmative action is different than nondiscrimination. *Affirmative action* requires that specific things be done to offset the present effects of previous discrimination, even though the organization taking the steps has never been involved in discriminatory actions toward people protected by law.

The key players are the HRM manager, the EEO staff, attorneys, and all supervisors and managers.

The major HRM issues include procedurally correct selection of employees, appropriate orientation, effective training and education, a reasonable amount of adaptation time, and counseling as needed. The keys to being successful in this area include being objective about people and the organization's practices and ensuring that there is absolute equality of treatment among employees. The HRD practitioner can contribute directly in this area by training supervisors and managers in legal issues of compliance and also by increasing their sensitivity to the needs of protected class employees. It is possible to reduce legal costs and exposure through appropriate internal practices. There is a direct effect on organizational performance if financial penalties are avoided, such as disbarment from bidding on government contracts or an unfavorable court award. Certainly, every organization's management would want to avoid a reversal of a management decision made to improve organizational performance.

Safety and Health Activities

The major goals for this function include:

Obeying the law

Cutting lost time and financial losses

Avoiding painful injury or death

Managing any citations that are issued in a particular setting

Offsetting tendencies toward *occuphobia* (fear of working in an occupation)

Typical activities include monitoring the workplace for hazards, providing periodic health examinations, developing statistics, conducting studies, dealing with complaints, accompanying inspectors, and making required reports.

The players include the HRM safety and health staff; the medical and safety staffs, if not part of the HRM organization; the environmental engineering staff; attorneys; and line operating supervisors and managers.

The major HRM issues include effective awareness programs, useful physical examinations, information systems to generate reports and track exposures, and liaison with contractors who might be in the plant and being exposed or exposing others. The key to success is clearly doing the right thing, which means spending money for prevention and investing management time to ensure appropriate results.

The HRD practitioner can contribute directly in this area by training supervisors, managers, and employees in various safety and health procedures. The line organization may take care of much of this in training, but the HRD professional still should consult with the line organization to ensure the delivery of effective training. This area has a direct performance payoff, as the organization obtains a reputation of being a good place to work. It is easy to visualize what can happen to an organization's employment practices and compensation requirements if people are simply afraid to work there. In this area, we're also able to extend careers, avoid direct payments, and perhaps judgments for injury or death, and cut various insurance costs. We also can avoid penalties that may be assessed as a result of regulatory violations. While the dollar cost may be low, the public embarrassment (and its consequences) is high.

Discipline Administration

The goals of this function include:

Maintaining good order

Strengthening the organization

Minimizing legal exposure (as a result of discrimination charges, alleged union contract violations, or wrongful discharge litigation)

Typical activities include creating due process systems, administering a progressive discipline procedure, ensuring appropriate documentation of employee behaviors, record keeping, and handling termination procedures.

The players include the HRM safety and health staff; the medical and safety staffs, if not part of the HRM organization; the environmental engineering staff; attorneys; and line operating supervisors and managers.

The major HRM issues include accurately judging performance, achieving employee behavior change, and administering or coordinating with special programs, such as alcoholism counseling (see *Employee Assistance*). The keys to success are consistency of treatment and effective performance documentation, not only of offenders but of all employees, so that selected documentation will not suggest discrimination and thus be tainted at the source.

The HRD practitioner can have a direct impact in this area by providing training on appropriate procedures, including ways to help employees change behavior. There is a direct organizational performance implication as one corrects errors made in selection or copes with changes in individual employee motivation. We also can avoid the cost of litigation and potential financial penalties and reasonably ensure that management decisions having to do with employee discipline will be sustained.

PERSONNEL OPERATIONS

The essence of this area is effective and efficient HRM administration. The environment involved is largely internal; it includes the kinds of employees on the rolls, the geographic areas of organization's operation, organizational technology, the variety of operations, and the economic situation. Six activity areas will be covered.

Planning/Design

The goals of this function include:

Correct staffing levels
The right person at the right place at the right time
Effective design of jobs

Typical HRM activities include interaction with organizational planners and senior executives to learn what the organization's future looks like, computer modeling, development of information systems, evaluating the organization's environment, statistical calculations, and future analyses.

The key players are the HRM planning staff; other functional, short-range, and long-range economic planning staffs; and operating managers and senior executives.

The major HRM issues include planning expertise, effective job and work design (perhaps through sociotechnical methods), understanding and sharpening of the organization's HRM goals, reduction of employee turbulence, and rapid response to creation of organizational opportunities. The keys to success are tight staffing and no surprises.

The HRD practitioner, with an appropriate background, can make a contribution by consulting on job and organizational design, facilitating group-based planning, and tracking and communicating changes. There is a direct contribution to organizational performance in this area in the sense of keeping payroll costs in line. Organizational skill needs should be communicated to recruiters and HRD practitioners. It is a major contribution to ensure that the right skills are present in the organization in the right numbers at the right place and at the appropriate time. This involves keeping the organization competitive and effective as it evolves over time. Finally, there is the opportunity to design a highly effective organization. Much of this is accomplished by the line organization, but the HRM team is in an excellent position to provide consultation.

Recruiting

The goals for this function include:

An effective applicant flow (appropriate applicant-to-opening ratio)
Attractive organizational image
Efficiency and effectiveness

Typical activities include scheduling recruiting trips and interviews, advertising, preliminary screening of candidates, reproduction of recruiter documentation, internal referrals of candidate packages, coordination of offers, and development of statistics.

The key players are the HRM planning staff, HRM recruiting staff, designated interviewers, and operating supervisors and managers.

The major HRM issues are knowledge of job openings and understanding of job content, searching out the best potential resources, and providing an effective and efficient match of human resources to organizational positions. The keys to success are being able to fill positions continuously and to do so efficiently and effectively.

The HRD practitioner contributes in this area by training interviewers for campus and other recruiting activities. There are direct opportunities to contribute to organizational performance through cost effective administration, including central coordination of activities where that is economically justified. This enables effective scheduling of visits and monitoring of salary offers. The availability of an information system allows superior management of the entire process.

Finally, although somewhat abstractly, recruiting activities are the point at which future employees begin to form judgments about the organization's emphasis on performance and productivity. Brochures and other contacts can communicate this view of the organization and set performance expectations at a high level.

Orientation

The goals for this function include:

Delivering essential information on the employment relationship
Building an identification with the organization
Establishing high performance expectations

Typical activities include special new employee orientation programs and employee orientation publications that cover benefits and working rules. (Continuing communication will be covered under *Internal Communications*.)

The key players are the HRM professionals designated to conduct programs (usually a member of the benefits staff also handles this area), all supervisors, and new employees themselves.

The major HRM issues include clearly communicating various rights, obligations, and rules that constitute the employment contract; establishing an accurate psychological contract as to performance expectations; and creating favorable attitudes toward the organization. While the HRM staff will normally brief new employees (often in groups), the key to success is the new employee's supervisor. Success involves the development and sharing of performance expectations so that everyone knows the rules of the organization.

The HRD practitioner can consult an effective design for the group orientation program and, in some organizations, may conduct it. Supervisor training should develop skill in establishing expectations. Impact on organizational performance can be seen, however indirectly, when supervisors do a good job of establishing expectations, communicate objectives and standards, and frame an effective psychological contract with new employees.

Wage/Salary Administration

The goals for this function include:

Compensating employees based on management's philosophy
Establishing and maintaining an appropriate employee performance level
Retaining valued performers
Providing equity and fairness of administration

Typical activities include competitive surveys, job evaluations, general assessments of the economic environment, studies of labor settlements, reporting of time for payroll purposes, payroll processing, and payroll budgeting.

The key players include the HRM manager, wage and salary staff, union/labor staff, operating managers, various review committees, and senior executives for budget approval.

The major HRM issues include maximizing the exchange value of payroll dollars, establishing job contribution in economic terms, developing an appropriate "keep whole" component to wage and salary changes, establishing a recognition component to wage and salary changes, and establishing an appropriate level of economic security for employees. The keys to success are being competitive, affordable, and explainable.

The HRD practitioner can do much in this area by training supervisors in their company's wage and salary policies and practices. There is a direct opportunity to influence organizational performance by ensuring that payroll costs are reasonable. It is important to avoid litigation by ensuring that practices comply fully with applicable laws. This saves attorney's fees and possible adverse judgments. Use of behavioral science knowledge will optimize the motivational value of your systems and procedures. This is something that is not done as often as one might hope. Much of this function is handled by supervisors and managers, who decide what happens through the appraisal process (see *Appraisal/ Counseling*) unless there is a direct relationship between wages and salaries and performance, as might be the case with a sales incentive program.

Benefits/Policies/Records

The major goals for this function are:

Keeping costs reasonable

Retaining employees

Providing protection from disasters

Encouraging good attendance

Providing acceptable reduction in force programs

Being attractive to employment candidates

Typical activities include competitive surveys, general administration (e.g., records, requests, etc.), investment decisions for trusts and funds, government reports, and communications to employees (see also *Internal Communications*).

The key players are the HRM manager, benefit/policy staff, union/ labor staff, various committees, attorneys, and senior executives for budget approvals.

The major HRM issues involve interpreting social values and deciding on coverage to deal with security needs of employees and families. The keys in the area include being affordable, communicating clearly, and being effective in applying "handcuffs" to retain employees.

The HRD practitioner can be helpful in this area in designing training on benefits/policies for supervisors and employees. This is a significant area for organizational performance when experienced and talented people remain at work on a career basis. When benefit programs pay for preventive medical examinations, the organization stands to benefit from reduced periods of time away from work, by reason of fewer major health problems. When benefits/policies support individual activities to improve one's lifestyle, there is also a direct relationship to organizational performance (see also *Employee Assistance*).

Employee Assistance

The major goals for this function include:

Good attendance
Good safety
Mental concentration

Typical activities include diagnosis of needs, individual counseling, behavior modification programs, referrals to specialist, and education about effective lifestyles.

The key players are an HRM staff representative (employee assistance contact, if not in medical), the medical staff (if separate from HRM organization), external counselors, and employees themselves. *

The HRM issues include valid bases for extending longevity, effective behavior modification methods, good counseling approaches, and mechanisms for coping with organizational and extraorganizational stress.

The keys to success are a high level of professionalism and confidentiality in dealing with sensitive employee problem areas.

The HRD practitioner can work directly in this area by training employees in effective lifestyles and stress management. Organizational performance can be improved through improved attendance and improved performance at work. People who are distracted, mentally and emotionally, are not as productive as others and are prone to accidents. This function could lead to decreased cost of benefits and worker's compensation.

ORGANIZATIONAL PERFORMANCE

The focus of this area is optimization of individuals and their contributions to their organization. This is human resource management's highest leverage area for bottom line impact. Employee behavior and contribution are influenced directly. It is a very broad area and involves both the internal and external organizational environment and the interaction of the two. Appropriately, we will look at 10 specific activity areas.

Research

The major goals for this function are:

Improved understanding of human performance in organizations

Assessment of human resource-organizational interactions

Achieving a competitive HRM advantage (e.g., selection, advancement)

Typical activities include gathering and interpreting information about human resources, applying measurement methods, performing statistical analyses, interviewing, assessing, and reporting.

The key players are the HRM research staff interacting with the HRM planning staff, HRM manager, operating and senior managers, and employees.

The major HRM issues are the state of knowledge of the behavioral sciences, understanding individual differences, effective data collection, professionalism, and a good sense of what counts organizationally.

The HRD practitioner serves best in a consulting role with the research group. The HRD people should have a good understanding of what is going on around the organization and what research will be most beneficial. There is a direct contribution to organizational performance when the research staff helps to optimize the use of the human resources, understands employee interactions with their organization, and structures work to achieve a high level of output with a high level of satisfaction. There is a direct contribution in improving selection of supervisors and managers to continue as a successful organization. The research staff's ability to successfully conduct employee surveys allows an organization to get a jump on competition. Human resource research is not "blue sky." There is direct practical value.

Selection

The major goals for this function are:

Optimum employment decisions

Achievement of a competitive talent advantage

Effective regulatory compliance

Typical activities in this area are reviewing files of employment candidates, conducting interviews, administering tests and physical examinations, discussing and deciding on candidates, and making employment offers.

The players involved are the HRM recruiting and placement staff, the HRM research staff, designated interviewers, and operating supervisors and managers.

The HRM issues include developing valid bases for hiring decisions, avoiding discrimination, taking appropriate affirmative action, and getting a good placement match. Also at issue is employment candidate health and its interaction with legislation regarding the handicapped. Legislation supports hiring the handicapped, unless there is a bona fide reason why a particular job cannot be done because of the handicap involved.

The keys to success are a sound understanding of the competencies needed in various jobs and an ability to predict effective performance using a variety of measures and techniques.

The HRD practitioner can make a contribution by training supervisors and others in interviewing methods and, based on background, can also consult on competencies that are significant for success. There is a direct contribution to organizational productivity as the organization continues to grow, expand, and improve, as employees leave and new people replace them. There is also an impact in avoiding legal exposure to judgments and legal fees.

Appraisal/Counseling

The major goals for this function are:

Evaluating and ranking contributors for compensation and promotion purposes

Confirming decisions to retain employees on a career basis

Terminating poor performers as necessary

Typical activities include reviewing personnel files, completing appraisal forms, and assessing an individual's performance situation, discussing performance, and conducting follow-up reviews.

The key players involve the HRM research staff, the HRM development staff, the compensation staff, the HRM manager, all supervisors, and senior management for approval of procedures.

The HRM issues include tying performance to compensation, having appropriate bases for selection for advancement, being able to analyze performance, ensuring fairness, and having acceptable and appropriate termination procedures.

The keys to success are effective performance feedback and accurate, continuing, and relevant evaluation of employee behavior against organizational parameters.

The HRD practitioner provides training for supervisors and managers in the procedures that the organization uses and in performance counseling. In communicating performance feedback, there is a direct contribution to organizational performance, because human resources are the lifeblood of the organization, and their day-to-day performance sets limits on how well the organization will do. As supervisors encourage and reinforce high-level contributions, there is a direct effect on performance. If there are substandard behaviors present, it is possible to bring them up into line with the organization's requirements. This function also enables the organization to apply the merit and incentive elements of compensation administration. While the HRM staff is a major contributor in this area, supervisors and managers are the ones who actually do what must be done.

Leadership/Motivation/Reward

The major goals for this function include:

High output
Satisfaction with quality of work life
Effective interaction within the organization
Ethical standards

Typical activities include giving and getting information, structuring work assignments, getting work out, checking progress, getting involvement, building variety into activities, evaluating performance, and making pay and promotion decisions.

There are a number of human resource players involved, including experts on research, training, individual development, organization development, communication, and compensation. The management organization, starting with the chief executive and moving down, presides over this area. Interestingly, it is not tightly organized, in the sense that everybody is responsible for much of what goes on.

The HRM issues include identifying leader effectiveness factors, working with individual differences, coping with changing values, creating a climate of trust and openness, applying sociotechnical design principles, creating an effective organizational structure, and providing economic viability for the organization.

The keys to success include day-to-day, face-to-face interactions; goal-oriented assignments; the ability to match people with their preferred job design; and effective reinforcement of successful performance.

The HRD practitioner is depended upon greatly in this arena. While not responsible for what happens, the HRD people provide training for managers and supervisors in this function and help establish norms and values within the organization.

A direct organizational contribution is visible in the amount of energy that employees are willing to expend toward achievement of the organization's goals and their retention by the organization. Few, if any people, have been successful in developing accurate and reliable assessment measures in this area, but it is an area in which progress is being made. Productivity centers throughout the United States have a great interest in developing measures that will track performance. Historically, one of the best efforts made to establish what really counts for an effective leadership/motivation/reward climate was undertaken by Dr. Rensis Likert of the University of Michigan's Institute for Social Research. Dr. Likert devoted a large part of his professional life toward measuring and evaluating behaviors and processes that really make a difference in an organization. Dr. Likert's *New Patterns of Management* (1961) and *The Human Organization: Management and Value* (1967) are bench mark works in this area.

Internal Communications

The major goals for this function are:

Building an identification with the organization
Developing an appreciation of the organization
Counteracting rumors on the grapevine
Providing enhanced organizational performance

Typical activities include establishing programs and editorial policies, publishing or contributing to the publishing of company-printed materials, producing media, arranging bulletin boards, and sending letters to employee homes.

The key players include the HRM communication staff, public affairs staff (if used to produce materials), attorneys, and operating and senior managers for guidance and approval to release information.

The HRM issues include developing clear language versus legal jargon, finding ways to attract attention to the materials, acquiring authority to release information, knowing how to be credible, and understanding and communicating management values.

The keys to success include acquiring and sustaining credibility, being timely in releasing information, and responding to the important questions and concerns of employees.

The HRD practitioner can assist by consulting on issues that need attention within the organization, particularly rumors to which human resource development people have access. Some organizations may have the HRD staff provide formal training of supervisors about organizational communication issues. In some cases, the HRD staff may become responsible for internal communications because much of what is involved is a very familiar process to the HRD professional.

Some direct impact on organizational performance is possible as internal communication activities condition employees to economic issues related to compensation and bargaining, threats presented by competition, and changes in the marketplace. Also, it is possible to strengthen employee identification with the organization. Perhaps these HRM functions are new to some companies. Most companies publish employee periodicals, but, perhaps they do so with the public affairs staff taking the lead. It is different to have a communicator involved in editorial policy and preparation of materials and media.

The four topics that should follow next in sequence, training, individual development, management development, and organization development, are the focus of the rest of this book, and, therefore, will not be discussed here.

The productivity function has been saved for last because it could easily be the most important for HRM staffs in the future. For now, it is one that is not well organized. Much like leadership/motivation/reward, productivity tends to be everybody's job. However, it could easily be centered in the HRM organization and handled very effectively and efficiently with HRM as its home base.

Productivity Programs

The major goals for this function are:

Making a direct contribution to organizational performance
Making optimum use of human resources

Typical activities in this area include organizing special task forces, generating base line measures, establishing objectives for improvement, building involvement groups/quality circles, bargaining increased flexibility with unions, undertaking special learning programs, structuring incentives, conducting evaluations, providing feedback to the organization, and following up on an ongoing and iterative basis.

The key players include the HRM manager for sponsorship and coordination, all staff groups, operating managers (particularly middle managers), senior executives for direction and support, and, most importantly, employees.

The HRM issues are creating and maintaining trust in management, creating incentives to contribute, creating an atmosphere of sharing ideas, fostering a constructive union interface, and providing the learning necessary to enable full employee participation. The keys to success are employee acceptance, involvement, and cooperation in the process.

The HRD practitioner makes a direct contribution in training employees and supervisors in methods and procedures for improvement and in consulting on the improvement process. This function hits the bottom line directly. If the HRM staff is not responsible for this activity, the staff can nonetheless participate fully in organizational programs and make a singularly important contribution. Unfortunately, this is a function that many HRM organizations have not yet seen as a major one for their involvement, contribution, and leadership. This deserves some rethinking.

SUMMARY

This chapter has provided a quick tour of the human resource management function. The shift from the old *personnel* to the new *human resource* concept is more than just a label change. It is a significant sign of the times that reinforces the importance of this area. While various organizational structures will exist to carry out human resource management, depending upon size, operations, union situation, and management philosophy of an organization, you should be able to see more than just traces of each of the functions that we have outlined above. In every case, legal, computing, and behavioral science advances have influenced the modern, fully involved HRM organization.

Interestingly, human resource management accountability and stewardship belong largely to the line organization. At the beginning, it was noted that this area was important—an area that demanded the attention of exceecutive management and other members of the management organization. It would be a mistake to have it any other way. However, much is expected of today's human resource management staff in terms of contribution to the organization and its performance. The staff is expected to perform excellently in its area of expertise.

There have been many dramatic and exciting role transformations to bring us to the current state of human resource management. Today, dynamic and sophisticated contributions are the norm within HRM organizations. This means that it takes talented, well-prepared people, who are fully able to interact as equals with operating management and be influential with that group. Meanwhile, it is historical fact that the human resource management organization started off by being the representative and spokesperson for the employee and must not abandon that fundamental role. In any organization, there is, inevitably, the need for part of the management team to represent human resources and their needs, interests, and values. This continues to be the job of the human resource manager, regardless of how closely he or she is drawn into the management team.

Remember that as a member of the HRD team, you make a major contribution. This chapter has examined the areas where human resource development people can directly contribute to aspects of the HRM operation. If you are missing some of these opportunities, perhaps you will now be able to become involved.

BIBLIOGRAPHY

Carrell, Michael R., and Frank E. Kuzmits. *Personnel: Management of Human Resources.* Columbus, Ohio: Merrill, 1982.

Cherrington, David J. *Personnel Management: The Management of Human Resources.* Dubuque, Iowa: Brown, 1983.

Chruden, H.J., and A.W. Sherman, Jr. *Personnel Management: The Utilization of Human Resources.* 6th ed. Cincinnati, Ohio: South-Western, 1980.

French, Wendell C. *The Personnel Management Process.* 5th ed. Boston: Houghton Mifflin, 1982.

Glueck, William F., Revised by George T. Milkovich. *Personnel: A Diagnostic Approach.* 3d ed. Plano, Tex.: Business Publications, 1982.

Hememan, Herbert G. III, et al. *Personnel/Human Resource Management.* rev. ed. Homewood, Ill.: Irwin, 1983.

Megginson, Leon C. *Personnel Management: A Human Resources Approach.* 4th ed. Homewood, Ill.: Irwin, 1981.

Schuler, Randall S. *Personnel and Human Resource Management.* St. Paul, Minn.: West, 1981.

Organization Development

DAVID W. JAMIESON, DEBORAH BACH KALLICK,
AND C. EDWARD KUR

This handbook focuses on HRD. Realistically, however, HRD cannot serve alone nor isolate itself from other aspects of organizational life, such as organization development (OD).

There are those who contend that the fields are the same or that one is part of the other. Rather than become embroiled in this controversy, the authors of this chapter have enabled us to see that there are two fields. It is important, however, that practitioners of the two fields search for areas of cooperation, so that both can contribute to more effective organizations and more satisfied and competent individuals.

Part of the search today is to identify the competencies needed by practitioners in each of these fields. Preliminary work indicates that there are overlaps, but there are also differences. Practitioners in each field have something to contribute. As people in each field seek their own identity and improve their competencies, they should still search for areas of cooperation. HRD practitioners must engage in this search with all fields that relate to any aspect of human resources.

David W. Jamieson (Ph.D.) is president of Jamieson Consulting Group, an organization that provides a wide range of services related to HRD and organization development. He has worked extensively in both the public and private sectors, with a wide variety of clients and organization change situations. In addition, he serves on the adjunct faculty of the University of California at Los Angeles and the University of Southern California. He has held numerous offices in ASTD and will serve in 1984 as the president of ASTD.

Deborah Bach Kallick is associate product manager, Union Bank. She has many years of experience working in the nonprofit sector, principally with human relations organizations. She has been assistant director of the Anti-Defamation League for the Pacific southwest region.

C. Edward Kur (Ph.D.) is vice president of Phoenix Associates, a firm specializing in HRD and organization development. He has worked extensively in industry, as both a line manager and a staff specialist, and in the areas of survey feedback, strategic planning, productivity improvement, and HRD. He has also served on the faculty of Arizona State University, College of Business Administration.

INTRODUCTION

Most organizations engage in human resource development and organization development activities. Normally, these activities occur side by side and relatively independently of one another. This independence frequently minimizes the ultimate effectiveness of both HRD and OD. Often the diagnosis, analysis, design, and intervention for HRD and OD are not adequately coordinated. They are seen as dealing in different worlds, yet, often, they just deal with different aspects of the same problems and needs. In this chapter, we will differentiate HRD from OD, describe current forces that drive increased needs for each activity, develop a case for improved cooperation between these fields, and show how they can support and assist each other.

HRD and OD have developed separately. They derive from different roots and different disciplinary perspectives. Consequently, they tend to operate separately. Yet, the desirability of cooperation surfaces quickly if one recognizes the role each plays in improving the overall effectiveness of an organization. In reality, improved effectiveness is a key result desired by all who engage in HRD or OD activities.

Practitioners in each area have concentrated on their own theoretical bases and practical issues with little concern for the role of other professionals who contribute to similar results. While less than ideal, this separation may have been necessary in the beginning. However, much of the impact of each field may have been lost due to the lack of coordinated and supportive action. As a result, we have often fallen short of the goal of a productive and healthy work force within effective organizational systems.

In the next section, we will briefly describe HRD and OD and consider their similarities and differences in order to better understand the related role each activity plays in improving organizational life.

HRD AND OD—ROOTS AND REALITIES

HRD has evolved from roots in training. In 1970, *HRD* was introduced as a more definitive term for *training and development*. Its meaning broadened to "an organized learning experience within a given period of time with the objective of producing the possibility of performance change."[1] This field focuses on increasing the competencies of the work force within the context of organizations. HRD focuses first on individual learning and then on methods for multiplying or spreading the individual learning across the entire pool of people in the organization.

HRD is based on learning theory. Its roots are in the learning disciplines. Through its various formats, methods, and strategies, HRD enables individuals to perform current and future job duties effectively.

OD also relies, in part, on learning, yet its focus is more on overall human systems than on individuals within systems. OD is concerned with long-term, planned changes in the culture, technology, and management of a total organization or at least a significant part of the total organization. Its disciplinary roots and targets are different from those of HRD.

OD has evolved to increase the effectiveness and quality of work life within organizations. The field began many decades ago, and its significance, utilization, and popularity have become prominent. From its beginnings, OD had experienced an identity crisis.[2,3] Its proponents and practitioners have engaged in an unending search for acceptable definitions and boundaries of the field. This changing identity is understandable given the extent to which OD values assessment, diagnosis, and experimentation. Its evolving identity is also related to the changing nature of organizations, the developments in behavioral and organizational science, and the growth of practical experience in changing and improving organizations.

OD has employed many types of strategies, interventions and approaches over the years. It originally grew out of laboratory learning and survey feedback in the United States and sociotechnical analysis in Europe. Early laboratory learning focused on self-awareness and interpersonal relations and effectiveness. Behavioral scientists then applied laboratory methods to relationships in work settings, and OD was on its way in the United States. Meanwhile, survey research and feedback efforts were undertaken. They centered on data collection and feedback. The data usually were from employees and concerned attitudes, working conditions, and satisfaction. The survey researchers utilized and extended Kurt Lewin's action research philosophy of data collection, feedback, joint analysis, action planning, and subsequent data collection. OD also grew out of work at the Tavistock Institute in Europe, which focused on discovering the impact of technology on people, their relationships, and their identities. The Tavistock researchers ultimately developed an approach for studying and changing organizations. Together, these roots provide the essential elements of OD today.

Eventually, interpersonal, intragroup, and intergroup relations efforts led to work on organizational systems for decision making, planning, communication, and conflict resolution. Data collection on attitudes and job satisfaction led to systematic collection of data on additional aspects

Item	HRD	OD
Professional thrust	Individual growth and learning to enhance their contribution to the organization	Joint optimization of organizational subsystems with emphasis on organizational effectiveness
Client	Individuals, singularly and collectively	The organization or its subsystems
Intended outcomes	More effective people who do more effective work	More effective organizations in which people can work more effectively
Diagnostic approach	Task analyses Competence assessment Performance factors	Organizational effectiveness models System models Organizational climate
Primary technologies	Workbooks Classroom instruction Media-based programs Participative exercises Programmed instruction Counseling sessions OJT	Team-building sessions Group problem solving Action research Survey feedback Role clarification Work systems design Organizational structure change
Disciplinary roots	Learning theory Instructional design Individual psychology	Organizational behavior Social psychology Organizational design Management

Figure 29.1. A comparison of human resource development and organizational development.

of the organization, such as role conflict and ambiguity, accountability, resource adequacy, planning, and so forth. The Tavistock work led to new concepts of the managerial process and to organizational design methods that respect the relationship between the technology and the people in an organization. While OD has never claimed to replace or subsume the role of other disciplines in organizational improvement, it has attempted to develop an umbrella philosophy, focusing on the needs of the total organizational system and recognizing that real improvement involves technical, personal, group, structural, and managerial considerations.

Today, it is most useful to think of OD as both a philosophy and a collection of methods for organizational improvement. Both philosophy and methods are characterized by an emphasis on collaborative participation in data collection and in planning organizational changes, in order to improve the entire organization. OD draws upon many disciplines and uses many kinds of interventions to integrate efforts to improve organizations. Strategic planning, team development, organizational design, human resource development, industrial engineering, and sociotechnical work design are increasingly combined in any given OD effort.

By assuming an umbrella perspective, OD practitioners approach change and problem solving through an integration and linking of the methods and skills of various disciplines geared to improving organizational effectiveness. Managers of change are increasingly recognizing the complex interrelationships of people, structure, technology, and managerial processes that create the dynamics of organizational behavior. Consequently, OD will continue to evolve and integrate improvement efforts to address the changing needs of organizations.

HRD and OD can be compared along several dimensions, as depicted in Figure 29.1.

A look at the roots and realities of both HRD and OD highlights their differences and similarities. Each is influential in improving the functioning and outcome of organizational operation, by working on separate but related causes of poor performance or inefficiency.

While each of these fields has been valuable in the past, the contemporary organizational world is quite different. The needs for each are growing as changes accelerate and business philosophies change. The next section outlines some key forces that drive increased needs for both HRD and OD and their cooperation.

CONTEMPORARY ORGANIZATION ISSUES: DRIVING FORCES FOR HRD AND OD

Our organizational world has changed so much and so rapidly in recent years that it has left many managers and professionals in a state of confusion and turmoil. However, many of the changes and trends are truly driving new needs for HRD-related and OD-related activities. It is possible that there has never been a time when HRD and OD needs have been greater. While this may be a wonderful opportunity for the respective fields, it is also a major and significant challenge, as each has had limited effectiveness, historically, in improving the effectiveness of the organization and the productivity of the work force. However, by combining focus, values, and technologies, one might have the necessary leverage to be effective in improving the way organizations function.

A number of key issues have surfaced and have been highlighted in recent years. They have created new and significant challenges for organizations. The following six issues have the greatest potential impact on HRD and OD and appear to be surfacing renewed needs and opportunities for increased cooperation between HRD and OD. These six issues are

1. The environment of change
2. The increase of specialization and need for integration
3. The technological imperative
4. The changing nature of the work force
5. The productivity dilemma
6. The changing management culture

The Environment of Change

Most of the work force has been working in organizations during periods of relative stability. There was growth with some change, but major changes were something that came only from time to time and usually created anxiety, turmoil, and resistance. However, change was not seen as a way of life.

In recent years, an environment of change has developed. Change is commonplace, and more people have come to recognize that change is a way of life. Many things are changing. The time frame within which people operate, the structure, the operational procedures and processes, and the nature of the tasks and jobs that people perform have all been changing much more rapidly in recent years. This is due in part to the accelerated pace of change in the organizational environment, our society at large, the changing marketplace, the economy, changing forms of competition, and the influx of new technology.

Organizations have been increasingly responding with numerous internal changes. Reorganizations are commonplace. The use of centralized-decentralized, functional, and matrix concepts are proliferating. Along with that come streamlined operating procedures, new uses of technology, and the elimination of some and addition of other kinds of jobs and roles.

HRD can be particularly helpful in responding to the proliferation of change. Individuals will need to develop greater skills in coping with change—in processing the change in their terms and managing the stress and anxiety often created by change. OD can play a particularly important role in helping organizational leaders plan and implement the changes they desire. It is never possible to fully plan changes, as subsequent effects and changes in events will occur. There is still room for improvement; we can get much better at diagnosing, targeting, planning, and implementing changes in a systematic and accelerated way. OD is in the position to look at changes from a systems perspective, envision the many interconnections that will occur throughout the organization, plan for those, and systematically work through the necessary interventions to facilitate the realization of effective change.

The Increase of Specialization and Need for Cooperation

The information explosion that Alvin Toffler cited in *Future Shock* in 1970 has become a reality. The expanded base of information, coupled with the complexity of tasks we have to accomplish, has led to a proliferation of specialists and specialized fields within management. New information about individual learning and social change processes has supported specialization and division between HRD and OD, each of which has its own skill and knowledge base as well as its own history. The pressure of an ever-expanding base of information not only enhances the split between HRD and OD, but it also puts a strain on many of the relationships between what has traditionally been known as line and staff, because the number of specialists required to solve problems or get the job done has increased.

The continuing growth of information in such a wide variety of fields supports the need for continuous learning both within and across disciplines. The nature of work and the problems to be solved require more coordination of effort among specialities. On the OD side, this leads to development of new structures, temporary systems, matrix project management systems, development of new teams, and the building of communication systems and work relationships among people with different backgrounds, languages, and perspectives. People need additional skills and ways to manage within these kinds of structures that lead to new emphases in HRD.

The Technological Imperative

Nearly everyone is affected by the accelerated growth of technology in the workplace and the speed with which it has become a driving force in changing the way we do work. Technology in the workplace is not only becoming commonplace but is also creating a number of issues that must be resolved. Such technology includes word processors, microcomputers, telecommunications equipment, and other electronic gadgetry that is capable of assisting the worker. There are two major implications that occur from the technological imperative.

On one hand, people need new skills to utilize the various pieces of equipment, requiring an increased need for HRD. On the other hand, technology has become a catalyst for changes in our systems, workflow, jobs, and communication patterns. These changes generate resistance, surface new issues, create disruption and turmoil, and basically require well-planned programs for managing and implementing. This requires an increased need for OD. For example, in automating certain aspects of office functions, one is faced with some systems analysis problems, some technical problems, some facility layout and workflow issues, and many human resource problems, in terms of acceptance, utilization, and skills. In addition, one may be dealing with many social system issues, involving people's relationships, status systems, norms for work, and communication patterns. There may be job displacement, impact on compensation systems, and the general fears and turmoil created by something new. HRD and OD need to be central in these change processes.

The Changing Nature of the Work Force

We are experiencing significant change in the nature and composition of our work force. The change is greater than ever and is affecting more than just the work force; it has permeated all of society. Such changes focus on the workplace, however, since we spend at least half of our lives there.

There is evidence that the basic demographic mix of the work force has changed significantly. An increasing proportion of people are, in many ways, different from the typical worker of the past. This is particularly true when one looks at average age, the number of women in the work force, the increase of minority and immigrant populations, the basic dissolution of traditional family patterns, and the creation and acceptance of new living and family relationships. In addition, there are significant differences in school levels, mobility patterns, and professional loyalties.

In a related vein, there are significant shifts in the attitudes, values, and beliefs of the work force. These are, in part, driven by the influx of younger workers into the work force during the past 10 years. Those born during the baby boom have grown up. However, shifts in attitudes and values are increasingly accepted and adopted by many other generations as well. These shifting attitudes and values tend to fall primarily into the following key areas:

Focus on self and self-fulfillment

Changing success ethic

Shift of priority from work to leisure

Resistance to authority and control

Emphasis on choice

Demand for participation and rights

Changing sex roles

Changing morality

Decreasing job satisfaction

The changing mix of the work force and the shifts of values and attitudes are encouraging signs for HRD and OD. There is a growing necessity for new management and supervisory systems, changed work schedules, and new career concepts. New skills for managing the changing work force and a growing emphasis on personal development drives new HRD needs. Many problems, issues, and conflicts are created by the clash of generations and cultures. In addition, as previously disenfranchised people enter the work force, more basic learning is required to help people gain necessary work skills.

Changing Management Culture

The philosophy, practices, and values of management—its culture—are changing. A new era for management has begun.[4] Driven, in part, by growing economic concerns, increasingly competitive worldwide market-places, and the increased use of technology in all levels of work, the profession of organizational management is adopting new models.

These changes are most readily evidenced by

An increased emphasis on accountability

A renewed entrepreneurial spirit

The "leaning" of corporate structures

The shrinking middle management ranks

The merging of line and staff

The more fluid, temporary structures

The use of multidisciplined teams

The shifting toward incentive and merit-based compensation and reward systems

These trends highlight numerous needs for HRD and OD. At the core is the need to redefine management competence and to develop new skills for success. Teaching existing and potential managers the values, practices, and skills to operate effectively in such a changed environment is a critical priority. Simultaneously, helping people to change culture, structures, and operating systems, is central to the practice of OD. This shift in philosophy puts in motion large-scale movements of people into and out of existing and new roles, groups, and organizations. The process of transition draws heavily on career development expertise, team formation, and HRD. Institutionalizing change through OD intervention, as a necessary aspect of management, strengthens the need for HRD within and across professional arenas.

HRD AND OD—THE CASE FOR COOPERATION

A number of writers have addressed the lack of or need for cooperation between HRD and OD.[5] Clearly, this thrust has been recognized, yet the practice of cooperation is slow.

HRD and OD each provide part of the perspective, expertise, and solutions needed to face the many needs in today's organizational world. Mutual understanding, support, and coordination are needed to effectively implement needed transformations. The issue is not whether one wishes to do one or the other, but that each can contribute to the improvement of organizational effectiveness and the quality of work life.

A number of statements concerning the cooperation of HRD with OD are listed below and are followed by an example.

HRD Needs Assessments Often Uncover OD-Related Problems

The department manager had done everything to improve output and efficiency, but nothing worked. Eventually the manager invited the HRD coordinator to develop some learning programs that would help. The HRD coordinator conducted an informal needs assessment, which indicated that the people in the department seemed to have all the skills needed for their jobs. Many were senior people, with excellent records on their current jobs or on similar jobs. Furthermore, very few procedural or technical changes had occurred during the past year to require new skills. The coordinator advised the manager that if people were not performing properly, it was not because they did not know how to perform. The coordinator concluded that the problem was not a learning problem. Perhaps the department was getting low-quality materials from the supply group, or perhaps interpersonal relationships within the department were not conducive to good performance. These are problems that might be addressed through OD techniques, but not through HRD techniques.

A Change in Organizational Structure/Systems Often Needs HRD Support

A long-term change effort in a consumer product company resulted in decentralizing into new divisions. Each division included its own staff groups (e.g., personnel, purchasing, product planning, etc.) as well as line manufacturing, distribution, and sales. The internal staff groups were to operate in a consultative mode, as advisors to the line managers of the divisions. Previously, the staff groups had made company policy, and line managers in the divisions had followed the dictates of these corporate groups.

The change was traumatic for many staff specialists who moved from positions steeped with power to positions in which their success was based on influence and on the cultivation of trust and confidence of line managers. Wisely, the change strategy included extensive training in consultative skills for these staff specialists. This training was necessary if the staff people were to perform effectively in their new roles.

Changes in Organizational Strategy and Structure Lead to HRD

An electronic components manufacturer undertook a comprehensive strategic planning process and determined that it should enter a highly specialized technical equipment market that could benefit from the quality of their components. This decision led top management into a reorganization, forming a new product group with an integrated technical support and sales function. The reorganization involved exploring numerous organizational design alternatives, interdepartmental conflict over the lead function, and a massive effort to educate some existing technical personnel in sales and technical support consultation.

Productivity Improvement Requires Systems, Technology, and Skill Changes

A large order-processing operation experienced high backlog, numerous delays, declining productivity, and increasing customer dissatisfaction. They classified the problem as a productivity problem and launched a widespread productivity improvement effort. Early diagnosis uncovered low morale, fragmentation of accountability, long average-per-order processing times, and other issues contributing to ineffectiveness. A team was organized to develop changes. This team consisted of experts in industrial engineering, data processing, HRD, and OD. They coordinated an integrated change and implementation strategy that incorporated:

A new organizing concept, teaming order takers with order processors, integrating the transition from sales to completed shipment

A change in the processing system, eliminating two steps and shortening the work flow system and time

Installation of an on-line inventory and shipment scheduling system, using distributed processing computer terminals at the point of sale

A comprehensive training and education program in sales, order processing, use of the computer, and the application system

A unique team-building program for all sales and processing employees as well as each two-person team

A change in the physical facility, bringing the sales and processing people together in the same building

An incentive commission system, based on volume, transaction time, and customer satisfaction

Utilizing HRD and OD in an Organizational Cutback

A multidivision company experienced a declining market and profits in a few of its product lines. The company could no longer afford to carry the structure, overhead, staff, and work force of the declining divisions, yet they wanted to retain the products, even at a lower volume, to stay in those markets. They decided to eliminate some jobs, merge the manufacture and sale of the products into other existing divisions, and integrate staff functions into the new divisions with fewer total positions. They utilized both OD and HRD resources to accomplish the transition. The integrated program included:

Career assessment and counseling for management and workers to ascertain placement in the new division, corporate headquarters or "out placement"

Training and education for incoming and existing workers in new skills for multiple product lines

Merger and team-building meetings for integrated staff functions

New job designs and classifications for workers, supervisors, and managers completing education in multiple-product knowledge and skills

Additional training for the continuing divisions' sales force in new product knowledge and cross selling

While each of these cases makes some assumptions, they are reality based. In each situation, the needs suggest both HRD and OD solutions or highlight the connection between them.

They are used only for illustrative purposes, in order to base HRD and OD in real organizational situations. Organizations repeatedly face similar dilemmas and need to respond in multiple ways, yet, too often, our HRD, OD, and other perspectives are applied separately, intermittently, or sequentially, and the potential impact and effectiveness are lost.

CONCLUSIONS

One of the most valuable approaches for improving cooperation between HRD and OD people in an organization is to develop an HRD and OD plan for the organization. Such a plan should specifically support the organization's strategic or business plan. A joint planning process involving line managers, HRD staff, and OD staff not only builds cooperation among the specialists, but it further integrates their activities into the overall management of the total organization. These HRD/OD plans typically have a two-year to four-year outlook and are updated at least once each year. From an HRD perspective, the plan should focus on major job categories and on each general level within the organization. From an OD perspective, the plan should provide professional services to each major division of the organization as well as to the total system.

Looking beyond specific organizations, the HRD and OD fields themselves can become more cooperative by ensuring that university programs and other programs designed for professionals in one field include exposure to the other field. It is common for students of HRD or training to have little exposure to OD, and students of OD frequently have no exposure to the HRD field in their programs—they concentrate instead on social psychology, psychology, sociology, organizational theory, and management theory.

Overall, the opportunity for cooperation between HRD and OD is substantial, and achieving that cooperation is highly desirable.

NOTES

1. Leonard Nadler, "Defining the Field—Is it HRD or...?" *Training and Development Journal* 34 (1980): 66–68.
2. W. Warner Burke, "Organization Development in Transition," *Journal of Applied Behavioral Science* 12 (1976): 22–44.
3. Frank Friedlander and Dave L. Brown, "Organization Development," *Annual Review of Psychology* 25 (1974): 313–41.
4. "A New Era for Management," *Business Week*, April 25, 1983, pp. 50–82.
5. See, for example, S. Applebaum, "Management Development and OD: Getting It Together," *Personnel Managment* (1975); David W. Jamieson, "Training and OD: Crossing Disciplines," *Training and Development Journal* 36 (1981), pp. 12–17; Gordon Lippitt, "Developing HRD and OD: The Profession and the Professional," *Training and Development Journal* 36 (1982), pp. 18–31; and Morris S. Spier, et al., "Predictions and Projections for the Decade: Trends and Issues in Organization Development" and Patrick M. Williams, "Management Development and Organization Development: Twin Cornerstones of Human-Resources Management," both in *Trends and Issues in OD: Current Theory and Practice*, edited by W. Warner Burke and Leonard D. Goodstein (San Diego, Cal.: University Associates, 1980).

BIBLIOGRAPHY

"A New Era for Management." *Business Week*, April 25, 1983, pp. 50–82.

Applebaum, S. "Management Development and OD: Getting It Together." *Personnel Management* (1975).

Argyris, Chris. *Intervention Theory and Methods: A Behavioral Science View*. Reading, Mass.: Addison-Wesley, 1970.

Beckhard, Richard. "The Confrontation Meeting." *Harvard Business Review* 45 (1967): 149–155.

Beer, Michael. *Organization Change and Development: A Systems View*. Santa Monica, Cal.: Goodyear, 1980.

Burke, W. Warner. "Organization Development in Transition." *Journal of Applied Behavioral Science* 12 (1976): 22–44.

French, Wendell L., Cecil H. Bell, and Robert A. Zawacki. *Organization Development: Theory, Practice, and Research*. Plano, Tex.: Business Publications, 1983.

Friedlander, Frank and Dave L. Brown. "Organization Development." *Annual Review of Psychology* 25 (1974): 313–341.

Goliembiewski, Robert T., Carl W. Proehl, and David Sink. "Estimating the Success of OD Applications." *Training and Development Journal* 36 (1982): 86–95.

Hersey, Paul, and H. Marshall Goldsmith. "The Achieve System: A Human-Performance Problem-Solving Model." In *Trends and Issues in OD: Current Theory and Practice*, edited by W. Warner Burke and Leonard D. Goodstein. San Diego, Cal.: University Associates, 1980.

Jamieson, David W. "Training and OD: Crossing Disciplines." *Training and Development Journal* 36 (1981): 12–17.

Jamieson, David W., and Kurt Motamedi. "Organization Development." *Handbook of Business Administration.* New York, McGraw-Hill, in press.

Klatt, Lawrence A., Robert G. Mordick, and Fred E. Schuster. *Human Resource Management: A Behavioral Systems Approach.* Homewood, Ill.: Irwin, 1978.

Kur, C. Edward. "OD: Perspectives, Processes and Prospects." *Training and Development Journal* 35 (1981): 28–34.

Lewin, Kurt. *Field Theory In Social Science.* New York: Harper and Row, 1951.

Lippitt, Gordon. "Developing HRD and OD: The Profession and the Professional." *Training and Development Journal* 36 (1982): 18–31.

Nadler, Len. "Defining the Field—Is It HRD or OD, or...?" *Training and Development Journal* 34 (1980): 66–68.

Porras, Jerry I. and P.O. Berg. "The Impact of Organization Development." *Academy of Management Review* 21 (1978): 249–266.

Rush, Harold M.F. *Organization Development: A Reconnaissance.* New York: The Conference Board, 1973.

Schein, Edgar H. *Process Consultation: Its Role in Organization Development.* Reading, Mass.: Addison-Wesley, 1969.

Shepard, Herbert A. "Rules of Thumb for Change Agents." *Organization Development Practitioner*, November, 1975, pp. 1–5.

Spier, Morris S., Marshall Sashkin, John E. Jones, and Leonard D. Goodstein. "Predictions and Projections for the Decade: Trends and Issues in Organization Development." In *Trends and Issues in OD: Current Theory and Practice*, edited by W. Warner Burke and Leonard D. Goodstein. San Diego, Cal.: University Associates, 1980.

Tichy, Noel M., Charles J. Fombrun, and Mary Anne Devanna. "Strategic Human Resource Management." *Sloan Management Review* (1982): 47–61.

Williams, Patrick M. "Management Development and Organization Development: Twin Cornerstones of Human-Resources Management." In *Trends and Issues in OD: Current Theory and Practice*, edited by W. Warner Burke and Leonard D. Goodstein. San Diego, Cal.: University Associates, 1980.

Zenger, John H. "Organization Development and Management: Friends or Foes?" In *Organization Development: Research Theory and Practice*, edited by John Thompson. Washington, D.C.: American Society for Training and Development, 1980.

Career Development

THOMAS G. GUTTERIDGE AND
PEGGY G. HUTCHESON

Since the early 1970s there has been an increased interest in human resources, and, consequently, there has been an increase in the number of areas that relate to those human resources. Career development (CD) is one such area.

It is not that CD did not exist before, but it did not exist in quite the same dimension. It has been a rapidly growing field and appears destined to become even more significant as robotics changes the workplace.

CD and HRD are related, as Gutteridge and Hutcheson explain so well in this chapter. CD and HRD should not be in conflict. It is not a question of which is more important. They are complementary activities, both concerned with the individual and the organization.

These authors explain CD and the symbiotic relationship that must exist between CD and HRD.

Thomas G. Gutteridge (Ph.D.) is dean of the College of Business and Administration and professor of administrative science at Southern Illinois University—Carbondale. In addition, he conducts short workshops on career planning in organizations and human resource planning and forecasting. He has served as director of the Career Development Division of ASTD and as president of the Niagara Frontier chapter of ASPA. Among his numerous publications is *Organizational Career Development: State of the Practice (ASTD)*.

Peggy G. Hutcheson (Ph.D.) is a principal in Atlanta Consulting Associates and has more than 10 years experience in HRD and career development. After working as manager of training for Rich's Inc., she moved to working externally with a wide range of different organizations, helping them to develop or improve their career management and HRD systems. In ASTD, she has been a member of the executive committee of the career development division and the HRD careers committee. She has written numerous articles about career development.

Human resource executives face the continuing challenge of integrating a number of different management functions into a single, coherent whole. Finding a consistent philosophy and framework around which to build this kind of human resource function is difficult. Career development has a unique perspective that may well assist this purpose. The organization and the individual are viewed as separate systems that interface in a single career system. This "career system," as depicted in Figure 30.1, holds the promise of bringing together the individual and the organization for mutual benefit.[1]

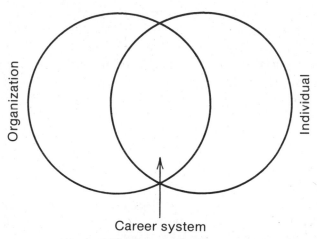

Figure 30.1.   The organizational career system.

The term *Career Development* means different things to different people. Moreover, there is only limited consensus regarding the distinctions between career development and such related processes as career planning, career management, career counseling, and the like. This definitional problem becomes even more complex in clarifying the relationship between Career Development and Human Resource Development.

The objective of this chapter is to present a conceptual model of the career development process and to articulate the ideal relationship between Career Development and the overall subject matter of this book—Human Resource Development. In so doing, this chapter will review some of the forces underlying the growing individual and organizational interest in Career Development and will outline the principal components of a comprehensive system.

OVERVIEW OF CAREER DEVELOPMENT PROCESSES

It is logical to presume that Career Development means the development of an individual's career. However, the term *career* itself connotes a variety of different meanings, and it is clear that societal and organizational forces as well as individual factors shape the development of employees' careers.

To some, the term *career* is reserved for certain high-status occupations, such as lawyer and doctor while other occupations, such as secretary and assembly line worker, are considered "only jobs." To others, a career connotes the notion of upward mobility and the achievement of certain external success criteria, such as income, status, or high-level responsibility. In recent years, however, a more neutral, less value-laden definition of a career has attained widespread usage and support. According to this definition, a career is seen simply as the sequence of a person's lifelong, work-related experiences and related attitudes and behaviors. Thus we can talk prospectively about the aspirations, job choices, and career activities individuals might engage in as their work life unfolds, or we can refer to career experiences as they are occurring. We can also retrospectively discuss how a person's career has evolved over time.

In addition to this individually focused past, present, and future time dimension, the emerging career perspective also acknowledges that an employee's career occurs within an institutional framework. Clearly, an individual can seek to develop his or her career unilaterally, as when a university student establishes a career strategy to be implemented upon graduation or when a housewife returns to college to enhance her chances of rejoining the labor force. In both these instances, however, as in the case of an employed individual, the objective is to pursue a career within an organizational context. As Tim Hall has stated:

> The career is a property of both the individual and the social structure. It is the individual who processes the occupational information, develops career attitudes, values, and experiences, and makes career choices. Yet it is the institutions and the social structure which provide training and occupational opportunities, recruitment, rewards, shape the person's attitudes, values, and experiences, and provide occupational information. The career is a mutual influence process of individuals choosing occupations, organizations, and positions and of institutions recruiting and selecting individuals.[2]

Given the preceding discussion, Figure 30.2 presents a model of the Career Development process as it occurs within an organizational setting.[3] As illustrated in Figure 30.2, organizational Career Development is viewed as the outcomes created by the interface between individual career planning and institutional career management processes. Some of the possible individual outcomes include better self-understanding and the identification of ideal career goals. Examples of desired organizational outcomes might include communicating career opportunities to employees and obtaining a better match between individual career interests and institutional career opportunities.

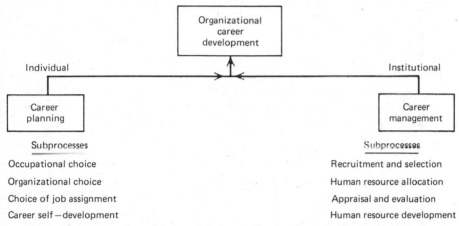

Figure 30.2.   A working model of organizational career development.

As suggested by this model, Career Development is comprised of two separate but related processes: (1) Career planning, which is an individual process, and (2) Career management, which is an institutional process. In turn, career planning includes those activities individuals must engage in to make informed choices as to occupation, organization, job assignment, and self-development. This includes such activities as self-assessing interests and abilities, examining available career opportunities, and establishing an appropriate career strategy, together with an implementation plan.

Career management refers to specific human resource activities, such as job placement, potential appraisal, counseling, training, and education. These activities are designed to help match individual interests and capabilities with organizational opportunities and to achieve other desired institutional outcomes. Typically, these functions are provided through various career systems, such as job posting, career path planning, and the like.

Important as this distinction between individual career planning and institutional career management is, it must be acknowledged that this model does not totally mirror organizational reality. In some organizations, systems such as replacement and succession planning, skills inventories and career ladders are established in the name of career development. All too often, however, these systems neither provide for nor encourage employee input regarding their own career aspirations. Consequently, in these institutions, the career development function is a one-sided process that simply substitutes one autocratic—albeit benevolent—career system for another. A less frequent but equally harmful case occurs when the organization encourages the employee to assess his or her capabilities and interests and to prepare a career strategy, but then it fails to provide any vehicle whereby these plans can be implemented. Thus an exclusive emphasis upon the individual career planning dimension can lead to employee frustration and, ultimately, excessive turnover among valued performers. Clearly, career development is most effective as a joint individual-organizational process.

Of course, there is and should be some overlap between individual and organizational career development responsibilities. For example, organizations may decide to encourage individual career planning by sponsoring a self-assessment and goal-setting workshop on company time or by establishing a career counseling service. Similarly, individuals contribute to their own career development and to organizational career objectives by participating in such career management programs as job posting and skills inventories.

RELATIONSHIP OF CAREER DEVELOPMENT TO OTHER ORGANIZATIONAL HUMAN RESOURCE PROCESSES

Although the relationship between Career Development and Human Resource Development will be addressed later in this chapter, it is important to explain the differences between career development and two specific human resource activities—HRD programs for managers and human resource planning.

In most organizations, HRD programs for managers consist of a combination of selected job assignments together with appropriate training (for those who are managers) and education (for those preparing to be managers). The programs are designed to strengthen the managerial competencies of a select employee group. By this definition, then, conventional HRD programs for managers are a subset of the career management process, which is only one-half of the Career Development process. This distinction is not intended to downplay the importance of programs for managers. Instead, the point is that these programs are not a synonym for Career Development; rather, they are an important component of a total Career Development system.

Neither is Career Development synonymous with human resource planning. Rather, as illustrated in Figure 30.3, these activities are complementary processes, and both should be subelements of a comprehensive human resource management system. As the term is generally used, both in the literature and in practice, *human resource management* is seen as a strategic, comprehensive, integrative approach to the utilization of organizational human resources. As such, *human resource management* is slowly superseding the reactive, paper pushing, transaction orientation of more traditional personnel departments.

As depicted in Figure 30.3, the basic objective of human resource planning is to enable organizations to anticipate their future human resource needs by forecasting the expected demand, projecting the

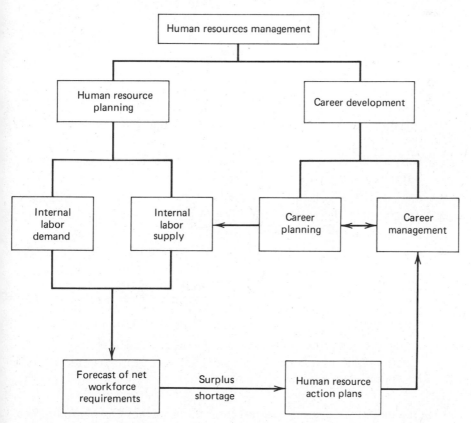

Figure 30.3   Interface between career development and human resource planning.

available internal supply, and identifying the difference between what will be needed and what is likely to be available. The results of this human resource forecast are used to formulate the personnel action plans (e.g., recruitment, allocation, HRD plan) required to fulfill the net human resource requirements. In turn, these personnel action plans are an input to the career management process. They are integrated with employee goals to establish specific individual/organizational career activities. It should be noted that, in addition to being linked with the career management programs, the employee career plans also can serve as a useful input in the forecast of available internal supply.

Human resource planning and career development are designed to fulfill different objectives, although they may utilize some of the same tools and techniques (e.g., skills inventories, promotability forecasts, and replacement planning). Human resource planning is intended to identify and provide ways to fulfill the organization's aggregate employment needs; whereas Career Development focuses on matching specific institutional career opportunities with individual interests and needs.

PRESSURES FOR CHANGE

The increased interest in Career Development from individuals and organizations alike is by no means accidental. Some of the individual factors accounting for this heightened concern include:

1. the well-documented, changing social values emphasizing a better balance among personal life, family life, and work life;
2. an unwillingness on the part of many employees to abdicate control over their career destiny to the whims of organizational politics and the vagaries of blind luck;
3. a growing awareness among many individuals that successful careers do not just happen; they are almost always the result of significant planning, preparation, and goal setting;
4. an expressed desire by many individuals for a better way to relate their changing selves to their changing environment; and
5. a recognition that career planning can be an effective way of anticipating and resolving individual-organizational career conflicts.

In some instances, organizational interest in Career Development is a direct response to expressed employee concerns. In addition, however, a diverse set of external and internal pressures motivate many organizations to consider implementing a Career Development effort. For example, some organizations have established Career Development in response to continuing pressure to improve the career progression opportunities for minorities and women; while others have utilized Career Development to enhance employee relations. In other cases, Career Development is designed to alleviate excessive turnover rates, especially among high talent, junior personnel. In addition, Career Development is sometimes a response to the organizational dilemmas created by professional obsolescence, plateaued and overpromoted managers, and related midcareer employee issues. In many organizations, Career Development reflects an increased commitment to the concept of promotion from within coupled with a perceived shortage of high quality, promotable talent. Finally, some organizations are persuaded that Career Development will increase employee commitment and help ensure that the right person is in the right job, both of which are presumed to have a positive relationship to work force productivity.

It should be emphasized that Career Development is not a panacea and cannot, by itself, solve all of the problems discussed here. However, there is empirical evidence that a formal career development program can improve an employee's opportunity to find career satisfaction and enable an organization to better cope with a variety of pragmatic human resource concerns. Moreover, there is considerable evidence that the 1980s will witness a continuation of the economic pressures, technological changes, demographic shifts, and social transformations that characterized the 1970s. Thus the pressure on organizations to do a better job of planning for and managing their human resources is likely to continue unabated. It seems apparent that career development is one technique for accomplishing this, and it has a payoff for all parties concerned.

Although a general discussion of the forces underlying the need for Career Development is illuminating, it is necessary for each organization to identify the specific forces, unique to its own institutional setting, that may be triggering an interest in Career Development. In turn, these organizationally specific factors will influence the objectives that a Career Development program may be expected to achieve and the tools, techniques, and processes that might be utilized. Figure 30.4 presents a comprehensive but by no means exhaustive listing of some of the individual and organizational goals that a Career Development program might be designed to address. These goals represent general purposes rather than specific objectives. However, organizations should not find it difficult to translate a general purpose into a specific objective and, in turn, into a program component.

Organizational

Identify and develop high potential employees

Orderly succession planning

Improve individual/organization match

Response to governmental pressures

Improve employee productivity

Increase employee retention

Communicate career opportunities to employees

Ensure adequate supply of employee talent

Humanistic image

Improve cost effectiveness of human resource decisions

Accelerate work force adaptation to change

Enable managers to aid career development process

Individual

Identify career goals, options, developmental needs, action plans

Exercise greater self-determination

Understand self

Implement career plans and evaluate outcomes

Figure 30.4. Illustrative career development purposes objectives.

COMPONENTS OF CAREER DEVELOPMENT SYSTEMS

Thus far, this chapter has outlined what Career Development is and why its importance is increasing. Next, we will examine who is served by these Career Development programs and how (i.e., what tools and techniques are commonly utilized).

Career Development has been applied at all levels of the organization, from nonexempt employees through executives. Figure 30.5 provides an overview of the range of possibilities, in terms of employee groups served and the geographic range of this coverage. The Career Development program should be a reflection of the individual and organizational objectives of the system, so that a decision can be made as to which employees and which organizational units should be included in the CD system. In general, however, most Career Development programs, at least at the outset, are designed to achieve a limited set of objectives and to focus on the unique needs of targeted employee groups, rather than to be implemented across the board. Likewise, Career Development is normally established on a decentralized basis, rather than on a company-

Employee Group
_____

All employees
Production/operative employees
Clerical workers
Supervisors
Professional/technical employees
Middle managers
Executives
Special interest groups
    —Women   —Plateaued workers
    —Minorities   —Mid-career workers
    —New hires   —Pre-retirees
    —High-potential employees   —Handicapped workers

Scope of Coverage
_____

Entire enterprise
Single geographic location
Particular function, department or unit
Major division
Multiple locations

Figure 30.5. Coverage of career development programs.

wide basis (the program may be started first at company headquarters). Typically, as the career program demonstrates its effectiveness, it may be expanded throughout the company and made available to a variety of employee groups and organizational levels.

In general, the heaviest concentration of formal organizational Career Development programs appears to be among managerial, technical, and professional employees. Perhaps this is a reflection of both the substantial level of organizational commitment among these workers and their perceived high value to the organization. Most Career Development programs are voluntary, in that employees are not required to participate, although they may be encouraged to do so. In fact, the level of employee participation generally varies, depending upon the technique involved. The level of participation ranges from a low of about 20% of the eligible individuals who enroll in a group workshop to the almost 100% participation in supervisor-subordinate discussions of career potential.

Although they may be available to all employees, generally particular Career Development tools are better suited to certain employee groups. Figure 30.6 provides a list of the basic tools and techniques that might be incorporated into a comprehensive organizational Career Development

Self-assessment Tools

Career planning workshops
Career workbooks (stand-alone)
Pre-retirement workshops

Individual Counseling

Supervisor or line manager
Personnel staff
Professional counselor
a. Internal
b. External
Outplacement

Internal Labor Market Information Exchanges

Job posting
Career resource center
Career ladders
Other career communication formats

Organizational Potential Assessment Processes

Assessment centers
Promotability forecasts
Replacement/succession planning
Psychological testing

Human Resource Systems

Skills inventories
Human resource planning

Developmental Programs

Job rotation
In-house HRD
External seminars/workshops
Tuition reimbursement
Supervisor training in career counseling
Dual-career programs
Mentoring systems

Figure 30.6. Organizational career development tools.

program. A detailed discussion of these techniques is beyond the scope of this chapter, but a brief review of the types of tools available is appropriate.[4]

Some Career Development techniques, such as career planning workshops and career workbooks, primarily focus on the individual career dimension and are designed to assist employees in assessing their individual goals, abilities, and self-developmental needs. Other tools, such as succession planning and career ladders, mainly focus on the identification and fulfillment of organizational career requirements. In addition, organizational career management also includes a matching function (e.g., job posting and skills inventories) that emphasizes the integration of employee career plans with institutional employment needs. Finally, some techniques, such as career counseling and career resource centers, are intended to encompass both the individual and the organizational dimension.

As suggested, the primary objective of organizationally sponsored career workshops is to provide employees with a systematic way of identifying and working toward their individual career preferences within the context of the institutional career structure. This is accomplished, in a group setting, by means of exercises and other structured activities that require participants to formulate, share, and discuss personal data regarding career activities, concerns, and plans. The workbook format is intended to fulfill the same basic objective as the group workshop and typically utilizes a similar series of exercises and reference materials to guide users through the individual career planning process. In contrast to the group approach, however, the workbook is designed to be completed by the individual working alone and thus is self-paced. The preretirement workshop is another form of career workshop that focuses on the life/career concerns of employees nearing retirement age (e.g., finance, health, and the transition from work to retirement). Although nominally available to all employee groups, career workshops and workbooks tend to be most heavily utilized by nonexempt employees and technical/professional and supervisory employees.

In a generic sense, career counseling involves discussing with employees their current job activities, individual skills and abilities, personal values and aspirations, and appropriate Career Development objectives and action plans.

In real terms, however, career counseling means different things to different people. Moreover, there are a variety of approaches for providing this counseling. Not surprisingly, the most common form of employee career counseling is provided by personnel staff members on a part-time basis. The employee's immediate superior is also an important link in the career counseling process in many organizations, although the available literature suggests that the supervisor-subordinate career discussion process is fraught with difficulties.[5] Only a few organizations, but a growing number, now provide career counseling by professionally prepared, specialized staff counselors. An even smaller number of organizations refer employees to external counselors. Probably as a consequence of the current economic climate, a substantial number of organizations utilize outplacement counseling, on an as-needed basis, to assist terminated employees in making the transition to a new job. Overall, career counseling is one career tool that seems to be provided in one form or another for all employee groups, with the possible exception of upper-level executives.

There are many different methods of providing employees with career information. Job posting, which is a common tool for internal staffing, is an excellent way to communicate job vacancy data and can be utilized to provide feedback to those employees responding to posting notices. While job posting is still most prevalent at the nonexempt employee level, its use as a career development tool has expanded in many organizations to include positions through middle management.

Some organizations maintain a career resource center as the distribution point for any information that concerns career development. In these cases, the career information center serves as a minilibrary and is typically stocked with a variety of company materials, reference books, learning guides, and self-study tapes.

Another, more focused means of providing career information is the use of detailed career ladders, or career path charts, that diagram the organization's internal progression routes. Some organizations have carefully analyzed their internal career structure and publish booklets describing traditional career paths, in terms of the types of jobs available in various units or departments and the most likely routes for advancement in these areas.

There is a tendency to gear both the career resource centers and the career path handbooks primarily toward professional, managerial, and technical employees. In addition, most companies have a variety of brochures, manuals, fliers, and other printed materials to communicate a wide array of career data to employees, concerning such matters as tuition assistance, developmental programs, and the like.

The assessment of employee career potential is one of the less well-developed career tools. The use of psychological testing, once an important technique for executive selection, has been discontinued by many organizations. However, a number of organizations utilize introspective tests and inventories to aid individuals in assessing their own interests, aptitudes, values, and so forth. There is also a growing use of the assessment center for developmental purposes. In an assessment center, the employee is interviewed and completes a variety of situational exercises, both individually and in a group setting. An evaluation panel, usually comprised of high-level corporate managers, observes the behavior of each participant and draws conclusions about his or her management potential and developmental needs. Based on this feedback, the individual, in consultation with the human resource staff and sometimes his or her supervisor, establishes and embarks upon a developmental program.

As part of their human resource forecasting system, a number of organizations require that supervisors evaluate the career potential of their subordinates and/or identify possible successors for key management positions. Typically, the potential appraisal process encompasses all professional, managerial, and technical employees through middle management, while the succession planning process is restricted to senior management positions. While promotability forecasts and succession planning have long been used for human resource planning and staffing purposes, there is a growing tendency among organizations to integrate these assessment processes into a comprehensive Career Development framework. In this manner, high potential employees and identified successor candidates have an opportunity to factor their career interests into the staffing decisions being made and to participate in a variety of developmental activities designed to enhance their ability to handle higher level responsibilities.

Another human resource system that can be utilized for Career Development purposes is the *skills inventory*, sometimes known as a *career information system*. Basically, a skills inventory is a computerized storage and retrieval system that contains a vast array of factual data about each employee included in the system—data such as work experience, schooling, employment skills, language capabilities, career interests and the like. Typically, participation in this system is voluntary, and the employee is responsible for providing the requisite input data. In most organizations, the career information system is restricted to exempt and salaried employees, and the system is primarily used to identify likely candidates for internal placement. In addition, the system can pinpoint shortages of critical skills needed by the organization and analyze the need for specific types of programs necessary to provide the skilled work force.

Besides the career tools previously discussed, there are also a variety of approaches available to actively implement employee growth. There is growing agreement among researchers and practitioners that the employee's current job is often an overlooked source of growth. As discussed, Career Development does not necessarily imply advancement. For many employees, this process is best fulfilled by restructuring the present job so that it provides challenging goals that are stretching, meaningful, and psychologically fulfilling for the individual involved. The use of cross-functional, lateral transfers is another technique for introducing variety and growth into an employee's career, especially for those senior personnel who have become functionally overspecialized and obsolete.

There are also a variety of in-house and external activities, including tuition reimbursement-supported degree granting programs, that can provide for growth. Other activities that can support employee growth include training, education, and development. It is equally important to reward supervisors for career planning skills and to complement the career counseling process by encouraging mentor-protégé relationships. Finally, organizations that are concerned with facilitating the Career Development process must find better ways to manage the conflicts introduced by the growing number of dual-career families.

Presently the available Career Development methodology far exceeds the utilization of these techniques by U.S. organizations. While many organizations view Career Development as a desirable, integral component of human resource management, there are many more organizations in which Career Development has not yet arrived. In those companies in which Career Development does exist, it is often largely an informal, experimental, and fragmented activity. All the available evidence, however, suggests that the future of Career Development is indeed bright as more and more companies are likely to implement such programs, and those companies that already have a Career Development system in place are likely to continue and refine such efforts. The need for improved human resource management practices is well documented, and Career Development has been shown to be an effective means of accomplishing this objective. The necessary career tools are readily available. The challenge is to apply them in a fashion that meets the needs of both the organization and the individual.

Based on this overview of Career Development, we will now review how this process is and should be related to Human Resource Development and how Career Development can be used to integrate the organization's entire human resource effort.

Career Development serves as a natural bridge, connecting the individual, the organization, and the HRD function. Career Development activities help uncover information about individuals that is needed in planning HRD programs. In addition, career-related interventions (e.g., workshops, workbooks, counseling, or career discussions) provide a logical forum for sharing information about the organization and about the training, education, and development opportunities that are available. Career Development and Human Resources Development share common goals and function most efficiently when they work as a team. Working together, these units prepare the individuals within the organization to perform the tasks and to fulfill the responsibilities of their present and future work assignments. Career Development adds a somewhat different dimension to traditional Human Resource Development activities, providing a new focus and a new impetus for HRD.

CAREER DEVELOPMENT AS A FOCUS FOR HRD

The roles and functions within Human Resource Development have undergone major changes in recent years. At one time, in many companies, job skill training was the major purpose of HRD. Later, the emphasis on management and executive programs added another dimension to HRD. More recently, emphasis on matching individual interests and goals with the skills needed and directions anticipated by organizations has created yet another role for the HRD function. This rapidly evolving role of liaison between the individual (who needs training, education, and development to achieve his or her goals) and the organization (which needs skilled, capable, and prepared employees to accomplish organizational goals) is a new and increasingly relevant focus for Human Resource Development.

Needed Information

A major part of this new focus is the additional information uncovered and shared through career-related programs. Information about the individual's work history and experience, schooling, training, and education should be available in a traditional human resource information system. When career development information is added to this set, the organization has specific data on the individual's career plans and goals, relevant experience and skills gained away from work, interests, and aptitudes to add to the existing data.

If the Career Development system is to work effectively, information about the organization must be shared with employees. Accurate, timely information regarding the organization's structure, projected changes in products, markets, technology, and career opportunities likely to be available in a given time period must be available. Information about policies and about procedures concerning access to positions available or to training, education, and development opportunities must also be disseminated to participants in Career Development programs.

The effectiveness of the individual components in a career development program is largely dependent on the quality of the information generated by the participants and the quality of the information disseminated through the activity. Having a systematic way to process and use information from participants and to share information about the organization is critical. Human Resource Development is an important part of this information system. HRD is a vital link, both as a user of additional data collected from Career Development program participants and as an ongoing channel for disseminating needed information to employees. Figure 30.7 provides one way to depict this needed career information linkage.

With a career development-related HRD system, decision making about training, education, and development for each employee is shared. The individual has the opportunity to express desired moves and goals (these may be expressed in terms of skills, knowledge, and abilities as well as in terms of desired target positions). The organization has the opportunity to react to those growth-related goals, providing feedback on their operational reality and assisting in identifying learning strategies to help the employee reach those goals supported by the organization.

The individual's interests, goals, and desired growth strategies are usually expressed through a developmental plan. Sometimes, the individual may complete this during a career-related workshop or after completing exercises in a career planning workbook. In many Career Development systems, this information is given a reality check by a career-related discussion between the employee and his or her immediate supervisor. The result of this discussion is a mutually agreed-upon plan for the employee that specifies, in addition to long-range position targets, some specific areas for the employee's improvement and strategies for reaching these developmental goals. This developmental plan then enters the human resource management system. Here, it may become part of the information used in a number of human resource functions, including human resource development. Figure 30.8 provides one example of a career developmental plan.

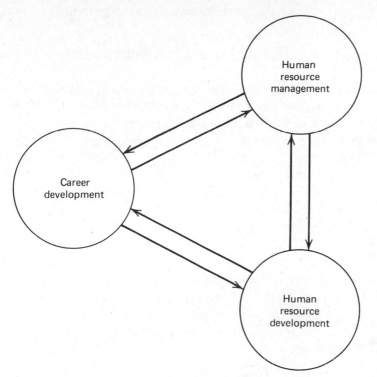

Figure 30.7. Career Development Information System.

Date _____

Development Plan for _____

Part 1   What are your long-range goals within the company?_____

_____

What shorter-range goals must you accomplish to move toward your
long-range career objective? _____

_____

_____

Part 2   List those specific skills, knowledge, and experiences you believe you
need to enhance your performance on your job and/or move you toward
your short-range goals. Beside each, indicate appropriate developmental activities to acquire the skill, knowledge or experience.

Skill, Knowledge, or Experience   Activities

Figure 30.8.   Individual development plan.

CAREER DEVELOPMENT AS A PLANNING TOOL FOR HRD

This additional information sharing, made possible by Career Development activities, offers Human Resource Development opportunities for increased responsiveness to existing and future needs. Program offerings can be planned, consistent with the perceived needs of employees and their supervisors. Training for the present job and education for a future job are seen as highly beneficial by both participants and supervisors, since attendance is designed to meet both individual and organizational goals. When developmental plans are submitted on a regular basis, they become an invaluable planning tool for those responsible for designing Human Resource Development programs. Since the developmental plan is *outcome based*, that is, it focuses on the skill, knowledge, ability, or experience desired, it provides a micro view of the needs of individuals within the organization. Collectively, the developmental plans represent an accurate view of the perceived training, education, and development needs within the organization. Careful content analysis of these documents may provide:

Information based on the need to update, revise, or maintain the content of existing training, education, and development programs

Needs analysis, to determine how frequently existing in-house programs should be offered

Data on additional topics, programs, or formats to be developed

A reading on how well current HRD programs are meeting perceived needs

A tool for marketing program offerings to those who have expressed needs

INDIVIDUALIZED TRAINING, EDUCATION, AND DEVELOPMENT

In addition to providing information to use in helping individuals grow in needed directions, Career Development programs highlight the need for individualizing these programs. For certain groups of employees (e.g., middle managers, highly skilled specialists) growth needs can be very specific and unique. Their needs may be difficult to meet in a traditional or structured way. Yet, in a Career Development system, which encourages highly specialized individuals to identify areas for growth, there is the implication that organizational resources will be made available to help them achieve their goals through learning. For these individuals, a skilled and resourceful specialist in Human Resource Development is needed to identify opportunities for learning experiences that will meet each person's unique needs.

Career Development and Human Resource Development share common goals. Fundamental to both is the desire to help individuals grow and develop to meet the changing needs brought about by the interaction of individuals with their work roles throughout life. Meeting this goal is a challenge. It is best accomplished by collaborative teamwork on the part of those responsible for career-related programs and for Human Resource Development. The next sections describe how this might take place, by examining the relationship of career development with training, with education, and with development.

RELATIONSHIP OF CAREER DEVELOPMENT AND TRAINING

Both training and career development begin with a focus on the individual's present job. Training provides, maintains, and enhances skills to perform the job. Career Development encourages excellence in performance on the current job as a practical prerequisite to movement within the organization or to an increased sense of satisfaction on the job.

Since training is the initial contact with the company for many new employees, orientation programs are an important link between Career Development and Human Resources Development. Understanding the organization's career system—what the organization's structure looks like; policies regarding movement within the organization; and definitions of roles for the employee, the supervisor, and the organization—must occur before the new employee can participate in this system effectively. Training can make important contributions to career development by transmitting information that describes this career system, emphasizing that the primary responsibility for the employee's career belongs to the individual, and providing lists of resources to assist the individual when he or she feels help is needed.

In addition, the assessment processes used in career workshops, workbooks, and some counseling programs reinforce for employees the positive aspects of their current jobs. In assessing self and work, Career Development program participants identify those factors that they seek or prefer in work situations (e.g., opportunity to use certain skills, visibility, autonomy, challenge). Similarly, they identify which of these factors are present in their current job. Confirmation that this job is a good one for them to have (at least for now) is the most common response to this type of exercise. This positive attitude is likely to lead to greater receptivity of opportunities to increase skills for the present job. In much the same way, developmental planning in Career Development typically includes some employee-identified, supervisor-supported, additional training, desired for improved performance on the job.

One major goal of Career Development is improving the person-job match. To achieve this goal, individuals are encouraged to seriously examine their own skills, interests, and preferences, and to evaluate jobs in light of this information. Intraorganizational moves are calculated to enhance the payoffs that the job has for the individual and to optimize the individual's contributions to the organization. The resulting improved person-job match has training implications. Depending on the nature of the work and the policies of the organization, the skill levels required of entry-level employees might change considerably; hence, the requests for additional training or advanced training might increase dramatically. Operating in isolation, neither training nor Career Development can be as effective as is possible with a mutually supportive team.

RELATIONSHIP OF CAREER DEVELOPMENT AND EDUCATION

Education is the portion of HRD that is generally associated most closely with Career Development. Educational activities are those that focus on developing the individual beyond the scope of job duties currently held. Education may include any number of different kinds of programs, ranging from in-house or public seminars to participation in degree-related programs at colleges and universities. Recent surveys have indicated that tuition refund or tuition aid programs are among the most prevalent Career Development practices for organizations.

Many activities in an individual's developmental plan are educational activities. Some of these are designed to prepare the person to move from his or her current position to another position somewhere else in the organization. Other educational programs enable the individual to prepare for emerging opportunities within his or her present work unit.

When an employee has participated in career planning activities, has identified areas of interest, and has specified moves to be made or developmental activities to be accomplished, educational activities take on relevance and personal meaning. The content of educational programs is not intended to be immediately applicable. Without the future orientation provided by a planned career, individuals tend to wonder "Why do I need to know this?" Career Development provides a clear link between education and future contributions anticipated for the individual.

RELATIONSHIP OF CD AND DEVELOPMENT

In recent years, organizations have become concerned with functioning effectively in a rapidly changing environment. Strategies that plan and manage change for continued or increased effectiveness in an uncertain future have become a basis on which an organization provides development. Career Development offers an individual the same forward looking perspective that development offers the organization when HRD is provided. Both take a macro approach to growth and change in that both seek to identify potential for a total system, rather than to focus on parts of the system. Career Development helps the total person identify life goals and establish ways of moving toward those ideals. The career is only one part of the whole person.

Increasingly, we are recognizing how futile it is to expect employees to segment themselves, that is, to abandon all other parts of self, except the career self, while at work. Career Development offers a framework for assisting workers to examine themselves, make realistic and meaningful plans for change and growth, and accept responsibility for their own lives. In this framework, the individual is not independent, but interdependent. This type of individual seeks development that can be provided through non-job-related learning.

CAREER DEVELOPMENT: AN INTEGRATING FORCE

Not only does Career Development have the potential for linking together the diverse functions within human resources, but without these links, Career Development programs cannot be as sound and credible as they might be. As Beverly Kaye, career development researcher and consultant, recommends,

> A major task of the career development practitioner...is to conceptualize the career development program as a logical, step-by-step framework and to determine how human resource development efforts can be supported by and supportive of each step.[7]

Career Development can offer a new focus to each aspect of HRD and management. With this new focus, each of the in-place human resource units is able to conceptualize programs, policies, and communications as part of the total career system (i.e., to consider the needs and goals of the organization and the needs and goals of individuals). Some of the potential differences in traditional human resource activities and in these same activities carried out with a Career Development focus are presented in Figure 30.9.

Activity	Traditional Focus	Career Development Focus
Human resoruce planning	Analyzes jobs, skill, tasks-present and future; projects need; uses statistical data	Adds information about individual interests, preference etc. to data; provides career path information
HRD	Provides opportunities for learning skills, information, attitudes related to work	Adds individual growth or "learning by objectives orientation"
Performance appraisal	Rating and/or rewards	Adds development plans...; individual goal setting
Recruiting and placement	Matching organizations needs with qualified individuals	Matching individual and jobs based on a number of variables
Compensation/ benefits	Rewards for time, productivity, talent, etc.	Adds non-job related activities

Figure 30.9.   Impact of career development on traditional human resource activities.

It was pointed out earlier that the techniques and methods available for use in Career Development far exceed their use. Similarly, the potential for integrating all human resource activities with Career Development is only beginning to be understood. Human Resource Development has many natural and necessary links with Career Development. These should be pursued to maximize the impact of both CD and HRD.

Organizations are able to grow, change, and adapt to an extent that is at least partially dependent on the ability of its human resources to grow, change, and adapt. Career Development is a major means of preparing individual employees for this process.

NOTES

1. To pursue this idea, see F. Otte and P. Hutcheson, "Career Development: Fact or Fad," *CTM: The Human Element*, December 1980, pp. 26–28.

2. D. Hall, F. Hall, and R. Hinton. "Research of Organizational Development: Where Are We and Where Do We Go From Here," *Human Resource Planning* 1, (4), 204 (1978).

3. This model draws upon some prior work done by one of the authors and others in the career development area. See W. Storey, *A Guide for Career Development Inquiry: State-of-the-Art Report on Career Development* ASTD Research Series, Paper No. 2 (Washington, D.C.: American Society for Training and Development, 1979) and T. Gutteridge and F. Otte, *Organizational Career Development: State-of-the-Practice* (Washington, D.C.: American Society for Training and Development, 1983).

4. For a more detailed discussion of organizational use of these various career development techniques, see J. Walker and T. Gutteridge, *Career Planning Practices* (New York: AMACOM, 1979) and "Career Development Activities: Practices, Focuses, Concerns," *The Career Development Bulletin* 1 (1979): 6–7.

5. For an elaboration of this problem see Walker and Gutteridge, pp. 12, 36.

6. To pursue this idea, see F. Otte and P. Hutcheson, *CTM: The Human Element* December 1980, pp. 26–28.

7. This work is drawn from materials developed by Peggy Hutcheson and Fred L. Otte for a workshop sponsored by the Career Development Research Project, Department of Vocational and Career Development, Georgia State University, Atlanta, Georgia.

BIBLIOGRAPHY

Bolles, R. *What Color Is Your Parachute.* Berkeley, Cal.: Ten Speed Press, 1981.

Burack, E. and N. Mathys. *Career Management In Organizations: A Practical Human Resource Planning Approach.* Lake Forest, Ill.: Brace-Park Press, 1980.

Hall, D. *Careers in Organizations.* Pacific Palisades, Cal.: Goodyear Publishing, 1976.

Jelinek, M. *Career Management: For the Individual and the Organization.* Chicago: St. Clair Press, 1979.

Kaye, B. *Up Is Not the Only Way.* Englewood Cliffs, N.J.: Prentice-Hall, 1982.

London, M., and S. Stumpf. *Managing Careers.* Reading, Mass.: Addison-Wesley, 1982.

Morgan, M. *Managing Career Development.* New York: Van Nostrand, 1980.

Schein, E. *Career Dynamics: Matching Individual and Organizational Needs.* Reading, Mass.: Addison-Wesley, 1978.

Storey, W., ed. *A Guide for Career Development Inquiry: State-of-the-Art Report on Career Development,* ASTD Research Series, Paper No. 2. Madison, Wis.: American Society for Training and Development, 1979.

Walker, J., and T. Gutteridge, *Career Planning Practices.* New York: AMACOM, 1979.

THE FUTURE OF HRD

CHAPTER THIRTY-ONE

Projections, Paradoxes, Paradigms

ANTHONY O. PUTMAN AND CHIP R. BELL

The *future*—just the word sounds exciting. We have seen an increasing interest in the future of HRD since the early 1970s. It is important that we never lose sight of the possibilities and challenges of the future.

In this chapter, Bell and Putman help us look at futuring and the future. This is not an easy task, but it is a necessary one. The future holds many possible traps, but there are also opportunities that can lift HRD above the ordinary.

Do not expect the authors to show you the future. There are too many soothsayers among us now. Instead, they offer ways of looking at the future and emphasize that this should be a continuous, ongoing process.

Anthony O. Putman is chairman of the board of Management Support Technology, Inc., an organization that develops and markets knowledge support tools for managers. Since the early 1970s, he has focused on making organizations more effective in productivity improvement and human system design. He is past president of the Society for Descriptive Psychology and a frequent conference speaker on HRD topics. He coined the acronym *AIDE* (artificial intelligence device) while writing a science fiction novel.

Chip R. Bell provides HRD services to a variety of clients in the areas of instructor of instructors, leadership learning, and team building. He was formerly a partner of LEAD Associates, Inc., an HRD firm, director of management development and training for NCNB Corporation (a bank holding company), and a staff officer with the Instructional Methods Division of the U.S. Army Infantry School. He has contributed to many professional journals. Among his books are: *Managing the Learning Process* (1983), *Influencing: Marketing the Ideas That Matter* (1982), and *The Client-Consultant Handbook* (coeditor, 1979).

What lies around the corner for HRD? Will the field grow, prosper, swell in influence and importance? Will it be consigned to the corporate backburners—or be taken off the stove altogether? What new technological wonders lie in store—or will it be business as usual? What will we be doing? How? When? Why?

The future holds an unshakable fascination for most of us. Gazing into the future in hopes of revelation is probably the world's second oldest profession (and, in some quarters, scarcely more respectable than the oldest). From princes plotting invasions to peasants looking for the auspicious time to plant onions, the human race has a long-standing conviction that, if only we would get a glimpse of what is to come, everything would turn out, if not fine, at least better.

Methods have changed, of course. We no longer poke through mounds of steaming chicken entrails, seeking omens from the gods. Now we poke through mounds of demographics and leading indicators in search of the projectable trend. But the end remains the same—to guide present actions by knowing future circumstances. This dilemma was first expressed by the Delphic oracle herself: "Beware! I am absolutely right half of the time and absolutely wrong the other half—but even I don't know which is which."

With that ringing caveat, we would like to offer a guided tour of the future of HRD, to be exact, the *futures* of HRD. We have no intention of offering the definitive version of how things will be, for as the late Ed Lindemann was fond of saying, "That is the business of fortune-tellers, not futurists." Instead, we would like to stimulate your thinking and imagination by offering a variety of futures, some straightforwardly conservative and probable, a few blatantly provocative and perhaps unlikely, and some in between.

Our task is to help you think productively about the future of HRD and how it might affect you; if we prove also to be right about some of these scenarios—well, you can't lose them all (we hope). The task is complicated by the fact that there are almost as many ways of examining the future as there are futures. Even after eliminating those methods that promise direct access to the truth (e.g., astrology, Ouija boards, supply-side economics), we are left with many different possible approaches, each with its advantages and advocates. A number of approaches will be examined. We will not mandate our favorite as *the* method.

This chapter is divided into three main sections, each employing a distinctive way of examining the future of HRD. They are:

1. *Projections.* This section embodies the most conservative approach, that of projecting, from currently available information (demo-

graphic data, technological trends, etc.), the imaginatively foreseeable implications for the future. This sound approach, favored by many futurists, helps ensure that the foreseeable is foreseen. The implications in this approach tend to be sensible, practical, and usually reliable. The drawback to this approach is that the future never turns out quite as expected on the basis of current data; therefore, important twists and turnings will be overlooked.

2. *Paradoxes.* The unpredictable nature of the future requires us to take a different approach. We suggest that surprises, in retrospect, frequently turn out to be a case of taking one of the present givens and standing it on its ear. Things that, at first glance, seem paradoxical or even nonsensical, viewed from the proper angle, suddenly make perfect sense, and the future veers off in an unpredicted direction. In this section, we stand several givens of HRD on their ears and ask, "What would the future of HRD be if *this* basic assumption were altered in *that* way? (Thanks to our friends and colleagues at Ron Lippitt Associates for helping brainstorm these.)

3. *Paradigms.* The first two sections are evolutionary approaches. This section, for the more adventurous, is revolutionary. It raises the question, "What if a *paradigm shift*—a fundamental change in the nature of the game—occurs in HRD?" Better yet, "What if it is occurring already—and we can see glimpses of it now?" We intend this to be provocative, challenging, and, we cheerfully admit, just possibly pure fantasy. (But, just possibly, it is not.)

First, a cautionary note about the present. We are living in interesting times. (Lest we be too self-congratulatory about that, recall that an ancient Chinese curse translates, "May you live in interesting times.") HRD professionals today are confronted with major challenges that are real, present, and virtually certain to extend into any version of the near future. Rather than identify these as *future trends*, we chose to simply list a few here as facts of life that must be taken into account now and in the future.

1.   The massive influx of new technology into the workplace presents great challenges to HRD. In particular, the task of keeping the work force's skills and knowledge base current, avoiding work force obsolescence, is a substantial and growing concern in almost every industry. We count on this to continue.

2.   Technological and economic changes have created a growing wave of the technologically unemployed. What is your company's policy for handling this, and how does HRD contribute?

3. New tools often disrupt traditional work patterns and communities—sometimes with devastating impact on morale and productivity. (Where is the water cooler in the electronic cottage?) We suggest that there is clear, present, and continuing need for HRD professionals to become corporately proactive in assessing and planning for the introduction of technology into the workplace.

4. Managers are demanding and will continue to demand more "bang" for the HRD buck. An emphasis on creating high-performance work units and demonstrating results from HRD efforts are part of the fabric of the 1980s.

These are some of the issues that face us today. What about tomorrow?

PROJECTIONS

Projections can be important data sources for examining the future. Such data represent the most plausible scenario, since projections take known data or present trends and chart them into the future. For instance, demographic projections state that if people continue to have babies, move, become more educated, and so forth, at the present rate, the future will look like this. Such projecting can be useful in many ways.

Demographic Projections

Demographers often remind us of the post-World War II baby boom—that huge crowd of people born in the late 1940s and 1950s. Their aging through this century has been visually compared to a python snake digesting a pig—a moving bubble. The baby boom has had its impact on schools and is now beginning to shape the character of work life.

Figure 31.1 shows the percentage change of certain age groups in each decade from 1960 to 2000. The age groups representing the largest percentage increase in each decade are indicated by a box. A second look reveals that each box represents the same group of people moving through time. As a result of this phenomenon, the 1950s were characterized by a large percentage of young children, the 1960s by a large percentage of teenagers, and the 1970s by a large percentage of young marrieds. Likewise, the 1980s and 1990s are characterized by a large percentage of middle-aged adults.

The most significant aspect of this population phenomenon is that the average U.S. worker's age will rise from 28 (in 1975) to almost 40 by 1990. This is the first time that the average American worker will be so old. In

Age	1960-1970	1970-1980	1980-1990	1990-2000
Under 20	+11%	-5%	+6%	+4%
20-24	+54	+23	-15	+8
25-34	+10	+46	+13	-15
35-44	-5	+10	+46	+13
45-54	+13	-4	+10	+45
55-64	+19	+13	-3	+11
65 and over	+20	+20	+15	+4

Figure 31.1. Population shifts in the United States, 1960–2000. *Source:* William Lazar, "The 1980s and Beyond: A Perspective," MSU Business Topics. Michigan State University School of Business, Spring 1977, p. 24.

fact, never in history has the average age exceeded 32. You can begin to appreciate why the Social Security Administration continues to be restless. When the baby boom crowd reaches retirement age, just after the turn of the century, their numbers may be so great that younger employees may be unwilling or unable to fund Social Security. Health care, welfare, and housing for the aged will, no doubt, suffer similar strain.

There are other important demographic trends impacting on HRD. The participation of adult males as a percentage of the work force is dropping, while that of women—especially mothers of small children—is climbing rapidly. Retirement age is climbing. The percentage of the American population over 65 was 11 percent in 1981. It will grow to almost 20 percent by the beginning of the next century—a tribute to our increasing life expectancy. Continual immigration pressure will add a social/cultural complexity to HRD activities.

What impact will all this have on the HRD field? As the work force of America "matures," will it alter the type of offerings provided by HRD? How will it change the way in which these offerings are provided? What education will be needed for future jobs? What can we expect for HRD practitioners of the 1990s?

The 1990s learning specialist and curriculum builder may need to become even more sensitive to the physiology of the learner. Visual acuity may become a larger issue in audiovisual-assisted instruction. As the industrial classroom is dominated by mature adults rather than children, the differences between *pedagogy* (learning as a child) and *andragogy* (learning as an adult) will be dramatized.

This may necessitate a more rapid shift in the learning specialist's approach from content dispenser to facilitator. A delivery orientation to learning will be subservient to a discovery orientation. HRD practitioners involved in training will have to focus on practical, immediate application of what is learned, rather than on theory attached to delayed gratification. HRD activities will need to help learners solve problems, rather than simply add to their knowledge. Since older learners will have more life experience, learning specialists will need to find better ways to capitalize on that experience in a learning arena.

The rapid change in most occupations and increasing technological advances will continue to shorten the time between skill acquisition and skill obsolescence. This, coupled with people changing careers several times during their lives, will make lifelong learning a necessity. The space between academic education and corporate HRD will blur. Credentials will be secondary to competence. In fact, the swing toward more conservatism stirring in the 1980s may result in a major shift in the way knowledge and skill are measured, monitored, and maintained.

HRD and Work Values

Most of us who grew up before 1960 viewed work as a duty and a responsibility. Adages such as "An idle mind is the devil's workshop," "All things come to him who waits," "Work now, enjoy later," peppered our language. We viewed people as either lazy or weird if they refused to work the traditional 9 A.M. to 5 P.M., Monday through Friday. Delayed gratification was an unquestioned way of life. A good paying job with demeaning responsibilities was more valued than meaningful work at meager wages.

The labor force of tomorrow, whose values were shaped in an era of affluence, liberalism, and varied life styles, will be unimpressed with organizational environments that place quantity of work output over quality of work life. Many will not be enticed to achieve a high personal-economic end when the means to that end take a toll on their self-esteem. The day of the worker as passive child is giving way to a time of the worker as an assertive adult.

The implications of this work-values shift touch many fronts in the HRD field. In the 1990s, there will be a continued surge for industrial democracy. Workers will demand and get a larger, more autonomous role in decision making, market selection, product identification, work planning, and even supervisor selection.

The current interest in quality circles is an indication of what is to come. While the "do your own thing" liberalism of the 1970s will be replaced by a more serious, results-orientated conservatism, it will still be concerned with the human need aspect of work.

Managers will need continual training in participative leadership, conflict resolution, interpersonal communication, and matrix/task force managment. Likewise, HRD professionals will be viewed as the experts of the human system and will be expected to play an internal consulting role to line managers struggling to cope with decreasing productivity and increasing worker demands. Participation as a means to "keep the troops happy" will be replaced by participation as a method to harness worker competence and creativity. HRD practitioners will exert more effort on organization development in the 1990s than they have in the 1980s.

HRD and the Workplace

The workplace will increase the challenges to the HRD practitioner. Alvin Toffler, in his book, *The Third Wave*, promises the growth of the "electronic cottage."[1] Given our movement toward an information technology society, more employees will be able to work at home via computer hookup with the office. However, few workers will be exclusive "work at home" employees. Instead, "at home" will be alternated with "at the office." The pursuit of leisure will fuel a demand for flexible work schedules. Peter Drucker has estimated that between two-fifths and three-fifths of all workers will be permanent, part-time employees by 1990. Flexitime and flex-place have an impact on HRD.

For example, the system for scheduling and delivering learning will become extremely complex. The use of work-to-home video telecommunications may make transmission of learning programs easier. But, what do we do about those classes requiring group process as a part of the learning, if people are working at home? Some have indicated that the laser beam and its offspring, the holograph, may be an answer to having many people at different locations projected into one location.

Learning specialists may be wise to add a leisure dimension to job-required training, as a way to heighten interest and broaden application. For example, a course in cost accounting designed for company auditors might include components related to personal income tax. Leadership training might have a module on effective parenting. Preventive maintenance classes on heavy equipment and company-sponsored instruction on how to overhaul the family car may carry equal legitimacy. Learners of the 1990s will expect holistic learning. Learning how to cope with stress and burnout will continue to be popular topics.

Organizations are expected to continue to decentralize the administration of HRD and to seek ways to more efficiently integrate working and learning. This will require supervisors and managers to be closely involved in training, education, and development, including actual classroom facilitation. Tested, tailored, training packages (turnkey learning programs) designed to enable supervisors and managers to train their own subordinates will increase in demand. Follow-up training and self-directed programs will be priority items. Additionally, HRD practitioners will have to don many hats to respond to various needs in a comprehensive, cost-effective fashion.

Decentralization and a more productivity-minded employee are expected to increase the requirement for cost-effective HRD in the 1990s. Economists predict only moderate economic growth for the remainder of this century. Learning programs with minimal cost justification or speculative in their developmental purpose are likely to be quickly whittled out of a strained budget. More than ever, HRD pros will need to understand how their business works, in order to appropriately position HRD as a valued tool to enhance organizational effectiveness.

HRD and Technology

HRD practitioners have always been fascinated with technology. That fascination has led to valuable breakthroughs in the field of learning. The teaching machines of the 1960s and the current interest in teleconferencing and the videodisc are examples. Other examples of projections related to technology that could influence HRD follow.

1. *Wristwatch Size Televisions.* Sony has already developed a pocket TV with a two-inch screen that weighs 12 ounces. The next step will be TVs with interactive capability, a learning tool.

2. *Pocket Telephones.* By the 1990s, a new network—"Skynet 2000"—will enable people to communicate from anywhere to anywhere, without physical connections, via a pocket telephone with a three-inch antenna.

3. *Holographic Instructors.* By the end of this century, it will be possible to transmit "celebrity instructors" to countless classrooms (including the electronic cottage) simultaneously.

4. *Library on a Computer Chip.* Some are predicting that at the current rate of computer software development it will be possible, by the beginning of the next century (maybe sooner), to store the contents of 20,000 books on a storage chip the size of an aspirin tablet.

5. *New Careers.* The 1990s will bring career opportunities reflecting changes in our world. Energy technician, housing rehabilitation technician, industrial laser processor, robot production specialist, genetic engineer, bionic-electronic technician, geriatric social worker, and holographic inspector are a few such careers.

Robotics

Robots represent a recent technological advancement that is expected to grow astronomically. Some forecasters predict a $3 billion to $4 billion market for industrial robots by 1990. The Society of Manufacturing Engineers predicts that by 1990 50% of the direct assembly of an automobile will be done by robots. One Ford Motor Company study stated that by the year 2000 most farm work will be done by robots. They will plow the ground, sow the seed, and harvest by honing in on wires or sensors buried in the soil.

Newsweek estimates that "from 50 to 75 percent of all U.S. factory workers could be displaced by smart robots by 2000."[2] Already the number of lower skilled jobs is declining for a host of reasons.

Are robots on Orwellian nightmare or an HRD opportunity? As robots do more jobs and do them more cheaply with each new generation, how will employees be impacted? As the predicted robot work force approaches 100,000 by the end of this decade, displaced workers will look to HRD to provide new, more relevant skills. The unemployment created by robotics will be an opportunity for creative HRD responses. What would you do differently today if your flawless crystal ball revealed that half of your company's output was going to be accomplished by robots in the next 10 to 15 years? The tin collar worker may need to be factored into your long-range planning.

PARADOXES

The most significant impact on the future is likely to be the serendipitous, sudden, left turns, which were unpredictable and, thus, unplanned. Such "left turns" frequently are caused by someone asking questions "backward," so to speak. For instance, the question "What would happen if we let people remain stationary and move the steps instead?" led to the discovery of the escalator. Another question, "What would happen if we got inside a clogged artery and vacuumed it out instead of bypassing it with a normal artery?" led to the laser heart vacuum currently under development.

We thought you might profit from several HRD questions "turned on their ear." While by no means predictions, they represent possibilities. We hope you begin your own list of questions that, paradoxically, may be future left turns.

1. *What Would HRD Be Like in the Future If We, in the Field, Were To Proceed from the Conviction that People Already Know Everything They Need to Know in Order to Perform Well on the Job?* What we are suggesting here is similar to those "is it a vase or is it a face?" eye-puzzlers of Gestalt psychology; we are suggesting a reversal of the figure and ground that ordinarily form the HRD Gestalt.

The current *figure* in HRD, that is, that which most practitioners are aware of and that to which we pay the most attention, is comprised of the knowledge and skills of a person. The predominance in our field of such words as *training, education, development,* and *learner* prove this. The *ground* of HRD, that is, that which we primarily take for granted and pay little attention to, is comprised of all those other factors that make a difference in a person's on-the-job performance (e.g., motivation, status, permissions, expectation, reinforcements, etc.). Suppose we were to reverse that figure and ground? What would HRD be like if we took knowledge and skills essentially for granted and concentrated on creating circumstances that maximally promote actualizing those competencies in performance?

For example, what would training be like if we assumed people already knew the material? Who, under these circumstances, would most appropriately be seen as the learner—the worker or the HRD professional? What would take the place of training as the reflex panacea when performance problems are encountered? Would ASTD run Motivate the Motivators workshops? Perhaps training sessions would shift their focus from concepts, principles, and skills to action planning, trouble shooting, and sharing of successful practices.

2. *What Would the Future of HRD Be Like If We Were to Discover that Learning Is Fundamentally a Matter of Subtraction, Not Addition?* There is a famous Zen story about a learned professor of philosophy who one day visited a master to be instructed in Zen. The master received his distinguished visitor cordially and, as is the custom of the country, invited him to have tea. The master filled his visitor's cup and then kept pouring. The professor watched the tea overflowing until he could no longer restrain himself, "The cup is full! No more will go in!" The master replied, "Like this cup, you are full of your own opinions and speculations. How can I show you Zen unless you first empty your cup?"[3]

What if we were to discover that the most useful learning was a matter

of "emptying your cup" to get your erroneous ideas out of the way? One of
Peter Ossorio's famous maxims says, "Things go right unless they go
wrong in one of the ways they can go wrong."[4] What if we assume that our
task was to help people to stop going wrong, rather than trying to instruct
them as to how to make it go right? Would we then take it that, for
example, successful performance precedes learning, rather than the
other way around? (This, by the way, is not far from the assumptions
underlying behavior modeling.) Perhaps we would emphasize centering
techniques to free up performance, as do many teachers of martial arts.
Would workshops end with a reflection on or celebration of things we
unlearned?

3. *What Would the Future of HRD Be Like If There Were to Be
Widespread Agreement that the Mission of HRD Is Legitimately and
Fundamentally Spiritual?* Why does HRD exist in the first place? If the
top brass is listening, most of us will forthrightly respond, "to contribute
to the success and profitability of the company." But, when we are honest
with ourselves and each other about our fundamental motivations and
values, a more diverse picture emerges, often a mixture of pragmatic
values and humanistic concerns.

What if we were to discover conclusively that the only HRD efforts that
made a genuine contribution to the bottom line were those that placed
primary emphasis on increasing the sense of meaning, purpose, and
satisfaction in an individual's life? What if we were to recognize that
HRD must be done for its own sake, in order to further these fundamental
human concerns, or else it does not really work? How would the form and
focus of our efforts change? Would our influence and the role in our
corporations increase? Decrease? Remain the same? How would we deal
with managers who were misguided and continued to insist on a bottom
line focus? What new ethical demands and constraints would this
approach introduce into HRD?

4. *What If We Devoted As Much Effort to Preventing Forgetting
(Deterioration of Skills) As We Did to Promoting Learning?* The
research related to learning has largely been devoted to fostering
additional skills or to the alteration of skills, knowledge, or attitudes. We
all appreciate the impact of the *law of disuse;* that is, if behavior is not
used and reinforced, it fades. Have we sufficiently studied forgetting?
What would be the impact on the field if we discovered a way to ensure
eternal retention?

"Ah," you say, "that could be a curse; there are things I'd like to
eternally forget!" But, what if you could choose at any time what was
remembered and what was forgotten? What if you could erase a negative

memory (a painful experience) and retain a useful memory (how to calculate the circumference of a circle in centimeters)?

5. *What If Learning Could Be Done as an Implant?* Learning is complex. Given that people have invested many years developing their personality, behavior change is frequently awkward and typically slow. All of us who have had to unlearn deeply entrenched habits appreciate the difficulty.

What would be the impact on the HRD field if someone devised a sure-fire way to mainline learning—a pill, a brain implant, a brain scan, a potion, a pattern of electronic charges to the nervous system, an alteration of DNA molecules in the body, genetic engineering, whatever? Bionics makes entertaining television material, but what would learning be if we discovered a shortcut to skill acquisition? While the fountain of knowledge or professorburgers may seem way out, variations on the theme may revolutionize our role.

6. *What If Someone Found a Foolproof Method?* We are a creative profession, frequently driven by the latest fad. It is a tribute to our pioneering spirit and a recognition of the complexity of HRD. But, did you ever wonder what would happen if someone discovered a method that was foolproof?

Pick any method—how to teach, how to enrich jobs, how to set objectives, how to lead, how to select employees. We have always been able to add to, replace, or change almost any method for a newer, more effective model. It is true that we are in the business of change, since life itself is a moving target. Think, for a moment, of the effect of a breakthrough that was universally acknowledged as the end of development in that area. How would a foolproof method affect HRD?

7. *What If HRD Totally Became a Line Function?* We have always acknowledged HRD as a staff or support function. While some may administratively treat it as a profit center (as opposed to an expense or cost center), it is perceived as a unit with a support mission. What if that changes?

We are becoming an information society. John Naisbitt, in *Megatrends*, describes the impact of reducing "information float" (the lag between sender and receiver).[5] But what if learning became the medium of exchange? What would be the impact on HRD if learning was bought and sold in the marketplace? What if the traditional line functions supported the bartering of learning? What if employees made widgets to enhance learning, rather than the other way around? What if learning became an end rather than a means?

We hope that our collection of paradoxes has stirred your thinking and your search for a potential left turn that might revolutionize the future. Others might include:

What if performance preceded learning rather than vice versa?
What if HRD became a research and development function?
What if HRD focused on problem making and decision solving?
What if HRD focused solely on training customers and clients to use companies?

Add your own set of paradoxes and ponder their impact on the HRD field and your role in it.

A PARADIGM SHIFT

If there is ever a Futurists' Hall of Fame, we should like to nominate for charter membership a certain stockbroker who lived around the beginning of the twentieth century, whose predictions of the future were as wrong as his reasoning was right. This man looked at the infant automobile industry in the United States and concluded that it had very little profitable future. After a careful consideration of the labor market, he concluded that it would simply be impossible to educate the necessary number of chauffeurs to drive them. This was actually an astute analysis, considering the fact that automobiles were quite expensive and that, of course, no one with that kind of money drove his own carriage. How could he know that Henry Ford was just about to change all the rules of the game by introducing the Model T, thereby throwing the automobile market open to the unwashed masses, who relished the chance to drive their own carriage—horseless or otherwise? The stockbroker got caught by that most powerful and unpredictable factor in assessing the future—the paradigm shift.

Previously, we talked about "turning questions on their ear," that is, coming up with a fresh or different way of looking at some familiar issue or question that leads to new insights and new practices. A paradigm shift, by contrast, is substantially more profound and radical. More than just a different way of looking at familiar things, a paradigm shift is a revolution in what we see, how we see it, and, most importantly, in what we do with it. That revolution can have profound implications.

Consider, for example, the famous paradigm shift that Christopher Columbus sold to Ferdinand and Isabella of Spain. Saying that the world was round and not flat was not just a neat new way of looking at things, it completely changed the rules of the game ("Sail west to go east! Are you mad?") and opened up a whole new world for exploration and exploitation. Before Copernicus, a major occupation of astronomers was computing the epicycles, which accounted for the apparent discrepancies of the motions of the planets around the earth. After Copernicus replaced the earth with the sun as the center of the universe, not only was our view of the central place of the human race profoundly and permanently altered, there was also no longer any need to compute epicycles.

Anyone predicting the future of HRD would do well to add a caveat stating that in the event of a paradigm shift, all bets are off. Projections and paradoxes of the sort we have already discussed presume that the basic enterprise called HRD will remain much the same, while certain of the forces it must contend with and the resources it has may change. But a paradigm shift in HRD would sweep the certainty aside. It would call into question our basic assumptions about what HRD is, how we go about doing it, and the fundamental place HRD has in the corporate universe. Indeed, from the viewpoint of a new paradigm, many of our current activities in HRD might well seem as quaint as computing epicycles would to a modern astronomer.

By now, many readers are raising the sensible objection—granted, paradigm shifts make a profound difference, but so what? Until one happens, why not stick with talking about HRD as we currently know it? Our answer to this sensible objection is simple and direct. We suspect that a paradigm shift in HRD has already begun. It is plausible that, within 10 years, the field itself will be transformed almost beyond recognition.

Our belief that a paradigm shift may soon occur (or indeed may already be in the process of occurring) stems from our recognition that today we are witnessing an influx of new technologies of historic proportions into the workplace. Indeed, it hardly seems an exaggeration to say that never before in history have so many different, powerful technologies converged in the workplace at one time. We believe the paradigm shift in HRD, if it occurs, will stem from the convergence of three powerful and parallel technological developments: the microcomputer, knowledge representation, and artificial intelligence.

There is no need for us to belabor the impact of microcomputers in the work world; that has been the topic of countless articles and books in the last few years. It is sufficient to note that the most recent projections say that 15 million microcomputers will be installed in the workplace by 1986, and to remember that, historically, projections of the rate and size of computer installation have invariably wildly underestimated the reality. The microcomputer is unquestionably one of the power tools of management and business in the future—and the future is now.

Perhaps the most significant implication for HRD in the microcomputer boom is that, at least in principle, it makes possible a previously impossible but highly desirable goal of HRD professionals, that is, getting real time, on-the-job access to people who need support. Instead of investing substantial time and expense in pulling people off the job and putting them into an artificial environment where we can train them in things we hope they can use on the job, the microcomputer makes it possible to bring training support to the individual on the job. Further (again, at least in principle), the microcomputer makes it possible for learning to occur at the convenience of the learner. The key difference that the microcomputer makes in this regard is collapsing the distinction between the place of work and the place of learning; with the microcomputer, for the first time, these two can be substantially the same.

But even the most sophisticated and exciting computer hardware is nothing more than an expensive piece of high-tech office decoration without equally sophisticated software. And, as those of us who have grappled with the various forms of computer-assisted instruction can attest, such software has been extremely hard to obtain. Although we, as HRD practitioners, have available to us an immense pool of human knowledge from which to draw, the techniques and methods for representing this knowledge in computer-usable form have been sorely inadequate. However, that appears to be changing at a rapidly accelerating pace.

In research labs all over the country, new and powerful forms (essentially high-level computer languages) are being developed and tested—forms that vastly expand the ease with which complex human knowledge can be represented in computer-usable form. This makes it possible to capture (and, therefore, make available by a computer) expert knowledge about how things work and how to get things done.

For example, one project at Bell Laboratories succeeded in creating a computerized mentor for newly hired technical employees on a large computer software development team (several hundred people were involved). This mentor was capable of answering questions ranging from the biggest picture down to the most minute detail—even down to how to fill in the various boxes on forms. Its purpose was to supplement the technical person's already developed competencies in developing software in general, with knowledge and skills about how to get that job done in this particular environment. (It will come as no surprise to those who have operated in complex technical environments that the nitty-gritty, "here's how it works around here," knowledge formed a very substantial data base.)

The third converging technology, artificial intelligence, has gained enough momentum that it is being hailed in some quarters as "the second computer revolution." These advances in artificial intelligence make possible computer programs that can interact in reasonable simulation of human functioning as experts on topics of critical interest. For example, several medical diagnosis programs are functioning. These programs do an excellent job of taking a medical history from a patient and supplying the human physician with shrewd diagnostic hypotheses.

Digital Equipment Corporation, the large minicomputer manufacturer, developed an artificial intelligence program to help put together specific systems, combining their thousands of potential components and troubleshooting the installation of the system. The aforementioned mentor program from Bell Laboratories is so advanced that it creates and sustains the uncanny illusion that one is communicating with another human being who is responding to one's inquiries by displaying answers on a computer terminal screen.

We believe that from this historic convergence of three powerful technologies will emerge the first of many generations of artificial intelligence devices (or AIDEs, as one of us termed them a number of years ago). An *AIDE* is a computer program that has expert and reliable knowledge about important topics. It is capable of interacting with human beings in a flexible, responsive way that closely simulates interacting with another human being. In short, speaking metaphorically, an *AIDE* is an expert person who lives in a computer. We believe that this is the breakthrough that might completely transform human resource development.

AIDEs, as their name punningly implies, exist solely to be of assistance to persons in accomplishing their work. The role of an AIDE is essentially that of an on-demand expert consultant (or, in appropriate cases, tutor). It directs the learner on what to do and how to do it. Since the AIDE is a part of the microcomputer on your desk, talking to it will be as easy as calling up a human expert on the telephone—but with AIDE, the line is never busy, the consultant is never out to lunch or in another meeting, and it does not matter how dumb or repetitious your question might be. And, for comparatively routine matters (e.g., filling out standard forms, pulling a document out of storage and routing it to your subordinates, rotating the artillery piece 74 degrees, etc.), once you have decided something needs to be done, an AIDE can do it for you if it is plugged in to the other computers and computer programs that accomplish these tasks. That is, an AIDE can be both an expert mentor on how things are done and a useful assistance in doing those things.

As these examples suggest, artificial intelligence devices would seem to be useful to virtually anyone who has work to do, from the soldier with an eight-grade education or equivalent operating a weapon system too complex for most college graduates to understand, to the executive who knows the banking business inside out but is not too sure exactly how to delegate responsibility and make it stick. AIDEs are useful because everyone has gaps in their knowledge and experience that lead to poorer quality decisions and execution than we would ideally like. However, it is recognition of precisely this same fact that puts HRD in business. An AIDE exists for exactly the same reason that HRD exists—to help fill in these gaps of knowledge and skill, wherever they might be.

What would an AIDE look like in actual practice? Here's a brief scenario that illustrates in condensed form the functioning of an artificial intelligence device for managers (called *Aide-de-Camp*) that has been developed by one of the authors for use on microcomputers.

Ed Black, project manager, has just attended a staff meeting that left him worried. One of his key team leaders, Jack Garvey, has been doing an outstanding job in a vital position but has become increasingly and obviously bored with the assignment. Ed is concerned about losing Jack, which would put the overall project badly behind schedule. Ed turns to his AIDE for consultation.

The AIDE first leads Ed through a series of multiple choice questions to determine what kind of help is needed. First, is it action planning or troubleshooting? Does the problem lie in customer relations, sales, finance, productivity, subordinates, or elsewhere? Which subordinates? Does the problem involve performance, cooperation, meeting deadlines, job satisfaction, or another issue? Having zeroed in on the problem, the AIDE then probes for details. Has Garvey's performance been slipping recently? Is he overqualified for the assignment? (At any point, Ed can interrupt the flow and check what point his AIDE is making. When this is done, the AIDE switches momentarily from consultant to tutor and explains, for instance, that to a strongly achievement-oriented person such as Jack, it is extremely frustrating to have skills that are not being utilized on the job.)

Exploring options and constraints, the AIDE helps Ed locate data on the current job market for people in Garvey's position. As feared, Garvey very likely could be hired away for a good increase and promotion. It then helps Ed pinpoint the skills Garvey has that are being underutilized and asks Ed to think through possible supplemental responsibilities for Garvey as a temporary fix. The AIDE helps Ed develop an action plan for moving Garvey into a bigger and more responsible position. The plan includes enlisting Garvey in training his own replacement and in establishing a specific developmental timetable with milestones to be achieved. Finally, at Ed's request, his AIDE helps him decide how to communicate these plans in terms that make sense to Garvey himself.

What, then, does all this mean for HRD? We suspect that AIDES will cause HRD professionals to profoundly rethink and alter their approach to accomplishing their objectives. Consider the objective of providing a particular worker with the knowledge needed to accomplish a given job, for example, the job of supervisor. The major and in many cases the only components of such a HRD program typically are some form of supervisory training, supplemented with policy and procedural manuals.

We would be the last to suggest that training does not make a difference or that manuals are a waste of time. It is, however, widely recognized in our field that training has certain irreducible difficulties.

1. Since we can never take supervisors off the job long enough to train them in everything they need to know, it is necessary to make some more or less arbitrary decisions about what portions of the whole we will cover.

2. Even with the best design and presentation skills, not everyone will grasp all of the material during the session.

3. Of the material actually grasped, unfortunately, a very large amount is forgotten shortly after the session.

4. It is often difficult for the learner to see how to apply the general principles or concepts learned in their own specific on-the-job situations.

By contrast, consider the use of a supervisory AIDE. Since we do not have to take supervisors off the job to use the AIDE—on the contrary, they use it on the job—there is no need to give them an incomplete set of knowledge and skills. They use the material at precisely the time and under precisely the circumstances that make for quality learning, that is, when they need to know the material in order to accomplish a task presently at hand. And, if they forget or are uncertain about a particular area, they can go over it repeatedly, quickly, and easily. In a nutshell, having an AIDE is equivalent to having the supervisory skills instructor chained to your desk, available for instructing at all times. Our hunch is that this will prove to be a substantially effective and efficient means of accomplishing our objectives.

Predicting the effects of a paradigm shift in advance virtually requires stepping out of the cautious disciplines of futuring into those of science fiction or fantasy. For instance, knowing that the flat earth paradigm would soon be transformed into a round earth, who could have predicted that one of its direct consequences would be to spread tobacco smoking throughout the world?

If artificial intelligence devices do revolutionize HRD, however, there are certain logical consequences that seem likely. In order to develop an effective AIDE, for example, the tools and techniques of performance analysis will need to be developed and emphasized. HRD professionals will be required to specify in detail the knowledge, skills, and judgment necessary to do a particular job as it is actually done, in contrast to how it is done theoretically or in principle. Performance observation and description in technically useful detail might well become HRD competencies. The capability of directly supporting a worker's performance on the job might become translated into a mandate that gives HRD professionals direct accountability for productivity. Indeed, the use of artificial intelligence devices might lead to HRD becoming a line function.

The more one contemplates the potential impact of artificial intelligence devices in our field, the more plausible it seems that it could indeed bring about a paradigm shift. We suspect that the nature of the shift would be from human resource development to human resource support (HRS). In most corporate worlds, development is not considered to be an end in itself. It is a means to the end of ensuring that the knowledge, skills, and judgment required to keep the company viable are present in the right places and at the right times. We may discover, when we look back on our field, that human resource development was what we did before we gained the tools for human resource support.

What would be the impact of such a paradigm shift on HRD professionals themselves? Again, while the answer to that question remains mostly unknown, there are certain fairly clear-cut implications that we can see now. A new profession within HRD will be central to the development of artificial intelligence devices. This professional, known as the *knowledge engineer*, will interview experts and observe them in action in order to capture their knowledge and translate it into computer-usable form. In the very near future, we will all need to become very familiar and comfortable with computers; an HRD professional who is not may be like a surgeon lacking in scalpel literacy. If HRD is to evolve into HRS, a part of the transformation will consist of moving HRD professionals into a substantially more proactive and central role in their organizations. The primary products of HRS activities—artificial intelligence devices—will be seen as necessary tools, rather than dispensable luxuries. (For most of us, this contrasts refreshingly with management's attitude toward current HRD activities.)

For consultants, a paradigm shift from HRD to HRS may be a mixed blessing. On the one hand, AIDEs dealing with management and personnel matters would almost certainly reduce the need for routine consultation on such matters, and many consultants may find themselves among the technologically unemployed. On the other hand, those consultants who remain in the field would be much less frequently asked to cover the same familiar ground with a succession of managers. Instead, they would be asked for help on matters that are so complex or require so much experience and judgment that it would be unfeasible to build an AIDE to deal with them.

Paradigm shifts are rare occurrences. They are impossible to predict accurately and, like the end of the world, are more often anticipated than they are actually seen. In even raising such a possibility for consideration, we realize that we are at risk of joining our patron saint stockbroker in the Hall of Fame of Bad Guesses. However, before dismissing the whole idea, suppose that the technology of artificial intelligence devices was well developed and widely available. How could you use them to make a difference in your own organization, and how significant would the difference be?

LOOKING FORWARD

This chapter has examined three scenes, three perspectives, and many implications. Our goal has been to offer you a range of alternatives, all of which cannot be correct, and to trigger as many "what ifs" as we could. We believe the more you can anticipate the future, the better planning you do, and the less reactive you become.

What will you be like in 1990, in 2000? How old will you be? What challenges, concerns, passages does one experience at the age you will be those years? Avoid reading this over without reflection. Stop and ponder. How might the future impact on you? Will you still be in the HRD field? What role will you be playing? What will you like? What will your industry or organization be encountering? What expectations will they have of you? As your own futurist, what do you believe is likely, probable, or possible in the next 10 to 20 years?

Everything we think and do from this second on will affect only tomorrow. Yesterday is gone, and today exists for only a brief moment. We spend the remainder of our lives in tomorrows.

An effective human resource development practitioner should function as an ally of change. Whether training employees to improve performance on their present jobs, educating them for a future job, or developing them to grow with the organization as it evolves, change is the common commodity.

Pursuing such a vital responsibility cannot occur effectively without one foot in the future. We are charged by our role to be serious purveyors of the future, not simply curious spectators. The more we are keenly aware of future projections and predictions, the better we are able to prepare ourselves and the clients we aid to successfully function over time.

NOTES

1. Alvin Toffler, *The Third Wave* (New York: Morrow, 1980).
2. James S. Albus, "Robots in the Workplace: The Key to a Prosperous Future," *The Futurist* (1983): 23.
3. Paul Reps, comp., *Zen Flesh, Zen Bones* (Garden City, New York: Anchor Books, Doubleday and Co., Inc., n.d.).
4. Peter G. Ossorio, "Notes on Behavior Description," ed. K.E. Davis, *Advances in Descriptive Psychology*, Vol. 1 (Greenwich, Conn.: JAI Press, 1981).
5. John Naisbitt, *Megatrends* (New York: Warner Books), 1982.

BIBLIOGRAPHY

Albus, James S. "Robots in the Workplace: The Key to a Prosperous Future." *The Futurist* (1983): 22–27.

Bell, Chip R. "Future Encounters of the HRD Kind." *Training and Development Journal* (1981): 54–57.

_____."Training and Development in the 1980's." *Personnel Administrator* (1980): 23–26, 38.

Cetron, Marvin, and Thomas O'Toole. *Encounters with the Future.* New York: McGraw-Hill, 1982.

Cornish, Edward. *Communications Tomorrow: The Coming of the Information Society.* Washington, D.C.: World Future Society, 1982.

Dickson, Paul. *The Future File.* Austin, Tex.: Learning Concepts, 1977.

Ferguson, Marilyn. *Aquarian Conspiracy.* New York: J.P. Tarcher, 1980.

Kornbluh, Marvin. "The Electronic Office." *The Futurist* (1982): 37–39.

Lindemann, E.B., and Ron Lippitt. *Choosing the Future You Prefer.* Ann Arbor: Ron Lippitt Assoc., 1979.

Mills, D.Q. "Human Resources in the 1980's." *Harvard Business Review* (1979).

Nadler, Leonard. "If You're Planning for Tomorrow, Remember It's Not What It Used to Be." *Management Review* (1978): 23–27, 37.

Naisbitt, John. *Megatrends*. New York: Warner Books, 1982.

"A Portrait of America." *Newsweek*. January 17, 1983, pp. 20–33.

Toffler, Alvin. *The Third Wave*. New York: Morrow, 1980.

Yankelovich, Daniel. *New Rules*. New York: Random House, 1981.

Index